Palestine & Palestinians

Guidebook

ALTERNATIVE TOURISM GROUP

74, STAR STREET, P. O. BOX 173, BEIT SAHOUR, PALESTINE
☎ +972 2 2772151, Fax: +972 2 2772211
E-mail: info@atg.ps
Website: www.atg.ps

First French edition prepared in 2003 by: Sabri Giroud & ATG Staff & others
English Translation by: Carol Scheller-Doyle, Walid Shomali
Edited and updated by: Angela Godfrey, Jawad Musleh

First English Edition: April 2005
Printed in Ramallah, Palestine

ISBN no: 9950-319-01-3

The Alternative Tourism Group is the only owner of the guidebook, and has the sole copyright of the guidebook in terms of translation, publication and marketing.

All rights reserved. No part of this publication may be produced, stored in a retrieval system or transmitted in any form by any means electronic, mechanical, photocopy or otherwise without obtaining prior written permission of the Alternative Tourism Group.

The authors and publisher cannot accept any responsibility for loss, injury or inconvenience arising from the use of information contained in this guide.

Readers are advised that whilst every effort has been taken by ATG to ensure the accuracy of this guidebook, changes can occur (permanently or temporarily) which may affect the contents. It is advisable to check locally on transport, accommodation, shops, etc. Also please be aware that roads and paths may alter or be eradicated by road building, wall building, landslip, settlement expansion, flash floods or change of ownership. ATG would welcome note of any such changes.

Photographic Credits:

A.Seri: Front Cover **Al-Watan Centre**: 217, 218, 219, 220 **Applied Research Institute - Jerusalem (ARIJ)**: XII, 186 **Atef Safadi**: XXIV, 394, 395, 399, 401, 402 **Badil**:139 **Bailasan**: I, II, III, IV, V, XIV, XVIII, XIX, XXII, XXVI, XXVII, 33, 34, 35, 37, 38, 39, 40, 44, 52, 53, 56, 57, 61, 64, 65, 73, 81, 83, 84, 92, 93, 96,110, 118, 121, 123, 127, 138, 139, 149, 150, 164, 171, 177, 182, 189, 190, 200, 201, 207, 213, 231, 233, 234, 236, 239, 240, 246, 251, 252, 262, 268, 295, 297, 302, 307, 311, 315, 327, 335, 338, 349, 371, 374, 379, 403 **Bernard Thuylié**: 42, 43, 45 , 50, 75, 76, 203, 204, 205, 227 **Bruno Marmiroli**: XX, 279 **Photos Central Bureau** (WAFA): 89, 234, 274 **Lakiya Negev Bedouin Weaving**: 388 **Defence for Children International - Palestine Section**: 200 **French Biblical and Archaeological Centre in Jerusalem**: 249, 250, 271, 272, 283 Garo **Nabaldian**: 21, 30, 78, 96, 99, 100, 103, 104, 107, 111, 116, 175, 185, 222, 336, 383 **Hanna Abu Sada**: VIII, 19, 97, 101, 118, 186, 206 **Kent Malmqvist:** Back Cover, VI, VII, IX, XI, XV, XXI, XXVIII **Latuff**: 73 **Maria Fialho**: XXV **Palestinian Ministry of Tourism & Antiquities**: 276 **Palestine Image Bank (Turbo Design)**: X, 59, 98, 122, 192 **Peter Makari**: 265 **Philippe Beutin**: 185 **Rev. Andrew Ashdown**: 229, 294, 299, 300, 317 **Riwaq - Centre for Architectural Conservation**: 67, 72, 148, 156, 173, 174, 176, 178, 181, 215, 248, 249, 256, 257, 258, 259, 273, 277, 338 **Sabri Giroud**: 91, 94, 140, 141, 152, 153, 154, 155, 300, 313, 314, 333, 342, 345, 350, 351, 355, 361, 362, 363, 365, 367, 369, 374, 375, 376, 380, 385, 400 **UNDP** XVI, XVII **UNFPA** XIII, XXIII

Preface

Dear Reader,

Publishing this Guidebook marks an important turning-point in presenting Palestine to visitors. Tourism to our country still relies mainly on Israeli guides and guidebooks. Besides distorting basic information about our history and culture, and introducing hostile views to our people, the domination that foreign tour operators have wielded over Palestinian tourism has meant that our own tour operators and vendors have seen little revenue from what is a major industry in the Palestinian economy. When foreign tourists, carefully shepherded by Israeli guides, venture into Palestinian areas - today limited to Bethlehem and Jerusalem — they zip in and out without spending a night in Palestinian accommodation, without eating a meal in a Palestinian restaurant and without patronizing Palestinian stores or cultural venues. Visitors receive a biased and superficial picture of the political situation, and seldom visit Palestinians or their many interesting sites. If they relate to Palestinians at all, most guidebooks accord them only a scant reference, an abbreviated chapter at the end. Worst of all, but most common, Palestine is presented as merely a part of Israel itself.

As this, one of the first Palestinian-oriented guidebooks, illustrates, Palestine possesses an ancient history, a rich society, exceptional tourist sites and a vital contemporary culture - all of which deserve to be promoted. This is a vital aim of the Alternative Tourism Group. Besides offering educational and tourist materials and programmes, the ATG strives to help develop the Palestinian tourism industry as a whole, notably by diffusing information on tours covering all aspects of Palestinian life. The idea of a tourist guidebook was born from the feeling that travellers to Palestine lacked essential information and a "Palestinian Voice." Our objective is to produce a professional, comprehensive and attractive guide to Palestinian life and sites. The guidebook is based on the contemporary approach of cultural tourism, which shifts the emphasis from merely visiting sites with a purely historical and impersonal narrative to creating opportunities for establishing contact between visitors and the local population. Palestine's history and its cultural patrimony go well beyond the religious sites (though an integral part of the visit, too). Cultural tourism facilitates meetings between individuals, specifically among visitors and their hosts, and it explores their hosts' history, as well as their social, political, cultural and environmental realities.

In this guidebook, as in all our activities, we endeavour to present Palestine from "the inside." The guidebook therefore covers such key topics as the Land, its geography and resources; Palestinian history from prehistoric times until the present day; Palestinian society in all its diversity; the holy and historical sites, sites of contemporary importance (neighbourhoods, villages, the destroyed villages of 1948, refugee camps and Israeli settlements); and contemporary culture. It contains information to facilitate encounters with the local population (including addresses of organisations, institutions and resource people), as well as practical information on internal travel, food, personal safety and the like. Not satisfying itself with simply providing long lists of sites, restaurants, hotels, taxis, and museums, the expertise of the ATG is harnessed to promote encounters of high quality, all carefully designed to connect with their particular agendas.

We at the ATG, together with all the people who contributed to this guidebook and who eagerly await your visit, would like you to consider the book you are holding as a personal invitation to come and visit Palestine. We realise that the tragic political conflict that has engulfed us hardly encourages tourism, but it is precisely at this time that your visit will be most appreciated and welcomed. In the midst of the conflict you will discover a truly warm and hospitable people inhabiting a fascinating and significant country, ingeniously finding ways to live in the midst of conflict.

We would like to thank the organisations who have supported this important project, in particular "CCFD" Catholic Committee Against Hunger and for Development in France and Firedoll Foundation in USA. We are also grateful to all the people who have helped and invested a lot of time in preparing the first edition of the English guidebook, especially Angela Godfrey, Carol Scheller-Doyle, Dr. Walid Shomali, and Bailasan, as well as the ATG staff (Ayman Abu Zulof, Samer Kokaly, Jawad Musleh), and others who must excuse us for not mentioning their names, who have all helped in bringing this book to fruition by translation, collation and updating of information, editing, designing, providing its photos, maps and all other forms of information.

We are proud of this guidebook, which we see as another step towards an independent Palestine that will find its rightful place among the peoples of the world. We hope you appreciate its significance as much as you learn from it. We look forward to seeing you in our country, to hosting you, and to hearing your comments on both our tours and this guidebook.

Salaam, In Peace,

Rami Kassis
Executive Director
Alternative Tourism Group

CONTENTS

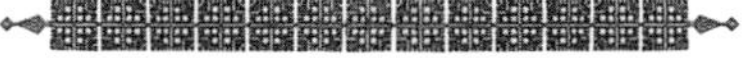

LIST OF FRAMED DOCUMENTS

INTRODUCTION

CHAPTER 1
LANDSCAPE

CHAPTER 2
HISTORY OF PALESTINE

CHAPTER 3
POPULATION AND SOCIETY

CHAPTER 4
CULTURE

CHAPTER 5
COLONISATION AND OCCUPATION

CHAPTER 6
RESTRICTIONS ON FREEDOM OF MOVEMENT

ITINERARIES

CHAPTER 1
JERUSALEM (AL-QUDS)

CHAPTER 2
THE WEST BANK

Jericho and the Dead Sea

Bethlehem

Hebron (Al-Khalil)

LIST OF TEXTS AND POEMS

LIST OF BIOGRAPHIES

LIST OF MAPS

INTRODUCTION

LOCAL MAPS

Introduction

CHAPTER 1
LANDSCAPE

Geography

Historical Palestine constitutes the western point of the arable lands of what is known as the Fertile Crescent, which curves around the Syrian Desert. Between the sea and the desert, the topography changes frequently, and often in sharp contrast, due to numerous movements in its surface formation and due to juxtaposition of its two very different subtropical climatic fronts: Mediterranean and desert climates. From the large fertile plains dominating the north, to the coastal plains in the west, the land relief rises suddenly in the east. The mountains of the West Bank, with their highest point at Jabal al-Assur (1015 m, in the Ramallah region), offer a wide range of landscapes. The mountain chain is grooved by deep valleys *(wadis)*, abundant for farming and wild vegetation. Further east, the rolling hills plunge into the depths of the Jordan Valley and the Dead Sea, which at 400 m below sea level is the lowest point on earth. Its record concentration of salt (290 g per litre at the surface) creates an unusual experience for swimming. To the south stretches the Negev (Naqab), a desert of rocks and mountains. The Jordan Valley is a continuation of the Afro-Syrian rift which separates the African tectonic plate from the Asiatic one. The shifting of these plates has created an extraordinary depression which has three parts: the East African rift, the Red Sea and the Dead Sea rift, which continues to the mountains of Lebanon. On either side of the Jordan River, the rock formations are sliding in opposite directions (1 cm per year). The correspondence between the geological formations is perfectly visible every 105 kilometres. A good illustration is the copper mines of Feinan in Jordan (north of Shobak) and their twin mines of Timna in the Arava (20 km north of the Gulf of Aqaba).

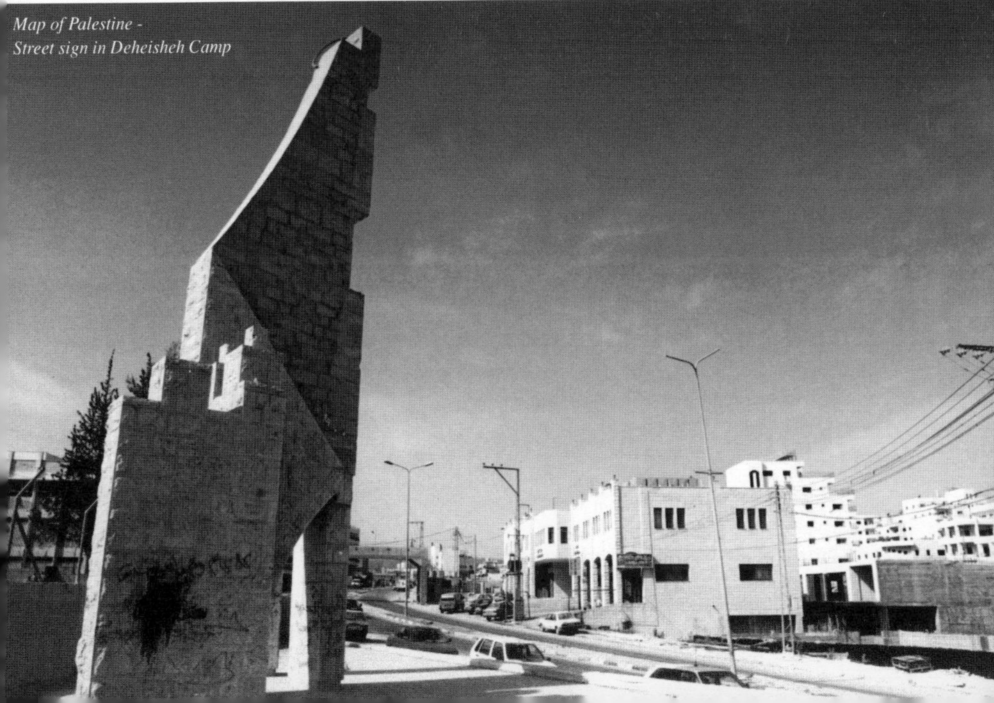
Map of Palestine -
Street sign in Deheisheh Camp

■ The Territories of the West Bank and the Gaza Strip

The Zionist movement was consecrated by the creation of the State of Israel on May 14, 1948. Its borders absorbed 78% of the territory of historical Palestine (26,000 sq. km); the West Bank and Gaza, with respective surface areas of 5,820 sq. km and 365 sq. km, constitute the remaining territories (22%). At its closest point to the West Bank at Tarqumia, the Gaza Strip is 50 km away, while the West Bank city of Qalqilia is less than 20 km from the Mediterranean. The coastal plain of Gaza is composed of sand dunes and fertile sandy sediments. Except for tufa (a porous limestone, *kurkar* in Arabic) there are no other rocks in this region. In contrast, the West Bank is dominated by low mountains: Mount Jarzim (881 m), Mount Nabi Samuel (875 m), and Mount Masharif or Mount Scopus (825 m). The rocks are principally composed of marine sediments (limestone and dolomite). The porosity of these rocks permits water to filter down to the non-porous strata, which supply water to the numerous aquifers in the region.

Administrative Divisions

The Declaration of Principles of the Oslo Accords on September 13, 1993, affirmed that *"the two parties* [Palestinians and Israelis] *consider that the West Bank and the Gaza Strip constitute one entire territorial entity, which shall be preserved as such during the entire interim period."* (Article IV)

Since 1993, however, the territorial integrity of the West Bank and the Gaza Strip has been increasingly depleted rather than reinforced! Following the Interim Agreement signed in Taba on September 28,1995, the West Bank and Gaza Strip were divided into three different administrative zones:

Area A: Here the Palestinian Authority (PA) exercises full sovereignty, representing approximately 3% of the West Bank and 60% of the Gaza Strip. Area A includes the territory of eight cities (Ramallah, Nablus, Jenin, Tulkarem, Qalqilia, Jericho, Bethlehem and part of Hebron) and some towns.

Area B: This area, 27% of the West Bank, includes rural zones (most of the villages and towns) where civil affairs are managed by the PA with the Israeli military authorities having security control over the territory.

Area C: This area corresponds to 70% of the West Bank and 40% of the Gaza Strip. Here, the PA has no authority. It includes sparsely populated areas (except for Hebron and neighbourhoods on the outskirts of Jerusalem), the peripheries of towns and villages, unpopulated land, industrial zones such as quarries, the Israeli settlement areas and the highway network.

This division has resulted in a "leopard skin" pattern of some 227 Palestinian islets or enclaves, which effectively separates the Gaza Strip from the West Bank and prevents the free circulation of goods or people between the autonomous Area A cities, which are thereby vulnerable to Israeli blockade at any time. East Jerusalem and its associated territories actually constitute a fourth unofficial zone, although the status of Jerusalem was postponed to a later stage in the Oslo Accords. Jerusalem having been annexed in 1980, the Palestinian population of Jerusalem has been subject to Israeli civil law ever since, although this status does not bestow citizenship or any such rights!

Oslo II (1995)

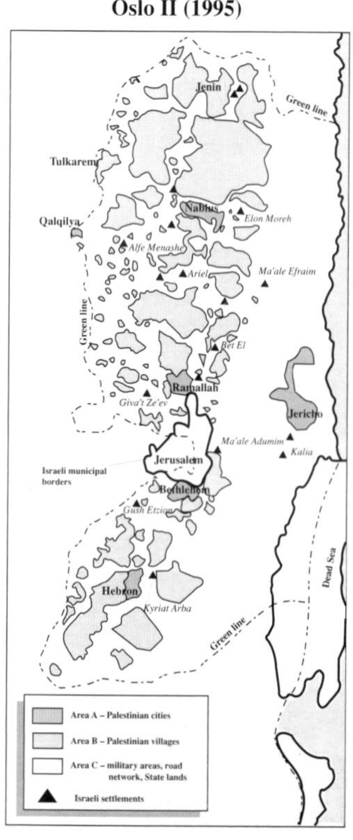

Flora and Fauna

"The olive tree wept, the pomegranate bent down, the lemon tree withered in the whole garden

The wind-swept seas, the rivers in fury, the birds lamented of love for free men (...)"

■ Rima Nasir Tarazi, *The dreams of my people*, 1985.

Adjusting to different habitats (Mediterranean, semi-arid, coastal plain) the flora and fauna are represented in all their diversity. Over 2,800 species of plants have been identified here on a comparatively small area. In the last century there were still large wooded areas, but they were sacrificed when the railway was built and wood was required for it. Today, fruit trees (olive, almond, orange, apricot ...) dominate the countryside while wild species such as pine, cypress, carob, acacia and turpentine trees are limited to certain regions (in the Galilee and on Mt. Carmel), on the edges of villages and in *wadis*.

The vast wild desert or semi-desert mountainous spaces are a refuge for various wildlife species of which some can be observed in the *wadis* in the early morning or at dusk. The Nubian ibex *(Capra ibex nubiana)* and the Dorcas gazelle *(Gazella dorcas)* are common on the hills of the West Bank. In Wadi Araba, another gazelle *(Gazella gazella)* and the rock daman *(Procavia capensis)*, a member of the marmot family, are amongst the most numerous and accessible animals. Predators also exist here: wolves *(Canis lupus)* are common in uninhabited areas, panthers *(Panthera pardus)* make their home in the arid mountains of the South Hebron Hills, and striped hyaena *(Hyaena hyaena)* live near remote villages where one sometimes hears their laughing cry.

The olive-tree

The supreme symbol of Palestine, the olive tree symbolises the deep connection of Palestinians to their land and has a primordial place in Palestinian agricultural activity. The cultivation of olive trees and the production of oil have been recorded since Neolithic times; ancient jars containing olive oil dating from 6000 BC have been discovered in Jericho. In the ancient city of Ekron *(Tel Miqne)*, over a hundred olive presses dating from the Iron Age have been discovered. The production capacity of this city of Philistine is estimated to have been half a million litres of olive oil annually. The very landscape has been sculpted by olive culture, in the creation of terraces to retain rain water. The traditional farming of the olive tree is a way of life as much in the West Bank as in the Galilee. In the West Bank, about 10 million olive trees cover the hills. Olive trees make up 80% of tree-covered land in the West Bank and Gaza. Olive oil comprises 15%-19% of the Palestinian agricultural output, depending on season. In 2004, 30,000 metric tons of oil were forecast to be pressed from 151,000 metric tons of olives, and 11,426 metric tons were to be processed as pickled olives; the export of Palestinian olive oil to Arab countries has nearly ceased, however, due to movement restrictions. Indeed, of the 277 olive presses in the OPT, only 215 are operating; as a result of the declining economic situation, 62 presses are temporarily closed.

Birds

Ornithologists are advised to bring bird guides with them, as Palestine is undoubtedly an ideal observation post for bird lovers. In spite of its scarcity of land, more than 470 species have been recorded. Thanks to the area's ecological diversity, various species either live here on a permanent basis or at least part of the year (349 species) or regularly pass through the coastal areas or the Jordan valley (121 species). The region is at the junction of the Asian, European and African continents and thanks to its wide variety of climate and topography, the region is a superb migratory route; ornithologists estimate that up to 500 million birds migrate in the spring and autumn. Peak migration time is between March 10 and April 20. The West Bank, blessed with many water sources, attracts the greatest number of birds. The Negev desert (Sahara en-Naqab) and the Jordan Valley also attract travellers thanks to their low barometric depressions or air thermals, which make it easy for birds to soar for long distances with a minimum of energy. The migration of storks is particularly remarkable and an impressive sight: Palestine and Israel are on the migratory route of 85% of the world's stork population.

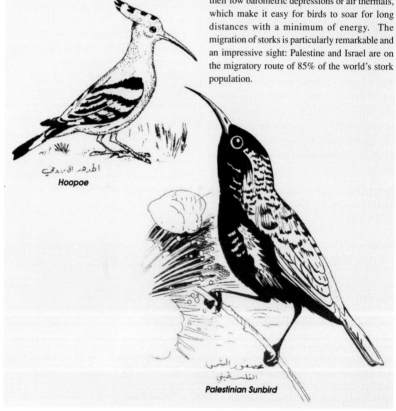

Hoopoe

عصفور الشمس الفلسطيني

Palestinian Sunbird

The Climate

One of the essential factors of the climate in Palestine is the sun, in summer as in winter. The climate is generally temperate with some variations depending on the region and altitude. If the days are hot or moderately warm for the entire year, the nights can be extremely fresh even in the summer. It should not be forgotten that most of the towns in the West Bank are at an altitude of about 800 m. It is important always to take suitable clothing. Winter is a season which can be rainy, but the rain never lasts for more than a few days. The spring sometimes brings hot winds which blow volatile sand storms from the Egyptian desert and the Saudi Arabian peninsula: this is the *hamsin*. Thus, temperatures remain cool at night in summer and during much of the winter, despite regular sunshine.

	Jan/Feb	**Mar/April**	**May/June**	**July/Aug**	**Sept/Oct**	**Nov/Dec**
Jerusalem	6/14	8/21	15/27	19/30	19/28	8/19
Gaza	9/19	10/22	17/28	21/31	16/30	9/25
Jericho	11/22	16/29	24/37	28/39	24/36	13/27
Nazareth	6/17	8/27	14/30	21/32	16/31	7/23

Minimum and maximum temperatures (°C)

"In Palestine, every summer night, when the south wind blows, dew descends like the water trickling down the gutters of The Distant Mosque [al-Aqsa]."

■ Al-Muqaddassi, tenth century.

CHAPTER 2

HISTORY OF PALESTINE

■ Prehistory

The most ancient traces of hominids in the Near East are bone fragments dating back 1.4 million years (Lower Palaeolithic), discovered in the Jordan Valley, at Tel 'Ubeidiya (north of Bissan). They are thought to belong to groups related to *Homo erectus*, who migrated from Africa to Asia and Europe along the Afro-Syrian Rift. Remains of *Homo erectus* are rare. The recent discovery of a skull fragment of the "Galilee Man" in the Zuttiyeh cave (north of Lake Tiberias) tells us something more about him. The fragment is between 300,000 to 250,000 years old, belonging - according to some scientists' opinion - to the ancient *Homo sapiens sapiens*. Far richer archaeological evidence exists from the Middle Palaeolithic Age (100,000 - 35,000 years) but this raises complex issues of the parallel and/or mixed evolution of Neanderthal man *(Homo sapiens neandertaliensis)* and modern man *(Homo sapiens sapiens)*. Over this long period, their material cultures were similar (use of fire - known to *Homo erectus*, flint, tools, burial rites, etc.). At Kebara (south of Mount Carmel), the bones of Neanderthals have been dated to as far back as 150,000 years; others, far more recent, again discovered at Kebara and at Amud, are 58,000 years old. These finds are therefore contemporary with modern man, while the oldest remains of modern man, approximately 92,000 year old, have been identified on the sites of es-Skhul cave and Jabal Qafzeh. These discoveries suggest a precocious differentiation of modern man *(Homo sapiens sapiens)* in Palestine - similar remains have come to light in Ethiopia and South Africa - and the simultaneous presence of Neanderthal man *(Homo sapiens neandertaliensis)*. Why the Neanderthals disappeared remains an enigma, although some specialist historians lean towards the theory of genetic absorption.

During the Upper Palaeolithic era, stone cultures diverged much more quickly. A new era succeeded it *circa* 12500 BC with the development of the Natoufian culture (see the *Shuqba Caves*, p. 240) which spread through the entire Near East. Natoufian communities settled down, forming the first permanent villages with permanent structures and round houses. Alongside these newly sedenterised people were itinerant (semi-nomadic) communities, mainly populating the peripheral regions (Negev and Transjordan). As they made their home in one place, these people began to domesticate their environment and produce goods necessary for subsistence. This phenomenon of the neo-Stone Age occurred at more or less the same pace throughout the entire Fertile Crescent. Between 9500 and 8000 BC, cereal crops were grown in Palestine. Later, in South Anatolia (south-eastern Turkey) and the Zagros (Iraq and Iran), animal domestication developed *circa* 7500 BC. Sedenterisation appears to have been the most decisive factor behind these changes; other significant innovations were the appearance of new techniques such as pottery making (*circa* 6000 BC), new social structures (the construction of large, rectangular houses, for example, reflects a more complex collective and hierarchical organisation than previously known), and a religion that worshipped gods.

■ The Chalcolithic Age (4000-3100 BC) and the Bronze Age (3100-1200 BC)

The Chalcolithic Age in Palestine was characterised by the introduction of copper extraction and manufacture, but also the reproduction of a model of socio-political organisation already present in Mesopotamia. With the first signs of urbanisation of Palestine in the Bronze Age, a social model that fostered new inequalities came into force; in traditional communities, a council of elders had maintained civic authority, but now an aristocracy replaced it and controlled a more or less extended area spreading out from the city-state. Antagonism between these economic and political centres (the city-states) and external power-seekers (the urban

centres of Egypt and Mesopotamia) as well as the semi-nomadic tribes (the majority of people in the region), manifested in reinforcement of the fortifications of those cities. Between 2200 and 1900 BC, incursions by these tribes put an end to this first urban experience, not only in Palestine, but in the entire cultural area that the Egyptians termed "Asiatic" - that is to say, the countries of Sham and Mesopotamia. After this interval, the urban network was reconstituted, striking a balance between areas governed by pastoral tribes and those administered by the cities. From the eighteenth to the fifteenth century BC, urban civilisation reached its peak, and its rulers, named the Hyksos (in Egyptian, "ruler of foreign countries") imposed their authority as far as the Nile Delta. In the fifteenth century BC, Pharaoh Thutmose III conquered the Hyksos and thus took control of the Syro-Palestinian region, appointing local suzerains as his intermediaries. Far from the influence of local-regional characteristics being dominant, the economic, diplomatic, literary and religious relations fell under the predominant influence of Egypt and Mesopotamia - whose Babylonian language became the *lingua franca* - which thus formed a single homogenous culture.

■ The Iron Age (1200 – 538 BC)

The arrival of the "Peoples of the Sea," as the Egyptians called them, on the shores of the Mediterranean, hastened the end of Egyptian rule in Palestine. This was also hastened by the breakdown of the old politico-economic city-state system. Amongst the new arrivals, the Philistines, the largest group, were installed in the south, in Egyptian territory. Their confederation of five cosmopolitan towns (Ascalan, Asdod, Gaza, Gath and Ekron) was ruled by a military and mercantile aristocracy. Their culture seems to have been a mixture of linguistic, political and religious traits which revealed Canaanite and Egyptian influences. The Philistines integrated harmoniously into the indigenous population. Unfortunately, not a single Philistine text is extant, which could otherwise shed light on the process of their fusion into the indigenous population, or their relations with their neighbouring powers, in particular the Egyptians, Judaeans and Israelites.

Whether in the interior of the land or in the mountains, power alternated between farmers settled in cultivated areas in the interior and tribes of semi-nomadic shepherds in mountainous areas or in the steppes or less fertile peripheries of the country. Palestine was divided into four distinct political sectors: the Galilee to the north, under Phoenician influence, the kingdoms of Israel and Judah in the centre and societies that were hard to administer but which were loyal to Arabo-Edomite control in the south. The towns' defences were fragile but guaranteed them an independent status for a while.

It is known today that the arrival of the Hebrews, coming in successive groups, came at the same time if not a little after that of the Philistines, and was peaceful. They were part of the waves of Aramaeans who settled all over the Near East, being accepted by the people already living there. The first millennium BC saw a profound evolution in politics and religion. One of the groups believing in Yahwism, or the worship of one God, Yahweh, supplanted the others: it became the official religion. It was this millennium that saw the birth and development of the Bible, created in different stages, and coming as a response to monotheism. Six hundred years earlier, Pharoah Akhenaton had had the plural of the word "God" obliterated in all Egyptian temples, an undertaking which had been only partially completed. The slow process of political and social maturity had - over time - stimulated religious and intellectual activity, of which the Old Testament offers some choice examples. *Circa* 1000 BC, King David established his authority in Jerusalem and the surrounding area. In their effort to establish a national identity, the different regions created an ideological and religious heritage which was inevitably influenced by their neighbours: dynastic genealogies and theories of the creation of the world owed something to Mesopotamian and Egyptian myth, as did the adaptation of certain rites and rituals, and so forth. The God of the Israelites (Yahweh) slowly emerged supreme over the multiple oriental divinities: *"You shall not go after other gods, of the gods of the people which are round about you."* (Deuteronomy 6:14) The Prophets were responsible for defining acceptable or unacceptable behaviour.

Royal scribes of the court sang the praises of the Jerusalem dynasty: *"And Solomon, the son of David, was strengthened in his kingdom, and the Lord his God was with him and magnified him exceedingly."* (2 Chronicles 1:1) The little kingdom was overshadowed for a long time by its more glorious neighbour Israel, until the final capture of the latter in 722 BC after repeated coups by the Neo-Assyrians (Israel lasted merely a little more than 200 years after its establishment).

At the time of the Neo-Assyrian conquest (722-586 BC), the Syro-Palestinian kingdoms were first obliged to pay tribute to the conqueror and were then transformed into Assyrian provinces. This event marked the end of their independence. Only Judaea and, further south, the Arab kingdoms maintained some autonomy. The coastal principalities and the kingdom of Samaria were destroyed, and their populations suffered deportation carried out in proportion to their resistance. As to Samaria, the Old Testament suggests that 27,000 people were deported, while most of the population were allowed to stay. This policy of deporting the population, common practice throughout the empire, enabled the conqueror to reinforce the Assyrian campaign by crushing local power. Population transfers, however, were practised in two senses. The kingdom of Judaea, for example, gained much by offering asylum in 722 BC to the banished Samarian aristocratic class which had been dispersed after the crushing of Israel, during the fall of Samaria. Jerusalem became a dynamic intellectual and religious centre based on the theme of an ingathering of the Diaspora by divine protection: *"Thou shalt have no other gods before me."* (Exodus 20:3) In the second half of the sixth century BC, the monotheism affirmed: *"Look unto me, and be ye saved, all the ends of the earth: for I am God, and there is none else."* (Isaiah 45:22)

Politics unceasingly reinforced religion. Moreover, influences coming from across the sea, from the Greek world, intensified. Cultural and religious exchanges followed in the wake of commerce. The idea of one unique god became progressively forged; the different kingdoms centred their official religion on the worship of one national god. Israel associated its God with the national temple, and the other kingdoms also consecrated a sacred place to their god. Popular religious practices inherited from the old Canaanite roots had not disappeared, however, and continued to perpetuate the antique religious unity of the Orient. Ancient agricultural rituals and fertility rites were deeply ingrained in local tradition everywhere. Even in Israel, nature religions jealous of the unique God continued to be practised for a long time alongside the worship of Yahweh. The exact moment when monotheism triumphed in the form we know it today is the object of lively discussion among historians of religion; some say that it appeared only in the Hellenistic period, with the encounter with Greek philosophy.

The neo-Babylonian conquest precipitated the fall of proud Jerusalem in 586 BC, sending its inhabitants into the Exile to Babylon. The kings of Gaza and Jerusalem (Zedekiah), with their families, priests and other officials thus came into contact with the highest civilization of their time. Those who returned in 538 BC brought precious political and religious knowledge back with them, which those who had stayed did not possess. They re-established Jerusalem on a strong ideological base in the midst of a changing world: the mixture of populations had given a new unity to the Orient. Aramaic had become the empire's *lingua franca*. But the Greek world was preparing to descend on the Levant...

This is the period when the traditions found in the Torah or Pentateuch (Genesis, Exodus, Leviticus, Numbers and Deuteronomy - also known as the Five Books of Moses), as well as the "historic" revisions of the texts (Joshua, Judges, Kings and Samuel) were compiled. Jewish culture was strengthened by its opposition to the increasingly pervasive hellenisation. The priestly hierarchy put an unprecedented emphasis on the sanctity of Jerusalem and the centrality of the (Second) Temple. Their intolerance of pagan religions took the form of the destruction of ancient places of worship which were dedicated to traditional deities in Judaea and threatened even the Samaritans who had no intention of giving up, despite all, their temple on Mt. Jarzim.

■ The Persian period (538 - 332 BC)

The Persian Achemenide kings struck up alliances with exiled aristocrats in order to oust the regional authorities loyal to their Babylonian rulers. This strategy was common throughout the vast Persian Empire from Egypt to present-day Pakistan. The Persian desire to take political, economic and spiritual power did not pass without arousing much resistance in the region; the most striking example was the conflict between the Judaeans and the Samaritans. During the two centuries of Persian domination, the region was divided into small provinces amongst which the most prosperous were undoubtedly the maritime cities, open to Mediterranean trade, particularly with Greece. At this time, the Phoenician suzerains (Tyre and Sidon) controlled the entire Mediterranean Levantine coast, with the exception of Gaza — the most important urban centre in the region, whose longstanding links with Greece were a prelude to its later hellenisation.

■ The Hellenistic Period (332-63 BC)

With the constitution of the Hellenistic Empire by Alexander the Great, and then its dismantling, Palestine became a buffer zone between the Ptolemaic and Seleucid monarchies. Ptolemy and Seleucus, Alexander's longstanding Greek generals, took control of Egypt and Syria respectively, while Palestine rotated between the two. A process of hellenisation was engaged: Greek became the official language of the administration in Palestine, and the use of a Greek name together with a Semitic name became common, at least among the elite; cities were founded or reorganised on the lines of the Greek state or *polis*, but although the elite class embraced Hellenisation, the people were more reserved. During the second century BC, a social and political crisis gave rise to an expansionist movement issuing from Judaea, the only region of Palestine where the majority of the population was Jewish. The cities along the coast and in the interior (Gaza, Samaria and the north of Transjordan) fell provisionally under the dominance of the Maccabee and then the Hasmonean dynasties. Judaism was imposed as the sole religion of the kingdom. During the reign of the Maccabees, the "purification" of territory was effected by deportations, massacres and forced conversions (children had to be circumcised). The Kingdom of Judaea under the Hasmoneans was more open-minded in religious matters and accorded with the hellenisation of the region, as indicated by the use of Greek certificates, names, and the Greek language. Greek remained the official administrative language; Aramaic, the language in daily use; Hebrew the religious language, reserved for the study of holy texts and religious services.

■ The Roman Period (63 BC - 324 AD)

Rome conquered Palestine after it had first become involved in internal political struggles there during the Hasmonean dynasty. Pompey reduced Judaea to the state of a client state. From 37 to 4 BC, the Roman Empire supported a man, loyal to Rome and whom they trusted, who ruled the province under the title of king (having been crowned in Rome in 40 AD by the Senate): Herod the Great, the son of an Arab princess and an Edomite. Herod kept Judaism as the official religion of the royal court, while also allowing the worship of Graeco-Roman gods and the imperial cult. He was a great patron of Graeco-Roman culture and was especially famed for his construction of palaces, temples and cities. On his death, his kingdom was absorbed by the Roman province of Syria, and Caesarea became the capital of the Roman governor. Herod had spent state money lavishly; he also confiscated and divided up the land for his veteran soldiers and the Roman generals, causing a general impoverishment of the peasant masses. Popular revolts, tinged with messianic overtones, increased during the first century AD. In 132 AD, Hadrian announced the restoration of Jerusalem as a Roman colony, renamed Aelia Capitolina, dedicated to Jupiter Capitolina, and his prohibition of circumcision of infants then detonated a new revolt in the province of Palaestina Prima. The measure banning circumcision was not applied, but Jews were banned from entering Jerusalem, now named Aelia Capitolina, except for one day each year when they were permitted to wail at the ruins of the temple. Palestine became the scene of frequent religious confrontations between pagans, Samaritans, Jews and the emerging Christian sects. From the end of the first century AD, Pharisee rabbis excluded Nazarenes, (the disciples of Jesus), from the synagogues. Still an obscure period, nevertheless it was a decisive time for the development of Christianity, which was seeking its identity and spreading with varying success. Critics of Christian currents note that conflicts between different groups of converts (whose interpretations were influenced by Judaism or paganism) was characteristic of this period of the formation of Christianity.

■ The Byzantine Period (324-638 AD)

In 324 AD, Emperor Constantine made Byzantium the capital of the new Eastern Roman Empire. The policy in favour of Christians marked a major shift in the empire and confirmed the edicts of tolerance towards Christianity made by Emperor Galeius (311 AD), and Emperor Constantine's Edict of Milan in 313 AD. This decision contributed to the rapid development of Christian religious communities, bringing a vast wave of pilgrims to Palestine, which began to be known as the Holy Land of the Christians. The large numbers of pilgrims boosted commerce and the development of handiwork by artisans (silk, leather, etc.) and agriculture, which was controlled by the religious foundations - churches and monasteries, the land owners of vast properties. However, pagan rites lasted until Emperor Justinian forbade freedom to those cults; finally, at the end of a long process, towards the middle of the sixth century, Christianity was imposed by imperial command when Justinian in 529 AD ordered all pagans to be baptised.

■ The Islamic Period (638-1516 AD)

The victory of the Arab-Muslim armies at the battle of Yarmuk (636 AD or 14 of the Hegira) sounded the end of Byzantine rule in the Near East. Yarmuk heralded a new era: a large number of the region's inhabitants (Christians, Samaritans and Jews) progressively converted to Islam, and the almost complete adoption of Arabic as the language of the region.

Palestine, together with its Moslem, Christian, Jewish and Samaritan components, from now on was assimilated into the Arab Empire, as Palestine was integrated into the vast Umayyad Caliphate (661-749) and then ruled by its successor, the Abbassid Caliphate (750-969). It remained important because of the numerous pilgrimage routes across it and because of the statute of the holy city of Jerusalem (Beit al-Maqdis - the House of the Sanctuary). The political and cultural structures were maintained and the new rule was greatly strengthened by the support of the well-established Christian landowners. At the end of the tenth century, the power base was reinstated to the interior of the country as the Fatimid dynasty began its conquest of Palestine, taking it from the Baghdad-based caliphate: local powers also rebelled, most notably the Bedouin tribe of Banu Jarrah who tried to create an independent state. But new outside forces were preparing to conquer Palestine. In 1070, the Seljuks, a Turkish Sunni dynasty, took Jerusalem and tried to create a kingdom in Palestine and in southern Syria, in the name of the struggle against the Fatimid Shiites.

Palestine under the Umayyads and Abbassids (661-970)

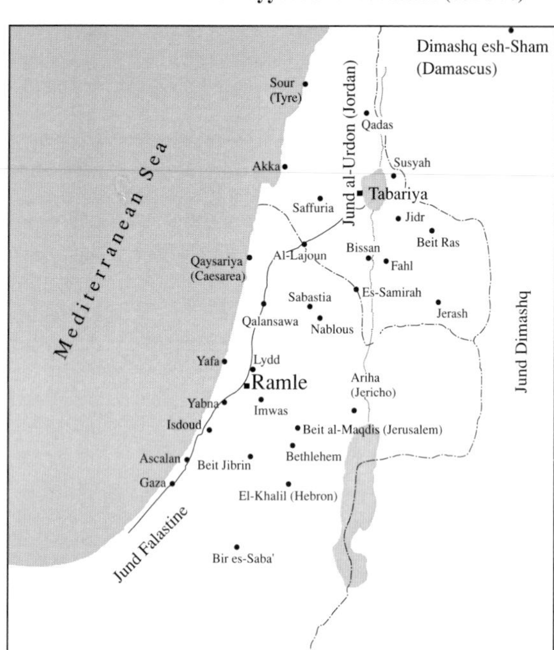

These power struggles and the parcelling out of territory created favourable conditions for Western ambitions in the Near East and the formation of Latin states. The Crusades, launched by the papacy and supported by many kings or European lords, were promoted under the title of a "holy war," but they had political motives, whether to expand the power of the church in Rome, to establish a fiefdom, or to divert attention from the misery and violence in Europe. "*The crusades will turn the thirst for eternal salvation into plundering ardour.*" (G.Duby). In 1187, the forces of Salah ed-Din al-Ayyubi al-Kurdi (Saladin) (1138-1193), a Muslim leader originally from Kurdistan, put an end to the first Latin kingdom in Jerusalem (1099-1187). After defeating the Crusader armies, in July 1187, at Hittin (near Tiberias), he liberated Jerusalem and all the ports of Palestine. During the Third Crusade (1189-1191), the king of France, Philippe Auguste, and the king of England, Richard the Lionheart, in 1191 took St. Jean d'Acre (Akka in Arabic), creating the kingdom of Acre, though they were not able to take Jerusalem. During the next century, Palestine was at the mercy of conquests, treaties, and still more conquests, and was partially occupied until the fall of the last Crusader fortifications (Jaffa in 1268, Ascalan in 1270, and Acre in 1291). After Mameluke Sultan Baybar took St. Jean d'Acre, Palestine remained under Mameluke rule (1250-1516); the Mamelukes were a military aristocracy which for two and a half centuries ruled over a prosperous state ranging from Syria to Egypt, in which Palestine was relegated to the status of a province of no political importance, and was far from any power struggles.

■ The Ottoman Period (1516-1918 AD)

From 1515 to 1517, the Ottoman armies under Sultan Selim I Yavuz ("the Cruel") seized power from the Mamelukes in Syria-Palestine, in Egypt, and in Western Arabia before extending their territory as far as the Maghreb (Morocco). The Ottomans (or Osmanlis), originally from Anatolia, took their name from one of their leaders, Othman, who died at the beginning of the fourteenth century. As a general policy, they respected existing political and religious structures wherever they conquered. Local leaders, the aristocracy and the different religious communities maintained their privileged status and were integrated into the Ottoman administration on condition that they pledge allegiance to the Sultan. Palestine was at first part of the administrative province of Damascus but became an independent province *(pachalik)* at the beginning of the eighteenth century; it was itself divided into three *sanjaks*: Acre, Nablus and Jerusalem. It was on these administrative bases that the pashas, or governors, supported by the local farmers, imposed order and collected taxes. During this period, the Palestinian countryside, and also the cities in the interior experienced a general decline. The diversion of commercial routes in favour of the Atlantic, after the discovery of the Cape Route (Vasco da Gama), diminished the commercial importance of the Palestinian ports (Acre, Haifa, Jaffa, Gaza) while the Sultan of the Sublime Port pursued a foreign policy of capitulations (economic and political concessions to the European powers and merchants) commencing in the sixteenth century. A first treaty of this kind was signed in 1535 between Suleyman the Magnificent and Francis I of France. The viceroy of Egypt, Mohammad Ali, took advantage of the Ottomans' weak defences and he governed Palestine from 1832 to 1840. The European powers supported the Ottoman Empire against Egypt, using their position to have an increasingly greater say in Turkish internal affairs. The ostensible need to *"protect"* Christians in the Orient and other minority groups became a favourite device to consolidate European presence on the ground. In the nineteenth century, Ottoman reforms on land ownership permitted a semi-feudal class to become owners of immense fiefdoms. Independent farmers and especially the ports Jaffa and Haifa and the towns, essentially Jerusalem, experienced an economic boom based on increased exports, soaring numbers of pilgrims and the establishment of European religious communities. *Circa* 1900, Palestine's population was 600,000 (87% Muslim, 10% Christian, and 3% Jewish). During World War I, the Palestinian population suffered from Turkish repression, forced mobilisation and requisitions. These final years of Ottoman domination contributed to fix in the collective memory the image of the Ottoman authority as parasitical and brutal.

Administrative borders of Syria and Palestine during the Ottoman period (second half of the nineteenth century)

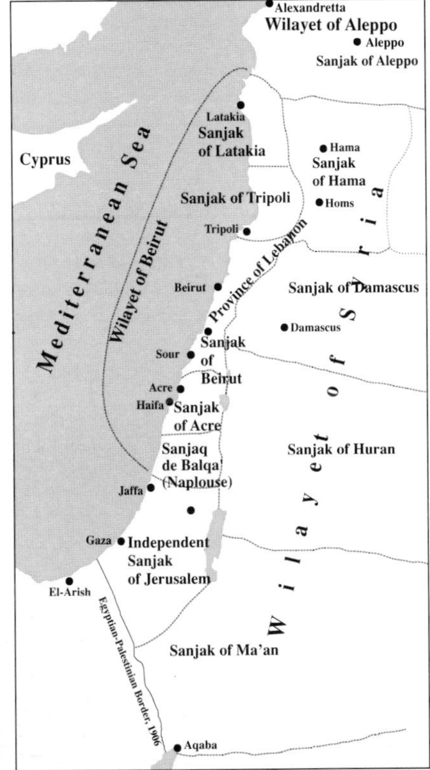

Zionism

Ever present in Europe in certain literary and political circles that were essentially Protestant, on the theme of "neo-Crusades," the idea of a Jewish colonisation of Palestine developed in the middle of the nineteenth century. Zionism emerged rapidly as a political movement reflecting the nationalist climate of opinion prevalent at that time with theories of the "non-assimilation of races," the inferiority of the native Arab population, and colonial expansion. In August 1897, Zionists gathered in Basel under the presidency of Theodor Herzl and adopted the basic programme of the Zionist movement; its central component was the colonisation of Palestine with the aim of creating of a Jewish state. Zionism justified itself by the alleged "Jewish right to the ownership of Palestine." With Zionism, the Palestinian people *"were destined to become foreigners in their own country, when admitting that they were permitted to remain where they were."* (Nathan Weinstock) The Zionist movement's major political ally was the United Kingdom. The Balfour Declaration of November 1917 was introduced by Balfour with "much pleasure in conveying ... our sympathy with Jewish Zionist aspirations which has been submitted to, and approved by, the Cabinet... His Majesty's Government view with favour the establishment in Palestine of a national home for the Jewish people, and will use their best endeavours to facilitate the achievement of this object, it being clearly understood that nothing shall be done which may prejudice the civil and religious rights of existing non-Jewish communities in Palestine..." . This declaration ignored the fact that the population at that time was more than 90% Arab Palestinian. In addition, the promise, in total contradiction to earlier promises made by the British in 1916 to support an independent Arab state on Arab land, naturally including Palestine, provoked consternation among Palestinians, and indeed Arabs in general. Between 1949 and 1953, the State of Israel gave judicial substance to Zionism by promulgating the "law of return," a law which gives the right to every Jew, whatever his origin, to settle in the State of Israel and to acquire Israeli citizenship. In 1975, Zionist ideology was condemned by the Assembly of the United Nations as "a form of racism and racial discrimination" (Resolution 3379, passed on November 10, 1975). However, Israeli Prime Minister Yitzhak Shamir managed to obtain the annulment of the resolution on December 16, 1991, at the final stage of the Madrid Conference, and to re-establish diplomatic relations with the republics of the former USSR: Zionism emerged victorious and a million Russian Jews immigrated to Israel in the following ten years.

In August-September 2001, international human rights organisations attending the International Conference Against Racism and Racial Discrimination in Durban, South Africa, condemned Israel as "a state practising racial discrimination" against its own citizens (the Palestinian citizens of Israel), and against the Palestinians in territories occupied since 1967.

■ Palestine under British Mandate

"Palestine presented a unique situation. We are dealing not with the wishes of an existing community but are consciously seeking to re-constitute a new community and definitely building for a numerical majority in the future..."

■ Lord Arthur J. Balfour, 1919.

In April 1920, the Supreme Council of the League of Nations put the Middle East under the guardianship of the two main colonial powers at that time, Great Britain and France. This year was designated by the Arabs as the Year of the Catastrophe. Great Britain supported a policy in favour of Zionism, against the indigenous (Palestinian) Arab people who, although representing 90% of the population in the 1920s, were simply referred to as the "non-Jewish community!" Representatives of the British Mandate tirelessly promoted Jewish immigration to Palestine and helped train Zionist military brigades. In this context, Winston Churchill declared: *"I challenged Wavell,* (an English general opposed to the idea of training a Jewish army) *and wrote to Dr. Weizmann authorising this army. Nevertheless, not a dog has barked!"* Representing 10% of the population of Palestine in 1917, the Jewish population increased to 17.7% in 1931 and to 28% in 1939. The Palestinian National Movement, in the hands of traditionally elite families, opposed these developments very ineffectually. Internal rivalries, and fear of losing favoured status or prerogatives in any direct confrontation with the mandatory powers, considerably weakened the movement. Nevertheless, popular resistance was expressed in frequent demonstrations against the British authorities and the Zionist settlers, with the principal demands being an end to Jewish

immigration and the repeal of the Balfour Declaration. Such revolts always voiced the Palestinians' fear of being dispossessed of their land; the purchase of land by European and American Zionist organisations (the Jewish National Fund and the Jewish Agency for Palestine) always involved the expulsion of peasants who had been farming the land according to traditional law; they would pay rent to an Arab absentee landowner in order to farm his land. For those landowners, their land was primarily a speculative investment. Zionist organisations built up population centres of farmers and soldiers on land they purchased, often using the collective structure of the kibbutz to develop the land. In 1929, following many expulsions of Palestinian peasants, on the one hand, and violation of the *Status Quo* concerning access of Jews to the Buraq Wall (Wailing Wall), on the other, a general revolt took place throughout Palestine. The Anglo-Zionist alliance was reinforced and British authorities increased their support for immigration more than ever. In Europe, anti-Semitism reached its climax in Nazi Germany, leading to an unprecedented genocide in which more than five million Jewish men, women and children were annihilated in concentration camps. Most, but not all Jews, especially those from central Europe, supported the Zionist movement. Jewish immigrants flowed into Palestine continuously while the Western powers closed their doors to them. Between 1932 and 1948, approximately 350,000 Jews immigrated to Palestine.

The Peel Partition Plan (1937)

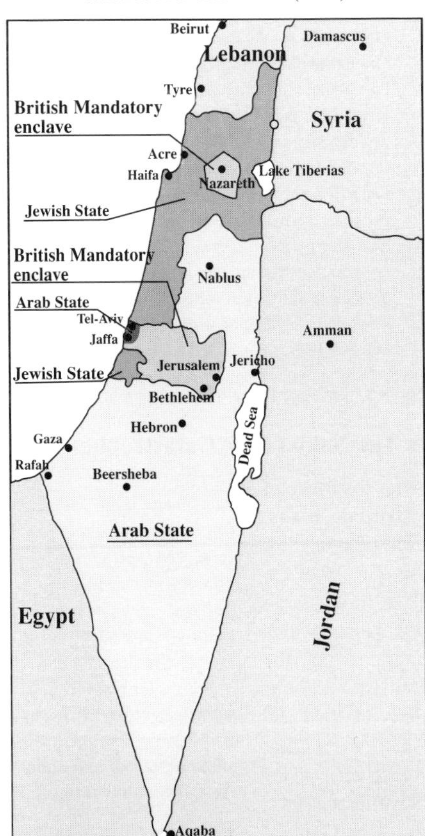

The Palestinian Revolution (1936-1939)

On April 21, 1936, a general strike was called in Jaffa. It was immediately adopted throughout Palestine. The Arab Supreme Council, founded the same month by the principal Palestinian political parties (The National Bloc, The Arab Palestinian Party, and The National Defence Party, among others) and led by the Mufti of Jerusalem, Haj Amin al-Husseini, directed the strike. In addition to advocating civil disobedience, underground resistance was formed by supporters of armed struggle which had been set up by the movement of Izz ed-Din al-Qassam, at the end of 1935. In 1938, numerous villages and even the Old City of Jerusalem were in the hands of the Palestinian resistance, supported by Arab volunteers under the command of Fawzi Qawuqji.

The Arab Supreme Council, for its part, increased its demands: it called for immediate independence for Palestine and an end to Jewish immigration. However, after rejecting the Council's idea to create a Palestinian Legislative Council in which all religious communities would be represented, the British mandatory forces, supported by the other colonial powers, developed a partition plan for Palestine. The first such plan was in 1937 (The Peel Commission); this partition plan suggested the creation of a Jewish state on 33% of the land in Palestine (Jewish property in Palestine at that time amounted to only 5.6% of the total territory). Lord Peel, chairman of the commission, proposed that the Palestinian inhabitants be expelled from all territories designated for the Jewish state.

From the beginning of the general strike and the boycott of all British institutions, the occupation authorities increased the measures of collective repression. These measures included mass arrests (5,679 Palestinians were put in prison or detention camps in the year 1939 alone), demolition of thousands of houses (amongst them, those of Jaffa's Old City), closure of schools, requisitions, and other harassments. For its part, the Zionist movement took advantage of this climate of repression to reduce the quota for Arab workers and build a port on the outskirts of Jaffa called Tel-Aviv. Zionist authorities worked closely with the British army, who trained a special Anglo-Jewish Alliance in June 1938; together they conducted night raids against Palestinian villages. In 1939, the British trained and armed a Jewish police force for the Jewish settlements. Helpless to stop the Palestinian uprising, and on the brink of conflict in Europe, the British authorities decided to appease Arab opinion by inviting representatives of the various Arab countries to a conference organised in London in February 1939. New recommendations were released there in a government White Paper. It notably called for restraint in Jewish immigration to Palestine, and fixed a quota of 15,000 people per year; it envisaged the possibility of the creation of a unitary and independent State of Palestine, after a transition period of 10 years. These restrictions on Jewish immigration met mounting hostility from Zionist organisations towards the mandatory authorities. In October 1939, the paramilitary Stern Gang, led by Yitzhak Shamir, even called for an alliance with the Axis powers (Berlin-Rome-Tokyo); but, however, it was finally an alliance with the United States, whose president in August 1945 backed the immigration of 100,000 Jews, that created a level of cohesion among all Zionist organisations.

■ The Nakba (The Catastrophe)

"[...] While those who had fled in the early days of the conflict had been able to take with them some personal effects and assets, many of the latecomers were deprived of everything except the clothes in which they stood, and apart from their homes (many of which were destroyed), lost all furniture and assets and even their tools of trade."

■ Count Folke Bernadotte, UN Mediator for Palestine, and representative of the Red Cross in Europe during the Second World War.

After a variety of partition plans, even proposals for the transfer of the Palestinian Arab population (which came from the British Labour Party in 1944 and American President Roosevelt), on 29 November, 1947, the UN General Assembly approved a partition plan - Resolution 181. Although Jews owned in private or collective property holdings only 6.5% of the lands in Palestine, the Jewish state was awarded 56.5% of the territory of Palestine, and the Arab state, 42.9% in the November 29, 1947 UN partition plan. The Zionist policies were victorious. The second stage of their strategy - a policy of terror and military conquest - would lead to the creation of the State of Israel. In December 1947, the Zionist movement launched a policy of terror, known by the code name "Plan C" (in Hebrew *"Tochnit Gimmel," gimmel* being the Hebrew alphabet's third letter. Attacks against the Palestinian civil population became frequent but were also mounted against British troops; on January 4, 1948, the Lehi (which included the notorious Stern Gang) killed 26 Palestinians in a car bomb attack on the Old Government House in

I

II

III

IV

Exile 1948

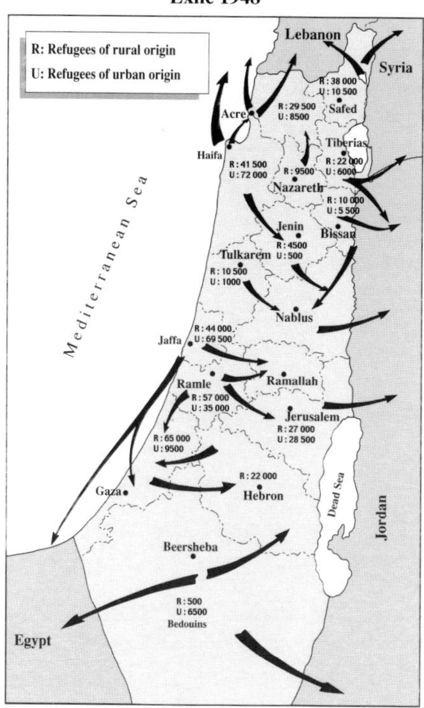

Jaffa. On January 5, 1948, an assault by the Hagana on the Semiramis Hotel in the Jerusalem neighbourhood of Qatamon killed 20 people, mostly Palestinian.

The most notorious and murderous attack was committed by the Irgun, with Menachem Begin in command, on July 22, 1946, when it blew up the headquarters of the British army, which had been established at the King David Hotel in Jerusalem: ninety-three British, Arabs and Jews died in the blast. Shortly before cessation of the British Mandate and the effective departure of British troops, a large-scale offensive was launched in April 1948 throughout Palestine under Plan D (in Hebrew: *"Tochnit Dalet,"* *dalet* being the fourth letter of the Hebrew alphabet). The Zionist "War of Independence" was accompanied by the systematic ethnic cleansing of Palestinian towns and villages. This first war for Palestine (April 4, 1948 - May 15, 1948) was fought against some 2,500 Palestinian combatants, reinforced by 4,000 Arab volunteers, by 50,000 Hagana soldiers. Massacres of Palestinian civilians increased. On April 9, 1948, between 100 to 254 Palestinians (depending on conflicting reports) in Deir Yassin, a village on the outskirts of Jerusalem, were massacred and the survivors deported to the other side of the Demarcation Line [see *Deir Yassin*, p. 146]. The shock was immense, especially since Abd al-Qader al-Husseini, commander of the Palestinian resistance in the Jerusalem region, had been killed the day before at Qastal, a strategic point on the Jerusalem-Jaffa road. By the time of the declaration of the establishment of the State of Israel (May 14, 1948), some 350,000 Palestinians had become refugees, followed by 500,000 additional refugees in the following months. For Palestinians, 1948 was the year of the Catastrophe (en-Nakba), the year of the destruction of the land and the year of exile.

The Arab coalition states held back from any military commitment until the day after the declaration of the State of Israel. Only then did

they intervene and only in the regions not yet under Zionist control, and so the first Israeli-Arab war broke out (May 15, 1948 - January 1949). However, the power balance remained fundamentally unequal in terms of men mobilised (less than 14,000 on the Arab side), equipment and strategy. The Stern Gang, led by Yitzhak Shamir (leader of the Likud Party in the 1980s and Prime Minister several times between 1983 to 1992), - intending to overcome all obstacles in the path of the Zionist project - claimed responsibility for the assassination of the UN Mediator in Palestine, Count Folke Bernadotte, on September 17, 1948: Bernadotte having voiced strenuous objections to the Zionist policy of ethnocide. At the time of the Armistice Agreement with Egypt in February 1949, the State of Israel was in control of 78% of historical Palestine, much more than had ever been projected by the 1947 UN partition plan. The remaining part was annexed by King Abdullah of Transjordan and known as the West Bank, while a strip of land south of Gaza (the Gaza Strip) was placed under Egyptian military administration.

UN Partition Plan for Palestine (1947) and Armistice Line of 1949

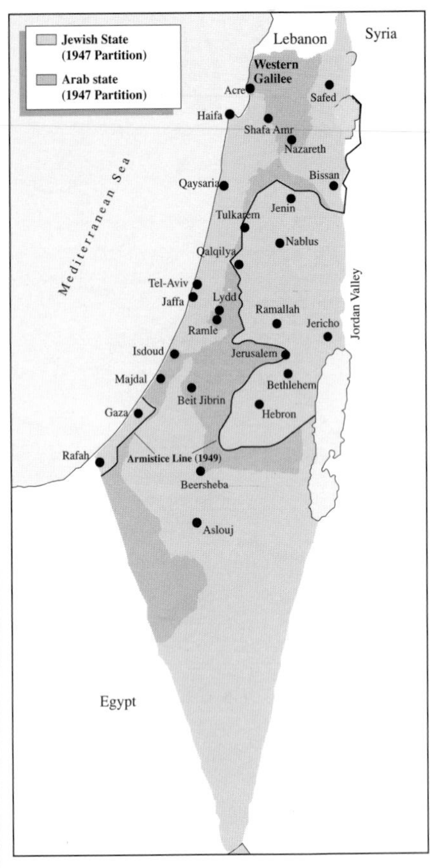

■ The Palestinian resistance and the creation of the Palestine Liberation Organisation (PLO)

> *"With our souls and with our blood, we offer you our lives, martyr. With our souls and with our blood, we offer you our lives, Palestine"*

During the 1950s, the expulsions and massacres continued: as examples, there was the expulsion of the people of 13 small villages in Wadi 'Ara (to the south of the Galilee) in February 1951, and the people of al-Majdal town (Ashkelon has been constructed on its site) in April 1951. In October 1953, 53 Palestinians were killed when houses in the village of Qibya (in the district of Qalqilya) were bombarded. In 1956, Palestinians enthusiastically supported Egyptian president Jamal Abdul Nasser and the nationalisation of the Suez Canal. The tripartite (Anglo-Franco-Israeli) aggression against Egypt permitted the State of Israel to occupy the Gaza Strip and part of Sinai for several months. On November 3, 1956, Israeli forces massacred more than 273 Palestinian civilians in the refugee camp of Khan Younis and on November 12, 1956 over 100 Palestinian civilians were massacred in the Rafah refugee camp. At this time, there was a bloody repression carried out against Palestinians of 48 (the massacre of 49 Palestinians in the village of Kufr Qassem, near Tel Aviv, in October 1956), who had rallied to the cause of Arab nationalism. [see *Kufr Qassem*, p. 358].

From 1949 onwards, small groups of resistance fighters carried out military operations against the State of Israel, whose soldiers increased their attacks on border villages and Gaza. In 1959, a group of fighters formed a project to unite militants in different places into one organisation which would take up the fight for freedom. They hoped to push the Arab states into action on their behalf and to stimulate an armed struggle on the model of the Algerian and Vietnamese liberation struggles. These men, who bore the names Yasser Arafat (Abu Ammar), Khalil al-Wazir (Abu Jihad), Salah Khalaf (Abu Iyad) and Yusef en-Najjar founded the underground Fatah movement. Its military branch, al-Assifa (the Storm), carried out its first operation on January 1, 1965. In the same years, the Arab Nationalist Movement (ANM) also embarked on the path of armed struggle. These military organisations had such names as "The Heroes of Return," or "Youth Organisation for Vengeance." Key figures in the Palestinian section of the ANM, among them Dr. George Habash (al-Hakim), Dr. Wadi' Haddad, Mustapha Ali Zabri (Abu Ali Mustapha) and Ghassan Kanafani, inaugurated the Popular Front for the Liberation of Palestine (PFLP) after the Arab defeat of 1967.

■ The Naksa (the Tragedy)

In June 1967, the State of Israel launched a new war by unleashing a surprise attack against Egypt, Jordan, and Syria, and occupied the West Bank, Gaza, the Sinai and the Golan Heights. More than 300,000 Palestinians became exiles, one-third of whom were refugees of 1948. A brutal repression

fell on Gaza and on the West Bank. In response to this new occupation, the UN passed Resolution 242 on 29 November, 1967 (20 years after the Partition Plan!), a vague document which neither stated which territories Israel should withdraw from nor gave a time frame for a withdrawal, and which implicitly accepted as borders the armistice lines of the 1948 war (in total contradiction to Resolution 181). The defeat of the Arab armies led to an unprecedented development: Palestinian resistance groups started to take up the war of liberation. They rejected *en masse* Resolution 242 which *"ignores the national rights of the Palestinian people. It does not mention the existence of these people"* (Fatah Central Committee). On March 21, 1968, the Palestinian resistance movement, at the cost of heavy losses, repulsed an Israeli attack on the Karameh refugee camp (on the eastern bank of the Jordan Valley, north of Shuneh). This Palestinian victory produced a strong psychological effect. The myth of Israeli invincibility was shaken. Shortly after the 1967 occupation, the resistance groups joined the same direction as the Palestine Liberation Organisation (PLO) (created by an initiative of Nasser in 1964), and elected Yasser Arafat (Abu Ammar) as president in 1969. The resistance took root in Jordan, Syria and Lebanon, and took part in all functions of life of Palestinians in exile: education, health, economy, local police, trade unions and military training. The fate of the Palestinian people was ignored by the international community; the Palestinian organisations brought their struggle to the international scene with three objectives: to remind the world of the Palestinian people's existence by spectacular actions (hi-jacking planes and hostage taking), to rally progressive forces and to threaten the State of Israel's interests wherever they existed. Palestinian militant Leila Khaled, insisted: "*He* (my oppressor) *is not in a position to make an impartial judgment (...) inasmuch as it is he who stole my house, and drove my people and me out of our land. I feel absolutely no obligation to listen to someone who defines morality and legality on his own terms and who, because he has the power and the means to justify his inhuman conduct, decides to impose his conception of law and ethics (...). On the other hand, if I feel morally obliged to do something, it is to resist and fight to the death against the moral corruption of this enemy.*" The repression of these resistance movements came to a head in Jordan in 1970. The American "peace" plan, called the Rogers Plan, which called for a cease-fire, also laid the ground for crushing Palestinian resistance, which had become too pre-eminent in Amman. King Hussein of Jordan used it to kill thousands, mainly Palestinians, in September 1970 (Black September), then in 1971 attacked the last Palestinian guerrilla strongholds in the Ajloun mountains. The United States, but also the Israeli army, threatened to retaliate should any progressive Arab government dare to intervene in favour of the Palestinians. Defeated, the resistance movement moved to Lebanon, the last remaining front outside Palestine.

■ From the Lebanese Civil War to the Israeli invasion

> *"They crucified a woman alive. I saw her body, arms stretched out, covered with flies, but especially at the ends of her two hands, on the ten holes of black coagulated blood: they had cut off her fingertips, her phalanxes; could that be the origin of their name, I wondered?"*
>
> ■ Jean Genet, An Amorous Captive

In 1975, the Lebanese civil war broke out, largely stimulated by Israel and the United States. Palestinian refugee camps around Beirut were besieged in 1976 and systematically bombarded; many were entirely destroyed by Phalangist soldiers and Israeli forces under the command of the Israeli Minister of Defence, Shimon Peres.

The Israelis invaded the south of the country on March 15, 1978, hoping to strike a fatal blow to Palestinian and Lebanese resistance in Lebanon; after turning over the positions they had captured to the Phalange militias, they withdrew. At the same time, Egyptian President Sadat, paying no heed to the united Arab front, negotiated and signed the Camp David Agreement with his Israeli and American partners in September 1978, accords which allowed Israel to concentrate all its military forces on the northern border. Having done so, in June 1982, the State of Israel invaded Lebanon again with the objective of "cleansing" Beirut of the PLO and the Lebanese national movement, and to place an ally as the head of state. The siege was horrendous: fragmentation bombs were dropped on the cities and camps; some 70% of the houses in Rashidiya and Ein al-Hilweh refugee camps were entirely destroyed. The war cost, according to estimates, between 10,000 and 30,000 Lebanese and Palestinian lives. In August 1982, the major powers evacuated a group of PLO fighters from Lebanon; its leaders went to Tunis, where they established their headquarters. At the end of August, UN forces withdrew from the Lebanese capital, Beirut, leaving the field open to a new wave of Israeli aggression. On September 15, the Israeli army entered West Beirut "to keep the peace." From September 16-18, the horror culminated in the camps of Sabra and Shatila, where over 3,000 unarmed Palestinian refugees in the refugee camps of Sabra and Shatila were massacred by the Lebanese militias, under the direction and supervision of the Israeli army, which controlled all entrances to the camps.

The camps of South Lebanon remained under the control of the Israelis and the Lebanese militias until 1985, when the Israeli army withdrew farther south. At the same time, the conflict between the different Arab factions increased, culminating in 1987. Several refugee camps were destroyed.

Faced with the Occupation and its corollaries (repression, deportation, land confiscation, settlements, humiliations, etc.), the Palestinians in the Occupied Territories relit the torch of their struggle. On December 9, 1987, the Intifada (in Arabic "shaking off") erupted.

The entire Palestinian society took part in it, responding to the orders of the Unified Command of the Intifada or to the calls of the Islamic Resistance Movement (Hamas, which was founded on December 14, 1988). This struggle

■ Intifada

I call you, I shake your hands
I kiss the earth under your shoes
And I say: I sacrifice myself for you

I offer you, in my eyes, the light
I offer you, of my heart, the warmth
The tragedy that I live
Is my part of your tragedies
I call you....

In my country, I have never humbled myself
Nor bent my shoulders
Against my oppressors I have stood tall
An orphan, deprived and barefoot
I call you ...

In the palm of my hands, I have borne my blood
I have never lowered my colours to half-mast.
I have kept the grass green
On the tombs of my ancestors
I call you ...

■ Tawfiq Zayyad

This poem has been a hymn to resistance since the First Intifada.

”

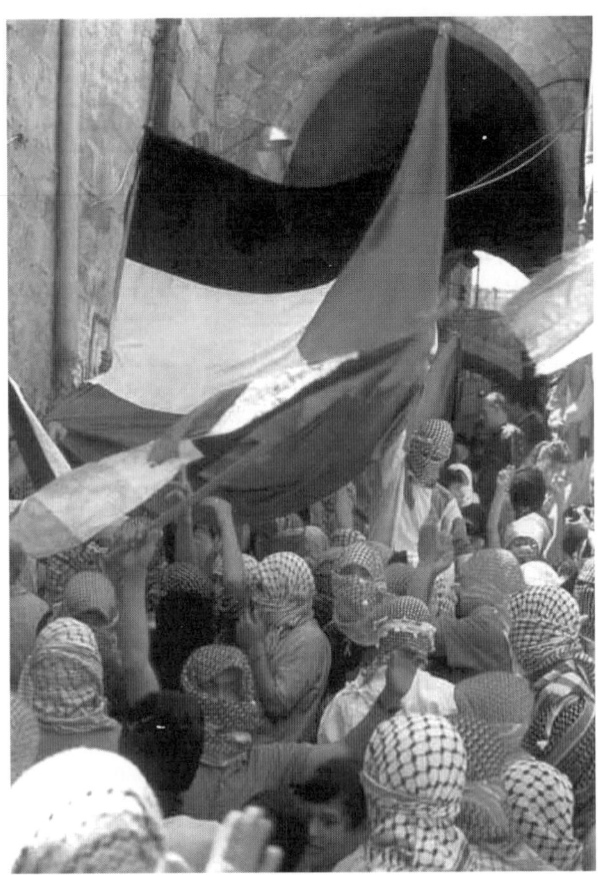

against Israeli occupation included a policy of confronting Israeli soldiers and settlers, actions of civil disobedience (refusal to pay taxes or fines, strikes, boycott of Israeli products, etc.) and a reorganisation of civil society through popular committees of solidarity and mutual assistance, responsible especially for food supplies, education, and health.

- **Repression**

To what the Israeli government labelled as "subversion," Yitzhak Rabin as Minister of Defence, then as Prime Minister of the coalition government - Yitzhak Shamir and Ariel Sharon of the Likud Party and Yitzhak Rabin and Shimon Peres of the Labour Party - applied a policy called "force, power and blows" or the policy of "broken bones ." A state of siege was declared, giving the occupying powers a free hand to apply military law with force in the West Bank and Gaza. Curfews were increased; tens of thousands of Palestinians were beaten, imprisoned and tortured, including children; the houses of militants were demolished under guise of reprisal. Some 1,400 Palestinian civilians were killed, and tens of thousands injured, many handicapped for life. The repression touched all areas of life: the closure of schools and universities, clinics and hospitals.

Human rights violations (December 1987 to June 1994)

Palestinians killed:	
Bullets	1 222
Tear gas	94
Beaten to death	73
Victims :	
Children (< 16 years)	362
Women (> 16 years)	40
Men (> 16 years)	987
Injured	130 787

Deported	489
Imprisoned	18 211
Curfews[1]	17 488
Trees uprooted or cut down	185 489
Lands confiscated[2]	41 205
Houses demolished	2 019

1. Total number of days of curfew in the West Bank and the Gaza Strip
2. In hectares (10 dunums = ~ 1 hectare = 2.47 acres

In 1990-91, most Palestinians condemned the collusion of Kuwait and America in the war against Iraq, and viewed this international intervention as applying a double standard: even when at the same time Israeli repression in the territories occupied after '67 was redoubled. One of the longest curfews since the beginning of the Intifada was imposed on Palestinian cities, camps and villages. When many Iraqi Scud missiles hit the Tel-Aviv region, Palestinians reacted enthusiastically; despite their repeated pleas for Arab or international intervention, those pleas had gone unheard.

■ Israeli-Palestinian Negotiations

The Madrid Conference (October 1991) reaffirmed the primacy of the Palestine Liberation Organisation (PLO) as the institutional body representing the Palestinian people. For his part, the Israeli Prime Minister, Yitzhak Shamir, resumed diplomatic relations with Moscow and obtained abrogation, under American pressure, from the General Assembly of the UN, of the UN resolution which had condemned Zionism as a "form of racism and racial discrimination" (Resolution 3379, November 10, 1975). Secret negotiations which had taken place in Oslo led to a signed agreement in Washington on September 13, 1993. This predicted the constitution of a Palestinian Council to manage the transition to autonomy (for an interim period of five years), the transfer of power in matters of education and health, the creation of a Palestinian police force, and the withdrawal of the Israeli military from the West Bank and Gaza; negotiations over refugees, settlements, Jerusalem and borders were scheduled to begin in the third year of the interim period. Yasser Arafat entered Gaza and Jericho, the first autonomous cities, in July 1994. On September 28, 1995, the Oslo II Accords divided the West Bank into about a hundred enclaves (Areas A, B, C, H1, H2). (See p. 20.) The Israeli army withdrew from the eight largest cities in the West Bank and Gaza Strip. However, the Israeli policy of accelerated building of new settlements in the West Bank and Jerusalem rapidly led to a loss of illusions. The massacre of 29 Palestinians in the Tomb of the Patriarchs/Ibrahimi Mosque in Hebron in 1994 reinforced Palestinian opposition to a process which neither ended the Occupation nor the humiliations. In November 1995, Prime Minister Yitzhak Rabin was assassinated by an Israeli extremist, Yigal Amir.

> *"However, municipal autonomy is not a compromise; it is the solution Israel prefers. What could be better than having political control and sovereignty over East Jerusalem without having to spend a penny on health care, basic municipal services and education for the local Palestinian population? During the last six years, Israel has been able to experiment with this approach in the West Bank and Gaza."*
>
> ■ Michael Warschawski.

In 1996, Shimon Peres ordered, for electoral reasons, even though a truce had been concluded, the assassination of Yahya Ayyash, known as "The Engineer" and commander of Ezz ed-din al-Qassam Brigades (the military wing of the Islamic Resistance, Hamas). The Islamic resistance movement retaliated with a series of attacks described as "the response to fifty years of terror and Zionist crimes perpetrated against the Palestinian civil population." Criticised for not being able to assure the security of his fellow-citizens, Shimon Peres, in the middle of the election campaign, sent troops into southern Lebanon. At Qana, near Tyre, a UN camp was shelled. More than 100 civilians, mostly women and children who had taken refuge in an administrative building of the UN, were killed. The brutality of this short but intense campaign heightened the bitterness of the Palestinians. More peace agreements followed: the Wye Plantation Memorandum, Sharm al-Sheikh, Camp David II, etc. All were limited in scope at their inception, and their application was partial, null or indefinitely postponed.

Yasser Arafat (Abu Ammar) 1929 - 2004

Born in Cairo in 1929, to a mother originally from Jerusalem, Chairman Yasser Arafat spent a brief part of his childhood in the Old City of Jerusalem, Palestine. In 1948, he interrupted his studies in order to join resistance groups based in Gaza. At the war's tragic end, he returned to finish his studies in engineering at the University of Cairo, where he helped found the Palestine Students' Federation of which he was president until 1957. During the Suez War in 1956, he volunteered in the Egyptian army. That same year, he moved to Kuwait, where he established a public works business whose profits financed his militant activities as he built up a resistance movement modelled on anti-colonial movements. Yasser Arafat remained president of Fatah until his death in a Paris military hospital on November 11, 2004. On April 19, 1968, at the height of Fatah's popularity, its leader Abu Ammar emerged from the underground and showed his face for the first time. In 1969, he assumed leadership of the Palestine Liberation Organisation (PLO), making the Palestinian national cause its priority. After the battle of 1970, he moved to Beirut, which became the headquarters of the resistance fighters. He stayed there until the Israeli invasion in 1982, leaving Beirut in 1982 under international protection for Tunis, where the different organs of the PLO were established. On November 15, 1988, Arafat pronounced the Declaration of Independence of the State of Palestine and was elected its first president by the PLO's central council, on April 2, 1989. After secret negotiations with the Israeli authorities, he authorised a controversial series of clandestine meetings that resulted in the signing of the official "Declaration of Principles" on September 13, 1993. He returned to Palestine on July 1, 1994, and assumed leadership of the new political institutions established in the autonomous Palestinian territories in the West Bank and Gaza Strip.

Although often criticized both by his opponents and his closest associates for his unilateral decisions and his strategic choices, Yasser Arafat remained a symbolic figure, an icon, of the Palestinian people until his death, and indeed thereafter. His story is of a man who dedicated his entire life to the Palestinian cause, living in secret for years, never sleeping two nights in the same place, escaping numerous assassination attempts and a 'plane crash in which others died, whilst firmly placing the Palestinian cause on the international agenda, he remained single until a late age, gladly claiming he was already *"married to the Palestinian cause."* His death has left a huge vacuum in the Palestinian leadership, since there is no single leader of the Palestinians who so unquestionably commands the loyalty of all, whether at street level, amongst other militants or amongst other leaders. Time alone will judge whether his constant declarations of seeking peace for both Palestine and Israel were opportunities Israel consistently missed (there are doubts any other Palestinian has similar credibility to make historic compromises) or whether the consistent demonisation by Israel of Arafat will follow him through the ages. His fellow peace-activist, Israeli Uri Avnery, has predicted that from a purely Arab perspective Arafat will be remembered on an equal with Saladin.

■ The al-Aqsa Intifada

> *"We need to put pressure on the weaknesses of the Palestinians so that they come crawling to us, begging us to cease our fire."*
>
> ■ Rehavam Ze'evi, former government minister in the Israeli 2001 coalition

On September 27, 2000, Ariel Sharon's provocative visit to the Temple Mount (Haram al-Sharif or al-Aqsa) sparked the beginning of a new Palestinian uprising against the Israeli Occupation. Immediately, Prime Minister Ehud Barak ordered harsh military repression of civilian Palestinian demonstrators, including Palestinians who were Israeli citizens. Within days, dozens of Palestinians of all ages were killed (most often by covert snipers of elite units) or wounded. The wave of repression launched by Barak's government actually allowed him to extract himself from the impasse of the meeting at Camp David II (July 2000). In fact, at the very moment of the Camp David II talks behind closed doors, the Israeli army was preparing a new plan of intervention. Its code name was to be *"Magic Air"* if there was *"low intensity conflict;"* or *"Distant World"* in the case of an occupation of all the Palestinian towns. This action did indeed take place, but under other names. The plan named *"High Tide / Low Tide"* was implemented in the first days of the al-Aqsa Intifada by the Barak Government; the total re-invasion of all Palestinian towns in April 2002 by Israeli occupation authorities after the Park Hotel "Pesach" bombing, bestowed on it the name: *"Operation Defensive Shield."*

Named in reference to the "visit" of Sharon and the bloodbath which accompanied it, the al-Aqsa Intifada was, well beyond the provocation of Sharon, an expression of Palestinian rejection of the Camp David II Accords, which had attempted to impose a political solution ignoring all the Palestinians' basic rights and which imagined a future "state of Palestine" in the form of a mere protectorate. During the talks in closed session,

Barak set the same "red lines" already laid down since the signature of the Oslo Accords in preceding negotiations by all his predecessors (Rabin, Peres and Netanyahu): no UN resolution to be applied, neither the Right of Return of Palestinian refugees to their town or village of origin (Resolution 194) nor the creation of a Palestinian state on the pre-1967 boundaries (Resolution 242); no independent Palestinian state sovereign within its own borders was envisaged; Jerusalem was the main stumbling block: it was to be an open city, undivided, placed under Israeli sovereignty.

The al-Aqsa uprising was also a response to eight years of a "peace process" during which for eight years Israeli colonisation, affirming *de facto* Israeli sovereignty on Palestinian land occupied since 1967, was established on the ground. Israeli government policy in the eight years after Oslo concentrated not only on developing settlements in East Jerusalem, the West Bank and the Gaza Strip, but also on carving up Palestinian land into isolated enclaves, curtailing freedom of movement for Palestinians, the isolation of Jerusalem, the imposition of economic dependence, daily humiliations and other abuses of basic human rights. Given the reality of the Oslo Peace Process, members of the PA who had determined the lines to follow in the peace talks were the object of much criticism as to the merits of their strategy, even despite their condemnations of the Israeli "acquisitions" during the "peace process" years. In addition, the PA was accused by its people of corruption and nepotism as well as disrespect for human rights, particularly the repression of opposition and the absence of freedom of expression. Palestinians were deeply distressed by the ambivalence of the international community, especially the United Nations, which had not intervened on their behalf on the basis of its own resolutions, neither before nor after the Oslo Accords. Their expectations of justice had been betrayed: the role of international law seemed to boil down to the innocuous statement *"to support the peace process in the Middle East."*

Mustapha Ali al-Zabri (Abu Ali Mustapha)

Born in Arraba (in the district of Jenin) in 1938 to a father who was a railway worker for the Haifa railways; Abu Ali Mustapha completed primary school in Amman. At the age of 17, he joined the Arab Nationalist Movement (ANM). As soon as King Hussein of Jordan declared martial law, he was condemned to five years in prison for "subversive activities." On his release in 1961, he returned to the ANM and became one of its leaders in the northern West Bank, responsible for social and military activities. In 1965, he trained at the al-Shata military school in Egypt; on his return, he took on the training of *fedayin* in the West Bank. In 1966, he was again imprisoned in a huge operation of arrests by Jordanian intelligence of Palestinian resistance movements. After the defeat of 1967, he continued the armed struggle against the forces of occupation and was one of the founding members of the Popular Front for the Liberation of Palestine and the commander of its military wing. In 1971, he settled in Lebanon, after the Palestinian *fedayin* retreat from Jordan. In September 1999, he returned to Palestine; shortly afterwards, he was elected Secretary General of the PFLP. From the beginning of the al-Aqsa Intifada, he was in favour of reinforcing national unity in democratic ways and set up a unified command of the uprising. On August 17, 2001, he was assassinated in his office in Ramallah.

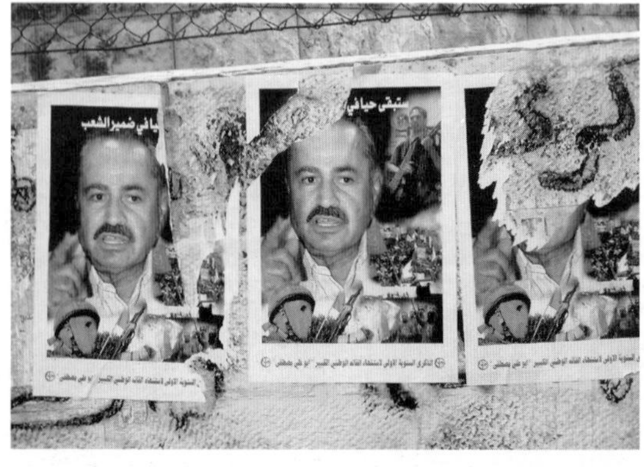

The Forms of Israeli Repression

• **Restrictions on movement:** closures, sieges, curfews, raids, checkpoints, Wall, permit system and mass arrests, etc.

• **Choking of the Palestinian economy:** restrictions on the circulation of merchandise (imports, exports, movement of goods internally), prevention of Palestinian workers' employment and refusal to issue work permits inside Israel, destruction of infrastructure whether for manufacturing or for farming, including groves or orchards, and irrigation systems, etc.

• **Deliberate creation of a humanitarian crisis:** The combination of punitive measures and restrictions on the free movement of people and goods has led to an unprecedented level of poverty, lack of basic food items and medical supplies. The absence of access to medical care and vaccination restrictions have led to a noticeable rise in infant and child (under the age of 5 years) mortality.

• **Military attacks on civilians:** Bombardments – by heavy artillery, assault vehicles, Apache helicopters, jet bombers (F15 and F16) – on residential areas, as well as on schools, hospitals, ambulances, etc; assassination of civilians (amongst them, a high proportion of children) by snipers at the time of demonstrations at the entrances to towns; firepower directed at medical personnel and journalists; extra-judicial assassinations of political figures.

• **Arrests and raids:** arbitrary mass arrests followed by inhuman treatment and torture.

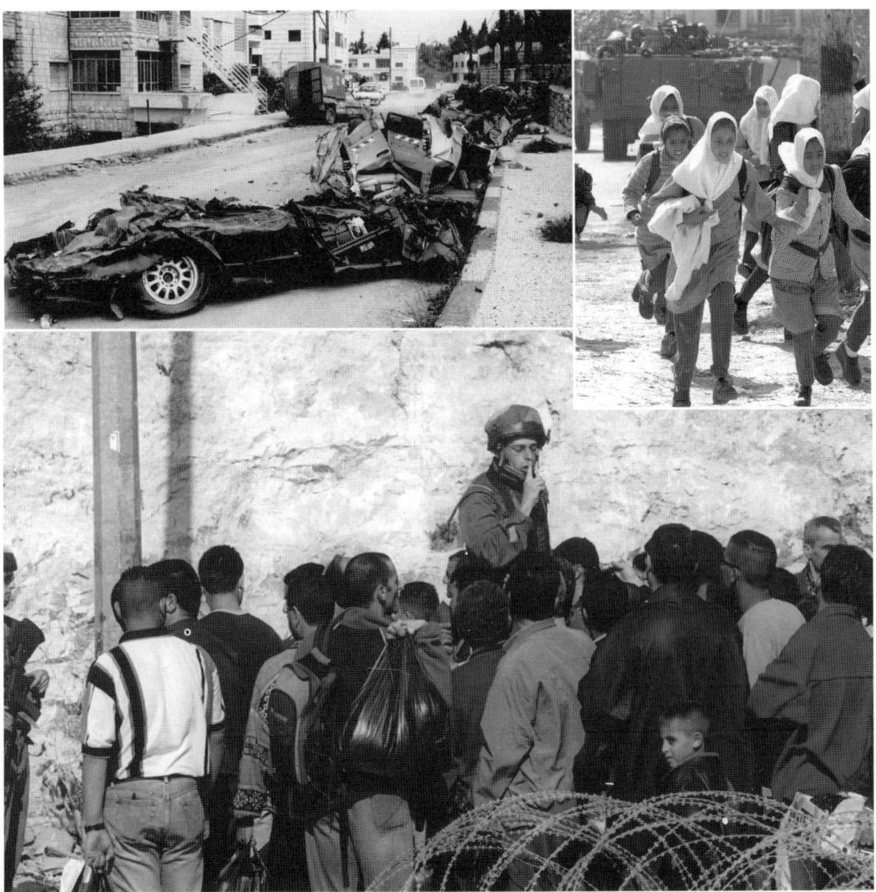

Hanan Ashrawi

Hanan Ashrawi was born in Ramallah in 1946, one of five daughters of a Christian Palestinian doctor. She has been an exceptional representative of her people both in her roles in academics and in national and international politics. After receiving her B.A. and M.A. (English) from the American University of Beirut, Dr. Ashrawi earned her Ph.D at the University of Virginia, USA. She established the Faculty of English at the University of Birzeit in 1973, when that West Bank university was being transformed into a 4-year institution. From 1973 to 1995, Dr. Ashrawi held various posts at the University of Birzeit, authoring many works of literary criticism. During this time, she and her husband raised two daughters. Dr. Ashrawi was caught up in politics as early as 1974, when Israeli closures made life hard for Birzeit professors and students. In 1988, she joined the Intifada Political Committee, while from 1991 to 1993 she served as the Official Spokesperson of the Palestinian Delegation to the Middle East Peace Process and was a member of the Leadership/Guidance Committee and Executive Committee of the delegation. Dr. Ashrawi served her country in different capacities from the beginning of the Oslo Accords, resigning as PA Minister of Higher Education and Research in 1998 because of concerns about corruption. She is Secretary-General of Miftah: The Palestinian Initiative for the Promotion of Global Dialogue and Democracy, a Palestinian NGO founded that year to monitor the situation in the Occupied Territories, and whose specific agenda covers democracy, public debate, networking, information and reinforcing the Palestinian nation-building process. Dr. Ashrawi is a member of the Independent International Commission on Kosovo and the United Nations Research Institute for Social Development, to mention only a few of her activities, whilst remaining the most widely respected woman in Palestinian society.

Violation of human rights committed by Israeli occupation forces or by Israeli settlers between 28 September 2000 and November 2004

Palestinians killed by the army or by Israeli civilians:	**3,899**
Ages of these victims or "martyrs":	
Under 8 years old	91
From 9 to 12	113
From 13 to 15	232
From 16 to 17	229
Over 18	3,234
Babies born dead at checkpoints:	31
Wounded	**28,189**
By live ammunition	7,538
By rubber / plastic bullets	6,279
By tear gas (various types)	6,334
Other causes (incl. shrapnel)	8,038

Attacks on journalists:	
Palestinian journalists killed	12
Foreign journalists killed	2
Palestinian and foreign journalists wounded	472
Unemployment rate:	
Gaza Strip	67%
West Bank	48%
Palestinians living under the poverty line	
Gaza Strip	70%
West Bank	55%
Families that have sold belongings in order to buy basic foodstuffs	16%
Families that depend entirely on humanitarian aid	30%
Malnutrition in Palestinian children:	
Children suffering from malnutrition	41.3%
Children suffering from anaemia	36.6%
Demolished homes & uprooted trees:	
Homes demolished	7,613
Estimated number of trees uprooted	1,176,431
Expropriated & razed lands (dunum = 1000 sq.m.):	
Lands expropriated	225,067
Lands razed	73,465

Educational statistics	
School students killed	516
University students killed	198
Teachers killed	28
School students injured	3,471
University students injured	1,245
Teachers injured	54
School students detained	669
University students detained	720
Teachers detained	167

Sources : Miftah (The Palestinian Initiative for the Promotion of Global Dialogue and Democracy) (www.miftah.org) and Defence of Children International/ Palestine Section - DCI (www.dci-pal.org)

CHAPTER 3

POPULATION AND SOCIETY

Population and Society

Write!
I am Arab.
Card number: 50,000
Number of children: eight.
And the ninth will arrive after the summer.
And you are furious!

Write!
I am Arab.
I work in the quarry with my companions in hardship.
And I have eight kids
Their flat bread
Their clothes and their schoolbook,
I pull them all out of the rocks ...
Oh! I will not go begging for charity at your door
I will not make myself small on the steps of your palace.
And so you are furious!

Write!
I am Arab.
Without a family name - I am my first name
"Infinitely patient" in a country where everybody
Lives on the embers of Anger
My roots ...
Before the birth of time they were growing deep
Before the overflowing of steadfastness.
Before the cypress and the olive
...before grass started to grow
My father ... comes from a family of labourers
And has nothing to do with gentlemen
My grandfather was a peasant - a person
Without value - or noble descent
Who taught me the pride of the sun before teaching me to read books
My house a caretaker's hut
Made of reeds and branches
See who I am - does it please you?
Without a family name - I am nothing but my first name

Write!
My hair... colour of coal
My eyes ... colour of coffee
Distinguishing marks:
On my head a kuffiya with its cord tightly knotted
And my palm is rough as a stone
... it scratches the hand that shakes it
The food I prefer is olive oil and thyme

My address:
I am from a remote village ... forgotten
Where the streets have no names
And all the men ... to the quarry as once to the fields
...
Write!
That I am Arab
That you seized the vines of my fathers
And the land I farmed
Me and my children together
You have taken everything from us except
The survival of my grandchildren
These rocks here
But your government is going to seize them, too
...from what they say!

SO!

Write!
At the top of the first page
That I have no hate for people
That I attack no one
But that ... if I am hungry
I eat the flesh of my Usurper
Beware! Beware! Beware
My fury!

■ Mahmoud Darwish, 1966
Identity Card

”

▪ Identity

> *"They want to seize Palestine, the heart of the Arab world and the central link between the Arab Peninsula and Africa. Their goal is to destroy this link and to divide the Arab nation, to prevent it from acting as one. A people must know it has a land and language of its own. If you want to destroy a people, cut its tongue out and occupy its land."*
>
> ▪ Khalil Sakakini, 1917

Before European colonialism imposed its borders, a great part of the Arab world formed a single unit under the Ottoman Empire. Its frame of reference was not the nation, but the town or the administrative province. In the nineteenth century, the Nahda (renaissance) cultural movement reasserted reference to Arab identity and a united Arab consciousness. Despite compromise in its dealings with the Ottoman federal empire, the nationalist response of the Young Turks in 1908 followed the replacement of the Arabic alphabet by the Latin alphabet (a negation *par excellence* of Arab culture), which developed the emergence of a distinct Arab consciousness. Although it proved impossible to establish a united Arab political entity, the struggles to construct an Arab nation and especially the struggles for the liberation of each Arab country created at least an Arab cultural nation *(Umma arabiyya)* where there was inter-Arab solidarity. In this context, British colonialism and the Zionist invasion contributed to the development of a specific sense of being Palestinian, amplified by the feeling of belonging to the Holy Land. The identity of the Palestinian people was heightened by the sense of being a single nation (over and above questions of religious identity of Muslims and Christians) whose defined borders were threatened by foreign conquest. The struggle to protect their land and then to recover their rights contributed to the defining of the identity of the Palestinian people, an identity deeply attached to the land.

Today, of the over 8 million Palestinians, some 4 million live within the boundaries of historic Palestine; half of those people are refugees in their own land (45.5%, without referring to the internally displaced refugees within the borders of the State of Israel). In the Gaza Strip, the

proportion of refugees reaches 76.5%. The other half of the Palestinian people are scattered all over the world, a large percentage in neighbouring Arab states. There is a high rate of natural growth among the population (3.5% in 2004), which makes Palestinian society a young one: 52.6% is under the age of 17. At the present rate, the population of the West Bank and the Gaza Strip will have doubled by 2025. The position of youth and its needs in terms of education, social infrastructure and housing as well as the aspiration to end the oppression and injustices they endure explain their strong commitment to the Palestinian national struggle.

Palestinian Population	
In historical Palestine (mid-2003)	**4,624,385**
West Bank and Gaza Strip*	3,364,495
48 Territories[º]	1,259,890
Outside Palestine (2001)*	**4,797,317**
Jordan	2,598,104
Syria	394,695
Lebanon	387,766
Egypt	57,500
Libya and Iraq	78,884
Saudi Arabia	287,499
Kuwait and other Gulf countries	151,959
Other Arab countries	113,359
North and South Americas	216,196
Other countries	511,355

*Palestinian CBS [º]Israeli CBS

Palestinian refugees

"We did not choose to be refugees; that was something imposed on us by force and terror. We have the right to personal security, to our homes, and to our land and to freedom. We do not intend, nor do we accept, remaining refugees forever. We do not accept that our children continue to be refugees."

A refugee from Deheisheh Refugee Camp

The majority of Palestinians are refugees. In the Occupied Territories of 1967 and the countries bordering on them alone, UNRWA listed over 4 million refugees in 2003, which is the largest refugee population in the world. Of these, over 32% live in the 59 refugee camps scattered across the Middle East.

UNRWA defines the Palestinian refugees in this way: *"To qualify for UNRWA registration, refugees must have been resident in Palestine between June 1946 and May 1948 and to have lost both their homes and their livelihood as a result of the 1948 Arab-Israeli War. The descendants of 1948 refugees are also eligible for registration with UNRWA, but only refugees living in its five fields of operations (Jordan, Lebanon, Syria, West Bank and Gaza Strip) are eligible for the Agency's services."* The figures, based on this minimal definition by UNRWA of a refugee, represent far less than the real number of Palestinian refugees. Several categories of refugees, nonetheless, are omitted by this definition: those who are refugees in countries outside UNRWA's mission, such as Egypt and Iraq; those Palestinians who were outside Palestine in 1948; those refugees who were not registered by UNRWA; internally displaced refugees inside Israel (more than 300,000 people) [See p. 325]; those made refugee by the 1967 war - approximately 300,000 in only six days; those expelled after 1967.

UNRWA

UNRWA (United Nations Relief and Works Agency for Palestine Refugees in the Near East) was created by the UN General Assembly in December 1949 to provide emergency assistance to the Palestinian refugees. The agency was only supposed to be temporary, but, 50 years later, is still functioning. The refugees are still waiting for the application of their rights. Employing a staff of 24,000 (of whom more than 99% are Palestinian refugees), UNRWA provides education (656 schools and 8 technical training centres), health services and social services (assistance to families that have no income, youth centres, and so on).

Today, the agency spends an average of US $71 per year per refugee to cover the cost of education, health care and food. But the Oslo Accords have meant that the plight of the refugees is no longer top priority, and financial resources have dwindled at an alarming rate. In 2003, the budget was $344 million, the largest donors being the United States, the EU and some member states of the EU. In December 2002, UNRWA launched an Emergency Appeal to cover the needs of the refugees in the OPT during January - June 2003, requesting $93.7m; only $38m was pledged.

The Nakba (The Catastrophe)

Palestinian refugees were created by two waves of expulsions: the first in 1948, the second in 1967. In 1948, over 800,000 Palestinians fled from their towns and villages following the policy of terror conducted by Zionist organisations. Initially, villagers and city dwellers did not take refuge far away, taking with them only a minimal means of subsistence and the key to their house. No Palestinian imagined that he was leaving his home for good. They had already lived through the same situation during the Anglo-Turkish battles in 1916-1917; when the danger and fighting was over, everyone had returned home. However, the hope for the arrival of Arab troops was in vain. The collusion of King Abdullah of Transjordan with the Zionists, aggravated by the military weakness of the Palestinian resistance, allowed their land to be taken from them. Until the early 1950s, some refugees tried to cross back and return to their villages or neighbourhoods, through unsecured borders, if only to retrieve some of the belongings they had left behind. Thousands were killed in such attempts, and any return very soon became impossible. The State of Israel demolished over 400 towns or villages, whether partially or completely. In the towns, the residences were immediately reoccupied by the Jewish new immigrants. Between 1949 and 1953, the State of Israel regularised these expropriations, in defiance of all international law, by enacting the Absentee Property Law (1950) (the refugees being the "absentees"), which denied Palestinians who had fled the right to return or to claim restitution of their property. Parallel to this law was the Law of Return (*aliya* in Hebrew) (1950), guaranteeing every Jew in the world the right to settle in Israel. The Development Authority (Transfer of Property) Law on land acquisition stipulated that land once belonging to a Jew could never be sold to an Arab. In 1967 the same policy of mass transfer of Palestinians was repeated. Palestinians call it the Naksa, (Tragedy). In less than 6 days, some 300,000 Palestinians living in the West Bank and the Gaza Strip were forced to leave their homes. One third had already been refugees since 1948; the other two thirds became refugees for the first time. Since these two mass transfers, the repression, demolition of houses and colonisation of land have not ceased.

Testimonies

"Every person had a piece of land at that time. Us, we had 4 dunums. We grew wheat, lentils, chick-peas. It was our source of income. In 1948, I was in high school when the war broke out. We left because of shelling from the air and the sea... We walked through the fields, thinking that they were the only safe place. We went all the way from Haifa to Jenin on foot. The only things we took with us were some clothes... It was summer, we stayed in two places: under the trees or in the mosques. The Red Cross gave us clothing and food; 3 kilos of flour per family. The Red Cross stayed until the United Nations arrived, they took a census and gave us ration cards... I returned to my city after the war of 1967, and I found that the 4 dunums had been turned into a huge stable. Some years later, they demolished the stable and the house that was still there when I first visited in 1967 and they were replaced by an Israeli settlement."

■ Bachar from Haifa, a refugee in Jenin Refugee Camp

"I'm from Jaffa. Before 1948, it was the largest port in Palestine. I was a child in 1948, but I'll tell you what my father told me. My father left with the hope of returning quickly to his town. He kept hens, and when he left, he locked them up and gave them enough feed to last 7 days, thinking he would soon be back... After 1967, I went back to my village on which they had built a military base. I brought back some soil from my village with me and gave it to my children so that they would remain attached to it."

■ Khaled, a refugee in Jenin camp

"I can still remember - I remember it perfectly. One summer night, while we were sleeping on the porch of our house, as was the village custom in summer, my mother woke me up in a panic, and I found myself running through the woods with hundreds of other people from my village. Bullets whistled over our heads, and I did not understand what was going on. After a night of walking and running, the whole family arrived in a strange village with strange kids. So I innocently asked: where am I? And I heard the word Lebanon for the first time in my life. I now know that that night put a violent end to my childhood."

■ Mahmoud Darwish, a native of the village of Birwa in the Galilee, near the ruins where Kibbutz Yas'ur was inaugurated on January 6, 1949.

■ Palestinians in exile

Palestinian refugees in Jordan

More than 40% of the Palestinians registered as refugees, as defined by UNWRA, live in Jordan (1,1740,170). Most of them (82%) do not live in refugee camps. The principal country of refuge, more than half of the total population (75%) of the Jordanian kingdom is Palestinian. Palestinians work in every economic sector and have played an essential role in the development of the country's economy. In Jordan, they have the full rights of any Jordanian citizen; this has been the situation since 1949, when Jordan annexed the West Bank and East Jerusalem. Those refugees originally from the Gaza Strip (150,000 people), which was never under Jordan's control, have only partial Jordanian citizenship. For example, they are not allowed to be employed in the public sector.

Palestinian refugees in Syria

413,827 Palestinians are refugees (according to UNRWA's criteria) in Syria. They have not been granted Syrian citizenship, but they are allowed to work in every sector, including the public sector. Twenty-nine percent of these refugees still live in the camps.

Palestinian refugees in Lebanon

394,532 Palestinian refugees (according to UNRWA's criteria) live in Lebanon. Unlike Jordan and Syria, the Lebanese constitution explicitly forbids integration for Palestinian refugees in Lebanon. In fact, Lebanon has instituted a policy of isolation of Palestinians and there are draconian restrictions in all domains of life in Lebanon - work, health, education and freedom of movement. Government decree (the most important being N° 38/11, April 5, 1983) gives Palestinians no access to anything except menial work, often paid by the hour or by the day. They are not permitted to work in any qualified work, which makes 72 job categories prohibited to them. The unemployment rate is consequently high - between 40% and 60%. In addition, Palestinians have no access to public health services or other services provided by the state, such as education. Restrictions also apply to construction in and around the camps, where most Palestinians in Lebanon live; this has led to extreme overpopulation and deplorable sanitary conditions. Since the Oslo Accords, conditions have become worse because PLO funds and international aid has been prioritised to be invested in development projects in the West Bank and the Gaza Strip.

Remembering and resistance

"He felt that it was time to leave: it was all over, there was nothing more to say. All his love for Khaled suddenly overwhelmed him, and he wanted to run to him, take him in his arms, hug him, cry on his shoulder and even exchange places with him. "That is our homeland," he said to himself, smiling, and he turned towards his wife:

"Do you know what homeland means, Safia? Our homeland is that nothing like this should happen."

A little alarmed, she asked,

"What's the matter, Said?

"Nothing, nothing. Nothing at all. I was just wondering, that's all. I was looking for the real Palestine. A Palestine that would be more than remembering, more than a peacock feather, or a son, or a scrawl in pencil on a staircase wall. And I was saying to myself: what is Palestine for Khaled? He has never seen the vase, the photo, the staircase, or al Hallisa or Khaldoun, and yet he believes that it is right to fight and die for it. While for us, for you and me, it's just a question of something we look for in the dust of our memories. And just see what we have found under that dust ... another layer of dust! We made a mistake when we thought that the homeland was only our past; for Khaled, our homeland is the future, and that is the difference between him and us. That's why Khaled wanted to fight. And there are tens of thousands like him; the tears that flow from the eyes of men rummaging through their defeat to find the rubble of shields and wilted flowers, these tears will not stop them. Them, they are looking towards the future, that's why they will correct our mistakes and the errors of the whole world ..."

■ Ghassan Kanafani, Return to Haifa

International laws that guarantee the Right of Return of Palestinian Refugees

I. UN General Assembly Resolution 194 :
"Article 11. "[The General Assembly] *resolves that the refugees wishing to return to their homes and live at peace with their neighbours should be permitted to do so at the earliest practicable date, and that compensation should be paid for the property which, under principles of international law or in equity, should be made good by the governments or authorities responsible."*

II. Article 13 of the Universal Declaration of Human Rights (December 10, 1948)
(1) Everyone has the right to freedom of movement and residence within the borders of each State.
(2) Everyone has the right to leave any country, including his own, and to return to his country.

III. The Fourth Geneva Convention (1949) affirms the right of return of all those who have been chased from their land because of the outbreak of war.

IV. Resolution 3236 of the UN General Assembly (1974) affirms the right of the Palestinians to self-determination, national independence and sovereignty, and the inalienable right of the Palestinians to return to their houses and their lands.

■ Society

Certain basic social characteristics are unique to all Palestinian society, regardless of religion or domicile. Undoubtedly, the family is the primary social unit, but not just a nuclear family; it is always a family which is extended in the plural: the appropriate term for this extended family is *hamula*, a veritable family network whose members can be very distantly related. Members of a *hamula* who identify themselves as being of the same family often number in the thousands. Social ceremonies such as weddings and funerals serve to bind members of the *hamula* together, as do economic ties. On the level of a single family, bonds are solid and it is rare for children to leave home before marriage. Usually, one of the sons stays with his parents while the others settle down nearby, adding additional housing to the family home. The women, on the other hand, join the husband's family, very often relatives, members of the same *hamula*, or at least from the same village or neighbourhood. Most homes house one family (parents and children); however 28% of the families in the West Bank are extended ones, in which case the paternal grandparents, and single brothers or sisters, as well as widows or widowers, live in the same house. This is especially common in villages, where traditional structures are stronger.

Palestinian society is young: the average age is 16. Couples have an average of 6 children per couple (5.4 in the West Bank and 7.4 in the Gaza Strip) and on average more than 7 people live in one household. The birth rate is variable from one city to another and sometimes from one neighbourhood to another. Jerusalem has the lowest birth rate (3.9 children per family), while the highest rate is 6.8 children per couple in the cities of Gaza and Hebron. Traditionally, there is a preference for boys. The eldest son guarantees the continuity of his family line and gives his parents a new social status. If a boy's name, for example, is Khaled, his father is called Abu Khaled, the father of Khaled; his mother is called Um Khaled, the mother of Khaled. In Muslim families, people recite the call for prayer *(athan)*, which includes the profession of faith, in the ears of the new-born baby. A few hours or a few days later, boys are circumcised. It is also quite usual for Christian families to have their children circumcised, too.

Important ceremonies

Marriage is a major event in Palestinian society. The decision is mainly made by the future spouses, but members of the family (parents, brothers and sisters) also express their opinion. This consultation is usually a formality, but it must not be neglected. Other practices are, in contrast, dying out; this is the case of double marriages *(badal)*, when a man (A) marries a woman (B) and that woman's brother (C) marries B's sister (D), i.e. a brother and sister marry the brother and sister of another family. One other such marginalised tradition is polygamy: this concerns less than 4% of all couples, while this was common two generations ago. Nowadays, polygamy is more a subject for ridicule than a current practice.

When a death takes place, the *muezzin* announces it from the top of a minaret, even if the deceased person no longer lives in the country. The ritual which accompanies death reunites the whole family, as they come together. For three days, the family receives relatives, friends and neighbours *('aza)*. The women receive their visitors in the residence of the deceased while the men get together at the home of a close relative (a son or a brother). When the time comes for the funeral, only the men (Muslim or Christian) take the deceased to the cemetery. On the fortieth day, there is a special ceremony to mark the end of the period of mourning *(ta'bin)*.

Martyrs *(Shuhada)*

All Palestinians who die for the national cause are honoured as martyrs *(shuhada)* regardless of their religion. The word *Shahid* (martyr) means "witness." Martyrs are thought to receive a two-fold reward: national dignity and spiritual recognition. Every mourner keeps this comforting verse in mind: *"All who obey God and the Apostle are in the company of those on whom is the Grace of God, of the Prophets, the lovers of Truth, the Witnesses, and the righteous: Ah! What a beautiful Fellowship!" (Koran, An-Nisa, 69)* The bodies of martyrs are neither washed nor changed, thus keeping intact the marks of honour. Their funerals override the family ceremony. The entire population, men and women, accompany the body of the martyr, holding flags and chanting words heavy with emotion that call for the continuation of the struggle: *"The martyr is beloved by God," (al-Shahid habib Allah)*, and *"God is mightiest" (Allah u-Akbar)*.

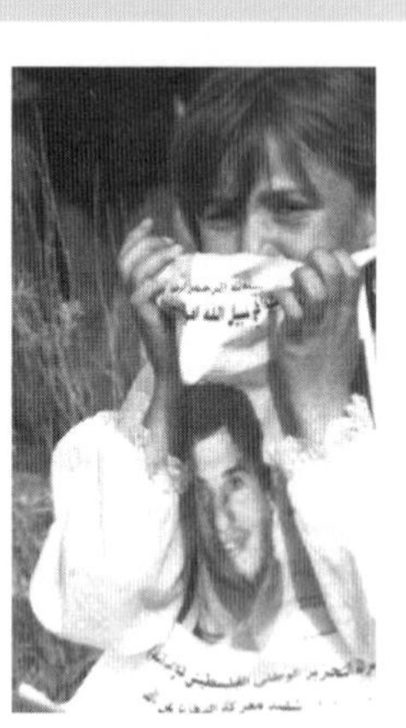

▪ Education

Despite the political context and the large number of young people in schools, the literacy rate in the Occupied Territories of Palestinian East Jerusalem, the West Bank and the Gaza Strip is quite high: 93.5% of the boys and 98.6% of the girls complete primary and elementary school. On the other hand, only 51% continue in secondary school (the same percentage of boys and girls). Palestinians value education as a privileged way to achieve a better future, and educated Palestinians have provided the Gulf States, Saudi Arabia, and Jordan with qualified personnel for the development of all sectors of their economy since the 1950s.

Schooling is obligatory until the age of 16. There are 4 divisions: nursery school for the youngest children (4-5 years); primary and elementary schools (6-16 years); secondary education (16-18), with three tracks: vocational, science, and arts; the final secondary school diploma, the *tawjihi* is the equivalent of GCE or *baccalaureate*. Until the PA took on the organisation of the schools, beyond the public, private and UNRWA school systems, the curricula in Palestinian schools were a patchwork that reflected the physical division of Palestine: a Jordanian curriculum in the West Bank, an Egyptian curriculum in the Gaza Strip, an Israeli curriculum in Jerusalem public schools and Jordanian curriculum in Jerusalem private schools, all subject to Israeli approval. The creation of Palestinian textbooks by the PA Ministry of

Education in collaboration with educational associations at least establishes the same programme for all Palestinian schools. Amongst the problems facing the Palestinian education system is the ever increasing number of students: the number of school children per class is relatively high - 38.9 students on average per class. In UNRWA schools, the average is 44.3 (50 in the Gaza Strip); 39 as stated in government schools and 25.7 in private schools.

UNRWA Schools

Since its creation, UNRWA has been in charge of the education to *tawjihi* standard of all Palestinian refugees in Palestine and the countries of the Palestinian Diaspora. UNRWA runs almost every second school in the Gaza Strip, and one in ten of the schools in the West Bank. With limited resources at their disposal (very basic equipment), schools in refugee camps are faced with too many pupils and insufficient buildings, which force them to operate most of the time on two or sometimes three shifts.

▪ The Economy

Sectors of activity

Agriculture has an important place in the Palestinian economy; it employs 12% of the workforce. A large variety of fruits and vegetables is produced in the West Bank and the Gaza Strip (citrus fruits, zucchini, sweet peppers, tomatoes, celery, cucumbers, eggplants, dates, almonds and grapes). Of all agricultural production, the most important is the cultivation of olive trees (25% of the value of agricultural production). Israeli restrictions on water consumption and land use, as well as on export, force farmers to limit their produce to the crops which bear a high return, destined for the international market, such as strawberries, flowers, etc. Actually, a number of agricultural products are exported via Israeli intermediaries, who label the products "Made in Israel." Palestinian producers prefer to pay for this Israeli commercialised service to avoid delays at the customs that could be fatal to perishable goods. The secondary sector (manufacturing and construction) employs 37% of the working population. Palestinian industrial production, often operating as family businesses, is characterised by small workshops employing 5 people on average. This applies to farm products (food, drinks, olive oil) and the manufacturing sector (shoes, furniture, plastic products, and construction materials). In the latter, Palestinian enterprises usually subcontract from Israeli businesses, which increases their dependency on the Israeli market. Construction and services expanded considerably since 1995, when there was a big need for housing after the return of tens of thousands of Palestinians to the West Bank and Gaza at the time of the Oslo Accords, and the new Palestinian Authority required new administrative buildings. There was also a construction boom and extension of Jewish settlements in response to the immigration of some million Russian Jews over a 10-year period and the economic prosperity that Israelis experienced during the "peace process" years. During the four years of the al-Aqsa Intifada, however, these expansions have ceased: currently unemployment averages over 40% and closures have made it impossible for many Palestinians to reach their workplaces.

Lastly, the tertiary sector is the most important one, contributing more than 73% of the Gross National Product (GNP) of the Gaza Strip and approximately 60% in the West Bank. The public sector employs 24% of the work force in the Gaza Strip and about 15% of the work force in the West Bank.

An economy of dependence

The Paris Protocol (1994) on Economic Relations obliged the Palestinians to co-operate on customs and excise affairs with Israel, in principle to guarantee freedom of movement of capital and goods. Taxation rates were fixed by Israel, which was to remit to the PA the VAT and customs duties on goods transported to the West Bank and Gaza Strip. In 1998, duty represented 60% of PA revenue. In this sense, Israeli control over custom duties works as a means of pressure on the PA, Israel periodically refusing to transfer taxes owed to the PA. Dependence on Israel is apparent in the fact that 90% of Palestinian import and export takes place with Israel; this dependence has disastrous consequences on the Palestinian economy because of the frequent sieges or total closure imposed on the Occupied Palestinian Territories, especially since the al-Aqsa Intifada. In 2002, the PA's fiscal deficit was financed by US$464 million of donor budgetary support, mainly from the Arab League states, the EU and World Bank. Nevertheless, the PA had debts with the private sector of $415 million and with domestic banks of US$65 million. At the same time, Israel had withheld clearance revenues of US$700 million.

Restrictions on independent economic development has led a high proportion of Palestinian workers to look for work in Israel, which profits from this cheap labour force and means of wielding pressure. Before the First Intifada, Israel employed 180,000 Palestinian workers every day, compared to 83,000 in 1993 and 22,250 in 1996 (due to a long period of closure and the import by Israel of foreign workers from Thailand, China, Romania and Eastern Europe). Since the beginning of the al-Aqsa Intifada, 110,000 Palestinian workers have directly lost their jobs because they have been forbidden entry into the State of Israel. The median monthly income had decreased from NIS2,800 before the al-Aqsa Intifada to NIS1,600 in June 2003. Some 71% of Palestinian households suffered some form of decrease, of which 45.4% lost more than 50% of their monthly income. As of August 2003, 38.6% of surveyed households were receiving humanitarian assistance (West Bank: 26.3% and the Gaza Strip 63.3%), whereas 79.3% of the households said they needed assistance. Some 44% of the total assistance was provided in the form of food supplies, 30% in cash. By 2004, the percentage of Palestinians living below the poverty line had reached 64%.

CHAPTER 4

CULTURE

Culture

The Arts

Until the early twentieth century, the different forms of Palestinian art were heavily influenced by artistic work in the Arab world. The negation of the Arabs of Palestine by succeeding phases of foreign occupation meant that all art became a means to express national identity and ever the fight to try to preserve it. Theatre, cinema, painting, music and literature, all rooted in living tradition, oriented themselves towards a culture of resistance based on popular education, by expressing the suffering and the struggle of the Palestinian people.

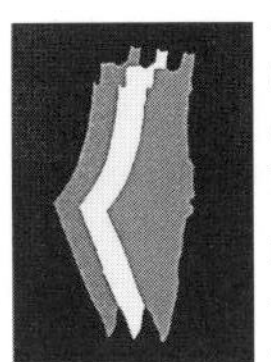

Music

Palestinian musical art finds its sources in contemporary Arab music, both classical and traditional. The main musical centres (Egypt, Syria, Lebanon, and Iraq) which continue to dominate the musical field, have imposed their mark. After the 1967 war, Palestinian musicians reoriented their music and production towards traditional and rural music. This helped to advance the creation of many folkloric groups which mixed music, dancing *(dabka)* and resistance music.

Palestinian Folklore

Music and popular songs belong to the oral tradition and are usually learned on the occasion of ceremonies or in special evenings. A Bedouin or peasant *sha'er* (poet, composer and singer) combines two musical genres, in which traditional music is mixed with improvisation. The long and repetitive singing about nostalgia for the past, love, or homesickness is sometimes accompanied by the *rebaba* (a sort of violin - a rectangular box with two strings made of horse-hair played with a bow). The syllabic chant has short verses and a refrain sung first by the *sha'er*, then by the audience. This often accompanies traditional dancing and wedding ceremonies. Hand-clapping and percussion *(darbouka* or *tabla)* keep the rhythm of the song lively. Sometimes, there are other musical instruments such as the *shebaba* (a small flute with or without a mouth-piece), and clarinet with double reeds of two types: the *mijwez* (two tubes of equal length) and the *yarghoul* (where one of the pipes can be as much as two metres long, to produce a humming sound).

Some Arab Musicians and Album Titles

Abdel Halim Hafez (Egypt)
Qare' et al-Finjan (The Fortune Teller)

Abu Arab (Palestine)
*Hadi ya Bahr Hadi (Be calm, oh sea)**

Ahmad Qa'bour (Palestine)
Unadikum (I call upon you)

Al-Founoun esh-Sha'abiyeh (Palestine)
Zaghareed (Ululations)
Majd al-Quds (The Glory of Jerusalem)

Palestinian Songs and Music (compilation)
*Palestinian Sounds** ▼

Palestinian Patriotic Songs
Iqa' at al-Intifada (Notes of the Intifada)
*Watan (Homeland)**

Fairouz (Lebanon) ▼
Keifak Inta (How are you?)
Al-Andalousiyat (The Andalusians)
'Qud Rannan (The Lute Vibrates)
*Zahrat al-Mada' in (The Rose of Cities or Jerusalem in My Heart)**
Wahdoun (Alone)

Fairouz / Shamseddine / Wadi' es-Safi (Lebanon / Syria)
Sahret al-Hob (Evening of love)

Farid al-Atrache (Lebanon)
Aktoub a-waraq a-shajar (I write on the leaf of a tree)

Firket Es-Soumoud (The Troupe of Steadfastness) (Palestine)
Jiser al-Aouda (The Bridge of Return)

Ilham al-Madfai (Iraq)
Khuttar
Julia Boutros (Syria)
Wein al-Malayin? (Where are the Millions?)

Marcel Khalifeh (Lebanon)
*Ahmad al-Arabi (Ahmad the Arab)**
Tousbihoun ala Watan (Dawn of a Homeland)
Wou' oud min al-Assifa (Promises of the Storm)

Mohammed Abdel Wahab (Egypt)
Min Ghair Lai (Without Asking Why)

Sabreen (Palestine)
Maout en-Nabi (The Death of the Prophet)

Samih Shqair (Syria)
Za' er al-Roman (Flower of the Pomegranate)

Sheikh Imam (Egypt)
Oh Palestinian, Nixon

Um Koulthom (Egypt)
Enta Omri (You Are My Life)
Ba' id Annak (Far from You)
Ya Maseherni (You keep me awake)

Ziad Rahbani (Lebanon)
Bala Ishi (Without Anything)
Abu Ali

* Five highly recommended albums

Literature

The distinctive characteristics of Palestinian literature developed under the British Mandate and during the Great Revolt of 1936. A number of Palestinian and Arab writers were involved in this popular uprising (1936-1939), amongst them Bishara al-Khoury. The adoption of prose written in verse form was a hallmark of the new generation of Palestinian writers such as Ibrahim Touqan, Rashid Hussein, and Abdel Rahim Mahmoud. After the Nakba, deep sorrow over the loss of the land and the separation of its people dominated Palestinian literature. Beginning with the Sixties and especially after the defeat of 1967, literature became "self-criticism" (Samih al-Qassem, Mahmoud Darwish, Fadwa Touqan, Ghassan Kanafani) and then documentary or historical record during the first Intifada. Fadwa Touqan published *The Martyrs of the Intifada* and Ezzet Gazawi *The Letters that Never Arrived,* where they describe the torture and life in Israeli jails. With the "Oslo Peace Process," the literary movement was first stifled, but then it was influenced by the feeling of defeat and frustration specific to the "peace process."

Mahmoud Darwish

An immense literary work of art, a land in itself. His poems have become popular hymns; some have been set to music, one of his most famous interpreters being Marcel Khalifa. Born in 1941 in Birwa (a village in the Galilee 9 kms from Akka), Mahmoud Darwish was thrown on the road to exile in 1948. After a year as refugees in Lebanon, he and his family secretly returned to what had become the State of Israel. In the meantime, his native village had been demolished and replaced by a settlement. A refugee in his own country, Darwish settled in the village of Deir al-Assad, where he lived a semi-clandestine existence for a while. He became, in Israeli judicial terminology, an "absent-present" person, a refugee living in his own land. After completing secondary studies, he settled in Haifa and joined the Israeli Communist party. He worked for two of its magazines, *al-Ittihad (The Union)* and *al-Jadid (The New)*, which were the only ones open to Palestinians. His involvement in politics and his poems earned him several prison terms. In these years, he became involved in the revolutionary and patriotic tendency called "the Literature of Resistance." In 1971, Mahmoud Darwish moved to Cairo, then Beirut, the capital of Palestinian resistance, where his reputation had preceded him. In his new exile, he pursued a more aesthetic approach. The Israeli invasion of Lebanon drove him into a new exile. Since then, he has gone from one Arab capital to another, sometimes living temporarily in Paris or London, where he can maintain a level of anonymity. A member of the executive committee of the PLO and president of the Union of Palestinian Writers, Darwish founded the literary revue *al-Karmel*. In 1993, he resigned from the PLO in protest against the Oslo Accords. Since then, he has been living either in Amman or Ramallah. His last collection of poems *"State of Siege"* describes the siege of Ramallah and the Palestinian territories during the al-Aqsa Intifada, evoking daily life and its many facets:

"Under siege,
Time becomes a space
Accustomed to its own Eternity.
During the siege, space becomes
A time
Delayed by the day before and
Late for tomorrow."

Palestinian Literature: A Bibliography

Badr (Liana),
A Compass for a Sun, 1992.
Stars over Jericho, 2001
Balcony over the Fakihan

Darwish (Mahmoud),
The Palestinian Poems of Mahmoud Darwish, 1970
Palestine, My Country; the Business of Poems, 1988.
Roses Are More Scarce, 1989.
Palestinian Poems, 1989*
Chronicle of Ordinary Sadness, 1989.
Why did you Leave the Horse Alone? 1996.
The Last Evening on this Land, 1994
A Memory for Oblivion, 1994.
The Land Hems Us In, 2000
Unfortunately it was Eden
Adam of Two Edens

Fawal (Ibrahim)
On the Hills of God

Habibi (Emil)
*The Extraordinary Adventures of Said the Pessoptimist.**
Forgotten Sins, 1991
Soraya daughter of the Ogre, 1996.

Jabra (Jabra Ibrahim)
Searching for Walid Masud, 1988.
The First Well, 1993.
The Fortieth Piece,1997.
The Ship, 1996.
Hunters in a Narrow Street

Kanaaneh (Sharif)
Speak Bird Speak Again

Kanafani (Ghassan)
Tales of Palestine, 1979
Men in the Sun, 1990.*
Return to Haifa, 1997.

Khalifa (Sahar)
Chronicles of the Wild Fig Tree, 1978.*
The Faith of Sunflowers, 1988.
The Impasse of Essaha Gate, 2001
Wild Thorns.

Muhawi (Ibrahim) and Kana'ana (Sharif)
Once Upon a Time, Palestinan Folk Tales, 1997

Nabulsi (Layla)
Vacant Land, 1990
Arise, Dead Ones, 1994

Qassem (Samih)
I love you unto death, 1988
A handful of light, 1997 *

Shammas (Anton)
Arabesque, 1988

Souss (Ibrahim)
Flowers of the Olive Tree, 1985.
Far from Jerusalem, 1987
In the Beginning Was A Stone, 1993.

Touqan (Fadwa)
The Rock and Sorrow, Memory I, 1997.
The Cry of the Stone, Memory II, 1998.

Yakhlif (Yahya)
A Lake Beyond the Wind

* Five highly recommended books

Painting and Drawing

In the beginning of the last century, some icon painters, portraitists and even landscape artists, influenced by orientalist painters in the West, initiated painting as a new Palestinian art form. Emphasis on painting grew during the Sixties, taking its inspiration from themes of exile and the loss of land. Paintings tended to evoke either a sense of nostalgia or a call to resistance.

Naji al-Ali
1936 - 1987

Born in the village of al-Shajara in the Galilee, and then a refugee in the Ein al-Hilweh refugee camp in Lebanon, in his work Naji al-Ali expressed with biting and mordant sarcasm the situation of refugees and the complicity between unscrupulous businessmen and the Arab regimes with the Zionists and American imperialists. The New York Times once said, *"If you want to know what the Arabs think of the United States, just look at Naji al-Ali's cartoons."* Naji al-Ali signed his drawings with a 10-year-old boy called Handala (colocynth or bitter apple). Handala always had his back towards the viewer, his face turned towards Palestine and *"his hands crossed behind him to show his rejection of the current situation in the region, and the solution offered by the United States and the system"*. Handala would show his face only when *"there is no longer any threat to Arab dignity"* and he would be able to return to his native land.

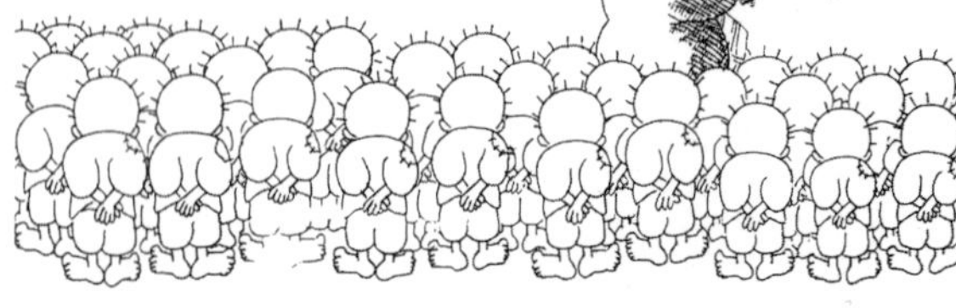

"WANTED - *dead or alive*"
"My country, my country *(biladi)* ...I give you my love and my heart"

Discovered by Ghassan Kanafani, Naji al-Ali published his first cartoons expressing "hope, revolution, and the birth of a new man." In his words, his caricatures were *"the expression of an oppressed people who pay dearly for their life, carrying on their shoulders the burden of errors committed by the powers that be. Everything they possess has been earned at a high price, under the unremitting siege of hardship and cruelty. They fight for their lives and die young, buried in the simplest of tombs. They are always on the defensive to stay alive. I live with them in their hiding places, observing them and burning to the beat of their hearts, to the flow of the blood which runs in their veins (...)"* Author of more than 40,000 cartoons published daily in several Arab newspapers, Naji al-Ali was assassinated on July 22, 1987, in the centre of London.

Caricatures by Naji al-Ali may be viewed at www.handala.org

Palestine our country, Palestine our country

The settlements

▪ Food: The Pleasures of the Table

Bread

Bread has a very specific, special importance. A basic food, it is also a product of the land and the symbol of people's attachment to the land, to their village and the lost homeland. Three kinds of bread are served with meals: the traditional bread, *taboun* (originally baked in clay ovens called *taboun*, hence the name) is used to make *musakhan; shrak*, a large, thin dough which is baked quickly on a half-circle of heated metal and is used to make *mensef* and sometimes to prepare *shawarma;* and *khobez* (which means "bread"), the bread most often eaten, usually accompanying salads and *mezzes*. It is used for the preparation of "sandwiches" and is especially good fresh from the oven or reheated, and may be eaten with olive oil and *za'atar* (a mixture of fresh, ground thyme and sesame seeds).

▪ Recipe for musakhan

Ingredients:
2 small chickens, each cut in two
3 tablespoons of olive oil
Juice of one lemon
Nutmeg
Pepper
Cinnamon
2 large onions
4 tablespoons of *sumac*
1 teaspoon of salt
2 tablespoons of pine nuts
4 *taboun* breads

1. Clean the chickens and cut them in half.
Pour lemon juice and a tablespoon of olive oil over the chickens and rub them with salt and spices (nutmeg, pepper and cinnamon), and a tablespoon of *sumac*.
Place in a very hot oven for 30 minutes.
2. Finely slice the onions.
Salt and add 3 tablespoons of *sumac*.
Brown the onions in the remaining olive oil.
3. Put half the onion slices and the oil on the bread.
Place a chicken piece on each piece of bread and cover with remaining onions.
Moisten the bread with water or meat bouillon.
Cook in a very hot oven for 20 minutes.
4. Sprinkle the pine nuts over the chicken.
Serve with green salad.

▪ Taboun Bread

Ingredients
1 kg of flour
1 tablespoon of active yeast
1 glass of olive oil
water

Sift the flour.
Dilute the yeast in water and oil.
Make a hole in the flour and add the diluted yeast.
Knead, adding a little water until the dough is elastic.
Leave the dough to rise for two hours.
Prepare several balls of dough and leave to rise.
Preheat the oven (very hot).
Knead the dough fairly thin, and make small holes in it with your fingers (do not pierce the dough - see photograph)
Place the dough in the preheated oven.

▪ Appetizers *(mezzes)*

Felafel: Small fried balls of ground chick peas and parsley, often served in a sandwich with mixed salads.

Foul: Mashed beans served with lemon, garlic and olive oil.

Hummus: Ground chick peas mixed with sesame cream *(tahina)*, lemon and garlic.

Kebab: Skewers of ground, grilled meat, usually served with grilled onions and tomatoes.

Kubba: A mixture of meat and chopped onions coated with cracked wheat batter, then fried. Served with lemon.

Labana: Soft white cheese, sprinkled with olive oil.
Mutabbal: (Known by its Turkish name: *Baba Ghanoug*): pureed, grilled eggplant, mixed with lemon, garlic and olive oil.
Sambusek: Baked dough, stuffed with spinach, or cheese, or meat.
Sfiha: A type of pizza covered with a thin layer of ground meat, tomato, green pepper, onion and parsley. Originally an Armenian dish.
Shawarma: Sandwich of roasted, thinly-sliced meat (lamb, beef or turkey).
Tabboula: Cracked-wheat (bourghoul) salad, mixed with finely chopped parsley, mint, cucumber, tomato, lemon juice and olive oil.

■ Main dishes

Kedra: Rice with saffron and pieces of lamb traditionally cooked over steam in a pottery jar (*a kedreh*); a speciality of Hebron.
Kussa Mahshi: Zucchini stuffed with rice and meat.
Makluba: ("Upside-down"): Layers of rice or potato, broiled meat, and vegetables (fried cauliflower, eggplant, and potato).
Mashawi: Grilled meat served with various salads.
Mansaf: *"Shrak"* bread covered with rice and pieces of broiled lamb, served with cheese soup and grilled pine nuts. Originally a Bedouin dish, it is these days served in all places, particularly grand occasions such as marriages or births.
Musakhan: Roast chicken served on *taboun* bread and covered with olive oil, thin-sliced onion, and *sumac*, a slightly acid soft spice.
Mulukhiya: Boiled leaves of *mulukhiya* (a sort of spinach).
Waraq Dawali: Stuffed vine leaves.
Waraq Malfouf: Stuffed cabbage leaves.

■ Desserts and Pastries *(halawiyat)*

Baklawa: Thin leaves of dough layered on each other, filled with ground pistachios and covered with honey or syrup.
Kenafa: White cheese baked in a delicately poached orange-coloured layer of pasta, covered with syrup; a speciality of Nablus.
Ma'amoul: Cake stuffed with dates, walnuts or white cheese. It is usually prepared in both Muslim and Christian religious feasts.
Qatayef: A sort of pancake, stuffed with baked cheese, or a combination of walnuts, coconut and cinnamon, then baked in an oven and glazed with syrup; a speciality at Ramadan. In Nablus, it is available throughout the year.

■ Drinks

Arak: Aniseed-flavoured alcoholic drink, similar to Greek *ouzo* or French *anis*. Local variations produced in the Ramallah and Bethlehem regions.
'Assir burtukal: Orange juice.
'Assir kharroub: Carob juice.
'Assir loz: Almond juice.
'Assir sous: Liquorice juice.
'Assir taza: Fresh fruit juice.
Taybeh beer: Beer from Taybeh. (See p. 238.)
Shai: Tea.
Qahwa: Arab coffee (Turkish or Greek). Usually, a few cardamom seeds are mixed with the coffee, which is prepared in water brought just lightly to boiling point.
Nabid: Wine (made by the monks at monasteries in Cremisan and Latrun).
Tamer hindi juice: Tamarisk juice, from the fruit of the tamarind tree.

CHAPTER 5

COLONISATION AND OCCUPATION

Colonisation and Occupation

■ The Zionist colonisation of Palestine

From the first hours of Zionist colonisation in Palestine in 1880, the appropriation and expropriation of the land was a major objective; the stated aim was: the creation of a Jewish state. Palestine was portrayed as a "land without a people" and Jews everywhere were encouraged to become real pioneers and to settle there. The Jewish National Fund (JNF), established at the time of the Fifth Zionist Congress in Basel (Switzerland) in 1901, was the principal institution established to acquire land, which then became the "inalienable property of the Jewish people." Lands bought from the large, feudal owners, mostly absentee landlords living in the cities of Lebanon, Turkey or Syria, were systematically cleansed of their Palestinian smallholding peasants, who farmed them only according to customary law. The British never ceased encouraging immigration and colonisation, sending their troops to help evacuate lands acquired by the JNF. In 1925, the JNF was replaced by a body still functioning today, *Keren Kayemet L'Israel BM*. (National Fund for Israel Ltd.). When, on November 29, 1947, the UN voted for its partition plan (Resolution 181), "Jewish"-owned land was only 7% to 8% of the total surface area of Palestine. The UN recommended the creation of a Jewish state on 56% of the country, leaving 43% for the Palestinian majority, while the region of Jerusalem (including Bethlehem) was to become an international zone.

Palestine (1945): Palestinian and Zionist property holdings by district (in percentage)

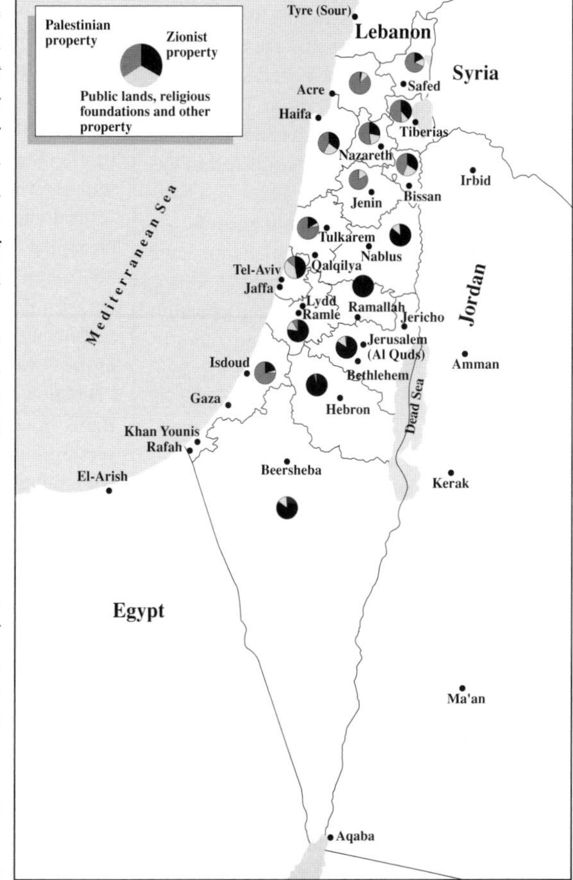

■ Confiscation of land in the 48 Territories

The Palestinian population of the 48 Territories (the present State of Israel), while it avoided transfer, has nonetheless incessantly witnessed the systematic confiscation of its lands for more than 50 years. Although Palestinian Israelis represent 20% of the population of the State of Israel today, they own no more than 3%

of the land, while 93% of the country's land has been declared "State Land." With its Absentee Property Law (1950), the State of Israel has given itself a "legal" framework for the seizure of lands and possessions of refugees, who have not been allowed to return to their property. Similarly, new "legal" measures, both military and civilian, have been instituted; among these have been the "arrangement of territory" law as one of the most efficient means. Thanks to this law, entire territories previously under Arab municipal administration have been integrated into the new borders of the Jewish municipalities, which limit construction on them (by control of building permits by urban planning) or reserving them for projects of "general interest." In addition, huge areas have been declared "military zones." One of the most pernicious methods of confiscation consists of simply not recognising the existence of dozens of Arab villages and thus depriving them of their property and basic services (water, electricity, health services, etc.). The steady growth of settlements in the Territories of 48 prompted strong protests that culminated in the Seventies (Land Day in 1976), and which have repeated themselves since the Oslo Accords. At Ein Mahil (Nazareth), Umm al-Fahm, and Tarshiha (a village on the Lebanese border), hundreds of hectares are in constant jeopardy. The dispossession of land and bureaucratic measures of restricting housing have, for their part, resulted in a correlating development of illegal construction.

All these measures are part of the Israeli policy code named "The Star of David" plan whose goal is to obtain a Jewish majority in regions predominantly Arab (Upper and Lower Galilee, the Triangle and the Negev). The plan also seeks to eliminate territorial contiguity between zones of Arab population. To effect this demographic change, the Trans-Israel Highway Project (Highway No. 6) presently under construction allows for the Jewish population to be more concentrated to the east, reinforcing links between the settlements on the other side of the Green Line - that is, in the West Bank. The cost for the Palestinians of Israel: one third of their lands will be confiscated! (See *Trans-Israel Highway*, p. 357.)

■ In the Territories occupied in 1967

Israeli colonisation in the Palestinian territories occupied in 1967 has responded to Israel's strategic military interests as well as economic and ideological ones (control of the principal roads in the Jordan valley and elsewhere, control of the aquifers, the Palestinian market, and the Palestinian cheap workforce) and the realisation of the Greater Land of Israel. These actions are a continuation of policies in the Territories of 48. From 1967 to 1977, 35,000 Jewish settlers were installed in the West Bank and Gaza Strip. Plans to colonise and populate new areas were enacted as a regular phenomenon but were sharply accelerated during the "peace process." There were 75,000 Jewish settlers in the West Bank at the time of the Madrid Conference in 1991, 95,000 at the time of the signature of the Oslo Accords in 1993, 147,000 at the end of the Rabin and Peres governments in 1996, while 29,496 hectares of land were confiscated to bring to fruition the settlement policy. In 2001, 180,000 settlers lived in the West Bank, 190,000 in East Jerusalem, 5,000 in Gaza and 17,000 in the Occupied Syrian Golan Heights. In January 2000, there were 209 Israeli settlements: (190 in the West Bank and 19 in the Gaza Strip); over 74 settlements were established after the signature of the Oslo Accords and 27 more after the Wye Plantation Accord in October 1998. Under the Barak government, 3,499 housing units in the settlements were approved and 2,270 constructed. State subsidies reached almost $17,000 for buyers and land tax exemptions for land owners was spread over a period of up to 10 years. Since the beginning of the al-Aqsa Intifada, some 15 new Jewish settlements have been given the green light.

Since the beginning of the settlement enterprise, according to Shimon Peres, $80 billion has been spent on settlements by the State of Israel, largely subsidised by the American government. Figures are hard to cite, since much has been buried in defence budgets. *[see Peace Now Settlement Watch - www.peacenow.org.il and ARIJ "Eye on Palestine" www.arij.org for up-to-date statistics.]*

The phases of Israeli Colonisation

The Allon Plan guided the politics of settlement building from 1967 to 1977, by aiming both to take control of as much of the West Bank as possible by seizing the strategic zones (the Jordan Valley and mountain aquifer sources) and to restrict the demographic evolution of Palestinian East Jerusalem. Since 1978, the colonisation plan had set out to obliterate the Green Line (the Armistice Line of 1949) and to settle the heart of the West Bank along an east-west axis. The plan was to create territorial contiguity and prepare for a future annexation of the West Bank, and even Gaza. In 1991, the Seven Stars Plan affirmed this territorial contiguity. The construction of seven cities on the Green Line *(Modi' in Illit, Ofarim, Elkana, Sal' it, Rehan…)* must effectively erase every notion of borders between the State of Israel and the West Bank. Today, 21 settlements have been developed close to the Green Line where more than 72,000 settlers live. This plan applies equally to Jerusalem *(Gush Etzion, Giv' at Ze' ev, Ramot…)*. During the Oslo Accords, the Israeli state advanced its settlement efforts at an unprecedented pace, around the Palestinian autonomous zones, whose contours depend on the military occupation authorities. The West Bank, cut off from Jerusalem and the Gaza Strip, is carved up by settlement blocs and a major road network or grid under Israeli control and to which access is granted only to Israelis. The geographic and demographic growth of every Palestinian locality, city or village, autonomous, semi-autonomous, or non-autonomous, is being stifled.

Allon Plan (1967)

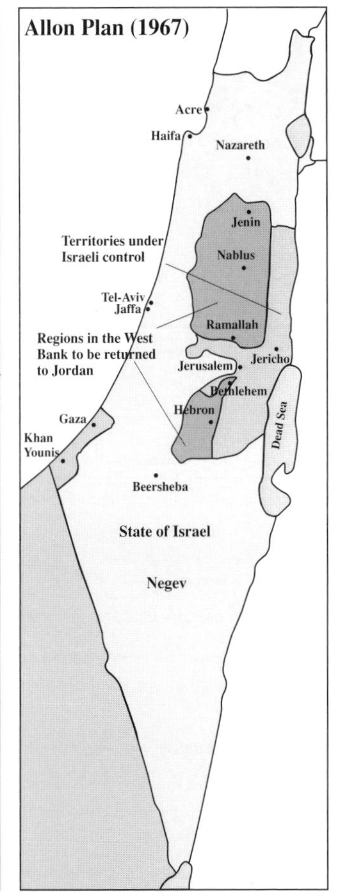

Plan of the Israeli Labour Party (1976)

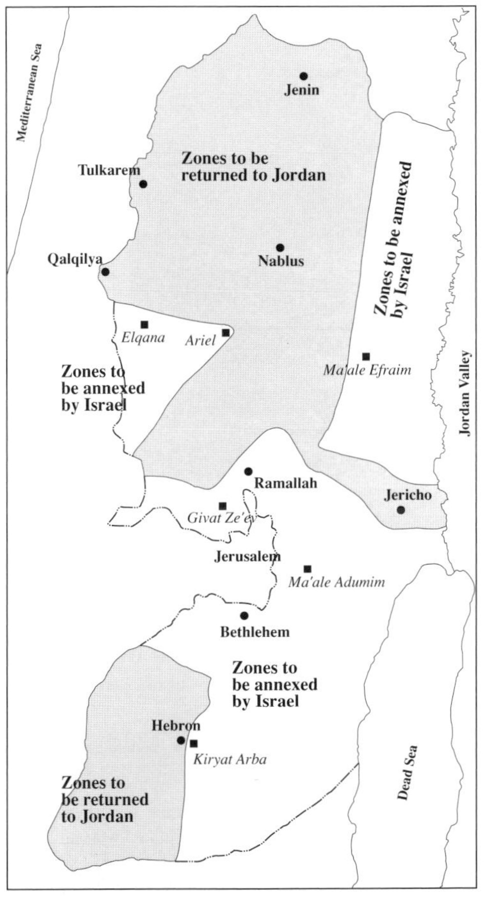

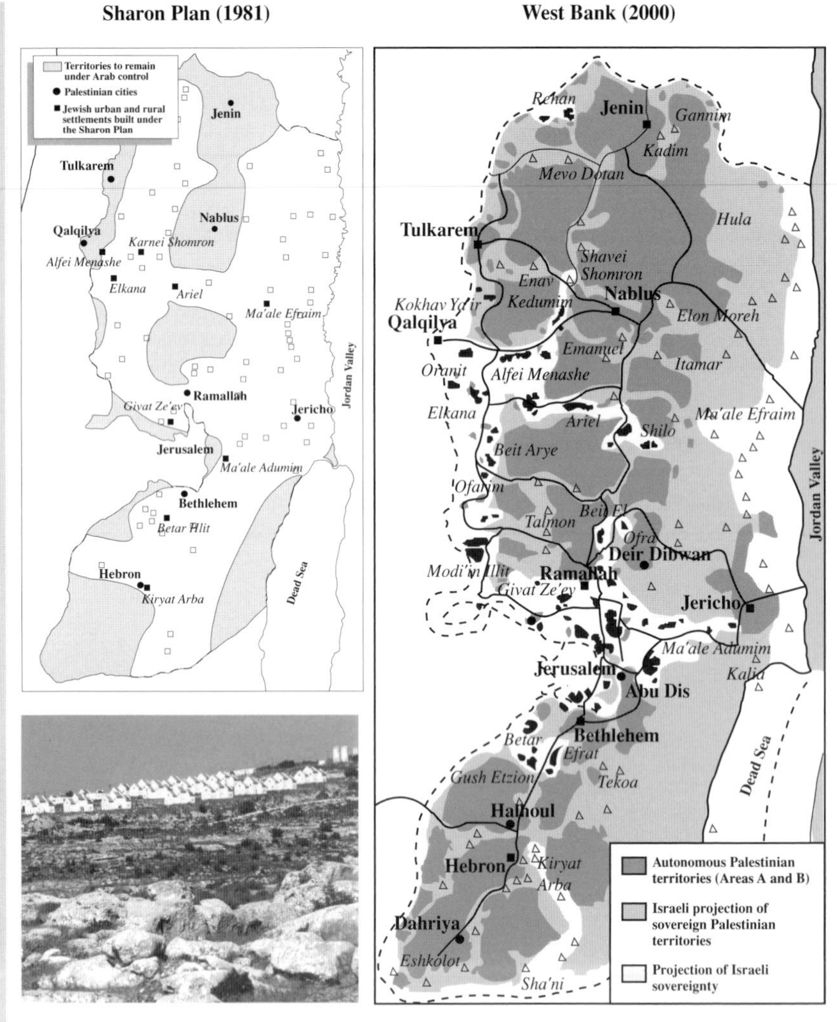

Techniques of land confiscation

To this day, land is being expropriated in the 1948 and 1967 territories under pseudo-legal arrangements.

- "Abandoned" property: The Absentee Property Law (1950) and military order 58 (1967) permit the seizure of lands and possessions "abandoned" by their owners who became refugees at the times of the wars in 1948 and 1967.
- "Government land" - expropriation of state land (Ottoman, British and Jordanian).
- Land seized for military purposes: Appropriation by virtue of vital and urgent military needs. In the West Bank, until 1980, this measure permitted the appropriation of land for settlements, openly considered as an integral part of military defence.
- "Government property" - Reactivating Ottoman law and that of successive authorities in Palestine

make a piece of land that is not officially registered, or not cultivated for a certain time, state property. About 40% of the West Bank has been confiscated under this law.

- "Closed" lands: Lands designated for military training.
- "General interest" - Lands expropriated for the general good: roads for settlements, infrastructure under Israeli control (water towers, electricity plants, etc.).

What does a settlement look like?

The characteristic feature of all settlements is their urban planning; their location and construction are subject to the preliminary approval of several ministries (Ministry of Defence, Ministry of the Interior, and Ministry of Housing and Infrastructure, among others). A mixture of civil and military architecture, they fulfil a double function, both aggressive and defensive. Usually built in concentric circles on hilltops, their position guarantees them territorial and military control of the surrounding areas. The uniform aspect of the buildings, built close together in neat rows, answer all these requirements as well as financial ones.

■ The By-Pass Road System in the West Bank

Since 1993, the State of Israel has invested over 3 billion dollars in the construction of a grid of new roads for settlers in the West Bank. The new road network's aim is to create infrastructure that facilitates the expansion of settlements, reduces the military presence to these highways only, and leaves partly-autonomous Palestinian enclaves in the entire West Bank which are under the jurisdiction of the Palestinian Authority, divided up by the grid of settler-only ("apartheid") roads with each enclave or ghetto separated each from the other and the single exit road from each ghetto easily monitored by Israeli military checkpoints or other control mechanisms (gates, earth mounds, "flying" checkpoints (roving jeeps), etc.). At the end of 1994, the Rabin government launched a programme of construction of 400 kms of new roads, linking the settlements directly to the Israeli state or connecting them to each other. The project required the confiscation of 1600 hectares of land, often extremely fertile. Since the al-Aqsa Intifada, large stretches of roads have been closed to Palestinians, who have been forced to take many time-consuming detours, sometimes using dirt roads, and to wait hours at the military checkpoints, whether fixed or temporary, which regularly punctuate the roads.

THE APARTHEID WALL, SEGREGATION BARRIER

(See Wall map - coloured photo no. XII)

On February 20, 2005 Israel's Cabinet approved a revised route of the West Bank Wall. Once completed, the total length will be 670 kms; 209 kms has been completed. Israel claims the Wall is primarily about security, but the "new" route runs over twice the length of the 1967 "border," making it much more difficult and expensive to patrol.

A concrete Wall with watchtowers in Bethlehem, Qalqiliya, parts of Tulkarem and the Jerusalem "envelope," there it is 9 metres high. Elsewhere it is a fence with a buffer zone 30-100 metres wide including electronic fences, cameras, military patrol roads, layers of razor wire, sand paths to trace footprints, ditches, surveillance cameras and agricultural gates; these do not provide any guarantee for farmers to access their land but instead strengthen Israel's strangling system of permits and checkpoints. Israel is constructing 24 "tunnels" throughout the West Bank to form the only points of connection within the ghettoized West Bank. Almost entirely built between Palestinians, only 20% is on the Green Line between Israel and Palestine. It is a unilaterally imposed border; international terminals are now being built by Israel in strategic places on its route, such as Qalandia-Ramallah and Bethlehem.

The Head of the Knesset Economics Committee has estimated the Wall will cost $3.4 billion; some $5 million per kilometre. Israel says its Wall is temporary, despite a projected lifespan of 35 years.

Already suffering from land lost to massive settlements, Israeli-only roads and military expansion, Palestinians are progressively being deprived of freedom of movement, work, agricultural land, hundreds of thousands of uprooted olive trees, water, roads, access to health facilities, educational institutions, markets, family connections and religious sites.

Despite inaccurate Israeli claims that the new Wall route "only" takes 7-8% of the West Bank, the Wall and planned settlement expansion will enable Israeli control of 46% of the Occupied West Bank. The new Wall route incorporates 9.5% of the West Bank including the Latrun Valley, East Jerusalem and the Ariel Bloc. Settlement blocs east of the Wall incorporates an additional 8.0% of the West Bank. Israel's incorporation of the Jordan Valley accounts for an additional 28.5% of the West Bank. The Wall facilitates expansion of the most damaging Israeli settlement blocs, all of which the International Court of Justice unanimously deemed illegal on July 9th, 2004. Days after announcing the new Wall route, Israeli plans were revealed for 6,391 new West Bank illegal settlement units, to accommodate an additional 25,000 settlers. Almost half of these units are slated for the Jerusalem area. The revised Wall route effectively incorporates 355,783 illegal settlers, or 86.6% of the Israeli settlement population.

PASSIA's "Settlements and the Wall" (www.passia.org) says: "Israel not only reduces the land area, territorial contiguity and economic viability of a Palestinian state, but also pre-empts the establishment of a viable independent Palestinian state and the possibility of a two-state solution."

Percentages are deceiving; the value and location of land is crucial. The Wall and planned settlement expansion incorporate many of the West Bank's most valuable water productive zones, effectively pre-empting future fair and equitable allocation of the West Bank's water resources, as required by international law. In the "first phase," Israel confiscated 36 groundwater wells.

East Jerusalem accounts for only 1.3% of the West Bank, but represents the economic, cultural and religious hub of the Palestinian economy. The "Ariel Finger," which stretches 22km into the northern West Bank, accounts for 2.1% of the West Bank, but sits atop the most valuable regional water resources. The new Wall route still effectively excises East Jerusalem from the rest of the West Bank and together with Jerusalem-area settlements sever East Jerusalem from Bethlehem and Ramallah, while dividing the West Bank into north and south. Historically, these communities have been culturally and economically interdependent. The illegal Adumim settlement bloc and its Wall prevent the future Palestinian capital, East Jerusalem, from having a direct, unimpeded link with Jordan. Reaching 14km into the West Bank at its narrowest section, Adumim will effectively slice the West Bank in two.

Incorporation into Israel of three major settlement blocs surrounding East Jerusalem - Givon, Adumim and Etzion-eliminate areas critical for natural expansion and Palestinian economic development. With the fragmentation of the Christian and Muslim Palestinian communities of East Jerusalem and surrounding areas, Jerusalem risks losing its historic character of housing vibrant communities of Christians, Jews and Muslims.

The Wall almost completely encircles towns such as Qalqilya, Habla, Azzun Atmeh, Bir Nabala, and Shuafat, while nearby settlements, illegally built on their lands, continue to expand. Salfit, the most fertile area of the West Bank, is losing over 70% of its land. North of Salfit, incorporation of the Ariel bloc cuts 22km into the West Bank, separating the central West Bank from the North. Bethlehem-area villages Wadi Fukin, Walaja, Battir, Nahalin, Nuaman and Husan (19,000 Palestinians) will now be walled in ghettos.

By Israeli military order, only Israelis-including immigrants to Israel under Israel's Law of Return-may enter, live or work in areas between the Wall and Green Line without permits. Thousands of Palestinians trapped in this Seam Zone must obtain and renew permits to remain in their homes. Palestinians with land or jobs on the other side of the Wall must obtain and renew permits from the Israeli military to access fields or places of employment. Within the "first phase," 16 villages west of the Wall were de facto annexed to Israel and some 50 villages separated from their lands. [For further info: www.stopthewall.org]

Timeline

- November 2000: Ehud Barak approves first project to build a "barrier."
- June 2002: Construction of Wall, land confiscation, uprooting of trees, west of Jenin.
- September 2002: First map of Wall, a portion of northern part, is made public.
- July 2003: Israeli Defence Ministry announces completion of "first phase" of Wall.
- October 2003: Israel issues military orders declaring all lands west of Wall's "first phase" a "seam zone," forcing permit system and de facto annexation of these lands.
- July 2004: ICJ declares Wall illegal and to be dismantled immediately.
- February 2005: Israeli Cabinet presents "modification" plans of Wall. World Bank plans to finance construction of Wall gates.
- March 2005: UN Secretary-General visits Palestine, failing to visit Wall or call on Israel to abide by international law and dismantle Wall.

CHAPTER 6

RESTRICTIONS ON FREEDOM OF MOVEMENT

Restrictions on Freedom of Movement

From 1948 to 1966, Palestinians of '48 living inside Israel lived under military law. All movement outside an official place of residence, no matter what the reason (medical, family or professional, etc.), required a "special permit" provided by the Israeli military authorities. Any Palestinian moving around or sleeping elsewhere and caught outside his or her own house at night without the proper permit was subject to a fine and prison sentence. In the first years of the creation of the State of Israel, house searches and the hunting down of refugees who had returned illegally to their homes were frequent. This regime continued for twenty years or so; a year after military law was lifted, the Israeli army occupied East Jerusalem, the West Bank and the Gaza Strip, and freedom of movement was strictly curtailed there.

From 1972 to 1989, a "general permit" authorised Palestinians from the West Bank and Gaza Strip to enter Israel and Jerusalem during the day and evening. However, they were forbidden to spend the night there (between 1.00 a.m. and 5.00 a.m.). In June 1989, the Israeli authorities added new restrictions to this "general permit," refusing it to any individual they considered "a risk." Then, in January 1991, an "individual travel permit" replaced the "general permit."

The Oslo Accords perpetuated this system of segregation and restraints which prevented the free circulation of goods and persons. Every infraction brought a fine of between 400 and 15,000 shekels and a prison sentence ranging from a few days to nine months. In the Territories occupied since 1967, the main highways remained under exclusive Israeli control so that

Israel maintained the right to allow or forbid access to Palestinians.

Since the outbreak of the al-Aqsa Intifada, restricted movement has been even more enforced. Each Palestinian town and each main highway has been put under real siege. Travelling between villages and cities has become a permanent challenge. Alternative routes have been improvised (ways across fields or on dirt paths, exchanging taxis when passage is closed, and much walking), which Israeli forces have responded to with new obstacles: new ditches, kilometres of huge rolls of razor wire, and even solid walls.

Another stage in the restriction of freedom has also transpired: the necessity to ask the occupation authorities in advance for permission to travel from one town to another or from one "canton" or "Bantustan" to another; (this same measure was imposed on those Palestinians living inside Israel from 1948 until 1966).

The Palestinians of Jerusalem - a right in danger

In 1993, nine permanent check-points (*mahsoum* in Hebrew) were set up on the main access roads into Jerusalem, predating the Hamas policy of bus-bombs (which had responded to Baruch Goldstein's 1994 massacre of 27 Palestinians while they prayed in the Ibrahimi Mosque or Cave of the Patriarchs, in Hebron). From April 1994 on, Jerusalem was permanently closed off: the nine checkpoints all were provided with infrastructure: watch-towers, lighting and strategically-placed cement blocks. From this time on, only persons with a card showing they were residents of Jerusalem (a blue card) could enter the city. Many Palestinians originally from Jerusalem, but living outside the municipal borders and therefore without a blue card, were forbidden entrance to their own city.

In December 1995, a new law was passed by the government of Shimon Peres which put holders of blue cards to a further test: they now had to prove (under threat that they would lose their card and their right to live in Jerusalem) that the centre of their life was within the city boundaries. In addition, this law was declared to be effective retroactively. And so, between 1995 and 2000, the authorities revoked 2,000 blue cards. Children whose names were recorded on the card of an adult whose card was taken back automatically lost their right to live in Jerusalem, too. However, after a decision by the Israeli Supreme Court in March 2000, this law is no longer in effect; but with the erection of the so-called "Jerusalem Envelope" or Wall, the issue has become - once again - critical. East Jerusalemites are already having more problems than previously in entering nearby Ramallah, which is being deliberately severed from its contact with Jerusalem.

Travel regulations from one territorial location to another depend on the place of residence of each Palestinian

- **A Palestinian from Jerusalem** (whose Jerusalem residence card is issued by the Israelis) may travel to the West Bank or to the 1948 territories (inside Israel); however, an East Jerusalem Palestinian wanting to enter the Gaza Strip must give an acceptable reason to the authorities in order to receive a special permit, which is given for a period usually limited to one day. It is also becoming increasingly complex and Kafkaesque for East Jerusalemites to enter Ramallah, especially by car.

- **A Palestinian from the West Bank** (with a West Bank residence card) must apply for and receive special authorisation in advance to go to Jerusalem or the State of Israel (48 Territories). He cannot receive this unless he shows a work contract or a certificate from a hospital. In the latter case, the patient must travel to the hospital alone, unless a family member has also applied for and received a permit. It is out of the question to go to Jerusalem for family or religious reasons without a permit. This means that it is not generally possible to visit the al-Aqsa Mosque (the third most sacred site for Muslims) or the Church of the Holy Sepulchre to pray, not even on important religious holidays (Ramadan, al-'Isra wa al-Miraj, Easter or Christmas), unless this often impossible, often Catch-22 bureaucratic process has been completed.

- **A Palestinian from Gaza** must obtain special permission in advance to go to Jerusalem or the State of Israel. He must go by way of Egypt, and then Jordan, in order to enter the West Bank by crossing the Allenby Bridge. (Gaza is otherwise actually less than an hour's travel from Hebron.) Another way was opened in 1999 [See *Tarqumia*, p. 225]. But Draconian measures at the customs and the humiliations to which travellers were subjected decided many to take the "normal" route through Egypt and Jordan, taking days.

- **A Palestinian of 1948** can theoretically go anywhere in the territories under Israeli jurisdiction, with the exception of the Gaza Strip but Area A is out of bounds to them (as it is to Israeli Jews), which makes family visits problematic. There are also many restrictions for anyone originally from Gaza married to anyone who is a Palestinian Israeli. The spouse originally from Gaza may obtain an Israeli residence card, but remains with no nationality, which makes foreign travel extremely complicated, if not almost impossible.

UNOCHA Report of 1 September 2004: The Humanitarian Impact of the West Bank Barrier on Palestinian Communities:

Barrier Gate Definitions

Agricultural Gate: An agricultural gate is a gate that allows access to agricultural fields, green houses and orchards located on the opposing side of the Barrier. Farmers must obtain a green permit to cross the gate to their fields.

Checkpoint Gate:A checkpoint gate is a crossing point from the West Bank into West Bank areas (*de facto* placed under Israeli jurisdiction) and Israel. Checkpoint gates are typically manned by Israeli Border Police or the IDF, and are also used by Israeli settlers. Palestinians from the West Bank must have a permit to enter Israel. Since the Barrier lies inside the West Bank in most areas, many of these gates are not located on the Green Line.

Military Gate: These gates are not permitted for Palestinian civilian use, with the exception of those gates indicated as "seasonal."

Road Gate: In some cases, a gate is installed at the junction where the Barrier blocks a road. Permits are required to cross road gates to continue travelling on the road.

School Gate: In some places, the Barrier blocks a route used to reach a school. Here a gate is installed to allow Palestinian school children and teachers to cross. Opening times coincide with school hours twice daily. Often, the IDF supplies a school bus to transport the students through the Barrier gate. These gates are usually closed to green permit holders.

Seasonal Gate:A gate closed for Palestinian use with the exception of harvest time - can be as early as September and as late as November. No official dates or times have been posted for these gates. Otherwise gates are used for military access.

Settlement Gate: Primarily used by settlers, these gates are officially open to farmers with green permits. However, due to the proximity of the gates to settlements and the fear of harassment by settlers, farmers generally choose not to use these gates.

Itineraries

JERUSALEM (AL-QUDS)

القدس

Jerusalem (al-Quds)

For thee I pray, oh city of prayer.
For thee, city of beautiful homes,
Flower of Cities,
Jerusalem, Jerusalem
I pray, oh city of prayer.

Our eyes turn to thee each day,
They follow, winding down the alleyways of oratories,
Hold ancient churches in their gaze,
Endure the melancholy of mosques.

Oh, night of the Nocturnal Journey ['Isrâ']
The path of those who have risen to the skies,
Our eyes gaze on thee each day,
And I pray.

The child in the cave,
His mother, Mary,
Two tearful faces,
Weeping for those who have gone astray,
Weeping for the children without homes,
For those who would defend the gates
And fell as martyrs at the start.

Peace martyred in the land of peace,
Justice silenced at its gates,
The child in the cave,
His mother, Mary,
Two tearful faces,
And I pray.

Fury thunders,
Faith lifts me up,
Fury thunders,
I will rise above my woes,
They come from every way,
On fearful steeds of war,
Like the Visage of our God of old,
It comes, it comes...

The gate of our city shall never close,
For I shall go to pray,
I will knock upon the gates,
I will open up these gates,
And you, Oh River Jordan,
With your holy waters: you will wash my temples clean,
And you, Oh River Jordan will wash away
All traces of barbarian feet.

Fury thunders,
On fearful steeds, it storms.

■ Poem by the Rahbani Brothers, sung by Fairouz

The Names of Jerusalem

Jerusalem was first mentioned in two of the so-called Egyptian "Execration Texts" of the nineteenth century BC at the time of the pharaohs. These texts were ritual lists of Asiatic and Nubian places Egypt at least theoretically controlled, recorded on dishes, vases and figurines, smashed in a symbolic act of domination. The two inscriptions were on a piece of pottery and a clay figurine. Jerusalem's name here is Rushalimu, the Egyptian form of the Canaanite word Urushalimu: "Uru" means "foundation," while "Shalim" or "Salem" (Genesis 14:18) was the name of the Canaanite god of plenitude. The Semitic roots of the word reappear in the Hebrew "Shalom" and the Arabic "Salaam," meaning "peace," but also implying "plenitude" or the blessings of life in a wider sense. In the fourteenth century BC, the name Urushalimu appeared again in the Egyptian Amarna Letters. The name survived over a long period of time that followed, a testimony to the stability of the population and its traditions. Jerusalem is mentioned in neo-Assyrian sources, in cuneiform writing on tablets of the eighth century BC, as Ursalimmu. On the other hand, it is named on the list of cities conquered by Nebuchadnezzar in the sixth century BC as "the City of Judah," which meant the capital of the territories belonging to King Judah. The original name never disappeared,

for it appeared in ancient Hebrew as Yerushalim (or -em) ("bear peace") and in Greek, Yerusalim or Hierosolyma (*hieros* = holy).
After putting down the revolt against the Romans, Hadrian established the colony of Aelia Capitolina here in 135 AD. Its Greek name prevailed during the Byzantine period, but was usually preceded by the name Agia Polis, meaning "the holy City." Jerusalem's Roman name is kept alive in the collective memory, and is also found in classical Arab poetry from the beginning of the Arab-Islamic period in its abbreviated, Arabised form, Iliya. In the Arabo-Islamic period, its name took on a religious significance. It became "Beit al-Makdas" (The House of Holiness or the Sanctuary) and later became "**al-Quds al-Sharif**" (The City of Holiness or The Noble). This last name prevails today, most often in its abbreviated form, **al-Quds.**

■ Historical Background

The discovery of stone tools in the region indicates that it has been inhabited by humans since the Palaeolithic age. After the first encampments or Chalcolithic villages appeared in the area (4000-3000 BC) identified at the edges of the Kidron Valley, a fortified town was built on the site of Jerusalem in the Middle Bronze Age (2000-1500 BC). No other local, written source refers to it, except Egyptian sources at the beginning of the second millennium, which mention the existence of a town, known as Rushalimu. The fourteenth-century BC Letters of Amarna - also of Egyptian provenance - provide more information; in one of the letters (dated *circa* 1000 BC) sent to Pharaoh Akhenaton, Abdi-Heba, the ruler of the region, begged for protection against Bedouin incursions. To that end, the town was fortified in *circa* 1000 BC for a second time. According to the Bible, King David, the ruler of the south of Judaea (Judah), incorporated the town into his territory [kingdom], and made it his official residence. Solomon succeeded his father, David, and continued his building programme, extending the city to the west and erecting a temple to Jehovah (1 Kings 1:1-38). However, neither archaeological evidence nor any text from that period has confirmed what the Bible says - nothing has been found except traces of an urban centre, not even a fortress or any monumental buildings that could have been the Temple or Solomon's palace.

When the Assyrians took the city in 732 BC, the aristocrats of Judah who lived in Jerusalem pledged allegiance to the Assyrian king in order to save the city from destruction and to escape deportation, the frequent fate of people in other territories in the Near East such as Samaria and the majority of the maritime city-states. During the reign of King Hezekiah (719-699 BC), Assyrians were expected to lay siege to Jerusalem (having destroyed the capital of the northern kingdom, Shomron or Samaria). The Bible says it was at first protected by an epidemic that took its toll on Sennacherib's army as well as on the entire region. The city finally fell to Nebuchadnezzar in 586 BC; as was usual, all elite citizens were deported - 4,600 people according to the Book of Jeremiah (Jeremiah 52:28-30), over 8,000 according to the Book of Kings (2 Kings 24:16), still a very small proportion of the total population of Judah at that time. For two entire generations, this exiled Jewish aristocracy was to create the myth of the primacy or pre-eminence of Jerusalem, their promised city (Psalms 137:1-6). Then, in 538 BC, the young Persian emperor, Cyrus, allowed the descendants of these exiles to return to Jerusalem. The city walls were rebuilt, as was the temple to Jehovah, which was also enlarged.

During the Hellenistic period, the city was a modest centre: only a few thousand people lived here - a Jewish, hellenised aristocracy and Seleucid mercenaries who worshipped Graeco-oriental gods. In the second century BC, the hellenisation process caused divisions in the practice of the Jewish faith; there were religious conflicts between different schools of Judaism and between some of these schools and other religious communities (such as the Hellenistic and oriental religious communities). Jerusalem's name was changed to Antiochia at this time. However, the Greeks lost Jerusalem to the Maccabees, who then founded the Hasmonean dynasty, which led to the imposition of Judaism as the state religion. The

Samaritan temple on Mount Jarzim, considered by the Samaritans as the sacred place where Abraham was asked to sacrifice his son Isaac, was a natural rival to the temple in Jerusalem. Yohanan Hyrcanus destroyed that temple in 124 BC, and Jerusalem became the capital of his new kingdom, which Rome formally recognised.

In 63 BC, Pompey conquered Jerusalem. Herod the Great, proclaimed king of Judaea by the Roman Senate, took over in 37 BC, thus ending the Hasmonean dynasty. Herod beautified the Jewish temple and greatly extended its platform. Throughout its history, this temple had been a disputed symbol or a national religious symbol and as such was a rallying point at the time of the struggle in revolt against the Romans. Herod's monumental construction programme transformed Jerusalem, for the first time in its history, into a true urban centre. There was a good deal of social unrest, fertile soil for the growth of different religious movements. One of these movements recognised Jesus as the new saviour, which posed a challenge to other schools of Palestinian Judaism, as well as to the Graeco-Roman and Graeco-oriental cults. After Herod's death, Jerusalem lost its status as political capital in favour of Caesarea. In 66-70 AD, a revolt against the imperial Roman power was brutally repressed. Part of the city, notably the temple of Jerusalem, the essence of Judaean identity, was destroyed. Between 132 and 135 AD, another revolt erupted in Judaea. In reprisal, Hadrian expelled the Jews from Jerusalem and built, on the ruins of the city, the colony Aelia Capitolina. At the end of Roman rule, a particular event had a huge impact on the status of the city and its development: the adoption of Christianity as the state religion in 325 AD. Since that time, Jerusalem has been the sacred centre of Christianity. There are monuments throughout the city, celebrating the martyrdom of Jesus, and all the holy places linked to episodes in His life and Passion.

In 638 AD, five years after the death of the Prophet Mohammad, the Arabo-Muslim armies conquered Jerusalem, ushering in a new era and consecrating Jerusalem, Beit al-Makdas (The House of the Sanctuary), as a holy city of Islam. The pact concluded with the Christian religious authorities and the handing over of the keys by Patriarch Sophronius to the caliph in person entailed no demographic change or exodus from the city, but confirmed the political victory of Islam over the imperial Byzantine power. Following the example of Caliph Mu'awiya (661-680), founder of the Umayyad dynasty, the induction ceremony for each new caliph was held in Jerusalem. Henceforth, Christians were placed under the caliph's authority. Upon the insistence of the Christian Patriarch, because of Jewish participation in the Persian massacres of 614 and Jewish encouragement of the destruction of churches and monasteries in the Holy Land (in Arabic: *Ard al-Muqaddasa)*, Jews were banished from Jerusalem. The dynasties that succeeded the Umayyad caliphate (660-750 AD), the Abbassids (750-969 AD) and the Fatimids (969-1071 AD), both took special pride in the city.

In July 1099 AD, the Crusaders led by Godfrey of Bouillon conquered Jerusalem, in a terrible bloodbath, in which most of the city's inhabitants were slaughtered; the city and its vicinity were then repopulated by the Crusaders. However, less than a century later, in 1187, the troops of Saladin liberated Jerusalem and once again the city regained its status as a holy city for Islam. The influx of Muslim pilgrims added new features to

the city, whose prosperity reached its climax under Mameluke rule. The Mamelukes defeated the Mongols in 1260 and the Crusaders in 1291, thus bringing serenity back to the city, albeit provisionally. The population grew to 40,000, but the number again fell as a result of the plague of 1350 and the state of insecurity prevailing in the area at the time.

In December 1516, city officials handed over the keys to its holy places to Ottoman Sultan Selim I, who defeated the Mamelukes at Marj Dabic, in North Syria. Jerusalem found favour with the Ottoman sultans, who endowed it with large foundations and, above all, a new wall or rampart. However, until the middle of the nineteenth century, the population of the city remained modest (approximately 11,000 people in 1849). The conquest of Palestine by Ibrahim Pasha brought new administrative reforms at the expense of the Ottoman power. Jerusalem, awarded municipal status in 1863, became, after Istanbul, the second city of the Ottoman Empire. Simultaneously, new privileges were granted to European powers, whose rights included land ownership. Eager to exert their influence in the region, the Europeans reinforced the political role of Jerusalem, establishing diplomatic missions: the British consulate in 1838, the Prussian consulate in 1842, and the French consulate in 1843. They also supported the missionary activities of their respective religious congregations there. Jerusalem, a provincial city, was transformed into a political capital.

In 1874, the city received unique status from the Ottomans, becoming directly subordinated to the administration in Istanbul. These political and administrative reforms accompanied a programme of modernisation in which the area of the city was extended [See *Urbanisation of Jerusalem* p. 135]. The population of the city was then between 14,000 and 22,000 and had increased to 80,000 people by 1915. Communication networks also developed: the expansion of the main road between Jaffa and Jerusalem in 1869 cut the length of a journey on muleback or by horse-drawn carriage in half: from 24 to 12 hours. Routes connecting the city with Syria and Iraq were constructed, a telegraphic line between Jerusalem and Istanbul was installed in 1865 and the Jaffa-Jerusalem railway line started operating in 1892. Care was especially paid to improving the infrastructure: roads were paved, camels were banned from the Old City in 1894, and public lighting on the streets (kerosene lamps) was introduced in 1905. In addition, the supply and purification of water was prioritised by the authorities, to combat the malaria and cholera that continued to plague the region - there was a cholera epidemic in 1900.

The acceleration of Jewish immigration rapidly kindled vigorous Palestinian protest, which found an echo in demands of the young Arab nationalist movement. While early Jewish immigrants lived in harmony with their Palestinian neighbours, the newer immigrants, mostly from central Europe, settled apart as a distinctive community with a zeal for colonisation.

On December 9, 1917, British forces entered Jerusalem, ushering in a new period in Jerusalem's long history, in which it became the administrative and political capital of the British Mandate in Palestine, created after World War I. Despite their loyalty to the Ottoman authorities, the status of the elite families of Jerusalem was confirmed by the British authorities as an expediency to exclude the younger generation, both Muslim and Christian, which was sympathetic to the cause of Arab national unity; although they kept on good terms with the British colonial authorities, the aristocrats of Jerusalem did not hide their hostility to Zionism and were the spokesmen for that cause.

The Palestinian most influential in shaping the political life of Jerusalem and that of the entire area of Palestine under the British Mandate was the Grand Mufti of Jerusalem, Haj Amin al-Husseini. Coming from one of the leading middle class families of Jerusalem, he promised to maintain public order (an over-riding concern for the British), and the interests of the Palestinian middle class, all the while pursuing a position as leader of the more radical Arab nationalism of the lower classes. Following the Great Revolt of 1936-1939, the British exiled the Haj, cracked down on his supporters and put forward the partition plan in 1937 without consulting a single Palestinian.

The international community promised the Jews a homeland in Palestine by the terms of its UN Partition Plan of November 1947, but the Palestinians, who aspired to liberation from colonialism, and independence, refused the plan, whereupon Zionist forces made an assault on Jerusalem, in April 1948; the ensuing flight of refugees, accelerating after the massacre in the village of Deir Yassin on April 9, 1948. The British Mandate in Palestine ended officially on May 14, 1948; on that same day, the newer part of the city of Jerusalem and 39 villages to the west of the city were occupied and their entire populations cleansed of their populations, without the least action of British intervention. All this, despite a British commitment to maintain public order until British departure. Neither the United Nations nor the surrounding Arab kingdoms intervened to prevent this occupation, terrorism and ethnic cleansing. The first decision made by King Abdullah the following day was to disarm the Palestinian partisans, ordering them inside the walls of the Old City, despite the fact that some armed Arab forces were holding many positions in the new part of the city. On July 18, 1948, the city was *de facto* divided into two halves that were designated from that time on as West Jerusalem and East Jerusalem. This surrender and the ensuing annexation of East Jerusalem to the Hashemite Kingdom, combined with repression of Palestinian resistance organisations, inspired a profound animosity towards the king, leading to his assassination in the heart of Jerusalem on May 20, 1951.

Israel carried out a total ethnic cleansing in the area it controlled west of Jerusalem, which was placed under Israeli sovereignty with the exception of the village of Abu Ghosh. More than 90,000 Palestinians of the Jerusalem district, including 30,000 people who had lived in different neighbourhoods of the municipality of Jerusalem, in various parts of the new city, lost all their possessions and the right to live in their own properties. The internationalisation of the city under the aegis of the United Nations, according to the partition plan of 1947, was reaffirmed several times, notably on September 16, 1948, by the United Nations special mediator Count Folke Bernadotte. The latter was assassinated the very next day after this reaffirmation, by the Stern Gang, a Zionist group led by Yitzhak Shamir, who later became Prime Minister of Israel.

Months later, Jerusalem was divided into two parts, controlled by Israel and Jordan, and underwent distinctly different development. Israel defied the entire international community by declaring West Jerusalem its capital on December 11, 1948, flaunting a decision made by the UN General Assembly only two days earlier. In parallel with Jerusalem's new political status and Israel's urbanisation policy for the municipality, the Jewish population increased from 100,000 to 197,000 between 1950 and 1967. Despite its change in size and status, Jerusalem retained its provincial character for a long time. East Jerusalem was formally annexed to the Hashemite Kingdom of Jordan in April 1950. The city preserved intact its historically Arab character, and business and tourism gave it a certain dynamism, although development efforts were concentrated in favour of the capital of Jordan, Amman.

On June 7, 1967, Israeli military forces occupied East Jerusalem. The bitterness caused by this event was enormous: despite the 5,000 Jordanian soldiers stationed in and around the city, no plans for its defence had been made. Over and above this, the years of surveillance and repression of Palestinian resistance movements had left the population unarmed and defenceless. On June 27, Israeli law was imposed on East Jerusalem, which was extended and annexed to West Jerusalem the following day. On July 30, 1980, the Israeli parliament declared Jerusalem to be "the eternal, united capital of Israel."

■ Which Jerusalem?

When one thinks of Jerusalem, the picture most people have is of the Old City inside the sixteenth century wall built by Sultan Suleiman al-Kanouni (Suleiman the Magnificent). However, the Old City represents less than 1 square kilometre of the entire 123 sq. kms of land Israel has treated as part of the entire municipality proclaimed a "united" city since 1967. The city borders have been extended greatly over the years, on the basis of strategic and diplomatic interests.

The municipal boundaries of Jerusalem (1947-2000)

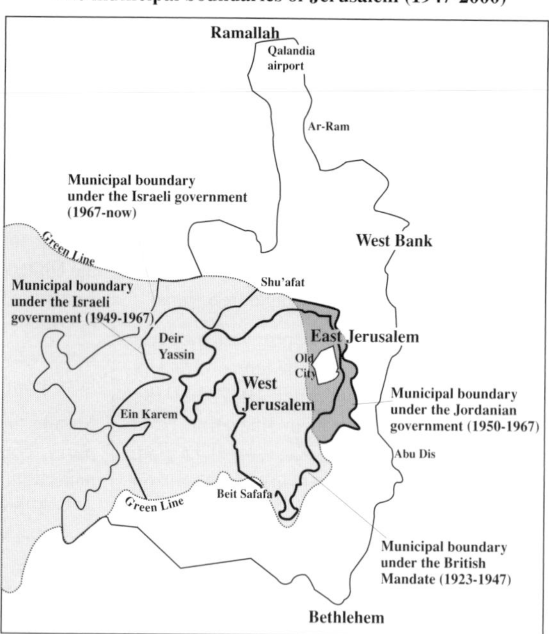

The boundaries of Jerusalem, which were originally promised a status under international protection in 1947, followed a strange logic that ignored the previous administrative area (the district of Jerusalem). Even Bethlehem was included in the new international zone of Jerusalem. When Zionist forces took over the region of Jerusalem and its surrounding area, in the First Arab-Israeli War of Palestine, and made West Jerusalem their capital in 1950, the members of the United Nations symbolically rejected the new state in various resolutions and based their embassies in Tel-Aviv or Haifa (still the case, to this day). From 1948 to 1967, Israeli authorities extended the municipal boundaries to the west, building on top of the ruins of destroyed or re-occupied neighbourhoods and villages, so that the total municipal area of West Jerusalem became 38 sq.kms. After 1967, they pushed municipal boundaries farther, judaising the newly conquered territories and legitimising their actions by referring to religious myths and the unique spiritual attachment of the Jewish people to Jerusalem and the "Greater Land of Israel."

■ The Municipality of Jerusalem since 1967

A few weeks after the 1967 conquest, the Israeli government defined new boundaries for Jerusalem, which thereby increased to a total area of 70 sq. kms, including Palestinian East Jerusalem (an area of 64 sq. kms was appropriated to the north and south of the city). Around 36% of this Palestinian land was confiscated for the construction of huge Jewish settlements, while 54% of Palestinian land was designated "open green space," which in effect kept it vacant for future Jewish use, (leaving only 10% accessible to Palestinians - land already densely built on). Previously, the area of the municipality of Jerusalem was 44 sq. kms (6 sq. kms in East Jerusalem and 38 sq. kms in West Jerusalem). Twenty-eight Palestinian villages or parts of their land were integrated into the new municipality. The city borders were defined in response to political and demographic considerations: to include the *maximum* amount of uninhabited Palestinian *land* and the *minimum* Palestinian *population*. As a result, villages were arbitrarily cut in half (Anata and al-Issawiya), while others such as Abu Dis, al-Azariya, Hizme, Dahiyat al-Barid and A-Ram were deliberately excluded from the municipal boundaries. This over-riding development policy explains the curious layout of the city. In May 1988, another area of 15 sq. kms west of the city was annexed to the municipality. With its 123 sq. kms, Jerusalem has now become the largest metropolitan area in Israel. The total area of Tel Aviv is only 51 sq. kms. The dozen or more Israeli settlements: *Ramot, Ramat Shlomo, Pisgat Ze'ev, Neveh Ya'akov, Atarot, Ramat Eshkol, French Hill, Ma'alot Dafna, Ras al-Amud, East Talpiot, Gilo and Har Homa* have a combined population of some 250,000 settlers (as opposed to the 200,000 Palestinians of East Jerusalem who are now recently and newly outnumbered because of that increase in settlers), all part of an "inner ring" of satellite settlements which consolidate the borders of the Jewish municipality. This "Greater Jerusalem" defines Israel's future borders and prejudices Palestinian rights in any peace plan, while judaising formerly Palestinian East Jerusalem by putting irreversible facts on the ground. Under the Sharon Government, new Israeli settlements (e.g. *Kidmat Zion* in Abu Dis, *Nof Zion* at Jabel Mukaber) are still being pushed ahead, despite the Road Map's strictures that Israel freeze all settlement building, especially in East Jerusalem, which all peace plans project as the future capital of Palestine. Israeli peace activists regularly demonstrate against such developments and have lobbied the Americans to enforce the Road Map's strictures on new settlements and to freeze new settlement building. To no avail.

■ "Greater Jerusalem"

In 1983, in order specifically to tighten control over Jerusalem and a large part of the West Bank, the Israeli government developed the concept of a "Greater Jerusalem." Its implementation, however, started only after the Oslo Accords had been signed; construction work then accelerated fast: a number of settlements now form an "outer satellite ring" beyond the expanded municipal boundaries of Jerusalem. Among these satellite settlement cities are: *Har Adar, Givat Ze'ev, Givon HaHadasha, Kiryat Sefer, Ma'ale Adumim, Efrata, the Etzion Bloc, and Beitar*. These peripheral settlements are planned to accommodate more than 250,000 settlers within the next 15 years. The largest, Ma'ale Adumim, has a population of some 30,000 (15,000 in 1991) but current new building is expected to swell the population by next year, 2005, to 45,000 and this is planned to more than double within five years to 71,000 by 2010. Its land on a Master Plan (55 sq.kms. - more than Metropolitan Tel Aviv) now stretches all the way through to Jerusalem, a mere ten minute drive away, through a new settler-only *(apartheid)* tunnel blasted under Mt. Scopus. This settlement, more than any other, is the most serious, major stumbling block to the viability of a future Palestine, cutting the West Bank into two separated "bantustans" as it does, with neither contiguity nor road system joining those Palestinian northern and southern blocs, and preventing Palestinians from gaining access to Jerusalem, while restricting the natural growth of Palestinian East Jerusalem.

■ "Metropolitan Jerusalem"

The regional map of Jerusalem shows the ultimate stage of the settlements that will eventually incorporate a vast territory of which only 30% lies inside the Green Line. The projected metropolitan map includes the agglomerations of the autonomous areas of Ramallah and Bethlehem. This new territorial entity is expected to include 75% of the Jewish settlements constructed in the West Bank. Since the construction of 142,000 housing units was approved for the "Jewish sector" of the Metropolitan Area when Binyamin Netanyahu was Prime Minister, work has proceeded under the governments of Ehud Barak and now Ariel Sharon, if anything at an accelerated rate.

The Plan to Isolate Jerusalem: A Step Forward towards Greater Jerusalem

In 2002, there was a new initiative taken toward the establishment of new municipal boundaries. Motivating their actions by reference to the emergency law of 1945 (issued under the British Mandate), Israeli government and military authorities approved the construction of new checkpoints, roadblocks, barbed-wire fences and walls. Under guise of "security needs," the city boundaries were extended beyond where this metal and concrete curtain was marked on the map. Municipal boundaries have thus been extended to the north and east, following the plan for a "Greater Jerusalem." The "Separation Barrier" in the Occupied Palestinian Territories, which the government prefers to call "the barrier" is designed to finish off the isolation of the city, and to justify further transfer of Palestinians from their homes.

■ Israeli Demographic Planning:

"I don't like the growth of the non-Jewish population in Jerusalem."
Ehud Olmert, Mayor of Jerusalem, May 1997.

Demography dictates all Israeli policy, in Jerusalem as elsewhere. The priority in Jerusalem is, at a very minimum, to maintain the demographic balance existing in 1967: 28% Palestinians to 72% Jews. All government policies have been formulated with the following objectives in mind:

1 To assure a Jewish majority.

2 To prevent contiguity between Palestinians of East Jerusalem and those in the West Bank.

3 To reduce, at all cost, the number of Palestinians living in the city.

To these ends "*the municipality uses a thousand tricks so that Palestinians are unable to make use of their land.*" (Sarah Kaminker, formerly in charge of The East Jerusalem Master Plan, June 22, 1999.)

■ Discriminatory measures:

1. For Israelis:

Since the occupation of East Jerusalem in 1967, 80% of all Jewish housing within the city's boundaries has been financed by public funding, compared to just one building project for Palestinian residents, which was built at the beginning of the 1970s. Public housing built by the government is considered "state property" and so automatically accessible only by Israelis.

> *"From 1967 to 1997, less than 12% of all new housing units in Jerusalem have been built in Palestinian neighbourhoods (and most of those built were done so on private initiative). By contrast, a minimum of 40,000 subsidised housing units have been built for Jews in expropriated zones."*
>
> ■ Marwan Bishara

Successive Israeli governments and the Municipality of Jerusalem have pursued a policy strongly encouraging new Jewish immigrants to settle in the city. Advertising campaigns, loans at very low interest rates, as well as municipal tax reductions over five to ten years, all aim at inducing Israelis to live in the settlements of East Jerusalem.

2. For Palestinians

● Restrictive Urban Planning

Since 1967, more than one third of Palestinian property in East Jerusalem has been confiscated for "public use," that is, for quasi-exclusively Jewish use, mainly housing and infrastructure. As for the rest of the appropriated land, some is already constructed upon (blue zones), while 40% has been classified as "green" (or "agricultural") in order to hamper Palestinian development and freeze the land for future Jewish settlements. Jabal Abu Ghneim, for instance, was classified as a "green zone" until the controversial establishment of *Har Homa* settlement (designed originally during the Oslo days to accommodate over 30,000 Jewish and Palestinian residents living together), was authorised on the site; *Har Homa* now is a strictly Jewish settlement. Palestinian requirements for both housing and land are purely and simply ignored and excluded from urban town plans. Although Palestinians represent one third of the population of the Municipality of Jerusalem (200,000 residents, who are full tax-payers), a mere 3.5% of the entire urban area is available for their housing and community needs.

● Obtaining a Construction Permit

To obtain a permit to build a house, there must first of all be an urban plan zoned for building, for the area. If there is such a plan, it is subordinate to a demographic quota, rather than the needs of the population. Indeed, all Palestinian neighbourhoods are subject to severe building restrictions. Even when the "legal" conditions for construction are met, sky-high land prices (caused by the scarcity of land available for Palestinian building) and construction permits represent a major obstacle. A construction permit costs approximately $30,000, and the waiting period is usually a minimum of five years. Only 150 to 200 applications are accepted for consideration annually! If construction is authorised, the residence may only be one or two floors high as opposed to eight floors allowed for Jewish builders. The building density allowed to Palestinians is 3.3 units per dunum (0.09 hectares) as opposed to 8.6 for Israelis. This restrictive building policy has led to a housing shortfall estimated at over 25,000 housing units.

● Illegal Construction:

Illegal construction is a natural consequence of building restriction. Sometimes, an entire building is illegal, whereas in other cases, only the added-on floors are regarded as unlawful. In all, since 1967 12,000 Palestinian houses have been demolished. In 1999, 131 Palestinian Jerusalemites saw their homes demolished before their eyes, including among them 68 children. Since the start of the al-Aqsa Intifada, in September 2000, over 500 "illegal" homes have been demolished by Court Order (and over 3,000 by IDF action, including 1,411 in Gaza, leaving 12,712 people homeless).

"The Quiet Transfer"

The presence of Palestinians in Jerusalem has no legal basis but depends on the good will of the State of Israel. When East Jerusalem was conquered in 1967, the Israeli authorities conducted a census. All Palestinians living in Jerusalem (some 66,000 people at the time) received the status of a permanent resident, whereas those who were out of the city at that time were deprived of this status. Since 1995, any Palestinian resident unable to prove that his or her life revolves around residency in the city has his status withdrawn or is threatened with the loss of that right of residence. This policy is the final step of the restrictive housing policy intended to force Palestinians to live in the cheaper, more available housing units on the outskirts of the city of Jerusalem, but not within its boundaries (i.e., A-Ram, Daret al-Barid, Abu Dis, and al-Azariya and other such suburbs). Between 1996 and May 1999, 2,200 ID cards were cancelled, forcing 8,800 Palestinians of Jerusalem to leave the city, or to live there clandestinely. (See *Ministry of the Interior in East Jerusalem,* p. 127.) This phenomenon is called by its critics: "the quiet transfer." Whilst ultra-right

wing settlers trumpet their policy of transfer (attempting to move the Palestinians to Jordan) under the banner "Jordan is Palestine," the ethnic cleansing of the quiet transfer has been taking place over the past 37 years, hidden behind the banal, insidious bureaucracy of town planning. This issue is especially urgent now that the Separation Barrier is being built, as it cuts through the centre of many of those Palestinian neighbourhoods where Jerusalem residents had moved, in order to be able to afford housing; now they are moving back into more expensive Jerusalem just so that they can keep their Jerusalem IDs, for all the benefits entailed such as work opportunities, National Insurance, family and cultural attachments, hospitals, education and so on.

● Minimal Services :

Even though East Jerusalemite Palestinians pay 30% of the total municipal taxes, less than 11% of the city budget comes back to them in the form of public services or jobs; only 17% of all the municipal employees are Palestinians of East Jerusalem, of whom two thirds are maintenance workers, and the others work in services catering exclusively to those Palestinians, whether in administrative and social sectors or garbage collection, among others.

"I have done many things for Jewish Jerusalem during the last 25 years. But for East Jerusalem, nothing at all! - neither sidewalks nor cultural institutions. Ah! We did install a sewage system [for them], *and we improved water distribution. But that wasn't for their good. It was simply because there were some cases of cholera there, and the Jews were afraid of contagion..."*

■ Teddy Kollek, former Mayor of Jerusalem.

Infrastructure is totally inadequate: many Palestinian neighbourhoods have no paved roads - the neighbourhood of Silwan is the best example - or have been paved by the residents themselves; street lighting is minimal; garbage collection is irregular and insufficient to the needs, so residents have no choice but to incinerate the garbage themselves. In 1986, 60% of all Palestinian neighbourhoods had no garbage collection. There is also an acute shortage of health care and cultural facilities. Medical institutions have been particularly affected by the policy of isolating the Palestinians of Jerusalem. Before 1991, 90% of the patients and 70% of the medical staff in city hospitals came from the West Bank and the Gaza Strip. Since then, potential patients have been obliged to obtain a permit from the Israeli military authorities ("Civil Administration") in the West Bank, to receive treatment in Jerusalem. Likewise, medical workers must obtain a permit. Obviously, patients' relatives also need a permit to visit them. These difficulties have led patients from the West Bank and Gaza to seek treatment in cities nearest their place of residence, since the infrastructure in Palestinian hospitals has witnessed an unprecedented development since the arrival of the Palestinian Authority; but Palestinian hospitals in Jerusalem (Mokassed on the Mount of Olives, mainly) are losing clients from the territories and from Jerusalem itself. The Wall has exacerbated this problem: many patients cannot reach the hospital; nor can many doctors. Jerusalem Palestinians are covered by Israeli national health insurance, but can be treated only in Israeli-managed hospitals for expenses to be reimbursed.

As for cultural life, every visitor swiftly realises there is a scarcity of cultural and recreational centres: only two public libraries and 33 sports centres are at the disposal of the Palestinian community as opposed to 26 libraries and 531 sports centres for the Jewish community. Until the beginning of the First Intifada, Salah ed-Din and Zahra streets were the bustling centre of East Jerusalem. Today, however, most cinemas, cafes, exhibition halls and auditoria there are closed. "In the past, Ramallah was a suburb of Jerusalem. Today, it's just the opposite." The closure of Jerusalem has made Ramallah the place where culture is alive and thriving. Thus, too, Israel has co-opted Jerusalem for its sole use, and forced the Palestinians to use Ramallah as their centre, or capital. Another element of control and quiet transfer.

East Jerusalem

East Jerusalem constitutes the oriental part of Jerusalem. As a result of the Israeli conquest of the western part of Jerusalem in 1948, the city was divided and a new designation came into being: East Jerusalem. Until 1967, East Jerusalem extended over an area of six square kilometres, encompassing the walled Old City and its immediate neighbourhoods, Silwan, A-Tur, Wadi Joz, and Sheikh Jarrah, among others. Today, the place denominated as "East Jerusalem" extends over a far more vast region, due to the Israeli municipality's spread over the lands of the West Bank. It reaches from Kufr Aqeb, past Qalandia checkpoint in the north, to Beit Safafa in the south.

The Old City

❑ The Walls

Damascus Gate and Jaffa Gate (two entrances). Open Saturday-Thursday 9:00-16:00, Friday 9:00-14:00, admission NIS 10.50. Ticket valid for two days.

One of the best ways to have a good view of the entire Old City and its surroundings is to take a walk along its ramparts. There are two optional walks: from the Citadel to the Gate of the Moors (Maghribi or Dung Gate) or from Jaffa Gate to the Lions' Gate (Damascus Gate lies halfway along this walk). The section between the Gate of the Moors to the Lions' Gate along the Haram al-Sharif is closed to the public. One may leave the walk at each gate, but one may ascend onto the ramparts from three points only: **Damascus Gate** (*via the Roman Plaza, below the gate*), **Jaffa**

Gate (*from outside the Citadel for the southern section of the wall*) and **Jaffa Gate** (*for the northern section*). The contemporary four-kilometre wall is a copy of the Ottoman-built military wall, erected between 1537 and 1541 in the time of Suleiman the Magnificent. The wall followed traces of older, preceding walls in some places. The huge blocks of stone with their bevelled edges in the southeast corner date from the days of Herod's Ramparts.

Ottoman Medallions

In the sixteenth century, decorative Mameluke architecture bowed to a more sober style. Ottoman architecture then abandoned or simplified the hitherto typical architectural features of Mameluke buildings, such as *ablaqs* and *muqarnas* and it then favoured medallions bearing floral or geometrical motifs. In Jerusalem these medallions or raised roundels, circular ornaments, decorate the ancient buildings beautifully, notably the ramparts of the Old City (especially gates, entrances and towers). There are 120 in number on the ramparts alone. Among the existing motifs, one may note the six-pointed star, known as Suleiman's Seal (or in the Arabic, *Khatem Suleiman*). In addition to their purely decorative aspect, these distinctive stone circles were believed to be invested with protective and magical qualities to ensure protection.

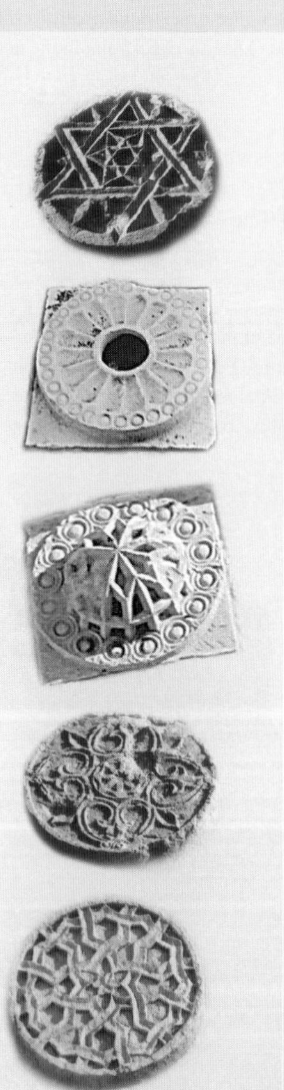

■ The Muslim Quarter

❑ Damascus Gate (Bab al-Amud)

Damascus Gate is the heart of East Jerusalem; it is the place of arrival and departure of all Palestinian public transport (Musrara Square and Nablus Road). In Arabic, the gate is called Bab al-Amud (Gate of the Column), in memory of the Roman square once found there, which had a column at its centre, on which stood an enormous statue, probably of Emperor Hadrian. According to the Madaba Map, the column was still there in the sixth century although the statue of the pagan emperor had long since disappeared. The present day gate, built by the Ottomans in 1537, stands on Hadrian's Arch, which has been partially brought to light by archaeologists *(entrance beneath the principal passage of Damascus Gate, open Sunday-Thursday 9:00-16:00, Friday 9:00 2:00; closed since the beginning of the Intifada)*. Today, you can see the side gate of the huge Roman entrance as well as part of the original pavement. An entrance from the Roman plaza leading to the wall has been created for the benefit of visitors. It is a journey back in time which leads one to one of the most beautiful observatories of the Old City.

Al-Wad Street

Al-Wad Street is the principal way leading from Damascus Gate to the Haram al-Sharif (Temple Mount) and then to the Western Wall (al-Buraq). It follows the ancient Valley of Tyropoeon. During the Friday *al-Dohour* or mid-day prayers, a dense throng fills the narrow alleys. Somewhere between spirituality and temporality, this movement of the crowds leaving their place of prayer is one of the most impressive moments of a trip to Palestine.

Just down the road, a group of apartments overhanging a roofed passage *(quantara)* has belonged to Prime Minister Ariel Sharon himself, since December 15, 1987. Their physical location perfectly symbolises Israeli state domination over Palestinian Jerusalem. Although Sharon does not live here, the **House of Sharon** is heavily guarded: as proof is the omnipresence of soldiers, armed settlers and surveillance cameras (more than 500 in East Jerusalem). At the end of the road, Jewish settlement in the Muslim Quarter reaches its

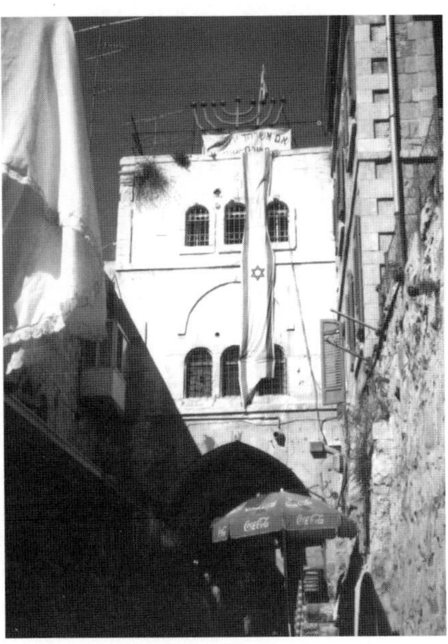

climax. The road is full of tourist shops alternating with Jewish religious seminaries *(yeshivot)* and apartment buildings occupied by these Jewish settlers fired by religious nationalism, who are obsessively colonising the Old City, Sheikh Jarrah, al-Musrara, Silwan, Abu Dis, Ras al-Amud and Jabal Mukaber, in order to pre-empt Palestinian viable statehood in East Jerusalem, and to judaise the city by this form of bloodless ethnic cleansing.

Jewish Settlers in the Muslim Quarter

Although there are settlers all over the Old City, there is a higher proportion especially at the end of al-Wad Street and at Herod's Gate. At the beginning of the 1970s, Jewish settlement was initiated in the Muslim Quarter by ultra-Orthodox, messianic settlers who occupied a building and transformed it into a bookshop *(Ben Arza bookshop, al-Wad Street, near an underground tunnel leading to the Western Wall)*. The Labour municipality permitted Jewish settlement around the new Jewish Quarter (the old North African quarter). At the end of the 1970s, groups of settlers belonging to an organisation called *Ateret Cohanim* (the "priestly crown" or "crown of princes"), and the

"Movement for Young Israel," among others, accelerated Jewish colonisation of the Muslim Quarter. Such groups received more or less discreet support from the government - ministries, the Municipality and the Supreme Court - in terms of financial help, the purchase of properties through umbrella organisations and policies encouraging the eviction of Palestinians. Their presence is forever increasing, especially under the current government, which is so sympathetic to settlers. They receive massive funding from American billionaires such as neo-conservative bingo-king, Irving Moskowitz (see: www.stopmoskowitz.com).

❑ The Souks (Markets)

Souk Khan ez-Zeit is the busiest, most picturesque and colourful shopping street in the Old City. Above all, the *souk* is a popular market selling all the food products used in Palestinian cooking - spices, dried fruit, herbs, coffee, and pastries - as well as more ordinary food supplies. Halfway along, the market street splits into two roofed passages; **Souk al-Attarin,** where there are many clothes shops, and **Souk al-Lahmin**, the meat market.

Ala' ed-Din (Aladdin) Street

Ala' ed-Din Street leads to the **Haram al-Sharif** and the **African Quarter** via the **Inspector's Gate** (Bab al-Nazir). The African Quarter is actually inside two ancient Mameluke hospices: **Ribat Ala' ed-Din al-Basir** *(to the left, opposite the en-Nazir Gate)*, and **Ribat Mansuri** *(to the right)*. The former was founded in 1267 by a blind person, Emir al-Basir, who was widely respected for his wisdom (in Arabic, *basir* means clairvoyant). He was the superintendent *(nazir)* of the Haram al-Sharif and the Haram al-Ibrahimi (Cave or Tomb of the Patriarchs) in Hebron. Since this hospice was one of the earliest Mameluke buildings, it was not built using the polychrome style (red, white and black-striped *ablaq* masonry) typical of Mameluke architecture, as this was not yet in use. The second hospice probably owes its name to Mameluke Sultan Mansour Qalawun (1279-1290). At the end of the Ottoman period, the two buildings were transformed into a prison, nicknamed "the prison of blood." The metal gate on the left opened onto the cells of prisoners condemned to death *(the bars on the gate are still there)*, while the door on the right led to the cells of those sentenced to lengthy prison terms. The prison continued to operate under the British Mandate until it was transferred to the former Russian hospice, al-Moskobiya ("the Russian Compound") (See p. 142).

The African Community

Over 40 Muslim families (descendants of African Muslims originally from the Sudan, Chad, Nigeria and Senegal) settled in Jerusalem, mainly at the beginning of the twentieth century, after making the traditional pilgrimage to Mecca. Some can trace an even earlier origin, when Africans from the Sudan worked for the Ottoman governor in the sixteenth century to guard the entrance to the Haram. Their descendants settled here in 1948. They fought as volunteers in various Arab and Muslim contingents to defend the holy city against the Zionist conquest. Their involvement in defending the integrity of Palestine earned them full integration in the Palestinian community. Their militancy has continued: a member of the African community, Osama Jiddaha (aged 21), was the first martyr of the Old City when the al-Aqsa Intifada broke out.

For further information, contact **The African Community Association** *(Ribat Mansuri Gate: ☎ 02-628 8915)* or visit the association's cafeteria for a warm welcome and inexpensive meal: it is located in the old entrance hallway of the Mameluke hospice. Ali Jiddah, nicknamed "the mayor," is a local personality and official alternative tourism guide here, who can help you discover a less conventional perspective of Jerusalem *(☎ 02-628 4216 or 0522-975 982; $100 per group for a three-hour tour).*

Aqabat et-Taqiya

The Tunshuq Palace

Lady Tunshuq, the wife of an aristocratic Kurd of the Muzaaffarid Iranian dynasty, who lost all his possessions to Tamberlain *circa* 1387 AD, settled in Jerusalem, where she had this luxurious palace built. In the sixteenth century, the building was annexed to the residence of the Ottoman Sultana Khassaki Sultan, wife of Suleiman the Magnificent. Three great doorways decorated with *muqarnas* of floral or geometrical motifs are an indication of the palace as an architectural masterpiece; unfortunately, some of the decorated panels are badly damaged.

Turba es-Sitt Tunshuq

Lady Tunshuq also had her tomb or *turba* constructed, opposite the palace. According to Mujir ed-Din (1456-1522), she died in July 1398. Here, too, the building is overwhelming in its design. Notice particularly above the two windows protected by grillwork, the different colours of marble *ablaq*, making a stunning impression. Today, the top floors of the mausoleum's annexes are inhabited.

Bab al-Hadid (Iron Gate) Street

Follow a covered alleyway to a quiet road with houses on both sides, dating from the Mameluke period.

Madrasa Muzhiriya was built in 1480 by Abu Bakr ibn Muzhir, secretary at the Egyptian Chancery. Ibn Muzhir died of a fever in Nablus in 1488 while he was preparing an attack on the Ottoman sultan.

Madrasa Jawhariya was founded by an Abyssinian eunuch in 1340. He was given the name of a precious stone (*jawhar* means jewel), as was the custom for eunuchs at that time; Jawhar was chief guardian of the royal harem in Cairo.

Madrasa Arghuniya (1358) w;as the work of Arghun al-Kamali, who - as the plaque above the entrance explains - was Steward of the Royal Wardrobe and, later, Governor of Damascus and Aleppo before being exiled to Jerusalem.

The adjacent residence, **the Kurdish Riba,** *(open to visitors)*, was a hospice founded by a Kurdish Mameluke, cupbearer at the court. He was killed in battle against the Tartars at Homs in Syria, in 1299.

Souk al-Qattanin (The Cotton Merchants' Market)

Although Al-Qattanin Gate does not allow tourists to enter the Haram esh-Sharif, a visit to the place is still highly recommended.

Mameluke Prince Sayf ed-Din Tankiz was mainly responsible for the founding of this picturesque little **covered market** (*al-kaysariya* - the prince). He was Governor of Damascus in 1312 and later became the Viceroy of Greater Syria between 1315-1340. Two inscriptions, one on a bronze plaque on the Qattanin Gate and one on the lintel of Khan Tankiz, date the construction to 1336. The plaque on the lintel shows Emir Tankiz' coat of arms (a goblet), signifying that he was a cupbearer before attaining the rank of prince. Like all markets at that time, **Souk al-Qattanin** had shops with living quarters above it, public baths (**Hammam al Ein** and **Hammam al-Shifa**) and a *caravanserai*. Profits were shared between the Haram al-Sharif and Madrasa al-Tankiziya (see p. 97). The Hammam al-Ein, which is undergoing restoration, was operational until the 1980s.

Mameluke Architecture

The Mameluke period (1250-1517) left a remarkable and astonishing mark on the Palestinian architectural landscape. The opulence of both the Mameluke state and the court encouraged the undertaking of various types of buildings, with a particular enthusiasm for religious institutions. Due to this commitment, the holy city of Jerusalem (al-Quds) particularly flourished. Forty four *Madrasas* (Islamic schools) and twenty *zawiyas* (buildings especially for Sufis, the mystic school of Islam) received generous donations. The construction of increased public facilities, such as khans, souks, and hammams, around the city was carefully planned. Inspired by the official status of both the philosophy and the message of Islam, artists and architects executed daring, delicate compositions where symmetry and geometry prevail. This technical and aesthetic perfection typified many examples of artistic creation at that time, including the calligraphy of Islamic manuscripts and the fabrication of gold pieces.

Many typical features allow the Mameluke style in architecture to be immediately identifiable, in the most lavish buildings. A typical façade, often the only place accessible to visitors, but also the most elaborate, is an ensemble of polished stones of several alternating colours (red, cream, and black) put together with consummate skill; the gates are deeply recessed and crowned by various decoratively worked arches - some chiselled, others multifoil - and sometimes with *muqarnas* or stalactites (honeycomb work). The play of decorative and architectural elements is endless, creating a unique pleasure for the viewer.

References:

- *Mamluk Jerusalem*, Michael Burgoyne, London 1987.
- *Mameluk Art, Exhibition Trail*, Palestinian National Authority, 2000.
- *Sharing the Sacred, Exhibition Trail*, Israel, 2000.

Street of the Chain Gate (Tariq Bab al-Silsila)

This street, an extension of David Street (leading from Jaffa Gate), goes to the Haram al-Sharif. Bab al-Silsila Gate is open to tourists.

Given the popularity of holy places in Jerusalem and the freedom of movement of people throughout the entire Arab world under the Mamelukes, many devout Muslims chose to retire to the city, at the end of their days: because of this phenomenon, this road is lined by a number of Mameluke buildings, especially *turba* - mausoleums.

Khan es-Sultan. Established on the site of an ancient Crusader market, which was renovated in 1386-87 by Sultan Barquq, the first Circassian Mameluke sultan of the al-Burj ("the tower") family line, who adapted it into a *caravanserai* (*khan* or inn for camelleers). The photo shows the interesting corbels that support the gallery.

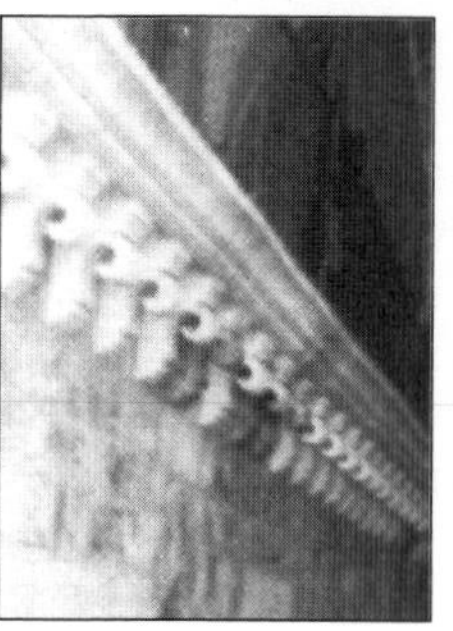

Madrasa Tashtumuriya. Tashtamur al-'Alai' was one of the most distinguished statesmen of his time; during his career he was appointed to the highest public functions of the state. He was successively appointed as First Secretary of the Mameluke state in the reign of Sultan Sha'ban, then General Commander of the Egyptian army before he fell into disgrace and was given less illustrious positions. He retired from the political scene in 1382, and settled in Jerusalem, where he oversaw the construction of his mausoleum. Apart from the funerary chamber, the complex he designed contained a *sabil* (a special building to house a pool), and a *kuttab* (a room where scribes and artists copied the Quran and illuminated Quranic passages) in addition to several other rooms dedicated to the *madrasa*. This interior is private: only the exterior gate may be seen by the public. Note the twentieth-century drawings on the Mameluke gateway's door (the Ka'ba, The Dome of the Rock, crescents, flowers and coloured dots), which illustrate the accomplishment of the sacred *haj* (pilgrimage to Mecca) made by the inhabitants of the building.

Turba Kilaniya houses the tombs of Jamal ed-Din Pahlavan, a prince from the Caspian province of Kilan, who died in 1352, and that of his nephew. There is a burial chamber behind each double window.

The al-Khalidiya Library was originally the mausoleum of Barka Khan, chief of the Khawarizmi tribe, of central Asia. Sultan Baybar made an alliance with Khan to protect the Mamelukes against the threat of Mongol invasion in the thirteenth century, despite misgivings as to the Khan's moral l standards. He was in fact killed in a

V

battle south of Homs, in central Syria, while he was drunk. His son, Badr ed-Din, erected a mausoleum to his memory in Jerusalem between 1364 and 1380. Later, the mausoleum was integrated into the residence of the Khalidi family. The burial chamber was transformed into the family's private mosque. In the eighteenth century, the Khalidi family undertook to collect the complete writings about Jerusalem, such as manuscripts and legal reports. With this written material, Sheikh Rajab al-Khalidi created the famous al-Khalidiya Library in 1901. Manuscripts in Arabic, as well as Persian (Farsi) and Turkish, both secular and religious, dating from the Mameluke period to the present day, are available to researchers.

■ **Turba Taziya** was built by the Mameluke Sayf ed-Din Taz, who rose from being a cupbearer to Governor of Aleppo, and then a prince. Ousted from his post, he was imprisoned in Alexandria in 1358 and blinded. He was allowed to settle in Jerusalem, where he built his tomb and a *madrasa*. When he fell out of favour and was stripped of his power, he also lost part of his fortune, as the modesty of his tomb indicates. In fact, his remains lie in Damascus, at the Sufi cemetery. Note on both sides of the inscription above the entrance gate, the presence of a goblet, which indicates his original profession as cupbearer to the sultan.

■ **Turba al-Jalaqiya.** Baibars al-Jaliq was a Mameluke of the Ayyubid Sultan al-Salih Najm ed-Din Ayyub, before being promoted to the rank of prince by Mameluke Sultan Baybar. When he died near Ramle in 1307, his body was laid in this mausoleum in Jerusalem in accordance with his last wishes. The main entrance is sealed and inaccessible to visitors, but nevertheless it is interesting to pause and admire the beautiful calligraphy visible from the street *(above the black door)*.

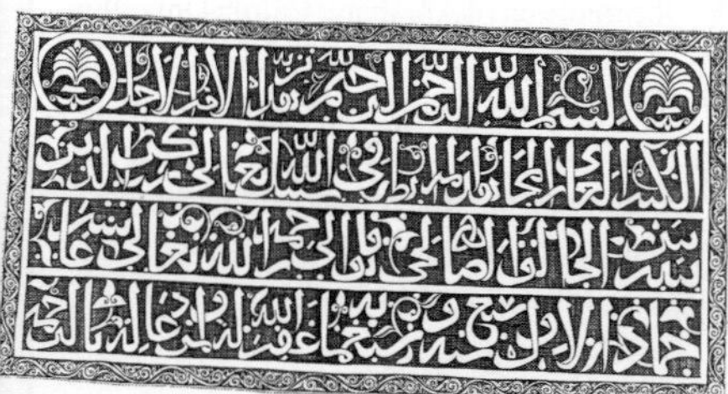

■ **Turba Turkan Khatun** is the tomb of a princess, the daughter of Emir Tuqtay Ibn Saljutay al-Uzbeki (from the central Asian dynasty of the Golden Horde Khans). She died in 1352 in Jerusalem while on pilgrimage to Mecca. The splendid decorations of panels of stars with truncated points are not only original but unique, as such decorations were prohibited in Mameluke art.

■ **Turba Sadiya** houses the tomb of *qadi* (judge) Burhan ed-Din, who died in 1311. Particularly impressive here are both the complex arrangement of coloured marble *ablaq*, and the *muqarnas* (the very first to be used in Jerusalem) decorating the entrance.

■ **Madrasa Tankiziya** was founded in 1328-1329 by one of the greatest patrons of the city, Sayf ed-Din Abu Sa'id Tankiz. Its decorative and architectural features are a good example of architecture of that time, as is the superb band of inscriptions bearing three coats of arms on the goblet. Al-Tankiziya was first a *Hadith* school (*hadith* is the study of the teachings of the Prophet), equipped with a hostel, then seat of the Judge or Qadi of Jerusalem in the middle of the fifteenth century, the city law court (al-Mukama al-Shariya) in the nineteenth century, then residence of the Head of the Supreme Muslim Council, Haj Amin al-Husseini, during the British

Mandate. It has been, since 1967, in the hands of the Israeli authorities, who have transformed it into a police station. [See photo, p. 97.]

■ **Sabil Bab al-Silsila** was constructed in 1537, as one of the five *sabils*, or covered pools, commissioned by Sultan Suleiman. It is a *sabil* of the recessed style. Like other contemporary *sabils*, it was crowned with a chevron (inverted V-shape) patterned arch (see *Birket al-Sultan*, p. 137). Note also the use of a sarcophagus as the basin of the fountain.

HARAM AL-SHARIF

Open from Sunday to Thursday 8:00-15:00, closed Friday from 8:00-10:00 during the month of Ramadan. Mosques are closed during prayer time: Salat ed-Dohour (around 12 noon) and Salat al-'Asser (at about 14:30). For more information about the Haram al-Sharif and about Islam, contact the Waqf Office (al-Qattanin Gate, ☎ 02-628 1222). A visit to the plaza is free of charge, but admission to the Dome of The Rock, al-Aqsa Mosque and the Islamic Museum costs NIS 26. Tickets may be bought at a kiosk inside Haram al-Sharif, near the Bab al-Maghribi (Gate of the Moors). To enter, one must use either Bab al-Silsila (Chain Gate) or Bab al-Maghribi. One may leave through any of the ten gates in the wall. While the Haram al-Sharif is without doubt a historical place of unique aesthetic value, it is also a place of spirituality and worship, and visitors are expected to dress and behave accordingly. Handbags and cameras are not allowed inside the mosque.

The Haram al-Sharif (The Honoured Sanctuary) is a vast promenade, at whose centre is the dominating, majestic Dome of the Rock; the al-Aqsa Mosque is nearby at its southern corner. This plaza takes up about one-sixth of the total area of the walled Old City. The al-Aqsa Mosque, *"the ultimate oratory"* or *"the distant mosque"* (Quran 17:1), referred to the entire area of the Haram in the seventh century, but in the Middle Ages this was restricted to the mosque alone. Ancient Judaean tradition identified the site as the *"Land of Moriah"* (Genesis 22), on which Abraham was ready to sacrifice his son Isaac. Muslims substituted a non-sacrificial cult - the Friday prayer.

According to the Bible, King Solomon built a temple on this hill, dedicated to Jehovah (the First Temple), from which came the name *"Temple Mount."* However, despite extensive excavations under the mosques' plaza, no proof of the existence of this temple has been found. There was a grandiose temple, the Second Temple, built under Herod the Great. The construction work continued for nearly ten years (from 73-74 BC to 64 BC). What remains are exceptionally important ruins: part of the southern wall, the Western Wall (also known as the al-Buraq Wall or Wailing Wall), Robinson's Arch, Wilson's Arch, and the Double Gate and Single Gate.

When Christianity triumphed as the official religion in the fourth century, the ruins of the temple were either abandoned or thoroughly plundered in favour of the construction of new Christian places of worship. Heir to the tradition of Abraham, Caliph Omar Ibn al-Khattab had the plaza cleaned in 638 AD and the first mosque built. The al-Aqsa Mosque was dedicated by Bilal the Ethiopian, the first muezzin of Islam, who called the people to prayer, but who had refused to do so after the Prophet's death. In 1099, the Crusaders seized Jerusalem and imposed their own symbols here until 1187. The al-Aqsa Mosque was known by them as the Temple of Solomon and the Dome of the Rock as the Temple of the Lord. Saladin, taking the city on the anniversary of the Night Journey of the Prophet Mohammad, proceeded to restore and sanctify the al-Aqsa Mosque: the principal of the two *qiblas* (the direction towards which prayers of the faithful are oriented), the second most sacred mosque, and the third holiest site after the two holy cities, Mecca and Medina. Under Saladin, the entire Haram resumed its sacred character as one huge mosque, with many Muslim shrines as part of it.

Masterpieces of Arab-Islamic Architecture

The Haram al-Sharif, a place for gathering and prayer, includes certain Arabo-Islamic architectural masterpieces, some monumental, others more modest. It is endowed with four minarets (Bab al-Maghribi, al-Silsila, al-Ghawanima, and al-Asbat), several domes (Qubbet al-Miraj, Qubbet al-Nabi, Qubbet Yussef, among others) and some pavements (al-Karak, Ala'a ed-Din al-Basri, and al-Ushaq). The Sufis or mystics used these pavements for prayer or teaching in summer months. Many fountains *(sabils)* are also located inside the sacred wall of which the most impressive is the Sabil of Sultan.

■ The Western Portico (er-Riwaq al-Gharbiya)

This monumental, massive portico occupies the entire western wing of the Haram al-Sharif. It was built under Mameluke Sultan Nassir ed-Din Mohammad Qalawun, during the years 1307 to 1337. The portico extends in an unbroken line from the al-Maghribi Gate to the Inspector's Gate (Bab al-Nazir). It also provides access to several Mameluke *madrasas*, including al-Uthmaniya, and al-Ashrafiya).

■ The Ghawanima Minaret

At the northwest corner of the Haram al-Sharif

This minaret is a Mameluke architectural masterpiece, erected in 1298 by Qadi (judge) Sharaf ed-Din Abdel Rahman, the caretaker of the Islamic properties: the *harams* of Mecca, Medina, Jerusalem, and Hebron. A six-storey minaret, it has survived many earthquakes which have shaken the region. It was constructed on the traditional model of towers in the Syrian style: quadrangular towers. The variety and quality of its ornamentation bestow on it a special splendour; notice in particular the corbelled *muqarnas* supporting the muezzins' gallery.

■ Madrasa al-Is'ardiya (Dar al-Ansari)

At the northern end of the Haram

Majd ed-Din al-Is'ari, a merchant born in what is now Siirt in Turkey, erected the building originally as a hospice, during the 1340s. The beautiful façade immediately above the portico was renovated in 1927. The *mihrab* or prayer niche jutting out from the façade is unique, being the only one of its kind in Jerusalem.

■ The Minaret of Bab al-Asbat

This minaret was constructed in 1367-1368 under the auspices of the caretaker of the Haram al-Sharif and the Haram al-Ibrahimi, Sayf ed-Din Qutlubugha. However, the cylindrical shape of the minaret, which is typically Ottoman, and the presence of motifs incised in the stone *(half-way up, on the level of the dormer windows)*, indicate that it must have been restored in the transition period at the beginning of the sixteenth century. After another restoration which was required in the

aftermath of the 1927 earthquake, an austere style was chosen for the *muqarna* corbels supporting the muezzins' gallery.

Madrasa al-Uthmaniya

Isfahan Shah Khatun, princess of a family originating in Asia Minor and member of the Ottoman dynasty, commissioned the building of this *madrasa*. She endowed it with revenue derived from several foundations in both Asia Minor and Palestine. Set above the portico *(on the al-Mathara Gate level)*, the building is distinguished by its double window surmounted by two circular medallions and a rose window.

Sabil Qaitbey

The *sabil* has a richness of exquisitely executed motifs, which deserve especial attention. Its intricately decorated sculptured stone dome is unique in Palestine. This is the handiwork of Egyptian mastercraftsmen stonemasons, and has no equal except in Cairo. The sponsor of this magnificent work, completed in 1482, was none other than Mameluke Sultan Qaitbey (Ashraf Sayf ed-Din Qaitbey, 1468-1496).

Madrasa al-Ashrafiya (or Sultan Qaitbey's Madrasa)

This *madrasa* was founded in 1482 during the reign of Sultan Qaitbey. Celebrated for his ascetic way of life, he initiated many religious foundations, in particular in the holy cities of Islam. The Royal Foundation of al-Ashrafiya owned several urban and rural properties (agricultural land and orchards in no less than 43 towns or villages), including in Jerusalem, Hebron, Ramle and Gaza. The academic and administrative staff numbered 55 people. The foundation definitely played a major educational role in Jerusalem during the Mameluke and Ottoman periods. Today, the building houses the al-Aqsa mosque library, and, on the upper floor, a religious school for girls and some private apartments. The entrance, which has been remarkably well preserved, has all the decorative features specific to the Mameluke period; for example, note the small blue stones embedded in the top lobe of the portal. It is hardly surprising that Mujir ed-Din considered this *madrasa* the third jewel of the Haram al-Sharif after the al-Aqsa Mosque and the Dome of the Rock.

Al-Kas Fountain

Built in the style typical of Ayyubid times (1171-1260), al-Kas is one of many fountains used for ritual ablutions before prayers. Sultan al-Adil Abu Bakr Bin Ayyub ordered its construction in 1193. It owes its name to the cup *(al kas)* standing at the centre of the circular basin of the fountain. The wrought iron screen was added as an embellishment by order of the Mameluke Governor of Greater Syria, Tankaz en-Nasri, in 1327.

Qubbet Musa

This four-sided monument is also called Qubbet al-Shajara (the Dome of the Tree), or Dar al-Quran al-Karim (the Dwelling of the Prodigal Quran). This quadrangular monument stands on a platform *(mistaba)*, while an octagonal drum supports its dome. Built in 1249-50 by al-Malik es-Salih Najm ed-Din Ayyub, (1240-1249), today the building houses a *quranic* school.

The Golden Gate (Bab er-Rahma - The Gate of Mercy)

This oriental gate, which is currently closed, was for a long time a mystery. Its origins have always been a subject of debate, but it is now believed to date from the Umayyad period (661-1171 AD). The floral motifs (particularly the acanthus leaves) and the geometric motifs alone deserve particularly observant attention. The most ancient Muslim cemetery of the city (*maqbarat* Bab er-Rahma) is located just outside this gate and the eastern wall.

Al-Aqsa Mosque (Masjid al-Aqsa or the Distant Mosque)

"Al-Aqsa" is the oldest name given to the plaza. Today the expression "Masjid al-Aqsa" (The Distant Mosque) applies to both the grand mosque itself and equally to the entire Haram al-Sharif. The al-Aqsa Mosque, located slightly behind the Dome of the Rock, was built between 705 and 715 AD under Caliph Walid, the son and successor of Abd al-Malik. With its many naves, it was initially able to hold some 5,000 people. The two earthquakes of 748 and 1033 destroyed several naves; the mosque was then rebuilt after its original model by Fatimid Caliph al-Dhaher in 1033. The mosaics above the arcade in the central nave and on the dome date from this time and are identical copies of the Umayyad mosaics, which may be seen on the Dome of the Rock.

Transformed into a church by the Crusaders, the mosque also served as the royal residence until 1128, and then became the headquarters of the Order of the Knights Templar. The women's mosque (Jam'a en-Nissa) and the second room of the Islamic Museum are the principal remaining buildings. The capture of Jerusalem in 1187 was the culminating point of the *jihad* (holy war) led by Ayyubid Sultan Saladin, who restored its Islamic identity and consecrated it as a major spiritual centre. Saladin gave the mosque its magnificent *minbar* (the pulpit from which the Friday sermon is preached), which was specially crafted for Jerusalem by Nur ed-Din and which was burnt in 1969; its remains are now in the Islamic Museum. Saladin also opened the Zakariya *mihrab (in the left alley opposite the Ka'ba).*

The Dome of the Rock

"The edifice is most marvellous and most solid and of the most extraordinary form. It has in abundance its share of beauties and has received much of everything marvellous. It is situated on an elevated place in the middle of the mosque and one ascends marble stairs to reach it (...) The eyes of those who see it are dazzled by its beauties, words elude those who gaze on it. At the centre of the chapel one sees the noble stone mentioned in Tradition; and one knows that from here the Prophet ascended to heaven."

■ Ibn Battuta, fourteenth century

The Dome of the Rock was built *circa* 691 by the Umayyad Caliph Abd al-Malik. The plaza and the sacrificial Rock of Abraham had already been cleared by the Caliph Omar Ibn al-Khattab, who insisted on Islam's attachment to the Abrahamic tradition (Abraham is recognised as the first Muslim because he submitted to divine will). In honouring this site, Omar Ibn al-Khattab bestowed on it sacred status as the first of the two *qiblas*. Until the emigration of the Prophet Mohammad to Medina, he and all other Muslims turned towards Jerusalem to pray. The holiness of the Dome of the Rock also has its roots in the tradition (today the most traditional anchor of Islam) surrounding the Nocturnal Journey *(al-'Isra)* and the Ascension *(al-Mi'raj)* of the Prophet Mohammad; during the course of the journey, he saw all the prophets who had preceded him and he assisted in the torments of hell and the delights of Paradise.

"Glory to God Who did take His Servant [the Prophet Mohammad] *for a journey by night from the Sacred Mosque* [Mecca] *to the farthest Mosque (Masjid al-Aqsa), whose precincts We* [God] *did bless, - in order that We might show him* [the Prophet Mohammad] *some of Our Signs! For He is all-hearing, He is all-seeing."* (Quran: Surat al-Isra 17:1)

It is hard to give a precise account of all the functions and rites that were initially practised inside the Dome of the Rock. It seems, however, that it had a particular function with regard to new converts. On the inside facade of the octagonal colonnade, there is a strip of mosaic inscriptions in Kufic calligraphy, contemporary with the construction of the Dome of the Rock, invoking the unity of God, the role of the Prophet Mohammad as God's messenger, and the messianic nature of Jesus (believed in Islam to be a messenger but not God Himself). The ecumenical appeal is evident; the fact that this long inscription is addressed to all "People of the Book," encouraging them to reject the divinity of Jesus and to accept the message of Islam, suggests that the Dome of the Rock was also intended for new converts (Christian, Samaritan, and Jewish).

Nor say of God aught but the truth:
Only that Christ Jesus the son of Mary
Was an apostle of God,
And his Word which he bestowed on Mary,
And a Spirit proceeding from Him
(...)
It is God who is my Lord and your Lord;
Then worship Him.
This is a Way that is straight.
There is no god but He:
That is the witness of God, His angels and those endued with knowledge, standing firm on justice.

-There is no God but He, the Exalted in Power, the Wise.

■ Extract from the mosaic calligraphy on the interior of the octagonal arcade - 72 Hegira / 692

Architecture and Ornamentation

The cupola made of wood and gilded with an alloy since the 1960s, restored and regilded in recent years as a gift from Jordan's King Hussein, reaches a height of 30 metres above the terrace. The size of the cylinder on which it rests was dictated in proportion to the size of the Rock itself (at the highest elevation of the hill), which can be distinguished inside the mosque. The exterior of the Dome of the Rock was decorated with mosaics until the sixteenth century. At this time, Sultan Suleiman the Magnificent began the first restorations; he had the lower section covered with coloured marble, and the upper section, with ceramic panels decorated with geometric designs and strips of calligraphy bearing long quotations from the Quran (Surat Yasin, 36). These were renovated at the end of the nineteenth century by Armenian craftsmen, and then again in the 1960s.

The arcades of the two colonnades, one octagonal, the other circular, are covered with the original mosaics dating from the end of the seventh century, and illustrate plant and jewellery motifs as well as inscriptions in Kufic style. On the ceiling, the wooden panels, overlaid in places with marble, offer a wealth of variations such as rosettes and intertwining patterns.

Inside the cupola, the sumptuous décor, of predominantly gold and red floral decoration, rises to the highest point, around which a splendid circular calligraphy from the Quranic

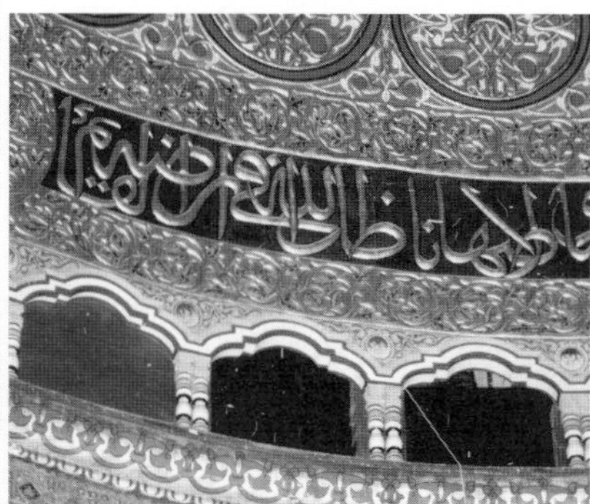

"Throne Verse" is inscribed (Quran, Surat al-Baqara, 2: 255). This work was carried out under the Ayyubid sultan, Saladin, who liberated Jerusalem from the Crusaders in 1187. Responsible for a number of renovations in the mosque and in the Haram al-Sharif, his exploits, too, are praised here in the long, golden-lettered inscription written on a black background. Under the cupola, emerging in all its simplicity, is the Rock: the site both of Abraham's sacrifice and the Ascension of the Prophet Mohammad. It is enclosed by a wrought iron grille, forged and erected by the Crusaders.

In the southern corner, a marble staircase leads down to a cave under the Rock. It is reserved mainly for private prayers and contains two *mihrabs*. The one on the left probably dates back to the Fatimid period (tenth or eleventh century).

The Terrace of the Dome of the Rock

Access to the terrace on which the Dome of the Rock stands is possible through eight flights of stairs leading to **eight arches** *(qanatirs)* called *mawazin* (scales). Islamic tradition has it that hearts will be weighed here on the Day of the Last Judgment. Built in the tenth century or in the Mameluke period, the arcades sometimes re-utilised older architectural elements. Thus the capitals of the unique oriental *qanatir* (Qanatir es-Silsila) date from Roman times although the *qanatir* itself was built in 1472 AD. As for the *qanatir* closest to Sabil Qaitbey, it is signed and dated 951. Near the *qanatir* in the south stands the **minbar of Qadi Burhan ed-Din** (the judge of Jerusalem). This building is also called **Qubbet al-Mizan** (The Dome of the Scales) or Minbar al-Saif (The Summer Pulpit). This *minbar*, which was restored by Qadi Burhan ed-Din in 1388, is the only outdoor *minbar*. It was used mainly on important Muslim holy days, when the al-Aqsa mosque proved too small to hold the throngs of the faithful. More occasionally, it has been associated with prayers for rainfall.

On the terrace, several domes are the object of a particular devotion: the **Qubbet en-Nabi** (The Dome of the Prophet), which was probably built on Umayyad ruins in 1620, was a gift of Farouq Bey, governor of the districts of Jerusalem and Nablus, and the person responsible for the caravans of pilgrimage. Since the ninth century, at least, this dome has been known as the site where the Prophet Mohammad prayed with the angels before his Ascension. Nearby, the inscription on the entrance to the **Qubbet al-Mi'raj** (The Dome of the Ascension) dates the restoration work undertaken by the Governor of Jerusalem, Izz ed-Din ez-Zanjabili, to 1200-1201. However, the foundations of this building commemorating the Nocturnal Journey of the Prophet Mohammad probably date back to the seventh century. The contrast between a multitude of delicate columns and large marble panels is remarkable. On the southern wall, the large *mihrab*, painted in green, is an Ottoman addition of 1781. In the northwest corner of the terrace, the **Qubbet al-Arwah** (The Dome of the Spirits) marks the place where, according to Islamic tradition, the spirits of all Believers will gather on the Day of the Resurrection. This building was probably constructed in the sixteenth century; eight columns of marble support its *qubbet*, which is unprotected. To the east of the Dome of the Rock stands the contemporary **Qubbet es-Silsila** (The Dome of the Chain), which was nevertheless renovated and remodelled under the Mameluke Sultan Baybar. Several stories are told about this building: according to one, it was here that Solomon passed judgment; he would suspend adversaries by a chain directly linked to the roof — anyone who lied would immediately be struck dead by lightning. **Qubbet en-Nahawiya** is the name attributed to the entire building rising to the dome itself, or *al-qubba*. It was commissioned by Ayyubid Sultan al-Malik al-Mu'azzam 'Issa in 1207-1208. A school of Arabic grammar (which had an important influence on the teaching of Arabic literature and linguistics) was located in this complex until the nineteenth century. The middle portal, whose twisted columns and capitals probably date back to the Crusader period, is unique. Today, the building houses the office of the Mufti of Jerusalem.

Attacks on the Sanctity of the Haram al-Sharif

"If I ever take control of Jerusalem," declared Theodor Herzl during the Zionist Conference in Basel in 1897, "I will take away all the holy places except the Jewish ones."

Inspired by Theodor Herzl and vindicated by the occupation of the Old City in 1967, the Zionist movement had never ceased its vigorous opposition to the *Status Quo* of the Haram al-Sharif, thereby encouraging individual as well as government attacks on the sanctity of the site.

August 15, 1929: Jews plant the flag of the Zionist movement, which later becomes the official flag of the State of Israel, on the al-Buraq Wall (in Hebrew, *HaKotel HaMa'aravi*) and demonstrate under the slogan *"The Wall is ours."* Until this incident, the site had been recognised as Islamic property and a holy place for Muslims; however, the Islamic authorities allowed the Jewish community to use the narrow area at the foot of the Western Wall of the Haram al-Sharif, on the sole condition that they make no modifications there.

August 16, 1929: Palestinian Muslims, joined by Christian Palestinians, hold counter-demonstrations. Clashes break out throughout Palestine.

1930: A British committee of investigation confirms the Islamic identity of the Wall (al-Buraq), including the pavement and a large part of the Maghribi Quarter. To this day, the majority of residences and shops in the Old City are religious property, belonging mainly to the Greek Orthodox and Armenian patriarchates, or the *Waqf* (the foundation that manages Islamic properties). Rights to these properties are passed down from heir to heir, while rents only slightly increase and remain very often of purely token value.

June 1967: Destruction of the al-Buraq Mosque and the Maghribi Quarter. The narrow pavement at the foot of the Wall is transformed into a vast area, or plaza. The plaza and Wall are declared *"inalienable property of the Jewish people."*

August 21, 1969: An attempted arson attack on the al-Aqsa Mosque by Michael Rohan, an Australian messianic tourist, who is convinced that the Messiah would never return until the *"Temple Mount is cleansed of its abominations."* Israeli forces deliberately delay the intervention of fire fighters, and the water supply to the mosque is momentarily cut off! The *minbar* or pulpit of Saladin, hand-crafted in Aleppo in the twelfth century, is ruined and the southern section of the mosque severely damaged.

May 1980: Israeli police discover explosives placed by the Meir Kahane group (a Jewish underground terror group, some of whose members are subsequently imprisoned) near the al-Aqsa Mosque.

August 21, 1981: On the anniversary of the attempted arson attack on the al-Aqsa Mosque in 1969, Israeli authorities start excavations to re-open the tunnel discovered by a British colonel, Charles Warren, in 1876 under the Haram al-Sharif.

April 11, 1982: An Israeli soldier of American origin opens fire on worshippers inside the Dome of the Rock; Israeli soldiers kill other Palestinians, when the latter mount protest demonstrations. Nine Palestinians are killed and more than one hundred injured.

March 10, 1983: Palestinian security guards arrest 49 Jews carrying explosives. Israeli authorities release them the next day.

October 8, 1990: Massacre of the Haram al-Sharif. Following a protest on the Haram against the attempt by a Jewish group ("The Temple Mount Faithful") to lay a cornerstone for the "Third Jewish Temple" here, Israeli forces enter the plaza, killing 20 Palestinians and wounding more than a hundred.

September 24, 1996: Opening of the tunnel under the al-Aqsa Mosque for the ninth time. Demonstrations break out throughout the entire West Bank and the Gaza Strip. The clashes result in 80 Palestinians killed and 1,200 wounded in the conflicts.

September 28, 2000: Having obtained Labour (Alignment) Party Prime Minister Ehud Barak's authorisation, leader of the Likud, Ariel Sharon, accompanied by other political figures and hundreds of riot police, enters the Haram al-Sharif. More than 3,000 Israeli soldiers and riot police are deployed in East Jerusalem. This provocation, aspiring - despite Camp David's recent focus on the Temple Mount or Dome of the Rock as being negotiable - to confirm Israeli sovereignty over the Haram al-Sharif and over East Jerusalem, detonates the al-Aqsa Intifada against the Israeli Occupation.

Museum of Islamic Art

In the south-west corner of the plaza. Admission is included in the admission ticket to the Haram al-Sharif.

Although the exhibition space is uninformative, and unattractively arranged, the Museum of Islamic Art has a good collection of mostly mediaeval, interesting pieces. In the first hall, which dates to the Ayyubid dynasty, are small exhibits: amongst them Quranic calligraphy and illuminated manuscripts, porcelain and other ceramics, vessels, coins, instruments of astronomy and swords. Particular attention should be paid to the relics of slain martyrs, killed by the Israeli army, and a variety of types of ammunition employed within the holy area of the Haram al-Sharif during the last decade.

The second hall, a former refectory built by the Knights Templar in the twelfth century, is devoted to architectural and decorative ornaments from the Dome of the Rock: monumental gates embossed with copper, fragments of Umayyad mosaics and a Crusader period wrought-iron screen from the al-Aqsa Mosque, which served until 1960 to protect the Rock. Here, too, may be seen Umayyad panels of carved cypress wood, and the remains of the magnificent *minbar* donated by Saladin, which was burnt in the fire of 1969.

From Herod's Gate to Lions' Gate

Herod's Gate (Bab al-Zahra)

The main access to the Muslim Quarter from Salah ed-Din Street, east of Damascus Gate.

The name Bab al-Zahra, "The Flower Gate," refers to the rosebush overhanging the Ottoman arch. Christian pilgrims, seeking biblical souvenirs in the sixteenth and seventeenth centuries, called it "Herod's Gate," mistakenly identifying the interior of a Mameluke house there as the palace of Herod Antipas, son of Herod the Great.

Lions' Gate or St. Stephen's Gate (Bab al-Asbat - The Gate of the Tribes)

This gate was once called the Gate of Mary, and indeed is still known in Arabic by this name: Bab Sittner Mariam. Another Arabic name for it, Bab al-Asbat, is the name also given to the access gate to the Haram al-Sharif, the nearest gate. Enigmatically, this refers to the Bedouin tribes who, originally from territories to the east of Jerusalem, used this gate when they came to the city. The names of the different tribes who shared these arid mountains until 1967 were given to their respective territories: Arab al-Hatimat, Arab al-Sawahra, and Arab Ibn Ubeid. The name "Lions Gate" refers to the two statues of lions that guard the entrance to the gate. According to legend, lions appeared to Sultan Suleiman the Magnificent in a dream, threatening to devour his father unless he built a wall around the city. According to another legend, Sultan Suleiman commissioned these lions in honour of the Mameluke Sultan Baybar, who drove the Crusaders out of Palestine: lions were a feature of his coat-of-arms. The gate was also once called the Gate of Jordan (Bab al-Ghor). Christian foreigners often call it "Saint Stephen's Gate" in memory of the first Christian martyr, who was stoned to death on this site. This was also the name used by the Crusaders, although in Byzantine times there was another St. Stephen's Gate (today's Damascus Gate) in the north of the city.

The defensive, L-shaped structure of the Ottoman gate was destroyed in 1917 by British forces in order to allow vehicles to reach the Austrian Hospice located on the Via Dolorosa in the Old City.

Church of St. Anne (es-Salahiya)

Via Dolorosa, Monday-Saturday, 8:00-12:00 and 14:00-17:00; in summer 14:00-18:00. Admission NIS 10. Annual celebrations July 13 or 14.

According to a tradition traced to the Byzantine era, the home of Saint James and Saint Anne, parents of the Virgin Mary, was in the crypt here (which is remarkable for its acoustic qualities). Today, it is the best-preserved Crusader building in Jerusalem, built in Romanesque style, whose rare architectural monuments have been integrally preserved. After its construction between 1131 AD and 1138 AD, the church underwent some remodelling. The enlarged facade was brought forward seven metres: the junction is visible in the first row of the columns. In 1192, Saladin transformed the church into a *madrasa* - whose foundation's inscription is to be seen over the lintel. Since that time, the building has been known as the **Madrasa Salahiya.** Religious foundations closed during the Ottoman period, so the building was abandoned and even used as a quarry after the earthquake of 1821. Finally, in 1856, Sultan Abd al-Majid donated the property to Napoleon III in gratitude for his support during the Crimean War. In the garden (once a cloister) stands the bust of Cardinal Lavigerie, founder of the "White Fathers," who were caretakers of the property. Since the church is the property of the French state, the national holiday celebrating the capture of the Bastille is held here every year. On this occasion, the French national anthem echoes inside the church walls, but remains curiously unsung. At the end of the garden are two large pools identified as the **Pools of Bethesda**, where Jesus healed a paralysed man (John 5:2-16). Belief in the miraculous power of this water preceded the miracle and continued afterwards: in the second and third centuries AD, curative baths were built here as well as a temple dedicated to the Graeco-Roman goddess of healing, Serapis Aesculapius. Thousands came here to take the waters in the hope of being cured.

■ Al-Khanqa ed-Dawadariya

On Tariq Bab al-'Atm Street. From the Haram al-Sharif, al-Khanqa ed-Dawadariya is visible above the northern portico between Bab al-Atem and Bab Hitta gates.

This large building, once housing a Sufi convent, was built by Mameluke Prince 'Alam ed-Din Sanjar ed-Dawadari in 1297. It has a splendid monumental gate bearing all the classical features of Mameluke architecture: *ablaqs* (alternating rows of red and cream-coloured stones), *muqarnas* and benches. Observe in particular its vault decorated with floral motifs which is truly a marvel. Today, the Khanqa houses a school, the al-Bakriya *madrasa*.

■ The Church of the Flagellation

The Second Station on the Way of the Cross, on the Via Dolorosa. Open every day 8:00-18:00, 8:00-17:00 from October–March. ***Museum of the Studium Biblicum Franciscanum****, open from Monday-Saturday 9:00-11:30; ☎ 02-628 0271.*

This Franciscan church commemorates in its two chapels (the Sanctuary of the Flagellation and the Chapel of Condemnation) the Passion of Christ (Matthew 27:26; Mark 15:15). The two chapels were reconstructed on their mediaeval foundations in the 1920s, the Sanctuary having been designed by Italian architect, Antonio Barluzzi.

The church houses the Studium Biblicum Franciscanum, a prestigious institute for biblical, geographical and archaeological studies, specialising in Byzantine mosaics. The museum principally exhibits objects discovered during archaeological excavations in Capernaum, Nazareth, Emmaus (Amwas) and Bethlehem undertaken by the Franciscans, who are the Catholic custodians of the Holy Land.

■ Ecce Homo Arch

Via Dolorosa. Convent of the Sisters of Zion. Open Monday-Saturday 8:30:-12:30 and 14:00-17:00.

The arch is all that remains of a triumphal gate built by Hadrian to commemorate the foundation of the colony of Aelia Capitolina in 135 AD. Today, its central arcade spans the street, while a lateral arcade has been integrated into the heart of the **Chapel of the Sisters of Zion**. The convent, built in 1868, also houses the **Struthion Pool** (Sparrow Pool); this is an old water cistern originally covered by a pavement *(lithostratos)* named the Pavement of Justice. Christian tradition has it that here Pontius Pilate brought Jesus out before the crowd, dressed in a purple robe and crowned with thorns, and declared to the people: *"Behold the man!"* (in Latin, *ecce homo*! John 19:5) Archaeologists, however, believe the pavement to have been built more than a century after this event.

■ Via Dolorosa

Every Friday, the Franciscan monks hold a procession here. All are welcome. The procession leaves at 15:00 from the Pilgrims' Reception Centre, 300 metres inside the Lions' Gate.

The Via Dolorosa or the Way of the Cross, according to Christian tradition, is the same path which took Jesus from the *praetorium* (tribunal) where he was judged, to Golgotha, the site of His crucifixion. Over and above questions of historical authenticity as to the way taken by Jesus, what has always guided pilgrims are religious traditions and beliefs; over the centuries, different religious groups have thus favoured different routes: from The Mount of Olives to the Church of the Holy Sepulchre via the Lions' Gate in Byzantine times; from the Garden of Gethsemane to Mount Zion and back from there to the traditional Way of the Cross and the Church of the Holy Sepulchre in the Umayyad period. During the Crusader occupation, two rival groups complicated the situation, each one maintaining that its route was the authentic one. In order to heighten the value of their religious property, each party claimed to own the place where Christ was judged (the procession's point of departure) - one on Mount Zion, the other north of the Haram al-Sharif. In the fourteenth century, the Franciscans established a new Way of the Cross, punctuated by eight stations (which may be identified in large part to this day), concentrated around the Holy Sepulchre. Finally, the route accepted as the genuine one today was defined in the eighteenth century. This inspired traditions of the Way of the Stations of the Cross, developed in Europe and repeated in the Holy City. The city once again, in the eighteenth century, became a centre of renewed Christian pilgrimage from the West.

The Way of the Cross

First Station: Jesus is condemned to death. The first station is located in the court of the Madrasa al-Omariya, opposite the Chapel of the Flagellation. It is popular belief that this is the site of the *praetorium* where Pontius Pilate condemned Jesus to death, at the residence of the Roman procurator (Matthew 27:11-24, Mark 15:1-15, Luke 23:1-25, John 18:28 and 19:16). Archaeologists, however, believe that the *praetorium* is underneath the Citadel, next to Jaffa Gate.

Second Station: Jesus receives the cross *(in the Franciscan Chapel of the Flagellation).*

Third Station: The first fall *(at the intersection of the Via Dolorosa and al-Wad Street, on the left of the entrance to the Armenian Catholic Patriarchate Hospice, marked by a small Polish chapel).*

Fourth Station: Mary's meeting with Jesus *(in front of the Armenian Church of Our Lady of the Spasm).*

Fifth Station: Simon the Cyrenian carries the cross *(to the right of the Franciscan Oratory on the corner of al-Wad Street and Via Dolorosa).*

Sixth Station: Saint Veronica wipes Jesus' face *(on the left-hand side of Via Dolorosa).*

Seventh Station: The second fall *(Souk Khan ez-Zeit Street, at the Franciscan chapel).*

Eighth Station: Jesus comforts the women of Jerusalem, lamenting over Him *(to the left of the Seventh Station Aqabat al-Khanqa Street).*

Ninth Station: The third fall *(ascend 28 stone steps and follow the alley to the entrance of the Coptic Chapel, Souk Khan ez-Zeit Street).*

***Tenth Station:** Jesus is stripped of His clothes.

***Eleventh Station:** The Crucifixion.

***Twelfth Station** Jesus' death on the cross.

***Thirteenth Station:** Jesus is taken down from the cross, and His body given to Mary.

***Fourteenth Station:** Jesus' body is laid in the tomb, and the Resurrection.

* The final five Stations of the Cross are at the Church of the Holy Sepulchre.

■ The Christian Quarter

❑ New Gate (Bab al-Jadid)

The New Gate, the most recent of the gates, was added in 1887 at the French Ambassador's request to Sultan Abdul Hamid in Constantinople. This was in order to improve the flow of traffic between the Old City and the French establishments developing west of the wall [see *Christian Foundations* p. 141].

❑ Museum of the Greek Orthodox Patriarchate

Greek Orthodox Patriarchate Street. Open Monday-Saturday 10:00-18:00, Admission NIS 10.☎ 0544-272859 (Undergoing renovation).

Located in the heart of the Patriarchate, around a pleasant garden of lemon, orange and olive trees, the museum has a collection of manuscripts, historical documents and treasures of religious art.

❑ Al-Afdal Ali or The Mosque of Omar

In the Christian Quarter, leading off Christian Quarter Road, Saint Helena Alley passes the Mosque of Omar, before rejoining St. Sepulchre Street and the Church of the Holy Sepulchre. The mosque was built in 1193 by al-Malik al-Afdal Ali, Saladin's son. In Ottoman times, the mosque was associated with the place where Caliph Omar Ibn al-Khattab chose to pray after he diplomatically declined an invitation from Patriarch Sophronius to pray inside the Church of the Holy Sepulchre. The traditional explanation for the Caliph's refusal was his respect for the integrity of Christian holy places, as evidenced by his protection of the Church of the Nativity in Bethlehem. (He is reported to have said: *If I had prayed in the church, it would have been lost to you, for the Believers would have taken it out of your hands, saying 'Omar prayed here.')* However, it should be noted that Muslim belief venerates Jesus as a prophet only, who did not die. They believe His image was substituted by His real presence on the cross. Like Christians, Muslims believe in Jesus' Ascension, but they believe it was a direct Ascension in which Jesus did not die, and nor was his body placed in a tomb. (Quran al-Imran 55). Thus, had Caliph Omar Ibn-al-Khattab prayed in the Holy Sepulchre, he would have been recognising a belief he did not share.

■ The Church of the Holy Sepulchre (Kanisa al-Qiyama)

Open every day 5:00-21:00 in summer, 04:30-19:00 in winter. A place of great spiritual importance, it also attracts crowds of tourists; to avoid them, it is advisable to visit the church either early in the morning or at the end of the day. [See *Map of the Holy Sepulchre*, p. 133]

The Church of the Holy Sepulchre, the most important Christian holy place in Jerusalem, is traditionally considered to be the site of Christ's Crucifixion (Calvary), burial (the Tomb) and Resurrection (the Anastasis). Emperor Constantine and his mother, the Dowager Empress Helena Augusta, built the original basilica between 326 and 335 AD, to honour these events; Empress Helena in fact supervised the work and authenticated the places of Jesus' life and Passion, on a visit to Jerusalem. At the time of Helena's pilgrimage, a Roman temple dedicated to Venus still stood on the site. The church was either damaged or destroyed several times over the centuries, and the present-day basilica is largely influenced by Emperor Constantine Monomac's constructions in the eleventh century and the Crusaders' in the twelfth century. The Crusaders inaugurated the church on July 15, 1149, to commemorate the fiftieth anniversary of the victorious Crusader conquest of Jerusalem. In the following centuries, however, the edifice was much neglected; the fire of 1808 and the earthquake of 1927 increased the urgent need for restoration. In 1959, the three principal religious communities signed an agreement dealing with repairs and maintenance; these recent restoration works, visible in the stones and in the modern iconographic works, contribute to the eclectic impression made by the basilica.

Since the days of the Crusaders, three religious communities - the Greek Orthodox, the Armenian and the Roman Catholic (Latin) - have shared the Church of the Holy Sepulchre. The Syrian Orthodox (Jacobite), Coptic and Ethiopian churches also participate, but their rights and proprietary titles are relatively minor. Since a preliminary consensus is required before any restoration work can be undertaken, it may be held up if agreement is not unanimous. The rights and privileges of the various religious communities in each holy place were established by the Status Quo of 1852 [See *Grotto of the Nativity*, p. 194]. This Status Quo was fixed according to the detailed minutiae defining each party's proprietary rights (space, walls, etc.); the agreement also laid down the timetable for the liturgy in shared places and especially the schedule of prayers for each community on the site of the Tomb.

The Atrium and Façade of the Church of the Holy Sepulchre

The *atrium*, or courtyard, of the basilica lies above a vast, vaulted subterranean cistern, which is supported by a retaining wall dating back to the second century. The *atrium* was probably part of the Temple of Venus, erected here by Hadrian; according to Eusebius of Caesarea, the Temple of Venus was actually built over the site of the Crucifixion and the Tomb. The bases of the eleventh century columns found at the entrance to the courtyard and in the western wing (which houses **the Chapel of Saint James, the Chapel of Saint John** and **the Chapel of the Forty Martyrs**) are attributed to Emperor Constantine. The **double portal** of the Holy Sepulchre is from the first half of the twelfth century, but the upper cornice utilises older, Roman decorative elements, which also served as models for all other cornices. To the left of the *atrium (near the entrance)* stands the mediaeval belfry, which lost its top at the beginning of the eighteenth century and which was not repaired in order to avoid dominating the minarets of nearby mosques, such as the Mosque of Omar. To the right, a flight of steps leads to the **Chapel of the Franks**, *(whose interior may be seen from a skylight in the Latin Chapel of Calvary)*. Entry into the Chapel of Calvary was, in Crusader times, through this small chapel, whose doorway was sealed in 1187; since then, the chapel has been used exclusively by clergy.

"In the courtyard, [the atrium of the Holy Sepulchre] *is a real marketplace where everything is sold - lemons, figs, grapes, bracelets, bottles, soap, halva, rosaries, candles, belts, pictures, clothes, crockery, glasses and carpets. (...) Moneychangers with many coins of little value sit on the bare ground. Some people change zolatas while others change gold. There are also hawkers of bracelets, incense, soaps and rings."*

■ *Extract from the diary of Zvar Jiyerjian*, an Armenian pilgrim from Istanbul, 1721.

The Byzantine Basilica

There are few elements of the Byzantine basilica visible today. However, archaeological excavations in the 1960s revealed the basilica's dimensions to have originally been much larger. At that time, the main entrance was on the same level as the Cardo *(Souk Khan ez-Zeit Street)*. Note that in the Byzantine era, access to the basilica and the Sepulchre (or Tomb) involved an ascent from the Cardo, which was at a lower level; later, access was through a side gate on the same level as the Tomb. (The Cardo was the principal Roman road in Aelia Capitolina; a large section of it was excavated in the Jewish Quarter in the 1980s.) The foundations of the old nave are still visible in the Chapel of Saint Helena *(walls to the left and right of the Armenian altars)*. To the north of the chapel *(on the left)*, there is a closed gate leading to a small underground space where foundations have been discovered of a primitive basilica built prior to the Byzantine one. On a stone block, a Christian pilgrim has drawn a merchant ship and written a Latin inscription: "O Lord, we came here!"

The Interior

Steep stairs, to the immediate right of the main entrance, lead to a hall built on the site known to have been **Calvary**. The hall is divided into two chapels: a Roman Catholic one on the right and a Greek Orthodox on the left, where there are four Stations of the Cross:

Tenth Station: Jesus stripped.

Eleventh Station: Crucifixion.

Twelfth Station: Death of Jesus on the cross.

Thirteenth Station: Jesus' body given to Mary.

Inside the **Latin Chapel,** is **The Altar of the Crucifixion**, on the place where Jesus was nailed to the cross (Eleventh Station). The Renaissance-style altar was crafted in Florence and bestowed on the church by Cardinal Ferdinand of Medici, in 1588. It has six panels of beaten silver (four at the front and one at each end) depicting scenes from the Passion of Jesus Christ. The mosaics on the ceiling date from the time of the 1937 restoration, except for a mediaeval medallion representing Christ's Ascension. In the chamber on the left is the altar of the **Greek Orthodox Chapel**, built around **The Rock of Calvary** (Twelfth Station). On the rock's righthand side, the **crack in the rock** is said to have been caused by the tempest and earthquake that followed the death of Christ (Matthew 27:51 and 28:2). The dim lighting unfortunately obscures the superb frescoes that decorate the ceiling of the chapel, which therefore requires specific focus.

Calvary or Golgotha

This is the site of Jesus' Crucifixion. Calvary, without doubt the place where execution by crucifixion was usually carried out, was outside the city walls in Roman times. According to the Apostle John: *"Then delivered he him therefore unto them to be crucified. And they took Jesus, and led him away. And he bearing his cross went forth unto a place called the place of a skull, which is called in the Hebrew Golgotha. Where they crucified him, and two other with him, on either side one, and Jesus in the midst. And Pilate wrote a title, and put it on the cross. And the writing was, JESUS OF NAZARETH THE KING OF THE JEWS. This title then read many of the Jews: for the place where Jesus was crucified was nigh to the city: and it was written in Hebrew, and Greek, and Latin."* (John 19: 16-20). Golgotha is actually an Aramaic word, being the language commonly used throughout the Near East at the time of Jesus. This place, venerated by almost the entire congregation of Christianity, is in the basilica of the Church of the Holy Sepulchre. (See *The Garden Tomb*, p. 126.)

Descending the steps again, one comes upon the **Stone of Unction** *(opposite the main entrance)*. This site was identified in mediaeval times as the place where Christ was taken down from the cross (the Thirteenth Station according to Greek Orthodox tradition), but the stone slab itself was only returned to its place here in 1810. The passage *to the left of the main entrance* leads to the **Rotunda**, originally an ambulatory, where a small, central dome covers the **Tomb of Christ** or the **Holy Sepulchre** (the Fourteenth Station: the placing of Christ's body in the Tomb and the Ascension). Despite so much destruction over the centuries, the Rotunda has retained its primitive, fourth century form. However, it must have been considerably loftier in the Byzantine era; during recent restoration work, it was discovered that the Crusaders had sawn off twelve columns (doubtless originally plundered from the temples of the Roman Forum) when they reconstructed the Rotunda. The Sepulchre itself was only built in 1810, the last in a long line of replicas made of the original tomb. In Jesus' day, the rock was much higher, but the site became a quarry when the Romans founded Aelia Capitolina in the second century AD. The Tomb is surmounted by a dark dome, whose shape has earned it the name "the Moscovite Dome." As the "holy of holies," it belongs to all the Christian religious communities represented in the basilica. The space allotted to each community and its prayer timetables are set out in the Status Quo on the Holy Places in Jerusalem of 1852, as concluded under the Ottoman authorities and guaranteed by Article 62 of the Treaty of Berlin, in 1878.

Beyond the columns, most of the space is closed and without specific symbolism. Only the dilapidated **Syrian Jacobite Chapel** is open. The external wall is part of the Byzantine Rotunda. At the back, there is a small Jewish burial chamber, (*circa* 40 BC or, possibly, AD). In any case, in 41 AD this part of the Holy Sepulchre was integrated inside the city walls.

Opposite the sepulchre, the vast rectangular space is now the exclusive property of the Greek Orthodox Church. This is the **Catholicon**, whose central point represents the centre of the world for the Orthodox faithful, in perpetuation of the Byzantine tradition; although visitors are not allowed here, it is possible to view it from outside. The religious services and plainsong chants continue throughout the day, creating a mystically spiritual atmosphere.

The space in the northern section, which once "belonged" to the Byzantine clergy, houses - ever since the eleventh century - **The Chapel of the Apparition** and **the Chapel of Saint Mary Magdalene.**

In the northwest corner, there is a small, partly Byzantine chamber, which has been identified since the eighth century as the **prison of Christ**, where He was held. At the far end of the church, a staircase leads to the underground **Crypt of Saint Helena**, which is used by the Armenian community. Take especial note of the crosses scratched all over the steps and walls of the staircase by pilgrims, and the mosaics on the mediaeval pavement, which depict the principal churches in Armenia. To the right, stairs lead down to **the Chapel of the Finding of the**

True Cross where one may see the cistern where Empress Helena (who was later sanctified) discovered the True Cross.

Near the exit, the **Chapel of Adam** is located exactly beneath the hill of Calvary and the Greek Orthodox Chapel. According to one Christian tradition, Jesus died here on the spot where Adam's skull was buried; an illustration of this is found in the mosaic fresco near the **Stone of Unction.**

Deir Es-Sultan or the Ethiopian Village
A small door *(on the atrium to the right of the main entrance)* leads to the Deir es-Sultan Monastery and the Coptic Patriarchate. A small Ethiopian chapel with beautiful colours is located on the intermediate floor. The iconographic work and many references to King Solomon and the Queen of Sheba are particularly interesting. The presence of stars of David and religious hassidic Jews in the pictures is quite curious. The southern part of the roof shelters the modest homes of the Ethiopian monks; to the north is the **Coptic Patriarchate**. A large cistern, **Saint Helena's Cistern**, is in the basement of the Coptic Church: ask the monk who supervises it to light your way.
From the Coptic Quarter, a small alley leads to **Khan ez-Zeit**, on the same level as the former main entrance to the church, in use in Byzantine days. The remain of the main doorway of Constantine's church, not open to the public at present, lies behind **Zaltimo's Sweets** shop, only a few steps from the stairway *(not open at the moment).*

❑ Alexander Hospice

Souk al-Dabbagha. Open Monday-Saturday 09:00-13:00 and 15:00-17:00. Ring the bell. ☎ *02-627 4952*

The Russian Orthodox Church built this hospice in 1859 on the ruins of the oldest church in the Holy Sepulchre complex. In 1882, Duke Serge Alexandrovich discovered the ruins of King Herod's second northern wall. This discovery was taken as proof of authenticity of the Holy Sepulchre's location on Calvary, which was situated outside the city walls under the Romans. There are ruins of a colonnaded street in the area open to the public and ruins of a triumphal arch erected during Hadrian's rule, in 135 AD, in the church administered by the White Russians.

❑ The Lutheran Church of the Redeemer

24 Muristan Street. Open Monday-Saturday 09:00-13:00, and 13:30-17:00. Ascent to the belfry costs NIS3. ☎ *02-627 6111. Frequent recitals of religious and classical music; ask for the programme.*

The Church of the Redeemer was consecrated by Kaiser Wilhelm II in 1869. It was built on the Crusader ruins of Saint Mary - Latine Church and the Islamic *madrasa* that had succeeded it. The new church integrated some elements of the older buildings: the entrance gate *(northern façade)* decorated with symbols of the months of the year, the mosque's thirteenth century entrance *(western façade)*, and a double window typical of Islamic architecture of the mid-thirteenth century, along the stairway which connected the patio's double tier of galleries *(on the southern side of the present-day Lutheran hospice)*. The highlight of a visit here must be ascent to the belfry, whose tower provides one of the most splendid panoramas of the Old City.

❑ The Muristan

Like the neighbouring streets of Tariq al-Silsila (Chain Street), David Street and Christian Quarter Road, the Muristan - a collection of tiny nameless streets - is full of cafes and souvenir, antique and handicrafts shops.

The Muristan quarter, near the oriental entrance of the Church of the Holy Sepulchre, is characterised by beautiful buildings in rose-coloured stone which surround an ornate fountain. The square formerly housed the Muristan, a Persian (Farsi) word meaning "hospital" or "hospice." It immortalises the legendary friendship between the Caliph Haroun al-Rashid and the Emperor Charlemagne, at the beginning of the ninth century. The caliph gave Charlemagne permission to build the hospice, which for centuries housed Latin-speaking Christian pilgrims. All that remains of the mediaeval complex is the **Greek Orthodox Church of Saint John the Baptist**, easy to recognize by its silvery dome. It was built in the eleventh century, and except for the two small belfries, the building has remained intact. *Services are held on Wednesday mornings in winter and on the feast day of St. John the Baptist, but it is otherwise closed to the public.* The order of the Knights of St. John (or the Knights Hospitaller) was founded here.

Jewish settlers live on the top floors of many buildings in the Muristan. On April 17, 1990, the gates of the Holy Sepulchre were even closed for the first time in eight centuries, in protest against the occupation of a Christian hospice.

■ The Armenian Quarter

The Palestinian Armenian Community

The Armenian presence in Palestine has roots in ancient times: Armenia was the first state to adopt Christianity as its official religion, after King Tirdat converted to Christianity, in 301 AD. At that time, the Armenian Patriarchate acquired properties near various holy places and established the Armenian Quarter in Jerusalem. When Caliph Omar Ibn al-Khattab defeated the Byzantines, he recognised the Armenian Patriarchate's properties and granted them freedom of worship. For centuries, 8,000 to 10,000 Armenian pilgrims would annually flock to the holy sites, assuring the prosperity of St. James' Monastery by their donations. At the beginning of the twentieth century, the Armenian community in Jerusalem numbered 1,500, but its population increased to 5,000 during the genocide of Armenians in Turkey in 1915; thousands of other Armenians sought refuge in Haifa and Jaffa. In Jerusalem, the new arrivals took up residence mainly in the new city, around Jaffa Road and Princess Mary Avenue *(today known as Shlomzion HaMalka or Queen Shlomzion Street)*, but in 1948, they were driven out of this area. Today, the Armenian Quarter of the Old City covers one-sixth of the total area inside the walls; half the Palestinian Armenian community of Jerusalem (over 1,000 people) live here. The Armenian community is well-known in Palestine for its technical and artistic innovations, among them the first printing press workshop in 1833, the first photography workshop established by Garabed Krikorian in 1885 and the first pottery works, in 1919 [See *Palestinian Pottery Works*, Nablus Road, p. 127].

❑ Jaffa Gate (Bab al-Khalil)

Jaffa Gate is one of the Old City's main entrances; its Arabic name clearly indicates that this meridional gate leads (via Hebron Road) to the second holy city of Islam in Palestine, al-Khalil (Hebron). The inscription above the gate (on the inside) reads: *"There is no God but Allah and Ibraham* [Abraham] *is his beloved son"* [Abraham or Khalil er-Rahman means the beloved of God]. The British authorities and Jewish immigrants chose the name Jaffa Gate in reference to the Jerusalem-Jaffa route, leading to the ancient port where they disembarked in order to reach Jerusalem. Above the principal entrance is a dedication in beautiful Arabic calligraphy commemorating its builder, Sultan Suleiman Ibn Selim, better known as Suleyman the Magnificent. A much more recent inscription in Hebrew takes you on a trip through time, linking the early years of the Israeli Occupation with the mythical times of the first city of Jerusalem: *"On the 10th of Teveth 5730* [December 19, 1969], *renovation of the city was completed."* The gate is wide enough for cars to pass: on the occasion of the triumphal arrival of Kaiser Wilhelm II's imperial cortege in 1898, the portals were destroyed, the entrance enlarged and the drawbridge filled in. Ten metres or so from Jaffa Gate, on the left, in a small garden protected by a railing, are two turban-capped Ottoman tombs, which legend says hold the bodies of the two architects of the rampart, beheaded for not including Mount Zion and David's Tomb inside the wall. It is more likely that these two sepulchres belong to two city dignitaries, who acquired the privilege of being buried inside its walls.

❑ Omar Ibn al-Khattab Square

At a crossroads just inside Jaffa Gate, Omar Ibn al-Khattab Square is one of the most active places and also one of the most cosmopolitan, in the Old City. It is on the shortest route by foot between West Jerusalem and the Jewish Quarter (the Maghribi Quarter). At the southern end of the Armenian Quarter and the northern end of the Christian, the square is ideally located as a centre of activity and a passage to the Palestinian commercial heart of Jerusalem at Souk Khan ez-Zeit in the Old City and outside at Salah al-Din Street.The number of cafés, restaurants, hotels, and handicraft and souvenir shops equally make this a favourite destination for tourists.

❑ The Citadel or David's Tower (Qala'a Daoud)

Jaffa Gate. Open April-October: Sunday-Thursday 09:00-17:00, Friday-Saturday 09:00-14:00 and November-March, Sunday-Thursday 10:00-16:00, Friday-Saturday 10:00-14:00. Admission NIS 35. Guided tours in English available daily except Saturday. Slide show; sound and light shows from April to October.

At the highest point in Jerusalem, the tower was fortified under the Hasmonean dynasty in the second century BC. Herod built a palace here, which followed the trend of his megalomaniac projects; according to Flavius Joseph, it was fabulous beyond imagination. The Roman Procurator lived in the palace on his visits to Jerusalem later, when Caesarea was the capital of the Province of Palestine. In the Byzantine era, one of three towers of Herod's Palace appears to have escaped destruction of the palace by fire during the Jewish Revolt (66-70 AD); it was then given the name David's Tower. The present appearance of the citadel is due to work ordered by Mameluke Sultan al-Malik en-Nasser in 1310; the minaret and the mosque were built between 1635 and 1655. In 1967, Israeli occupation authorities closed the mosque and transformed it into the Museum of the History of Jerusalem; although the Israelis tailored history to fit their understanding of it, the museum is superb. A visit takes at least two good hours and a sharp eye to appreciate all the exhibits: the ruins include a Roman cistern and Umayyad walls; the collections include the replica of an Ottoman *sabil* and an impressive model of Jerusalem made by a Hungarian artist in 1873.

❑ The Armenian Orthodox Patriarchate

Armenian Patriarchate Road, ☎ 02-628 2331

Stretching from Jaffa Gate to Zion Gate is a huge complex, home to some of the Armenian community, its holy places and its institutions. The Armenian Church received the status of a patriarchate in the fifth century; its first known patriarch was named Abraham. In the mid-seventh century, the first patriarch received assurance from Caliph Omar Ibn al-Khattab of his full guarantee for the integrity, rights and privileges of the Armenian Church in Palestine. This protection is reiterated in a beautiful inscription in Arabic calligraphy engraved on the wall opposite the church's main entrance: *"This decree is of our Lord, Sultan and King, al-Dhaher Abu Sayid Mohammed: Cursed are all those and their descendants and may God Almighty curse whomsoever causes any harm or inflicts any injustice upon this holy place. I, Abu Kheyer Razan, hereby guarantee the safety of the Armenian Convent of Saint James of Jerusalem. In the year 854 of Mohammed* [1488 AD]."

To make a pilgrimage to Jerusalem has always conferred particular social prestige on pilgrims; those Armenians who visited the Holy Sepulchre and saw the tomb of Christ with their own eyes earned the honorary title "Mahdesi," which signifies one who has seen death - referring to one who has seen the tomb of Christ.

❏ Saint James' Cathedral

Armenian Patriarchate Road. Open during services: Monday-Friday 6:30-7:30 and 15:00-15:40, Saturday–Sunday 6:30-9:30. ☎ 02-628 2331. The liturgical rites, canticles and prayers are one of the most moving moments of any visit.

Jewel of Jerusalem, Saint James Cathedral, was built over the tombs of both the apostle and martyr, James the Wise, patron saint of Armenians, and of Saint James the "Pillar," the brother of Jesus. Most of the main body of the building dates from the twelfth century, but the decorative elements were installed during the eighteenth century. In the small courtyard in front of the cathedral, there is a late nineteenth century fountain, dedicated to Ottoman Sultan Abd al Hamid. The large plaque at the entrance of the cathedral marks the tomb of the 94th Armenian Patriarch of Jerusalem, Guregh Israelian, who died in 1949 *"after witnessing the intolerable sufferings caused by the war of 1948."* During the war, the church served as a shelter. On one particularly unforgettable night, more than 1,000 bombs fell on the quarter without causing any casualties, a phenomenon which the faithful attributed to the holy protection of Saint James. Another inscription identifies the tomb of the Armenian Patriarch Abraham, a contemporary of Saladin. The cathedral has no bells: instead, wooden panels are struck with bronze mallets *(nakus)* to signal the beginning of services *(on the right-hand side of the courtyard)*. This system of calling the faithful to worship was invented in the ninth century in response to a Muslim ruling which forbade the ringing of church bells. On entry to the cathedral, one's gaze is immediately absorbed in a fairyland of suspended oil lamps *(ganteghes)*, centuries old: they are the unique source of light. Marvellous blue and white eighteenth century faience tiles and richly-coloured carpets on the floor add to the cathedral's mystic charm. The Armenian complex is located opposite the cathedral *(across the road)*. The buildings are private and include schools, a library, a seminary and a residential area.

❏ The Mardigian Museum

Armenian Patriarchate Road. Open Monday-Saturday 09:00-16:30, admission NIS 5; ☎ 02-628 2331. The Armenian Library may be consulted for research.

The museum, dedicated to Armenian history and culture in its entirety, is located in the ancient Armenian seminary. It has a very beautiful collection (cultural objects, manuscripts, costumes, robes and maps). Among the major pieces on display are the oldest books ever printed in Jerusalem (in 1833), and a picture of the Holy Sepulchre taken in 1861, when it was surrounded by open green space.

❏ Saint Mark's Church

On Ararat Road, between the Armenian and Jewish quarters. Open Monday-Saturday 9:00-12:00 and 15:00-17:00. Daily vespers at 16:00 in winter and 17:00 in summer.

At the heart of the Syrian Orthodox or Jacobite community, Saint Mark's Church is rich in evangelical tradition. The church is believed by the community to be where Jesus and His apostles celebrated The Last Supper and also where the Holy Spirit appeared to the apostles. On the northern pillar inside the church, a sixth century, Aramaic inscription states that here is to be found the house of Saint Mark and the mother of Jesus. A painting of The Virgin and Child is even attributed to Saint Luke, although art historians disagree. The painting hangs just above the baptismal font located where the Syrian community believe Mary was baptised by the apostles. The site's sacred nature is reinforced by a legend that the icon was robbed, but returned miraculously to the same place where it had been hanging.

■ The Maghribi Quarter (The Jewish Quarter)

The Jewish Quarter in the Old City today exists as a result of the Israeli conquest of East Jerusalem in June 1967. The first action the Israelis took was to destroy the historical Maghribi Quarter, which dated from the reign of Afdal ed-Din, son of Saladin, between 1186 and 1196, and was completed in the Mameluke and Ottoman eras. The second Israeli decision was to expand and develop a new quarter. Since the time of Saladin there had been a small Jewish neighbourhood between the Armenian and Maghribi quarters. The people living here in the first half of the twentieth century were Orthodox Jews - both pious and poor - who depended on donations from Western Jewish communities *(tzedaka)*. The community was divided into two ethno-religious groups with different cultures: Sephardi (in Hebrew, "from Spain") Jews, who originally followed Spanish Rabbi Nahmanides here in 1267 *(around the Meidan Road)*, and Ashkenazi Jews (Hassidic and Perushim) who immigrated here in the nineteenth century and organised around their own cultural centres.

During the 1948 war, the Arab Transjordanian Legion expelled the 1,500 Jewish residents of the Old City, along with the soldiers of the Hagana. In the first week following the occupation of the Old City in 1967, part of the historical quarter that dates back to the fourteenth century was demolished and more than 600 Palestinians were evicted to Shuafat Refugee Camp in N.E. Jerusalem. Two historically important mosques, al-Buraq and al-Afdaliya, were demolished. In April 1968, the area of the new Jewish Quarter was doubled by massive land expropriation and entirely replaced all the original population. Six thousand Muslim and Christian Palestinians were forced from 1,048 apartments; 437 workshops and shops employing 700 workers were also confiscated. All these people became refugees who, like all other refugees of 1967, are not included in UNRWA statistics.

After cleansing the area of its inhabitants, the Israeli Labour Party undertook the judaising of the Old City. By destroying the historical quarter and replacing it with an artificial residential area, Israel obliterated all signs of the Arab-Muslim heritage of Jerusalem. The quarter is now inhabited by wealthy Jews able to afford the extremely expensive apartments in this "Oriental style" neighbourhood, where the *lingua franca* is American English.

Since 1981, a decision of the Israeli Supreme Court has formally prohibited the purchase of any property here by all non-Jews. The area is extremely clean and well kept, contrary to the situation elsewhere in surrounding Palestinian East Jerusalem, since the municipal services give special priority to appearance here and the comfort of its 2,000 Jewish inhabitants. Only the ancient ruins or places important in Jewish history are carefully indicated and explained to visitors.

❑ Bab Harat al-Magharba (Maghribi Quarter Gate or The Dung Gate)

This gate was built in the sixteenth century and renovated by the Jordanian authorities after 1948 to make it possible for vehicles to pass through. It is known as the Dung Gate, in reference to a gate that was renovated under Nehemiah: *"But the dung gate repaired Malchiah the son of Rechab, ... and set up the doors thereof, the locks thereof, and the bars thereof."* (Nehemiah 3:14)

❑ The Ophel Archaeological Garden

Maghribi Gate. Open Sunday-Thursday 09:00-17:00 (Friday 09:00-14:00)

Located in the southwest corner of the Haram al-Sharif, at the entrance of the Maghribi Gate, this large archaeological park presents a historical panorama of Jerusalem. The oldest ruins of settlement in this sector date from the late-eighth century BC. Prior to that time, the town was limited to the southern end of the City of David. The most beautiful ruins, however, date from Herod's reign; (note in particular the beginning of Robinson's Arch emerging from the wall of the Haram, and which originally supported a staircase and the Double Gate in the southern wall). Also worthy of notice are the Byzantine House, the Umayyad Palace and the Triple Gate in the southern wall, creations from the Byzantine and Umayyad periods.

■ Al-Buraq Wall, the Western Wall, or the Wailing Wall

"The Prophet said: 'I was fast asleep when Jibril [the angel Gabriel] *appeared before me and brought me to al-Buraq, the horse usually ridden by the Prophets. This animal is like no other on Earth (...) I got on him, and in the twinkling of an eye, he took me from the Temple of al-Haram* (the Ka'aba) *to the Temple of al-Aqsa* (the Distant Mosque in Jerusalem). *I touched earth, and I tied him to the ring used by the Prophets.'"*

■ Hadith.

This monumental wall has long been thought to have been part of Solomon's mythical temple; in fact, it was the western wall around Herod's temple, built in 20 BC with its unmistakeably large stones. The upper levels were repaired under the Umayyads (661-749), and then the Fatimids (969-1071), after the devastating earthquake in 1033. After destruction of the Jewish temple by Roman General Titus in 70 AD, the Jewish community was only allowed to enter Jerusalem once a year, to lament at the ruins of the temple. However, with the conversion of many Jews

to Christianity and then to Islam, this tradition died out for a long time to be replaced by an Islamic tradition linking the wall to the Night Journey (al-Isra) of the Prophet Mohammed. In the sixteenth century, Sultan Suleyman the Magnificent allowed Jews to pray before the wall once again; before his time, it seems the Jewish faithful prayed in synagogues in the Jewish Quarter and, on public occasions, on the Mount of Olives. Jewish manoeuvres to monopolise the prayer space defined for them by the Status Quo of 1852 was a factor detonating the Palestinian Great Revolt of 1929. On June 11, 1967, Israeli authorities took sole control of the holy site and demolished adjacent Palestinian homes and al-Buraq Mosque, to create the Western Wall Plaza, which is now a space for religious and nationalist gatherings.

❑ The Western Wall Tunnel

Entrance near the Western Wall with exits on al-Mujahidin Street and the Via Dolorosa in the Muslim Quarter.

This tunnel under the Old City was opened to Israeli and foreign visitors in September 1996, authorised by Binyamin Netanyahu (in defiance of Israeli security warnings) as funded by American ultra-right billionaire, Irving Moskowitz. Its inauguration provoked violent reaction; Palestinians protested at Israeli lack of respect for Islamic holy places. The tunnel confirmed the continuation during the "peace process" of settlement expansion, including subterranean, and was seen as confirmation of Israeli claims to sovereignty over Occupied East Jerusalem. In Israeli historian Avi Shlaim's words: *"By giving the order to blast open a new entrance to the 2,000-year-old tunnel, Netanyahu blasted away the last faint hopes of a peaceful dialogue with the Palestinians (...) Most outside observers regarded Netanyahu's policy of bogging down the peace process as the underlying cause of this costly and bloody conflict."* Repression of demonstrations in Jerusalem and the Occupied Palestinian Territories was at a fatal, high cost: 80 Palestinians and 15 Israeli police killed, over 1,200 Palestinian civilians injured.

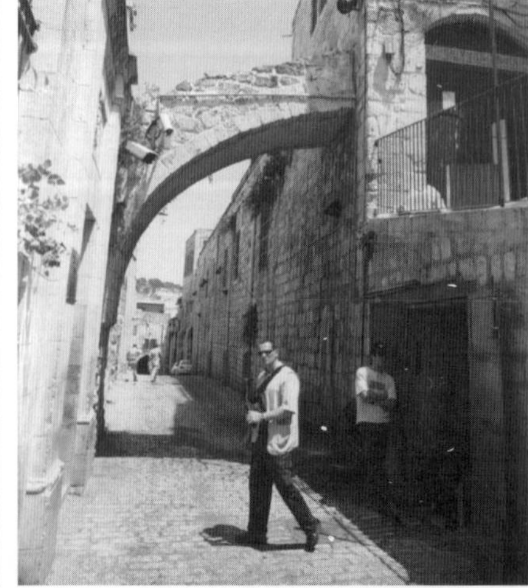

❑ The Cardo

Between Habad Street and the Jewish Quarter.

Transformed now into a commercial gallery, the Cardo was built in the Roman era, and rebuilt in the fourth century. It measured 12.5 metres wide. The Madaba Map indicates that in the sixth century, the Cardo was a principal city axis. Shops partially cut into the rock, whose ruins can be seen at the southern end, stood side by side on both sides of this colonnaded route.

❑ The Broad Wall

Plugat HaKotel Street

This 7-metre thick wall was free-standing over a distance of 65 metres. Erected by Hezekiah, King of Judah in the eighth century BC (II Chronicles 32:5), it was built at the same time as the city's extension, to protect the city from the Assyrians. Following the Assyrian victory over the Samarian kingdom in 722 BC, a considerable number of refugees (in particular the elite) settled in Judah.

❑ Hurva Arch

Hurva Square

Hurva Arch is a contemporary twentieth century reconstruction of the original synagogue built by Ashkenazi Jews in the eighteenth century. Shortly after its construction, it was set on fire by its Jewish creditors, only to be rebuilt in 1864. However, it was destroyed for a second time by the 1948 shelling of the Maghribi Quarter.

❑ Sidna Omar's Mosque (Minaret)

Hurva Square

Historical sources are specific about the minaret's renovation in 1397, but nothing indicates the period of its construction. The muezzin's balcony and the lantern are fifteenth century. Since the Maghribi Quarter's destruction in 1967, worship in the mosque has been prohibited.

❑ The Ramban Synagogue

Hurva Square. Open during morning and evening prayers.

In 1267, Andalusian Rabbi Nahmanides settled in Jerusalem, where he founded a community on Mount Zion near King David's Tomb. In the fifteenth century, the Sephardi community moved and built a synagogue on the site of the present one. However, in the late sixteenth century the synagogue was transformed into a workshop; its original function was not restored until the Israeli occupation of the city in 1967.

❑ Wohl Archaeological Museum

1 HaKaraim Street. Open Sunday-Thursday 9:00-17:00. Friday 9:00-13:00. Admission NIS 16, including entry to the Burnt House.

This museum was built on the ruins of six mansions of the Herodian period (37-4 BC) belonging to the religious aristocracy. Each house originally had several floors and was built around a central courtyard and ritual bath *(mikveh)* and cisterns. Only the baths in the Western Building survived: the floors are embellished with mosaics from the first century AD; the corridor that starts here leads to the ruins of two large mansions known as the "Middle Complex." During excavations, burnt wood was discovered by archaeologists on the pavement, probably being what remains of the destruction of the quarter by Titus in 70 AD. The "Palatial Mansion" contained a large number of baths and magnificent mosaic pavements. These mansions undoubtedly belonged to Jerusalem's nobility, headed by the High Priest of Jerusalem; some wish even to identify one of these mansions as his residence.

❑ The Burnt House (House of Kathros)

13 Tiferet Yisrael Street. Open Sunday-Thursday 9:00-16:30, Friday 9:00-12:30. Tickets available at the Wohl Archaeological Museum; 15 minute audio-visual show.

This burnt house in the quarter next to Herod's temple is a terrible reminder of how the Romans destroyed the quarter next to the Temple of Herod by fire when they took Jerusalem in 70 AD. This house probably belonged to an ecclesiastical dignitary, a certain "son of Kathros" mentioned in the Babylonian Talmud (a codification of Jewish law drafted in the third century AD).

❑ Saint Mary of the Germans Church

Misgav Ladach Street. Free entry. Spectacular view of the Dome of the Rock.

The walls of the German Church of Saint Mary, which lie under the terrace of the 'Quarter' café, are all that remains of the mediaeval hospital complex. The hospice and the hospital met the needs of German-speaking pilgrims who spoke no French, the language of the Latin kingdom. Following the liberation of Jerusalem by Saladin, the German community founded the Teutonic Knights, a military order independent of the Hospitallers. They established their headquarters in Monfort Castle in Upper Galilee.

❑ The Old Yishuv Museum

6 Or HaChayim Court. Open Sunday–Thursday, 9:00-14:00.

The museum derives its name from the term "old yishuv" (*yishuv* is the Hebrew word for "settlement"), as applied to the small Jewish community that lived in Jerusalem and throughout the country before the arrival of the first Zionist settlers in the 1880s. The museum occupies the former residence of a Jewish family, prominent members of the old *yishuv*, who lived here for five generations until the evacuation of the Jewish Quarter, after it fell in 1948.

The Mount of Olives

Take a Palestinian transit shared taxi from Damascus Gate to al-Tur village, on top of the Mount of Olives. The early morning light, when the air is still humid, guarantees photos of rare clarity. Panoramic view from the terrace beneath the Seven Arches Hotel.

The so-called "Security Wall" has recently smashed its ugly, concrete way through this entire, ancient and historically resonant area, which is significantly less beautiful, even vandalised, as a result. Nevertheless, from the top of the Mount of Olives (Jabal ez-Zeitoun), there is a splendid view of the Old City with the Dome of the Rock and the eastern arid hillsides of Jerusalem in the foreground, and, on the horizon, the Jordanian Mountains. Since time immemorial, the Mount of Olives has been a holy place where one graveyard has succeeded another, until our present time. The first Canaanite tombs were dug here around 2400 BC. A place of mystery, the Mount of Olives is also associated with important moments in the life of Jesus: *"And when He was come near, He beheld the city, and wept over it, ..."* (Luke 19:41). When Christianity was adopted as the state religion, in the sixth century, the mount was covered with no less than 24 churches.

❑ The Mosque of the Ascension

Open daily. Ring the bell if door closed. Admission NIS 3.

Also known as the Chapel of the Ascension, this small octagonal sanctuary, originally surrounded by a covered colonnade, or portico, and a fortified monastery, was built by the Crusaders in the Middle Ages; it was then transformed into a mosque after Saladin's victory in 1187, when the dome and *mihrab* were added. Islamic tradition holds that this was the place where Jesus, who is recognised by Muslims as a prophet, ascended into heaven: *"Behold! God said: O Jesus! I will take thee and raise thee to Myself..."* (Quran, al-Imran 55). A footprint inside the sanctuary is said to be the last mark Jesus left on earth. Franciscan priests celebrate mass in this mosque three days every year: it is one of the rare places in the world where the two religions coexist in harmony.

In a small crypt near the mosque is the tomb of a Bedouin woman, Rabia al-Badawiya, who died in the tenth century; despite the efforts of Ibn Battuta in the fourteenth century, her name was altered and eventually replaced by the name of a more celebrated female Muslim saint or mystic, Rabia al-Adawiya, who lived and died in Basra (in Iraq) in 801. Other traditions attribute the crypt to the prophetess Huldah (2 Kings 22:14-20) or as the burial place of Saint Pelagius.

❑ The Russian Church of the Ascension

Rabia al-Adawiya Road. Open Monday-Thursday, 9:00-12:00. ☎ 02-628 4373.

On the summit of the Mount of Olives, the tall square belfry of this convent stands out. Apart from a small museum and a fifth century Armenian mosaic pavement, discovered during construction work in the church between 1870 and 1887, one may enjoy the freshness and the fragrances of the delightful garden.

❑ The Pater Noster Church

Open Monday-Saturday, 9:00-11:30 and 15:00-17:00.

This church and its Carmelite monastery were built by Princess de la Tour d'Auvergne, between 1868 and 1872. Archaeological digs in 1910 and 1911 revealed the ruins of the Byzantine church commissioned by Emperor Constantine, the Eleona Basilica or the Church of Olives, built over a grotto which tradition held was where Jesus ascended into heaven. At the end of the Byzantine period, the site of the Ascension was declared rather to be the summit of the Mount of Olives. Since then, the grotto has been associated with Jesus' teaching of the Lord's Prayer to his disciples, a tradition which was revived in the twentieth century. The tiled panels *(in the cloister and outside it)* display the "Lord's Prayer" in over sixty languages.

❑ Bethphage (or Beit Fage)

Follow the Beit Fage Road toward the east, starting at the Pater Noster Church.

Bethphage is where Jesus started his triumphal entry into Jerusalem on Palm Sunday (Matthew 21:1-17). The Bethphage Chapel inside the Franciscan monastery was built on ruins of a Crusader chapel, in the late nineteenth century. *(Open 8:00-11.30 & 14:00-17:00, 16:30 in winter. Ring the bell at the gate or call ☎ 02-6284352.)* Notice the mediaeval paintings on the stone near the apse; this stone was thought to mark the place where Mary, Lazarus' sister, first met Jesus. This has always been the point of departure, every Palm Sunday, of a procession commemorating the final entry of Christ into Jerusalem. The Wall is preventing access to Jerusalem from much of this area, but the procession still follows this route.

❑ The Tomb of the Prophets

Open Monday-Friday, 9:00-15:30. Bring a torch (flashlight).

A huge Jewish graveyard covers the southern slope of the Mount of Olives. It is Jewish religious practice to place a pebble on a grave every time one visits it. This rite ensures that the person buried there will be among the first to rise from the dead on the Day of Judgment. Indeed, all three monotheistic religions share the belief that the final judgment will take place around the Kidron Valley, at the foot of the Mount of Olives. At the top of the graveyard are ancient catacombs said to be the final resting place of the final three prophets of the Old Testament - Haggai, Zechariah, Malachi, who lived in the fifth and sixth centuries BC. In fact, these tombs date from the first century AD and continued to be used during even the fifth century AD.

❑ The Chapel of Dominus Flevit ("The Lord Wept")

Open daily, 8:00-11:45 and 14:30-17:00.

A tradition established by the pilgrims of the Middle Ages says that, as he neared Jerusalem on Palm Sunday, Jesus wept here over the future fate of Jerusalem (Luke 19:41), and therefore the chapel is called Dominus Flevit (The Lord Wept). A Byzantine monastery was originally built here in the fifth century; *(ruins of its mosaic pavements may be seen outside the church)*, but it ignored the tradition attached to the site. In 1955, the Italian architect, Antonio Barluzzi, respecting the original scheme of the Byzantine chapel, designed the new church in the form of a tear. Underground is an ancient burial site that dates back to *circa* 1600 BC; the burial chambers at the entrance to the property are of more recent date: the first two *(on the right)*, are either first century BC or first century AD. It was customary in those days to leave the bodies to decompose naturally in the earth; the bones were then placed in small limestone ossuaries.

❑ Church of Saint Mary Magdalene

Open Tuesday and Thursday, 10:00-11:30.

The church's architectural and decorative style is typical of Moscovite religious monuments of the sixteenth and seventeenth centuries; with its seven golden cupolas, this church is one of the principal sights of the city of Jerusalem. It was consecrated in 1888 by the Grand Duke Sergei Alexandranovich (a brother of Tsar Alexander III) and the Grand

Duchess Elizabeth Feodorovna. After the grand duchess was executed in 1917 during the Bolshevik Revolution, she was buried here, and to this day, the church remains administered by the American White Russian community.

❑ The Church of the Agony, Gethsemane - The Church of All Nations

Open daily, 8:00-12:00 and 14:30-17:00 (18:00 in summer) ☎ *02 - 628 3264.*

This church consecrates the place, Gethsemane, where Jesus prayed the night before his arrest (Mark 14:32-42), and where He pronounced the painful words: *"My soul is exceeding sorrowful unto death. Wait here and watch."* The church, conceived by architect Antonio Barluzzi in 1924, was subsidised by twelve countries, as represented through the dome. On the pediment, the letters Alpha (A) and Omega (Ω) (the first and last letters of the Greek alphabet) appear below a representation of Christ, evoking the revelation of St. John the Divine: *"I am Alpha and Omega, the beginning and the ending, saith the Lord .. the Almighty."* (Revelation 1:8). Ruins of the Byzantine and Crusader churches can still be seen in places here, while plans of the churches succeeding them on this site are presented on a panel at the entrance to the church.

In the **Garden of Gethsemane** the venerable and ancient olive trees with their gnarled trunks were witness (or, if not, must be descended from those original trees) to the desolation of Jesus, and his anguished prayers.

❑ The Tomb of Mujir ed-Din

On the roadside above the Tomb of the Virgin Mary, there is a small tomb surrounded by a grille, the burial place of Jerusalemite historian and distinguished citizen, Mujir ed-Din al-Ulaymi (1456-1522). His writings are a precious source of historical information about a key period in the history of the city - the transition from the Mameluke state to the Ottoman empire.

❑ Church of Mary's Tomb - Qaber Sayeditna Mariam

Jericho Road. Open daily 8:00-12:00 and 14:30-17:00. One of the most ancient and most original churches.

The New Testament makes no mention of Mary's death. In the fifth century, two cities, Ephesus and Jerusalem, both claimed the honour of harbouring her burial site. After much controversy, Emperor Marcian was finally convinced by the Patriarch of Jerusalem, Juvenal, that the latter site was the authentic site. The present building stands on the site of a Byzantine church, whose cruciform crypt is still intact. Rebuilt in 1130 by Benedictine monks, only to be partially destroyed in 1187, the church's stones were used to repair the city ramparts.

The facade, the monumental stairway, and the royal tombs *(in the side niches half-way down the staircase)* are twelfth century. On the right of the mediaeval stairs *(as one descends)* is the tomb of Crusader Queen Melisende, who died in 1161. Her body was transferred to the crypt in the fourteenth century, and since that time, her tomb has also been identified as that of Saint James and Saint Anne, the parents of Mary, the mother of Christ.

Mary's tomb, found in the right-hand wing of the crypt, is venerated by Oriental Christians (Greek Orthodox, Armenian, Coptic, and Syrian Orthodox). In the same area, there is also a *mihrab* where Muslims have come to pray alone, apparently, since the dynasty of Caliph Mu'awiya (661- 680), founder of the Umayyad dynasty. According to Islamic tradition, as related by Mujir ed-Din in the fifteenth century, the Prophet Mohammad, during his Nocturnal Journey, saw a light above the tomb of his Sister Mary, where he stopped to pray. This incident shows the deep attachment and veneration Muslims have for Mary, the mother of Jesus Christ.

Behold! the angels said: "O Mary ! God hath chosen thee and purified thee - chosen thee above the women of all nations. (...)" Behold ! the angels said : "O Mary ! God giveth thee glad tidings of a Word from Him: his name will be the Messiah, Christ Jesus, the son of Mary, held in honour in this world and the hereafter and of the company of those nearest to God; He shall speak to the people in childhood and in maturity, and he shall be of the company of the righteous."(Quran: al-Imran III, 42-45).

The Kidron Valley

The Kidron Valley, a countrified space at the gates of the Old City, also contains a number of burial sites. The upper part of the Kidron Valley has been identified as the Yehoshaphat Valley, where all men are supposed to be assembled on the Day of the Last Judgment; since ancient times, it has been the favourite burial place for Jerusalem residents. There are three monumental tombs from the Hellenistic and Roman periods, there, the most remarkable of which is **Absalom's Pillar** (in Arabic, *tantour firaoun*, or "the Pharaoh's cap"), which looks like a bottleneck. Absalom, a rebellious son of King David, is supposed to be buried here, according to twelfth century legend. In fact, the tomb dates from the end of the first century BC (several hundred years after Absalom's death). In the nearby vicinity is a funerary compound with Hebrew inscriptions on two columns bearing Doric capitals, indicating that they once belonged to the **Bene Hezir**, a family of Jewish priests (Nehemiah 10:20). A few steps away is the curious second century BC **Tomb of Zechariah** with its distinctive pyramidal roof.

Silwan and The City of David

Light years away from any archaeological interest in Palestinian antiquity, Silwan is one of the poorest and most densely populated areas in Jerusalem. Here, the discriminatory policy of the Israeli municipality is only too obvious. Infrastructure (roads, and streetlights) - and public services (schools, garbage collection and social services) are totally neglected. Since the early 1990s, the neighbourhood has also become a target for Jewish settlers, who today occupy several buildings; this year they attempted to occupy the Yemenite Quarter there, amidst violence and massive Border Police support. Court decisions at the end of interminable, costly, legal procedures, which have in fact stipulated in the majority of cases that the occupation of Palestinian homes is against the law, have never been enforced. Jewish settlers claim they are "reappropriating" what was once David's capital - the City of David. This was indeed the place, south of the Haram al-Sharif, on this rocky outcrop of land overlooking the Kidron Valley *(oriented north-south)* and the Gihon Valley *(oriented east-west)*, where the ancient town of Jerusalem grew up. The defensive nature of the site, (set near three steep valleys) and the presence of water sources were two principal criteria for its value as a permanent settlement.

■ Archaeological Garden of The City of David

Ophel Road. Sunday-Thursday 9:00-17:00, Friday 9:00-13:00, entry NIS 5.

On this modest *acropolis*, impressive ruins are visible today of the walls of the original thirteenth century BC Jebusite town: from the foundations of David's fortress to the ruins which bear witness to the brutality of the Babylonian conquest of 586 BC, including the **Burnt House**. The steps -leading down the hill, a hundred metres or so from the *acropolis*, lead to a vertical tunnel named after the English archaeologist who discovered it in the nineteenth century: **Warren's Shaft** *(open Sunday-Thursday 9:00-17:00, Friday 9:00-13:00, admission NIS 7)* reaches a water basin fed by the Gihon Spring. The cistern, built by the Jebusites and originally a natural sinkhole, guaranteed a water supply to the city when under siege. From the eighteenth to the sixth centuries BC, access to this water source was protected by a wall, whose oldest part dates back to the eighteenth century BC. Its roughly hewed stone blocks make it easy to identify even at some distance.

■ The Shiloah Tunnel and Pool

Gihon Valley. A torch (flashlight) and appropriate clothing are recommended: the water is 20 to 30 cm deep. A trip from one end of the tunnel to the other takes approximately 20 minutes. Open Sunday-Thursday 8:30-15:00, Friday 8:30-13:00, admission NIS 5.

Confronted by the Assyrian threat at the end of the eighth century BC, King Hezekiah ordered this tunnel dug in order to direct Gihon's water towards the pool of Shiloah. (II Chronicles 32:2-4). **Hezekiah's Tunnel**, or the **Tunnel of Shiloah**, was cut out of solid rock over a distance of 533 metres. Near the end of the tunnel was an inscription describing its construction (now conserved in a museum in Istanbul). Halfway through the tunnel, one may see where the two teams working from either end met: there is a difference of 10 cm between the two sections of the tunnel. During the Roman era, the connection between the tunnel and the pool had already been long-forgotten; nevertheless, the **Pool of Shiloah** always attracts bathers despite frequent alterations. The pool was associated with Jesus' miraculous healing of a blind man (John 9); popular belief in the curative values of the water persisted until the early twentieth century. In 1890, the small mosque whose minaret is a local landmark was built over the pool. Until the nineteenth century, Silwan's inhabitants sold goatskin vessels of water, which they drew from a number of Kidron springs.

❑ Church of St. Peter in Gallicantu

On the eastern slope of Mount Zion, Malkei Tsedek Road. Open Monday-Saturday 8:00-17:00 ☎ 02-673 1739.

This church of the Assumpsionists was built here in 1931on the site of the house of the Roman Procurator of Judah, High Priest Caiaphas, where Jesus was imprisoned the night before he was condemned by Pontius Pilate, and where Saint Peter denied that he knew Jesus, thus fulfilling Jesus' prophecy: *"Before the cock crow twice, thou shalt deny me thrice."* (Mark: 14:72.) The church commemorates Saint Peter's repentance as he heard the cock crow (*gallicante* in Spanish). There are Byzantine and Herodian remains here at the entrance to the church (mosaics of a church and a monastery), and a beautiful view of Jerusalem's three valleys, Silwan and the City of David.

Mount Zion

The location of Mount Zion in the Old Testament, corresponded to a hill east of Jerusalem *"And the king and his men went to Jerusalem in to the Jebusites, the inhabitants of the land. (...)Nevertheless, David took the stronghold of Zion: the same is the city of David"* (II Samuel 5:6-7). Today's Mount Zion, however, is a hill south of the Old City, originally identified in the fourth century AD. Easiest to reach through Zion Gate (Bab en-Nabi Daoud), the hill was successively included or excluded from the city proper according to the strategic interests of the governors of Jerusalem. In the thirteenth century, the Ayyubid rampart surrounded the hill and the Tomb of David; the wall was then razed, and Mount Zion was left outside the reconstructed wall, at the beginning of the sixteenth century: legend tells that its architects paid for this oversight with their heads, by execution. The Nabi Daoud quarter developed here on Mt. Zion in the late-nineteenth century. It comprised: certain properties belonging to the Dajani Family, an English school, the Church of the Dormition (Dormition Abbey), three monasteries, a tomb attributed to David, the burial place of Sheikh al-Mansi, and two graveyards - one Christian, the other Islamic. Successive assaults by the Israeli army, in attempts to enter the Old City, have left indelible traces on Zion Gate; following the 1948 war, the neighbourhood of Nabi Daoud was annexed to West Jerusalem and became an Israeli military outpost.

❑ The Dormition Abbey

Mount Zion. Open Monday–Thursday 9:00-12:00 and 12:30-18:00, Friday 9:00-12:00 and 14:00-18:00, Sunday 10:30-12:00 and 12:30-18:00. ☎ 02-565-5330.

The Dormition Abbey is an imposing church in neo-Roman style, inspired by the Palatine Chapel of Charlemagne at Aix-la-Chapelle; Christian tradition holds that it marks the place where Mary lived her last days in an "eternal sleep." The Madaba Map shows a huge basilica on this spot in Byzantine times. The present church was erected between 1906 and 1910 by the German Catholic Church on land granted to Kaiser Wilhelm II by the Ottoman authorities. The pavement inside the church is inlaid with beautiful mosaics, while the walls are decorated with representations of biblical women personalities: Eve, Ruth, Judith, Esther.

❑ The Room of the Last Supper and the Tomb of David, the Prophet

Mount Zion. Open every day 8:00-20:00 (18:00 in winter).

A building located to the south of the Dormition Abbey contains two highly symbolic holy places: the Coenaeculum or Room of the Last Supper, where Jesus celebrated the Last Supper with his disciples, and the Tomb of David. The building is the work of the Franciscans who built it in late Gothic style in the fourteenth century, over a succession of older churches - Roman (The Chapel of God, erected in the second century), Byzantine (The Church of the Apostles in the fourth century and The Zion Mothers of All Churches in the fifth century), as well as Crusader churches. In 1524, the church was transformed into a mosque commemorating the tomb attributed to the Prophet David (Nabi Daoud). A *mihrab (in the southern part of the wall)*, a minaret and a small cupola were successively added later.

Byzantine Christians traditionally believed that the Gothic room upstairs, and not the Coenaeculum, was where the Last Supper took place (Matthew 26:17-29, Mark 14:12-25, John 13-17). Later, a tradition sprang up that placed King David's tomb here *(in the eastern part of the Gothic room)*. This tradition continued into the eleventh century, before becoming firmly established under Muslim influence in the fifteenth century; this controversial place has, since 1948, been under exclusive Israeli control. The low-roofed mosque has been transformed into a synagogue. A Jewish memorial to the victims in the Second World War has also been built here - the Chamber of the Holocaust.

Nablus Road and Bab ez-Zahra Quarter

If the historical, spiritual, and tourist heart of Jerusalem is the Old City, the neighbourhoods around Damascus Gate and Herod's Gate have been the active centre of the Palestinian part of the city since 1948: Salah ed-Din Street, Sultan Suleiman Street, ez-Zahra Street, Nablus Road and Musrara Square constitute the central area, outside the city walls, of commerce, shops, services, cultural centres and entertainment in East Jerusalem.

❑ King Solomon's Quarries or Zedekiah's Cave

Sultan Suleiman Road. Open Sunday-Thursday 9:00-16:00, Friday 9:00-14:00, admission NIS 10.

A gigantic network of underground galleries lies underneath the Old City between Damascus Gate and Herod's Gate; there is no evidence that it was built by King Solomon, to whom many monumental works have been attributed, nor can it be traced to the reign of King Zedekiah, who is said to have escaped in 586 BC from the Babylonian conquerors through these same subterranean tunnels. Yet it is almost certain that large amounts of stone from these quarries supplied Herod's intensive building programme. Whatever the case, this underground quarry provides a rare glimpse of antique methods of stone excavation.

❑ The Garden Tomb

Nablus Road. Open Monday-Saturday, 8:00-12:15 and 14:30-17:15. Free admission. ☎ 02-628 3402.

The tomb was discovered in 1867 by Dr. Conrad Schick, whose name was given to the path leading to the tomb. Then, in 1983, General Charles Gordon, the British commander and conquering coloniser of China and the Sudan, identified the site as the "authentic" tomb of Christ. He argued that the hill behind the tomb looked like a skull, bringing to mind the Biblical text: *"And they brought him unto the place Golgotha, which is, being interpreted, the place of a Skull"* (Mark 15:22). The Anglican bishopric supported this identification of the place, happy to revenge their exclusion from the Church of the Holy Sepulchre, where they had no rights, by creating their own Golgotha. Not all Anglicans, however, agreed that this was the true site. Gordon's Tomb came to be known as The Tomb of the Garden *(Garden's Tomb)*, perhaps due to a mistake in transcription.

❑ The Dominican School of Biblical Research in Jerusalem and Saint Stephen's Monastery

Nablus Road. Open Monday-Saturday 9:00-16:00. Ring at the small grey gate. ☎ 02-626 4468, www.ebaf.op.org

The Dominican monastery of Saint Stephen was built in 1891 on the ruins of a Byzantine church discovered during excavation work. The monastery houses the Dominican School of Biblical Research in Jerusalem; in this way, its founder, Father Lagrange, inaugurated the oldest biblical and archaeological research centre in Palestine at the time of an animated debate in Europe over the authenticity of the Bible. In 1891, the school founded the *Biblical Review*, a publication established as a counterbalance to German biblical scholars and English members of the *Palestine Exploration Fund* (1865). The institute is renowned for its photographic collection (taken in Palestine and the entire Near East from the late nineteenth century to the first half of the twentieth century), its archaeological and epigraphic discoveries and its exegetic work.

Exegesis and Archaeology

"History in the Bible was revealed as a series of selected events and the Bible itself, as a theological book unveiling the relation between a people and its God."

■ Jean-Baptiste Humbert.

Spinoza's reading of the chronologies of the kings of Israel and Judah in the Book of Kings and Book of Chronicles brought to light contradictions in a text previously held to be indisputable. He was excommunicated as a result. The Reformation, however, allowed different readings of the Bible and therefore unanimity in interpretation was no longer required; this development was at the origin of critiques of the Bible and the Vulgate of Saint Jerome (the Bible adopted by the Catholic Church). The critiques revealed a more urgent need to understand the text in its specific context: especially its background geography and history; their writers generally regarded the native people of the Bible lands with a contemptuous, at best indifferent, air unless they resembled a biblical figure, when that person was treated as an indigenous representative of the Holy Land. Scientific missions from Europe and North America came to discover this Eastern reality, eager to verify biblical history. As research progressed, the scope of biblical information (as opposed to more important discoveries in Mesopotamia, Egypt, and other great empires of that time) appeared relatively modest. Where had the powerful kingdoms of old, those of Samaria, Israel, the sumptuous constructions of King David, and especially Solomon, all disappeared? So many of the magnificent monuments in Palestine are synonymous with these historical periods; but archaeological research more than any other discipline questioned biblical tradition and replaced it with history. Over time, more and more differences between history as set down in the Bible and history as discovered by archaeologists have come to light.

❑ The Israeli Ministry of Interior

Nablus Road, opposite the Dominican School of Biblical Research in Jerusalem.

The office of the Israeli Ministry of the Interior is where Palestinians from annexed East Jerusalem must apply for all offical documents (residence cards, travel documents, etc.). It provides a clear picture of the discrimination reserved for Palestinians; this discrimination at the East Jerusalem Ministry of Interior has even been taken to Israel's Supreme Court, and is currently under much scrutiny. The office is open every day from 8 am to 12 noon. Palestinian Jerusalemites of all ages must wait hours in the street outside the office just to begin administrative procedures. People start queuing in the earliest hours of the morning (2.00 am); papers are processed for an average of 200 people per day. Moreover, since May 2002, family reunification procedures have been frozen by ministerial decision. Concretely speaking, this means that if a spouse from the West Bank marries someone from Jerusalem, that West Banker and any children will be forbidden to live in Jerusalem.

❑ The Palestinian Pottery Shop and Works

14 Nablus Road, opposite the American Consulate. Open 9:00-16:00. Closed on Sunday.

Established by an Armenian family in 1922, these works perpetuate a tradition in pottery-making originating in Kutahya in Turkish Anatolia, and brought to Palestine by David Ohannessian and his two assistants, Neshan Balian and Mekerditch Karakashian. The first works opened their doors in 1919 in the Muslim Quarter, dedicated to restoring the ceramics of the Dome of the Rock. Since then, this handicraft industry has inspired other such workshops. The retail outlet has objects on display of a high quality of design and range of forms; they are relatively expensive, and certainly worth a visit.

❑ Saint George's Cathedral

Nablus Road. Open 9:00-16:00. Free admission.

Built in 1890, this cathedral is the seat of the Anglican archdiocese. Its neo-Gothic architecture, inspired by the colleges of Oxford and Cambridge universities, makes it one of the most distinctive monuments in Jerusalem. The complex houses a school, a seminary, a small garden, and two guest houses (See *Pilgrim Guest House,* p. 167).

❑ The Tombs of the Kings

Salah ed-Din Street. Open 8:00-12:30 and 14:00-17:00. Admission NIS 5. Every summer, open-air concerts are held here as part of the annual Palestinian Jerusalem Festival.

Orientalists who visited the country in recent centuries considered this royal burial site the "eighth wonder of the world," because of its spectacular first century AD royal sepulchre; they concluded that the Old Testament kings were buried here. It is indeed a complex of royal tombs, but more recent investigation has proved that this is the family vault of Queen Helena of Adiabene, an exile from her native Armenian kingdom, who converted to Judaism on a pilgrimage to Jerusalem; in the nineteenth century, archaeologists discovered a sarcophagus bearing the bilingual (Hebrew and Syriac) inscription "Queen Saddan," the name by which Queen Helena of Adiabene was known. Her sarcophagus was sent to the Louvre Museum, while part of its cover is today in the Islamic Museum (See p. 105). Helena's Tomb was originally crowned by three obelisks, similar to Absalom's Pillar in Kidron Valley. In the open-air forecourt, a place for frequent rituals, a millstone door rolls aside to open onto the vault; inside, a central room leads to several chambers with banquettes on the sides, where the dead were laid, with another part reserved for tombs. At the end of this room there was probably an ossuary. This site was acquired by the Republic of France in 1886.

❑ The Museum of Arab Palestinian Folklore (Dar at-Tifl)

The museum is located in Dar at-Tifl al Arabi school, near Orient House. It has two entrances: the first from Abu Obeida Street (Dar at-Tifl School), the second from the American Colony. Open daily, 9:00-13:00.☎ 02-628 3251.

Although this museum of popular Palestinian tradition is not strictly professional, it is one of the best museums of its kind today. Its collection of Palestinian costumes and robes as well as its reconstruction of different handicraft techniques and scenes from traditional daily life in the first half of the twentieth century are the main attractions of the museum.

❑ Orient House

Abu Obeida Street.

This huge private house, built in 1897 by Ismail Musa al-Husseini, has a long diplomatic history. A year after its construction, it hosted Kaiser Wilhelm II of Germany (Kaiser Bill) for a tea party. The Ethiopian Emperor Haile Selassie lived here with his court from 1936 to 1937, during the Italian conquest. In 1949-1950, it became the temporary headquarters of the UN and UNRWA before being converted in 1967 into a hotel known as *The New Orient House*. In 1983, Faisal al-Husseini made it the office of the *Arab Studies Society*. Although Israeli authorities closed it from 1988 to 1992, it remained the official seat of the Palestinian political institutions in Jerusalem until the Israelis again closed it, in 2001. Today, it houses the offices of an aid organization, ANERA, American Near East Refugee Aid.

Faisal al-Husseini (1940-2001)

Son of Abdel Qader al-Husseini (see p. 149), and a grandson of Musa Kazem al-Husseini (a former mayor of Jerusalem), Faisal Husseini was born in Baghdad. He received his scientific and military education in various Arab countries. In 1964, he was named Vice-Director of the Public Affairs Department in the West Bank on behalf of the Palestine Liberation Organisation (PLO). In 1967, he graduated from the Damascus Military Academy and served in the Palestine Liberation Army. In 1979, he founded a research institute, The Arab Studies Society and was made a member of the High Islamic Council in 1982. The Israeli occupation authorities placed him under house arrest and surveillance from 1982 to 1987 because of his responsibilities on behalf of Fatah and the PLO. He was also imprisoned several times between 1987 and 1989, during the First Intifada. Subsequently, as of 1990, he led the Palestinian delegation charged with preparations for the Madrid Conference and, later, for the Oslo Accords. In 1994, he was promoted to the High Command of Fatah in the West Bank, then became a member of the PLO Executive Committee and Palestinian Authority minister in charge of Jerusalem affairs; these functions he fulfilled until his death. During the first official PLO visit to Kuwait after the Gulf War, Faisal al-Husseini died of a heart attack, on May 31, 2001; to this day there are recriminations levelled at Israel that his heart attack, stimulated by his acute asthma, was in turn exacerbated by excessive use of tear gas on his office at the Orient House, during the al-Aqsa Intifada.

❑ The Palestine Archaeological Museum (Rockefeller Museum)

Sultan Suleiman Street (near Herod's Gate, Bab ez-Zahra). Open Sunday-Thursday 10:00-17:00, Friday-Saturday 10:00-14:00. Admission NIS 14. ☎ 02-628 2251.

Founded in 1927 by an American-Jewish oil magnate, the museum was called the **Palestine Archaeological Museum** until 1967; it contains archaeological treasures from Palestine and the entire Near East, dating from prehistoric time until the eighteenth century. Amongst the masterpieces in the museum's collection is a sculptured lintel from the Church of the Holy Sepulchre (Crusader period), carved wooden panels from the al-Aqsa Mosque (ninth century), *stuccoes* from the Umayyad Palace of Hisham in Jericho (eighth century), and some fragments of the Dead Sea Scrolls: the remainder having been transferred to the Israel Museum after the occupation of East Jerusalem in 1967. Going further back in time, the museum also has on exhibit a skeleton of ancient man *(homo carmeliensis)*, dated 100,000 BC, which was discovered near Atlit, on the coast near Caesarea.

Wadi al-Joz Neighbourhood (Walnut Valley)

At the end of the nineteenth century, the upper class of Jerusalemites lived near Herod's Gate (Bab ez-Zahra). Their sumptuous mansions were conspicuous in the lands farmed by peasant day-labourers, or market gardeners, from nearby villages. Under the British Mandate, the valley became an urban area, whose population rose drastically with the influx of refugees fleeing West Jerusalem in 1948 and then the exodus from the rural areas, from 1950 to 1960. The inhabitants' different origins explain the social and architectural diversity of the neighbourhood. In the late sixties, the last Palestinian mayor of Jerusalem, Rawhi Khatib, abandoned an urban renewal project intended to upgrade the area and to provide it with a bus terminal. Instead, he established an industrial zone, much of it on land his family owned here, in a lucrative "deal" for them; today this industrial zone specialises in motor mechanics' workshops.

In the 1980s, a 400-year-old, fortified agricultural building *(qasr)*, whose owner was planning to transform it into an agricultural museum, was demolished by the Israeli authorities. It was condemned as illegal! The majority of recent buildings are also illegal: the slopes between Wadi al-Joz and the Hebrew University on Mount Scopus (built on land confiscated from owners in Wadi al-Joz at the time of the British Mandate) are officially classified "open green space" or "state land." On the other hand, housing projects for the exclusive use of the Jewish population are being given the green light from the Israeli authorities. This explains why the Municipality of Jerusalem has forbidden the construction of a girls' secondary school for 800 students, (pressured by the Hyatt Regency Hotel) on the pretext that the school would develop into a "point of confrontation." A second project for a centre for 200 handicapped people was then submitted and rejected for "security reasons." An Israeli parliamentarian, Yigal Bibi, argued: *"...the youngsters may be handicapped, but that doesn't mean that they have no arms to throw stones."* At the time of going to press, the Israeli Mayor of Jerusalem, Uri Lupoliansky (a religious Jew) has proclaimed the need to "judaise" Wadi Joz and rezone it for Jews...

The Tomb of Simon the Just

A nineteenth-century Jewish tradition identifies the tomb at the bottom of this valley in Sheikh Jarrah as that of Simon the Just (Shimon HaTzadik), a fourth century BC High Priest. An association of Sephardi Jews became interested in acquiring it in 1890, and the tomb has become a place of daily devotion since 1967; dozens of Orthodox Jews visit here daily and settlers pursue their agenda to take over the area by all means: force, the lawcourts, dubious land deals, etc.

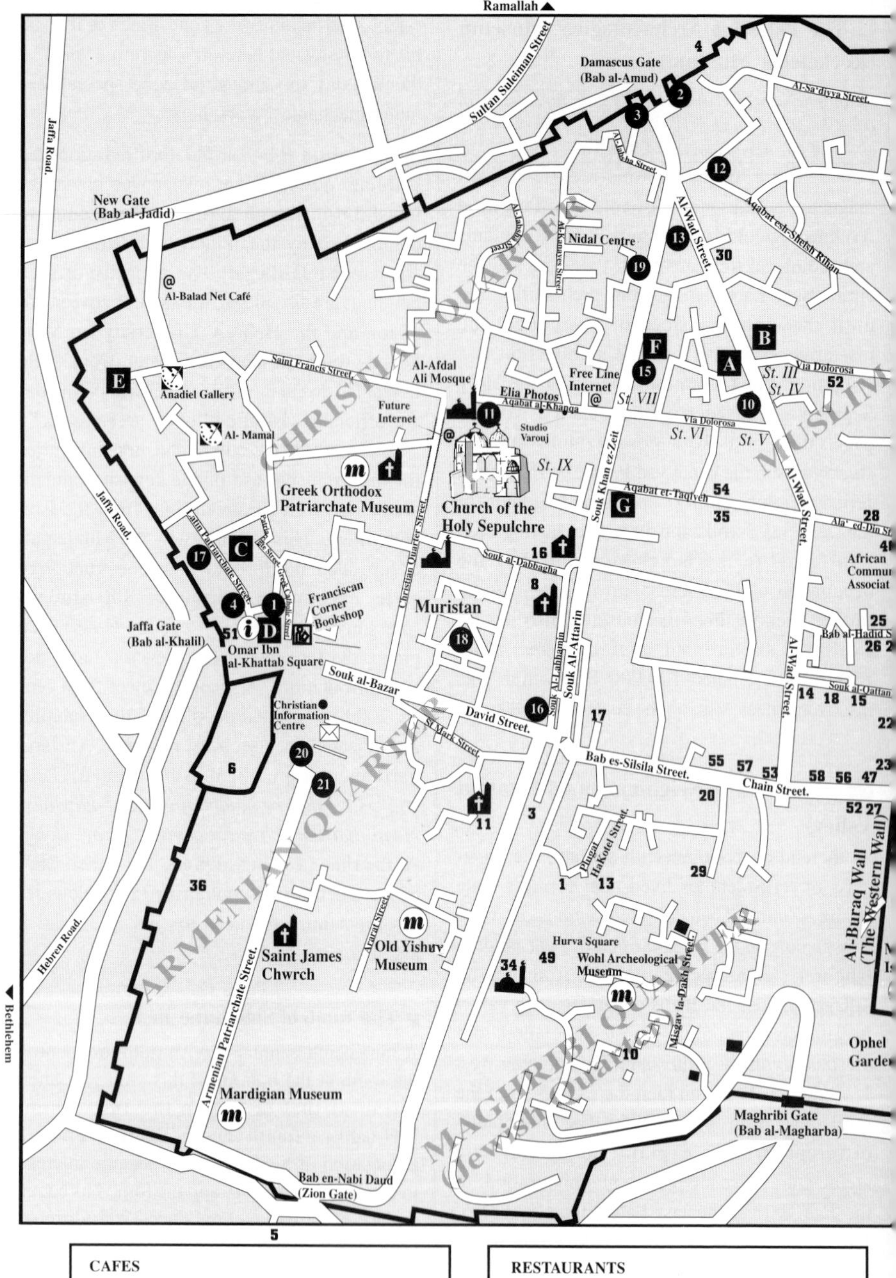

CAFES

1. Cappucino Café
2. Gate Café
3. Princess Cafeteria
4. Al-Moukhtar Cafe
5. Jaber Cafe
6. Biat al-Balad Cafe

RESTAURANTS

10. Abu Shoukri
11. Costa's Greek
12. Fouroun Abu Ali
13. Jerusalem Star
14. Abu Shenab
15. En-Nasser
16. Sha'in
17. Nafoura
18. Papa Andrea's
19. Jaffar Sweets Shop
20. Select
21. Armenian Tavern

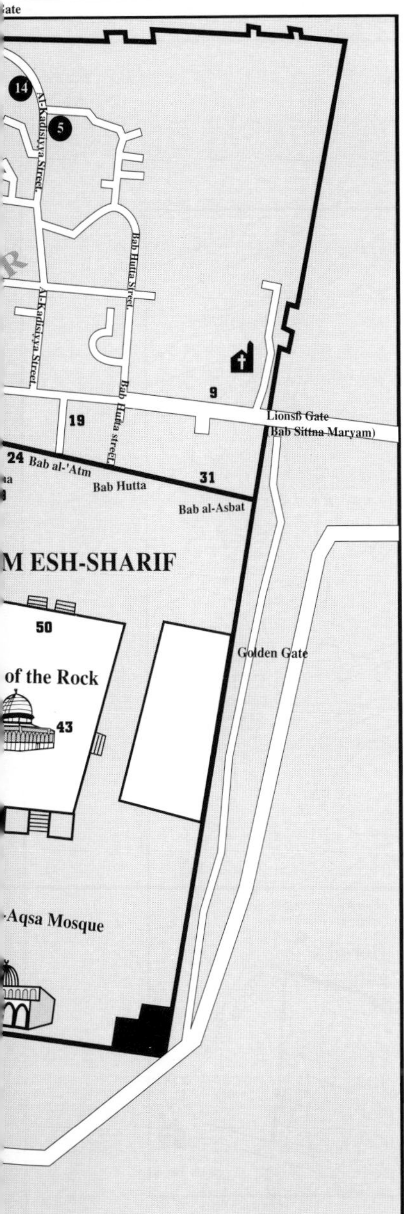

HEBERGEMENT

A. Al-Ahram
B. Austrian Hospice
C. Gloria Hotel
D. New Imperial Hotel
E. Knights' Palace - Latin Patriarcate
F. New Hashemi Hotel
G. Tabasco Hostel

Jerusalem: The Old City

ACCOMMODATION

1. Hurva Arch
2. Ecce Homo Arch
3. Cardo
4. King Solomon's
5. Coenaushun
6. The Citadel (David's Tower)
7. Church of the Flagellation
8. Lutheran Church of the Redeemer
9. Church of St Anne (Es-Salahiya)
10. Saint Mary of the Germans
11. Saint Mark's Church
12. Al-Kas Fountain
13. Broad Wall
14. Hammam al-Ein
15. Hammam esh-Shifa
16. Alexander Hospice
17. Khan es-Sultan
18. Khan Tankiz
19. Khanqa ed-Dawadariya
20. Al-Khalidiya Bookshop
21. Arghuniya School
22. Al-'Uthmaniya School
23. Al-Ashrafiya School
24. Al-Is'ardiya School (Dar el-Ansari)
25. Al-Jawhariya School
26. Al-Muzhiriya School
27. At-Tankiziya School
28. At.-Tashtamuriya School
29. Burnt House
30. Ariel Sharon's House
31. Bab al-Asbat Minaret
32. Ghawanima Minaret
33. Qadi Burhan ed-Din Minbar
34. Sidna Omar Mosque
35. Tunshuq Palace
36. Armenian Orthodox Patriarchate
37. Western Portico (Er-Riwaq al-Gharbiya)
38. Qubbet Musa
39. Qubbet al-Arwah
40. Qubbet al-Mi'raj
41. Qubbet an-Nabi
42. Qubbet an-Nahawiya
43. Qubbet es-Silsila
44. Kurdish Riba
45. Ribat Ala' ed-Din al-Basir
46. Ribat al-Mansuri
47. Sabil Bab es-Silsila
48. Sabil Qaitbey
49. Ramban Synagogue
50. Terrace of the Dome of the Rock
51. Ottoman Tombs
52. Western Wall Tunnel
53. Turba al-Jalaqiya
54. Turba es-Sitt Tunshuq
55. Turba Kilaniya
56. Turba Sadiya
57. Turba Taziya
58. Turba Turkan Khatun

East Jerusalem

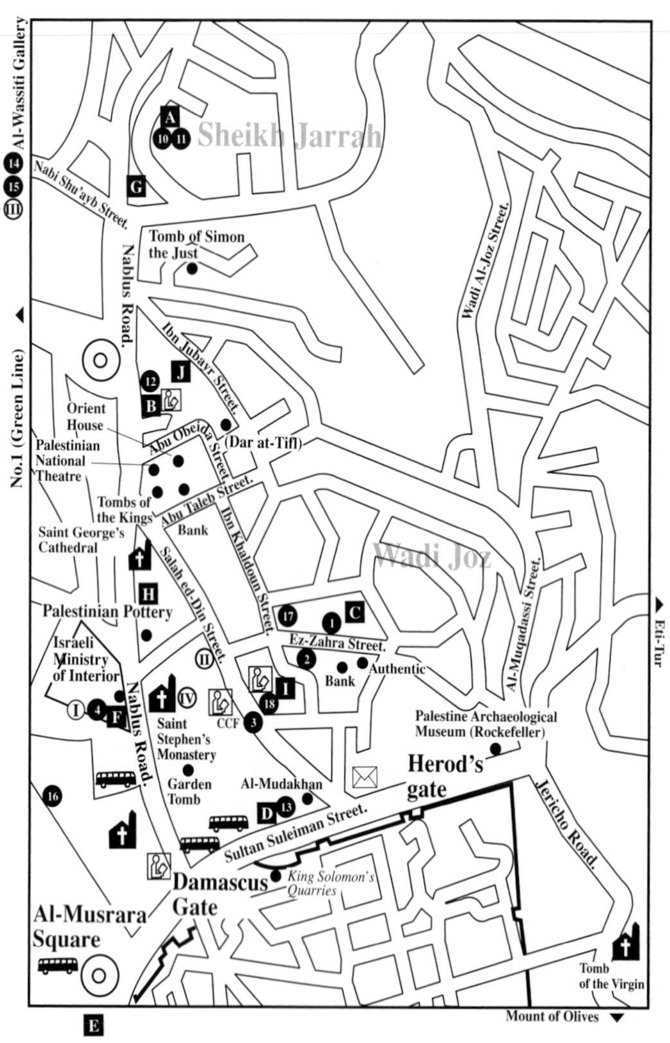

Church of the Holy Sepulchre

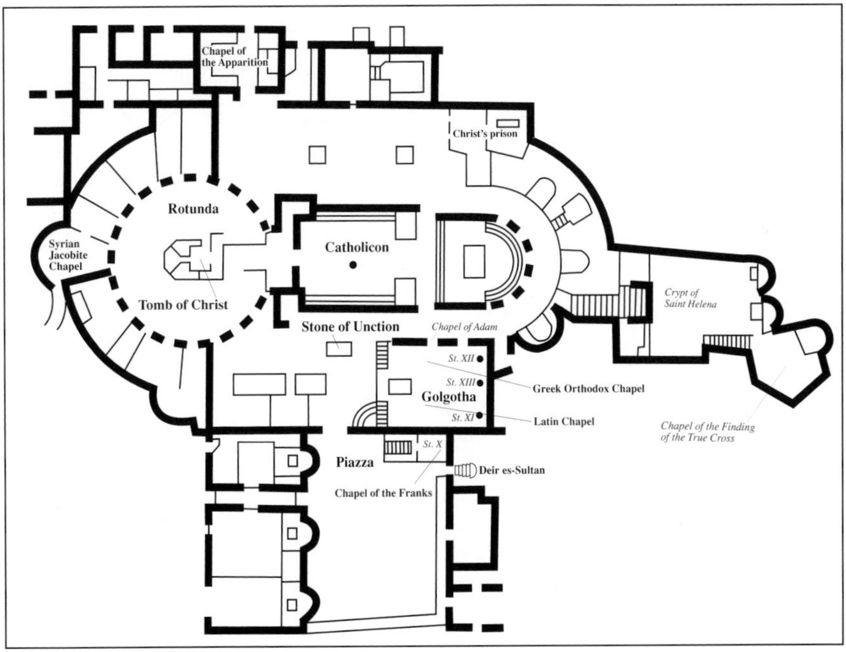

Chapel of the Apparition
Christ's prison
Rotunda
Syrian Jacobite Chapel
Catholicon
Tomb of Christ
Stone of Unction
Chapel of Adam
Crypt of Saint Helena
St. XII
St. XIII
Greek Orthodox Chapel
Golgotha
St. XI
Latin Chapel
Chapel of the Finding of the True Cross
St. X
Piazza
Deir es-Sultan
Chapel of the Franks

The Mount of Olives

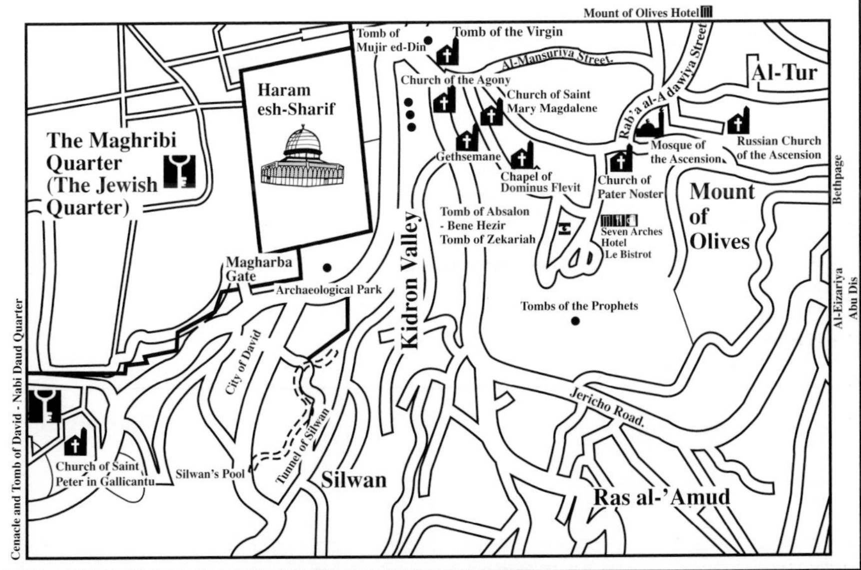

Villages destroyed and emptied of their populations in the district of Jerusalem (1948)

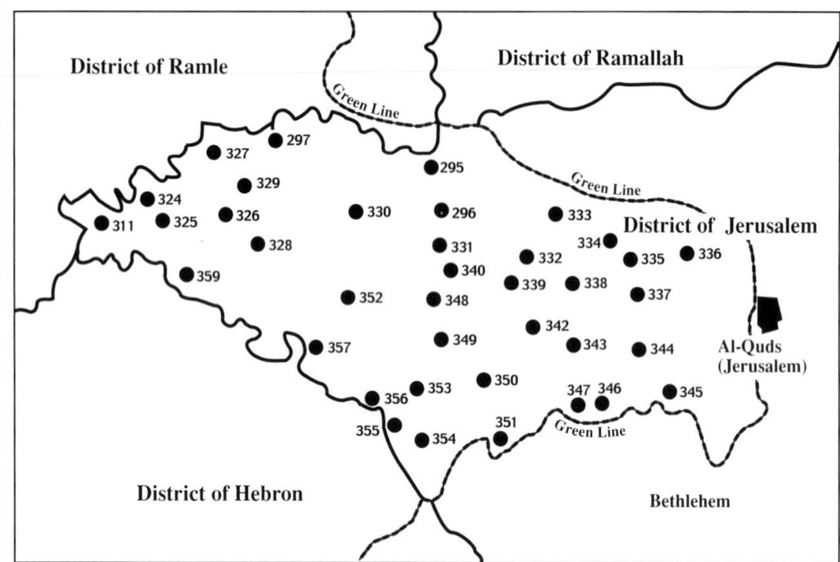

395 Nitaf
296 Beit Thul
297 Deir Ayyoub
311 Khirbet Beit Far
324 Khirbet Ism Allah
325 Deir Rafar
326 Sar'a
237'Islin
328 Artuf
329 Ishwa
330 Beit Mahsir
331 Saris
332 Khirbet el-'Oumour
333 Beit Naqquba
334 El-Qastal
335 Qalunya
336 Lifta
337 Deir Yassine
338 Suba
339 Deir 'Amar
340 Beit Oum el-Mays
341 Kasla
342 Khirbet el-Lawz
343 Sataf
344 Ein Karem
345 El-Maliha
346 El-Jura
347 El-Walaja
348 'Aqqur
349 Deir esh-Sheikh
350 Ras Abu 'Ammar
351 El-Qabu
352 Deir el-Hawa
353 Beit 'Itab
354 'Allar
355 Khirbet et-Tannur
356 Sufla
357 Deir Aban
358 El-Bureij

West Jerusalem

West Jerusalem and East Jerusalem came into existence as a result of the partition of the city, in 1948. The Zionist conquest of the western part of the city in 1948 imposed a division *de facto* on the national character of Jerusalem, a city that had already been divided in many ways on previous occasions by various criteria: ethno-religious, familial, professional, social and so on. Mixed quarters of the city (Jaffa Road, Musrara, Shamma, Romema) sprang up between 1920 and 1940. However, the implementation of the Zionist and colonial ideology by most Jewish immigrants, combined with the fact that few of them spoke Arabic, reinforced the divisions between Palestinian Arabs and Jews. If ethnic diversity exists today in West Jerusalem, it is exclusively within the Jewish population itself.

With the policy of ethnic cleansing practiced by Israeli forces in 1948, all Palestinians were driven out of the new part of the city. There, on the western side of the new city, about 10,000 Palestinian homes were totally ransacked between March and June, 1948.

Although the names of the streets and neighbourhoods have been replaced, the Palestinian architectural heritage is still visible, in spite of the growth of this western part of Jerusalem. These days, there is even heavy Israeli property speculation involving "Arab" homes, and the term "Arab house" is given as an added incentive for the sale, or for the location.

The Urbanisation of Jerusalem (1850-1948)

In 1841, Jerusalem was nothing but a provincial town surrounded by a wall. However, from the second half of the nineteenth century on, the city grew substantially beyond its walls towards the less hilly west, reaching eight times its former size by 1914. For obviously practical reasons, the city developed west, where the topography is less accentuated. Greater security allowed expansion beyond the walls, while the Ottoman land reforms *(tanzimat)*, in 1839 and 1856, stimulated private investments and authorised non-Ottoman citizens to buy property; these reforms would have far-reaching consequences. Three types of urbanisation developed the surrounding countryside. Rich Palestinian families (Christian and Muslim) moved to the airy outskirts of the Old City and built houses with a distinctive character: these are remarkable properties. As for foreign establishments - these tended to be institutions, religious congregations and Christian or Jewish philanthropic associations. The Christians built monumental compounds destined for worship or social services, while the latter, the Jews, built modest but denser housing, to accommodate the wave of Jewish immigrants.

Palestinian Neighbourhoods

The neighbourhood of al-Musrara

Landmarks: Heleni HaMalka Street and Ha-Ain Chet Street (West Jerusalem), al-Musrara Square (East Jerusalem).

To the west of Damascus Gate, the al-Musrara Square neighbourhood was one of the first to be built outside the city walls by the extended well-established Muslim families of Jerusalem. In 1948, it was partly destroyed *(Musrara Square and the main road, or Highway No. 1)*, then divided. The most beautiful residences became part of West Jerusalem in 1948 and are today in one of the most expensive Jewish areas in Jerusalem - known as *Morasha* in Hebrew or Musrara, its original name. On the other side of the main highway, which was a "no man's land" from 1948 to 1967, there is a popular Palestinian market area that extends to Damascus Gate.

Mamilla

Landmarks: Agron Road (Mamilla Road), Shlomo HaMelech Street, Shlomzion HaMalka Street.

Mamilla is a deformation of the Arabic name "Ma'miat Allah" (God's Sanctuary). This area grew in an arc around a graveyard and along three principal arteries - Julian Road, Jaffa Road, and Princess Mary Avenue. The roads were renamed after 1948: *HaMelech* (King) *David Street*, *Yafo* (Jaffa) *Road,* and *Shlomzion HaMalka* (Queen Shlomzion) *Street*, respectively. Under the British Mandate, the area was the commercial centre of the new city, incorporating government and private administrative offices, the municipality, banks, shops, cinemas and cafes. The population was mixed here, and the architecture was inspired by contemporary European urban styles. A good example of this tendency is the old **Palace Hotel**, at the crossroads of Julian and Mamilla Roads, designed by architect Nahas Bey; the inscription on top of the building reads : *"This hotel was built by the Supreme Islamic Council of Palestine - 1348 Hegira / 1929 AD."* Many details were borrowed from Mameluke decorative art, others from Art Deco. Along Princess Mary Avenue *(Shlomzion HaMalka Street)*, the Armenian Patriarchate owned a large number of shops and apartment buildings rented to the Armenian community, whose number increased with the arrival of refugees in 1915, fleeing Armenian genocide. The **Post Office** on Jaffa Road (still in service) was built by the mandatory authorities, on property given to them by the Armenian Patriarchate.

The Islamic Graveyard of Mamilla

Along Mamilla Road (today, Agron Road).

The old Islamic graveyard of Mamilla was demolished by the Israelis in 1948 and converted into a green space named Independence Park. Among the rare tombs that survived destruction was the al-Kubakiya mausoleum, whose crowned dome contains the tomb of Mameluke Prince al-Kubaki. Successively the governor of Safad, then Aleppo, **al-Kubaki** was exiled to Jerusalem, where he died. One may read on the inscription above the entrance to his tomb: "*...this is the tomb ... of Prince Ala' ed-Din Aydughdi bin Abdallah, known as al-Kubaki. He died on Friday, 5 Ramadan 688* [September 22, 1289]." In the middle of the graveyard or Independence Park one finds the ancient **Mamilla Pool**, built by Pontius Pilate.

The Mamilla Parking Area

Hillel Street carpark, at the corner of Independence Park.

Israeli archaeologists made an unexpected discovery when work for this parking area began in the early 1990s - a mass grave dating from 614. It marked one of the bloodiest pages in the history of this land; the parking area was quickly completed over it. The macabre cavern was marked by a cross and an inscription : *"God alone knows their names."* The grave dated from the Sassanid invasion of 614, which saw the systematic destruction of Christian holy sites, churches and monasteries, terrible massacres of the population, and repression most often committed by order of the Persian Jewish elite, allied with their co-religionists in Palestine. There, Strategius of Saint Sabas relates: *"The Jews paid the Persian soldiers a high ransom for capturing the Christians. Then they massacred them with delight at Mamilla Pool, which overflowed with blood."*

The YMCA

24 King David Street, open Monday-Saturday, 8:00-18:00. Visit to the tower: NIS 3. ☎ 02-569 2692. A luxury hotel, the YMCA has a cosmopolitan terrace café, a restaurant, a sports centre and a swimming pool.

A mixture of oriental Byzantine, Roman, Islamic, and Art Deco styles, this sumptuous and imposing complex was built between 1926 and 1933; it was the work of the American architect Arthur Loomis Harmon, equally celebrated for having built the Empire State building in New York City. There is a magnificent view of the city from the tower, which rises to 90 metres.

King David Hotel

23 King David Street

This hotel was built in classical, colonial style in the 1930s by an Egyptian Jewish family. It became the privileged meeting-place for diplomats, and then the general headquarters of the British occupation forces; its name is inextricably associated with the attack committed on July 22, 1946, by the Zionist Irgun organisation, led by Menachem Begin (Prime Minister of Israel, 1977-1982). More than 90 people were killed, and hundreds injured. The building was partially destroyed. The attack was among several that took place against Palestinian civilians and British forces in the 1940s.

Birket es-Sultan (Sultan's Pool)

Below Jaffa Gate.

Sultan's Pool was built by Sultan ez-Zaher Barquq in 1399 and was renovated in the sixteenth century by Ottoman Sultan Suleiman the Magnificent (1520-1566). It is now an Israeli open-air theatre. The Sultan's Sabil, a fountain to the south of the pool *(half buried under the present street)* is precisely dated June 29, 1536. Note in particular its arch, pointed with chevrons (V-shaped mouldings) typical of that period.

Abu Tor Neighbourhood

A soldier in Saladin's army, Sheikh Ahmad al-Tori, gave his name to this hill where he was buried, as well as to the village here. As the Jerusalem elite settled here in the nineteenth century, the village grew in two directions: small village houses spread out on the eastern foothills, while huge middle-class villas were built along planned roads which led to the Bethlehem Road and the railway station. The suburb was considerably developed in the 1930s. In 1948, the western part was occupied and renamed *Givat Hanania*, while the eastern part was annexed to East Jerusalem, under Jordanian administration.

South of Abu Tor, a sparsely-inhabited plateau is the site of the United Nations general headquarters. Until 1967, this hilltop was a huge "no man's land." A recreation area here, the **Haas Promenade** *(Daniel Yanovsky Street)* offers a splendid panorama of Jerusalem and the Old City. The Israeli government has instructed all official, licensed tour guides to show tourists the Wall (deceptively called the "Jerusalem Envelope"), which is being built in East Jerusalem. Rather than take groups of tourists to the actual 9m high Wall, they take them to this lookout point, from where it can be seen in the distance, suitably remote so that tourists need not be involved in the huge human suffering it is causing.

The Katamon Neighbourhood

Landmarks: Rachel Imenu Street, Kovshei Katamon Street, Tel Chai Street, Hahish Street, Hizkiyahu HaMelech Street

Like Talbiya and Baq'a, Katamon (renamed *Goneim*) was mainly (but not exclusively) inhabited by wealthy Christian Palestinians (lawyers, teachers and merchants). The Greek Orthodox Patriarchate, owner of a considerable amount of land in Jerusalem to this day, encouraged development here, selling land to compensate the church for losses it had suffered in the Russian Revolution. The neighbourhood was close to the railway station, so it became a cosmopolitan quarter: many diplomatic missions were established here, amongst which were the Lebanese Consulate *(32 Kovshei Katamon Street)*, the Italian Consulate *(16 Kaf Tet Be-November)*, and the Iraqi Consulate *(28 Hizkiyahu HaMelech)*. There were also many cafes and hotels, including the famous **Semiramis Hotel** *(10 HaHish Street, but the present building was built in 1989)*. The hotel no longer exists and with good reason: it was totally destroyed by a bomb planted in the heart of the hotel by the Hagana on January 5, 1948. The toll was over twenty-six civilians killed in the attack, and mostly Palestinian but also some foreigners, while an additional 60 were injured. The bombing marked the commencement of terror and exile for residents of this area.

Khalil Sakakini
(1878-1953)

A native son of Jerusalem, Khalil Sakakini was one of the pioneers of the Arab nationalist cultural movement in Palestine. A Greek Orthodox Christian, Sakakini initiated a reform movement and the Arabicisation of the church, thereby infuriating the Greek ecclesiastical hierarchy. In 1913, he was excommunicated for publishing his pamphlet *The Orthodox Renaissance in Palestine*. Soon after, he took up the fight against Zionist colonisation of Palestine. In 1917, he was jailed by the British authorities for having shot at a Jewish Polish immigrant known to be a spy for the United States. A zealous defender of the Arabic language, he founded the En-Nahda School, where all lessons were in Arabic, unlike the tendency in the elite schools where most classes were taught in foreign languages (English, Italian or French). His school applied the first modern method for teaching Arabic, based on the alphabet. An active member of the Arab nationalist cultural movement, Sakakini was also the author of many pamphlets and political and patriotic poems. In 1948, he left Katamon to seek refuge in Egypt, where he became allied with Arab writers such as Taha Hussein.

The house of Khalil Sakakini, one of the great Palestinian national and literary figures, is at *9 Yordei Hasira Street.*

The Talbiya neighbourhood

Landmarks: Ze'ev Jabotinsky, Hovevei Zion, Benjamin Disraeli, David Marcus and Yitzhak Elhanan Streets.

South of the YMCA, Talbiya (in Hebrew, *Komemiyut*, or uprising) is a neighbourhood of extremely beautiful, large Arabic villas built in the 1920s and 1930s. Development here started as a protest against the Greek Orthodox Patriarchate's sale of a parcel of land to a Zionist organisation which then established the *Rehavia* area. As a result, wealthy Christian Palestinians of Jerusalem, Bethlehem, Beit Jala, and Ramallah built the Talbiya quarter. The majority of villas were built between 1924 and 1937. Several different schools of architecture influenced their design, especially the International Style of the 1920s and 30s. The stone, which was quarried and then worked by stonemasons in the area around Jerusalem, blends harmoniously with the Art Deco-style wrought-iron gates and railings which ornament most of the houses.

Talbiya's charm and luxury have attracted many foreign diplomats, especially among the British. Among the most impressive residences is the **Villa of Constantine Salameh** *(Orde Wingate Square)*. This villa was the Belgian Consulate after 1948. A wealthy businessman, Constantine Salameh (1897-1999) commissioned French architect Marcel Favier, who specialised in building public buildings and national palaces. In a totally different style is the **Villa of Haroun er-Rashid** *(18 Marcus Street)* built by Ibrahim Bishara in 1926; between 1938 and 1948 it was leased to the British Air Force. In the early 1950s, Golda Meir, then

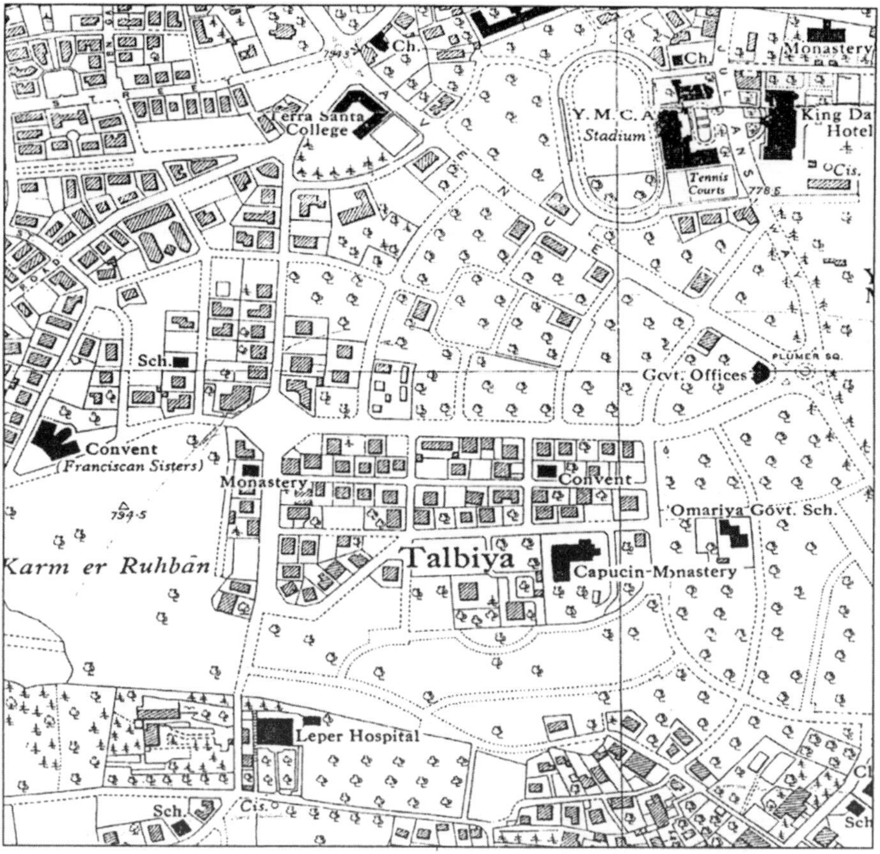

Ch.
Monastery
Ch.
Terra Santa
College
Y. M. C. A.
Stadium
King Da
Hotel
Cis.
Tennis
Courts
PLUMER SQ.
Sch.
Govt. Offices
Convent
(Franciscan Sisters)
Monastery
Convent
Omariya Govt. Sch.
Karm er Ruhbān
Talbiya
Capucin-Monastery
Leper Hospital
Sch.
Cis.
Sch

Minister of Labour and Housing, lived here for a while. At this time the villa was no longer known as the villa of the Abbassid Caliph Haroun al-Rashid. At what is now *21 Hovevei Zion Street,* is the villa of Khalil Haddad, which he built in the 1930s. Between 1939 and 1948, it was a hotel named **Jasmin House Hotel** after Dr. Tawfiq Kana'an's daughter, Jasmin, its manageress. In 1947, UN staff members charged with preparing the partition plan of Palestine lived here. On the edge of the neighbourhood was the **Jesus Hilfe Hospital**, originally a leprosarium *(17 Marcus Street)*; built by the German architect Conrad Schick in 1887, it originally housed a hospital for lepers. Dr. Tawfiq Kana'an, a native of Nablus, was director of the hospital from 1919 to 1948. After 1948, the hospital was re-named **Gerhard Hausen Hospital** in honour of that leprosy specialist. *At 10 Brenner Stree*t is the **family home of the late Edward Said**, built in 1932. During the days of the British Mandate, the first floor was leased to the Persian Consulate, then to the Yugoslavian Consulate. After 1948, the building was occupied by Martin Buber (1878-1965), the philosopher of Austrian origin, and today, by the International Christian Embassy.

Edward Said

Born in Jerusalem in 1935, a leading contemporary intellectual and university professor at Columbia University in New York died in 2003, leaving the Palestinian cause without its most respected and influential international voice. Ilan Pappe, an Israeli peer, wrote: "His insight and input on the global reality in general - and the Palestinian one in particular - will guide us all for many years to come. Above all, we shall miss Edward's unique ability to articulate in the public sphere the evil inflicted upon the Palestinians in the past and the continued efforts in the Western media to sideline, if not altogether eliminate, the plight and tragedy of Palestine. We should be grateful, however, that so many of our colleagues have followed in his footsteps, drawing on his brilliant deconstruction of the power bases and sinister interests behind the production of knowledge in the West about the Orient in general and the Middle East in particular."

Recommended Works of Edward Said:

- *Orientalism - the Orient Created by the West, Vintage, 1979.*
- *Covering Islam- How the Media and the Experts Determine How We See the Rest of the World, Vintage, 1981, revised 1997.*
- *The World, the Text and the Critic, Harvard, 1983.*
- *The Question of Palestine, Vintage 1992.*
- *Culture and Imperialism, Vintage, 1993.*
- *Peace and its Discontents: Essays on Palestine in the Middle East Peace Process. Vintage, 1995*
- *Intellectuals and Power, ed. Seuil, 1998.*
- *Israel — Palestine, Equality or Nothing, 1999.*
- *The End of the Peace Process: Oslo and After. Vintage, 2001.*
- *Out of Place, Memoirs, ed. Serpent, 2002.*
- *Reflections on Exile and Other Essays.*

The Museum of Islamic Art

LA Mayer Memorial Museum for Islamic Art. 2, HaPalmach Street. Open Sunday-Monday, Wednesday-Thursday 10:00-15:00. Tuesday 10:00-18:00, Friday-Saturday 10:00-14:00. Admission NIS 12.

This museum has a very beautiful collection of objects including ceramics, miniatures, glass, calligraphy, jewellery and textiles, mostly from the seventeenth and eighteenth centuries, provenance of the entire Islamic world ... except for Palestine.

"At the end of 1948 (...) all the vacated houses in the Arab suburbs had been entirely vandalised, and anything valuable [even the doors and windows] *stolen. Our nerves were really on edge, and as one observer put it, we lived as if we were in a concentration camp on the edge of a battlefield."*

■ John Melkon Rose

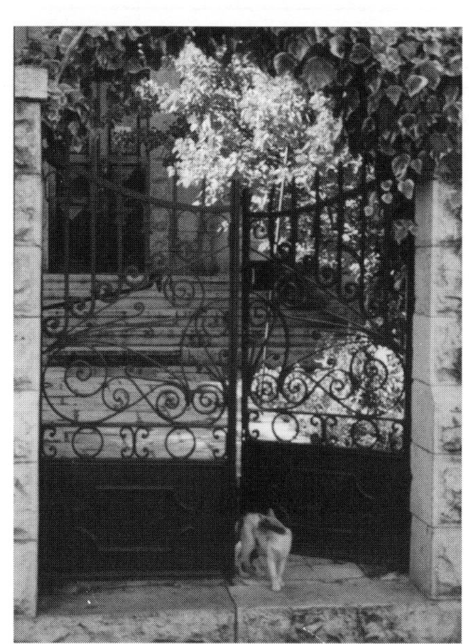

The Baq'a Neighbourhood

Landmarks: Bethlehem Road, Efrayim Street, Reuven Street

Baq'a (renamed *G'eulim*, which signifies liberation in Hebrew) was one of the first neighbourhoods established outside the walls of Jerusalem. At the end of the Ottoman period, Christians and Muslims originally from the Old City settled here; the neighbourhood remained a mixed quarter (Muslims, Christians, foreigners) until the eviction of its inhabitants in 1948.

■ Christian Foundations

In the second half of the nineteenth century, Christian congregations from western and eastern Europe, with the diplomatic and financial backing of their various countries, launched a campaign of land acquisition, provoking inflammatory prices of properties in and around the Old City. The Christian congregations brought with them a specific architectural culture linked to the religious importance of the holy city, where they established monuments of a spiritual or philanthropic nature, such as hospitals, schools, and orphanages. There was undeniably a good deal of competition. Whoever got closer to the holy places of the Old City, especially the Holy Sepulchre, had an advantage over others. Foundations established west of the Old City, like the external counterparts on the eastern side, especially on the Mount of Olives, all vied in the same spirit.

Between 1870 and 1890, the French undertook several construction projects near the Old City walls. **Saint Louis Hospital** *(at the junction on the other side of the road from the New Gate)* replaced the French Hospital, built in 1851 inside the Old City. The new hospital was built thanks to the legacy of **Count Paul-Amédée de Piellat,** a young French noble from France's Midi region and a fervent Catholic who loved the Holy Land, where he died in 1924. Next to the hospital, the hospice **Notre Dame de France** and the convent of the Marie-Réparatrice Sisters were built in 1888. A large statue of the Virgin Mary was erected above the chapel as the final touch to this work, in 1906; with its 410 cells, the hospice had a capacity for more than 1,000 pilgrims. The hospice and the Church of Saint Vincent de Paul, constructed in 1911, comprised the "French Quarter." The same period saw other convents and French institutions built outside the Old City: **Saint Stephen's Monastery to the north** [See *French School for Biblical and Archaeological Studies in Jerusalem*, p. 126) and Saint Peter of Zion-Ratisbonne Monastery to the west, built under the auspices of Marie-Alphonse Ratisbonne, a Jewish woman from Alsace who converted to Christianity, who became a missionary and was involved in converting Jews to Christianity.

The Germans too took part in the frenzied building contest between various foreign religious groups: in 1898, they built the **Dormition Church and Abbey** on a piece of land offered by the Sultan of the Sublime Door to Kaiser Wilhelm II, while the Empress supervised the construction of the **Augusta-Victoria hospice** (today a hospital) on Mount Scopus (which more than amply reveals the pretensions of the Crown Prince, who inaugurated it in 1910). Other German settlements of a different nature were founded by a millenarist sect in Jerusalem [See *German Colony* p. 143], as well as Jaffa and Haifa.

Yet other countries joined the race, albeit on a lesser scale. The Ethiopians acquired lands opposite the Russian Compound, thanks to funds provided by Negus Johannes IV and Menelik II; they built the Ethiopian Church in 1874 *(Ethiopia Street, open every day, March-September 7:00-18:00, October-February 8:00-17:00, free admission).*

❑ Al-Moscobiya (Russian Compound)

Built on a tract of land purchased by Tsar Alexander II between 1857 and 1858, the Russian Compound represents an excellent example of the inseparability of politics and religion. The complex has housed the Russian Consulate and the Russian Orthodox bishop's palace since 1860. The cathedral *(open Monday-Friday 9:00-13:00),* distinguished by its green dome, the hospital, and the religious and educational institutions attached to the compound, received thousands of Russian pilgrims every year. After the inauguration of the British Mandate in 1917, most of the complex became the general headquarters of the British administration. In 1967, the Israeli authorities converted it into a police station better known as al-Moscobiya. Two steps away from the bustling cafes of West Jerusalem, the centre became a centre of "interrogation," where all Palestinians from Jerusalem were taken when arrested. However, in 2004 a Border Police and General Security Services (Shin Bet) base was built in Anata, next to East Jerusalem, to replace al-Moscobiya; it has been erected on a hilltop near Ma'ale Adumim and Anata, while the old prison has become a museum.

❑ Nahon Museum of Italian Judaica

27 Hillel Street; Sunday-Tuesday 9:00-14:00, Thursday 9:00-13:00, Friday 9:00-16:00. Admission NIS 15. Guided tour in English every Thursday at 12:00.

This elegant nineteenth-century building, built by German missionaries, shows the influence of Arabo-Islamic architecture. Today a museum of Jewish Italian art, it holds a famous collection of ceremonial art. The centrepiece of the museum is the **synagogue of Conegliano Veneto**, built in 1701 and transported to Jerusalem in 1952 from its original location in a town 35 miles from Venice. The synagogue functions as a place of worship for Jerusalem's Italian Jewish community.

❑ Thabor

58 HaNevi'im Street.

Built in 1882, the original building belonged to the German architect and Protestant missionary, Conrad Schick; today it houses a Swedish theological institute. It is not officially open to the public, but one may ask to visit the garden and its archaeological ruins; if entry is impossible, it is nevertheless worth admiring the originality of the gate.

The Greek Colony

Landmarks: Beit Safafa Road (today Emek Refaim Street), Greek Colony Street (today Rachel Imenu Street), and Katamon Street (today Elazar Hamoda'i Street). These three roads marked the limits of the quarter until 1948.

The area was originally built by the Greek Orthodox Patriarchate, for the benefit of Greek Orthodox Palestinian families and the Greek families who accompanied the exclusively Greek clergy. The first houses were built along Eftimos Street (today Yehoshua Bin Nun Street), named after Patriarch Eftimos (1843-1917), who established this neighbourhood in 1902. At the time of the British Mandate, Palestinian Christians of various orders, Muslims, Greeks and British officials settled here; during the 1948 war, only international expatriates, safeguarded by consular protection, dared to stay in their homes.

"Towards the end of April 1948, the situation had deteriorated to a point where it became unwise to go outside except in case of absolute necessity. The number of inhabitants remaining in the Greek Colony decreased every day. Friends and neighbours told me they intended to stay, but eventually left. Families rented vans to transport their luggage and furniture. There was no time for goodbyes; everyone preferred to sneak out unseen at dawn. Mohammad, the milk-man, stopped making his usual deliveries. His customers had gone, and it was also too dangerous for him to leave the Old City. Villagers stopped bringing their vegetables and fruit for sale. From now on, the Greek Colony was almost abandoned - only five Greek families were still there. Houses were locked up and shutters closed; there were Greek flags on the doors of the houses (it would have been crazy to display an English flag on my house) [The author had an English father and an Armenian mother from Jerusalem], *in the hopes that foreign properties would be protected - after all, everyone thought that they would be returning in two or three weeks."*

▪ John Melkon Rose, born in Jerusalem

The German Colony

Landmarks: Emek Refaim Street, Lloyd George Street, Jan Smuts Street, Bethlehem Road.

This neighbourhood was established in about 1860 by a German millenarist sect from Wurtemberg whose goal was *"to create the ideal Christian community in the Holy Land."* By the end of the nineteenth century, over 40 families lived here; because the colony was near the railway station, some of its inhabitants specialised in railway freight transport between Jerusalem, Bethlehem and Jaffa. The houses were of a relatively modest design, but each had a garden, which to this day gives the German Colony a rural charm.

▪ Jewish Neighbourhoods

From the middle of the nineteenth century on, European Jews fond of the idea of "reviving the Jewish race" and close to the Zionist movement or to Jewish philanthropic associations, inaugurated programmes to improve sanitation, education and health services in the small Jewish Quarter. These programmes also aimed at "protecting" the Jewish community in Palestine from Christian proselytising. Immigration of Ashkenazi Jews, mostly religious Jews from the Austro-Hungarian, Prussian and Russian empires, increased rapidly from 1880 onwards. The Old City was, at first, their principal destination, but they quickly started settling outside the city walls as well (*Mishkenot Sha'ananim* in 1860 and *Mea Shearim* in 1874, for example). These Ashkenazi communities were unfamiliar with Arabic culture or language and adhered to the prevalent theories of colonialism and racial superiority and so kept their distance from the local Arabic-speaking communities.

The Ottoman authorities, concerned by the acceleration of immigration and the rise of separatist movements, issued an edict in 1882 that prohibited Jews from Russia, Bulgaria and Romania from settling in Palestine or buying property here; they were only allowed a temporary stay, but corruption and consular support helped such immigrants to by-pass the law. Jewish immigrants usually chose to keep their original nationality, which guaranteed them consular protection and exemption from some taxes.

As of the end of the nineteenth century, secular Zionist immigration to Palestine made Jewish urban development programmes in the new city a real success. New neighbourhoods *(Mahane Yehuda* in 1887, *Shaarei Tzedek* in 1891, and the *Boukharian Quarter* in 1891) were concentrated more on the western side of the city, along Jaffa Road, while community, cultural and sports centres served as links between these different areas (such as Israelite Alliance and The Hebrew Gymnasia High School of the Zionist Spirit). If Jewish property holdings of the first phase of immigration were relatively modest, the continuing development of Zionism under the British Mandate accelerated Jewish immigration to Jerusalem, the extension of existing areas and the creation of new neighbourhoods *(Talpiot* in 1922, *Rehavia* in 1924, *Sanhedriya* and *Mekor Hayim* in 1927).

Yemin Moshe

Thanks to a grant from a Jewish American millionaire, Judah Touro, Sir Moses Montefiore sponsored the construction of *Mishkenot Sha'ananim*, the first Jewish neighbourhood to be built outside the city walls; it was built between 1857 and 1860 by the stonemasons of Bethlehem. The complex was destined for poor Sephardic Jews of Jerusalem, who were at first unhappy to leave the Old City. Mishkenot Sha'ananim was founded on the concept of the separation of communities and was meant to ensure in principal the autonomy of the Jewish community for whom it was built. It contained twenty apartments and an astonishing windmill that was never used; in 1892, it was integrated into the Yemin Moshe neighbourhood. Between 1948 and 1967, it was used as a military observation post overlooking the Old City; today, a small museum here is dedicated to its founder, Moses Montefiore *(open Sunday-Thursday 9:00-16:00).*

The Neighbourhood of Mea Shearim

This quarter was initially built for Orthodox Polish and Lithuanian Jews, who immigrated to Palestine at the end of the nineteenth century. Totally isolated from its surroundings, it was encircled by a wall which had six gates. Behind a uniformity of dress codes (a long black coat and black socks for men, wigs and scarves with hairnets on the head, most often shaved, for women), certain details such as the shape of the hat or the way in which trousers are worn, indicate the person's origins (Eastern Europe, Central Asia or North Africa) or their specific religious affiliation (such as the "Haredim" or Hassidic Jews). In *Mea Shearim*, many people still speak Yiddish in daily life, reserving Hebrew for worship or religious studies that are the principal activity of the inhabitants. The majority of residents follow an Israeli national religious party, Shas. This was not always the case and, to this day, the quarter includes an orthodox Jewish community (Neturei Karta), which strongly rejects Zionist ideology. According to them, Zionist ideology must be distinguished from the Jewish faith from a theological and moral point of view.

Rehavia

Unlike many Jewish neighbourhoods, Rehavia was conceived on the lines of private property. It was designed from the start to be "a Prussian island in an Oriental sea," which set the tone for this privileged neighbourhood. Since the 1930s, members of the Ashkenazi intelligentsia from Germany, Austria, and Czechoslovakia have made their privileged homes here. Architecturally, the individual houses and properties are characterised by the international style: a style stripped of decoration, with the exception of a few Art Deco motifs in wrought iron. Animated by strong Zionist principles, the residents hired only Jewish architects and masons to build their homes. This explains why decorative elements in bevelled stone are extremely rare, in contrast with their abundance in the surrounding Arab neighbourhoods.

To the West of Jerusalem

❑ The Monastery of the Cross

At the foot of the valley, dominated by the Israel Museum and the Israeli parliament (Knesset). Open Monday-Friday 9:00-16:00; admission NIS 5.

Hemmed in between motorways and scrublands, this fortified mediaeval monastery is most unusual. Built by King Bagrat of Georgia in the eleventh century, the monastery rests on the place where a tree was cut down to make the cross on which Jesus was crucified. The Georgian Christian community was relatively important during the Mameluke period because of the good diplomatic relations at that time between the Mameluke state and the Georgian kingdom. However, in 1685, during the Ottoman period, the community declined and was forced to sell its monastery to the thriving Greek Orthodox church. The interior decor and the frescoes are remarkable; observe in particular the presence of Christian saints next to Greek philosophers and ancient pagan gods.

❑ The Israel Museum

Ruppin Street, open Monday and Wednesday, 10:00-16:00, Tuesday, 16:00-21:00, Thursday, 10:00-21:00, Friday 10:00-14:00, Saturday 10:00-16:00, closed on Sunday. Admission NIS 37. (A second visit, during the fortnight after a ticket has been bought, is available for half-price, and a visit to the Rockefeller Museum is free.) ☎ 02-670 8811; buses 9, 17 , 24, and 99.

Located opposite the Israeli parliament *(Knesset)*, the Israel Museum is renowned for its excellent collection of archaeological artefacts and works of art. Its archaeological collection is unique in the country: notice in particular the treasure of Nahal Mashmar (Chalcolithic period) with its sceptres and "crowns" decorated with birds and animals; the anthropomorphic caskets discovered at Deir al-Balah (Bronze Age); and the bronze bust of the Roman Emperor Hadrian from Bissane *(Beth She'an)*. Many European and North American schools are represented in the fine arts section, as well as works by the Flemish artists of the seventeenth century, impressionists, cubists, surrealists, pop art and contemporary conceptual art. A third section is devoted to work that is both ethnologic and artistic, especially illustrating the life styles and artistic productions of Jewish communities of the world. Notice particularly the eighteenth century Yemenite prayer pulpit; the reconstruction of the Venetian synagogue of Vittorio Veneto (1710) and the German Horb Synagogue (eighth century). These exceptional collections and modern museography, under cover of scientific research, require a discerning, critical eye to identify the underlying need for Israeli archaeology to establish a certain national legitimacy and fulfil national needs at the expense of local history. Archaeology is not always conciliatory; the museum has managed to ignore two historical facts: the unbroken presence of the land's inhabitants and their traditions.

❑ The Bible Lands Museum

Opposite the Israel Museum. Open every day Sunday-Tuesday and Thursday 9:30-17:30; Wednesday 9:30-21:30 (November–March, 13:30-21:30); Friday 9:30-14:00; Saturday 11:00-15:00. Admission NIS 28. : ☎ 02-561 1066; buses 9, 17, 24, and 99.

The unique objects in this museum are the provenance of a private collector of Polish origin, who in the course of his career succeeded in discovering the most rare objects. The Bible Lands Museum is not intended only to teach; the museum is, above all, an exhibition of unique pieces belonging to the ancient civilisations of the Near East and the Middle East. Most, if not all, of the ancient systems of writing are represented here, from the first signs inscribed on clay tablets to complete alphabets.

■ Some Palestinian Villages West of Jerusalem

'Allar al-Fawqeh, Artuf, Beit 'Itab, Beit Mahsir, Beit Naqquba, Beit Thul, al-Bureij, Deir Aban, Deir al-Hawa, Deir Rafat, Deir al-Sheikh, Deir Yassin, 'Ein Karem, Ishwa', al-Jura, al-Lawz, Lifta, Kasla, al-Malha, Nitaf, Qalunya, al-Qastal, Ras Abu 'Ammar, Sar'a, Saris, Sataf, Suba, al-Walaja...

Deir Yassin

The village was named after a respected local personality, Sheikh Yassin, whose tomb is found in the village mosque. In the 1920s, quarrying work at Deir Yassin replaced much of the agricultural activity. The villagers made an important contribution to the construction of the new neighbourhoods in Jerusalem. In about 1945, only 15% of the population worked full-time as farmers; between 1931 and 1948, the population of the village increased from 428 to 750 people. On the outskirts of Jerusalem, the village was modernised. In 1946, it had two schools, many shops, a club, a savings and loan committee, and a bus company that connected Deir Yassin and Lifta to Jerusalem. In contrast to the neighbouring Jewish implantations of *Givat Shaul, Montefiore,* and *Beit Hakerem*, among others, Deir Yassin, like Lifta, was classified as being outside the Jerusalem municipal boundary, and consequently deprived of the supply of electricity and potable water.

The Village Today

Landmarks: Givat Shaul B, around Rabbi Yisrael Nagara Street.

In autumn 1949, the colonisation department of the Jewish Agency approved the settlement of the village, which it officially named *Givat Shaul Bet*. Houses which had not been destroyed were given to Orthodox Jews, mostly from Poland, Czechoslovakia and Romania. Today, many former Palestinian homes in Deir Yassin are visible from Rabbi Yisrael Nagara Street; some of these houses have been transformed into warehouses or workshops.

Deir Yassin or "The Guernica of Palestine"

At the end of 1947, raids started against the Palestinian towns adjacent to Deir Yassin: Lifta and several Palestinian quarters in Jerusalem (Sheikh Badr, Romema and others). In February 1948, these neighbourhoods were entirely emptied. In view of the alarming situation, a crisis committee was formed in Deir Yassin to organise the defence of the village; the weapons, which the inhabitants clandestinely bought from Egypt, were paid for by selling their most precious belongings, even the jewellery received as a dowry by the women of the village. Veterans of the 1936-1937 revolution trained young men how to handle arms and together they organised night patrols to keep watch. On April 4, the Hagana attacked all the Palestinian villages along the Jaffa - Jerusalem Road. On the night of April 8, two Zionist organisations - the Lehi and the Irgun Zvai Leumi ("Etzel") - took the initiative of attacking the village, hoping for a quick victory. Although they were much better armed, the Zionist militants were unprepared for the organised resistance they met and faced a critical situation at daybreak, unable to advance or to evacuate the wounded. They were saved by a unit of the Hagana, who arrived with heavy artillery. A veritable massacre followed: over 120 of the 750 villagers were murdered - men, women, children and old people. The survivors were loaded onto trucks to be paraded through the streets of Jerusalem, which were then under Jewish control, before being transferred to a buffer zone. In addition to bulletins describing the massacre which were broadcast on the radio, the story appeared in all the newspaper headlines, in a deliberate attempt to demoralise Palestinian inhabitants. The figure of 245 Palestinians killed, quoted by the Zionist organisations, was intended to terrorise Palestinians, and in fact Palestinians from the new city (West Jerusalem) progressively started leaving, emptying those areas of their population.

Friday, April 9, 4 a.m. in the morning

"We started to scream: 'The Jews, the Jews!' Then we started to run in all directions. I heard a woman cry: 'They threw the baker into the oven.' Our house was quite far from the oven. I ran with some other women to seek refuge in the house of the Moukhtar, Mohammad Ismail Sammour. A few moments later, Mohammad Mahmoud Sammour, armed with a rifle, joined us. There were five of us inside the house: Mahmoud Jawdah, his wife, and their son Mahmoud, Mohammad Mahmoud and me. Outside, the shooting and explosions were terrible. Then we heard a great noise that made the whole house shake, followed by shots and the screams of a woman. They started pounding on the door: 'Open up! Open up!' I moved forward and shouted: 'Will you kill us if we open?' A voice answered: 'No. Are there any men with you?' -'Yes' - 'How many?' - 'Three.' 'Open.' 'Swear by your ten words [the ten commandments] *that you will not kill us.' He swore. I opened the door and went out first. They immediately threw a grenade inside, killing the four other people in the house. I started running, and I saw the dead body of the Moukhtar's wife Hajja Fudiyya (60 years old) lying on the doorstep beside her grandsons, Sammour Khalil (12 years old) and Ismail (15 years old)."*

■ Zaynab Atiya

Friday, April 9, in the afternoon

"I saw with my own eyes three trucks slowly moving at 2 o'clock in the afternoon up and down King George VI Street in Jerusalem. Men and women were packed in the vehicles with their hands on their heads, surrounded by Jewish soldiers pointing machine guns and rifles at them ...The village sheikh was in one of the trucks with a group of women with a child in front, his inert hands resting on his head. Their faces expressed exhaustion and their haunted looks gazed into the far distance."

■ Harry Levin, an English journalist, a high-ranking official at the Israeli Ministry of Foreign Affairs at the time

Saturday, April 10, in the afternoon

"The Jewish Agency and Hagana general headquarters tell me they didn't know anything about this business, and that it is impossible for anybody to go inside the 'Irgun Zone.' They discourage me from pursuing the issue and warn me that our mission might run the risk of being cancelled if I persist. Not only do they refuse to help me, but they decline any responsibility for the dangers I would be taking. I reply that I am going and that the Jewish Agency, which everyone knows exercises authority over all the territory under Jewish control, is responsible for my safety as well as for my freedom of movement within the framework of my mission."

■ De Reynier, a delegate of the International Committee of the Red Cross

Sunday, April 11

The delegate of the Red Cross was not authorised to enter the village until Sunday. "The troop is in field dress, wearing helmets. All young people and even adolescents, men and women, are armed to the teeth: pistols, machine guns, grenades, but also huge knives that they hold in their hands, most of which are covered with blood. A young girl - beautiful, but with the eyes of a criminal - shows me her knife, still dripping with blood, which she flourishes like a trophy. This is the cleaning crew that has done its job thoroughly and conscientiously. I try to enter one of the houses. I am surrounded by a dozen soldiers, pointing their machine guns at me, and the officer orders me to stay where I am. 'We are taking the dead if there are any,' he says (...) Then, I shake off the individuals holding me back and go into the house. The first room is dark, everything is in disorder, but there is no one there. In the second room, in the middle of the furniture, which has been slashed, bed covers, and all sorts of debris, I find several cold corpses. They had done the cleansing with machine guns, then with grenades, they finished with knives. It is the same in the next room, but just as I am leaving, I hear something like a sigh. I search everywhere, moving every single piece of furniture, and finally find a small foot that is still warm. It is a little girl of ten, seriously injured by a grenade, but still alive. As I want to take her with me, the officer forbids it and stands in front of the door to block me. I push him aside and pass with my precious burden."

■ De Reynier, a delegate of the International Committee of the Red Cross

Lifta

At the entrance to Jerusalem; the ruins of Lifta may be seen on the way into Jerusalem from Highway No. 1 (the Jaffa/ Tel Aviv-Jerusalem highway). They are found below one of the enormous road networks (Golda Meir Highway) that connects the settlements to the north and east of Jerusalem. A walk around the village and the valley takes about an hour and a half.

Nephto was the name of this village in the Byzantine period, when it was identified with the site of the Biblical spring of Nephthoa (Joshua 15:9, 18:15). It was later called Clepsa under the Crusaders before becoming known as Lifta. Zionist armed forces annihilated the village on December 28, 1947. Afterwards, its villagers sought refuge, soon after, in Jerusalem. On February 7, 1948, David Ben-Gurion was able to make this statement: *"When you enter Jerusalem from Lifta - from Romema, from Mahane Yehuda, King George Street, and Mea Shearim, there are no foreigners. One hundred percent Jewish."* With over 2,500 inhabitants, the village was considered a suburb of Jerusalem. Cereal crops were still important, but more and more men had been giving up farming for employment in the city or as construction workers.

The Village Today

Although dilapidated, a number of houses in the village are still intact. Some architectural details indicate its former prosperity; many houses have a dedication and the date of construction on the lintel above the front door. In the late 1980s, the Israeli Nature Reserves Authority planned a field centre here for studies and history, in the open air, in order to *"deepen Jewish roots on the site."* However, the project was never carried out. Instead, a large two-level by-pass road above what remained of the village was recently built to facilitate traffic flow to and from Israeli settlements to the north and east of Jerusalem.

Qastal

Jerusalem - Jaffa Highway. National Park, open 8:00-16:00. Admission NIS 10. There is little to see on the site, which is of interest because of the historical battle in April 1948.

Because of its key position on the main route between Jaffa and Jerusalem, Qastal was the "key to Jerusalem." For this reason, this small village of 90 people was stormed by the Hagana on April 3, 1948. The barbed wires and ditches are still visible. The Palestinian resistance managed to recapture it on April 8: *"With 200 men equipped with four mortars, one of which was of local manufacture, and some grenades, Abd al-Qader led his troops in an attack from three different directions ...."* (Walid Khalidi). Villagers from the area were also on the battlefield, but as unarmed spectators they were limited in helping the combat, which certainly had some effect on the Zionist soldiers. The official brochure on the site describes the situation as follows: *"Thousands of villagers swarmed to the battlefield."* In the fight, Abd al-Qader al-Husseini, commander of the Jihad al-Muqqadas brigades, was killed. In order to accompany his funeral cortege to Jerusalem, his men left the hill empty for the Hagana to follow up their offensive, to reconquer Qastal and control the road to Jerusalem.

Abd al-Qader al-Husseini

Born in Jerusalem in 1908. He joined the Palestinian resistance in the Great Revolt of 1936-1939. After being wounded, he was evacuated to Lebanon, before he rejoined the Iraqi Arab nationalist movement, which was in open opposition to the pro-British Hashemite monarchy. In January 1948, he returned clandestinely to Palestine and was named Commander of the Jihad al-Muqaddas brigades for the defence of Jerusalem by the Arab High Committee. He was responsible for 550 Palestinian volunteers. He died on April 8, 1948, while trying to recapture Qastal.

Abu Ghosh

Located 15 km from the Old City.

The village of Abu Ghosh is the only Palestinian village to the west of Jerusalem whose population was not ethnically cleansed. On the route that links the coastal plain to Jerusalem, for centuries the village has been a halt for travellers, pilgrims and merchants. The ruins of an Abbassid *caravanserai* and reservoir (ninth century), renovated in the Mameluke period, are a short distance from the monastery. Until the second half of the nineteenth century, the Abu Ghosh tribe collected a toll from all travellers entering their territory, which provoked outraged complaints to the Ottoman authorities from pilgrims and foreign diplomats. The Ottoman rulers, however, were mainly interested in discouraging the ambition of the tribal chiefs to establish a semi-independent state in their territory and start an open rebellion against the Ottoman central power.

The Crusader Church *Open 8:30-11:00, and 14:00-17:00, except on Thursday and Sunday. Free entry.*

In the heart of the village, the church is Abu Ghosh's main attraction. The victorious Crusaders identified the place with Emmaus and built a church here in 1142. The twelfth-century frescoes are still intact. The property was acquired by the French government in 1873. A "recycled" stone in the crypt indicates that the Tenth Roman Legion was stationed in the vicinity in the first century AD. At the top of the village, Mount (or Jabal) Deir al-Azhar is crowned by **the Church of Notre Dame of the Ark of the Covenant**, on which stands a monumental statue of the Virgin and Child. The church was built over a Byzantine church, which in turn was erected over an Iron Age village. The Byzantine church's mosaic pavement is still preserved. The village is thought to be Qiryat Yearim, where biblical tradition says the Philistines gave the Ark of the Lord back to the Israelites (1 Samuel 6:20-21; 7:1-2).

Malha

Located on a rocky plateau, the village is now annexed to a neighbourhood known as Manachat or Malha. A number of the houses and the mosque are still fully preserved.

The origins of this village are lost in the mists of time. In the sixteenth century, it was called Maliha es-Sughra and had 300 inhabitants. Under the British Mandate, the village soon became a suburb of Jerusalem. On the night it was attacked, it had a population of 1,940 (1,930 Muslims and 10 Christians).

En Nakba

The initial Zionist attack took place on March 6, 1948. Yet it was not until the day after the Deir Yassin massacre that the first group of villagers left and sought refuge in the centre of Jerusalem and Bethlehem. When the village was attacked again, the rest of the population (except for those who were armed) joined the refugees. Zionist forces finally occupied the village on July 22, after fierce resistance from irregulars from Egypt and Palestinian partisans.

Scale Model of Ancient Jerusalem

Bayit Vegan. Situated in the garden of the Holy Land Hotel. Open daily 8:00-23:00. Admission NIS 15. The model is on a ratio of 1:50. Bus 21.

The scale model displayed in the **Holy Land Hotel** is a version of what Jerusalem might have looked like in the Herodian era; it was made according to descriptions found in Flavius Josephus (1 AD) and the Talmud. Note that most of the materials used - limestone, marble, copper, wood and linen - are authentic.

The Biblical Zoo

Gan Hachayot Road. Open Sunday, Monday, Wednesday, and Thursday 10:00-17:00, Tuesday 16:00-18:00, Saturday 10:00-16:00. Bus 26 from the Central Bus Station (Jaffa Road). Admission NIS 32.

The zoo has a large number of animal species (mammals, birds, reptiles and fish). Not all these animals are mentioned in the Bible but they are all endemic species or have become extinct.

Ein Karem

Bus 19 & 27. Recommended for walks.

Ein Karem (the spring of the vineyard) was the birthplace of St. John the Baptist or Nabi Yahya (the Prophet John the Baptist), according to Christian tradition. This tradition justified a visit by Caliph Omar Ibn al-Khattab in the seventh century, who stopped to pray here. In the Crusader period, the village was renamed "**St. Joan de Bois.**" Ein Karem grew considerably in the late nineteenth century; although the majority of the population was Muslim, various Christian communities (the Franciscans, the Sisters of Zion and the Russian Orthodox) built monasteries and convents in the village and its vicinity. One of the village's Muslim residents was Sheikh 'Issa Mannum, who even taught at the famous al-Azhar University in Cairo, where he was promoted to the position of dean of the Department of Islamic Foundations. Until 1948, village life was stimulated by many sports and arts clubs; there was even an open-air space for theatrical and musical performances: the well-known singer Noor Ibrahim notably performed here in the 1930s and 40s. Coming from the north of Palestine, Noor Ibrahim was exiled to Ein Karem by the British mandatory authorities for his part in the Palestinian revolution or Great Revolt of 1936-1939. Protected by mountains and forests, Ein Karem was an important stronghold of Palestinian resistance; it was even freed of British occupation at one point. In 1945, the village had become a suburb of Jerusalem and the population had risen to 3,180 inhabitants - (2,510 Muslims and 670 Christians). Many of its inhabitants were prosperous businessmen or craftsmen.

En-Nakba

Many villagers fled from Ein Karem immediately after the massacre in Deir Yassin (only 2.5 km to the north-east), and after the Zionist offensives on the villages to the west of Jerusalem. The final assault on the village was launched by several Israeli military units (Irgun and Gadna - the battalion of Hagana Youth), in mid-July, 1948. Although the resistance received no support from either the Arab Legion of Transjordan or the Egyptian army, they managed to hold out for several days before being defeated. After the Israeli-Jordanian Armistice, the villagers, most of whom became refugees in the Aida Refugee Camp (Beit-Jala), continued their resistance by means of the Jihad al-Muqaddas organisation. But the movement was soon disbanded by the Jordanian authorities and its members arrested. Ein Karem was cleansed of its population; it was not destroyed, but occupied: commencing in December 1948, about 150 Jewish families were installed here.

The Village Today

Despite its integration into the Jerusalem municipality, Ein Karem has preserved its rural charm. Its traditional architecture indicates its unequivocal prosperity, which is in part due to the many religious foundations here, and its proximity to Jerusalem. It is hardly surprising that before 1948 the village had been given the honorary title "capital of the villages." Today, the temptation of its Jewish residents to change its identity is above all perceptible in the sight of Israeli emblems placed over the antique buildings' entrances. Some wealthy residents have even had their houses built on traditional Palestinian architectural lines, integrating their own national-religious symbols into them.

The numerous cafes and restaurants of Ein Karem are highly appreciated by West Jerusalemites, especially in the evenings and at weekends *(Friday and Saturday)*. A visit to Ein Karem during the week is even calmer. Surrounded by wooded hills, it is also a perfect place for invigorating walks to one's heart's content. A hiker may plan a full day out on the marked paths. For a shorter walk, follow the path that starts at the Mosque of Omar. Below the mosque runs Mary's Spring which, according to tradition, gushed up when Mary appeared to Elisabeth.

Church of St. John the Baptist

In the heart of the village, inside the walls of the Franciscan Monastery. Open Monday-Friday 8:30-12:00 and 14:30-18:00 (in winter, 17:00); Sunday 9:00-12:00 and 14:30-17:00. Free admission.

This church was built in 1674 on the site said to be where the house of Zacharias and Elisabeth (parents of St. John the Baptist) stood. The remains of a mosaic pavement from an old Byzantine church can be seen through an iron railing below the porch; an inscription in Greek on the pavement says: *"Salvation for God's Martyrs."* Inside the church, there are several darkish paintings from the seventeenth century; above the altar, the painting of The Visitation is attributed to the celebrated Spanish artist, El Greco (1541-1614). To the left of the altar, there are stairs leading down into a natural cave called the **Grotto of the Nativity of St. John the Baptist.**

The Church of the Visitation

Behind the Mosque of Omar (HaMaayan Street). Open Sunday–Friday 8:00-11:45 and 14:30-18:00 (in winter, 17:00). Free entry.

This is a recent church, built in 1955; it commemorates Mary's visit to her cousin Elisabeth (Luke 1:39-56). According to the Gospel of Luke, Elisabeth received Mary with these words: *"Blessed art thou among women, and blessed is the fruit of thy womb."* To which Mary replied with a hymn to the Lord, the Magnificat: *"My soul doth magnify the Lord and my spirit hath rejoiced in God my Saviour."* These words are written in many languages on ceramic tiles set out in the courtyard of the lower chapel. Inside the chapel, a mark *(to the right of the entrance)* is said to have been made by the footprint of the infant St. John the Baptist. According to pre-Byzantine legend, Elisabeth escaped to a hill to hide her child after learning that Herod was looking for all children under two years of age (Matthew: 2:16). Having found no place, she invoked *"the mountain of God"* which opened and offered them refuge.

Sataf

Road 395 leaving Ein Karem. Sataf National Park is a very pleasant place to walk in wooded, mountain foothills.

A Palestinian village of 540 residents in 1945, Sataf was occupied and destroyed by Israeli soldiers in the military campaign launched against Ramle and Lydda in mid-July, 1948. The terraces of olive trees and the ruins of the village are visible in what has become the nature reserve of Sataf (free entry). Several Israeli families settled in the west of the destroyed village and have made a specialty of producing goat cheese. The **Shai Selzer farm** is only 3 km away from the main parking area: *to drive there, follow the signs with a goat on them; the farm is open to visitors only on Friday (16:00-19:00) and Saturday (11:00-19:00) in summer; and only on Saturday in winter (11:00-16:00).*

Suba

The hilltop ruins of Suba are visible from the surrounding countryside. There is a good view from Sataf National Park (Road 395). From there one may reach the village by a short cut across the vineyards. To reach Suba from the opposite direction, on the Tel Aviv/Jerusalem highway, follow the signs for Ein Hemed and then Tzuva. A beautiful place to hike.

The village has been identified by some as Rubut, a town mentioned in the Amarna Letters in the fourteenth century BC. However, archaeological excavations have found no evidence for the existence of a village here before the Persian period (sixth - fourth centuries BC).

Under the Romans, the village bore the Aramaic name Seboim, which the authorities hellenised to Soba, or Sobetha. During the Crusader period, the Franks built a fortified village here which they called Belmont. The fortress and the walls survived until 1832. This system of fortification was even used by the Abu Ghosh tribe, which controlled several villages west of Jerusalem and which resisted domination by Egypt and, above all, its centralised government. When the troops of Ibrahim Pasha captured the village, they destroyed both the fortress and the walls. *(Parts of the fortress are still visible.)*

En-Nakba

In 1944, Suba, which was a part of the district of Jerusalem, had a population of more than 600 people. After the first Zionist shelling on April 3, 1948, most of the villagers fled to the outskirts of Jerusalem and Bethlehem. Palestinian resistance forces remained in the village until mid-July, when Zionist groups occupied Ramle, Lydda and the group of Palestinian villages west of Jerusalem.

➡ The Village Today

Although much of the village is in ruins, a number of houses still stand - a testimony to the solidity of traditional village architecture; others, unfortunately, were totally demolished. A kilometre to the west of Suba, Kibbutz Tzuva was established on village lands in 1948.

Saris

Signs clearly indicate the Shoresh forest (or Yitzhak Rabin Park) on Highway No. 1, about 20 kilometres west of Jerusalem. Amateur hikers will find a wonderful place for strolls. The entrance to the park is marked by several memorials dedicated to Zionist soldiers killed during the 1948 conquest of Jerusalem. The village of Saris is 500 m to the west. Opposite a vineyard topped with a red and white antenna (on the right-hand side), a small gravel road - accessible by car - on the left-hand side leads directly to the village. The presence of fruit trees, and the ruins over-run with vegetation, indicate the site.

En-Nakba

In 1945, the village had a population of 500, most of them peasant-farmers. On April 13, 1948, it was occupied and demolished soon afterwards. Before its occupation, the highest military commander of the Hagana called for settlements to be built "as quickly as possible" for reasons of "security." The settlement project was adopted by Israeli authorities in August, 1948 when Shoresh (southwest of Saris) was founded, followed by Sho'eva (to the northeast) in 1950.

The Village Today

Today, Saris is covered by the Shoresh Forest, which was planted by young women sponsored by the Jewish National Fund of Johannesburg, South Africa. A few ruined houses and metal girders overgrown with vines and other plants indicate that there was once a village here; like all demolished Palestinian villages, the presence of familiar village trees also indicate the past: almond, fig and cypress. One may still find many of these trees in the middle of the pine tree forest planted after 1948.

To the North of Jerusalem

Nabi Samuel (The Tomb of the Prophet Samuel)

Six kms. from Jerusalem on Road 443. Village council, Abu 'Ala Barakat.☎ 02-234 6069 or 0545-735550.

The place corresponds to the site where Solomon offered sacrifices to his God. *"And the king went to Gibeon to sacrifice there; for that was the great high place: a thousand burnt offerings did Solomon offer upon that altar."* (I Kings 3:4-15) In the sixth century AD, the hill was identified as the biblical site Rama (which was until then thought to be in the region of Mount Carmel!), where the prophet Samuel was buried (1 Samuel 25:1). Putting all his weight behind this Christian tradition, the Emperor Justinian built a monastery on the site. This local tradition was apparently unknown to or neglected by the Crusaders, who, one day in 1099 were able to see Jerusalem, the goal of their mission, from the top of this hill. They named the place the "Mount of Joy" before descending on the holy city to give it one of the bloodiest days of its history. The Crusaders abandoned this place shortly after Saladin's victory at the Horns of Hittin. Then, in 1192, Richard the Lionheart led the Third Crusade as far as Nabi Samuel; however, reinforcements he had counted on never showed up, so he was forced to retreat. In the fourteenth century, a **mosque** (whose southern section and minaret are still preserved), and a Muslim religious foundation *(zawiya)* were built here. Islamic authorities also inaugurated an annual pilgrimage to Nabi Samuel's tomb. In the fifteenth and sixteenth centuries, there was also a synagogue here as well. During the First World War and later in 1948 and again in 1967, the hill became the arena of fierce battles for control of this strategic point of command over Jerusalem.

The Village Today

The population stagnates at some 200 people; there is no way for young couples to remain. With the present occupation, the village has been deprived of all basic infrastructure. The village was not linked to the water supply of Ramallah before 1986, despite the fact that Israeli authorities had requisitioned both its springs, its only source of water. The village was connected to the mains electricity network in 1981. The village **school** is only one room, measuring only a few square metres. A few years ago, the village council asked permission to buy a prefabricated building in order to create another schoolroom, but their request was categorically denied by the Israeli authorities. The villagers are also forbidden to make any improvement in roads or pathways or install public streetlights. Located in Area C, the village is totally isolated. Since the beginning of the al-Aqsa Intifada, villagers have not been allowed to go in their own cars to other parts of the West Bank. They are obliged to cross the military checkpoints on foot and continue by taxi. They say that a sword of Damocles is hanging over their heads, and that the Israeli authorities are just waiting for the right moment to make them leave the village. In fact a project for a nature park in Nabi Samuel is being studied. As in Hebron, part of the mosque has been confiscated and transformed into a synagogue. The village council and the Islamic authority *(waqf)* charter two buses each Friday in order to ensure regular attendance in the mosque.

A view from the top of the minaret, built in 1345, (or from the roof of the tomb) is splendid and painful at the same time. From this vantage point, the plan behind the Israeli settlements around Jerusalem is all too obvious. To the south, the settlements of *Ramot* (38,000 settlers) and *Ramat Shlomo* (11,300 settlers), among others, form an inner ring of satellite settlements around the Israeli Municipality of Jerusalem. To the north and west, the settlements of *Givat Ze'ev* (10,500 settlers), *Har Hadar* and others configure part of the outer ring of "Greater Jerusalem." In the middle of these settlements emerge Palestinian villages deprived of space for natural growth or geographical contiguity. To the east, a long built-up strip of land stretches from Jerusalem to Ramallah, starting at the Palestinian neighbourhoods of Shu'fat and Beit Hanina (Upper Beit Hanina) on the edges of the Municipality of Jerusalem. Farther north, the highly populated neighbourhood of A-Ram, and the Qalandia refugee camp are relegated to Area B of the West Bank: when annexing territory, Israel has always used the "maximum land, minimum population" rule, thus forcing the demographics of Jerusalem to remain 70% Israeli, 30% Palestinian. Further north lies Ramallah, in Area A. Israel is currently erecting the Wall down the middle of the main Jerusalem-Ramallah road, totally disrupting the commercial centre of A-Ram and cutting many schoolchildren off from their schools (leaving them without education), patients are also cut off from hospitals, workers from jobs, and families are being split up. Closures prevent West Bank Palestinians from getting to work in Jerusalem, and the works being undertaken in the entire region to build the so-called Jerusalem Envelope or Wall will lock most Palestinians into small enclaves or ghettoes. Meanwhile Israel is developing a hi-tech industrial estate nearby at *Har Hotzvim* (near Nabi Samuel and the settlements of *Givat Ze'ev* and *Ramot*), where hi-tech does not require Palestinian manual workers.

A Village Under Occupation

A visit to the village of Nabi Samuel (only a hamlet, these days) is an excellent opportunity to witness the Israeli occupation in detail. The village is on a hill 890 metres high, overlooking the entire north-west region of Jerusalem; one can see as far as the outskirts of Ramallah. Although the Zionists did not touch the village in 1948, it was one of the first villages in the district of Jerusalem to be occupied in 1967. The majority of its 1,000 villagers sought refuge in surrounding villages such as Bir Nabala and Beit Hanina and above all, in Jordan. In 1971, the Israeli authorities issued an order to demolish the village, whose houses were clustered around the mosque of the prophet Samuel. The village was completely demolished and its remaining residents evacuated to a dozen houses on the plateau east of the village. Since then, no construction has been permitted, with the exception of two new houses, at the entrance to the village, constructed on confiscated land; they belong to collaborators (Palestinians who work as spies in the pay of the Israeli authorities) originally from the village. The "owner" of the luxurious house lives there only during the day; at night, he sleeps in an apartment in nearby Ramot, the Israeli settlement, for fear of retaliation. On one side of the hill, a Jewish settler has also built a house on confiscated land; when the villagers complain about this to the military authorities of the area (the "Civil Administration"), they claim that as regards the settler, a demolition order has also been issued to destroy his home!

The Archaeological Site

The village having been demolished in 1971, the foundations of the village (especially the oldest parts around the mosque) were excavated in the 1990s by Israeli archaeologists. (Israel has the highest number of archaeologists per inhabitant in the world!) The archaeologists found Hasmonean, Byzantine, Crusader and Mameluke remains. Near the southern wing of the mosque, the floors of some Palestinian houses are still visible; among the extensive ruins at this archaeological park, there are also the remains of a public building from Hasmonean times (second century BC), a Byzantine wine press, a huge rampart (100m x 50m) carved in stone which was used to build a fortified monastery in the twelfth century, a huge Crusader stables (24m x 7.6m) and a Mameluke foundry.

Al-Qubeibeh Village

On Road 436, 4 km west of Nabi Samuel. Follow the signs for the village of Biddu.

Al-Qubeibeh (which means "the small dome") is located on an old Roman way that once led to the coastal plain. In the twelfth century, Crusaders established the village in order to farm the fertile land and lined the road on either side with houses. The village had a church and a modest castle; ruins, especially the foundations of three mediaeval apses, are still visible in the contemporary church (built in 1902). The church commemorates a sixteenth-century Christian tradition which identifies the village as Emmaus of the Gospels, where Jesus appeared to his disciples Simon and Cleopas after his Resurrection (Luke 24:13-32).

Al-Jib

Bir Nabala road, on Highway 437.

This village has seen the passing of thousands of years since the days of its Canaanite name Gibeon, mentioned in the Bible, to those of its current name al-Jib. Names of places in this region remind us of the permanent place of its people and its habitat in history. One of the most celebrated battles in the Old Testament was here. Gibeon's aristocracy was threatened by five allied city-states (Jerusalem, Hebron, Eglon, Lachish and Jarmut) and had made a treaty with the Israelite leader, Joshua. Joshua and his allies beat all the attackers when Joshua made the sun stand still in the middle of the sky over the city, in answer to his prayer (Joshua 10:12-14).

The ruins of al-Jib are on the hill at the far end of the village. An impressive cistern from the twelfth or eleventh century BC, with a spiral staircase of 79 steps, led to a spring outside the walls. Although it is prohibited to descend into the reservoir itself, it is still possible to walk along the ancient tunnel that led to the spring *(entrance near the cistern. Do not forget to take a torch/flashlight)*. Since the Bronze Age and especially since the eighth or seventh centuries BC, al-Jib has been famous for its wine (63 ancient wine cellars have been discovered). The presses and the old cellars that kept the wine at the right temperature are easy to identify on the tel.

To the East of Jerusalem

Shu'fat Refugee Camp

No road acknowledges the existence of this camp. Built on the eastern slope of the village of Shu'fat (incorporated into the city of Jerusalem since 1967), the camp is squeezed between two settlement blocs (French Hill to the south-west, Pisgat Ze'ev to the north). The popular committee of Shu'fat Camp organises informative meetings about their special situation as well as tours, especially inside the camp. Khader ed-Dibs ☎ 0522-287 811 or Khalid al-Khaldi ☎ 0522-741 233.

This refugee camp was built in 1965 and 1966, more than ten years after other officially recognised camps, for refugees living in extremely bad sanitary conditions in the Mu'ascar Camp in the Maghribi Quarter in the middle of the Old City. Mu'ascar Camp was closed, after the establishment of the camp in Shu'fat. After the occupation of 1967, Shu'fat was the only refugee camp included in the borders of the Municipality of Jerusalem. The official number of refugees is around 10,000, but the actual number of residents is over 15,000. People pay no land taxes here, and water is free, factors which attract the poorest of Jerusalem to live here, as well as the fact that land available for construction in Jerusalem is so rare that housing prices there are exorbitant. In addition, other refugees or non-refugees who had their homes outside the municipal boundaries of Jerusalem returned here in order to keep their Jerusalem residency card, since Shu'fat is inside the city boundaries. Therefore, residents have no choice but to construct both in an extremely cramped way, and also only upwards (3 to 4 storeys). Building foundations are dangerously fragile, and there are no security norms. People often try to extend the area of the camp even when threatened with demolition; for instance, on July 9, 2001, 17 houses were destroyed by Israeli authorities, after demolition orders were issued only the night before. On many occasions, the municipality hears of new houses being built from residents of the Pisgat Ze'ev settlement, illegally built during the Oslo Peace Process on the opposite hill, who complain that the building reduces the value of their property (a visit is recommended: Third World vs. First). As this book goes to print, the Wall has still not yet been built here; it is planned to be built around Shu'afat Refugee Camp, excluding its residents from easy access to Jerusalem despite their residency status (not full citizenship), trapping them in a ghetto with only one exit, which will have a military control there. Many of the Palestinian East Jerusalem neighbourhoods: Shua'fat, Anata, Azariya, Abu Dis, al-Jib, Bir Nabala, Walaja, Al Nuaman, Sheikh Saad, A-Ram, etc. are all destined for ghettoisation. In the name of security. Or land grab?

Anata - An Ordinary Village

Anata is next to Shu'fat refugee camp.

Originally an agricultural village, today this suburb of Jerusalem has 12,000 residents. Since the 1967 occupation, the village and its lands have been divided. Today, only a third of the population belong to the municipality of Jerusalem; the other two-thirds are in Area C. According to Israeli regulations, people in the West Bank's Area C do not have the right to go to the other part of the village without an official permit, which is extremely difficult to obtain. Since 1967, almost two-thirds of the village's lands have been confiscated. Four Jewish settlements have been built on part of them: *Alon, Kfar Adumim, Almon* and *Ma'ale Adumim*. Whilst Anata suffers from lack of infrastructure, a new Israeli prison (see p. 142) has been built there, on land illegally annexed during the Oslo "Peace Process." Ma'ale Adumim, on Anata and Azariya land, currently has a population of 31,000 settlers; building proceeds rapidly there (in spite of Israel's commitments under the Road Map to freeze all settlement building) and a population of 71,000 is projected by 2010; 45,000 by the end of 2005.

Al-Azariya (Bethany)

Village Council, ☎ 02-279 9273.

Officially al-Azariya has 25,000 inhabitants, yet the real population is far more. Many Palestinians from East Jerusalem have settled here because the town is next to the Jerusalem city boundaries, and rents are cheaper than in the city. Fearing to have their Jerusalem ID/ residence card (which allows them to live in the city, work or study or pray there, receive National Insurance payments such as child allowances, and state health care) confiscated by the Israeli authorities, residents of al-Azariya often have a second, official address inside Jerusalem. However, since January 2004, a 9 metre high concrete wall has cut al-Azariya off from the city, ghettoising this once prosperous, largely middle class suburb and many people have therefore moved back into Jerusalem proper, even though it is so expensive.

The Arab name of the town originates from the Greek "Lazarion," or "place of Lazarus," as Bethany was known during the Byzantine period. Evangelical tradition has it that it was here that Jesus raised his friend Lazarus from the dead (John 11). This same tradition is shared with Muslim residents of al-Azariya, where the **al-Ozir Mosque** honours Ozir, who is thought to have been the brother of Lazarus. The two churches next to the mosque commemorate the resurrection of Lazarus. The Franciscan Church of the Province or **Saint Lazarus Church,** consecrated in 1954, is the work of the ubiquitous architect Antonio Barluzzi. *(Open 8-11:30, and 14:00-17:00 in winter, 18:00 in summer; ☎ 02-279 9291).* Designed without any windows, the church is definitely unique. In fact, Barluzzi wanted to contrast the semi-darkness, symbolic of Lazarus's death, with the hope of resurrection, symbolised by the opening in the dome, the unique source of light. The Latin inscription at the base of the cupola reads : *"He that believeth in me, though he were dead, yet shall he live; and Whosoever liveth and believeth in me shall never die."* (John 11:25-26.) On the walls are impressive mosaic panels representing the different scenes of Jesus' visit to Bethany. Outside the church are the remains of mosaic pavements with geometrical motifs which belonged to a Byzantine church of the fourth century.

Above the mosque, stairs lead to the **Tomb of Lazarus,** which consists of a vestibule and a burial chamber.

The **Greek Orthodox Church of Saint Lazarus** is further up the street. This church was built in 1965, but the interior was only recently completed. The iconostasis (screen with icons) created by Greek cabinet-makers and the extremely beautiful modern icons are of particular interest.

The Arab al-Jahalin Charitable Society

Sheikh Khalil is the contact for the society, ☎ 0522-408856. Field trips and meetings can be organised. No fee is charged, but you are requested to spread the word about the local situation and the programme providing material assistance .

The society offers legal aid and material assistance (to purchase water tanks and electric generators, for example) to the Bedouin community. It is also an interesting information centre and organises meetings and tours for visitors. The Bedouin of the al-Jahalin tribe, 1952 refugees from the Negev, were evicted from lands they were originally moved to, at what is now the huge settlement, *Ma'ale Adumim.*

Practical Information

Travelling in Jerusalem and away from it

The best way to discover Jerusalem is on foot. Most of the historical, cultural, and religious sites are concentrated inside the Old City or in close proximity to it.

- If you have to take public transportation, the area around **Damascus Gate** is the arrival and departure point for all destinations in East Jerusalem and the West Bank. However, the current traffic complications make several vehicle changes necessary to get to a desired destination. Buses and service taxis (which take several passengers at a time) operate regularly all day long. The only means of transportation to the Gaza Strip is by private taxi, which costs NIS 200.

- If you have to take a private taxi, make sure that the mileage metre is on. The average cost of a trip is approximately NIS 15. However, prices go up at night (21:00-05:30).

- In West Jerusalem, public transport is provided by the Israeli *Egged* bus company. A map for *Egged* bus lines is available at the **Israeli Tourism Office** at Jaffa Gate. To use public transport inside Israeli, go to the **Egged Central Bus Station** at Jaffa Road, *(just after the neighbourhood of Mahane Yehuda, ☎ 02-530 4555)*. The central bus station has routes for the following cities: Ashqelon *(every hour, a journey of 1h15)*; Beersheba *(every half hour, ~ 2h)*; Ben Gurion airport *(every 35 minutes, ~ 45 minutes)*; Eilat *(four buses a day, ~ 5h30)*; Ein Gedi *(ten buses a day, ~1h30)*; Haifa *(every 30 minutes, ~ 3 hours)*; Massada *(8 buses a day, ~ 2 hours)*; Nahariya *(3 buses a day, ~ four hours)*; Qumran *(seven buses daily, ~ an hour)*; Ramle *(every 25 minutes, ~ 1h30)*; Tel Aviv/Jaffa *(either to the Central Bus Station or the Central Railway Station) (every 15 minutes, ~ an hour)*; Tiberias *(every hour, ~ 3h30)*.

Tourist Information

Since there is no Palestinian tourist information office in Jerusalem, the English publication ***This Week in Palestine*** is an essential source of information on cultural events in East Jerusalem, the West Bank and Gaza. It also has a complete list of restaurants, hotels and car rental offices as well as much other useful data. The brochure is free and easily found in many of the public places such as hotels, in Jerusalem. In addition, it contains very useful maps of Bethlehem, Jericho, Ramallah and Jerusalem as well as general Palestinian statistics and other useful information. The **Christian Information Centre** is the best place for information on Christian holy places, times of different church services and the many Christian hospices which accept guests. *(Omar Ibn al-Khattab Square near David's Tower next to the Jaffa Gate. Open Monday-Saturday 8:30-13:00. ☎ 02-6272692. Email cicbarat@netmedia.net.il)*. A good selection of brochures and maps is available for visitors. Upon request, the centre also issues "Pilgrimage Certificates." There is a Tourism Office managed by the Israeli municipality of Jerusalem located at Jaffa Gate, *(open Sunday-Thursday 8:30-15:45; Friday 8:30-12:45)*. Other **tourist information centres** are located at the *Jerusalem Municipality at 34 Jaffa Road and at 24 St. George's Street.*

The Post Office and Communication

The **main post office** in East Jerusalem is at the intersection of Salah ed-Din Street and Sultan Suleiman Street *(open Sunday-Thursday 8:00-18:00, Friday 8:00-12:00, Saturday 8:00-14:00)*. To send a parcel or buy stamps, stand in the line on the left-hand side; for letters or postcards, it is simpler to buy stamps at the tobacco shop **al-Moudakhan** on the other side of the street, which is the only place other than the post office where one can get stamps. There is also another **small post office** located inside Jaffa Gate opposite the entrance to David's Citadel *(open Sunday-Thursday 7:30-14:30, Friday 8:00-12:00)*; another post office (the **central post office** of West Jerusalem) is at 17 Jaffa Road *(Sunday-Thursday 7:00-19:00, Friday 7:00-12:00)*.

@ Internet Cafes

In the Old City

Albalad Net Café: New Gate : Open Monday-Saturday, 9:00-21:30, NIS 6 per hour.

Free Line Internet: Aqabat Khan al-Aqbat; open 10:00-24:00; NIS 10 per hour.

Future Internet: Christian Quarter Road, *opposite a large billiards hall;* open 10:30-24:00; NIS 10 per hour.

Outside the City Walls

Eldorado Internet café: 19 Salah ed-Din Street; open daily 8:30-22:00; NIS 20 per hour.

Money-changers and Banks

Money-changers always offer the best rates and charge very low commissions or none at all. Most money-changing offices are along Salah ed-Din Street and around Damascus Gate. Rates are more or less similar, but do not hesitate to compare the rates offered by different offices. For bank transactions (travellers cheques or pensions, etc), there is little choice in East Jerusalem. **Bank Hapoalim** *(az-Zahra Street, open Sunday-Thursday 8:00-14:00, Friday until 12 noon, closed on Saturday)* has an automatic teller installed inside the bank. Be careful to note closing hours. **Mercantile Discount Bank** *(at the junction of Salah ed-Din Street and Abu Taleb Street, open Sunday-Thursday 8:30-14:30, Friday 8:30-12:00)* allows you to withdraw money with a card at any hour; it is the only outdoor automatic teller in East Jerusalem. There are many banks along Jaffa Road in West Jerusalem.

Bookshops and Places To Buy Newspapers

East Jerusalem:

At the foot of Nablus Road, opposite Damascus Gate, there is a well-stocked kiosk selling local and international newspapers and magazines. It opens early in the morning and closes at 1:00 p.m.

On Salah ed-Din Street, facing the French Cultural Centre, the ***Educational Bookshop*** *(open daily 7:30-19:30)* also sells local and international newspapers and magazines, as well as a good range of books about Palestine (society, culture, history and the Israeli-Palestinian conflict). Most of the books are in English or Arabic. The bookshop also sells tour guides, postcards, maps and manuals on the basics of Arabic (Syro-Palestinian dialect or classical Arabic).

The Bookshop *(open daily 9:00-12:00)*
This bookshop at the American Colony Hotel is considered one of the best for books on the Israeli-Arab-Palestinian conflict (mainly in English) and for English literature generally.

The Franciscan Corner Bookshop *(Ibn al-Khattab Square - Jaffa Gate; open Monday-Saturday 10:00-13:00 and 15:00-19:00)*. This bookshop stocks works on the archaeology of Christian sites, studies on Christianity in the Holy Land and monographs on the Christian holy places. Publications in English, French and Italian.

West Jerusalem

Mayer Bookshop *(4 Shlomzion HaMalka Street. Open Sunday–Thursday 8:00-13:00 and 15:00-19:00, Friday 9:00-13:00).* This multilingual bookshop specialises in reference books in English, Hebrew, German, Russian, and French. There is a large selection of English reference books on archaeology, history, politics, literature and philosophy. There are also some reference books on the Arab world. Next door, **Dayla,** an activists' centre, has recently opened, with an intriguing programme of events.

Points of Cultural Interest (East Jerusalem)

Al-Wasiti Centre of Contemporary Art

Nabi Shu'ayb Street, ☎ 02-582 2859, www.alwasiti.org.

This contemporary art gallery is located next to the **al-Pasha Restaurant** (see p. 164).

Al-Mamal Foundation

Latin Patriarchate Street, ☎ 02-628 3457. Periodic exhibitions of photography by young Palestinian amateurs or by professionals.

Al-Mamal Foundation opened in 1997 with the aim of stimulating cultural life in East Jerusalem. Among its main activities, the centre organises photography workshops for young people; their work is regularly displayed here alongside photographs by professionals, in local newspapers and in the *Shoufi* (Arabic) magazine and its English version, *What's Up?*

***Dar At Tifl Museum**, near The Orient House:* ☎ *02-627-2477 Open daily: 9:00-13:30.*

Black and White Photography

In the nineteenth century, the enthusiasm for Palestine of the orientalists and Christian pilgrims accompanied the early introduction of photographic equipment. The Armenian community marked the second stage of photography's development here by establishing the first photography studio in the precincts of the Armenian monastery in Jerusalem. As photography grew more popular, a second studio was set up near Jaffa Gate, in 1885. Until 1948, the Armenian community had a quasi-monopoly on black and white photography, which they shared with several religious institutions. However, most of the studios were located outside Jaffa Gate at that time. With the destruction of this area in 1948, most collections were either destroyed or confiscated by the Israelis. But photo buffs are welcome to browse and can even buy antique monochrome photographs, available in some small studios whose owners are, unsurprisingly, Armenian: **Elia Photos** and **Varouj** *(both in the Old City on Aqabat Khanqa Street)*; **Authentic** *(az-Zahra Street).*

***Qalandia Camp Women's Handicraft Co-operative**:* ☎ *02-656-9385 Email: qalandia@palgate.net*

The Anadiel Gallery

New Gate, Jack Persekian. ☎ 02-628 2811. Periodic exhibitions of photography and paintings.

The Palestinian National Theatre (al-Hakawati - The Storyteller)

Abu Obeida Street ☎ 02-628 0957, Fax 02-627 6293. Email: tdp@palnet.com

Founded by the al-Hakawati theatrical company in 1984, this theatre is the cultural centre of Jerusalem. Programmes include pieces of theatre, concerts, films, shows for children and puppet show festivals.

***Yabous Productions**: For current productions: www.yabous.org* ☎ *02-626-1045* This company aims to return to East Jerusalem some of its past cultural glory and traditional ambience; it promotes Palestinian artists and productions locally in festivals and promotes them both regionally and internationally. Its annual music festival is a major attraction.

Places to eat

Cafes

Inside the Old City

Herod's Gate

Jaber's Café *(inside Herod's Gate; open 8:00-211:00)* is a popular café exclusively frequented by men. Card players and backgammon *(Shesh Besh)* enthusiasts will enjoy spending time here.

Damascus Gate and al-Wad Street

Inside the gate, there are two cafes behind the main road. The terrace of the ***Gate Café*** *(to the left of the entrance)* is raised up and has a view over the busy street. On the other side of the gate, the ***Princess Cafeteria*** has a roofed terrace. Entrance is through a small door inside Damascus Gate.

Around Jaffa Gate

A pathway below the ***Hotel New Imperial*** leads to ***Cappuccino Café***, which has been entirely renovated and is very cosy.

Of all the roads around Jaffa gate, the Latin Patriarchate Street has the greatest number of cafes, restaurants and bars; all of them serve alcohol. Amongst them, the ***Moukhtar Café*** is the most picturesque. Although there is no name outside, it can be identified by the beer cases stacked up on the sidewalk. The café is rather dirty but the atmosphere here is friendly. There is a small garden at the back of the room, which merits better care. On Saturday, the street becomes a rendezvous for Romanian "foreign workers." Farther up the same street, the ***Nafoura*** (Fountain) café-restaurant is much more chic. One can have a drink on the terrace here at the foot of the wall or at the counter of a bar, where there is a good wine selection.

Outside the Walls

Kan Zaman Restaurant (*kan zaman* = "once upon a time") *Jerusalem Hotel, Nablus Road.* ☎ *02-628 3282.*

The garden and the diwan (downstairs) guarantee a pleasant setting at any time of year in what has become a well-known rendezvous, or meeting place. Grapevines shade the terrace in the summer; there is a buffet every Saturday evening (NIS 60 per person) with music - usually, oud (lute) or piano.

Salah ed-Din and az-Zahra Streets

Eldorado Internet café *(19 Salah ed-Din Street, near French Cultural Centre, open every day 8:30-22:00; Internet NIS20 per hr)* The speciality of this café is the preparation of coffee; thus all varieties of expresso coffee from most of the coffee-producing countries of the world are served here.

Gondola Café *(Az-Zahra Road)* This café is closed for the moment, hopefully temporarily, but it definitely deserves a mention. It is the most original café in Jerusalem, designed in the 1950s by master cabinetmakers from Damascus. The interior decor is entirely in wood, evoking the splendid popular cafes of Damascus.

Café Europe *(Az-Zahra Road)* This café is cozy and comfortable, especially in winter. It has plain cooking: omelettes, steaks, chips and so on.

Sheikh Jarrah

Askadinya *(11 Shimon Hazadik Street; open every day from 12 noon on, (Tuesday from 7 pm) 02-532 4590* [See p. 164.]*)*

In the summer, the small green, half-open door covered by climbing plants is easily missed or unnoticed. This is one of the rare places in East Jerusalem that stays open quite late. Located in an old renovated mansion, the interior is cool and pleasant and helps to make Askadinya one of Jerusalem's most popular restaurant-cafes.

Restaurants

Inside the Old City

Around Jaffa Gate

Costa's Greek (Yunani) Restaurant *(28 Aqabat al-Khanqat, open 12:00-18:00. ☎ 02-627 4480)* This is a small, popular restaurant. Do not judge this restaurant by its modest décor: its cuisine is first class and it has one of the best reputations; the speciality here is stuffed young pigeon as well as Armenian meats: pastrami *(basturma)* and sausages *(sujuq)*. Upon request, stuffed rabbit is also served.

En-Nafoura *(18 Latin Patriachate Street; rather expensive)* With a large terrace running along the city wall, this restaurant is one of the most pleasant places in the Old City. The attention which has been paid to its décor contributes much to its atmosphere. Grilled à la carte and Armenian specialities are first choice, while the marinaded chicken is also recommended.

In the Muristan, ***Papa Andreas Restaurant*** *(near the fountain)* offers a classical cuisine of grilled meat and various types of salads *(mezze)*. The restaurant is strictly self-service. The terrace on the roof has a splendid panoramic view of the Old City. The large building next door, which used to belong to the Greek Orthodox Patriarchate, has been occupied by Jewish settlers since the 1990s.

In the Armenian Quarter, the ***Select*** or ***Mata'am Abu Ali*** *(Armenian Orthodox Patriarchate Street, near the police station)* is one of the best-known Palestinian restaurants in the neighbourhood, with prices corresponding to its reputation.

The ***Armenian Tavern*** *(79 Armenian Orthodox Patriarchate Street; closed Monday; ☎ 02-627 3854)* is located under street level; its setting is particularly charming. The cuisine is indistinguishable from Palestinian cooking except for certain specialities such as sausages *(sujuq)* and pastrami *(basturma)*.

Souk al-Lahmin (the Butchers' Market). There are a few small, simple restaurants in the Butchers' Market. ***Mata'am Sha'in*** *(north of the crossroads of al-Silsila (Chain) and David streets)* has a modest appearance, yet its kebab is superb.

Souk Khan ez-Zeit

There are some large restaurants on this street. ***Mata'am en-Nasser*** serves delicious grilled meat. For wonderful Arab pastries, the huge ***Jaffar*** Oriental pastry shop is a must; the knaffes are especially good. *(Place your order first, then pay at the cash desk, and then enjoy the pastries.)*

Al-Wad Street

Abu Shoukri *(63 al-Wad Street, next to the Fourth Station of the Cross, closes at 16:30)*. This small popular restaurant serves amongst the best hummus in Jerusalem.

Backpackers are ***Fouroun Abu Ali's*** best customers. The décor is really unusual, and the choice is limited, but one may order pizza made in front of you. This place is not for fussy people, as it is not the cleanest kitchen.

Jerusalem Star *(al-Wad Street, near "Sharon's house")*.

The décor here is nothing special, but prices are good, so the restaurant merits a visit. Do not hesitate to discuss there the presence of Jewish settlers in the neighbouring building.

Herod's Gate

Mata'am Abu Shenab *(inside Herod's Gate, Bab az-Zahra)*

This is a small, popular restaurant which serves delicious hummus and ful. It is not on the main tourist routes; the atmosphere is pleasant.

Outside the Walls

Al-Musrara Square and Nablus Road

Fouroun Musrara *(al-Musrara Square)*.

This isn't really a restaurant, but a bakery and grocery all in one. There is a wide variety of garnished bread here (bread with olive oil and thyme - *za'atar* or bread baked with meat -

sfiha and other specialities) as well as biscuits. Ideal for satisfying a hungry stomach. The shop remains open until late in the evening.
Kan Zaman Restaurant [See ***Kan Zaman*** *Café* and ***Jerusalem Hotel***, p. 162 and p. 166].

Around Salah ed-Din Street
Arabesque Restaurant *(American Colony Hotel, Nablus Road. ☎ 02-627 9777)*. This is an excellent but very expensive, restaurant. The European dishes are served in rather small portions; oriental cuisine -- somewhat larger.
Candy restaurant *(Suleiman Road, near the post office)* has a small room that opens onto the street and another on the first floor. In addition to traditional sandwiches, it prepares a special dish every day as well as different chicken and meat specialities (meat cuts, *kubbeh, sfiha* and others).
Mata'am al-Ikirmawi *(Ibn Khaldoun Street, near the Ritz Hotel)* is a tiny little place that serves first class *felafel, hummus* and *ful*. It is more take-away than sit-down, as there is just one counter and two seats.
Mata'am al-Shuleh *(Salah ed-Din Street)*. This cheap popular restaurant is only open during the day. Its delicious meat and meat cuts either in *shawarma* sandwiches or on plates with chips and salads are recommended. It is reasonably priced.

Sheikh Jarrah
Askadinya Restaurant *(11 Shimon Hazadik Street: ☎ 02-532 4590; open 12 noon except Tues. from 19:00. Gastronomic restaurant; reservations recommended; expensive.)*
This is one of the most interesting café-restaurants in the city. Apart from its ideal setting, its reputation comes from its original fine cooking. The dishes are all based on traditional Palestinian recipes and ingredients prepared in a contemporary way. Among the gourmet meals to choose from are eggplant roulees, *sumac* salad made with *jarjir* (a slightly bitter herb), cheese and pine kernels, *fteereh* (*shrak* stuffed with spinach), steak with pomegranate sauce and asparagus - all mouthwatering creations.
Al-Pasha Restaurant *(Nabi Shu'ayb Street, al-Wasiti Gallery)*
In addition to the traditional salads and grilled meat, the ***al-Pasha*** serves traditional Palestinian dishes such as *musakhan* and *mansaf*. The terraced room is heated in winter. Inside the house, a visit to the ***al-Wasiti Gallery*** of contemporary art is recommended.

Yahya Ibn Mahmoud al-Wasiti

Al-Wasiti lived in Iraq in the thirteenth century. He was one of the masters of a group of artists called the "Baghdad School." Of his *oeuvre*, ninety-one of his paintings on wood have survived; apart from their artistic value, these works are a rich source of information as much about the ethnology as the architecture, daily life, interiors of buildings and homes, architecture, costume, flags and social ceremonies at that time.

The two restaurants ***Addiwan*** and ***Tent*** are both found at the ***Ambassador Hotel*** in Sheikh Jarrah. The surroundings, whether inside or out on the terrace or in the garden, are beautifully designed. Middle Eastern food is the main choice; Italian and French cuisine follows; there is a wide range of choice and everything is first class.

Mount of Olives
The ***Bistrot*** is at the ***Seven Arches Hotel***; it has been designed to resemble a Parisian café. Meat and shellfish cooked on stones are among the specialities served here.

Accommodation

A premier tourist destination, East Jerusalem offers a wide variety of accommodation - youth hostels, guesthouses and hotels. A considerable number offer very beautiful views of Jerusalem, while others lack more attractive decor.

The Old City

Al-Ahram Youth Hostel *(Al-Wad Street, opposite the Austrian Hospice, closed at the moment).* The warm welcome here, its proximity to the calls to prayer, and the unique view over the Dome of the Rock from the private rooms on the top floor, compensate for the rather run-down condition of the rooms.

Austrian Hospice *(At the junction of al-Wad Street and Via Dolorosa, ☎02-6274636 office@austrianhospice.com. Sgl, dbl or tpl $49, $78 and $111. The doors close at 22h, so ask for a key if you expect to come back late; bar, restaurant.)*
A real haven of calm in the heart of the Old City, this building was built in 1869 and was successively the Austrian Consulate, a convent and a hospital until the mid-1980s. Since then, it has been transformed into a hospice and a café-restaurant. The rooms are clean and comfortable. The peaceful terraced garden, away from the noise of the street, is in itself worth a visit. The restaurant serves Austrian and other specialities.

Gloria Hotel *(33 Latin Patriarchate Street. ☎ 02-628 2431. gloriahl@netvision.net.il Sgl, dbl and tpl $50, $80 and $90, bar, cafeteria.)* The hotel is located on a busy street; evening is the busiest time. The rooms are clean and comfortable and much favoured by pilgrims. There is a panoramic view of the Old City from the rooftop.

Knight's Palace *(Latin Patriarchate Street; ☎ 02-628 2537 kp@actcom.co.il Sgl, dbl and tpl $50, $70 and $100, bar, restaurant.)*
This charming nineteenth-century building was once a seminary; the rooms were actually the former cells of young students studying for the priesthood. They have very high ceilings, and are elegant and comfortable; some family rooms have a mezzanine. In the restaurant, there are stone blocks that were part of the wall around Jerusalem in Roman times.

New Hashemi Hostel *(73 Souk Khan ez-Zeit, Via Dolorosa ☎02-628-4410. Email: salehhasimi1107@hotmail.com Dormitory beds cost NIS 20. Sgl, dbl and tpl $25, $35 and $45; cafeteria.)*
Recently renovated, the hostel has real character, and the rooms are comfortable. The cafeteria and the common area on the roof have an absolutely splendid view of the Old City and the Dome of the Rock.

New Imperial Hotel *(Omar Ibn al-Khattab Square. The entrance is to the left, up an alley, under the hotel's sign: ring the bell. ☎ 02-628 2261-627 2000 (imperial@palnet.com). Sgl, dbl and tpl $30, $50, and $65, cafeteria, @ and CB.)* Built in 1884, the hotel is a little dilapidated, and its decoration is, to say the least, eclectic. It still has a definite charm. Ask for a room with a balcony looking onto Omar Ibn al-Khattab Square and the Citadel; some family rooms have a mezzanine. Every room has a toilet and shower en suite.

Tabasco Hostel *(8 Aqbat et-Taqiya, near the Ninth Station of the Cross on the Via Dolorosa. ☎ 02-628 1101, Fax: 02-628 3461. Bed in a small dormitory NIS 20, in a large dormitory, NIS 15. Individual rooms with shower NIS100 and NIS60 without shower, bar, cafeteria, @ and a CB.)* The rooms are clean and comfortable and there is an Internet café, (NIS 10 per hour). The arches and natural stone walls lend a special charm to the small, recently renovated dormitories. On the other hand, the large dormitory on the top floor is much more anonymous, with a lot of bunk beds almost on top of each other.

Outside the Walls

Ambassador Hotel *(Sheikh Jarrah ☎ 02-582 8515* *amb@netvision.net.il. Sgl, dbl and tpl $120, $135 and $150, bar, cafeteria and CB.)* The hotel is very comfortable and spacious, with a beautiful view. It has several common rooms (lounges and gardens). It also has two excellent but expensive restaurants: ***Addiwan*** (Arab specialities) and ***Tent***, a garden restaurant ; there is also an excellent patisserie shop at the entrance to the hotel. The place is lively because it is frequently used for press conferences and meetings. Nevertheless, one can always find an island of calm amidst all the activities here.

American Colony Hotel *(Nablus Road.☎ 02-627 9777 reserv@amcol.co.il. $100 to $200 single and $140 to $240 double room. Bar, restaurant, gift shop, bookshop, swimming pool, sports centre and CB.)* The principal house in the neighbourhood, it originally belonged to Selim al-Husseini, Mayor of Jerusalem (1882). In 1896, it was rented to a Swedish-American messianic group, led by Horacio Spafford; later, the house was purchased by Baron Ustinov, who transformed it into a hotel. This luxury hotel is the preferred rendezvous for diplomats and journalists; with its rooms, gardens and cafes, the *American Colony* offers outstanding comfort and atmosphere. Its cosmopolitan ambience bridging the gulfs between Israel and Palestine, the Middle East and Europe or America, hints at how life in this troubled part of the world could have been different and yet still may be.

Az-Zahra Hotel *(Az-Zahra Street. ☎ 02-628 2447. azzahrahotel@shabaka.net. Sgl, dbl and tpl $70, $100 and $130, bar, restaurant and CB.)* Originally a residence built at the beginning of the twentieth century, it has been a hotel since 1948. The neighbourhood is quiet; the rooms are simple but comfortable, and some have a large balcony. Its café and restaurant are popular with Jerusalemites. There are musical evenings every Thursday.

Golden Walls Hotel *(Sultan Suleiman Street. Tel: ☎ 02-627 2416, info@goldenwalls.com Sgl, dbl and tpl $70, $90 and $110, bar, cafeteria and CB.)* This hotel overlooks the city walls. The decor of the rooms is classic, and the rooms are very comfortable: air conditioning, satellite TV, hair dryer and safe. The hotel also has a large restaurant and a bar.

Jerusalem Hotel *(Nablus Road. ☎ 02-628 3282. raed@jrshotel.com. Sgl, dbl and tpl $75, $85 and $95. Free for children under six. Discount for members of associations, journalists, etc. Reservations essential. Bar, restaurant, CB.)* The highly advantageous geographical location near Damascus Gate, the architecture and ***Kan Zaman*** café-restaurant *(two rooms: one a terrace and one underground)*, its prices which are considerably less than for similar accommodation at the American Colony, make this hotel a favourite rendezvous. The oriental character of what was once a private home adds to the charm of your stay here. The rooms are spacious and the surroundings refined (Egyptian furniture and exposed stone walls); each room has a unique decor. Excellent service.

Mount Scopus Hotel *(Sheikh Jarrah. ☎ 02-582 8891, mtscopus@netvision.net.il. Sgl, dbl and tpl $60, $80 and $110, bar, cafeteria and CB.)* Comfortable, spacious rooms with large balconies and a superb view.

Notre Dame Hospice (*Opposite New Gate. ☎ 02-627 9111 Fax 02-627 1995. Sgl, dbl and tpl $55, $94 and $140, bar and restaurant.)* Owned by the Vatican, this large complex receives mainly pilgrims, but all guests are welcome. The rooms are simple with TV and air conditioning; there is also a terrace café *(open 9:00 to 23:00)* and a good *(rather expensive)* restaurant "La Rotisserie."

Saint George's Cathedral Pilgrim Guest House *(8 Salah ed-Din Street. ☎ 02-627 7232 sghostel@netvision.net.il Sgl, dbl and tpl $80, $100 and $130, bar and cafeteria.)* The architectural setting and the garden more than compensate for the austere but clean rooms here. The bathrooms have recently been renovated.

Victoria Hotel *(Massudi Street.☎ 02-6274466, fax 02-627 4171. Sgl, dbl and tpl $60, $80 and $110, bar, cafeteria and CB.)* The rooms are calm and both comfortable and well-equipped.

YWCA Hotel *(Ibn Jubayr Street, Sheikh Jarrah. ☎ 02-628 2593 ywca@ywca-palestine.org Sgl, dbl and tpl $35, $42 and $56, bar, cafeteria and sports centre.)* The rooms are comfortable and charming and some have been renovated recently. The hotel's profits are reinvested in various YWCA (Young Women's Christian Association) projects, which include the professional education of young women and child care centres in the refugee camps of Jalazon, Aqbat Jaber, and Qalandia.

Mount of Olives

Mount of Olives Hotel *(53 Mount of Olives Road, near the Mosque of the Ascension. ☎ 02-628 4877 info@mtolives.com Sgl, dbl and tpl $54, $78 and $98)* Most of the clean, calm rooms have a superb panoramic view.

Seven Arches *(Mount of Olives. 02-626 7777 svnarch@trendline.co.il Sgl, dbl and tpl $100, $130 and $150 but during the al-Aqsa Intifada, prices have fallen to $45, $55 and $80. The hotel has bar, restaurant, CB, and phones operated by cards purchased in the hotel.)* This hotel offers a spectacular view of the Old City and Haram al-Sharif. Slightly old-fashioned, its large common rooms (lounges and corridor) are comfortable although they are so large -- the fashion in the 1960s when the hotel was built. The rooms are comfortable, very well-equipped and very well-lit, and some have been recently renovated. The **Seven Arches Hotel** also has a Parisian-style café-restaurant, the **Bistrot**, which serves excellent meat cooked on hot stones.

Contacts

Alternative Tours

An agency based at the Jerusalem Hotel.☎ 0522-864 205 or 02-628 3282. raed@jrshotel.com Day tours: Jerusalem 3 hours, $13 per person. Nablus and Ramallah, $23, Jericho (half a day), $18, Gaza, $35, Nazareth and Tiberius, $30, Dead Sea and Massada, $25. Minimum of 5 persons per group.

In keeping with the philosophy of alternative or cultural tourism, this agency opts for realities of life in Palestine: history, sites, culture, society and the political situation.

The Community Development Centre - Nidal

Christian Quarter.☎ 02-628 2815, nidalc@palnet.com, visits to the city (a fee may be charged).

This centre was created in cooperation with the UHWC (Union of Health and Work Committees) to meet the need for social and medical programmes in the Old City, which has over 32,000 Palestinian residents. The centre holds many educational and cultural activities for children and adolescents to encourage equality between the two sexes, to stimulate learning and to instil progressive values.

The Centre for Jerusalem Studies - Al-Quds University

Souk al-Qattanine.☎ 02-628 7747, fax 02-628 0297. Guided tours in English, $20 ($10 for students).

The centre organises thematic tours on the architectural and cultural patrimony of Jerusalem. Tours are usually on Saturday from 10:00-13:00. Al-Quds University also offers courses in Arabic dialect and classical Arabic during the school year and intensive classes in the summer.

Alternative Information Centre (AIC)

4 Shlomzion HaMalka Street, West Jerusalem. ☎ 02-624 1159, www.alternativenews.org aic@alt-info.org. Conferences and guided tours, particularly in relation to the Israeli plan to control "Greater Jerusalem." There may be a minimal charge for tours.

The centre publishes a monthly political magazine in English: *News from Within* [See *AIC, Beit Sahour* p. 208].

The Israeli Committee Against House Demolitions (ICAHD)

7 Ben Yehuda Street, West Jerusalem. ☎ 02-624 5560 www.icahd.org info@icahd.org Tours of the Occupation, including settlements, Wall, checkpoints, and other points of control, all focussed on Prof. Jeff Halper's thesis: The Matrix of Control, which is available online at the website. A charge for tours.

A coalition of Israeli peace groups, ICAHD works to end the Occupation and advocates for a just, viable peace for Palestine and Israel. As such, it has concentrated largely on issues of Israel's house demolition policy and violations of Palestinian human rights by Israel; its tours are extended to journalists, diplomats, VIPs, peace groups and Israelis.

The Palestinian General Federation of Trade Unions (PGFTU)

Salah ed-Din Street, ☎ 02-628 2737. This trade union holds meetings to inform people of workers' conditions.

Established in 1965, the Palestinian General Federation of Trade Unions is heir to the Trade Union Movement of Palestinian Workers (1925-1948). The federation today is an umbrella body for more than 10 sectors of employment - in public administration, construction work, teaching, media and publishing, the agro-food industry, the metallurgic industry, catering and tourism, among others. In 1999, the union had more than 80,000 members. A trade union has to conform to a complicated multiplicity of work legislation: Jordanian, Palestinian, and Israeli. The situation of Palestinian workers in the West Bank and the Gaza Strip who work inside Israel is difficult and it is almost impossible to defend their rights. Since the beginning of the al-Aqsa Intifada, Palestinian workers with work permits have lost all their rights including unemployment compensation, social security and retirement pensions. In litigation with Israeli or Jerusalemite employers, PGFTU cannot intervene directly because it is not officially recognised by the Israeli authorities. Its only resource is to give legal advice with the help of lawyers.

Sabeel (The Ecumenical Centre of Liberation Theology)

Near Nabi Shu'ayb Street, in Sheikh Jarrah. ☎ 02-532 7136, www.sabeel.org. Lectures or tours - $50 minimum per group.

The English equivalent of "Sabeel" is "the road" or also "a fountain." Founded by Palestinian Christians, the centre has a vocation to share the daily life of Palestinians under occupation from a theological and a secular point of view. Sabeel organises frequent conferences, lectures, meetings and cultural evenings.

The Union of Palestinian Medical Relief Committees (UPMRC)

Beit Hanina, on the main road. ☎ 02-583 4021, Fax: 02-583 0679. www.upmrc.org; contacts and field trips.

A non-government organisation, UPMRC was founded in 1979 to compensate for the lack of adequate structures for medical care in the Palestinian territories since their occupation twelve years previously, in 1967. The UPMRC offers medical services of all kinds and is particularly active in the field of preventative medicine. Since 1996, the society has initiated a first-aid programme, which has proved of great importance and efficiency since the beginning of the al-Aqsa Intifada.

Swedish Christian Study Centre

Jaffa Gate, Old City Jerusalem. ☎ 02- 626 42 23, scsc@bilda.nu, www.bilda.nu/scsc

The study organization, Bilda, enjoys longstanding contacts and exchange with Palestine. Since the 1960s Bilda's work in the Holy Land focused on study trips, research projects, cultural exchange and dialogue between people, religions and cultures. Bilda's permanent presence in the Holy Land, the Swedish Christian Study Centre (SCSC) was established in 1991. The Study Centre enables visitors from Sweden and other countries to research and study local cultures, religions, history and politics. One of the SCSC's main aims is to promote and support the local people in Palestine and to provide an interface for people from Sweden and those of the Middle East. The meetings and discourse that ensue, provide new understanding and insights which build bridges across cultural, religious, ethnic and political divides.

THE WEST BANK

الضفة الغربية

JERICHO

Jericho

Getting to Jericho

To drive to Jericho from Jerusalem, simply follow Route 1, in the direction of *Ma'ale Adumim* settlement taking the left highway down towards Jericho as marked. Unfortunately, there are no service taxis that go directly from Jerusalem to Jericho. They leave from the central station in Abu Dis; from there, the fare in a service taxi is NIS 6. From Qalandia's central taxi station to Jericho in a service taxi, the fare is NIS 8. From Qalandia or Nablus checkpoint (Huwwara), one may take a taxi all the way to Jericho without changing vehicles.

■ Between Jerusalem and Jericho

The Israeli settlement of *Ma'ale Adumim*

Founded in 1978, this settlement is easy to spot with its white, block-like apartment buildings, typical of other Israeli settlements encircling Jerusalem. Ma'ale Adumim is the largest settlement in the West Bank, currently accommodating over 30,000 settlers but projected to reach 70,000 by the year 2010 (45,000 by late 2005 - housing built during the Road Map peace process, during which Israel committed itself to freeze all settlement building, even natural expansion). It is a key link in the chain of settlements east of Jerusalem called the "outer ring," which was conceived both to isolate East Jerusalem from Jericho, and to cut the West Bank in half, separating the north from the south. The Ma'ale Adumim Bloc is intended by Israel (as ratified by the Bush-Sharon Letter of Understanding of April 2004) to remain Israeli even after any Final Status Agreement; its impact is huge, as it is such a threat to viability of any future Palestine. If visiting, look for the ancient olive trees recently planted everywhere; they are trees uprooted from Palestinian groves, during the erection of the Separation Wall, whose bark even still has white "wounds" showing bulldozer damage to them.

❒ The Monastery of Martyrius

An archaeological site in the Israeli industrial estate Mishor Adumim. Open Sunday-Thursday 8:00-16:00, Friday 8:00-13:00. Egged bus 174, Jerusalem-Mishor Adumim.

Martyrius, originally from Cappadocia, became Patriarch of Jerusalem in 478 AD and founded this monastery at the end of the fifth century. The foundations of the monastery were rebuilt thanks to generous donations. Not much remains of the buildings themselves, yet one gains a good idea of the complete plan of the Byzantine monastery, as well as that of a farm built on its ruins under the Omayyads, before its destruction in an earthquake in 749.

❒ The Inn of the Good Samaritan (Khan al-Hatruri or al-Khan al-Ahmar)

The ruins of this old *khan* (inn) of the sixteenth century are next to the road; the site, where the two banks of the Jordan River meet, used to be a halt for merchants and many Muslim pilgrims bound for the holy city of Jerusalem (al-Quds). Today, it is squeezed between two Israeli settlements: *Mizpe Yericho* and *Mishor Adumim*. At the beginning of 2000, Israeli authorities closed the souvenir shop and tent-café here despite the fact that they managed a profitable business with Christian pilgrims who came to the place where Christ supposedly preached the parable of the Good Samaritan (Luke 10:30-36). Above the *khan* are the ruins of a Crusader fortress (Qala'at ed-Dam or the Castle of Blood), which subsequently became a Mameluke stronghold.

❒ The Monastery of Saint Euthymius

This site is opposite the Inn of the Good Samaritan. It is no longer open to visitors, but the ruins of the monastery are visible from the road.

Built in the fifth century, this monastery was one of the most important centres of its kind in Palestine until the end of the Crusader occupation. Euthymius, an Armenian monk originally from Cappadocia, settled in Palestine *circa* 405; he and Theoctistus founded this coenobite monastery and several *lauras* (monasteries with a group of cells for the monks, who met for meals and worship). Gerasimus and Sabas modelled their monastic communities (Deir Hajla and Mar Saba) on this one. Destroyed in the earthquake of 660, the monastery was reconstructed at the beginning of the Islamic period and again during the Crusades. In the thirteenth century, Mameluke sultan Baybar had a *caravanserai* built on the ruins here, halfway between Jerusalem and Jericho.

The Bedouin Encampments

*Meetings and visits to Bedouin encampments are organised by the 'Arab al-Jahalin charity, an association in al-Azariya (Bethany [*see p. 157*]), which also shows the documentary film, Jahalin, produced by the AIC. [*See Contacts, p. 208*]. Rabbis for Human Rights has a project here, too, working with the children and community.*

Makeshift encampments are dispersed all along the road. Most of the Bedouins who live here belong to the al-Jahalin tribe ('Arab al-Jahalin). Originally from the region of 'Arad in the Negev, they were expelled at the beginning of the 1950s and resettled mainly east of Hebron and around al-Khan al-Ahmar, between Jerusalem and Jericho. However, as of 1967, they have been constantly displaced towards the worst land, and far from water sources. The occupation authorities confiscated their land under the pretext that it was uncultivated, although it was clear that it was Bedouin pastureland. First transformed into military zones, many of these territories were later used for Jewish settlements, the first of which was *Ma'ale Adumim*. In 1997, in the middle of the "peace process," new expulsions gave this settlement more room to grow. Hundreds of people were forcibly resettled on the outskirts of al-Azariya, overlooking the municipal garbage dump. Others, in Anata, are now losing land to the Wall there and many of their shacks have recently been demolished by the Israeli authorities.

The pastoral way of life of the Bedouins continues, but on a much smaller scale because of the drastic reduction in pastureland. Flocks once numbering over 20,000 head are now less than 4,000 and the Bedouin who used until recently to provide 60% of the meat and dairy produce of the Palestinian economy are now hard hit. In addition, water scarcity (water has to be bought from tankers) limits the number of animals that can be raised. Besides this, the sale of animal products of any kind in Jerusalem or Israel proper is forbidden, and a sanitary cordon prevents distribution of animal products to the West Bank and Gaza, effectively outlawing the chief source of Bedouin livelihood. As a result, Bedouin men now work in factories in Israel or as construction workers in Jewish settlements if they can obtain the necessary movement permits, but such access has been seriously restricted of late. For example, Bedouin are forbidden entry to nearby *Ma'ale Adumim*.

Wadi al-Qelt

Take Route 1 and then the old Jericho road at the settlement of Mitzpe Yeriho.

Wadi al-Qelt is a spectacular place for hiking. There are impressive aqueduct ruins here, some of which date from Hasmonean times; these aqueducts were re-used, and others built, in the Herodian, Roman, Omayyad and Ottoman periods. Signposts indicate the way up to the springs of Ein Qelt, Ein Farah and Ein Fawwar, whose waters either irrigate Wadi al-Qelt, or flow down to Jericho. The landscape is exceptional, with unusual and varied fauna and flora (especially in the spring). Bring binoculars, because the animals usually take refuge on the steep, inaccessible hillsides. The route itself is relatively easy except for the heat, particularly in the summer. To prevent dehydration, cover yourself, and carry a good supply of water (several litres if you want to reach Jericho). There is drinking water available at the monastery of Saint George of Choziba, at the beginning of the route, but only during opening hours. Water from the springs is unsafe to drink. In the winter, beware of dangerous flash floods. It is preferable to go into the desert with a guide. *[Abdullah Shahine is a Bedouin providing such services: 0522-650-988 for a wide range of possibilities, including jeep or camel.]*

The monastery of Saint George of Choziba

Fifteen minutes' walk from parking area. Open Sunday-Friday 8:00-12:00 and 15:00-17:00, Saturday 8:00-12:00. Closed on holidays; free admission. Drinking water available.

According to Christian tradition, the prophet Elijah stayed in one of the caves here on his way to Sinai and here Saint Joachim learned from an angel that Anne, his barren wife, was to give birth to the Virgin Mary, Mother of Jesus Christ.

The monastery was founded by Saint John of Thebes *circa* 480 AD and became an important spiritual centre in the sixth century under Saint George of Choziba, a Cypriot. The monastery permitted hermits in the numerous caves in cliffs nearby to meet for a weekly mass and communal meal. The history of the monastery is similar to that of most monastic foundations: devastation in 614 (Saint George of Choziba was even held prisoner for some time), a decline in the first centuries of the Islamic period, reconstruction by the Byzantine emperor in the twelfth century, and, at the end of the Crusader occupation, another decline in monastic life until the end of the nineteenth century. Restoration undertaken in 1878 and 1901 revitalised the Greek Orthodox monastery, which today has a modest, active community.

The decorative elements are for the most part recent; there are, however, ruins of a sixth century

Byzantine mosaic pavement in the chapel dedicated to Saint John and Saint George, as well as the relics (skulls) of 14 monks killed in 614. In the Church of the Blessed Virgin, a polychrome pavement features the two-headed Byzantine eagle. It is attributed to Emperor Manuel I Komnenos (twelfth century).

Nabi Musa

Open every day 8:00-sunset; free admission, but donations are appreciated.

The complex of Nabi Musa was erected under Mameluke sultan Baybar (1260-1277); guest rooms for pilgrims were added on progressively until 1475. Muslim tradition has it that this is the burial place of the prophet Moses (Nabi Musa). An inscription announces that Baybar "*... ordered the construction of this handsome maqam on the tomb of Moses, our Lord the Sultan, the king al-Daher ... Abu al-Fatah Baybar...during the months of the year 668* [1269 - 70 AD] *of the Hegira.*" The title "Abu al-Fateh," which means "the conqueror," was the battle name of this famous leader, who re-conquered Palestine in the thirteenth century. The Nabi Musa compound is designed in typically austere, impressive Islamic style; its buildings have two floors, surmounted by white domes which stand out against the starkly arid surroundings.

A *mawsim* or *mouled* which travelled from Jerusalem to Nabi Musa, which seems to have been inaugurated under Saladin, began as a celebration of the triumph of Islam over the Crusaders. The *mawsim* was also an occasion for amusements (horse races, theatrical performances, traditional storytelling, or games). Under British colonialism in Palestine and the threats weighing with it, pilgrimage turned into a political issue and an occasion to demonstrate against Zionism; for this reason it was forbidden by British military authorities, in 1937. The ban was maintained after 1948, and the *maqam* was transformed into a Jordanian, then an Israeli, military camp. In 1987, the annual event was authorised once again, but this did not last long. The Intifada broke out, and the occupation authorities prohibited almost all public gatherings, as much as possible. When the Palestinian Authority took over, the pilgrimage to Nabi Musa was again authorised, in 1997. It usually commences every Good Friday (by the Greek Orthodox calendar) with a long procession, from al-Aqsa Mosque, via the Lions' Gate, all the way to Nabi Musa, a procession which proceeds to the rhythm of religious refrains, accompanied by drums and flutes. Since the beginning of the al-Aqsa Intifada (September 2000), the week-long event has again been banned. Israeli authorities have declared the area a "military security zone," but tourists continue to visit here.

❐ Herod's Winter Palace (Tulul Abu al-'Alayiq)

At the exit of Wadi al-Qelt, 2 kms southwest of Jericho. Hikers who follow the wadi from the Monastery of Saint George of Choziba will find it at the end of their trail. Free admission.

Ever since prehistoric times, Man has exploited these fertile lands and their water resources; in the Hellenistic and Roman periods, scattered estates were agricultural

and centres of craftmaking, as well as places of entertainment and prestige. Nothing remains of the Hasmonean palaces on either bank although their ruins add substantially to the height of the tels; only the Herodian ruins give an idea of the past splendour of these palaces.
Herod built no less than three in all: the first, in 35 BC, when the famous Egyptian queen Cleopatra reigned over the whole Jordan valley; the second, after the earthquake and Cleopatra's suicide in 31 BC; the third, the most beautiful and the best preserved to this day, *circa* 10 BC. It is the only one of the three to have been built in dried brick; ornamental fountains, superb gardens and colonnaded porticos on both sides of the wadi produced a dazzling mirror effect. Only the foundations of this fairy-tale palace still exist to be seen today. The *triclinium* (dining area) opened onto a vast peristyle courtyard overlooking the wadi. The brick columns were coated with plaster and decorated to look like marble. The floor was covered with tiles of inlaid coloured limestone - white, orange, pink - and grey or black bituminous limestone, cut in squares, diamond shapes and rectangles. There was a *podium* or pool in the centre of the courtyard. The neighbouring room, a throne room, was surrounded by three

colonnades. At the centre, one may imagine a luxuriant garden and not the dusty ground visible today. To the side of the show rooms, and there were several of them, Roman-style baths added to the comfort and luxury.

The Jordan River Valley

The scenery down into the valley from the mountains (Road 1 or Road 449 - Tariq al-Ma'arajat) is full of extreme contrasts. The valley itself is extremely fertile; many orchards cover its hillsides. The oasis of Jericho emerges from an ocean of arid land and mountains. There is nothing to indicate the presence of a river concealed at the bottom of the valley, a river whose size and volume have been extremely diminished. Like the rest of the West Bank, the Jordan valley, a fertile and strategically vital area (albeit less strategic as an eastern front if Iraq and Jordan no longer threaten Israel), is part of the land conquest plan of Israeli colonisation. Over 30 farms and military settlements are scattered throughout the valley. Palestinian villagers must make do with a limited water supply and continuous land confiscation; of the 85 wells used in the early '70s, only 17 are viable today. Huge quantities of water are rerouted to the verdant settlements (whose green is deliberate, so settlers feel no subconscious, temporary status). The majority of people here survived on agriculture in the 1960s, when the area's population was maximal; today, only a minority of Palestinians can make a living from farming their own land. Fluctuating prices, generally low, make farming a poor investment: certain products no longer find a foreign outlet and internal transportation is almost impossible with the road and permit systems. Jordan, which with the Gulf states imported 60% of the farm production of Jericho in the 1960s, has a protectionist policy ever since the signature of the Jordanian-Israeli Peace Treaty of 1994, which reinforces dependence of Palestinian producers on the Israeli market. The case of Jericho's bananas, which Jordan is now forbidden to import, is typical: prices have slumped, and production has collapsed. Israeli farmers, on the other hand, benefit from a guaranteed minimal price for all their products. Many Palestinians now have no choice but to work in nearby settlements as agricultural workers, which ensures them a minimum income, if they are allowed in. **The village of Fassayel**, *(Mahmoud al-Abayat, member of the Village Council, ☎ 0505 305 669)*, 20 kilometres north of Jericho, is a prime example. Most of its land has been confiscated by neighbouring Jewish settlements *(Tomer, Peza'el, Gilgal* and *Yafit)*, and today only 5% of the working population can make a living from farming their own land; 25% work in the neighbouring settlements.

The Aqbat Jaber Refugee Camp

UNRWA office, ☎ *02-232 2411.*

This camp was established in 1948 on a piece of arid land located 3 kilometres southwest of Jericho. When the war broke out in 1967, most of the 30,000 people living in the camp had no choice but to become refugees once again. Today, less than 3,000 people live here, so crowding is no problem; the available free space has attracted many poor families who have no refugee status. In the camp, the problem of water is critical because of the aridity of the desert land. The Israeli national water carrier *(Mekorot)* controls the major water sources, so people have to adapt all the time to a miserly, irregular water supply. This permanent water shortage contrasts dramatically with the generous amounts of water available in the agricultural settlements of the Jordan valley, where most of the Palestinians from Aqbat Jaber work: people who are refugees without land and farmers without water.

Jericho

The Biblical name for Jericho, "city of palm trees," like its Arabic name Er-Riha, or "the perfume," indicates the striking contrast the oasis makes to the surrounding desert; luxuriant greenery and fragrant flowers flourish here; its subtropical climate makes it an extraordinary garden, ideal for winter vacation, when wealthy families of Jerusalem, Ramallah and Bethlehem come to enjoy the warmth. Situated on the west bank of the Jordan valley, eight kilometres north of the Dead Sea, Jericho owes its fertility to cool, abundant springs. In ancient times, there were already isolated farms on the valley's fertile land. Cleopatra was undoubtedly the most famous of Jericho's landowners; her estate here was a gift to her from Mark Antony in 35 BC.

Until 1948, Jericho was a large, peaceful country town; in 1948, tens of thousands of Palestinians from Lydd, Ramle, and villages west of Jerusalem

took refuge here. Three camps grew up around Jericho: Aqbat Jaber (30,000 residents), Ein es-Sultan (25,000 people) and Nuama (20,000 residents). The remaining refugees settled outside the camps. The village of Jericho became a city with official municipal status.

In 1952, after the Conference of Jericho, the Emirate of Jordan and the annexed West Bank were renamed the Hashemite Kingdom of Jordan. At the same time, the Palestinian national liberation movements (Fatah, the Arab Nationalist Movement, and the Communist party) were fostering resistance against the state of Israel from inside the refugee camps. The 1967 war forced people out again, on a new flight to the east; not one person in the entire governing body of Jericho was left - the camp of Nuama was totally demolished. When the Oslo (Oslo II) Accords were signed, Jericho became, in May 1994, the first Palestinian city in the West Bank with autonomous status, like the Gaza Strip. Despite frequent closures, the city invested heavily in tourism development. Since the al-Aqsa Intifada, Israeli forces have placed Jericho under a total siege and closed it to Palestinians from Jerusalem, Palestinians from the West Bank, or foreigners. The casino is also closed. But in the wake of the 2005 Sharm al-Sheikh Summit, there is talk of transferring Jericho and Tulkarem to the Palestinian Authority again, and re-opening the casino, which is jointly Israeli-Palestinian owned.

Sites of interest

❒ The tree of Zacchaeus

Ein es-Sultan Road, north of the Hisham Palace Hotel.

This tree looks like any other tree, but Christian tradition has it that this is the very sycamore that Zacchaeus, a patrician of Jericho, climbed to see Jesus better, who was walking through the city followed by a large crowd (Luke19:4). Jesus spent the night in Zacchaeus' house and converted the tax collector to charitable deeds.

❒ Tel es-Sultan (ancient Jericho)

Two km north of the city centre. Open daily 8:00-17:00. Admission NIS12.

Irrigated by the Ein es-Sultan river, the ecosystem of this area made it an ideal place for the early development of the first agricultural societies. Man first settled here in the second half of the tenth millennium BC (Epipalaeolithic period). Groups of hunter-gatherer-fishermen established seasonal camps and, for the first time, experimented with the cultivation of wild plants. In the Neolithic period (before pottery was made - between 8500 and 6000 BC), a sedentary agricultural community developed here. Farming and raising of livestock provided essential needs, supplemented by the traditional hunting of gazelle. The settlement's surface area was some 4 hectares for a population estimated at 3,000 people. The prosperity of the community and the building of a defensive wall (6m high with a tower 8.5m in diameter and at least 8m high) - unique at that time - have led experts to call Jericho "the oldest city in the world." There are also indications of a complex social organisation which worshipped different gods than those of their forefathers: skulls moulded with clay and lime, as well as sepulchres under the floor of the dwellings.

It was during the Early Bronze Age (3100-2450 BC) that the first towns in Palestine were created. The city of Jericho developed along the regional model: first, an unfortified town between 3100 and 2900 BC, then fortified between 2900 and 2600 BC, and then enlarged between 2450 and 2300 BC. In this latter phase, a new rampart was raised while the ancient, more imposing one was consolidated with wooden girders. Archaeologists have been able, with the help of radiocarbon dating, to place the destruction of the city at *circa* 2300 BC. Contrary to biblical tradition, according to which Joshua conquered Jericho in *circa* 1200 BC (Joshua 5:13-25), the destruction of Jericho came a millennium earlier, and moreover, archaeological remains show no disturbances at all in 1200 BC. The discovery deals a serious blow to the historical contents of the Bible, which has increasingly become known as a far more recent historical source than the events it records. Towards 2000 BC, the city was reconstructed along the model then in use from Mesopotamia to Egypt. It extended well beyond the *tel* itself. Towards 1550 BC, Jericho was abandoned, like many other cities in Palestine, following the conquest of Pharaoh Amosis I. The site was not inhabited again until the seventh century and then only for a limited duration.

❒ Hisham's Palace (Khirbet al-Mafjar)

Open 8:00-17:00; admission NIS8.

In the heart of hunting and farm land, the Hisham Palace was one of the most impressive country residences of the Omayyad period, so archaeologists call it "the Versailles of the Middle East." The palace was built at the beginning of the eighth century by Omayyad Caliph Hisham Ibn Abd al-Malik (724-743), only to be partially destroyed 20 years later in an earthquake. Reconstructed, it was in use until the tenth century. The complex included a palace, a mosque, a monumental fountain and thermal baths.

[According to Hamilton]

The living quarters were organised on two floors around a courtyard; a corridor of archways went through a garden and led into a large hall with multifoil columns. The room had three apses on either side, with the northern side opening onto a *diwan* and thermal baths. The walls were covered with elaborately chiselled stuccos, and the mosaic floors were exceptionally fine, their motifs typical of the Omayyad period: geometric shapes, complex knot-work and above all, rosettes and designs made to look like textiles and carpets covering the ground. The most famous, enigmatic mosaic, called "the tree of life" or "the tree of human cruelty," illustrates the extraordinary ability of its artisans to create the impression of a real carpet in stone. Exquisitely beautiful samples of these stuccos are on display in the Palestine Museum of Archaeology, or Rockefeller Museum [see p. 129]; dominant among them are a procession of partridges and nude busts of women supporting the vault. To the north of the palace, there was a courtyard with service and handicraft workshops grouped around it. Open canals fed by local springs supplied the palace with its water. A balustrade of small arches is all that remains of the monumental fountain.

❒ The Monastery of the Qurantul (the Forty)

From the parking lot near Tel es-Sultan, it is a 400 metre climb to the monastery. There is a cable car, inaugurated in 1999, which allows for effortless access. Open every day 8:00-21:00, $8.00; ☎ 02-232 1590, www.jericho-cablecar.com. Transport possible to es-Sultan panoramic restaurant ☎ 02-232 4025, a few minutes' walk from the monastery.

The monastery, perched on the side of the Mount of Temptation, offers a stunning panorama over the Dead Sea, Jordan Valley and Jericho. Tradition has it that this mountain was where Jesus fasted for 40 days and was tempted by the devil (Matthew 4:1-11). Christ's example inspired monks to brave the Judaean mountains, whose isolation and challenging terrain test the faith of even the most devout. During Byzantine days, numerous Christian hermits settled in the bare caves around the monastery. The name *Jabal Qurantul* is the Arabic transliteration of the Latin *Mons Quaranta* ("the Mount of the Forty").

The monastery dates from the twelfth century; it has two churches associated with the temptation of Christ: one constructed near a cave, the other, on top of the mountain. The present day chapel in the monastery only dates to the end of the nineteenth century (1874-1904); it has an exceptional collection of eighteenth and nineteenth century icons. There is a footpath from the monastery entrance to the top of the mountain, to the ruins of the **Diouk fortress**, originally built by the Seleucids (second century BC), and also a strategic place for the Hasmoneans and Romans. The fortress was part of a large surveillance network of lookout towers and smaller forts, in which homing pigeons were the communication. This site witnessed a harsh power struggle: here, high priest Simon was assassinated by his adopted son, Ptolemy. In the fourth century, the monk Chariton founded a prosperous monastic centre here.

❒ The Sugar Mills (Tawahin es-Sukkar)

Near the tel of es-Sultan. Under restoration. Free admission.

Production of sugar here dates to the Omayyad period (seventh–eighth centuries) but was at its height during Crusader days. There is a mediaeval mill east of the Mount of Temptation where remains of the hydraulic system, a forced conduit, or flying aqueduct, are partly preserved. Calcite deposits on the inside walls reveal the force of water from the Ein Diouk springs. The pottery workshop here specialised in ceramic vessels for use in sugar production: shards are strewn on the ground.

Ein es-Sultan Refugee Camp

This camp was established in 1948 on lands of the Mount of Temptation. On the eve of the 1967 war, about 25,000 refugees lived here. Their number decreased to just over 2,000 after the new exile in 1967 forced them into and beyond Jordan. **Independence Park** and the **Memorial to the Martyrs,** in the camp on Bissan Street, were inaugurated on April 16, 1997, in memory of combatant Khalil al-Wazir (Abu Jihad), the Fatah leader assassinated by Israeli secret services in Tunisia, on April 16, 1988.

❐ Khirbet Na'ran

Four kms NW of Jericho on Road 449. Open daily 8:00-16:00. Admission NIS7/10.

An arch spanning Wadi Ein es-Sultan marks the site of the aqueduct that brought water to Hisham's Palace. Ruins of a Byzantine synagogue were discovered under a house here, so it was placed under Israeli military protection. It has a beautiful mosaic floor with ornamental patterns similar to those found in Christian churches of this period. Unsurprisingly, fifth century BC mosaic artisans decorated places of worship for different religious communities. Instruments of Jewish religious practices are mixed with other religions' symbols here: a menorah, or seven-branched candelabra of Judaism, a palm leaf of both Christianity and Judaism and an incense scoop of Christianity and pagan worship as well as a Zodiac circle in the Graeco-Roman tradition, representing the sun and the personification of the seasons on the four corners of the mosaic carpet, as well as the remains of a picture of Daniel in the lion's den.

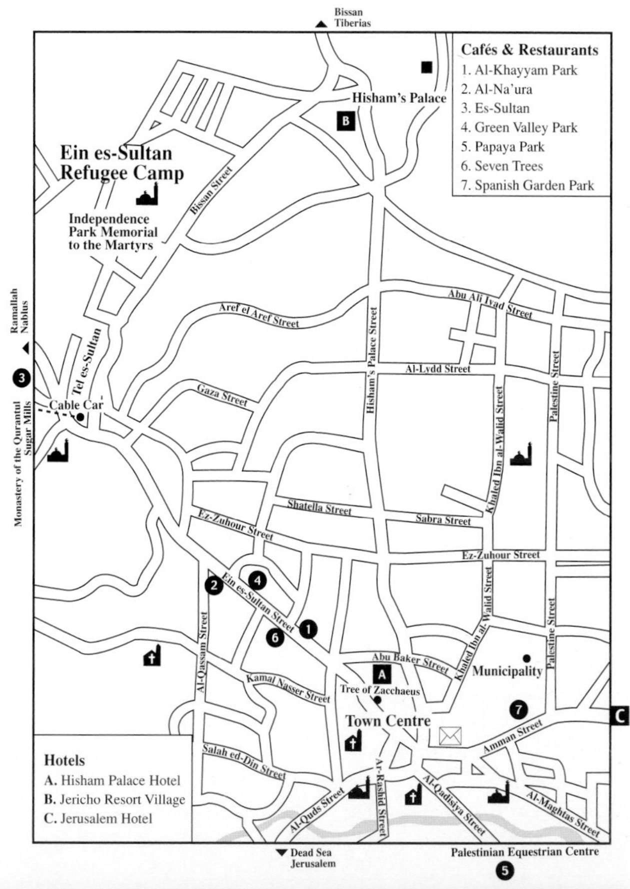

Practical Information

There are banks, a post office and taxis available within the perimeter of the city centre. Ancient Jericho (Tel es-Sultan) is about 2 kms from the centre of the city. The cost of a journey in a private taxi is NIS5 or NIS1.50 in a service taxi (going towards the refugee camp of Ein es-Sultan). One may also rent a bicycle in the city centre as a means of inexpensive and practical transportation (NIS3 per hour, and NIS15 for the day).

Cafés and Restaurants

There are many inexpensive restaurants where one may find appetizers, salads, and grilled meat, but what really makes the reputation of the city is its seasonal fruit juices. Ein es-Sultan Street, which leads to the historical site of old Jericho, is lined with most of the cafés and restaurants. One of the best is the ***Seven Trees*** *(10:00-midnight, reasonably priced).* Next to it, the ***Green Valley Park*** *(11:00-23:00, moderate prices)* and ***al-Khayyam Park*** are very popular. A short distance away, ***al-Na'ura*** *(8:00-19:00, reasonable prices)*, also known as the Bedouin Tent, has recreation areas for children. This restaurant is particularly famous for its brochettes *(shishlik).*

Several parks offer entertainment and recreation areas. The popular ***Papaya Park*** *(admission NIS 15, musical evenings Saturday and Thursday; ☎ 0505 286 067)* is both an agricultural and a tourist project with a forest of papaya trees, pools and slides, a small zoo and a restaurant. ***The Equestrian Centre of Palestine*** is next to it *(one hour of riding inside the ring or outside, NIS 40; ☎ 02 - 232 5007)*; horseback riding is an original way to discover Jericho's unique countryside. The ***Spanish Garden Park***, in the city centre, is one of its newest developments.

An unusual place for dining is the ***Es-Sultan*** panoramic café-restaurant, suspended on the Mount of Temptation *(☎ 02-232-1590, cable car).*

Accommodation

In the city centre on Salah Khalaf Street, ***The Hisham Palace Hotel*** *(☎ 02-232 2414)*, looks like an old colonial residence. Somewhat dilapidated, it has the advantage of being inexpensive. ***The Jerusalem Hotel*** located on al-Furat Street *(☎ 02-232 2444, sgl, dbl, and tpl $60, $80, and $100)* is more expensive, but much more comfortable. Close to the Hisham Palace, ***The Jericho Resort Village*** *(☎ 02-232 1255)* is a modern luxury tourist complex, complete with swimming pool.

South and East of Jericho

Deir Hijla (Saint Gerasimus Monastery)

East of Jericho, on the road to Abu Bakr or by-pass Road 90. The monastery has a guest house, rooms NIS50 per person; ☎ 02-994 3038. Advisable to reserve in advance.

There is only a small community here today in what is one of the most ancient Greek Orthodox monasteries in Palestine. Founded by Saint Gerasimus *circa* 455, the monastery was built on the site where Jesus was baptised. The Greek Orthodox Church three kilometres to the northeast of the monastery sponsors a pilgrimage to al-Maghtas and baptisms here, every year on January 19, commemorating the baptism of Christ by Saint John the Baptist (Matthew 3:13-17). The site is inside a closed military area open to the public only on this occasion, and upon prior reservation *(ask at the **Christian Information Centre** at Jaffa Gate in Jerusalem, ☎ 02-627 2692).*

Khirbet Qumran

20 kms south of Jericho. Open daily from 8:00-16:00 (15:00 in winter); Admission NIS 16.

This site gains its reputation as the place where the Dead Sea manuscripts were discovered in caves in the surrounding cliffs. In 1947, a young Bedouin first accidentally came upon some terracotta jars containing manuscript scrolls of copper. Three types of documents were discovered: original Old Testament texts from the second and first centuries BC (1,000 years older than other existing manuscripts), biblical commentaries and writings describing the organisation of the Essene community, an eschatological religious sect which observed strict rules in order to ensure the second coming of the Messiah.

The oldest ruins on the site date from the Iron Age; these are the remains of a fortress that belonged to a system spread over the Judaean desert in the seventh century BC. During the Hasmonean period (late second century BC), there seems to have been a villa here associated with the fortress of Hyrcanus.

At the end of the second century or during the First Century BC, the Essenes split from what they saw as the corrupt official Judaism of Jerusalem (or possibly even another dissident Essene group) and settled in small communities in the oases along the Dead Sea as far as Ein Gedi. Qumran and its buildings (designed to accommodate group activities) appears to have been their cultural centre, as a substitute for the temple in Jerusalem. Rituals associated with holy days were celebrated here by a permanent community of priests and farmers and craftsmen who lived nearby.

In an atmosphere characterised by messianism, ritual baths held a primordial status. An imperative need for water led to the construction of a system of dams and canals to bring water to cisterns. Several places in Qumran appear to have been destined especially for sacrifices, libations and offerings, confirming its cultural centrality. When a Roman garrison took possession here in 68 AD, the Essenes fled but not before hiding their precious manuscripts in the neighbouring caves. The scrolls became forgotten until their accidental discovery in 1947. Fragments of the manuscripts and the jars containing them are on exhibit today in the Archaeological Museum in Amman, and in the Palestine Museum of Archaeology (Rockefeller Museum) and the Israel Museum, both in Jerusalem.

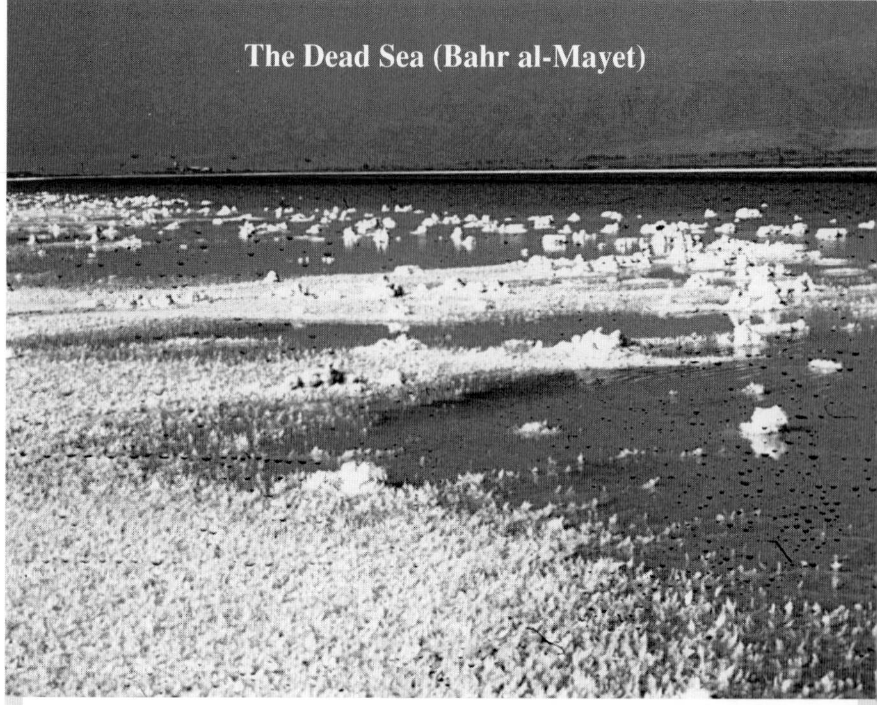

The Dead Sea (Bahr al-Mayet)

Except for very rare micro-organisms, neither flora nor fauna can survive in this lake, a fact which explains its name. Fish carried here by flood waters in tributary rivers die immediately because of the high salt content; one may see them on the shore, stiff with salt. The lake is also sometimes known by its Biblical name, Bahr Lot, the Sea of Lot.

The Dead Sea lies at the lowest point of the great Afro-Syrian divide (the Great Rift); over 400m below sea level, the surface of the Dead Sea is the lowest point on earth, its base being 800m below sea level. This huge salty lake extends over 80 kms and 18 kms at its widest point. It is actually the residue of the ancient Lisan Sea which, a million years ago, stretched from south of the Dead Sea to the Hula Valley, north of Lake Tiberias. The Dead Sea is unique for the high concentration of salt in its water: 20%-26% compared to only 4% in most other bodies of salt water. There are signs of instability in its *substratum*: lumps of pitch occasionally escape from submarine fissures and come to the surface; in the past, this pitch was collected either to waterproof roofs or to be burnt as fuel. Other intense natural activity *substrata* is responsible for hot sulphur springs on the eastern bank (Zerqa Ma'in and Hammamat Ma'in in Jordan). The lake's water level has dropped considerably since ancient times and continues to recede by 18 cms or more per year. The natural phenomenon of evaporation is no longer compensated by a fresh supply of water, due to the system regulating water flow to the Jordan River from its sources. Dams have substantially reduced the amount of water flowing into the Jordan River, and the effects of the drop in its water level are accelerating. Environmentalists warn that the Dead Sea is dying, partly due to the lack of freshwater inflow, but mainly due to the bromide industry which has taken over, on both sides of the shore (Jordanian and Israeli), especially the huge Israeli factories. Sink holes are an increasing sight and worry, if not danger; excessive pollution from emissions from these factories is also troubling.

Where to Swim?

Swimming in the Dead Sea is a unique experience; because there is so much salt in the water, it is easier to float than to swim. In fact, attempts to swim may even be dangerous, especially if you are at all overweight. Warning: the water can be extremely painful for eyes or any open cuts. For this reason, 'swimmers' need fresh water to rinse any irritated areas, including the eyes if they have contact with the salty water. There are many unsupervised, open and wild beaches along the shores, but most visitors prefer the official beaches where there are showers. Buses from Jerusalem stop here, en route to Eilat or elsewhere in the south.

❑ Ein Feshkha

Three kms south of Qumran. Open daily April-October 8:00-17:00, November-March 8:00-16:00. Admission NIS22-25.

The site is now far from the beach (because of the receding level of the lake); this reserve is usually less crowded than the popular Ein Gedi and has the advantage of being located where the fresh water spring of Ein Feshkha comes down from the hills. This natural reserve is an ideal place for hiking.

❑ Ein Gedi

50 kilometres from Jericho and 80 kms from Bir es-Saba' (Beersheba). There are frequent Egged buses: to Jerusalem (10 buses daily, 1.5 hours' ride), to Massada (3 buses daily, journey 30 minutes), to Arad and Bir es-Saba' (5 buses daily, 1 and 2 hours, respectively). Nature reserve: open Saturday-Thursday early morning to 17:00 (16:00 in winter).

Praised in the Bible for its beauty (Song of Songs 1:14), the natural reserve of Ein Gedi is an enchanting place for walks with its canyons, caves and waterfalls. In winter, hikers must watch out for flash floods. The combination of a hot climate and fresh water springs in the middle of desert creates ideal conditions for the development of luxuriant tropical and desert flora. There are many species of wild animals here, some such as the ibex and daman have even become accustomed to visitors and are therefore very accessible. There is a public beach here on the river. *(Showers NIS5.)*

❑ Mount Sodom

On Road 90, 50 kms south of Ein Gedi.

The depravity of the people of Sodom and Gomorrah and their divine punishment is legendary (Genesis 19:24-25). According to biblical tradition, a rain of sulphur and fire devastated this region, transforming it into a desolate landscape. One of the statues in rock salt on the side of the road here can only be Lot's wife, who, disobeying the angels, looked back at the city and was transformed into a pillar of salt.

BETHLEHEM

بيت لحم

Bethlehem

Getting to Bethlehem

Bethlehem is 10 kilometres south of Jerusalem, as indicated by frequent road signs. From Jerusalem, there is a bus from Musrara Square, opposite the marketplace at Damascus Gate *(NIS 2)* or service taxis *(Ford transit)* near the same bus station *(NIS 3)*, which drop one at the western entries to Bethlehem (CP300, Beit Jala or Al Khader). A private taxi *(NIS 30, at night NIS 50)* or rented car from Jerusalem may take the regular road, which is the shortest way. It is also possible to drive to Bethlehem on the road running north to south in the West Bank. This road was designed to by-pass Jerusalem, not to avoid traffic build-ups, but simply because West Bank residents are forbidden to enter the Municipality of Jerusalem; nevertheless there are various checkpoints (Container, DCO and other flying checkpoints) which often make this a difficult journey. The name of this route is Wadi Nar (The Valley of Fire), and the name is especially significant in the summer. In any season, the scenery is spectacular - steep, rolling desert hills in summer, floral in spring. To reach Bethlehem from Jerusalem go by taxi from Damascus Gate to Abu Dis taxi station *(NIS 2.5)*, then by service taxi, with green West Bank licence plates, to Bethlehem *(NIS 5)*.

"For the first time in centuries, there will be no occupation forces in Manger Square."
■ George Abu Khazen, Catholic priest of Bethlehem, Christmas 1995

■ From Jerusalem to Bethlehem

❑ Mar Elias

Open every day 8:00-11:00 and 13:00-17:00, free admission, ☎ *02-676 0966, advance reservations necessary for the hospice and restaurant for pilgrims.*

Shortly before the Israeli CP300 (Gilo) checkpoint, the Mar Elias Greek Orthodox Monastery stands alone at the foot of a hill from which there is a panoramic view of the Bethlehem region, Jerusalem, the Israeli settlement *Har Homa* and the sinister grey cement of the ubiquitous Wall, running through the desert like a post-Christo profane Running Fence¸whose dual purpose is the ghet-toization of Palestinians and further landgrab; already it is forcing people into the bantustans of the largest population centres and off the fertile village lands, which settlements greedily absorb.

The monastery was built by Emperor Manuel I Comnenus around 1160 AD, on the ruins of a fifth-century Byzantine monastery destroyed by an earthquake then. This is said to be where the prophet Elias or Elijah, hungry and thirsty, stopped on his way to Mt. Horeb, when fleeing Jezebel's anger (Kings 19:1-8). There is a rock opposite the monastery venerated by the Greek Orthodox who believe that here an angel brought Elias bread and water; other traditions are also associated with this spot: this is also said to be the site of the tomb of an Egyptian monk who became Patriarch of Jerusalem in 494 AD; another claims it as the burial place of an Orthodox bishop from Bethlehem who died in 1345. Today, the annual Christmas Day procession from Jerusalem to Bethlehem starts here and it is where various Christian Patriarchs pay their respects to the leading families of Bethlehem.

Near the monastery there is a raised stone bench dedicated to the memory of an English painter William Holman Hunt (1827-1910), known for his scenes from the Bible and the life of Jesus leader of the pre-Raphaelite movement, Hunt lived for several years in Palestine, the inspiration for his work.

Jabal Abu Ghneim and the settlement of *Har Homa*

Soon after the signature of the Oslo Accords and the Gaza-Jericho Accord, the State of Israel ordered the confiscation of this land, which belonged to villagers from Beit Sahour and Umm Tuba. The very day Prime Minister Ehud Barak and President of the Palestinian Authority, the late Yasser Arafat met for the first time, on July 12, 1999, Israeli authorities burnt down one of the last forests in the district of Bethlehem to start the construction of a new settlement, thus ignoring three years of protest on the part of Palestinian and international organisations and at the time on the sole understanding that it develop as a joint Israeli-Palestinian housing development. The settlement of *Har Homa* was the final link in the chain of colonies which, together with the ubiquitous Wall, separates Bethlehem from Jerusalem. Since then, building has continued apace. The new apartment buildings will soon house some 30,000 settlers. *Har Homa* plans to develop tourism, especially hotels for tourists interested in local tourism sites, the major attraction being Bethlehem and its holy sites.

❑ The Field of Chick Peas

This pebbly field is on the northeastern outskirts of Mar Elias; its name comes from an ancient legend. Tradition has it that Jesus met a peasant planting chick peas here and asked him what he was sowing. The man retorted sarcastically that he was planting pebbles. So he was told, *"You will reap what you have sown."* Ever since that day, the field has been covered by stones resembling peas. A warning to the sarcastic!

❑ The Tantur Estate

Open Monday -Thursday 8:00-16:00, Friday 8:00-14:00, Saturday 8:00-12: 00, free admission,☎ 02-676 0911, ***www.come.to/tantur***

This property, on the hill next to the Israeli checkpoint separating Jerusalem from Bethlehem, was acquired in the nineteenth century by the Knights of Malta, who founded a hospital here. When Pope Paul VI visited in 1964, the site was transformed into a religious centre: an ecumenical university was inaugurated in 1971; the Israel-Palestine Conflict Resolution Institute (IPCRI) is also based here.

■ Bethlehem

There is evidence that hominids lived in the Bethlehem area dating from the Lower Palaeolithic era. Local springs, particularly al-Ain, near the Church of the Nativity, encouraged habitation and, later, a Canaanite population developed a village here. The first historical mention of the town was in the fourteenth century BC, in one of the Amarna Letters (diplomatic communications from the Canaanite princes to the pharaohs of Egypt); the king of Jerusalem claimed the town, which evidently was seeking to set itself up as a city-state called Beit Lahmu, the name of a protective goddess. Much later, it was mentioned in the Old Testament as Ephrata, where, according to the Bible, ruled King David who was an Ephrathite of Bethlehem-Judah. Bethlehem was subsequently just another ordinary Palestinian village or town until the day when the birth of a child made powerful King Herod tremble; his reign was already threatened by the growing popularity of various messianic religious movements. Only several centuries later did the prophetic message of Jesus become the state religion. After Constantine's Edict of Tolerance in 313 AD, Bethlehem quickly became a popular place for Christian pilgrims; many churches and monasteries were built in the region, and Bethlehem became a prosperous, fortified city, as is shown in the sixth-century Madaba Map. In 638, Caliph Omar Ibn al-Khattab conquered Bethlehem and signed a treaty with Patriarch Sophronius guaranteeing Christians the right to own property, to enjoy freedom of worship and to maintain religious property. With the exception of the periods of Crusader occupation (1099-1187 and 1228-1144), Bethlehem reverted to being a small prosperous market town, continuing to welcome occasional pilgrims, until the nineteenth century. In Crusader times, kings were crowned in Bethlehem, and its unpretentious parish was promoted to the rank of an episcopal seat in 1110 AD, as the town found itself at the heart of the invaders' ambitions.

In the second half of the nineteenth century, colonial powers vied for a foothold in Bethlehem, promoting the establishment of different religious orders here. Bethlehem flourished, but its prosperity was over-dependent on outsiders. The Christian institutions contributed to improvements in health and education in the Palestinian Greek Orthodox and Roman Catholic communities, but these positive initiatives proved to be double-edged: the influence of the mother foundations abroad, particularly in North America, much encouraged emigration. Confronted at close quarters by the injustices of the British colonial system as well as the Zionist threat, the residents of Bethlehem firmly took up the cause of Arab and Palestinian nationalism. In the 1920s and 1930s, the Palestinians of Bethlehem and Beit Jala mounted numerous public campaigns against the British law that repealed citizenship of many Palestinian emigrants but granted citizenship to Jewish immigrants after a mere two years of residence. At the same time, the British cracked down hard on representatives of Bethlehem and its vicinity. In 1938, Issa Bandak, the mayor of Bethlehem since 1935, and co-founder of The Reform Party, was deported by the British

Bethlehem

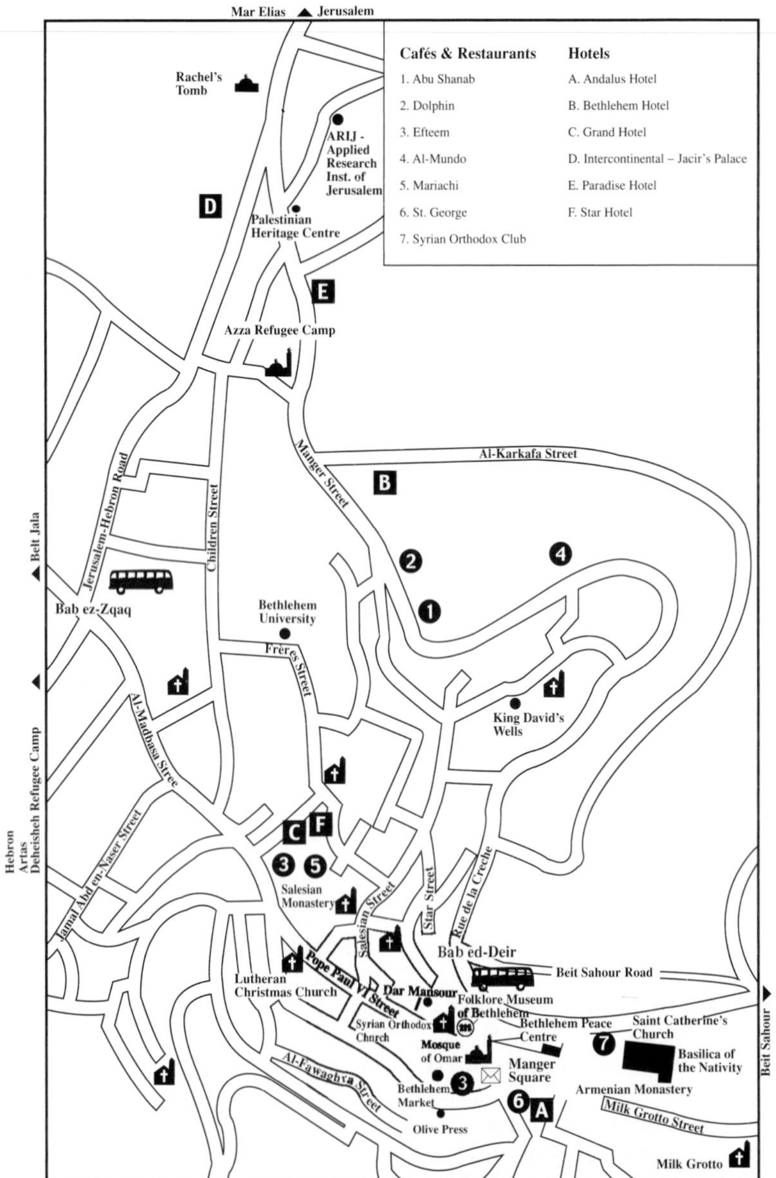

Mar Elias
Jerusalem
Cafés & Restaurants
1. Abu Shanab
2. Dolphin
3. Efteem
4. Al-Mundo
5. Mariachi
6. St. George
7. Syrian Orthodox Club
Hotels
A. Andalus Hotel
B. Bethlehem Hotel
C. Grand Hotel
D. Intercontinental – Jacir's Palace
E. Paradise Hotel
F. Star Hotel
Rachel's Tomb
ARIJ - Applied Research Inst. of Jerusalem
Palestinian Heritage Centre
Azza Refugee Camp
Al-Karkafa Street
Manger Street
Jerusalem-Hebron Road
Children Street
Belt Jala
Bab ez-Zqaq
Bethlehem University
Frères Street
King David's Wells
Al-Madbasa Street
Hebron
Artas
Deheisheh Refugee Camp
Jamal Abd en-Naser Street
Salesian Monastery
Salesian Street
Star Street
Rue de la Creche
Bab ed-Deir
Beit Sahour Road
Lutheran Christmas Church
Pope Paul VI Street
Dar Mansour
Folklore Museum of Bethlehem
Syrian Orthodox Church
Bethlehem Peace Centre
Saint Catherine's Church
Mosque of Omar
Manger Square
Basilica of the Nativity
Al-Fawaghra Street
Bethlehem Market
Olive Press
Armenian Monastery
Milk Grotto Street
Milk Grotto
Beit Sahour

occupation authorities. In Deheisheh, a suburb of Bethlehem, one of the last armed victories over the Zionist movement and its military forces took place on March 27, 1948. In that battle, 25 Jewish settlers were killed, 149 others were evacuated by British forces and 22 vehicles were destroyed. Bethlehem subsequently became a sanctuary for countless Palestinian refugees expelled from their villages. Population figures rose from 9,000 to nearly 20,000, while an additional 40,000 refugees stayed temporarily in Bethlehem on their way into exile.

The town today

Clinging to a rocky spur, Bethlehem dominates a vast hinterland, some of which is desert. To the east, arid hillsides plunge steeply into the Jordan Valley. In the distance, the horizon is formed by the high Jordanian plateau. Bethlehem (27,000 residents) constitutes, together with the towns of Beit Sahour (to the east) and Beit Jala (to the west) and the three refugee camps, Aida, Beit Jibrin or 'Azza, and Deheisheh, an agglomeration of over 61,000 people. The Bethlehem district, encompassing the surrounding villages, numbers over 136,000 people. Dominated by minarets and bell towers, the city affirms its religious diversity: it has a Muslim majority (65%) and a strong Christian minority (35%). Almost every Christian community is represented: Greek Orthodox, Roman Catholic (Latin), Armenian, Lutheran and Syrian, all sharing the same Arab Palestinian culture. The local economy is heavily dependent on tourism, which employs up to 20% of the working population. Since the Second Intifada, this tourism has been badly hit and the Wall and surrounding checkpoints imprison Bethlehem, Beit Sahour and Beit Jala.

❑ Rachel's Tomb

Jerusalem-Hebron Road. Open Sunday -Thursday 7:30-16:00. Friday 7:30-13:30.

A long high wall with watchtowers rising at each end guards the main road here. This is an Israeli military post and new Israeli settlement and yeshiva, previously in the Palestinian autonomous Area A, under full Palestinian Authority control according to the Oslo Accords but recently annexed to Israel: the Palestinian checkpoint lies past it (the Wall and checkpoint before it) on the Bethlehem side of the road. Behind the wall is an ancient *maqam* dedicated to Rachel. Tradition has it that Rachel died in childbirth here while en route to Hebron. *"And Rachel died, and was buried in the way to Ephrath, which is Bethlehem. And Jacob set a pillar upon her grave: that is the pillar of Rachel's grave unto this day."* (Genesis 35:19-20). There was a pyramid-shaped mausoleum here in the Byzantine period and at the beginning of the Islamic period. The Crusaders also left their mark. The present-day building was constructed during the Ottoman period. In 1841, an Anglo-Jewish philanthropist, Sir Moses Montefiore, financed the rebuilding of the dome as well as the addition of a vestibule with a *mihrab*. Montefiore's generous gesture was intended to mollify the Muslim community, for whom the site was of major importance (housing both a mosque and a Muslim cemetery), and who did not take kindly to the crowds of Jewish pilgrims who habitually disturbed their ceremonies. Venerated by Muslims, Christians and Jews, the shrine was until 1977 an Islamic property administered by the Department of Islamic Affairs *(waqf)* and accessible to all. At the end of 1995, shortly before the withdrawal of the Israeli army from Bethlehem, an Israeli military camp was set up on the other side of the street, and the wall and its watchtowers were built. In 1998, the dome and the vestibule were destroyed. Since, the maqam and the Bilal Ibn Rabah mosque have been made inaccessible to Palestinians. Foreigners may enter if they honour the exclusively Jewish nature of the shrine by wearing a skullcap. The annexation of this area to Jerusalem, proposed in 2002 by then Mayor of Jerusalem, Ehud Olmert, has now been finalised: a huge wall of 9 metres height has surrounded the Rachel's Tomb complex, attaching it to Jerusalem. A national border is almost finished at the new checkpoint and Dr. Irving Moskowitz has funded the purchase of surrounding buildings; there is now a yeshiva in the basement of the shrine. The road is controlled by the Israeli army, which frequently resorts to force; in the early days of the al-Aqsa Intifada, snipers on the roof of Rachel's Tomb shot and killed local children.

❑ The Palestinian Heritage Centre

At the crossroads of Manger and Caritas streets. Open Monday-Saturday, 9:00-21:00, free admission;☎ 02 274 2381. One can arrange a display of traditional costumes.

At the entry to Bethlehem, the centre has a small museum *(one may try on traditional Palestinian clothing)*, and a gift shop with extremely beautiful embroidery work, among other products. Proprietress Maha Saca, an embroidery expert, will gladly present her collection.

Al -Azza or Beit Jibrin Refugee Camp

The 'Azza refugee camp is straight ahead, approximately 200 metres beyond the Palestinian military post at the entry to Area A, on the Jerusalem-Hebron road.

The typical architecture of a refugee camp - concrete buildings closely packed together - distinguishes this camp from the surrounding residential areas. With 1,700 inhabitants, 'Azza refugee camp is the smallest of all refugee camps. Most residents are originally from Beit Jibrin. Remains of a Roman aqueduct, whose excavation has revealed inscriptions dating it to 195 AD, may be seen under the foundations of houses which border on the camp.

❑ Applied Research Institute of Jerusalem

Caritas Street ☎ 02-2741889 www.arij.org

The website is a superb source of information covering aspects of the Occupation.

❑ Bethlehem University

University Road.☎ 02-274 1241/6 www.bethlehem.edu

Founded in 1973 by Pope Paul VI, Bethlehem University was created to give all young people from the south of the West Bank, both Muslim and Christian, the opportunity to pursue higher education in their region, and to minimise Christian emigration. Michel Sabbah, the current Catholic Patriarch of Jerusalem, has directed the university for some years; it has over 2,000 students and offers a wide choice of studies: Fine Arts, Sciences, Education, Business, Nursing (especially midwifery), Tourism, and so on. The creation of Bethlehem University answered a longstanding problem: since the mid-nineteenth century, European religious communities recently established in Palestine had founded educational institutions primarily for Christians. The development of this education was, however, also intended to facilitate emigration of these young Christians, in search of El Dorado in Europe or Latin America. In the early twentieth century, Palestinian Christians represented over 20% of the population; today they represent only 2-3%, although they have an inordinately large influence on Palestinian society (some 30% of all Palestinian health institutions are Christian funded and run, as an example of this trend). The British Mandate and subsequent development and victory of the Zionist movement (together with its consequences) contributed much to the Christian community's diaspora; indeed, since the outbreak of the al-Aqsa Intifada, some 200,000 Palestinians have emigrated, many of them Christians. By making it possible for young Palestinians to pursue higher education in Palestine, Bethlehem University proved to be an excellent means of stemming the emigration of qualified citizens.

■ The Old City

Pope Paul VI Street, which starts at Bab ez-Zqaq taxi station, leads down to Manger Square in the heart of the Old City. The numerous convents and churches built by European religious congregations have firmly marked the urban

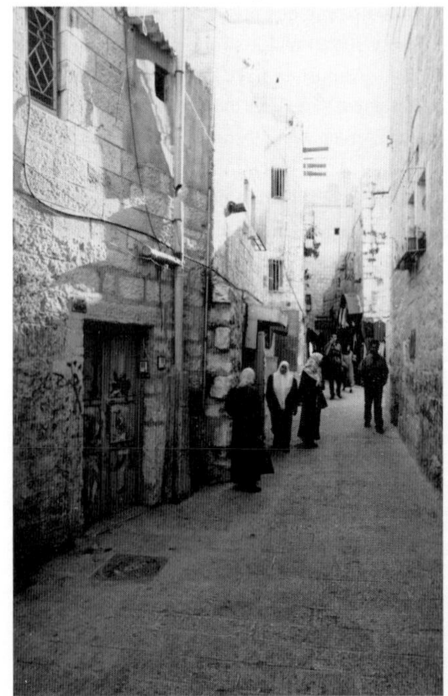

landscape, but Bethlehem is above all an oriental city. The neighbourhoods around Paul VI, Star and Farahiya streets offer visitors a model of Arab architecture typical of the Ottoman era.

Dar Mansour, the "House of Mansour" *(Star Street)*, is a good example of the architectural style of bourgeois homes at the end of the nineteenth century. Following the line of the hill ridge, the streets converge on Manger Square. Contrasting with the activity of the town's main arteries, the sleepy narrow side streets run between houses arranged in close clusters on the steep slopes around the Old City. Most of these alleyways have stone stairs that are sometimes overhung by passageways in order to connect two dwellings belonging to the same family. During the First Intifada, Israeli forces blocked many of the tiny streets with piles of metal barrels cemented together to ensure military control of the Old City. These traces of Israeli occupation, in the very heart of the city, were erased by recent restoration of the old quarters of the city. One of the distinctive features of the houses in Bethlehem is their orientation. They almost always face the scenery and the valley; despite the fact that the houses are arranged around a closed space, the traditional interior courtyard often has a *liwan* (a vaulted living room open on one side) looking out over the cultivated land. The tremendous variety of architectural openings, doors, windows and the *liwan* greatly adds to the picturesque charm of old Bethlehem.

❑ The Salesian Convent and Church

Salesian Street, ☎ *02-2742421*

This convent was built between 1872 and 1892, on the initiative of an Italian priest, Antonio Balloni. He arrived in Bethlehem shortly after a terrible cholera epidemic had struck the region, leaving many orphans. Balloni collected the funds he needed by selling religious articles made of olive wood, a standard means of money-raising resorted to by many religious foundations in Bethlehem. To this day, the church has an orphanage as well as a technical school.

❑ The Lutheran Christmas Church

Paul VI Street. Open 9:00-16:00; ☎ *02-277 0047; workshop and handicrafts shop (glassware and pottery)*

This church was built thanks to an endowment from the Empress Augusta Victoria to Lutheran Pastor Ludwig Schneller in 1886. It has served the Bethlehem Lutheran congregation since 1854.

❑ The Syrian Orthodox Church

Paul VI Street. Opening hours 9:00-17:00; ☎ *02-274 4757 (Father Yacoub Isa'ac).*

Built in 1955, this church is also known as the Church of the Virgin. Without doubt, the best time to visit is Sunday morning *(9:00)* for the weekly mass celebrated in Syrian.

❑ **The Green Market** has existed since 1929 on the square opposite the Syrian Orthodox Church. Tradesmen and farmers from the Bethlehem area and even Hebron come here to sell their fresh produce. This picturesque spot was renovated in 1999 as part of the Bethlehem 2000 project.

❑ **The Olive Press Museum** The olive press *(al-Najajra Street)* is the property of the Giacaman family. It is the only press conserved in the Old City and dates back to 1792. It is a reminder of the all-importance of the olive tree in the life of Bethlehem and of Palestine as a whole.

❑ The Old Bethlehem Museum

Off Paul VI Street on Star Street, near Manger Square. Open Monday-Saturday 10:00-17:00, NIS8, ☎ *02-274 2589, www.arabwomenunion.org, bawu8@hotmail.com. Embroidery made and sold here.*

A museum dedicated to the arts and popular traditions, the Bethlehem Museum is located in a traditional house dating to the seventeenth century. Inside, the rooms recreate a typical home at the end of the nineteenth century, with a reception room, kitchen, *taboun* (oven) and other artefacts typical of that time. The museum also has a beautiful collection of traditional embroidery and costumes; photographs of Palestine during the 1920s and 1930s complete the collection. **The Embroidery Centre** on the first floor was created in 1971 by the ***Bethlehem Arab Women's Union***; for gifts: its standard is exquisite yet inexpensive.

❑ The Mosque of Omar

At the corner of Paul VI Street and Manger Square

This mosque was built in honour of the second Caliph, Omar Ibn al-Khattab. A companion of the Prophet Mohammed and his father-in-law, he

Bethlehem

entered Bethlehem after taking Jerusalem and prayed in the southern aisle of the Basilica of the Nativity. However, he guaranteed that the Basilica would remain a Christian place of worship in the Pact of Omar, which stipulated that Muslims would be allowed to pray here only individually and which prohibited calling for prayer *(al-Adan)* from the church walls. In fact, the Muslim community in Bethlehem developed rather late, and the need for a place of worship of its own was not felt until the nineteenth century. The Muslim quarter in the city was destroyed by the Egyptian troops of Ibrahim Pasha in 1834.

The land on which the Mosque of Omar was built in 1860 was a gift to the Muslim community from the Greek Orthodox Church. It is the only mosque in the Old City of Bethlehem; it was enlarged in 1954 to answer the needs of the Muslim refugees exiled in 1948. At that time, many Christian families left their run-down traditional houses in the town centre to live in new homes on the outskirts of Bethlehem. Palestinian refugees who had been expelled from coastal towns or the central region (Beit Jibrin, Jaffa) rented these old homes.

❑ Manger Square

Bab ez-Zqaq to Manger Square in a private taxi (NIS 7).

This vast esplanade between the Mosque of Omar and the Church of the Nativity constitutes the tourist centre of Bethlehem. The square as well as much of the Old City underwent renovation from 1998 to 2000. Many events throughout the year take place here, culminating in Christmas Eve, or eves, since the birth of Jesus is celebrated three times: on December 25 by Catholics, January 7 by the Orthodox, and January 19 by Armenians. There are frequent cultural exhibitions, concerts and conferences at the **Bethlehem Peace Centre** at the square *(☎ 02-276 6677 www.peacecenter.org)* and at the nearby **International Centre of Bethlehem** *(www.annadwa.org: ☎ 02-2770047)* just off the square, housing the **Al-Kahf Gallery** and the **Dar Annadwa Arts & Crafts Centre** *(open daily except Sunday 9:30-19:00)* which are well worth a visit: indeed, at a time when Bethlehem is under such threat and siege, international and local art flourishes here, despite all. The **Tourism Office** (☎ 02-276 6677) and a bookshop (most books in English) also selling some souvenirs are on the ground floor of the peace centre.

X

SEGREGATION OF THE WEST BANK, February 2005

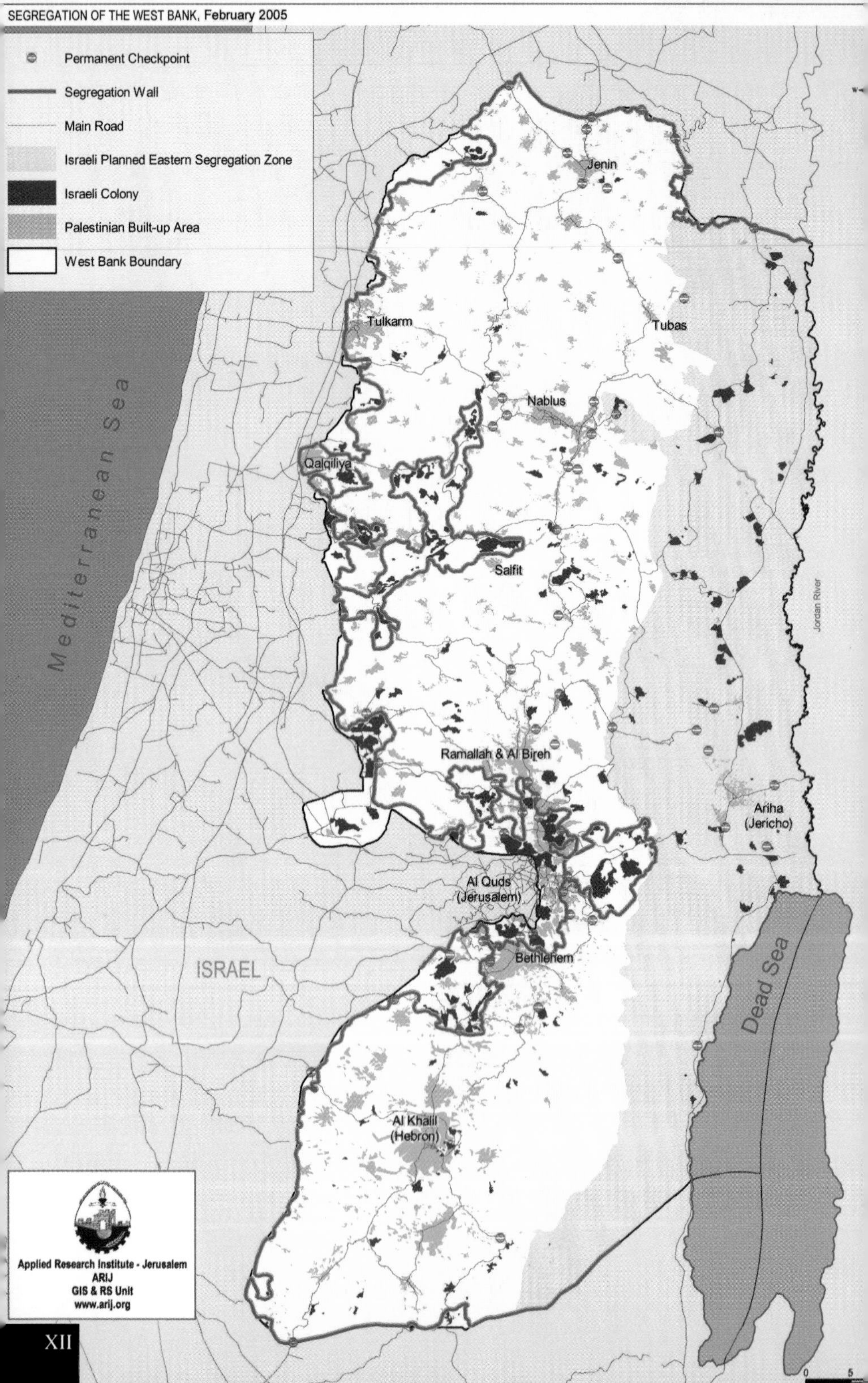
Permanent Checkpoint
Segregation Wall
Main Road
Israeli Planned Eastern Segregation Zone
Israeli Colony
Palestinian Built-up Area
West Bank Boundary
Jenin
Tulkarm
Tubas
Mediterranean Sea
Nablus
Qalqiliya
Salfit
Jordan River
Ramallah & Al Bireh
Ariha
(Jericho)
Al Quds
(Jerusalem)
Bethlehem
ISRAEL
Dead Sea
Al Khalil
(Hebron)
Applied Research Institute - Jerusalem
ARIJ
GIS & RS Unit
www.arij.org
0
5

■ The Basilica of the Nativity

Open daily 5:00-19:30, 18:30 in winter; free admission; ☎ *02-274 2425*

The Church of the Nativity, and the religious buildings around it, make an imposing, austere monument. In the second century AD, in the reign of Emperor Hadrian, this was a place consecrated to the cult of Adonis. To efface all pagan practice, Emperor Constantine, a convert to Christianity, built the basilica, a rare example of the religious architecture of that great era. Helena Augusta, mother of the emperor, personally supervised the first work in 326, while on pilgrimage to the Holy Land. The basilica was consecrated in 339 and subsequently underwent many substantial modifications.

Built in the imperial style, the square basilica fronted onto a spacious courtyard *(atrium)*, designed to accommodate large crowds of worshippers. The main body of the church consisted of a central nave (9m), surrounded by four large lateral aisles. The octagonal apse, of which only the base remains, was imposed over the Grotto of the Nativity. The fourth-century **mosaic floor** was discovered in 1934 under the level of the present-day floor *(it may be seen through the wooden props that protect it)*. The mosaics are rich in variety: decorative borders of interlaced

Basilica of the Nativity

Paintings on the Pillars

1. The Crucifixion
2. Saint John the Apostle
3. Virgin and Child
4. Saint Catald
5. Saint Cosma
6. Saint Damien
7. Saint Leonard [from Limoges]
8. Saint George
9. Saint Euthymius
10. Saint Antony
11. Saint Macarius the Great
12. Saint Margaret
13. Saint Fosca
14. Saint Onophrius
15. The Prophet Elias
16. Saint John the Baptist
17. Saint Vincent
18. Saint Olaf
19. Saint Canute
20. Saint Stephen [the first Christian martyr]
21. Saint Sabas
22. Saint Theodosius
23. Virgin and Child
24. Saint Margaret (Saint Marina)
25. Saint Leo the Great (Pope from 440 to 461). He established the orthodox doctrine at the Ecumenical Council of Chalcedon in 451.
26. Saint Anne, the mother of Mary
27. Saint Blaise
28. Virgin and Child
29. Saint Bartholomew
30. Saint James the Great

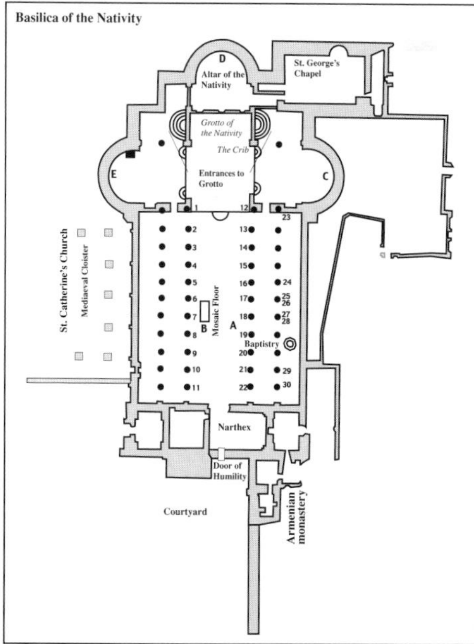

Mosaics on the Walls (from the middle of the twelfth century)

A. Genealogy of Jesus as recounted by Saint Matthew the Apostle. Above this, the ecumenical councils of Nicaea (325), Constantinople (3981), Ephesus, (431), Chalcedon (451), Constantinople (680), and Nicaea (787).

B. Genealogy of Jesus as recorded by Saint Luke the Apostle. Above this, the councils of Ancyrus (314), Antioch (272), Sarde (347), Gangrus (fourth century), Laodicius (fourth century) and Carthage (254).

C. The triumphal entry into Jerusalem.

D. Knot-work designs. Date of restoration work (1169).

E. Doubting Thomas (the Apostle). The Ascension.

garlands and leaves, floral motifs featuring vines, flowers and fruit and representations of animals (a rooster and a partridge) as well.
In the aftermath of the Samaritan revolt in 529, in which the church was destroyed, Byzantine Emperor Justinian (527-565) had it rebuilt and enlarged, to make it the most beautiful church in the Holy Land, and similar to the Church of Saint Helena in Constantinople. In order to show respect to the original design, the **huge colonnades** of polished red limestone streaked with white (a local stone, quarried in Bethlehem), and their capitals, were restored to their place. The new edifice has survived over the centuries.
Justinian lengthened the Basilica by adding a *narthex* and the octagonal apse was replaced by a vast apse with large transepts on both sides (46m wide). The main door of the original entranceway (originally there were three) is still visible, framing the **Crusader gate** and the **Door of Humility**, the entrance used today, dating to Ottoman times. A chronicler relates that the Emperor, unhappy with the new basilica, which he had imagined as more majestic and well-lit, had the architect beheaded.
In 614, the basilica miraculously escaped the Sassanian invasion which ravaged Palestine. The Persians spared the church when their eyes fell on the scene of the Adoration of the Magi, dressed as Persians and wearing pointed Phrygian caps, said to be worn by the Persian god Mithra, which commanded their respect and clemency.
Although Caliph Omar Ibn al-Khattab had promised his protection to the basilica, fights between the oriental and occidental churches for control of the church became more and more serious after the Schism of 1054.
During the Crusader era, the basilica became a coveted shrine. The Frankish kings were crowned here (Baldwin I in 1101, Baldwin II in 1122) following in the footsteps of King David. To choose Jerusalem for their coronation - Jerusalem, where Jesus Christ was made to wear a crown of thorns - was outright sacrilege! Between 1165 and 1169, Franks and Greeks renovated the Church of the Nativity and built a high wall around it, giving the complex its fortress-like appearance. The construction work between 1165 and 1168 was ordered by Manuel I Comnenus, Emperor of Constantinople, Amalric, King of Jerusalem at that time and Ralph, the Latin Patriarch of Bethlehem. This joint Byzantine-Latin venture accounts for the mixed decorative character of the church, where both influences are visible. The building was inlaid with cedar wood and lead, and new pavements of marble. The **columns** were repainted with murals representing saints, churches and inscriptions, some in Greek, others in Latin, while new **polychrome mosaics** on a golden background *(along the central nave)*, depict the genealogy of Jesus Christ and the essential decrees establishing the theological and doctrinal foundations of Christian dogma, as well as the heresies they opposed. After the victory of Saladin over the Crusader army (1187), the Orthodox again took control of the Grotto and the basilica. There followed a period where keys to both changed hands frequently, at the beck and call of political intrigues and power struggles. In the succeeding centuries, the basilica progressively fell into disrepair despite attempts to maintain it. The main entrance was modified during the Ottoman period, to end the habit of soldiers who rode horses into the church. The Door of Humility is so low (120 cm) that it forces anyone who enters to bend over in order to enter the holy place. The roof was repaired in sturdy English oak by King Edward IV of England, a sign of the high regard in which the basilica was held by Christianity in the West.

■ The Grotto of the Nativity

Two stairways on either side of the altar lead to a crypt venerated as the place of Jesus' birth. A **fourteen-pointed silver star**, a gift from France in 1717, is embedded in the holy floor here and bears this inscription: *Hic de virgine Maria Jesus Christus natus est. (Here Jesus Christ was born of the Virgin Mary.)* Fourteen represents the number of generations separating Adam from Abraham, Abraham from King David, King David from the exile in Babylon, and the Babylonian exile from the birth of Christ (Matthew 1:17). Fifteen lanterns are kept burning around the clock in the crypt (six belong to the Greek Orthodox, five to the Armenians and four to the Catholics).

In another corner of the grotto, the Chapel of the Manger replicates the crib scene; the Altar of the Adoration of the Magi in a chapel facing it commemorates the visit of the Three Kings. Nineteenth-century tapestries on the walls here depict the birth of Jesus. Although the grotto is a place sacred to all Christians, it has been the object of bitter dispute between the different Christian communities. In 1847, the star was stolen, and the Sultan in Istanbul was asked to arbitrate: he chose to freeze the controversies with a *Status quo*, recognising the existing allocation of space and customs of the three religious communities then represented in the grotto. This decision satisfied no one - neither France, "the custodian of the holy places", nor Tsarist Russia, which demanded recognition as protector of all Orthodox subjects in the Ottoman Empire. The star was replaced by a copy. However, prolonged disagreement over custody of these holy places even served as pretext for hostilities between the great imperialist powers which led to the Crimean War of 1853-1856, with England, France and Turkey opposing Russia.

Today, the *Status quo* still holds. It itemises minute details which must be respected regarding ownership of each square metre, the walls and religious objects as well as hours of opening and various ceremonies, the organisation of feast day celebrations and other observances. The Orthodox, Armenian and Catholic communities must all agree on restoration plans. Needless to say, restoration work is extremely rare.

The Christmas Crib

Veneration of the birthplace of Jesus and various representations of it date back to the first centuries of Christianity. Near the end of the fourth century, Saint Jerome expressed regret that the authentic, modest clay crib had been replaced by a silver one. Since then, the mystery of the birth of Christ has become an international tradition with countless versions. The palm tree is at the heart of local Palestinian Muslim and Christian tradition: *"And the pains of childbirth drove her to the trunk of a palm-tree: (...) The child which was found at her feet spoke to her: 'Grieve not! For the Lord Hath provided a rivulet beneath thee; and shake towards thyself the trunk of the palm-tree: it will let fall fresh ripe dates upon thee. So eat and drink and cool (thine) eye.'"* (Quran, Maryam 23-26) In Bethlehem, the theme of the crib inspires many delicate, dynamic handicrafts in olive wood and mother of pearl. Thus it comes as no surprise that the late President Yasser Arafat would give privileged guests mother-of-pearl replicas of the Crib of Bethlehem (Bethlehem 2000) and the Dome of the Rock.

■ Saint Catherine's Church

Open: Monday-Saturday 5:00-12:00 and 14:00-19:30, Sunday 14:00-19:30.☎ 02-274 2425

In 1212, disciples of Saint Francis of Assisi, whose vows dedicated him to a life modelled on the life of Christ, took up residence in Bethlehem. They established their convent next to the Church of the Nativity. The convent and the Church of the Nativity were placed under their jurisdiction and care from the fourteenth century on (1347-1634 and 1690-1757). In 1757, their custodianship of the holy places was revoked in favour of the Greek Orthodox Church.

A small door in the lateral wall of the Church of the Nativity allows access to the Franciscan cloister, in the middle of which stands a **statue of Saint Jerome (Jeremy) and from there to Saint Catherine's Church,** built in 1881. The **mediaeval cloister** is the oldest part of the Franciscan convent, built in Crusader times on ruins of the Byzantine convent of the enclosed Franciscan nuns of Saint Paula. The convent was renovated in 1947 by Italian architect Antonio Barluzzi.

Since then, the Church has become world

famous for its Christmas Eve midnight mass, televised all over the world. The Church has three small chapels dedicated to Saint Francis, Saint Antony, and the Immaculate Conception of Mary. Every year at Christmas, the Baby Jesus in the Chapel of the Immaculate Conception is carried in a procession to the grotto of the Church of the Nativity, from the altar of the chapel. A stairway near the altar leads to an underground complex whose oldest room dates back to the fourth century. There is a side altar commemorating the dream Joseph had telling him to depart with his family for Egypt (Matthew 2:13) to escape the massacre of the infants ordered by Herod (Matthew 2:16-17). In the same chamber, a chapel is dedicated to the Holy Innocents, all the children under two years of age slaughtered by Herod. Further along is the altar of St. Eusebius, and tombs of St. Paula, her daughter St. Eustochium and St. Jerome. The underground complex ends in a room believed to have been St. Jerome's office.

Saint Jerome and the lion

One evening Saint Jerome and his companions were listening to a reading from the Scripture, when a limping lion suddenly entered the monastery in Bethlehem. Everybody ran away in fear; only Jerome faced the lion. He examined its wounded paw and called his companions back to ask them to take care of the injured paw of the lion. They did so. The lion recovered and lived with the community as a tame pet and the protector of Saint Jerome.

Saint Jerome

A native of Dalmatia, he was educated in Rome; Saint Jerome (347 - 420) or Hieronymus, an ascetic of Egyptian origin, settled in Palestine in 385. He was accompanied by two wealthy patricians, Paula and her daughter Eustochium. Paula founded a convent of women, while Jerome established a monastery said to have been on the site of the present Franciscan monastery. At the request of Pope Damasus I, Saint Jerome gladly made a translation of the Bible. The Latin version of the Bible, which existed until then, was a translation of the Greek version. St. Jerome translated most of the books of the Old Testament directly from the Hebrew and the Greek version of the New Testament. This version, called the Vulgate, was formally authenticated in 1546 until the second Vatican Council (1962-1965).

▪ The Armenian Monastery

On the other side of the Door of Humility, a second door on the right leads to the monastery, built on the Byzantine ruins identified as the *atrium* of Justinian. The columns of the *atrium* are still visible on the facade. Today, only six Armenian monks live here and tend to Bethlehem's small Armenian community (approximately 300 people). They are heirs to the monastic order which flourished in the seventeenth-century, a period during which the community specialised in transcribing and illustrating the Bible.

▪ Around the Basilica of the Nativity

❑ The Milk Grotto

Milk Grotto Street. Open every day 8:00-11:00, 14:00 - 18:00; free admission.

A chapel built by the Franciscans in 1872 houses the Milk Grotto, venerated by all Palestinians, both Christian and Muslim. It is said that the Holy Family made a stop here on their flight to Egypt so that Mary could nurse the baby Jesus. While he was nursing, a few drops of his mother's milk fell on the ground and turned the red rock white. Since, women of both faiths have come here to pray, especially those who have a fertility problem or a shortage of milk for breastfeeding. They must only, after praying, chip off a little piece of the chalky rock and swallow it.

❑ David's Wells

Star Street. Open every day 7:00-12:00, 14:00-19:00; free admission.

At the end of Star Street are three wells called Bir Daoud, or "David's Wells," whose water runs into a large cistern (14m x 4m). Tradition thought to be from Byzantine times associates the place, as is customary, to a biblical episode that illustrates how essential control over water supplies was during battles and sieges. David, parched with thirst, asked for water from this well, which belonged to the Philistines. Three men risked their lives to bring the water to him; but David would not touch it when he realised that he had endangered the lives of his men, instead, he offered it as a libation to his God (2 Samuel 23: 14-17). Archaeologists have brought to light the nearby church, built in the time of Justinian. Pilgrims in the sixth and seventh centuries are said to have identified in the crypt underneath this church the sepulchres of King David and King Solomon.

Practical Information

The Bab ez-Zqaq Square is the departure point and terminus of most transport lines, whether bus or service taxi. Service taxicabs to Jerusalem cost NIS 3, NIS 6 to Hebron, NIS 1.5 to al-Khader and NIS 1.5 to Beit Jala. A minibus regularly goes to Bab ed-Deir, at the foot of Manger Square, to Beit Sahour (NIS2), Obeidiya (NIS3) and Za'atara (NIS3). The journey to Beit Sahour is more expensive in a private taxi, between NIS10-15. It is easy to find a return service taxicab (NIS 2).

All basic public services are located near each other, in the perimeter of Manger Square or nearby. The **Tourism Office** *(☎ 02-276 6677)* is located on the ground floor of the **Bethlehem Peace Centre**. For information on events at Christmas, ask here. A post office, the town hall, and banks and moneychangers are also located in the city centre near Manger Square.

Cafes and Restaurants

There are many restaurants on Paul VI Street, in the Old City, and on Manger Street. Except for some popular restaurants, prices are in general higher than those in the neighbouring towns of Beit Sahour and Beit Jala. Manger Street offers a wide range of restaurants. Despite its modest appearance, the **Abu Shenab Restaurant** *(☎ 02-274 2895)* is a good place for classic dishes such as *mezzeh* or grilled meat, and the service is excellent. The two **Efteem** restaurants *(Madbasa Street; ☎ 02-277 0157* and *Manger Square; ☎ 02 274 7940)* have been reputed in the city for more than 40 years for their superb felafels. The **Dolphin** restaurant *(☎ 02-274 3437)* specialises in quality fish and shellfish. **Al-Mundo** Restaurant *(☎ 02-274 2949)* is recommended for pizza. In the **Grand Bandak Hotel** *(Madbasa Street)* **Mariachi Restaurant** *(☎ 02-274 1440)* serves Mexican food. In the Old City, the **St George** *(Manger Square;☎ 02-274 3780)* serves gourmet cooking, but is expensive. More originally, the **Syrian Orthodox Club** *(Syrian Church Street;☎ 02-274 2805)*, features traditional cooking such as *musakhan* and an original lamb's head soup.

Accommodation

Bethlehem is the second most popular destination in Palestine after Jerusalem, and there are many hotels and guesthouses here. While the majority of these hotels tend to lack any originality in decor, the services and facilities usually meet high standards. This criticism does not include the **Intercontinental - Jacir Palace** *(Jerusalem-Hebron Road; ☎ 02-276 6777, www.intercontinental.com ; single, double and triple rooms $180, $230, and $270)*. This luxury hotel was developed around a manor built in 1910 and thereafter by a wealthy Bethlehem family who returned to Bethlehem having originally emigrated from there. It served successively as the headquarters for the British Army (1935), as a hospital, a school for boys and finally as a school for girls, before being enlarged and converted into a hotel. Those who prefer to spend some time in the hotel without staying overnight may choose either of two elegant restaurants, or simply stop for a drink at the **al-Makan** bar *(open 14:00–midnight; very expensive)* in the old *riwaq* (cloister) or smoke a cigar in the space reserved for this. For those with a smaller budget, the **Paradise Hotel** *(Manger Street, opposite the 'Azza Refugee Camp; paradise@p-ol.com, ☎ 02-274 4542; single, double and triple rooms for $35, $55, and $70)* despite its impersonal style, is 15 minutes on foot from Manger Square and one of the cheapest hotels. [The hotel has recently been renovated after being completely burnt down by the Israeli army in November 2001.] The advantage of the **Bethlehem Hotel** *(Manger Street; bhotel@p-ol.com; ☎ 02-277 0702; single, double and triple rooms for $50, $75, and $ 90)* is its location in a street with many cafés and restaurants. It is a popular place for large groups of American tourists. Perched on the top of a hill, the **Bethlehem Star Hotel** *(University St.; htstar@hally.net; ☎ 02-274 3249; single, double, and triple rooms for $40, $55, and $70)*, with its restaurant located on the roof, has a superb view of Bethlehem, especially on its eastern hills. Further down the hill is the **Grand Hotel** *(Madbasa St; khalid9933@hotmail.com ☎ 02-274 1602; single double, and triple rooms for $50, $80, and $115, respectively)*. Although it cannot be described as classy, the hotel is close to the market in Bethlehem, and the service is good. The **Andalus Guest House** *(Manger Square; ☎ 02-274 3519[u1]/ 1348; $25 per person)* in the centre of the city is very reasonably-priced, but nights can be noisy. Choose between a room overlooking the square and its night life or one at the back of the building for a quieter evening.

Contacts

Al-Liqa' (Centre for Religious and Heritage Studies in the Holy Land)

(Jerusalem-Hebron Road, ☎ 02-274 1639, email: al-liqa@ p-ol.com; open Monday-Friday 8:00-15:00, Saturday 8:00-14:00).

Founded in 1983 by Palestinian Muslim and Christian community leaders, Al-Liqa' ("the meeting" in Arabic) aims at furthering dialogue between the different religious communities. It organises and participates in frequent conferences and publishes a newspaper in English: *Al-Liqa*' Newspaper focuses on issues such as the Palestinian historical heritage and the religious patrimony of Muslims and Christians.

Citizens' Committees of the Refugee Camps in the Bethlehem District

Contact: Mohammed al-Laham (Abu Khalil) ☎ 0505-619385.

These committees provide visitors with an overall view of the situation of Palestinian refugees; they also organise visits and contacts in Aida, Beit Jibrin and Deheisheh camps to explain the role citizens' committees play in the internal organisation of the camps.

Around Bethlehem

The Deheisheh Refugee Camp

This camp was set up between 1949 and 1950 on land belonging to the Municipality of Bethlehem and rented to UNRWA for 99 years. The camp's refugees (10,000 in 1999) come originally from 30 villages in the region from West Jerusalem to Beit Jibrin. Most of these villages were totally annihilated by the Israelis during the early fifties; some such as Ein Karem were completely re-occupied by Jewish immigrants. In 1967, many people were obliged to flee again to safer areas. In all, nearly a third of the refugees left Deheisheh for Jordan and other Arab states.

With the Israeli occupation of the West Bank, two new words appeared in everyday use: *al-jeish* (the army) and *al-mana 'tajawoul* (curfew). Inaugurated in 1967, curfew became a common practice as of 1976; between 1979 and 1995 (the year in which the camp was placed under the jurisdiction of the Palestinian Authority), the camp was under curfew an average of 3.5 days a month, with a record of 84 consecutive days during the Gulf War. Military patrols, arrests and night raids became a daily practice. Israeli settlers also contributed to the constant harassment of inhabitants here. Rabbi Levinger, founder of the *Kiryat Arba* settlement, who also initiated the Jewish settlement in the heart of the Old City in Hebron, set up an encampment directly opposite Deheisheh which remained for several months under military protection. Deheisheh came under heavy surveillance. During the first Intifada (1987-1993), the Israelis installed a second military camp overlooking the camp and installed a six-metre high fence of barbed wire surrounding the camp. Destroyed each time by camp residents, the wire was then each time replaced and reinforced by the IDF (with no less than three separate parallel barbed wire fences). Thirteen of the fourteen entrances to the camp were barricaded. The metallic turnstile gate which was the main entry to the camp is exhibited today near the **Ibdaa Cultural Centre.**

Sixteen Deheisheh residents were killed during the first Intifada, and hundreds injured; many remain handicapped for life. More than 80% of the young people from Deheisheh were imprisoned for varying periods of time. After the waves of transfer and the occupation of their lands in 1948 and 1967, the refugees organised and developed a culture of resistance. Despite military law imposed on the occupied territories by the Israelis, arms and revolutionary literature were smuggled in, as were cassettes of patriotic songs and the forbidden Palestinian flag circulated clandestinely, fanning the flames of resistance.

As in all refugee camps, basic services are provided by UNRWA *(Hussein Shaheen, ☎ 02-274 2445)*. Deheisheh has two schools for its 1,100 students and one part-time doctor for 11,000 people. UNRWA has a very limited budget for social assistance. The camp also has a **citizens' committee** and the **Ibdaa Cultural Centre**, among the more active such centres. The committee, composed of representatives of all political persuasions, addresses itself to problems inside the camp (organising the distribution of assistance, choosing the poorest families in need of help, development of infrastructure, construction, etc.). In 1996, the committee organized a "telethon" and collected 600 tons of tar and $20,000 to make several asphalt roads in the camp.

The Ibdaa Cultural Centre

☎/fax: 02-277-6444 www.dheisheh-ibdaa.net; hostel rooms for $15 per person.

In Arabic, ibdaa means "creativity." Inaugurated in 1995, the centre offers a wide range of activities (day-care centre, bookshop, Internet centre, oral history project, to name a few) for over 800 children. Ibdaa also owes its reputation to the 60 young people in its famous folk dance troupe. It is a good place to meet foreigners, who come to learn more about the situation of the refugees, their status, rights and claims. The centre has recently started to show documentary or fictional films about Palestine and has an Internet centre ($1 per person), a restaurant and hostel rooms.

❑ Al-Khader Church (Saint George's)

(Jerusalem-Hebron Road, al-Khader Gate; ☎ 02-274 3233, daily 8:00-12:00 and 15:00-19:00. Free entry).

Every year on May 5, there is a pilgrimage to the al-Khader Church, which was built in 1600 AD and rebuilt in 1912. The pilgrimage is in honour of Saint George (in Arabic al-Khader), the soldier monk who slew the dragon; he is venerated for being able to ward off the evil eye. Islamic tradition has it that he left his native Lydda, where he was born, and settled here in this village which bears his name. Muslims and Christians come together annually on this day to celebrate their common protector, to whom many different blessings are attributed. Saint George is also the patron saint of farmers, travellers and the mentally sick. According to popular belief, lunatics were chained to a ring in the walls of the courtyard here in order for them to be delivered from their insanity due to the intervention of Saint George.

Schools under Attack

Since the beginning of the al-Aqsa Intifada, a large part of the land belonging to the **village of al-Khader** has been confiscated, and the inhabitants, particularly the schoolchildren, have been subjected to frequent aggression by the Israeli army. In October 2000 alone (on October 11, 14, 22, 23 and 28), six schools in the Bethlehem district came under fire. Tear gas grenades, rubber bullets (metallic balls covered with rubber) and live ammunition were used. In al-Khader, four of these schools have regularly received such "visits": the Said al-As Primary School for Boys, the primary school for girls, the secondary school for boys and the secondary school for girls.

■ *A Generation Denied*, Defence for Children International- Palestine Section, 2001. Report for September 28 - December 31, 2000

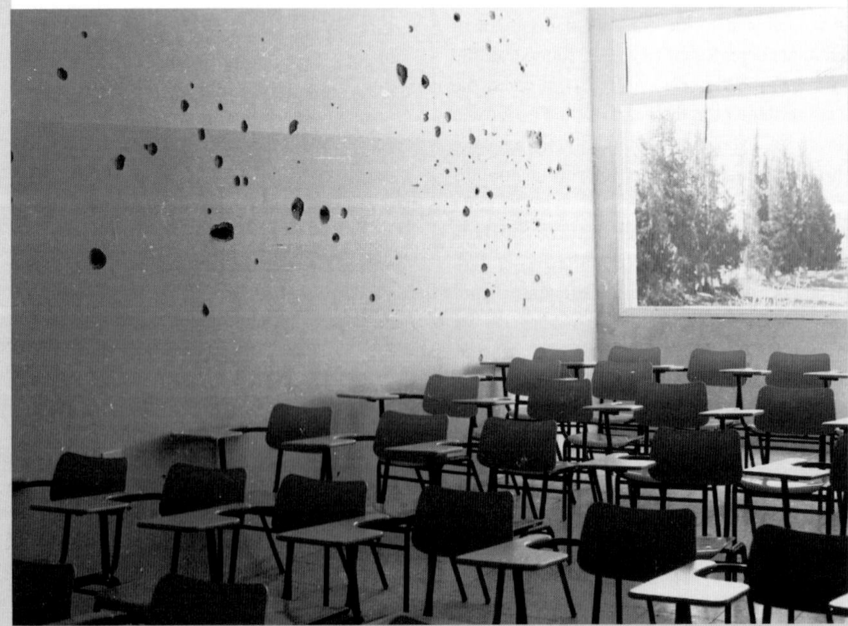

❑ Solomon's Pools

Near the village of al-Khader.

Solomon's Pools, near the top of a valley, are one of the main sights in the area. These three rectangular reservoirs are situated one above the other on a gentle slope. They were part of an ancient water supply system for the city of Jerusalem, dating back to the second or first century BC. Aqueducts linked them to Jerusalem and Herodion, and were still used to irrigate crops in the valley into the early twentieth century! Brooks and rainwater supplied the cisterns with up to 160,000 cu.m. of water. The three ponds measure 116 x 70 x 7m, 129 x 70 x 12m, and 177 x 83 - 45 x 12m. Every army intending to capture Jerusalem - such as the Crusaders in 1099 or Saladin in 1187 - first set up camp here. In the seventeenth century, the Ottomans built the **Qal'at al-Buraq** fortress and *caravanserai* on the site. With its crenellated battlements and a square tower on each corner, this fortress built under Sultan Mourad IV was home to soldiers who guarded the reservoirs and the canal system leading to Jerusalem. The fortress was also the penultimate halt for merchants or pilgrims on their way to the Holy City. Since the outbreak of the al-Aqsa Intifada, this historical site has been partially damaged by heavy Israeli shelling.

❑ Wadi Artas

Wadi Artas is a fine example of the fertility of Palestinian valleys. Its ideal landscape calls to mind the paradise lost, said to have been King Solomon's garden, which was said to have inspired The Song of Songs, or Song of Solomon, in the Old Testament *"A garden inclosed is my sister, my spouse. A spring shut up, a fountain sealed. Thy plants are an orchard of pomegranates, with pleasant fruits;"* (Song of Solomon 4:12-13). The name Artas, more recent, is derived from the Latin hortus, or *"garden."* Nowadays, the **Convent of the Sisters of Our Lady of the Garden** *(☎ 02-274 3622)* and the **Convent Hortus Conclusus** symbolically associate the image of Mary with her virginity and fertility.

As with all villages situated in Area A, there was a chaotic building boom in Artas after Israeli building restrictions were lifted when the area was

Bethlehem

transferred to the jurisdiction of the Palestinian Authority. In this new situation a villager, Musa Sanad, created the Artas Folklore Centre in order to preserve the local rural heritage *(☎/fax 02-276 7467)*. The centre, located just above the mosque, contributes to the preservation of customs and traditional practices, by producing documents on Palestinian culture and collecting archives. The Palestinian Ethnographic Centre *(museum: NIS 12)* is a fascinating part of the project. It is responsible for several old houses, recently renovated, on a site inhabited for thousands of years. In addition to a tour of the homes and museum, the Centre will also serve a traditional Palestinian meal and organise an evening with folk music and dancing *(for a minimum of 10 people)*. The Artas Lettuce Festival takes place every year from March 21 to April 11, featuring Palestinian *dabka* (folk dancing) contests and horse races.

A Stroll in Wadi Artas, from Qal'at al-Buraq to Herodion

Spring is without question the best season for a walk in Wadi Artas, when the scenery is at its greenest and flowers are everywhere. It is an easy three-kilometre walk in the wadi to Solomon's Pools. Between the second and third pool, one finds the old pumping stations first installed by the Germans, and then by the British at the beginning of the last century The road traverses a hill where there are ruins of a Roman village called *Khirbet al-Khoch*, which some think was the biblical village of *Etam*. Herodion is located twelve kilometres away from Artas. The road is not yet indicated, since this impressive architectural ruin is in Area C, but there is little risk of losing one's way as there is always someone to give directions.

Every spring, the centre organises day excursions to al-Buraq and Herodion or half-day excursions to the nearby mountains. *(For details:-Artas Folklore Centre ☎/fax 02-276 7467)*.

Jabra Ibrahim Jabra (1920-1994)

A native son of Bethlehem, Jabra Ibrahim Jabra won an international reputation as a distinguished Palestinian intellectual: novelist, poet, translator of Shakespeare and Faulkner, literary and art critic and painter. Born in Bethlehem, he studied in Bethlehem and Jerusalem. Later, he was a student at the Er-Rashidiya School in Jerusalem. His university studies took him to the Arab College in Jerusalem, Cambridge University and Harvard. After completing a Master's degree in literary criticism, he returned to Palestine to teach English in Jerusalem. In the year of al-Nakba in 1948, Jabra Ibrahim Jabra became a writer-in-exile in Iraq, where he died forty years later. In his lifetime, he received many awards including the Europe Award for Culture (Rome, 1973), the Award of Literature and Arts (Kuwait, 1987), the Literature Award for Stories and Novels (Baghdad 1988), and the Jerusalem Award for Culture and Arts (1990). He wrote some 65 books in Arabic and English, of which thirty are translations; he particularly enjoyed translating English works into Arabic. His own works have been translated into English, French, Spanish, Italian, Slovak and Croatian.

FOOTNOTE

In December 2004, the United Nations Office for the Co-ordination of Humanitarian Affairs (UNOCHA) and the Office of the Special Co-ordinator for the Peace Process in the Middle East (UNSCO) issued a report (available at www.ochaopt.org) entitled "Costs of Conflict: The Changing Face of Bethlehem." It states: "The glory of Bethlehem, a city of historical and religious importance for those of the Christian, Muslim and Jewish faiths alike is vanishing. Surrounded by Israel's Barrier on two sides and restricted roads and roadblocks on the other, urban Bethlehem has become isolated from the rest of the West Bank and most importantly, from Jerusalem." Bethlehem residents talk now of being in a prison. Christians are now less than 2% of the Palestinian population, (30% in 1967, over 40% in 1948). This is the price of occupation, which has slowly caused their "Quiet Transfer" - not due to any inter-Palestinian tension, but solely due to their mobility, as they represent the middle class, intellectual, educated leadership, deliberately forced out by Israel's policies and strategies.

Beit Jala

Beit Jala is one of the three towns which form Greater Bethlehem. It has a population of over 12,000 people: 7,000 Greek Orthodox, 2,500 Roman Catholics, 2,000 Muslims and 500 Protestants. Perched on a hill 930 metres high, Beit Jala was originally surrounded by orchards and vineyards; olives and apricots are the major crops. Beit Jala has lost much of its land to successive Israeli colonisation in the area. Three separate settlements *(Gilo, Har Gilo, and Giv'at Hamatos)* as well as two tunnels and two Israeli by-pass roads solely for settler use (and forbidden for Palestinian use) have been constructed on these agricultural lands. During the Oslo "peace process," the land of Beit Jala municipality was completely divided into various administrative zones. One quarter (25%) of the municipality is in Area A under Palestinian administration. The other 75% of the land is under total Israeli control (Area C) of which 7% has been annexed to Jerusalem. Beit Jala was systematically exposed to shelling by the Israeli army from the *Gilo* settlement, at the beginning of the al-Aqsa Intifada. Many houses were partially or totally destroyed and churches, mosques, schools and private homes suffered serious damage.

Israeli Settlements in Beit Jala

The settlement of *Gilo* was built between 1971-1979 on lands confiscated from Beit Jala and the villages Sharafat and Malha. *Gilo* and its 28,716 inhabitants act as a physical separation between Jerusalem and Bethlehem. The settlement of *Har Gilo* was built in 1976 to the west of Beit Jala, initially as a military base, on more than 350 dunums and then transformed into a civil settlement, following a time-honoured strategy. More than 350 settlers live here in individual houses, excluding any possibility for Beit Jala to expand towards the west; on the contrary, nearby Wallaje is losing its land both to the rapacious Wall and to *Har Gilo* (the same fate as Al Nuaman which is threatened by the Wall, as *Har Homa* tries to expand onto ***its*** land), as is Beit Jala itself losing its farm land in that area. Most houses in the part of Wallaje falling within Jerusalem municipal borders have demolition orders outstanding (after systematic denial of building permits, so Israeli demolition can be attributed to illegal building). The *Giv'at Hamatos* settlement (soon to be enlarged by Israel), visible from Mar Elias Monastery, was built in 1991 on a tract of land (310 dunums) confiscated from the Greek Orthodox Church in Beit Jala. 800 Ethiopian Jewish immigrants live here. The Israeli government plans to build another 3,600 housing units here to settle 99 more dunums of land confiscated from Beit Jala and Beit Safafa. All this expansion will accomplish the final severing of any direct contact between Jerusalem and Bethlehem, whilst ghettoizing Greater Bethlehem, locked in a huge prison, controlled at three checkpoints.

■ Saint Nicolas Church

Nijma Street; ☎ : 02-274 2493.

This church is said to be built on the site of the cave where Saint Nicolas lived. Nicolas was a monk originally from Cappadocia who came to Palestine in the fourth century and later became bishop of Myrrh in Turkey. Patron saint and protector of the town, it is to him that the faithful have addressed their prayers when bullets and missiles have rained down upon the city. He has been immortalised by Benjamin Britten in an oratorio.

■ The Cremisan Salesian Monastery

Cremisan Road; ☎ 02-274 4826/7. A visit to the cellars must be reserved in advance.

The monastery has, since 1925, housed an institute of philosophy and theology which has been affiliated with the Salesian Pontifical University of Rome since 1966. For laymen, Cremisan is above all the name of a famous albeit simple Palestinian wine produced by the Salesian community since 1885. The Cremisan wine cellars use the latest equipment to produce approximately 400,000 litres of wine every year.

Practical Information

Cafes and Restaurants

The Orthodox Club of Beit Jala, *En-Nuzha Street, ☎ 02-274 1935*. This restaurant has traditional family cuisine, with gastronomic Palestinian specialities such as *karshat* (stuffed tripe), *musakhan* (chicken with bread and onion), and *mouloukhiya*, a delicious Palestinian spinach dish.

Accommodation

The Nativity Hotel *(Main Street; ☎ 02-277 0650; nativity@nativity-hotel.com. Single $40, Double $70, and triple $80)* is new, well equipped and ten minutes from the Old City of Bethlehem. On top of Ras Beit Jala hill, the **Everest Hotel** *(☎ 02-274 2604)* was renovated in 1999, but it has been closed since Israeli occupation forces made the immediate area into a military camp.

Contacts

Badil (Resource Centre for Palestinian Residency and Refugee Rights)

Karkafa Street.☎ 02-274 7346, www.badil.org

Badil is a Palestinian community-based organisation that advocates the right of return for Palestinian refugees, providing alternative information and records concerning Palestinians refugees, their status, their claims and their rights. In addition, the centre organises regular awareness campaigns and activities in Palestine, specialising in solidarity visits and study trips to Palestinian villages demolished in 1948.

Environmental Education Centre (Children for the Protection of Nature in Palestine) (EEC)

☎ 02-2765574; eec@p-ol.com; www.eecp.com

The EEC is a leading provider of environmental and educational facilities as well as information on nature conservation issues for a wide base of Palestinian students and researchers through natural history museum with a rich collection of birds as well as a bird-banding station which facilitates constant observation of the endemic bird species as well as migratory birds.

Beit Sahour

Southeast of Bethlehem, Beit Sahour was once a small village of farmers and stone masons. Today it has a population of approximately 12,000. The majority of its inhabitants are middle-class and proud to live in a city that has the highest percentage of university-educated people in Palestine and, in fact, in the entire Arab world. Beit Sahour has the largest Christian population in the West Bank and Gaza Strip: 75% of the residents here are Christian. Many of them have returned to Beit Sahour after education and work experiences abroad, which is not the case in other Palestinian towns with a high percentage of Christian inhabitants. During the first Intifada, the city made a reputation for itself by the creative methods it used to resist Israeli occupation. The inhabitants refused to pay taxes imposed by the occupiers and went on to organise demonstrations, using the slogan (which remains in use): *"No taxation without representation - No taxes without a government."* In retaliation, the Israeli army made large-scale arrests, confiscated many goods and imposed a 45-day curfew.

Beit Sahour's recently renovated city centre is a beautiful example of traditional village architecture. The twinned windows, topped by relieving vaults, are typical of the region. Larger than a village, but not quite a city, Beit Sahour is a pleasant place for a stay and the proximity to Bethlehem is an added advantage.

Ibrahim Ayyad 1910 - 2005

Born in 1910 in Beit Sahour, Ibrahim Ayyad was ordained as a priest in 1937 after studying philosophy, canon law and theology at the Seminary of the Latin Patriarchate in Jerusalem. He was given responsibility for the parish of Ramallah, where he founded the al-Ahliya school. In 1946, he joined the Arab High Committee brigades and in 1948 took part in several battles; accused of participating in the assassination of King Abdullah in 1951, he was arrested and condemned to death by the Jordanian authorities. He owed his reprieve to the Vatican which intervened on his behalf; his death sentence was commuted to exile, which he underwent in Chile. As an active member of Fatah, Ayyad continued to promote the Palestinian cause in Latin America; he was a member of the highest Palestinian governing bodies - the Palestinian National Council, the Central Council and the Executive Council of the PLO. He returned to Palestine in 1996. In 1998, he was awarded the Legion of Honour by the Chilean president and died in 2005, on January 8.

■ The Shepherds' Field

This was the field, north of Beit Sahour, where, according to tradition, the angel appeared to shepherds to announce Jesus' birth (Luke 2:8-14). Many local hills claim to be the site; the Greek Orthodox celebrate the Annunciation at Deir er-Ra'wat; Catholics at Syar al-Ghanam.

Deir er-Ra'wat: consecrated in 1989, the new church was built next to the ruins of a Byzantine monastery; founded *circa* 454 AD by Abbot Marcion, it was devastated by Samaritans in 529 and again by the Persians in 614. The chapel, in a Byzantine cave which honours the tomb of the shepherds, is decorated with magnificent icons and murals. Further north, the **Franciscan Church of the Angels** is built over a cave where a Byzantine monastery, possibly Poimenian, preceded it; the ruins are called **Syar al-Ghanam** (assembly of the flocks). Although the Franciscan foundation dates back to 1859, the church was only built in 1953; designed by Italian architect Barluzzi, it is tent-like in form, to symbolise a shepherds' encampment. The beautiful light inside the church filtering through the translucent cupola is intentionally dazzling, to replicate the light that shone down upon the shepherds.

Practical Information

Cafes and Restaurants

The Shepherds' Valley Tourist Village** (☎ / fax 02-277 3875)* The Shepherds' Valley Tourist Village should be visited both for its atmosphere and its natural setting. It is both a cafe-restaurant *(under a tent)* and a campsite *(tents for groups, $15 per person, sleeping bags available)*. Local Palestinians come here for a drink or a meal, and the food is excellent. Traditional cultural activities (music, *dabke*) are regularly organised. Near the Catholic Church of Syar al-Ghanam, ***Ruth's Field Restaurant (☎ 02-2773505) serves good grilled meat and *shawarma* on its terrace. In the city centre, ***The Double Four Restaurant*** (☎ 0522-206892) is much appreciated by families for its open garden and its cuisine, ***Hakura Restaurant*** serves good grilled meat and chicken (☎ 02-2773335).

Accommodation

Beit Sahour has several different types of convivial, inexpensive accommodation: hotels, guesthouses, campsites or *bed and breakfast*. Two moderately-priced guesthouses are pre-eminent: **Saint Elias Guesthouse,** on a small hill in the south of Beit Sahour *(Oueina Street; ☎ 02-277 3614, fax 02-277 4095; $20 per person, traditional Palestinian meals)* with a very beautiful view, and **The Arab Women's Union** *(Isteih Street, ☎ 02-277 5507, single room $25, traditional Palestinian cooking)*, which donates its earnings to projects run by the association in Beit Sahour.

The Three Kings Hotel *(☎ 02-277 4325, single room $30)* in the centre of Beit Sahour, is a small, comfortable, new hotel near the Bethlehem Road, next to an Internet café. **The Golden Park Resort & Hotel** *(near Shepherds' Field, ☎/fax 02-277 4381, single room $50)* is a modern hotel with an outdoor swimming pool and a classical restaurant, although somewhat outside the city centre.

Bed and Breakfast

The **Alternative Tourism Group (ATG)** *(74, Star Street, ☎ 02-277 2151, fax 02-277 2211, info@atg.ps and www.atg.ps, for bed & breakfast arrangement: half board $25 per person, full board $30. A meal costs $11.)* ATG arranges for meals and/or rooms in private homes in Beit Sahour, Bethlehem, and Beit Jala, which provides a unique opportunity to discover Palestinian hospitality, to get to know a family and to learn about Palestinian Arab culture. Privacy is guaranteed for guests, with a separate entry and private bathroom.

Contacts

Alternative Information Centre (AIC)

Near the Beit Sahour bus station (in the Jadal Centre); ☎ 02-277 5444, www.alternativenews.org; there is another AIC office in West Jerusalem, 4 Shlomzion HaMalka Street ☎ 02-624 1159). Conferences, lectures and organised tours (cost to be agreed by the parties) [See p. 168.]

The Alternative Information Centre was created in 1984 by Israeli and Palestinian activists in order to provide critical information about the political, social and economic realities of the Israeli-Palestinian conflict. It publishes a monthly journal in English: *News from Within*, *Rouya Ukhra*, or "Another Vision," in Arabic, and *Mitsad Sheni* - "From the Other Side" - in Hebrew. It also posts a weekly newsletter on its website. The AIC is a resource centre for institutions as well as for individuals. It co-operates with the Alternative Tourism Group (ATG) based in Beit Sahour, organising specific tours such as on "Greater Jerusalem," "By-pass roads," "The Nakba and the destruction of Palestinian villages," "Problems of the Bedouin in the Negev" or "Palestinians living inside Israel."

□ Alternative Tourism Group (ATG)

74, Star Street, ☎ *02-277 2151, fax 02-277 2211, info@atg.ps,* www.atg.ps

The Alternative Tourism Group specialises in arranging and guiding stays in Palestine. It works closely with the Alternative Information Centre (AIC) and The Israeli Committee Against House Demolitions (see p. 168), offering travel programmes and detailed itineraries designed to give a complete picture of Palestinian realities, past and present: its society, history, culture, land, as well as the Israeli Occupation. The group facilitates contacts with official representatives, citizen committees, trade union leaders and members, religious institutions, social organisations, medical organisations, NGOs, associations, etc. Visitors are encouraged to participate in the individual planning of their stays. Additional trips to places in Jordan may be arranged on request. Visitors may take part in solidarity direct actions to support the Palestinian cause such as the olive harvest, or activities either in a visitor's home country or in Palestine or Israel. ATG sponsors a variety of conferences, for example, on Palestinian literature or the Israeli-Arab conflict or globalisation as it affects Palestine. They organise courses in Arabic for beginners. They are the publishers of this book.

Union of Health Work Committees (UHWC)

Beit Sahour Medical Centre, Dr. Majed Nassar, ☎ *02-277 4444, bsmc@p-ol.com*

The UHWC provides quality health service to all individuals and families, regardless of their economic situation. In 2000, the health committees treated more than 200,000 people in the West Bank, including East Jerusalem, and in the Gaza Strip.

There has been special emphasis on prevention programmes (vaccinations, women's health, school health programmes and decentralised medical centres) and preventative treatments. The Beit Sahour Medical Centre, the diagnostic centre of the UHWC, provides various medical services. Health has been a high priority since the beginning of the al-Aqsa Intifada and the devastating effects of the repression orchestrated by the State of Israel on the entire structure of Palestinian society. As a result of the critical situation, prevention is becoming a questionable priority, albeit a part of the UHWC's double commitment to preventative care and tending the wounded in emergencies.

Casualties and deterioration in health care in al-Aqsa Intifada's first year

- 35,000 Palestinians wounded
- 16 chronically ill Palestinians following therapy (e.g. kidney dialysis, chronic pathology) dead after being refused permission to travel to treatment centre
- 11 Palestinian medical staff killed
- 65 Palestinian medical staff wounded
- 250 cases of violence reported which involved mistreatment of medical staff at Israeli military checkpoints
- 34 instances of hospitals or clinics being targeted by gunfire or bombardment by the Israeli army
- Thousands of incidents where medical staff were refused access to wounded or ill people in villages or neighbourhoods under curfew

- 25% of all children without protection by vaccination
- Women giving birth at home increased from the previous 4% to a current 13%

Wall's Impact on Palestinian Health Care System *(Medecins du Monde-2005)*

- 32.7% of all West Bank villages denied free access to health care system
- 52% of doctors working in clinics are delayed or denied access to work place
- 117,600 pregnant women, including 17,640 high risk pregnant women may be unable to access antenatal care, hosptal delivery and postnatal care
- 10,000 chronic disease patients prevented access to essential medical services
- 133,000 children under 5 may not obtain vaccines on time or at all
- [In 2003, only 56,755 permits were issued in West Bank for a population of 2,313,609 Palestinians]

Jadal Centre for Culture and Development

Near the bus station in Beit Sahour. ☎ 02-277 5445. bsmc@p-ol.com Foreigners are welcome to attend talks and debates here.

The Jadal Centre aims to inform, by critical analysis and discussion, in order to develop and promote a plan for an open, forward-looking society. To this end, it organises debates, conferences and talks on a regular basis , round tables, poetry readings and readings of other texts, as well as presentation of films and musical evenings.

The Palestinian Centre for Rapprochement between People (PCR)

☎/fax 02-2772018 email: info@rapprochement.org www.rapprochement.org www.imemc.org

The PCR is a non-governmental, non-political organization that works in three different fields. Preparing youth and empowering them to take an active role in the society and to be young advocates for the Palestinian Cause, nonviolent resistance to the occupation, and information dissemination and media. Contact persons: Ghassan Andoni, and George N. Rishmawi

Young Men's Christian Association (YMCA)

☎ 02-277 2713 www.shepherdsfieldymca.org: camping by reservation

Beit Sahour's YMCA branch was established in 1955, and until the first Intifada had a youth hostel as well as a sports and cultural centre for youth. Since 1989, the YMCA has re-oriented its services to care for victims of Israeli repression. All in all, nearly 140,000 Palestinians were injured during the first Intifada, and 40,000 of them suffer from permanent disabilities. Between 1989 and 2001, the rehabilitation centre at the YMCA attended to more than 7,500 Palestinians handicapped by their injuries. The centre has a programme for physical rehabilitation and is developing a social service programme (providing ramps and railings for private and public centres, vocational training, and support at workplaces especially tailored to handicapped needs).

The YMCA property is also a religious and historical site: the renovated grottoes here belong to the Anglican Church, which has identified them as the real Shepherds' Field. There are campgrounds for tourists *(NIS 15 per person; tents not provided)* and there are high quality tourist facilities.

Joint Advocacy Initiative

The initiative participates in conferences, seminars and workshops on the local, regional and international levels. It carries out research and campaigns where dissemination of information through, newsletters, magazine, press releases and action alerts relative to the Palestinian issue and the work of the YWCA/ YMCA are shared with partners and friends. It hosts and arranges youth exchange and various delegations and fact-finding missions programs and events. Moreover, it cooperates, coordinates and networks for advocacy work with local organizations, including governmental, non-governmental and church-related organizations.

■ Outside the city of Bethlehem

❑ The Monastery of Saint Theodosius (Deir Ibn Ubeid)

Wadi Nar Road, 1 kilometre from the village of Ubeidiya, ☎ *02-276 6360.*

Like all foundations of the Byzantine period, the monastery of Saint Theodosius is associated with biblical history: the grotto under the monastery is believed to have sheltered the three kings returning from their visit to Baby Jesus in Bethlehem after being warned in a dream not to visit Herod, but to take another way home (Matthew 2:12). When Theodosius (423-529), the Coenobite, originally from Cappadocia, visited the grotto, he was deeply moved and decided to build a monastery here in the year 476, where he lived until the end of his days. He died here at the ripe old age of 105! In its heyday, the monastery housed some 690 monks of eastern religious orders (Greek Orthodox, Georgian, Armenian). Damaged more than once over the centuries, the monastery was totally abandoned in 1620. Towards the end of the nineteenth century, the Greek Orthodox Church partially restored it. A small religious community, a monk and a nun, watch over the tomb of the founder as well as the relics of the monks who were massacred by the Persians here in 614.

❑ Mar Saba

20 kilometres east of Bethlehem. From Bethlehem, a taxi ride costs between $20 to $25, which includes a visit to the monastery of St. Theodosius and Mar Saba. Open Sunday-Thursday 8:00-16:00; men only, suitable clothing, no entrance fee. Women are not allowed entry but may wait in the Women's Tower at the entrance to the monastery or, even better, on the opposite slope, which commands a magnificent view of Mar Saba.

Clinging to the face of a cliff, the Mar Saba monastery looks out over the Kidron Valley. If it were not for its copper-covered domes and its white houses with their blue windows, it would be hard to tell the monastery from the steep walls of the cliff. A wall that protects the cells, terraces and stairways inside the monastery forms a bastion against outside threats; the last time it was sacked was in 1835. Although the monastery was developed to house a hundred Orthodox monks, there are now only about a dozen living a life of prayer here. Displayed in vitrines behind the choir of the church are the skulls of the 120 monks massacred in 614. The body of Saint Sabas, stolen by Venetians but restituted by Pope Paul VI in 1965, lies in the second chapel of the main church, wrapped in a coat fringed with gold. Saint Sabas (439-533), originally from Cappadocia, lived in the late fifth century in Palestine, as an ascetic. Living reclusively in sparsely furnished caves, the monks united every Saturday evening in the monastery to attend mass together.

Monasticism in the Judaean Desert

The Judaean Desert stretches over the arid escarpments to the east of Jerusalem and Bethlehem. For the first monks who followed in the footsteps of Jesus, the severe climate here was a real test of their faith. Until the fourth century, Christian monastic centres existed mainly in Asia Minor and Egypt. The Egyptian Saint Antony was one of the great pioneers of monasticism in the third century. Among his disciples, some settled in Palestine, particularly in the area of Gaza and in the desert near Jerusalem. On a quest for perfection and renouncing material possessions, ascetic monks from all over the Christian world settled in caves suspended on the sides of the cliffs of gorges *(wadis)* in the desert. Choosing a life of solitude, they met only for Sunday mass and a dominical meal thereafter.

These coenobite communities welcomed pilgrims and travellers and actually grew very prosperous. The great figures of monasticism, such as Euthymius, Sabas, and Theodosius, to mention just the well-known monks, lived in the Judaean desert and played an influential role in the development of Christian liturgy and dogma; it was due to them that western monasticism developed. On the night of the Sassanian (Persian) invasion, in 614, there were no less than 10,000 monks living in the Judaean desert. Yet only three of the first monasteries are still active nowadays - the Monastery of Saint Theodosius, Mar Saba to the west of Bethlehem, and the Monastery of Saint George in Wadi Qelt.

❑ Herodion or Herodium (Jabal al-Furdeis)

From Bethlehem (Bab al-Deir), a service taxi (NIS 2.5) will take you to Za'tara, the nearest village. Ask the driver to leave you at the foot of the Herodion (off the usual route). A private taxi should cost NIS 50 at the most, including any wait. Open every day 8:00 - 17:30, NIS 23 entrance fee. The site, in Area C, is under the jurisdiction of the Israeli Ministry of Tourism.

Herodion standsd out against a background of arid hills and cultivated land like an artificial volcano and is undoubtedly the most impressive of all King Herod's palace-fortresses. The site has, over the centuries been named: Jabal al-Furdeis (the Hill of Paradise), Jabal Khreitoun (the Mountain of Saint Chariton), and Jabal al-Franj (the Mountain of the Franks). Built between 24 - 15 BC, the palace and city that extended to the foot of the mountain are material evidence of all the might of the royal power at that time. It seems that this palace was Herod's favourite and, according to Roman historian Flavius Josephus, this is where he was buried. A long funeral procession brought his body from his winter palace in Jericho to a mausoleum here which remains unlocated. The palace was occupied twice by Jewish rebels: the insurgent Zealots, from 66 - 70 AD; then the Revolt of Bar Kochba from 132 - 135 AD. In both cases, as at Massada and Macherus (Machor), the fighters are said to have chosen suicide rather than to die by Roman sword or crucifixion. The site was then abandoned for a long time, until the Byzantine and Crusader periods.

At the foot of the mountain is the **lower city**, whose homes have been partially excavated. Digs have uncovered a garden surrounded on three sides by porticos of smooth columns bearing ionic capitals. In the middle of the garden, there is a huge open pool (45 x 70 x 3 m) at whose centre is a small round islet (13.5 m in diameter) used as a pavilion of fantasy. Water for the garden and pool was diverted from Solomon's Pools, eight kilometres away, using a system of terracotta canals. In the Byzantine era, churches flourished and the lower city alone had three; the basilica in the east is best-preserved, with a mosaic pavement of vines and animals, typical of the sixth century.

The Herodion itself is the greatest artistic achievement. A generous third of the earth and gravel used to build the hill for the circular palace-fortress was used to make an earth rampart laid against the outer foundations of the fortification (62 m in diameter), raising the hill and giving it its distinctive conical shape. Such an arrangement was unique in its time. Three semi-circular towers and the round eastern one dominated the entire Herodion. An inner wall surrounded the palace and a hanging garden. There were private baths and reception rooms which gave onto the garden. Further inside, there were service rooms, storage areas and stucco cisterns. The Byzantine occupation of the fortress is marked by the ruins of a small church that could be the "Ephrata" mentioned on the famous Madaba Map. A well-known chronicler of the fourteenth century, Nicephorus Calliste, often using very ancient sources, said that there was probably a *leprosarium* on top of the Herodion in the fifth and sixth centuries. The mediaeval text describes the construction of a *leprosarium* by Empress Eudokia in the fifth century in a place called Prodisia. The discovery around the Herodion of tombs in which bones reveal traces of leprosy tends to confirm this conclusion.

❑ Wadi Khreitoun

Located less than two kilometres SE of Herodion. A torch or flashlight is essential.

Many caves, inhabited since the Lower Palaeolithic age, are scattered around the valley. The first cave, **Erq al-Ahmar**, whose entrance was walled up by Bedouins, was inhabited *circa* 80,000 BC. The second cave, **Um Qal'a**, is located above the river bed about one kilometre away from the first, and habitation began *circa* 8,000 BC. The third cave, most important, is **Um Qatfa**, excavated in 1930-1940, at a depth of over 12 metres, to reveal the first traces of the use of fire in Palestine, in the Lower Palaeolithic Age (500,000-120,000 BC). **Um Qatfa** cave is opposite the ruins of a Byzantine monastery on the same level as the cave. The monastery, known as "Old Laura," was founded by Saint Chariton *circa* 345 AD and was probably replaced by a monastery, fortified at the time of the Crusaders. Nevertheless, there is little information about the monastery, as archaeologists have never explored the site. Finally, there is the **Khreitoun cave**, four kilometres *(an hour's walk)* from the valley. The cave winds along under the mountain for 17 kilometres. The first 150 metres have been somewhat cleared. Take a torch (flashlight) and extra batteries!

The Segregation Wall around Bethlehem

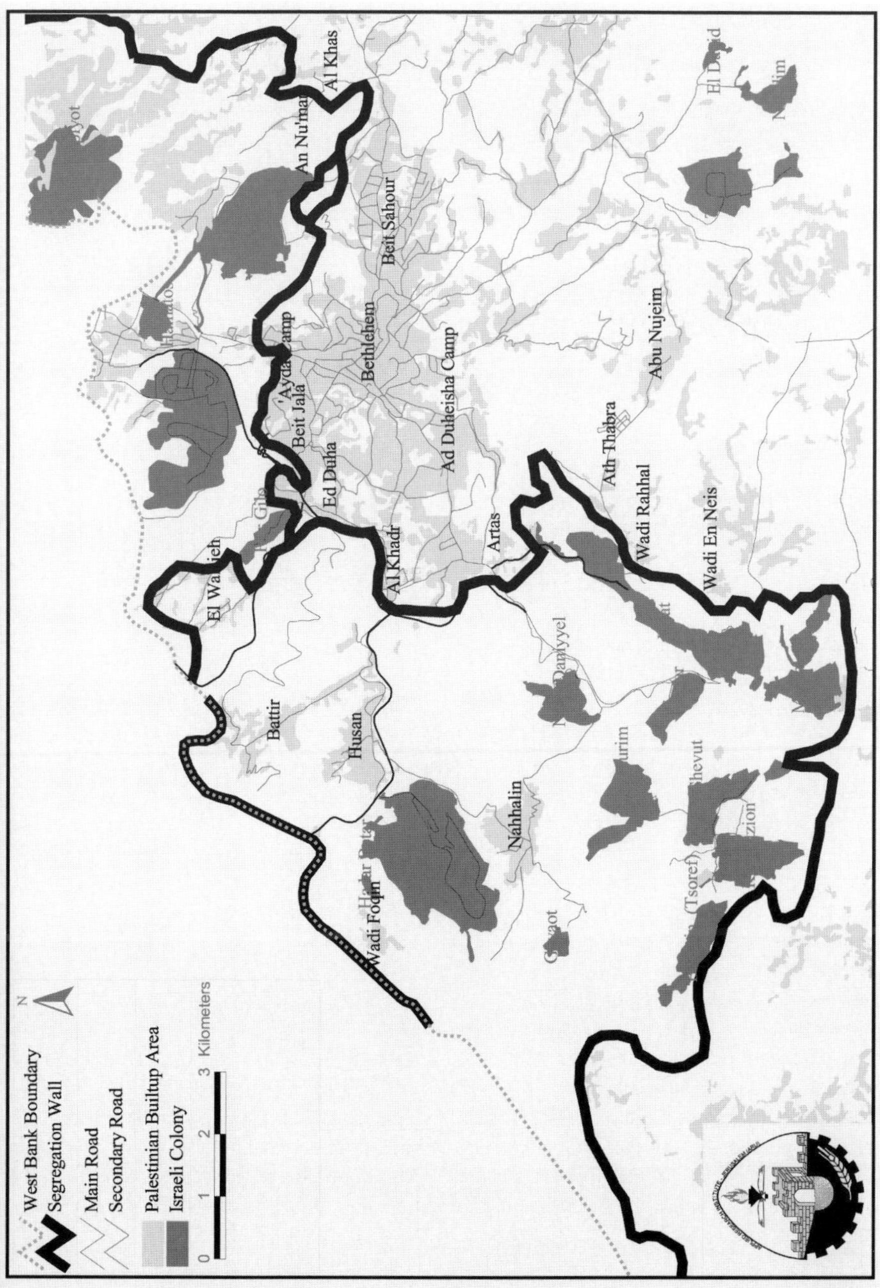

HEBRON

الخليل

HEBRON (AL-KHALIL)

■ From Bethlehem to Hebron

Getting to Hebron

■ *Departing from Jerusalem to Hebron take a "service" shared taxi from Musrara Square at Damascus Gate (NIS8) or from the taxi station at Bab ez-Zqaq in Bethlehem (NIS 4). From the central bus station in Beersheba (Bir es-Saba) in Israel to Hebron costs NIS 20.*

■ *For leaving Hebron, the Ford transit minibuses to Jerusalem are stationed at Malik Feisal Street. From Hebron to Bethlehem, the Ford transits are at the taxi station of Hebron. Taxis run regularly in the morning, but traffic in the evening is very light. It is preferable to be off the road by 18:00 because of the risk of waiting a long time for a shared taxi to be full, before departure. The nature of the Closure also means it is preferable to go through any fixed or "flying" checkpoint in daylight.*

The Jewish Settlements

Gush Etzion

Gush Etzion (the Etzion Bloc) is the name of a huge settlement bloc of 17 originally separate developments to the south and west of Bethlehem. The settlements of *Beitar Ilit* and *Efrata*, for example, act as barriers to prevent any contiguity between Bethlehem and Hebron. Gush Etzion and its over 40,000 inhabitants are in process of being annexed to "Greater Jerusalem." The integration of Gush Etzion into the outer ring of settlements guarantees the Jewish character of an entity called "Unified Jerusalem" on a territory as vast as possible, in the middle of Palestinian-administered autonomous areas in enclaves cut off from one another. The bloc guards, for Israeli use and control, the highly strategic Mountain Aquifer source in Gush Etzion: for this reason Israel has settled this entire bloc, which has been ratified by George W. Bush in his Bush-Sharon Letter of Agreement of April 2004, as ratified by Congress and Senate.

Kiryat Arba

Built in 1970 on 430 hectares of confiscated land, this settlement, where more than 7,000 settlers live, is the core of Israeli settlement projects around Hebron. Over 500 hectares have already been confiscated, and land appropriation will undoubtedly continue until finally the entire city is encircled, an ongoing process that can be observed at the moment around all the cities in the West Bank. It is expected that part of the Old City of Hebron will be expropriated to integrate it into the enlarged settlement of *Kiryat Arba* and a $5 million promenade, funded by Israel's Ministry of Tourism, is destined to link the two. Since 1974, the occupation policy of "outside control" was first implemented here, when vital elements of Palestinian infrastructure such as water pipes and electricity generators were placed inside the settlement. This practice has been proved as a particularly effective way to intensify the stranglehold on the Palestinian population. Mainly populated by Jews of American and French origin, the settlement of *Kiryat Arba* is known as a hotbed of Zionist and Jewish fundamentalism. Every year, the anniversary of the death of Baruch Goldstein, the perpetrator of the massacre at the al-Ibrahimi mosque in 1994 and a follower of Meir Kahane (whose political party Kach, for whom Kahane served as a member of the Knesset, was outlawed by the Israeli Knesset as a terror organisation), is commemorated as one of the major celebrations.

Arroub Refugee Camp

On Road 60, halfway between Bethlehem and Hebron; UNRWA representative, Issa Khayran,☎ 02-252 2289.

Arroub Refugee Camp was established in 1950, next to the main road and is closely monitored by Israeli occupation troops. At the beginning of the al-Aqsa Intifada, several houses located at the entrance to the camp were confiscated and turned into military bases and lookout posts. Sanitary conditions are extremely precarious, and the camp is still not connected to any sewage system. Its 8,000 residents must put up with draconian yearlong water shortages although there is an abundant water supply near the camp.

Some 200 metres east of Arroub is the vast reservoir of **Birket esh-Shatt**, built by Pontius Pilate, a Roman prefect, in the first century AD. It has a capacity of 20,000 cu.m. and was part of an aqueduct system linking the Hebron Hills to Bethlehem and Jerusalem. Today, the exclusive control of this water source is in Israeli hands.

❐ Mamre (Ramat al-Khalil)

In the area of Nimreh, 200 metres east of the road to Jerusalem, 3 kms north of Hebron. At the head of Nimreh Road, close to the Palestinian checkpoint (signalling the entry into Area A).

Tradition has it that Abraham pitched his camp on this hill under some oak trees where three angels appeared and told him that his wife, Sarah, would bear him a son in spite of her advanced age (Genesis 18:1-16). The site is an ancient one: its plants and stones were worshipped by the Canaanites long before Abraham honoured the place with his visit. The only visible ruins, however, are more recent: they date from the Roman period, when Herod built a haram here on the model of the temples in Hebron and Jerusalem. Archaeologists discovered a marble statue of Dionysus and an altar to the Edomite goddess Qos (unfortunately no longer on the site), examples of the religious syncretism and worship of the vine, a crop which contributes to this day to Hebron's reputation. All that remains of the Herodian temple are the enormous, perfectly-shaped stone blocks that were recycled to build a temple to Hermes *(eastern side)* circa 130 AD. One of the largest slave markets in the area was held here under the divine patronage of the god Hermes, god of commerce and the slave market. In the fourth century, this pagan temple was replaced by a basilica which is noted on the Madaba Map; it was built under the auspices of Eutropia, mother-in-law of Constantine.

■ Hebron

> *"Abu Horayrah says the following: The Messenger of God says: "When the angel Gabriel took me on the Night Journey to Jerusalem, we went over the tomb of Abraham, and he said to me, 'Get off and execute two rak'ahs of prayer, for here is the sepulchre of your Father Abraham.' Then we went over Bethlehem, and again he said: 'Get off and pray two rak'ahs, for this is the place where your brother Jesus was born.' Then he brought me to the rock* [of Jerusalem]."
>
> ■ Passage from the Hadith quoted by Ibn Battuta in his book *Journeys*.

Hebron is one of the first cities to develop in Palestine in the early Bronze Age. Islamic tradition holds that this was the first human establishment, where Adam and Eve lived after being driven from the Garden of Eden. The biblical name of Hebron is Kiryat Arba, or the "Village of the Four," said to be a reference to four giants who fell from Paradise. Another explanation refers to four biblical couples said to be buried here: Adam and Eve, Abraham and Sarah, Isaac and Rebecca, Jacob and Leah. The "four" are equally interpreted as the four hills of Hebron on which the four Canaanite tribes settled, in a confederation, to establish the first city-state. The founding of the city is even dated in the Old Testament, precisely: seven years before the creation of Tanis in Egypt, that is, in 1730 BC (Numbers 13:22). In fact, this date is attributed to a late Judaean tradition, (after the exile of the Jews to Babylon), which glorified David's first capital, Hebron, as being older than Tanis, then the Egyptian capital.

marks in the urban landscape apart from the blue eyes of many of its citizens, who may be descendants of those Crusaders who made their home here and converted to Islam.

At the end of the eighteenth century, Hebron became one of the most important commercial centres in Palestine, benefiting from trade with Egypt, whose caravans preferred the internal route through the hinterland, through Sinai and Bir es-Saba' (Beersheba), rather than the coastal route.

Archaeological excavations on Tel er-Rumeida *(partly covered by the cemetery, south of Shuhadeh Street - the Street of the Martyrs)* have shown the biblical description to be inexact (something scriptural interpretation had already foreseen) and fix the date of the founding of Hebron earlier, *circa* 2000 BC, a period when city-building increased in Palestine. According to the Bible, David was anointed king in Hebron (II Samuel 5:3), towards 1000 BC, but the area seceded from the kingdom of David and his inheriting son, Absalom (II Samuel 15:10) set up his headquarters in Hebron. During the Persian era, Hebron became one of the main cities in the Edomite province (Northern Negev). John Hyrcanus conquered the province in 134 BC, thereby acquiring full control over the trade routes between Arabia and the Mediterranean, routes which were a major source of prosperity for the region.

The prestigious Haram al-Ibrahimi monument is a heritage from Roman times, when it was erected by Herod, son of an Edomite father and an Arab princess (Transjordan), a marriage that perfectly reflected the close ties between Hebron and transarabian commerce. In the seventh century, the city became an important centre for Muslim pilgrims, as its Arabic name, al-Khalil er-Rahman, or "the beloved of the Merciful One," suggests. A *surah* in the Quran emphasises the importance of Abraham (Ibrahim): *"I will make thee an example for mankind to follow"* (Quran, al-Baqara 124). Hebron fell to the Crusaders, who named it Castellum; they left few permanent

During the British Mandate, the population of Hebron rose to between 10,000 - 16,000 people. The Zionist moves to create a Jewish state in Palestine caused several riots in reaction in Hebron. At the time of the national revolt in 1929, there was more than one cause; one main cause was the Zionist attempt to ignore the *Status Quo* agreement on access to the al-Buraq Wall (the Wailing Wall), Islamic property, which stirred up feelings particularly in Hebron, where there was also a holy shrine to the three Patriarchs (Abraham, Isaac and Jacob) venerated by Jews as well as Muslims. In addition, Jewish immigration brought new citizens with no inclination to assimilate, which was disrupting the balance between the two communities living in Hebron. The growing animosity exploded into violent clashes which left sixty-seven of the Jewish community dead and the British evacuated the Jewish community from the city. After the war of 1948, refugees flowed in from the southern areas of Palestine (Beersheba and the plains east of Majdal) and settled mainly in two camps, al-Arroub and al-Fawwar *(UNRWA representative, Yussef al-Haljawi, ☎ 02-228 2663)*. The 1967 war allowed for Zionist hopes of establishing *Eretz Israel* ("The Land of Israel" - i.e. Greater Israel) to become concrete. Rabbi Moshe Levinger, head of the National Religious Party, pioneered colonisation in the city; he and others rented the Park Hotel, protected by the army, in the city centre.

He did so as a protest against his government, which was reluctant to authorise a settlement in the centre of Hebron, fearing an uprising. However, from 1970 onwards, the Israeli government put its reservations aside and approved the construction of the first settlement on the outskirts of Hebron, giving it the city's ancient biblical name, Kiryat Arba. In March 1979, Miriam Levinger, leading a group of women and children, occupied an abandoned hospital in the city centre (Al-Dabawiya, renamed *Beit Hadassah*). This time they obtained authorisation for a permanent settlement. In reaction to increased colonisation, Palestinian resistance groups waged various attacks on Israeli settlers during the 1980s. The Israeli authorities responded by more repression and by deporting the mayor and the Qadi (religious judge) of Hebron as well as the mayor of the neighbouring town, Halhoul. In 1983, the authorities replaced the new mayor of the city, Mustafa Natsheh, with an Israeli military officer. He was, however, reinstated in this position by the Palestinian Authority. During the first Intifada, the people of Hebron were constantly harassed and subjected to ill-treatment by settlers and Israeli soldiers alike, in addition to the endless curfews. Far from changing the situation, the "peace process" was inaugurated, just six months after the Oslo Accords were signed, by a new massacre.

The Ibrahimi Mosque Massacre

Early on the morning of February 25, 1994, in the holy month of Ramadan, as hundreds of Palestinians were praying in the Haram al-Ibrahimi Mosque, Dr. Baruch Goldstein, a settler from Kiryat Arba and a member of the Kach party, wearing Israeli military uniform, burst into the mosque and opened fire at worshippers prostrated in prayer: 29 men and young boys were killed (mostly shot in the back) and almost 200 wounded. Demonstrations broke out all over the West Bank and the Gaza Strip, while the Israeli army killed 12 more Palestinians gathered near the Hebron hospital, wounding other Palestinian victims there and in other parts of the Occupied Territories. A curfew was imposed on the city, neighbourhoods around the Haram were closed down and declared "security zones." As for the Jewish settlers in the centre of Hebron, they had full freedom of movement. For nine months, Palestinians were forbidden to go to the Haram. Dr. Goldstein's widow subsequently tried to sue the surviving Palestinian survivors of the attack for killing her husband! To this day, his tomb is a central pilgrimage site for ultra-right-wing followers of the late Meir Kahane, many of them settlers in the most rabid West Bank settlements.

The City Today

The municipality of Hebron has 150,000 inhabitants, which makes it the largest city in the West Bank, after annexed East Jerusalem. The district of Hebron (over 400,000 people) is the most urbanised region: 67% are city dwellers, while 30% live in the rural areas as villagers or Bedouins, and 3% are refugees living in al-Arroub and al-Fawwar refugee camps. In spite of the settlers in its centre, Hebron is a highly dynamic economic and industrial centre, with diversified manufacturing including stone quarrying. Its inhabitants have a reputation as confirmed entrepreneurs, known for their generosity and hospitality.

Hebron today is divided into two sectors after an agreement on the withdrawal of the Israeli army on January 15, 1997. Sector H1 (80% of the municipality of Hebron) is under Palestinian autonomy (the PA); sector H2 (20%) is under Israeli control. In sector H2, which includes part of the Old City including the Tomb of the Patriarchs / al-Ibrahimi Mosque, live 40,000 Palestinians and some 500 settlers, most of whom come from the United States, but also from France. The presence of these settlers, and that of the 4,000 soldiers (CPT figures) here to protect them, explains the tension in the city. Harassment of the Palestinian population and even journalists is frequent, as are acts of vandalism. The international observers (Temporary International Presence in Hebron - TIPH and Christian Peacemakers Team - CPT), in Hebron since 1996, record all army and settler acts of harassment, including aggressions they themselves have experienced. In certain places, the boundaries are clearly indicated by fences, sometimes electrified, or more often by netting covering the streets (settlers occupy the upper floors there and throw many types of rubbish or detritus down onto these areas). In spite of the tense situation, foreign tourists receive as warm a welcome here as in all other Palestinian cities, and a tour around the city is guaranteed to be both educational and surprising. To quote a 2004 report by The Alternative Information Centre: *Occupation in Hebron*, "Israel's settlement policy, which supports the presence of radical Jewish fundamentalists with a strong anti-Arab ideology in the middle of a Palestinian city, is the proximate reason for the high level of violence in Hebron…"

Curfews

Year 2000*	Curfew
October 4 - November 15	Total (24 hrs)
November 16	Partial (lifted 8:30-13:00)
November 17 - November 25	Total (24 hrs)
November 26	Partial (lifted 12 noon-16:00)
November 30 - December 2	Total (24 hrs)
December 3	Partial (lifted 8:00-13:00)
December 4	Total (24 hrs)
December 5	Partial (lifted 8:00-13:00)
December 6 - 11	Total (24 hrs)
December 12	Partial (lifted 8:00-13:00)
December 13	Total (24 hrs)
December 14	Partial (lifted 8:00-13:00)
December 15	Total (24 hrs)
December 16	Partial (lifted 15:00-16:00)
December 17 - 24	Total (24 hrs)
December 25	No curfew
December 26 - 31	Intermittent

* First months of al-Aqsa Intifada. Source: DCI-PS, "A Generation Denied," 2001

■ The Old City

Since the Ayyubid period, the city has had no protective wall; yet its closely-built houses have been sufficient to guarantee safety to the inhabitants. Until the late nineteenth century, the only way into the city was through guarded entrance gates that were closed at night. **Bab al-Wakala** (Bab Khan Ibrahim) is the most beautiful surviving example of such a gate; at the southern end of the city, it opened directly onto a *caravanserai* and public areas, while the more private residential areas were located further away. Outside the gate, several historic buildings, now abandoned, serve as a reminder of the bustling activity here not so long ago. The vast pool named **Birket es-Sultan** was a major monument in its time. Built by the Mameluke sultan, Seif ed-Din al-Alfeh (1279 - 1290), this huge pool supplied water for city dwellers as well as visiting Muslim pilgrims. It was the arrival point for all caravans and a social meeting place facing out into the world, encouraging trade between inhabitants and visitors. Today, the old cistern can be viewed through a small attic window on the southern side, empty of water but inundated with detritus. To the northern side *(Shuhadeh Street)* stands the **Hammam al-Birka** *(currently closed)*. The reception hall inside the

hammam bears an enigmatic inscription ending in the following words *"If you want to know the date of this construction* [the date of the mosque], *date it and say: Pray for the one who builds the house of God. 1127 Hegira."* This is a curious game with words and numbers: the date mentioned, 1127 Hegira (1715), corresponds to the exact sum of the position or value of each letter in the Arabic alphabet.

According to accounts of travellers in the first half of the nineteenth century there is no mention of any building next to the reservoir at that time. This suggests that the *hammam* was built at the end of the nineteenth century for private use, also taking into account its small size, and that the inscription was probably originally found in an Ottoman mosque built by Rajab Pasha, an Ottoman administrator of the districts of Jerusalem and Hebron.

Today, the sector around Birket es-Sultan is under Israeli control (any restoration of buildings of historical importance is forbidden here), and its residents are under daily threat from the arrogance and menace of Israeli settlers and soldiers.

❒ The Market (Souq)

The *souq* alone justifies a visit to Hebron. The ambience, architectural surroundings and the diversity of wares sweep foreign visitors into a totally exotic world full of strong sensations. Above all, take time to observe, feel, discuss and take advantage of the choices on display in the stalls, if you are seeking original gifts.

Specialities of Hebron

A commercial centre for neighbouring villages and a major transit point for trans-Arabian caravan traders in the old days, Hebron developed a wide range of specialities. Celebrated for its growth of grapes since the days of early antiquity (Numbers 13:20-24), this ranks high among agricultural activities in the area. Until the occupation of 1967, Hebron was the principal exporter of grapes to the Arab world, especially to the Gulf States. In Hebron as well as throughout Palestine, grapes are consumed as jam, syrup *(dibes)* or sweets *(malban:* thin layers made from concentrated grape juice decorated with small dry pine kernels called *kresh).* Sweetbreads are another speciality served in many small restaurants.

Hebron is famous for leather, skins and carpets. Tanneries of Hebron had their day of glory at the time when caravans from Egypt and the Arab Peninsula passed through, and traders would purchase goatskin bottles for transporting their water. Today, leather is used mainly to manufacture the excellent shoes made in Hebron, and for the manufacture of fine-quality sheepskins. Superb woollen carpets are made throughout the Hebron region and are on sale in Old City shops.

One production especially captivating visitors: glass blowing. Of all colours, cobalt blue is the favourite. The technique was probably brought here in the fifteenth century by Venetian merchants who came to Palestine to buy cotton. The main glass-blowing workshops are not in the Old City, but are located around the northern entrance to Hebron. The **Hebron Glass and Ceramics Factory** is near a Palestinian checkpoint which marks the boundary between Area A (H1) and Area C (H2). The **al-Salam Glass and Pottery Factory** is located 200 metres further away towards Bethlehem, opposite Nimreh Road. In both places one may take photographs, observe ancient techniques of glass-making and buy exquisite glassware. The fixed prices are very reasonable.

Hebron

Cafés and Restaurants
1. Kawkab ash-Sharq Restaurant
2. Abu Mazen Restaurant
3. Geith al-Mashawi Restaurant

Accommodation
A. Hebron Tourist Hotel
B. Al-Mizan Hotel

Contacts
I. Mobile Library Association
II. Hebron-France Association for Cultural Exchange
III. (UGU) Hebron University Alumni Association
IV. Committee for the Rehabilitation of Hebron
V. Christian Peacemakers' Team
VI. Temporary International Presence in Hebron (TIPH)

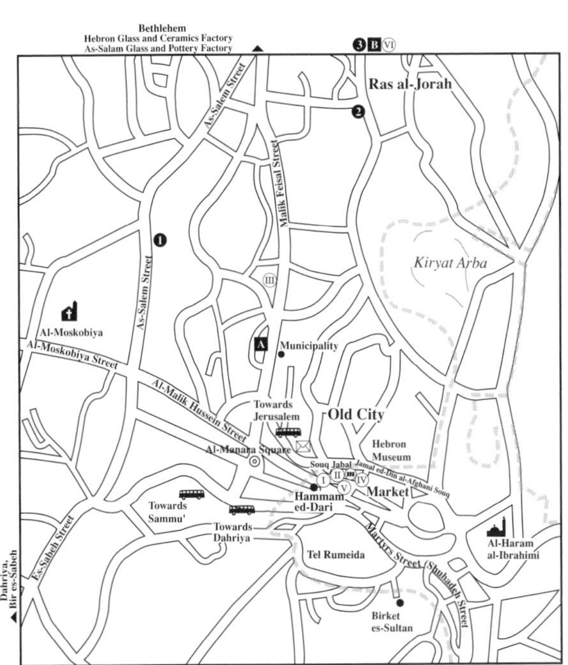

■ Al-Haram al-Ibrahimi or Haram al-Khalil (Tomb of the Patriarchs)

Open Sunday-Thursday 8:00-16:00, except during prayers, free admission; passport necessary at various checkpoints. Jewish settlers have prayed in the mosque since 1967; but division of the Haram into two spaces - one for Jews, the other for Muslims - followed the 1994 massacre. Waqf office; ☎ 02-222 8213/51.

The oldest and most venerated monument in the city, the Haram al-Ibrahimi or Haram al-Khalil is linked to the biblical account of the coming of the prophet Abraham to the region. The book of Genesis (Genesis 23:1-20) describes Sarah's death at the age of 127, and how Abraham bought the cave of Machpela from Ephron the Hittite, to bury his wife here. The bodies of Abraham, Isaac and Rebecca, Jacob and Leah, as well as Joseph, are said to rest here. This cave has consequently become one of the most sacred places in Palestine.

No archaeological artefacts have been found to indicate that the spot was a holy one before Herod built this impressive sanctuary. The holy precincts are 59 x 34 m vast. The wall, of the Herodian epoque, is 20 metres high, made of imposing stone blocks (the largest is 7.5 x 1.4 m). The crenellated band on top

was added later, in Mameluke times. The presence of regularly-spaced pilasters breaks the monotonous regularity of the structure; from close quarters, one unusual architectural detail stands out: each superimposed block is recessed an increasing 1.5 cms. Without this adjustment, the wall would appear on the verge of collapse. This optical illusion is even more interesting because, in defying the straight vertical line, the builders have given the impression of having built in reverse order, when the building is viewed from the ground. A number of other structures were subsequently added to the *temenos* ("sacred enclosure" in Greek), complicating visual appreciation of the site.

In 1099, the Crusaders conquered the city, and the Umayyad mosque was transformed into the Church of Saint Abraham; a stained-glass window above the main entrance dates from this twelfth-century period. The Crusaders rediscovered the caves as well as the bones inside them, attributed to the Patriarchs. They became a special object of worship for every pilgrim able to journey to the Holy of Holies. When the city was liberated by Saladin's troops in 1187, the vaulted church was reconverted into a mosque; two minarets were added to the compound. After 1250, the Mamelukes made rich donations to the Haram and added new mosques (ed-Dja'uliya and Joseph's Mosque), two minarets and five of the seven cenotaphs.

■ Inside the mosque, the *minbar* crafted in marquetry is considered one of its most beautiful ornaments; made in 1091, it decorated the main mosque in Ascalan until Saladin bestowed it on the Haram al-Khalil in 1191.

❒ The Hebron Museum

In the Old City; open daily 9:00-16:00 except Fridays. ☎ 02-222 3495. Frequent exhibitions and the architectural style of the museum merit a visit.

In the heart of Hebron's historical centre, near the Haram, the municipal museum recently opened its doors in the old Ibrahim al-Khalil Hammam. The *hammam* was constructed on the orders of Ala ed-Din al-Basir in the thirteenth century (see p. 84); the *muqarnas* in the hot room are the *hammam's* outstanding feature, typical of Mameluke gate decorations.

❒ ed-Dari Hammam

Opposite the cemetery, the Street of the Martyrs (Shuhadeh Street).

Although this *hammam* is contemporary - it was built at the end of the nineteenth century - its architectural style differs from that of adjacent buildings. It was inspired by the Mameluke architectural style, similar to that of the Ibrahim al-Khalil Hammam and the al-Pasha Hammam in Acre (Akka). This *hammam* has been closed since 1985 but is due to re-open soon.

❒ The Russian Orthodox Church (al-Moskobiya)

Entry al-Moskobiya Street or west of the small monastery. Open daily 8:00-16:00.

In 1871, the Russian Orthodox Church was built around an old sixteenth-century oak held up on supports. The Arabic name of the monastery is al-Moskobiya. According to a late tradition, the monastery is located on the biblical site of Mamre. The monastery not being open to the public, the only real attraction here is the tower in the garden outside, from which the view extends on a clear day to the Dead Sea.

Practical Information

Cafés and Restaurants

Any number of popular coffee shops and restaurants are open during the day. Do not hesitate to go in, even if the outside does not look particularly inviting, especially in the Old City. However, not many establishments stay open at night; one exception which we recommend is ***Kawkab al-Sharq*** (Planet of the Orient), which has an effigy of the legendary Egyptian singer, Um Qalthoum. The intimate ambience and songs of the Egyptian diva make it an agreeable place for a traditional evening out *(☎ 02-221 9144)*.

In the city centre, the ***Abu Mazen*** restaurant is known for its stuffed meat dishes *(next to Adoua al-Medina Club, ☎ 02-221 3833)*. ***Geith al-Mashawi*** restaurant, located at the entrance to the city in the Ras al-Jorah quarter, serves delicious local specialities such as sweetbreads or giblets.

Accommodation

There are only two hotels in Hebron: **Hebron Tourist Hotel** *(Malik Feisal Street, ☎: 02-222 6760; single, double, and triple rooms for US $35, $40 and $55)* is quite reasonable and located in the heart of the city (Area H1). Rooms are spacious and well-equipped, with satellite TV. **Al-Mizan Hotel** is much more luxurious, decorated in impeccable classical style *(northern entrance to the city, ☎ 02-225 7389/99; regency@hebronet.com; single or double rooms or a suite for $80, $100, and $170)*. It has two restaurants (Palestinian and Italian) and a *hammam*. For more domestic accommodation, **Abuna Ibrahim House** *(Ein Bani Salem neighbourhood, 3 kilometres northeast of the Old City; ☎: 02-222 4811; bed and breakfast $15 per person, lunch or dinner $6)*. The house has a huge vista over all the surrounding countryside… and the Israeli settlements *Givat Harsina* and *Kiryat Arba*.

Contacts

Mobile Library Association for non-violence and peace

Old City, Kantarat esh-Shallodi; ☎ 02-583 5146.

This association runs a mobile library for children over a hundred localities (Hebron, villages, refugee camps and schools) and offers programmes aimed at improving the general educational level through reading. A programme of books on cassettes for blind children is planned.

Hebron University Alumni Association

Ein Sarah Street, Taher Amro, ☎ 0599-205109. Visits to the University of Hebron and around the city.

Members of this association are from the city or its vicinity and happy to welcome any foreign visitor interested in learning more about the city's situation and the life of its residents. Information is also available on *waqf* property in Hebron, of which the Haram al-Ibrahimi is the prime example.

Temporary International Presence in Hebron (TIPH)

Ras al-Jorah, al-Zaghal Building. ☎ 02-222 4445, Fax 02-222 4333, www.tiph.org; easily identified by their armbands, the observers are present in the city at all times and happy to inform visitors and talk to them.

The TIPH is a civilian observer mission based specifically in the city of Hebron. It has 85 members from Denmark, Italy, Norway, Turkey, Sweden, Switzerland, etc., and despite its somewhat inappropriate name, its founders not having been particularly arabophone (*tif* in Arabic means "to spit"), the members of the mission report on daily misconduct on either side in the conflict. The Jewish settlers hardly welcome these observers with open arms, and they are the constant target of settler harassment. Their presence is welcomed by

Hebron

Palestinian residents of Hebron even though the efficiency of their role is questioned: "After the meticulous recording and reporting of repeated human rights abuses, when will there be a force on the ground to protect Palestinians, and when will there be enough international pressure to end the occupation?"

Christian Peacemaker Team (CPT)

In the Old City, near the chicken market and also in H1, ☎ 02-222 8485.

A Christian organisation from N. America has had a base in Hebron since 1995 (veteran CPTers now serve a similar mission in Iraq). CPTers regularly intervene as an intervention and accompaniment group in Hebron and the S. Hebron Hills, where militant settlers (some of whom are serving army or police officers) are a constant problem, which recently even hospitalised a CPTer (broken ribs punctured his lung). With its continuous presence in the city, CPT is a source of reliable information on military and civil Israeli human rights abuses and ongoing land confiscation.

Committee for the Rehabilitation of Hebron

In the Old City; ☎ 02-222 6993/4. Inventory of buildings and monuments in the city; guided tours (remuneration required).

The Committee works to renovate the Old City, as well as to bring people back to live in this part of Hebron and improving living conditions here. Pre-1967, 10,000 lived in the Old City; from 1967 to 1996, 85% of these homes were abandoned: Israeli restrictions on the restoration of historical homes led to their deterioration--as indeed did the development of a local market for stolen goods and drugs, encouraged by the occupation authorities - not to mention the problematic presence of Jewish settlers, all of which added to a general atmosphere of insecurity and fear. To improve this situation and discourage more large-scale settlements, the first Committee for the Rehabilitation of the Old City was formed in 1988, by a group of architects from the University of Hebron, who undertook a systematic study of the urban architecture of the Old City. In 1995, the committee was authorised to renovate, except buildings occupied by the Israeli army or settlers. From 1995 to 2001, the committee restored over 150 buildings, some thirty shops and many alleyways. This policy has given a new impulse to the Old City and allowed over 230 families to return to live here.

■ South of Hebron

Yatta

Yatta Municipality, ☎ *02-227 9502. Information and tours to study land confiscation and the deportation of Bedouins in the Yatta region.*

This old village has some particularly beautiful examples of traditional dwellings, which specialists describe as a living example of what could have been the Byzantine habitat, embodying an unbroken architectural continuity across the centuries. Some of these houses, which have recycled building materials previously found in the vicinity, bear inscriptions and designs from Roman and Byzantine times. Today Yatta, which has 35,000 inhabitants, covers an area much larger than the historical village. Although agriculture used to be the village's mainstay, only a small fraction of its working population now works on the land; Yatta's land has been regularly confiscated from the town to build the settlements of *Carmel, Ma'on, Otniel*... The majority of workers would daily cross the Green Line (5 kms away), often illegally, depending for their living on jobs in Israeli industry and agriculture in the north of the Negev; these days the closures, checkpoints and absence of freedom of movement have hit this area badly. Most of the 700,000 people are unemployed, subsisting on international food aid.

Samu'

Samu' Municipality, ☎ *02-226 8001.*

Seven kilometres south of Yatta, the village of Samu' looks out over fields of olives and vineyards. Small fields of wheat may be seen here and there on the arid hills to the southeast. The known history of the village dates back to the Bronze Age and Canaanite ruins are present everywhere inside underground galleries. Do not hesitate to ask the villagers how to get into the caves, which are used today as sheepfolds or storerooms. Situated on the road linking the Jordan Valley to Bir es-Saba' and Gaza, the village was a halt for Roman, Ayyubid, Mameluke and Ottoman caravans and troops. At the centre of the old village, the mosque has survived in its present-day form thanks to restoration work carried out in Saladin's time in the twelfth century.

For those interested in woollen carpets, a tour of carpet shops *(especially **Samu' Co-operative: Samu' Charitable Society** ☎ 02-226 8006, 200 metres from the mosque at the top of a steep hill)* is compulsory. Their quality carpets are woven locally.

Tarqumia, or the story of a "crossing" between the West Bank and Gaza

On Road 35. Since the beginning of the al-Aqsa Intifada, this crossing has been more or less closed, with permits for crossing rarely given. Palestinians from the West Bank cannot generally go to Gaza (and vice versa) through this point but must go through Jordan and Egypt.

Most of the agreements signed between the Palestinian Authority (PA) and the Israeli governments anticipated that there would be a passage for people, vehicles and goods between the West Bank and the Gaza Strip. The Wye Plantation Memorandum (October 1998) stipulated that the crossing here would be operational within a week. However, the passage between the Gaza Strip and Tarqumia (the West Bank area nearest to the Gaza Strip) started functioning only in October 1999, and then not on the principle of total freedom of movement. In the "Special Protocol" of October 5, 1999, the State of Israel reserved the right to authorise or deny passage to whomever they want. To travel from the West Bank (Tarqumia) to Gaza *(Erez)*, Palestinians have to pass through lengthy mandatory formalities: first they have to apply to the Israeli authorities for a special yellow card which allows them to travel inside Israel; a pink card is issued to those not allowed to go through without military or International Red Cross escort (for example, families visiting prisoners in Israeli prisons). At first, the passage was open daily to private and public vehicles, then only on Mondays and Wednesdays *(7:00-sunset)*. After a preliminary inspection, a passenger is subjected to "security investigation" at an Israeli checkpoint either in Erez or Tarqumia; such an investigation has turned a 45-minute trip into a 2 or 3-hour affair. Another permit is then delivered to the traveller indicating the date when return is compulsory, and usually this is on the very same day. Since the beginning of the al-Aqsa Intifada, this "safeguarded passage" is even more closely controlled.

RAMALLAH

رام الله

Ramallah

Getting to Ramallah

Ramallah is approximately 15 kms from Jerusalem. To go to Ramallah from Jerusalem, one takes a collective taxi (NIS 3.50) or a bus (NIS 3.50) from the bottom of Nablus Road, near Damascus Gate and travels to Qalandia checkpoint; after crossing it, yet another shared taxi to Ramallah will cost NIS 2.50. To return to Jerusalem, the transportation available (at Manara Square) depends on the situation. Service taxis or buses at the checkpoint are available and are more frequent from Thursday to Saturday. Note that Qalandia checkpoint closes at 24:00 for cars (open at 4.30h), although it remains open 24 hours for pedestrians! Take passports so that you may cross the Qalandia checkpoint.

Qalandia Refugee Camp

On the Ramallah Road just past Qalandia checkpoint. UNRWA office, Khalil Souss.☎ 02-585 7827. Contact the Medical Society of Qalandia (☎ 02-583 5731) and the Health Workers' Committee (HWC,☎ 02-583 3593) for information on the general deterioration in health in the area since the beginning of the "peace process" in 1995.

Qalandia refugee camp was founded in 1949. The 8,000 refugees came from Ramle, Lydd and demolished villages west of Jerusalem. Until 1957, refugees lived in tents here until small temporary housing units were built. In 1967, half of the population from here fled to Jordan; at the same time, new refugees arrived from Amwas, Beit Nuba and Yalo (all villages demolished and annexed to Israel); UNRWA does not consider those people as refugees, since they were not chased out of their villages in 1948. The refugee camp is under the shadow of the Wall (including the Wall down the centre of the main Jerusalem-Ramallah road at A-Ram and Beit Hanina) and Qalandia checkpoint; it has been the scene of many incursions by the army stationed at the checkpoint: often soldiers go "hunting" refugee camp kids who throw stones in defiance. Over ten children have died here in the last few years

Ramallah

since the checkpoint was instituted. People in the area know that disturbances depend on the mindset of the soldiers. A reasonable group means a quiet month; others who think they are heroes in a video game have kept locals on their nerve edges with live fire and daily teargas.

Example of the Israeli Matrix of Control: The industrial zone of Sha'arei Binyamin

View from the permanent Israeli military checkpoint (machsom in Hebrew) near the entrance to the Qalandia refugee camp.

This military checkpoint at Qalandia is an ideal point to observe the reality of Israeli colonisation down to its last detail.

To the north: the Qalandia refugee camp. [See previous page.]

To the west: Jerusalem's airport, built by the Jordanian authorities. International flights were in service until the beginning of the first Intifada (1989). A new airport is due to be built at the Ma'ale Adumim settlement city, east of Jerusalem.

A highway (Road 45/443), runs next to the airstrip; it is part of a $3 billion highway system approved by the Rabin government in the early Oslo Accord years and largely funded by American grants. It cuts across the West Bank to link Tel Aviv to the Jordan Valley; its West Bank routes are uniquely for Israelis living in the settlements. In 2003 it was estimated *[Haaretz - September 26, 2003]* that the section between Givat Ze'ev via Atarot to Jerusalem had already cost NIS 80 million and the entire road would cost NIS 1 billion.

To the east: Road 45 is vital for the demographic and economic development of the settlements east of Ramallah, which include *Adam, Kochav Ya'akov, Tel Zion* (which is spreading rapidly towards Qalandia), *Psagot* (the settlement towers over the urban area of Al-Bireh-Ramallah) as well as *Beit El, Ma'ale Mikhmas,* and *Almon,* further to the east. All these settlements are integral parts of the plan for "Greater Jerusalem," a huge administrative planning unit which embodies the Israeli definition of what constitutes the territory of Jerusalem, officially enacted in 2004.

The *Sha'arei Binyamin* industrial park (By-pass Road 60) is one of many industrial parks originally planned by The Peres Centre for Peace as CBIZ (cross border industrial zones). The park (and others such as at nearby Mishor Adumim, Tulkarem, Barkan, Ariel) fulfils several functions: it creates a centre for economic activity, stimulating the economic, demographic and geographic growth of nearby settlements; it is a source of low-income jobs for Palestinians, thus deepening their dependence on Israel (whilst competing directly with and impacting negatively on Ramallah as a place of business activity and labour pool) and it also moves Israel's most polluting industries (e.g factories manufacturing aluminium, plastics, chemicals, fertilizer and slaughterhouses and meat packing plants) into the West Bank and "Greater Jerusalem." This industrial park, planned as an integral part of "Greater Jerusalem," is consecrated by its name, which means "Benjamin's Door", an allusion to the original territory here of the Biblical tribe of Benjamin, the youngest of Jacob's twelve sons. *Tel Zion* is a new city settlement in this "sacred" space of "Greater Jerusalem" slated to be inhabited by 30,000 ultra-Orthodox Jews. It is vaunted by Israel as "natural expansion" of *Kochav Ya'akov* - a settlement of 3,000 religious nationalists of "Gush Emunim" who claim to be part of Greater Israel - *Judaea* and *Samaria,* whilst those of *Tel Zion* are ultra-Orthodox for whom Jerusalem is the holy of holies, hence inclusion of *Tel Zion* within the Jerusalem *"eruv"* - a thin, high wire which encloses religious areas, making it possible for women to walk their children in pushcarts on the Sabbath.

■ Ramallah and al-Bireh

On Road 60, 16 km north of Jerusalem.

Ramallah ("Allah's Mountain" in Arabic - at an altitude of 860m) and al-Bireh (*bir* means "well" in Arabic) were once two distinct villages, but have grown together into a built-up area of over 60,000 inhabitants; the entire district of Ramallah today has more than 200,000 inhabitants. Since the Palestinian Authority (PA) took office in December 1995, the district has evolved as the administrative, cultural and political centre. It has known the same urban growth as other autonomous Palestinian cities, but the development in Ramallah has had a particularly marked cultural and recreational flavour. Before its occupation in 1967, the city's cool temperatures during the summer, its fresh air, its cultural life and cafés made it a favourite summer resort.

The history of Ramallah was first recorded in the

sixteenth century, when the Christian tribe of Rashid, originally from Karak (Jordan), settled here. For a long time the village remained a simple farming town. Al-Bireh's origins are more ancient, traced to the Canaanite city of Beroth. The importance of Ramallah steadily increased from the end of the nineteenth century: in 1902, it became the administrative centre of the region, and in 1910, was declared an official municipality. After the tragedy of 1948 (Nakba), and an influx of refugees, the two towns of Ramallah and al-Bireh experienced a building boom. Ever since the occupation in 1967, resistance has been strong here. In May 1980, Karim Khalaf, the mayor of Ramallah, and the mayors of al-Bireh and Nablus were victims of car bombs placed in their personal vehicles by settlers with the help of the Israeli army. The mayor of Ramallah lost a foot and suffered paralysis of one leg; the mayor of Nablus lost both legs while the mayor of al-Bireh stopped using his personal car for some time. In 1982, all three were dismissed for refusing to collaborate with the Israeli administration and for "inciting the population to revolt." Between 1982 and 1986, an Israeli officer was named to manage affairs in the two municipalities. A closely-knit network of local committees and associations developed to see to needs of the population inadequately tended by the occupying authorities. These groups and other non-governmental organisations gradually developed in Ramallah after the arrival of the PA in 1995 in addition to numerous NGOs and several political institutions: the Palestinian parliament meets here and several ministries also have their offices here, albeit the new, unfinished Palestinian Legislative Council building stands in the closed ghetto of Abu Dis, East Jerusalem next to the Wall, a new settlement *(Kidmat Zion)* and a Palestinian West Bank hotel newly annexed by Israel as "absentee property" (named as theft by Israeli newspaper Haaretz, in an editorial), with another new settlement *(Nof Zion)* on the opposite hill.

❐ Tel al-Nasbeh

Located on top of a hill overlooking the southern entrance to Ramallah, this site has been identified as the Biblical city of Mizbeh. There are ruins here from the Bronze Age as well as those of a city built *about* 1100 BC. Incomplete excavations in the 1930s revealed part of the rampart, visible today. At the foot of the hill (to the south) are also modest ruins of a *caravanserai*. A walk along the hill is especially interesting for an overall view of recent urban development in Ramallah-al-Bireh and the equally recent development of the Israeli settlement *Psagot* (to the east).

❐ The Crusader Church

Al-Bireh - junction of al-Ein and al-Balad al-Qadim streets.

This church has been thoroughly excavated by archaeologists; Christian tradition has it that this was where Joseph and Mary lost twelve-year-old Jesus on their way to Jerusalem. They found him only later in Jerusalem, praying in the great temple there. This story originated in the late Crusader period and is not related in the New Testament.

Ramallah

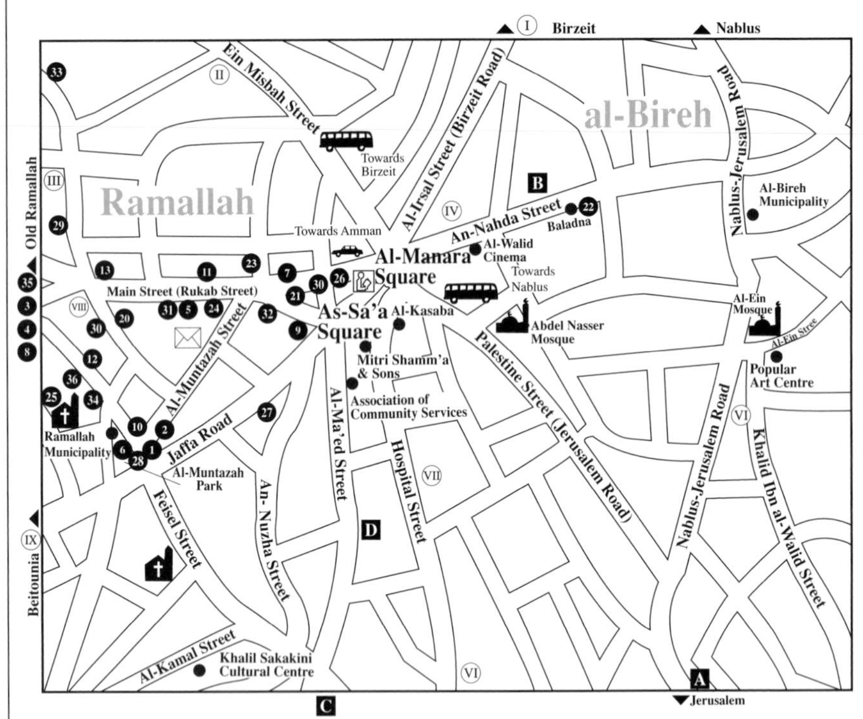

Contacts

I Addameer
II Teachers' Creativity Centre
III Al-Haq
IV Charitable Assoc. of Amwas
V PACE
VI PARC
VII UAWC
VIII HDIP
IX Ramallah Cultural Palace

Cafés

1. Beit Falastine
2. Black Horse
3. Al-Mattal Cinema-Café
4. Diwan
5. Al-'Asseel
6. Al-Muntazah Park
7. Kan Bata Zaman
8. Nadi es-Saraya
9. Privacy
10. Pronto
11. Sheish Beish
12. Stones
13. Zyriab Gallery

Restaurants

20. Angelo's
21. Antika's
22. Baladna-Urjuwan
23. Chinese House Restaurant
24. Damascus
25. Darna
26. Eiffel
27. Al-Bardoni
28. Al-Muntazah
29. Flamingo's
30. Jaffar
31. La Strada
32. Leili Falastine
33. Mandy Tatchi
34. Nefertiti
35. Taboun
36. Zarour

Hotels

A. City Inn
B. Al-Wihdah
C. Grand Park
D. Merryland

Practical Information

Ramallah is a fascinating urban centre for all visitors interested in political and social issues, since many institutions of Palestinian government and non-governmental organisations and diplomatic missions are based here. An effervescent cultural scene contributes to Ramallah's truly unique atmosphere. Ramallah has replaced Jerusalem as the cultural and political centre of Palestine, although Jerusalem represents 40% of Palestine's economy, due to tourism. Recently (in 2005) it is becoming harder for East Jerusalem Palestinians to visit friends and family in Ramallah because of checkpoint restrictions, as Israel increases its apartheid policies and forcibly separates Jerusalem from Ramallah. Despite all closures, at night the city remains lively until late.

All services are concentrated in a relatively small perimeter where everything can be easily reached on foot. An in-town taxi costs from NIS 7 to NIS 10 at night. There is no official tourism office as yet, but the **Ministry of Tourism and Antiquities** *(third floor, Palestinian Investment Bank Building, al-Bireh)* will answer any questions. A number of money-changing offices in the centre of town have the best exchange rates. The **British Bank** near Muntazah Park has an automatic teller outside, which accepts international credit cards (Visa, MasterCard, Cirrus, Maestro, etc.). At the top of al-Muntazah Street is a **post office**.

Cafés

There are several popular cafés on al-Quds Road. They are usually open from the early morning hours until late at night. They serve non-alcoholic drinks, and one can smoke a water pipe; cards or backgammon *(sheish beish)* are the two most popular games. Ramallah's cafés and restaurants are the soul of its night life. At the end of its main street, the ***Zyriab*** café *(on the 1st floor, ☎/Fax 02-295 9093)* is a café-gallery which features figurative art: Tayseer Barakat, the café proprietor is an artist, and one often finds him here, absorbed by the creation of a new work. Barakat was born in the Shati refugee camp in Gaza (www.art-barakat.4t.com).

Like many other cafés, ***al-'Asseel*** *(on the last floor of Tannous Building)* is located on the building's top floor; with a view over the main street, it is spacious with an attractive decor; no alcoholic beverages are served here. There are concerts every Thursday and Friday. A little farther along the main street is the ***KanBata Zaman*** café - small, modern and intimate. Near the centre of the Old City of Ramallah, on al-Tira and es-Saraya streets, the café-cinematheque ***al-Mattal*** and the ***Diwan café-restaurant*** are both located in old traditional residences with extremely beautiful interiors. Al-Mattal shows quality films in its small theatre *(☎ 02-298 6529, films at 16:00)*. Private showings of particular films for groups can be arranged *(There is a wide selection of films, usually subtitled in English)*. Nearby *(200 m to the right)*, the ***First Ramallah Group*** or ***es-Saraya Club*** has an outdoor cafeteria,

Zyriab
(Baghdad 789 - Andalusia 857)

Zyriab was a musician in the court of Haroun er-Rashid before he moved to Cordoba, where he founded a musical academy, where he introduced the lute *(oud)*. Ibn Khaldoun described his work, which became the basis of Arabo-Andalusian music, as "an ocean which flooded Seville and all Andalusia."

an outdoor swimming pool, a basketball court and sports rooms *(☎ 02-295 2706/2609, Fax: 02-298 2583; www.sirreyeh.org)*. Festivals of traditional dance and of music, as well as political reunions, are regularly organised here. The café-restaurants ***Pronto*** and ***Stones***, around the ***al-Muntazah Park*** are original and good; the service at ***Stones***, however, sometimes leaves something to be desired. ***Beit Falastine*** restaurant's ***Black Horse*** cafe, with subdued lighting, has a superb view of al-Muntazah Park and above all -- the entire west of Ramallah. ***Sheish Beish***, a tiny café *(opening hours: 8:30-22:00)*, should not be missed -- it's an ideal place for a traditional breakfast (cheese, *za'atar,* olive oil and fruit juice), at a very reasonable price. Its name refers to a Turkish game better known in Europe as backgammon.

Restaurants

There is a wide choice of small *falafel* and *shwarma* restaurants in the city centre; most are cheap and stay open late at night. ***Antika's*** *(Main Street)* is one of the best self-service restaurants. ***Fawanees*** ("The Lanterns" in Arabic) on Ben Bella Street (or Ministry of Culture Street), serves delicious garnished bread (with cheese and *za'atar*, spinach, or meat). Near Dowar es-Sa'a Square *(Ma'ahed Street)* the popular ***Leili Falistine*** restaurant *(Ramoun Building, 2nd floor - ☎ 02-295 8869)* serves traditional Palestinian dishes *(maklouba, kidra, bamia,* zucchini, and stuffed vine leaves, among others). The dishes are excellent "home cooking" and reasonably priced. ***Taboun*** *(in the Cairo-Amman Bank Building)*, ***Union of Palestinian Women Committees*** *(☎ 02-298 0505)*, and ***Baladna-Urjuwan*** *(☎ 02-295 8434, open 9:00 - 17:00)* also serve traditional dishes. ***Al-Bardoni*** (terrace), ***Flamingos, Zarour***, and ***Muntazah*** (terrace) are restaurants in another category: they serve mainly traditional Palestinian appetizers *(mezze)* and quality grilled meat. ***Bayt al-Falastine*** *(5th floor of the building overlooking al-Muntazah Park)*, and the ***Nefertiti*** *(Post Office Street)* have good *moloukhiya* and *musakham*. The best pizzas, cooked over a wood fire, are at ***Angelo's*** or ***La Strada*** (Italian cuisine), and ***Pronto*** restaurant (French cuisine); their high-quality pizzas are quite expensive. There are also two exotic Palestinian-Chinese restaurants: the ***Chinese House Restaurant*** and ***Mandy Tatchi***. The best oriental pastries are at ***Eiffel*** *(near al-Manara Square)*, ***Damascus*** and ***Jaffar***, on the main street. But the very newest restaurant in Ramallah, ***Darna*** *(☎ 02-295 0590, opposite the Melkite Greek Catholic Church, near the Municipality, at al-Sahel Street)* is a completely different experience. Opened during the past year, it is so luxurious people ask how the owner dares to be so brave in the current "situation" to open; his response is that in dark days, the people need and deserve the best and that Darna is therefore intended to grant people a moment's peace, escape and luxury. It is thus a divine retreat into its own world of graciousness.

Accommodation

City Inn Hotel is definitely the most famous hotel in the region. Situated near a roundabout at the northern entrance to Ramallah-al-Bireh (Area C), it was first requisitioned by the Israeli army in May 2000. The army moved in again after September 28, 2001, converting it into a regular fortress. Israeli snipers took over the top of the building, which overlooks the place where most Ramallah demonstrations congregate: a roundabout now called Martyrs' Square, whose name speaks for itself. There is a second very comfortable ***City Inn Palace Hotel***, which opened a short time before the beginning of the al-Aqsa Intifada, in the centre of Ramallah *(Jerusalem Street; ☎ 02-240 8080; www.cityinn-hotel.com; single, double or triple rooms at $70, $100 and $130)*.

The ***Grand Park Hotel***, a luxury hotel, is the favourite of international diplomatic delegations *(al-Mansyoun Heights; ☎ 02-298 6194 info@grandpark.com, www.grandpark.com; single (NIS 110), double (NIS 130) and triple (NIS 150) or suite (NIS 350)*. Some distance from the city centre, it has all the facilities of a luxury hotel (swimming pool, gym, coffee shop and restaurant, banquet and conference hall, bar, patio).

Al-Wihdah Hotel *(on al-Nahda Street, just opposite the police station, on the third and fourth floor-no elevator service; ☎ /Fax 02-298 0412; single, double, and triple rooms NIS 100, 150, and 180).* The rooms are clean and spacious and it is the least expensive hotel in the city.

The Merryland Hotel *(al-Ma'ahed Street; ☎ 02-298 7176, Fax 02-298 7074; single, double, and triple rooms, NIS 120, 170, and 200)* is good value, and also in the city centre. This hotel's furnishings are strictly utilitarian, but the rooms are well-equipped (television, shower).

The ***Pension Miami*** has eleven small rooms with a shower and a television *(on Jaffa Road, next to Muntazah Park; ☎ 02-995 6808, fax 02-995 5874¸ single, double, and triple rooms, NIS 130, 170, and 200).*

Palestinian Embroidery

One can find embroidery with original, high quality designs at the ***Association of Community Services*** shop on al-Ma'ahed Street; or ***Mitri Shamm'a & Sons***, at the main intersection where the al-Kasaba Theatre is located. Both are near Dowar es-Sa'a Square (Clock Square). The fixed prices are fair on embroidered work made especially for framing, trays, shawls, scarves, and other embroidered garments or table decorations. Another embroidery centre is at the Melkite Church near Ramallah Municipality (next to Darna restaurant), at al-Sahel Street, with the most gorgeous choice of colours - the thread is imported specially from France to this women's co-operative and is of the highest quality.

Cultural Centres and Entertainment

Al-Mattal Cinema

(See ***al-Mattal*** café-cinema, p. 231)

Al-Qassaba Theatre and Cinema

On al-Mughtaribeen Street, near Clock Square. ☎ 02-296 5292/3; www.alkasaba.org. Programmes available in public places as well as the Internet.

Films shown here are largely recent Hollywood productions, but there are occasional exceptions. *(Daily film showings start at 16:00. Theatre performances start at 19:00.)* Theatre here is more original than the films and proves a unique occasion to watch a play despite the language barrier. There is a pleasant café-restaurant

Al-Sharqi Turkish Bath

Al-Irsal Street, near the Ministry of Planning. Open 10:00-22:00, for men: Monday, Wednesday-Saturday; for women: Sunday and Tuesday; hammam and drink NIS 35; shampoo and supplementary massage NIS 25 extra. ☎ 02-240 8281.

Take a break here and emerge feeling relaxed and refreshed.

Al-Walid Cinema

At al-Nadha Street. One can watch three consecutive films for the price of one (admission: NIS 13, main auditorium, NIS 17, balcony). ☎ 02-295 2295.

This cinema specialises in American and Asiatic B-movies and recent Egyptian films. Dilapidated and none too clean, the cinema is typical of old neighbourhood movie theatres. People also come here to chat, eat and smoke.

Baladna (Our Homeland)

On al-Nadha Street, opposite the police station destroyed by Israeli missiles on 12 October 2000. ☎ 02-295 8434.The centre regularly holds shows and concerts, for children in particular. Films are shown occasionally. The ***Urjuwan*** *("purple" in Arabic) café-restaurant on the ground floor is open until 17:00. At lunchtime there is a different daily dish of the day.*

Khalil Sakakini Cultural Centre

On al-Raja' Street, near the Lutheran Church. Open everyday 8:30-15:00 except Friday. ☎ /Fax 02-298 7374/5, www.sakakini.org. Current programmes available in public places.

This centre opened in 1996 in a restored traditional mansion which was damaged when the Israel army broke in, in April of the same year. The centre promotes the visual arts and Palestinian heritage, past and present, with exhibitions of painting and photography, concerts, documentary films, historical information and on-going workshops for children and adults. Activities here are a living memorial to Palestinian writer Khalil Sakakini (portrait on p. 138).

Popular Art Centre

On al-Ain Street, on the second floor opposite al-Ein Mosque in al-Bireh; ☎ *02-240 3891; www.popularartcentre.org; programmes available in public places.*

This centre was established in 1987 by the al Funoun esh-Sha'abiyeh Palestinian Popular Dance Troupe *(www.el-funoun.org)*. It has a leading role in organizing cultural activities and events; it initiated the Day of Cultural Heritage celebrated annually on 7 October. Among its activities, the centre organizes music and dance festivals, workshops for children, folk dancing *(dabka)* courses, jazz, music, puppets and drama and ensembles of traditional Palestinian music. The centre sells audio and videocassettes produced by it, especially of the superb performances of the al-Funoun Troupe - *Zaghareed (Ululations)* and *The Jerusalem Glory*, for example. The art centre also houses a cinema which shows international films here daily *(beginning at 18:00 or 19:00; NIS 15)*.

Ramallah Cultural Palace

Tokyo Street, Ramallah ☎ *02-298 4704 www.ramallahculturalpalace.org*

Ramallah Cultural Palace opened in July 2004, with $6 million donated by the Japanese Government for this state of the art cultural centre and conference centre; it hosts music, dance, theatre and film programmes.

Contacts

Addameer ("conscience") - Prisoners' Support & Human Rights Association

Al-Irsal Street, Al-Isra' Building, 7th floor; ☎ *02-296 0446, www.addameer.org ; Reports on prisoners in Israeli and Palestinian prisons. Meetings with former prisoners and briefings on the situation of imprisoned Palestinians.*

Addameer was established in 1992 by a group of activists interested in human rights; it provides legal and moral support for Palestinian prisoners. Such support may include visiting the prisoners, following up their cases with their families, launching support campaigns and protests and working to end torture through monitoring and legal procedures.

Palestinian prisoners: prisoners of war

With the inception of the "peace process," the situation of prisoners greatly deteriorated. The transfer of detainees to prisons inside the State of Israel made family visits more difficult and since the al-Aqsa Intifada, almost impossible. The Oslo Accords did not address the issue of liberating prisoners: Palestinian negotiators mistakenly assumed that the "peace process" automatically meant the freedom of Palestinian political prisoners, defined by international law as prisoners of war.

Some prisoners were indeed released, but Israel reserved the right to define the criteria relevant for prisoner release, excluding any clemency for prisoners from Jerusalem or from the 1948 territories. Whilst the 2005 Sharm Summit was supposed to free up to 900 prisoners, currently only 500 have been released, and they were mainly prisoners anyhow due for release. There are over 8,000 prisoners: 4,124 detained without trial, 129 women, 340 children, plus 905 administrative detainees and 2,457 sentenced prisoners.

Of the 1,400 prisoners released between 1995 and 2000, 1,000 were serving short sentences: many were labourers condemned to several months for having entered Israel without a permit, while others were at the end of their term. Some even had their sentence lengthened in order to be qualified for release on a certain date, while others were simply common law prisoners.

In October 2002, the State of Israel detained over 5,000 Palestinians in prison, including 300 minors. Often arrested in their homes under extremely brutal conditions in front of humiliated families, and terrorised by soldiers, detainees are detained at interrogation centres. Israeli law stipulates that interrogators may hold Palestinians from the West Bank and the Gaza Strip for as long as 108 days. Torture and solitary confinement are common practice and lawyers' visits are very hard to negotiate. Detainees are tried and sentenced by military courts, and the procedures are bewilderingly arbitrary. Recently, Mohammad Abu Sukkar, who had been in prison for over 25 years, was the longest serving Palestinian prisoner. The youngest prisoner was a young woman, Sawsan Abu Tourki, arrested at the age of 14 on September 6, 2001.

Al-Haq Association ("The Right")

Main Street, ☎ 02-295 6421 www.alhaq.org

Established in 1979, al-Haq is affiliated to the International Commission of Jurists in Geneva, Switzerland. The association documents violations of basic human rights in the Occupied Territories, publishing studies on Israeli violations of international laws and giving legal assistance to Palestinian victims of violations committed by the occupation authorities (for example, the revoking of Jerusalem residence IDs, demolition of homes, administrative detention). It also addresses itself to abuses of human rights by the Palestinian Authority (e.g. prisoners arrested for their opinions or unfair trials).

DCI-PS - Defence for Children International - Palestine Section

Al-Khulafa Road, Es-Sartawi Building 2nd floor; ☎ 02-240 7530; www.dci-pal.org

Affiliated to Geneva-based Defence of Children International, the Palestinian section of the DCI was established in 1992. It concentrates its efforts on legal and social aid for children and gathers evidence on situations of Israeli violations particularly related to child rights: curfew, assassination, shelling of civilian houses and schools, imprisonment, torture.

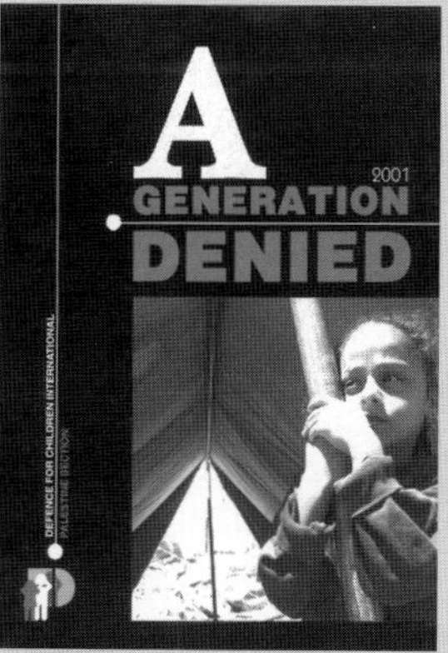

Military order # 132: Issued in 1967, invalid since 1993, this order to arrest 12-14-year-olds was reactivated in 1999 during the Barak administration, and was widely applied after the beginning of the al-Aqsa Intifada.

Child fatalities according to circumstances of death September 28, 2000 - October 31, 2004

	2000	*2001*	*2002*	*2003*	*2004*	*Total*
Clashes	80	42	30	36	31	219
Air or ground attack	4	17	67	37	69	194
Assassination attempt	0	12	19	14	7	52
Random gun fire	9	17	50	38	40	154
Closures	1	3	9	3	0	16
Unexploded ordnance	0	7	12	2	2	23
Home demolition	0	0	5	0	0	5
Total	***94***	***98***	***192***	***130***	***149***	***663***

DCI - Palestine Section, *A Generation Denied, 2001*

Health, Development, Information & Policy (HDIP)

☎ 02-298-5372 hdip@hdip.org

Founded in 1989 by presidential candidate, Dr. Moustafa Barghouthi, a social activist who also founded the Union of Palestinian Medical Relief Committees to focus on development and health issues. Palestine Monitor (palmon@hdip.org) is a news and information agency at HDIP: www.palestinemonitor.org.

In'ash al-Usra Society

Samiha Khalil Street (al-Bireh). ☎ 02-240 2876; folklore museum, open Saturday- Thursday 8:00-14:00. NIS 2 entry.

Established in 1965, In'ash al-Usra Society is the oldest women's organisation; its founder Samiha Khalil (Um Khalil), who was opposed to the Oslo Accords, was the only candidate to run in the Palestinian presidential elections against Yasser Arafat in 1996. The association runs a day-care centre and offers training sessions for women; it also has a reference library and a folklore museum (a dusty exhibition of pieces on display without documentation) and is pursuing a project of documenting Palestinian folk traditions.

Palestinian Association for Cultural Exchanges (PACE)

Near the al-Ain Mosque. ☎ 02-240 7610, www.planet.edu/pace. One day's guided visit costs between NIS 120-NIS 140 (for min. group of 5 persons).

This association organises tours to sites of archaeological and historical interest as well as urban and rural areas in the West Bank and Gaza Strip. The main focus is on the daily life of Palestinians living under occupation, the customary alternative tourism approach. Individuals can join PACE tours offered on its weekly calendar (depending on the situation). One of the most original tours is "A visit around Nablus followed by a cultural evening in the hammam" *(from 14:00-20:30. NIS 140).*

PARC - Palestinian Agricultural Relief Committees

Government Hospital Road, Ramallah. ☎ 02-295 2650; www.pal-arc.org; contacts with local farmers can be arranged.

Founded in 1983 by a group of agronomists, PARC has created various programmes in rural areas to oppose land confiscation and improve agricultural techniques, in particular by creating ways to compensate for cuts in energy and water and distribution. Ways to circumvent restrictions on freedom of movement are high on its agenda: it has developed a network of alternative roads and paths to help farmers reach their land, routes which the entire population resorts to due to the Israeli authorities' imposition of curfews and closure

Teacher Creativity Centre

Street for Bir Zeit taxis, ☎ 02-295 9960; www.teachercc.org

Teachers created the committee in 1995 to focus on educating and training teachers, and develop tools for teaching. It also promotes awareness of the specific needs of children and concepts of human rights and democracy. To this end, the committee was a principal creator of the civic education programme developed for public schools in co-operation with the PA Ministry of Education.

Union of Agricultural Workers Committees (UAWC)

Government Hospital Street, Ramallah, ☎ 02-295 4289; email: uawc@palnet.com [See also UAWC Gaza, p. 281] Field trips can be organised for groups on request (cost variable). From October to end-November, the union welcomes international volunteers in the villages to help with the olive harvest. This is a unique occasion for participants to share village life and learn about the difficulties of Palestinian peasant-farmers.

Founded in 1986, the UAWC is an active local non-government organisation (NGO) in the West Bank and Gaza Strip. Its main objective is to prevent further Israeli land confiscation and to increase agricultural productivity, particularly by growing crops in greenhouses and encouraging people to return to working the land. UAWC offers courses, including the amelioration of water resources, and the development of agricultural co-operatives, land reclamation and a programme for producing quality virgin olive oil for export.

Women's Associations: Women's Affairs Technical Committee (WATC)

Radio Street, Awwad Centre, ☎ 02-298 6497, watcorg@palnet.com,

The WATC works for women's empowerment on different levels through lobbying and networking, and is establishing a "National Government Body for Women." Various training courses are offered here.

■ North and East of Ramallah

Beitin

The village of Beitin is on the outskirts of al-Bireh, separated from it only by a huge Israeli military camp, HQ for the entire region around Ramallah (north and east).

Beitin is now a residential village near Ramallah on the slopes of what was once a flourishing city of religious importance. Archaeologists have found evidence that herding communities lived here, at the beginning of the Copper Age. *Circa* 3200 BC in the Early Bronze Age, animal sacrifice to the Canaanite gods was regularly practised. In the eighteenth century BC, Beitin was a significant fortified city-state. When the Egyptians captured it in 1550 BC, it went into decline, only to reassert its full splendour in the fourteenth century BC. The city remained a bastion of culture until the Assyrian conquest in 721 BC.

The oldest name for the city that has survived, Bethel ("House of God"), reflects the religious function of the site, with its reference to El, the supreme Canaanite deity. In the Iron Age, the worship of El, associated with agrarian fertility rites, gradually lost ground to the emerging worship of Yahweh, a religion of herders, and Bethel was known as a sacred city like Jerusalem and Mt. Jarzim. The Old Testament mentions Bethel in connection with the Patriarchs - Abraham, Jacob and Lot. Abraham built an altar "in the mountain region east of Bethel" on his way south from Nablus, while Jacob dreamed of a ladder reaching up to heaven. The city remained strong as a federation of different local groups, removed from fights for power, until its capture by the Assyrians in 721 BC. The city did not, however, disappear from the face of the map; it even saw prosperous periods once again in Roman and especially Byzantine times, but as an agricultural town. The name of the place was handed down over the centuries and finally written as Beitin in its Arabicised form, evidence of the continuity of the people and traditions here. Jewish settlers originally from Europe chose to call their colony here *Beit El*, like the Biblical name, in a poor attempt to erase the history of thousands of years and replace it with a deformed version, motivated by their politico-religious project.

Among the rare ruins of the old city still visible today are the **Hellenistic tower**, the church and **Byzantine monastery** in a place called Roujm Abu Ammar. The view from here gives an idea of the extent to which Israeli settlement has transformed the land. Beit El built on confiscated village land is home to more than 4,600 settlers.

❑ Tel et-Tal (Ai - or Tourmos Aya)

Between the arid hills to the east and the olive groves to the west, a large Canaanite city-state (10 hectares) grew up at the beginning of the third millennium BC. Protected by a fortified wall, the city possessed all the characteristics of an important Bronze Age urban centre: a residential area, an area for craft industry, a palace and a temple. Since it was destroyed *circa* 2400 BC, the city was never revived; a small village continued to exist on the site until it was abandoned *circa* 1050 BC. The Bible relates how Joshua destroyed the site Ai and slew all its inhabitants (Joshua 8:14-29).

The site is found on a small hill, dominated by the village Deir Dibwane; remains of the Bronze Age wall, and houses dating back to the Iron Age, can be seen on the site. But doubtless it is the rural setting which enchants visitors most; in the spring, the green countryside is, for hikers, an enticing invitation hard to resist.

Taybeh

Taybeh is a village with a population of 1,200 people, most of whom are Christian. It is mentioned several times in the Old Testament as Ophra and, in the New Testament, as Ephraim. When Saladin liberated Palestine from the Crusaders in 1187, he passed through the village of Ephron, whose name in Arabic means "demon." Saladin ordered the village to be renamed with a name that emphasised the beauty of the place, hence Taybeh al-Issem ("the Beautiful Name"). Today, the villagers are particularly proud of the Christian tradition that identifies Taybeh (Ephraim) as the place where Jesus chose to stay with his disciples on the night before his Passion (John 11:54). The villagers even claim to have perpetuated Christianity from its early roots here, even if, since then, many Christian families have converted to Islam.

The **traditional peasant home** inside the fence around the Roman Catholic (Latin) parish property shows that Christians and Muslims shared exactly the same way of life. The **al-Khader church**, originally Byzantine, then rebuilt by the Crusaders, was abandoned at the end of the Crusader occupation; now in ruins, it is still an object of special devotion where sacrifices are placed on important occasions such as the return of a native of Taybeh from abroad or the birth of a new baby. Archaeologists are currently working on the ruins; notice in particular the Crusader floor in the central nave: the pavement is made of stone alternating with bands of mosaic work. The baptistry is from the Byzantine period, but has occupied its present place only since the Crusader period when the church was rebuilt on a smaller scale and the baptistry moved. Byzantine mosaics with various motifs (rose buds, interlaced designs) have been discovered under the Crusader walls. At the top of the village, dominating the ruins of a Crusader fortification, is Saint Elias Castle, some of whose ramparts are visible.
In the twentieth century, the village saw an exodus of emigrants; yet one emigrant returned to Taybeh in 1994 to add a new element to its renown. Nadim Khoury founded the Taybeh Beer Brewing Company here in 1995, the only beer company in the Middle East. Taybeh is a high quality natural beer *(☎ 02-289 8868 or 02-289 9293; www.taybehbeer.net, tours of the brewery)* praised by connoisseurs and up to the standards of any German beer. In fact, there are now Taybeh breweries in Germany and in the United Kingdom. Taybeh beer (*taybeh* also means "delicious" in Arabic) is found in all Palestinian cafés serving alcohol.

The Hospice of the Sisters of the Holy Cross of Jerusalem *(☎/Fax: 02-289 8161; half board $29, bivouac $5 - bring your own sleeping bag.)* This hospice is located on the property of the Catholic church and it provides an opportunity to extend one's stay in the village. The rooms are simple and kept with care.

An association dedicated to the restoration of the local Palestinian historical heritage and stone cutting is in the process of being founded. The association will include the Taybeh community, the Palestinian Authority Ministry of Tourism and Antiquities and Friends of the Tour de France *(Call Mrs. Ferial Kurt, Women's Association of Taybeh:☎ 02-289 8450 or Fakher, ☎ 0522 680 154).*

The house *(ed-dar* or *al-beit)*

Traditional rural homes usually contained one large square room, 5 to 6 metres square, a stone ceiling with ribbed vaults and narrow windows. A small stairway led to a unique room in these traditional peasant homes - the *mastaba*, which was slightly raised. The *mastaba*, reached by a small staircase, was kitchen, living room and bedroom all in one. During the day, mattresses for sleeping were piled up in a large alcove *(qaws)*. On the lower level, the livestock (sheep, goats, donkeys or mules) were kept in a space, the *rawia*, where agricultural tools were also stored. The entrance to the stairs allowed heat from the animals to heat the family area on the upper level. Rooms were added on around the courtyard *(hosh)* when there were additions to the family.

Jalazone Refugee Camp

UNRWA office, Mahmoud al-Atharbeh, ☎ 02-281 0874.

Established in 1949 on rocky hills 7 kilometres from the city of Ramallah, Jalazone refugee camp has a population of over 8,000 refugees, most of whom come originally from the cities of Lydd and Ramle and from villages in the centre of Palestine. The camp, which is in Area B, is an enclave surrounded by Area C territories, making it particularly vulnerable to any form of closure decreed by Israel. As in most refugee camps, the infrastructure is minimal, and the lack of a sewage system poses a serious sanitary problem. There are two schools in the camp, one for boys (898 pupils) and one for girls (943 pupils): the number of children makes it necessary for the teachers to work double shifts. Situated on the main road from Ramallah to Nablus (now a by-pass road exclusively for Israeli settlers), the camp was very active during the first Intifada. Twelve teenagers have been killed by Israeli soldiers or settlers (living nearby in the hardline settlement Beit El, home to Israeli politician, Benny Elon - known as one of the most militant, rabid settler leaders).

Jifna

Village council, ☎ 02-281 1073.

At the end of the Hellenistic period, Jifna was already called a "small city," appearing as "Gofna" on the sixth century Madaba Map. Today, Jifna is a small village with a Christian majority, famous for it annual apricot festival (May 1-15). An old, fortified house of the Ottoman period, **al - Burj**, recently renovated, houses a cultural café-restaurant where there are conferences, musical evenings and recreational activities. It also has a museum and exhibitions. *(☎ 02-281 0801/2)* A hotel is under construction. The house is a charming place to spend an evening near Ramallah.

Birzeit

The village

The village of Birzeit *(2 km from the campus of the University of Birzeit)* is a lively place, thanks to its proximity to the university. There are restaurants, Internet cafés, shops and chemist shops and a hostel for foreign students and many rooms for rent. The university's Department of Archaeology is located in the centre of the village, providing the opportunity to visit a small **archaeological museum** *(open Sunday-Thursday, 9:00-14:30; ☎ 02-298 2000)*. Birzeit is equally famous for its international music festival every summer (cancelled since the beginning of the al-Asqa Intifada). The countryside around Birzeit is beautiful and an ideal point of departure for walks or hikes. With luck, you may surprise gazelles, partridges or even foxes in these stunningly beautiful countryside surroundings. Have a look at the many dry stone constructions you will find scattered around the farmlands. These constructions on two floors are known by the term *qasr* or *mantara*. The ground floor was used to store agricultural tools and harvested crops; the upper level was used to keep a lookout and was also where temporary help would sleep, notably during the olive harvest.

• Useful Addresses

Ein al-Hammam Swimming Pool *(☎ 02-281 0076; open 10:00 -19:30, mid-June - end-August, NIS 10 for children, NIS 15 for adults)* In the eastern part of Birzeit, this swimming area has several outdoor pools for wading and swimming, one indoor pool for women and refreshment areas. It is a pleasant, busy venue, full of children.

Al-Koukh café-restaurant *(☎ 02- 281 1018, open 11:00 - midnight)*, next to the the Ein al-Hammam swimming pool. The setting and view of its countryside surroundings are delightful; in the evening, the scent of flowers on the air gives a very special aura. Good grilled meats and salads are served here for reasonable prices.

The University

A linguistic programme is available (classical and spoken Arabic) for foreign students, as is one for Arab civilisation. ☎ *02-298 2153 www.birzeit.edu*

The history of the university dates to the year 1924 when the first school especially for girls was established here under the direction of Nabiha Nasir (1891-1951). The school grew into a community college called Birzeit College, which delivered a diploma after two years of study (lower diploma). To ameliorate the situation after the 1967 occupation, when students had to cope with travel restrictions imposed by the Israeli military authorities, the college established in 1972 a centre for higher education. Birzeit University was officially inaugurated in 1976. To this day, the occupation authorities have not ceased to affect life of the university and students. Between 1979 and 1992, the university was closed 75% of the time. Today, the Israelis no longer issue closure orders since the university is considered to be in an autonomous zone (Area A). However, the army controls all access routes.

To the west of Ramallah

The Shuqba Caves

15 km northwest of Ramallah. Village council head, Adam Shallah, ☎ *02-248 4201. Prehistoric caves on the northern side of* ***Wadi Natouf****. Bring a torch or flashlight for a visit to the caves.*

The discovery in 1924 in one of the caves of Wadi Natouf of human bones belonging to 45 individuals pointed to the existence of a community in the process of sedentarisation. Prehistorians were able to define another culture, known by the term "Natoufian." The Natoufian era dates from *circa* 12,500 BC, when it flourished from south to north of the Levant, with its centre in Palestine; it was a precursor of the Neolithic Age. Natoufian culture was characterised by many specific traits: sedentarisation and the formation of "villages" and an improvement in intensive hunting techniques, with a preference for the gazelle, which was a source of food, leather and bone. The people grew cereal crops - the sickle appears at this moment in history - and some vegetables. Dogs became the first animal to be domesticated at this time, and observances for burying the dead became recognised - for example, the dead were sometimes buried with decorated teeth.

Ras Karkar

Village of 1500 inhabitants. Village council, Rezek Nofal, ☎ *059-798 660.*

The fortified residence of Bani Harith Shamaliyeh, constructed in the eighteenth century, extends over 2430 sq.m of the hilltop here. Its monumental entry, galleries, stables and a spacious interior courtyard (330 sq.m), surrounded by a series of rooms, speak for the importance of this feudal village, which collected taxes from eleven nearby villages also belonging to the sheikh. Only part of this old village is still inhabited.

Qibya

Destroyed village to the west of Ramallah

The massacre of Qibya took place on October 14, 1953, when Israeli military forces led by Ariel Sharon attacked this West Bank village then under Jordanian control. The village was bombarded by artillery blocking all exits from the village or indeed from the houses (whose huge wooden doorways bear hundreds of bullet-holes to this day). Casualties numbered 67 men, women and children, some twelve of whose skeletons still remain in one of the village's dried out wells. In addition, 56 houses, a school, water reservoir, and mosque were deliberately blown up so as to preclude the return of survivors. Today, the village, near the "Green Line" (also known as the '67 Border or 1949 Armistice Line) is near the Modi'in settlement bloc to its south; the Wall to its west and south and a new settler-only bypass road to the east; thus, like other Palestinian villages, it is stranded in a ghetto with minimal access for its agricultural produce to markets.

Amwas and Latrun

On the Jaffa-Jerusalem Road, take the exit to Beersheba.

Emmaus or Amwas was first mentioned in the Bible in descriptions of the struggle between the Seleucids and the Maccabee dynasty (in 161 BC) for control of this strategic point between Jerusalem and the coastal plain (1 Maccabee 3:40, 3:57; 4:3-4). Its privileged location brought fortune to the village, as well as misfortune. In 221 AD, Roman Emperor Heliogabalus bestowed the status of city-state on Emmaus at the request of Julius the African, naming it "Nicopolis," in Greek meaning: "the city of victory." People here were early converts to Christianity and a Byzantine tradition says it was in Emmaus that Christ appeared to his disciples Simon and Cleopas after his resurrection (Luke 24:13-34). The visitation of Jesus at the village bestowed on it a rich religious iconography, which praised the hospitality and generosity of its people; the tradition died out towards the seventh century after an epidemic of plague broke out here, but was

successively kept alive in other places. In fact, the villages of Abu Ghosh, and Qubeiba and Qalunya (a demolished village in the district of Jerusalem, which had 910 inhabitants in 1944) also claim to be the place where the event occurred. In 1948, Zionist troops were forced to give up the conquest of Amwas. Nonetheless, 85% of the land of the village was taken, including the most fertile. The Amwas villagers who had become landless peasants found jobs either on other farms or in construction work in neighbouring cities, mainly Jerusalem and Ramallah.

"The houses in Beit Nouba were extremely beautiful houses built in stone. Some of them were even luxurious buildings. Each home was surrounded by olive trees, apricot trees and vineyards, as well as cypress trees and other majestic trees, which provided generous patches of shade. Every tree was carefully watered. There were rows of lovingly tended vegetables planted between the trees. Inside the houses, we found a wounded Egyptian officer and several elderly men and women. At midday, the first bulldozer arrived and advanced towards a house, the first one on the edge of the village. In one go, it tore up the cypress and olive trees. Ten minutes later, the house and all its modest furnishings and furniture were a heap of rubble."

■ Report sent to the members of the Israeli parliament (Knesset) by an Israeli soldier, Amos Kenan, a reservist in the battalion that took over the area.

I am from Amwas (Emmaus). I left Amwas on June 6, 1967, with my child, without taking anything with me ... Near Amwas, there were 60 soldiers in the Arab armed forces. My brother, who was mukhtar of the town, and I were in the street exactly at midnight. Our house was on the main road. We heard two cars approaching. Someone got out of one of them and called out to us, "Abu Deeb, Abu Deeb" (my brother's name). It was the captain of the Arab army in the region. He said to him, "Abu Deeb, we are pulling out. Take care of yourselves." The town of Amwas owned a bus. We got as many people into the bus as possible to take them to the parish house in Latrun. ... The shelling had started. My two cousins and I took refuge in the [Amwas village] church ... A patrol came to the parish house where the group in the bus had taken shelter. One of the soldiers said to them: "There's only one way open to you: the road to Ramallah. We don't want to see anyone going back to his home." An old man said to the soldier, "I want to go back home to get a pair of shoes," because he was only in sandals. The soldier replied, "If you stop at your house, you will be killed. You must take the road to Ramallah." [A cease-fire was ordered.] ...
It was about the 13th or 14th of June. Nadim ez-Zarrou, who was mayor of Ramallah and the military administrator of the town, announced that everyone should go back to his property. The people asked, "To Amwas, too?" "Yes," he said, "to Amwas, Beit Nouba and Yalou - you can return to your villages." Everyone who had heard the news started back along the road. When they arrived near Beit Nouba, which was before Amwas, they met a line of tanks "and were told not to go any further, or they would be shot. (...)"

■ Hikmat Deeb Ali

■ Amwas, Yalou and Beit Nouba

In 1967, approximately 12,000 people lived in these three villages. On June 11, the residents of these three neighbouring villages were expelled by armed Israeli forces, acting under orders of Yitzhak Rabin, and forced to flee towards Ramallah. Everything in the three villages was then systematically dynamited and bulldozed: around 539 houses in Yalou, 550 in Beit Nouba and 375 in Amwas were reduced to nothing. Today, the refugees from these villages and their descendants number over 30,000; most live in Jordan or on the outskirts of Ramallah. Strangely enough, Palestinians forced to leave their homes in 1967 are not considered refugees by the United Nations! For more information or a guided tour, contact the ***Charitable Association of Amwas*** *(Ramallah, Niad Abu Gosh, ☎ 02-295 1613).*

The demolished villages of Deir Ayyub (a village in the district of Ramle demolished in 1948, which had 320 inhabitants in 1944), Beit Nouba and Yalou (demolished in 1967) were all converted into an Israeli park with donations from the Canadian National Jewish Fund, hence its name

- **Canada Park**, recently renamed **Ayalon Park**. Traces of the demolished villages, covered by a pine forest, are scanty; only some tombs of the Amwas cemetery are visible still, at the foot of the village *(at the entrance to the park)*. Here and there, there are also a few reminders that not so long ago this was a place where people lived and farmed: carob, olive, and almond trees, Barbary figs, wells and so on. There are also ruins from the area's past history: oil presses and *maqams* from the Mameluke period. The **Abu Obeida *maqam*** can be seen in the middle of the cemetery; it was successively a Roman bath, then a Crusader storage area, then a *maqam* dedicated to Abu Obeida Amer Ibn al-Jarrah in the thirteenth century. The latter, a commander of the Arabo-Muslim armies in 638, is thought to have succumbed to plague. He was buried in the market town which Arab historians called by the name Amwas. Celebrating him as a champion of the struggle against the Byzantine armies, the Mamelukes created a new holy site, by building - on his supposed tomb - a *maqam*. On the top of the hill, another *maqam* built by the Ottomans honours the memory of Ma'ath Ibn Jabal, a companion-in-arms of Abu Obeida. The ruins of the village of Yalou are still visible to the west of the park, on a little hill.

The Community of the Beatitudes Estate

(Open Monday-Saturday, 9:00-16:00, NIS 1 entry) At the entrance to the park are the remains of a Byzantine church destroyed in the Samaritan Great Revolt of 529 as well as another church built by the Crusaders. Many archaeological finds from this site are on display in the Studium Biblicum Franciscanum in East Jerusalem.

■ Latrun

Fourteen kilometres from Ramle, the small Christian village of Latrun had 190 inhabitants in 1945. Until the end of the nineteenth century, its rammed earth houses were all inside the walls of the Crusader castle here. When Trappist monks bought the land and the old village, they built a new village for the residents, some 500 metres south of the monastery, in compensation. After the war in 1948, the abbey and the old village (in the district of Ramle) were placed under the administrative jurisdiction of Jordan, while the new village found itself in a no man's land. The houses in the old village remained empty until they were destroyed in 1967.

■ The Domain of Latrun

Latrun Abbey is renowned for its wine production and has its own shop where Latrun wines or liqueurs are sold *(open Monday-Saturday, 9:00 - 11.30 and 14:30-17:00 ☎ 08-922 0065)*. The abbey was built at the end of the nineteenth century by French Trappist monks, who founded a hospice for pilgrims and an agricultural school here. The gardens and vineyards are open to the public. On the abbey's land on the top of the hill are the ruins of the Crusader fortress, the Tower of the Knights, *(open to visitors)* which was constructed in 1133. Saladin had the castle dismantled; later, villagers took up residence inside.

NABLUS

نابلس

Nablus

Getting to and from Nablus

From Ramallah, you can take either a service taxi on the first floor of the bus station for NIS13 or the bus on the ground floor for NIS8. There are also shared "service" taxis to Nablus (Huwwara checkpoint) on the Jerusalem side of Qalandia checkpoint (NIS15). Service taxis from Nablus leave for Jenin and Tulkarem from Beit Iba checkpoint and for Jericho from Huwwara checkpoint. Because of the various checkpoints (seven around Nablus) and other Israeli control mechanisms (over 700 in the West Bank, including gates, roadblocks, earthmounds, watchtowers, etc.), the situation is not stable so always check with locals the best way to travel. For example, at the time of going to press there is talk of Israel returning both Jericho and Tulkarem to PA control, which may affect travel arrangements in those areas for the better. All Palestinian centres are severely crippled by the Closure and restrictions on movement but Nablus is the most seriously affected and transport is therefore often a problem.

My Country

Majesty, beauty, grandeur and splendour are in your hills
Life, liberty, happiness and hope are in your love
May I see you whole and overflowing with blessings,
Dignified and secure, may I see you
May I see you on your pedestal reach to heaven, may I see you
My country, my country
The young do not weary of calling for independence or death
We feed ourselves on hope, we will never be the enemies' slaves
We refuse eternal humiliation and a life of anxiety
We wish to restore our ancestral glory
My country, my country
Our device is the sword and the pen, and not discussions or arguments
Our pride, our commitment are duties to which we remain faithful
Our pride is an objective that brings honour like a flag billowing forth
Oh, up there, on your pedestal, overcoming the enemies
My country, my country

■ Ibrahim Tuqan, *Diwan Ibrahim*, 1930. Nablus (1905-1941).

Between Ramallah and Nablus

Sinjil

Road 4665

At the centre of the village whose name is the Arabic version of the name of a Crusader monk Saint Gilles, is a very old mosque, originally a Crusader church, and a *maqam* known locally as Nabi Yahya, the cenotaph of the prophet Yahya (John the Baptist).

Caravanserais

There are ruins of many Ottoman *caravanserais* on the road between al-Bireh and Nablus. Some of them, from the Ottoman era, merit a visit, for a good visual impression of these halts. In the past, *caravanserais* played a major role in the organisation of commerce. They were above all places where traders stopped to rest, sleep and take on provisions before continuing their journey. In addition, they served as postal relays and sometimes as military bases. Between al-Bireh and Nablus, the *khans* of Ein Sinya, Sinjil, al-Lubban, and Qabalan *(at the latter, there is now a store selling green plants at the side of the road)* attest to the former importance of this route, which continued on far beyond Nablus, to Damascus and the Mediterranean coast.

Tel Shiloh

Near the village of Turmus Ayya.

This site was first inhabited in the Middle Bronze Age (1750-1550 BC). Thought to have been a holy place which united a federation of different Canaanite groups, it kept its religious function until the Islamic period. In the Iron Age, the Israelites built a temple here containing the Ark of the Covenant (1 Samuel 3:2-15), where all the tribes used to gather every year. In the Roman and Byzantine periods, Tel Shiloh remained an important religious centre. During the fifth century AD, religious celebrations took place here in two churches: the Basilica and the Pilgrims Church, whose mosaic tiles were discovered at the beginning of the twentieth century. Near the churches' ruins two Muslim *maqams*, Weli Yetin and Weli Sittin, have succeeded them.

Nablus

The city of Nablus lies in a narrow gorge less than a kilometre wide between Mount Jarzim (880 m) and its counterpart, Mount Ebal (940 m). The road through the plain from Ramallah to Nablus crosses the industrial zone and Balata Refugee Camp before starting up the gorge, which runs from east to west. The old city of Nablus (Shechem) first grew up around a spring under what is now the Balata Refugee Camp.

"Then, I went to Nabolous. It is a magnificent city with many trees and rivers that flow abundantly. It is, moreover, one of the most important cities in Syria for its olive trees. They export olive oil to Cairo and Damascus from here. In Nabolous, they make carob paste and export it to Damascus and to other countries."

Ibn Battuta, fourteenth century

Shechem was destroyed in the second century BC by John Hyrcanus' army. In 70 AD, Roman Emperor Titus totally annihilated the ancient city and built the settlement of Flavia Neapolis (the Latin *neapolis* - "new city" - having also baptised the city Naples, similar to Nablus in its transliteration) at the foot of Mount Jarzim, in honour of his father Emperor Flavius Vespasian, whom he succeeded in 79 AD. Flavia Neapolis progressively acquired characteristics typical of

Nablus

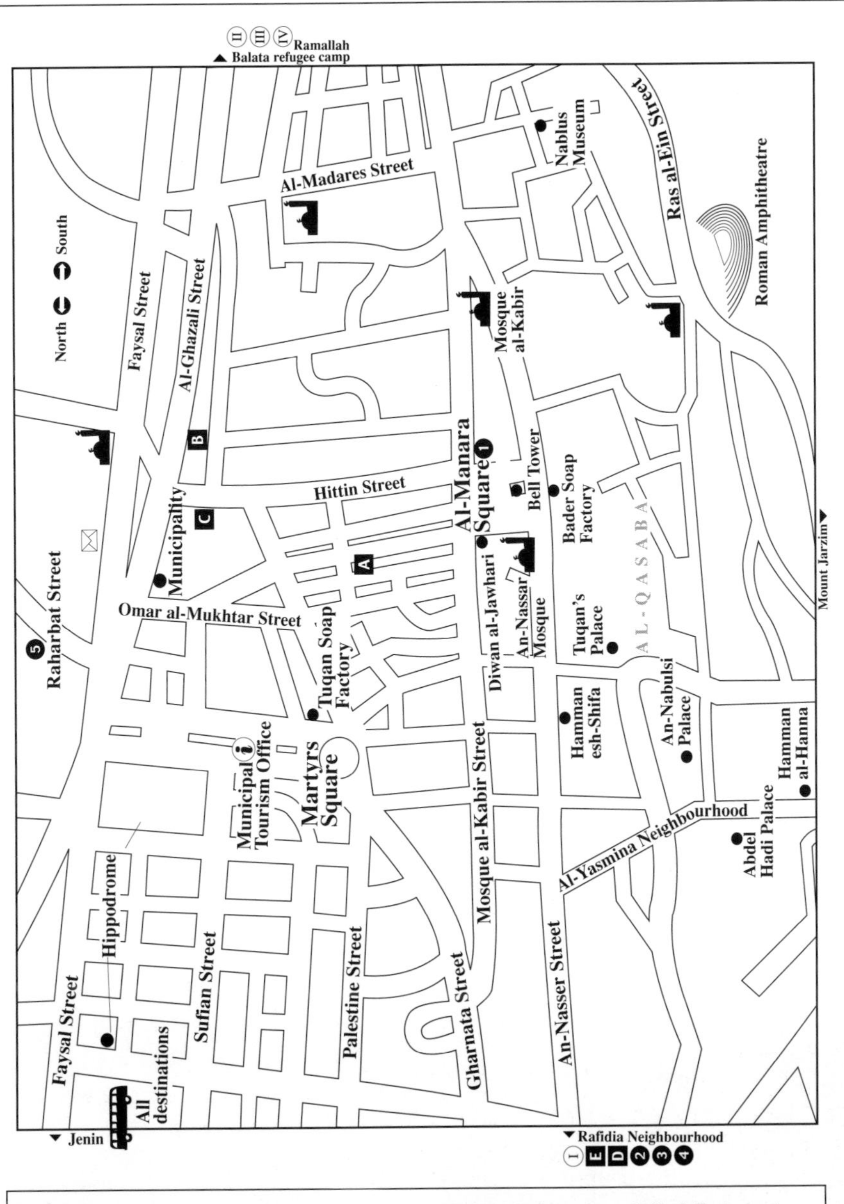

Contacts

I. An-Najah University
II. Committee for the Defence of Rights of Refugees
III. Yaffa Cultural Centre
IV. Women's Activity Centre

Accommodation

A. Al-Yasmeen Hotel
B. Crystal Motel
C. Al-Istiklal Hostel
D. Asia Hotel
E. Al-Qaser Hotel

Cafés & Restaurants

1. Halawiyat al-Aqsa
2. Halawiyat Arafat
3. Al-Madafa
4. Layali Zaman Roof
5. Salim Afandi Restaurant

a Roman city: a forum, amphitheatre, hippodrome and paved streets with colonnades; it was later surrounded by a wall.

Graeco-Roman religious cults developed in the region, but not without opposition from the Samaritans, who were among the principal victims of the Roman occupation. The subsequent growth of Christianity and its official recognition in the fourth century dealt a fatal blow to the Samaritan community. In 636, Nablus was conquered by Arab troops and went through a rapid process of Islamisation and Arabisation. Christian places of worship, often established on the same site as older Samaritan or Roman temples, were in turn transformed into mosques or Muslim shrines. Nablus developed on the model of Damascus, the Umayyad capital, to such an extent that the Arab geographer al-Muqaddassi (tenth century), nicknamed it "The Little Damascus," a title of which it is proud to this day. In the eleventh century, Nablus became the seat of a power struggle between the Abbassids and the Fatimids. This crisis left the field open for the Crusader conquest. Queen Melisende of Jerusalem, mother of Baldwin III, retained Nablus after her regency ended and lived here from 1152 to 1161. Saladin recaptured the city in 1187. In the following century, the city experienced a number of calamities: an earthquake in 1202, the Mongolian invasion in 1260 and Bedouin plundering in 1280, before retrieving prosperity again during the Mameluke period. Its production of soap, cotton cloth and pastries acquired a reputation in the entire Arab world.

At the end of the nineteenth century, Nablus became the political arena for the Arab national movement as it confronted three challenges: the Turkish national movement between 1909 and 1914, Zionist immigration and British colonialism. During the Palestinian national movement's revolt (1936), Nablus was even the first city to create a Palestinian National Committee. Its avant-garde position against colonialism and occupation earned it the name *Jabal en-Nar* (the Mountain of Fire). In spring 1963, the liberation movements of Palestine even declared, in Nablus, the "Republic of Palestine." It goes without saying that this prompted tighter control of the city by the Jordanian authorities of King Hussein. Subsequent Israeli occupation brought new forms of repression. Many Palestinian political leaders were victims of assassination attempts. In 1980, Bassam Shaka'a, mayor-elect of Nablus survived the explosion of his booby-trapped car. His two legs were blown off. Having survived the attack, he was dismissed from his position by the Israeli authorities and placed under house arrest. In 1995, Nablus became an autonomous Palestinian city (Area A), but totally surrounded by Jewish settlements. The economic situation of the city, where there are many small manufacturers (furniture and construction materials, among others), is paralysed

by Israeli restrictions on export and dependence on the Israeli market.

Named the "Mountain of Fire" by Palestinians in allusion to its strong resistance, the Israeli authorities have given it the name "capital of terrorism" since the outbreak of the al-Aqsa Intifada and have been merciless in their siege of the city, which has been repeatedly bombarded since the beginning of this Intifada. After the Israeli army entered the centre of the city in April 2002, the population - already besieged by seven checkpoints around it - was subjected to a more or less permanent curfew from July until mid-October. At that time, curfew was lifted for 79 hours, or just over three days.

"[During the first Intifada] *over 600 or 700 military orders controlled and monitored our daily life. All our schools and universities opposed these military orders. ...When I was mayor, the Israelis controlled my daily life. When I returned after my medical treatment, God gave me the chance to continue living, yet they tried to destroy my entire social life. A military patrol watched my house around the clock. No one could visit me without first being investigated. Not a single one! Not a single visitor whom I received didn't have traces of blood on his face. They hit them very hard, then they allowed them to enter, to put pressure on me.*"

■ Bassam Shak'a, [See p. 253]

■ Al Casbah (Qasaba - the Old City)

Most religious and civic buildings here date to the Ottoman period, but one can find earlier architectural elements from the Mameluke, Crusader, Byzantine and Roman periods hidden from visitors' eyes in the later constructions. Roman cornices, beautifully-designed Mameluke edifices with their characteristic geometric decorations around the doorways (do not seek the impressive entrances to *muqarnas* typical of Jerusalem: homes in Nablus are less ostentatious and more subtle) and stones with crosswork. These historic buildings and their labyrinth of tiny alleys running along the side of the hills are a scene of intense activity and a flourishing business of numerous shops, small factories, and other businesses often hidden behind an unassuming doorway which it is rarely possible to experience. The Old City is a world unto itself with the varied colours and smells of its stalls and their fruits, vegetables, spices, *za'tar* (thyme), *labaneh*, tobacco and popular cafes, where distinctive scents come from the water-pipes or various workshops (mattresses, wool blankets, soap factories, the preparation of sesame oil, ground *za'tar* or sweets).

A historical treasure proof against bombs

From April 3 until April 21, 2002, the Israel army supported by F16 fighter jets, helicopters, tanks and bulldozers attacked the residential neighbourhoods of Nablus, and particularly the Casbah in the Old City, killing dozens of its inhabitants and wounding hundreds. Some were buried alive under the ruins of their demolished homes; for the population this destruction revived painful memories of Palestinian cities in 1948 (Haifa, Jaffa, Lydda, al-Majdal, Ramle, Tiberias and others). Many historical buildings (religious, public and private, as well as factories) were hit. In all, over 500 buildings were damaged,

Nablus

60 totally demolished and 221 left on the verge of collapse. The city was placed under virtually permanent curfew during April, making salvage work impossibly difficult. Among the historically important religious sites destroyed or damaged were the al-Khadra Mosque (a mosque in Mameluke style), whose façade was destroyed by tanks and bulldozers; the Tomb of Sheikh Badr ed-Din; the Greek Orthodox Church of Saint Demitrios; the thirteenth-century Canaan and al-Nabulsi soap factories; the esh-Shifa Hammam; the al-Fatimiya school (an Ottoman building); some 60 traditional eighteenth and nineteenth century houses and the eastern gate of the eighteenth-century Khan al-Wakale.

❒ The Belfry

Al Manara Square

As with the belfries of Jaffa, Acre and Jerusalem (at Jaffa Gate), this bell tower was built in the early nineteenth century, opposite the en-Nasser Mosque, to mark the thirtieth birthday of Ottoman Sultan Abdul Hamid II (1876-1909). To the south, the **Diwan al-Jawhari** building was the seat of the Ottoman civil administration.

❒ The al-Kebir Mosque (Great Mosque)

The principal historical events of Nablus are inscribed on the stone of the mosque, successively a Roman basilica, erected by Philip the Arab in 244 AD; a Byzantine basilica; the Crusader Church of the Agony and the Resurrection of Christ, built in 1168; it became a mosque in the reign of Saladin. The 1927 earthquake destroyed the mosque, and it was rebuilt in 1935 on the original model; although the upper part of the mosque collapsed in 1927, certain elements survived, in particular the massive columns and the capitals of the Byzantine basilica, which are visible through the windows along the length of en-Nasser Street.

❒ Qaber (Tomb) of Sheikh Badr ed-Din

At No. 41, en-Nasser Street, west of the en-Nasser Mosque, there is a small, delicately executed window painted in green, behind which lies the tomb of Sheikh Badr ed-Din, who was one of Saladin al-Ayyubi's officers. Nablusis (people of Nablus) have a tradition of lighting candles here to the memory of this holy man, during the month of Ramadan.

The Hammams

The tradition of baths is ancient and has its origin in Roman times. The baths of that era are still preserved but are not open to the public. At the beginning of the nineteenth century, an important part of Nablus's social life revolved around its public baths *(hammams)*, of which there were several. Under the main room, a fire fed with olive pits was kept burning twenty-four hours a day. Today, most of these baths (which can be recognised by the open-work coloured glass in their ceilings) have lost their original function and been converted into warehouses, factories or shops. Nevertheless, two public baths renovated in the 1990s carry on the tradition. They provide an opportunity for a unique moment of escape and of well-being. In both *hammams*, bathers can prolong an agreeable moment with inexpensive refreshments and a smoke on a water-pipe.

Hammam esh-Shifa

En-Nasser Street, open daily 8:00-24:00 for men except Tuesday and Sunday, 8:00-17:00 for women and 17:00-24:00 for men. Bath NIS18, massage NIS10 and bath with camel's-hair brush NIS10. This hammam was built in 1624 by the Tuqan family. Musical evenings (classical Arab repertoire) are organised on request (☎ 09-238 1176; total cost NIS700).

Hammam al-Hana (es-Sumara)

Jadet al-Yasmina Street, open daily 6:00-23:00 for men except Tuesdays, 8:00-17:00 for women. Bath NIS20, massage NIS10, and bath with camel's- hair brush NIS5). This hammam is proud of its ancient history. Closed since 1928, it re-opened in 1995.

❐ The soap factories of Nablus

It is easy to understand, after a trip around the north of the West Bank, why the industry based on olive oil, especially soap-making, was established in Nablus. Its production is renowned throughout the Middle East. In the twelfth century it was sold as far away as Europe. Despite the development of the modern cosmetic industry, Nablus soap is still widely popular in the Arab world because of its natural properties. At the beginning of the twentieth century, Nablus had some 30 soap factories. Today, many are still active and open to the public. A visit is particularly interesting and allows every secret of the fabrication of this pure soap to be seen, before the truly artistic drying process.

The Manufacturing Process

In the first place, olive oil, nicknamed "green gold" in the Nablus region, is first mixed for several days with caustic soda. The mixture is then spread on the floor for three days to allow it to solidify. Then it is stamped with the mark of the manufacturer and cut into individual bars. Finally, the soap is piled up to dry, which takes from two to three months.

Tuqan soap factory: corner of Martyrs' Square

Bader soap factory: 20, en-Nasser Street, opposite the en-Nasser Mosque

[Olive oil soap, handmade in Palestinian villages around Tulkarem, may be bought at DAILA activists' centre in West Jerusalem at 4 Shlomzion HaMalka Street; ask if none is readily on view.]

❐ The Cardo and the Museum of Nablus

Remains of the Cardo, the principal road of the ancient city, were discovered inside the Zafer al-Masri School. The modest al-Qasaba Museum has on display artefacts from the city's past. Another curiosity to see here is a flight of stairs constructed on the paved way, leading down into the underground aqueduct that supplied the city with water. According to popular legend, it was through this underground passageway that the troops of Saladin entered the city in 1187.

❐ The Roman Amphitheatre

Free admission; ask for the keys from the owner of a small workshop to the left of the iron gateway.

This amphitheatre was built in the second century AD on the slopes of Mount Jarzim, during the reign of Emperor Hadrian (117-138 AD) and was rediscovered in 1979. With a capacity of 7,000 spectators, it was one of the largest amphitheatres in Palestine. Time has not been kind to it: at one point, it even served as a quarry. Only the lower portion of the amphitheatre is still visible today: the rest has disappeared under the foundations of a road and various houses. Notice the names of Graeco-Roman gods carved in Greek on the stone seats in the first rows and the numbers which probably served as place numbers for spectators. These places were reserved for the dignitaries of the city and each leading family, each of which had its own god attached to the Graeco-Roman pantheon of gods.

❒ The Hippodrome

Several parts, including the western end, have been unearthed. One part is alongside the alleyway that connects the site to Martyrs' Square.

The hippodrome is among the Roman era's monumental achievements; it was built in the second century AD in the western part of Nablus and remained in use until the third century. It was 420 metres in length and 76 metres wide.

Practical Information

Most sites of interest in Nablus are within walking distance of less than 15 minutes from the bustling city centre at Martyrs' Square. The **Municipal Tourism Office** organises guided tours *(open daily 8:00-16:00 except Fridays; NIS 200 for a two-hour guided tour in French, English, German, or Italian).* If the office is closed, contact the **Nablus Municipality** (☎ 09- 237 9313). The **post and telecommunications office** is located opposite the Municipality Building on Faysal Street.

Cafés and Restaurants

The **al-Aqsa** pastry shop, located on en-Nasser Street in the centre of al-Qasaba, is reputed for its quality *knafeh*, a speciality of Nablus. **Halawiyat Arafat**, another pastry shop located on Rafidia Street near the hospital, has an equally excellent reputation.

The Old City abounds in small popular restaurants and inexpensive cafes where one can also smoke a water-pipe; these cafés are generally for men only. Cafés and restaurants that cater to families are to be found along Rafidia Street. The **al-Madafa** café *(15 Rafidia Street, ☎ 09-238 4492, open from 9:00-24:00)* is one of the best. There are usually cultural evenings (poetry reading, music and such) here every Tuesday from 17:00-20:00. The **Roof**

Leile Zaman on Rafidia Street, in the same building as the Asia Hotel, has a panoramic view and pleasant setting, but the service can be slow *(music on Thursday evenings).* Near Martyrs' Square, on Raharbat Street, the **Salim Effendi Restaurant** serves excellent traditional dishes. The **Yasmeen Hotel** is located in the Casbah inside a building originally an Ottoman house; a café, restaurant and handicraft shop in the same style have been added: the restaurant here is more expensive than others in Nablus, but is one of the few that serve alcohol.

Accommodation

The **al-Yasmeen Hotel** *(☎ 09-233 3555, yasmeen@palnet.com; single and double rooms or a suite for $40, $50, $120)* is the hotel of Nablus with the most character. It also has the advantage of being in a central location in the heart of the Casbah and has a very pleasant café-restaurant.

The **Crystal Motel** *(Faysal Street ☎ /Fax 09-233 2485; single, double or triple rooms for $35, $50 or $60)* is located just outside the Casbah. The hotel is beautifully maintained, and its rooms are spacious, well furnished and new. The rates are more than reasonable. Nearby, on Hittin Street, the **al-Istiklal** ("Independence") **Hostel** is the least expensive accommodation *(☎ 09-238 3618; bed in a dormitory for NIS 25)*, and is ideal for male travellers on a low budget who do not mind a minimum of comfort; it is reserved for men only.

The **Asia Hotel** *(☎ 09-239 2321/2 Fax 09 239 2322; single and double, or suite for $40, $53, or $60)* and the **Qaser Hotel** *(☎ 09-238 5444 Fax 09-238 5944; single and double rooms or a suite for $55, $75, and $80)* are located in the Rafidia neighbourhood. Both are modest but comfortable.

Contacts

Bassam Shaka'a

Bassam Shaka'a, former mayor of Nablus, is happy to be available to any individual or group to share his knowledge and experience. *(☎ 09-238 4605).*

En-Najah National University

Department of Public Relations: ☎ 09-238 1113/7, www.najah.edu. The University offers intensive Arabic courses for foreigners in the summer or during the academic year. These courses are inexpensive and the ambience conducive to language learning. Lodgings in the city are provided for foreign students.

Started as a high school in 1918, en-Najah University was established in 1977; since its inauguration, the University has constantly developed the range of its educational facilities, especially in the faculties of medicine and science. Nearly 10,000 study here, making en-Najah the largest university in the West Bank; like the city that is its home, en-Najah has a history of active participation in the Palestinian resistance movement; from 1988 to1991, Israeli occupation authorities denied entry to faculty members and students alike: the university was declared a "closed military area." Since 1993, en-Najah University has been one of the major institutions to oppose the Oslo agreements consistently.

The Committee for the Defence of Palestinian Refugee Rights and the Yaffa Cultural Centre

Both institutions located on the same floor of a building in Balata Refugee Camp, near Jacob's Well. ☎ 09-232 4930. yafacult@hally.net. Visits to the camp may be arranged.

Established in 1998, the Yaffa Cultural Centre offers many cultural and educational activities, including courses in computer literacy. It is also in the process of developing a major research project to be carried out by young people from Balata interested in a career in journalism. They are in the process of tape-recording refugees' personal accounts of their experiences in the Nakba. The Yaffa Centre and the Committee for the Defence of Refugee Rights afford visitors the opportunity to learn more about the situation of refugees and their aspirations.

Centre for Women's Activities

In Balata Refugee Camp opposite the Committee for the Defence of Refugee Rights. "Programme Women's Centre" ☎ 09-232 4052.

This centre was established in 1975 to answer the specific needs of women. It provides training in different areas such as sewing and hairdressing, and a computer project is planned. There are also literacy courses and seminars on health, human rights and religion. In addition to its social activities, the centre mobilises women for peaceful political activities such as demonstrations against the Israeli occupation or in favour of the right of return.

■ In the Nablus Area

Balata Refugee Camp

UNRWA representative, Taysir Daoud, ☎ 09-238 8038.

Balata's refugee population of over 20,000 people makes it the largest refugee camp in the West Bank; it was built in 1950 on the outskirts of the ancient Canaanite city of Shechem. The majority of its residents are originally from Jaffa, the central plain of Palestine or the Galilee. Balata is known for its involvement in the first Intifada and its unremitting resistance to Israeli occupation. Military forces of the Israeli occupation besieged the camp during the entire period without being able to gain control inside the camp due to the organisation of the resistance. Military units would enter the camp regularly to arrest militants or to destroy homes of their families. Today the Nablus Municipality provides the infrastructure for this camp, in Area A: running water and electricity.

■ Jacob's Well

At the entrance to Balata Camp. Open Monday-Saturday 8:00-12:00 and 14:00-17:00; free admission, donations appreciated.

Christian tradition has it that it was here that Jesus appeared to the Samaritan woman and announced for the first time that He was the Messiah, in a parable: *"Whosoever drinketh of this water shall thirst again: but whosoever drinketh of the water that I shall give him shall never thirst"* (John 4:13-14). The feast day of Plotine, as she is called by the Orthodox Church, is celebrated every year on March 20. The twelfth-century church which is currently being restored here by a priest, who is working almost single-handedly, was built on the ruins of a Byzantine church destroyed during the Samaritan revolt in 529. The site was acquired by the Greek Orthodox Church in the nineteenth century. At the beginning of the 1980s, it nearly suffered the same fate as Joseph's Tomb, when a group of Jewish settlers claiming biblical ownership of the spot tried to occupy it. A monk was killed, but the settlers did not succeed in their endeavour. When visiting the church, do not hesitate to ask the monks for permission to see the private rooms where they burnt candles during the endless curfews during the first Intifada.

■ Qaber Yusef (Joseph's Tomb)

Just to the north of Jacob's Well.

The small tomb of Joseph the Patriarch and its white cupola were renovated in the nineteenth century. It is located on a piece of land that "... *Jacob bought of the sons of Hamor the father of Shechem for an hundred pieces of silver"* (Joshua 24:32). In fact, this tradition is recent; the site had been a Muslim *maquam* commemorating a Muslim saint for a long time. In the 1980s, Jewish settlers occupied the site; even after Nablus and Balata Camp were declared a Palestinian autonomous zone in 1995, the tomb remained in the hands of the Israeli army and settlers. At the beginning of the al-Aqsa Intifada, the tomb became a stronghold of the Israeli army of occupation, an unbearable affront to the rights of Palestinians for their freedom. The shrine became a target for demonstrators, of whom 17 were killed here during the first month of the al-Aqsa Intifada. When the Israeli army was forced to withdraw, the tomb or more exactly the *maqam*, a symbol of all their pent-up suffering, was destroyed by the demonstrators.

■ Tel Balata (Shechem)

Inside Balata Refugee Camp, free admission.

Tel Balata has been identified as the Canaanite city-state of Shechem. Mentioned first in Egyptian texts, Shechem means "shoulder" or a "high place." The city lay on a small knoll with a commanding view of the vast fertile plain of Askar and the commercial roads that crossed it; a strategic location which earned it the status of a regional capital. Although there were groups of sedentary Canaanites living here as far back as the fourth millennium BC, a real city developed only at the beginning of the second millennium BC. In the nineteenth century BC, Pharaoh Sesostris III captured the city, which was the leader of the Canaanite city-state confederation. In the next centuries, after this interlude, the city developed and flourished, as did the other city-states in Palestine.

Shechem's territories extended from the fertile plain of Marj Bin Amer (the Jezreel Valley) in the north to Jerusalem in the south. *Circa* 1550 BC, the Egyptians, led by Ahmosis I (1570 -

1546 BC), put an end to Hyksos domination and extended their territory until the north of Palestine. The fortress Shechem, one of the main strongholds in the region, was destroyed. However, in the twelfth century, the city regained its prosperity, which lasted into the eighth century. In 724 BC, the city was sacked by the Assyrians, who deported many inhabitants to Mesopotamia. The Assyrians then brought people from other captured cities to live in the region; many of them adopted the Samaritan worship of Yahweh. When Alexander the Great settled the veterans of his wars here in the fourth century BC, Shechem entered its very last period of greatness as a pagan Hellenistic city. The conquest of Shechem by the Hasmonean monarch, John Hyrcanus, in 117 BC sounded the death knell of the city.

Biblical Shechem

Biblical tradition fixes in Shechem many events in the Old Testament involving the Patriarchs of the Bible and refers to its political importance. This was the first city in Canaan where Abraham came after leaving the city of Ur in Iraq (Genesis 12:6-7) and where he built the first altar consecrated to Yahweh. Another story tells how Jacob's sons took revenge for the rape of Dina, Jacob's daughter, by Shechem (the king), killing all the men of the city (Genesis 34). Jacob's sons pretended to consent to Shechem's marriage to their sister and to forgive the crime, on condition that all the city's men undergo circumcision. The agreement was concluded and when he and his men were unwell after being circumcised, Jacob's sons took advantage of the situation and massacred them all. Shechem is also mentioned in the Old Testament as the place where a new alliance between all the tribes of Israel was established with great pomp (Joshua 24).

The Ruins

The massive wall and its triple gate date to between 1650 and 1550 BC. The huge stone blocks in the wall earned it the nickname "the Cyclopean wall." This access opened onto the main road and also onto the royal living quarters. The foundations of the Canaanite temple near the gate, dedicated to Ba'al-Berith, date back to the Late Bronze Age (1500 - 1200 BC). The huge stones from the foundations give a good idea of the temple's monumental proportions.

Mount Jarzim and the Samaritans

Mount Jarzim, of great historical and spiritual importance, is home to the last Samaritan community, custodian of the most ancient religious tradition in Palestine and indeed in the entire Middle East. Samaritan tradition goes back to the time of the Kingdom of Samaria (the name of their capital), or Israel, in the first half of the second millennium BC. After the Assyrians conquered Samaria in the eighth century BC, they brought inhabitants deported from Mesopotamia to live here. These people settled in the region, adopting their own religious beliefs and practices. In the sixth century, the Judaean community developed its own distinct branch of Yahwism (the origin of Judaism). By virtue of the Persian conquest in 538 BC, these elite Judaeans-in-exile were allowed to return to Judaea, where they became powerful allies of the new empire. They established their principal religious site for worship in Jerusalem, and vigorously opposed the Samaritans on theological and political grounds. Cultivating the notion of purity of "race," they rejected the Samaritans as a heretical rank who had mixed their blood, by intermarriage, with that of Gentiles (non-Jews) (2 Kings 17:24-41).

The Samaritans developed as a separate group which was strongest at the beginning of the Hellenistic period. Jesus, who was also despised by the Jews, scandalised his contemporaries by associating with Samaritans, whom he even sometimes cited as examples of virtue compared to the laxest Levites (high-ranking religious society personalities of Jerusalem), a particularly insulting criticism (Luke 10:29-37). In the Byzantine period, a well-established community of Samaritans thrived in the Nablus region. After the introduction of Islam in Palestine, the community lost the last of its faithful, as the family name "Samara" of some Muslims today indicates.

The Samaritans have perpetuated certain specific

traditions until the twenty-first century; Mount Jarzim remains for them a holy place of biblical tradition (site of the sacrifice of Isaac and the tomb of Moses), as described in the oldest texts of the Old Testament, namely the Pentateuch or Torah, revealed by God to Moses. On these very texts, there are over 6,000 differing details between the Samaritan and the Jewish Torah, although both are written in Hebrew; all the later books written during the exile in Babylon or afterwards are rejected by Samaritans. In their attachment to the foundations of the religion of the Patriarchs, the Samaritans affirm themselves as the direct descendants of Moses' brother, Aaron. They celebrate only the holy days mentioned in the Pentateuch, the most important of which is the Passover *(Pesach)*, which commemorates the sacrifice of Isaac by his father Abraham, a sacrifice which Samaritans believe took place on the sacred Mount Jarzim and which Jews place in Jerusalem. On the seventh day of Passover, they make a pilgrimage *(haj)* up the holy mountain.

The Samaritan community

The Samaritan community is one of the oldest religious communities in the world, yet also one of the smallest; today, it has 636 faithful, as compared to 146 in 1917. The community lives both in Nablus and in Holon, a suburb of Jaffa-Tel Aviv. The Samaritan community once had its time of glory - over a million followers in the fifth and fourth centuries BC. Their religious observances cement cohesion of the community and are strictly defined, with no tolerance for breaches. Women are particularly affected by laws to ensure their purity; they are not permitted to participate in any ordinary activity for the seven days of their menstrual period or after giving birth: 41 days if the baby is a boy, 80 days if it is a girl. Access to the group is extremely limited. Marriage outside the community is forbidden to a Samaritan woman, but a man may do so on the condition that his future spouse convert and submit to a six-month trial period under the direction and supervision of a priest who decides in the end if the marriage may take place. Aside from their religious traditions, Samaritans have the same secular traditions as Palestinian Arabs. Although the Israeli occupation authorities have granted them special status, Samaritans have remained attached to their Palestinian identity and institutions. There is a seat automatically reserved for them on the Palestinian Legislative Council (PLC).

The Samaritan community lives partly in the Samaritan quarter in the Old City and partly in the village on Mount Jarzim. The **Centre for Samaritan Studies**, 26 Omar al-Mukhtar Street and the **Samaritan Museum** on Mount Jarzim *(☎ fax 09-237 0249, open daily 8:00-14:00 except Saturdays; admission fee NIS4)* offer an opportunity to obtain further information on the community and its religious creed.

FAX
AGRI

Mount Jarzim

Magnificent panorama. A journey in a private taxi costs between NIS20 and NIS25. The Samaritan Museum is in the centre of the village.

This mountain has a special sanctity for Samaritans, who consider it the first piece of land created by God *(Har HaKedem* means "the First Mountain"). They also believe that Adam was created from the earth of this mountain and that this was also the sole site spared in the Flood. Samaritans also revere Mount Jarzim as the site of the Sacrifice of Isaac, an event celebrated after elaborate rites held throughout Easter/Passover every year. The entire community comes to live in the village on this occasion.

Just beyond the plateau, a pathway leads to Tel er-Ras, where a Samaritan temple was built during the Hellenistic period, converted into a Greek temple during the reign of Antiochus IV Epiphanes, and then destroyed by John Hyrcanus in 129 BC. In the second century AD, a Roman temple dedicated to Zeus Hypsistos was erected on the mountaintop: Roman coins with the inscription "Flavia Neapolis in Syria-Palestine," bearing an image of a temple on top of a mountain, have been found here, minted by the city during the reign of Emperor Antoninus the Pious (139-161 AD). After a long period during which it was forbidden (the community was not able to practice its rites on Mount Jarzim until the eighteenth century), finally only in the nineteenth century could it completely re-establish its practices after purchasing land here.

❒ Tel al-Far'a

Located 12 kilometres from Nablus in the direction of the Jordan Valley, on the edge of the al-Far'a Refugee Camp.

This picturesque road through fertile land irrigated by two sources (Ein Far'a and Ein Duleib) leads to the Jordan Valley. The ancient Canaanite city of **Tirza** built on this strategically located axis was the first capital of the Kingdom of Israel before the ascension of Samaria. Devastated at the beginning of the ninth century BC, Samaria took from it the status of capital. Tirza steadily declined and was finally abandoned in 600 BC, probably in the aftermath of a malaria epidemic. No sign marks the ruins, but they are easy to locate: archaeological excavations have unearthed several interesting remains: a beautiful underground sanctuary at the far northern end of the site, where animal sacrifices were practiced between 1750 and 1550 BC; various gates and walls, including the original rampart of sun-dried brick, reinforced in later times with a slope of stones, are also visible; and house foundations of a popular neighbourhood which is separated by a rectilinear wall from a royal quarter.

On the main road that continues along Wadi Far'a (towards the Jordan Valley), there are a number of centres of recreation (restaurants and swimming pools) offering refreshment from the cool spring water which is abundant throughout the area.

West and North of Nablus

The Village of Kur

Route 55 then 5506. Village of some 300 residents. Village Council, Khateb al-Jayousi, ☎ 09-268 0915.

To the west of Nablus, the architecture of the throne village of Kur has uniquely well-preserved Mameluke and, especially, Ottoman ruins. The excellent state of the buildings in this village is unique and gives a glimpse of social organisation during the Ottoman period. The simple peasant houses, each with its own courtyard, are overshadowed by three walled houses two or more floors high. One of these, which dates back to 1184 Hegira (1771 AD), belongs to the Jayousi family. Today, most of the old homes are now abandoned.

Traditional Villages

Most villages in Palestine, situated either on hilltops or on hillsides above farmland, overlook the plains and cultivated valleys. Built in the ubiquitous limestone of the West Bank, the common construction material in the West Bank, the traditional village *(qura')* was a compact mass of uniform houses surrounded by terraced orchards *(habayel)*. The village was built around a source of water to guarantee maximal protection from the possibility of Bedouin raids. Each family had its own special area *(hara)* made of a group of houses linked by interior passageways. Reflecting the social hierarchy, the leading families would have their homes at the top of the village. The most important often had a *diwan*, or a room where people gathered for important social occasions. Men would gather here to celebrate a birth, a wedding, to solve disagreements, or simply socialise after Friday prayer. There were other public places assigned to women, especially the village well *(al-'ayn)*.

The traditional architecture of villages is relatively simple. Only those villages designated under the name **throne village** *(qura' al-karasi)*, inspired by urban architecture, had a more sophisticated and more rich style. Throne villages were the property of rich rural landowners who worked closely with leading citizens in the cities, themselves owners of vast tracts of land.

Today, the structure of a village is not as carefully defined: old, run-down homes are often abandoned for simple, spacious modern constructions. The exterior walls in mountainous areas have a special character; house building is viewed as an efficient means of protecting land from confiscation and settlement building. Construction zones have been enlarged and permits widely issued by the Palestinian Authority (PA) in Area B, where most villages are located. Land in Area C, however, is still subject to restrictions imposed by the Israeli military authorities, who have defined much of this land as "open green spaces" zoned for agriculture only and "state land," which makes it the unique property of the Jewish state, despite the existence of Palestinian land deeds. Much of this land has been colonised in recent years by illegal settler outposts - illegal even by Israeli standards.

Tulkarem and Qalqilia

These two cities, located along the Green Line (a border established by the Armistice Line in 1949), are less than 20 kilometres from the Mediterranean Sea, to which residents are denied access. Until 1948, Tulkarem and Qalqilia were agricultural towns; Tulkarem was the main town in the district. In 1948, waves of refugees from 17 surrounding, totally destroyed villages, swelled Tulkarem's population. Qalqilia was slated for destruction in the '67 war: due to diplomatic pressure the army finally withdrew its bulldozers and each city now numbers over 40,000 residents; both are enclaves or ghettoes completely encircled by the Wall (disguised from the Israeli side at Tulkarem by a huge earth-bank) and in desperate economic circumstances. Unemployment runs at 95% and most families exist on foreign food aid. Closure means men cannot seek work outside the cities. Until the al-Aqsa Intifada, Qalqilia and Tulkarem had close ties with the cities in the Triangle, where they worked; however, since April 2002, a new fact on the ground has been added to the curfews, economic stranglehold and *Ariel* settlement bloc: thousands of hectares of prime farm and urban land have been confiscated and destroyed for construction of the separation wall and even more recently the landgrab of the seamzone area created between the Green Line and Wall, in favour of new settlement expansion. The Wall creates a new barrier near the Green Line, totally isolating many West Bank villages (e.g. Barta'a, Baqa a-Sharqiya, Nazlat Isa, Habla, Azzun Atma, Ras Tira, Daba, Wallaja, Nu'aman, Wadi Fukin). Industrial zones are planned here: serving Israel's settler economy.

Tulkarem and Nour Shams ("sunlight") Refugee Camps

UNRWA representative, Mohammed Haikal, ☎ 09-267 1106 (Tulkarem); ☎ 09-267 1116 (Nour esh-Shams). Popular Committee of Nour Shams, ☎ 09-267 8191.

Founded in 1950 and 1952, these camps are home to 15,000 and 8,500 refugees, respectively; because of their proximity to the Green Line, the majority of these refugees worked inside Israel until recently. The economic dependence is very strong: each closure or siege results in one of the highest rates of unemployment and added misery. During the al-Aqsa Intifada, the Israeli army made mass arrests here several times; in one such operation, prisoners were marked on the arm.

Sebastiya

Located 13 kilometres northwest of Nablus. Take Road 60, then 5715.

Ruins of an ancient city cover the vast plateau above the village of Sebastiya. Archaeological evidence proves the site was Chalcolithic Period. In the twelfth century BC, a small city grew up which acquired its economic and political power in the ninth century BC, when it became the capital of the Kingdom of Israel (or Samaria). King Omri, sixth king of the kingdom, elevated Samaria to his capital, open to the eastern Mediterranean cultural sphere. The influence of the Phoenician cities made itself felt in all aspects of life: material culture, commerce and religion. Threatened by the rise of Assyria, King Omri cemented an alliance by marrying his son Ahab to Jezabel, a princess from the powerful Phoenician city of Tyre. Ahab erected a temple to her gods, Baal and Astarte, in the city, thus infuriating the Judaeans who condemned this act as the work of an infidel. They looked upon the Assyrian conquest by the troops of Sargon II of the Kingdom of Israel in 721 BC as a divine punishment.

The city regained its status as a provincial capital during the Persian period. In 331 BC, Alexander the Great made it a Greek settlement; the city was under Hellenic cultural influence until its destruction by John Hyrcanus in 108 BC. Herod, the right-hand man in Palestine of the Roman Empire, rebuilt the city on the model of the Greek *polis*, or city. He renamed it Sebaste (Augustus in Greek), in honour of the Roman Emperor Caesar Augustus (27 BC - 14 AD). In the second century AD, Emperor Septimus Severus conferred on Sebaste city status with all the pertaining privileges. As the popularity of Christianity grew in the fourth century, this former centre of Graeco-Roman paganism went into permanent decline.

The Ruins

Two routes lead to this site, the first of which runs directly into the forum after crossing the village. The second route, accessible by car, leads to the western gate. Open April - September 8:00-17:00, October - March 8:00-16:00.

Of all the visible ruins, the Roman era constructions are the most impressive. The central square at the old Roman **forum**, to the east, is now a parking lot. The portico that enclosed it is partially preserved, particularly the western end, which opens onto a basilica. The **basilica** (68m x 32m) was divided into three naves, separated by a row of columns, some of which are still standing. To the north of the forum *(the platform behind the restaurant)*, there is a view of what was the hippodrome, marked by a few columns. Behind the restaurant a path leads to the **Roman theatre**, which dates back to the beginning of the third century AD. It is believed to have been built on top of the ruins of the Herodian theatre. A splendid Hellenistic **circular tower** located behind the terrace is a fine example of Hellenistic fortification. Another way around the theatre, through some orchards, leads to where the Acropolis used to be. Stairs (second century AD) lead to the podium which is all that remains of the Herodian temple dedicated to Augustus, renovated later by Septimus Severus. In the second century AD, its neighbour to the north was the temple to Cora, a goddess of harvest, built on the ruins of a Hellenistic temple, which had been dedicated to the goddess Isis.

From the location of the former Acropolis, the panorama is spectacular. Towards the south are the pillbox walls of an ancient Samarian palace (ninth century BC), as well as the ruins of the temple to Baal and Astarte which are visible, but somewhat hard to identify exactly. Some splendid pieces of ivory were discovered here, but are on display today in the Israel Museum in Jerusalem. Between the Acropolis and the colonnaded street are the ruins of a small Byzantine chapel, remodelled by the Crusaders, supposedly on the spot where the head of Saint John the Baptist was discovered. An old Christian tradition has it that Sebaste was where Herod Antipas, son of Herod, had John the Baptist beheaded for Salome, who demanded his head be brought to her on a platter at Herod's birthday celebration (Matthew 14:8). At the western end of the site is the city's western gateway and the ruins of a Hellenistic square watchtower integrated into newer structures in Herod's time and then again in the days of Septimus Severus. From the western gate, an impressive colonnaded street leads back to the forum. There are no less than 600 intact or broken columns standing here in the middle of olive trees, lining the entire 800-metre-long road. A roof originally protected the columns, which were over 5 metres high, with Corinthian capitals. Foundations of several small (4 m wide) Roman shops have also been discovered on the way here. The Roman road (12 m wide) was narrowed during the Byzantine period and the roofed areas were used in order to enlarge the shops.

The Village of Sebastiya

Sebastiya Municipality, ☎ 09-253 2430.

The **Sidi Yahya Mosque** on the village square is a memorial to Saint John the Baptist. Its main building was built by the Crusaders *circa* 1160, in the Burgundian style. The remains of the Prophet Yahya (John the Baptist) are here in a burial niche between the tombs of two other prophets, Elijah (Elias) and Obadiah. Built in the middle of farmland, Sebastiya was a throne village in the last centuries, the residence of the powerful al-Kayed family, as attested by the huge three-storey home here which extends over 875 sq.m. around a courtyard of 100 sq.m. The **al-Kayed** residence (Qaser al-Kayed, the Palace of al-Kayed) has a monumental entrance flanked by two symmetrical stone seats. The architectural details (geometric and floral decorations) give the edifice a special charm.

Jenin

For people interested in the history of place names, Jenin is a real treat: it is mentioned in various historical and mythical references as well as various travel chronicles: Gi-na (in the Amarna Letters), Qena (in the papyrus annals of Thutmose III), En Ganim (in the Bible), Ginea (Flavius Josephus), Genon or the Greater Gallius (by the Crusaders), or Jenin (the Mameluke period). Located in the heart of fertile plains, Jenin was also at the crossroads of important trade routes. In the thirteenth century, in order to forestall another Crusade, the authorities fortified the region. A relay station for homing pigeons was set up in Jenin; at the same time, a tower *(manwar)* relaying light and smoke signals was built in the vicinity. Damascus and Jenin always kept close contact. A fifteenth-century writer even describes how ice was transported by camel-back from Damascus to Jenin. In the sixteenth century, Fatima Khatun the wife of the governor of Damascus ordered the Izz ed-Din Mosque *(Talal Street)* built here, *circa* 1566, as well as a complex of public buildings *(hammam, sabil, souq)*. Jenin developed late as a large agricultural town, in the eighteenth century. During the First World War, German troops stationed nearby constructed an airport near the city, to help their Turkish allies. A memorial *(on the western side of the city)* honours pilots killed in the war. South of Jenin, there is another memorial to the memory of the Iraqi soldiers killed defending Palestine in 1948.

Practical Information

From Nablus (Beit Iba checkpoint) a service taxi to Jenin costs NIS6. From Nablus to Nazareth via Jenin is NIS 28. (The closure and checkpoints around Nablus and Jenin and elsewhere mean that these travel routes and prices may differ from those at the time of publication.) Although the city has few tourist attractions, it is still a pleasant place to visit.

It is possible to stay in the only hotel in Jenin: the **Garden Hotel** *(☎ 04-243 6151, bed in dormitory NIS30 per person, room NIS50 per person)* is not very attractive from the outside, but its rooms are inexpensive and clean.

Jenin Refugee Camp

UNRWA camp representative, Abdel Razek Abu Haija, ☎ 04-240 1113.

Jenin Refugee Camp was established in 1953 on land inside the city border. Most of its 13,000 residents are originally from villages in the large fertile plains of the Lower Galilee. Some of those former villages are actually visible from the camp. Today, there are still tight family ties between families in Jenin Camp and their relatives on the other side of the Armistice Line ("The Green Line"), in Israel. Since 1995, the camp has been under the administration of the Palestinian Authority (PA) (Area A).

The Jenin Massacre

"Operation Defensive Shield," a deadly Israeli offensive into major Palestinian cities and West Bank villages in the spring of 2002, (in retribution for the Park Hotel attack which killed over 40 family members celebrating Pesach there) subjected Jenin city and the camp to a total siege on April 3 when they were declared a "closed military zone." The camp was bombarded without interruption day and night for 13 days, while scenes of horror unfolded. Medical workers and journalists were categorically denied access to the camp. On April 10, the Israeli army gave the population one last warning to evacuate the camp. The attack that followed redoubled the intensity against those 4,000 who refused to leave. In all, over 50 Palestinian civilians were killed, many in cold blood by bullet or bulldozer. Hundreds of others were wounded, and more than 450 families (on average, 6 children per family) saw their homes destroyed. The award winning film "Arna's Children" has footage filmed of some of the Jenin fighters, who talk in it shortly afterwards of

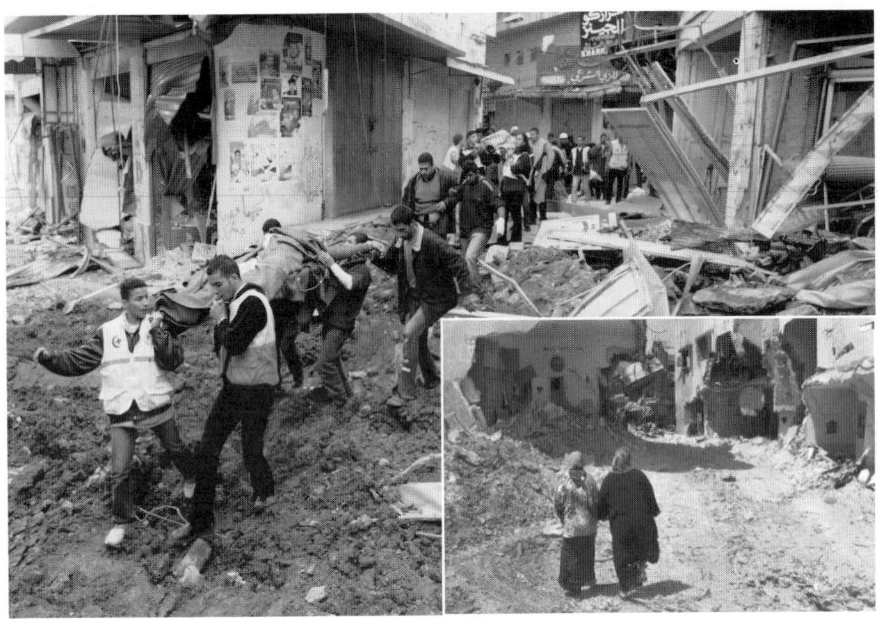

their resistance to the Israeli incursion. Whilst Israel denies a massacre took place, there is no doubt many were killed, the people unable to bury those dead for many days, and at least one bulldozer driver later boasted as to his ruthless devastation of as many houses as possible, even with people inside. Now some houses have been rebuilt by international development agencies; the roads have (controversially) been made wide enough for tanks, in an attempt to safeguard those houses in any future incursions or raids.

❒ Tel or Khirbet Belameh

Two kilometres south of Jenin.

This town has been called by many names during its long history: Ibleam in Egyptian texts of the second millennium BC, Issacher in the Bible, Belemoth in the Hellenistic era, Belemontus under the Romans and today Belameh. The view from this site takes in the most fertile plains of Palestine, including Marj Bin Amer (the Jezreel Valley), a source of prosperity for the ancient city-states of antiquity. Under the ruins here, which are mostly Mameluke and Ottoman, on the hill opposite the contemporary village, lies the Bir es-Sinjil spring, whose water supplised the town from a tunnel carved into the rock. Notice the large Roman vault renovated by the Crusaders; the tunnel can be traced along 115 metres; it is 3.20 metres wide and from 3 to 7 metres high. The steps are cut into the rock, as are the small niches made in the walls for lanterns that lit the tunnel. Changes are being made in the tunnel to make it safe for visitors.

❒ Burqin

Three kilometres west of Jenin, on Road 6155. A trip from Jenin to Burqin costs NIS2 in a service taxi.

Christian tradition has it that this village was the site of one of Jesus' miracles, where He miraculously healed ten lepers (Luke 17:11-19). Saint George's Church was built over an ancient Roman cistern where Jesus performed the miracle. Mass is said only once a month for the Christian community in the village. The gates of the church are usually locked, but villagers are happy to allow visitors to visit the church. The grotto and the small chapel in the church give every appearance of having been in existence since the early days of Christianity.

THE GAZA STRIP

قطاع غزة

GAZA

غزة

THE GAZA STRIP

Getting to Gaza

Visiting the Gaza Strip is an overwhelming experience. More than three quarters of the population are refugees, most of whom are from villages less than 50 kilometres away, but access to their place of origin is sealed off by electric fences on three sides and on the fourth side by the Mediterranean Sea, which is controlled by the Israeli navy. There are only two places where one can enter the Gaza Strip: Erez or Rafah (temporarily closed). If you are coming from Egypt or returning there, you can enter or leave Gaza at Rafah with Israeli customs approval. If you are coming from the West Bank or Israel, you must go through Erez. There is no legal thoroughfare between the West Bank and the Gaza Strip and no collective transportation (known as *service* taxis, where several passengers share the cost) available. The cost of a private taxi from East Jerusalem is about NIS200. Once you have gone through customs at Erez, the cost of a second taxi to the centre of Gaza City, 8 kilometres away, is about NIS35. Service taxis are much less expensive: NIS2 to the neighbourhood of Shuja'iya.

Erez and Karni crossings

Erez is the crossing place for workers; Karni, only for merchandise. During the so-called peace process, new restrictions were placed on men and goods. The shortest route to the West Bank, between Erez and Tarqumia (see Tarqumia, p. 225) was open during the entire "peace process" only from October 1999 to September 2000. The sole alternative was to go first to Egypt, then to Jordan, and finally into the West Bank by the King Hussein (Allenby) Bridge. Today, this is still the only way to travel between the Gaza Strip and the West Bank. The only Palestinians allowed into the State of Israel are workers in possession of a permit issued by Israeli military authorities, as well as a magnetic ID card, which stipulates the return time limit and also provides information on its bearer. Palestinian workers are not allowed to stay overnight at their places of work Israel, so they have to journey to work every day. So, in the middle of the night, from 2 a.m. on, one sees thousands of Palestinian workers lining up to wait to get to their jobs in Israel on time. Only after several hours of harrying procedures will they reach the other side of the passage they must take, where buses await them.

■ ***Erez*** (☎ 08-674 1605). There are two places to cross at Erez : one for Palestinians and the other for foreigners or senior Palestinian

Gaza

in Authority officials. The first is used daily by thousands of Palestinian workers. A 200 metre long passage, it is closed at either end by a wall and a wire fence several meters high. The passage leads to a series of massive cement blocks where the workers are checked, searched and sometimes questioned (particularly if they lack a permit or a card). These humiliations are just the first of more of the same reserved for these workers throughout their day. On the other side of the wall, the crossing used by foreigners or VIPs looks much like any other border control, except for the soldiers. But the treatment is quite another story. Just to see, try taking the passage for Palestinians. When you reach the cement blocks, you will be escorted through a tiny passageway into the corridor for foreigners, but this is enough to get a pretty good idea of how workers on their way to work in the Jewish state are treated.

■ ***Karni*** (south of Gaza City). This crossing point is "open" solely for merchandise, and together with Erez, is the only point of access to outside markets. Due to the restrictions imposed by Israel on imports and exports, the economy of the Gaza Strip is in a state of utter strangulation. Traffic delays and the frequent closures are often fatal to fresh produce such as strawberries, flowers and citrus fruit. To cut their losses, farmers sometimes call on Israeli food enterprises to buy their perishable produce at minimal cost, so that at least it arrives quickly on the market in Israel, the West Bank or abroad, such products being labelled "Made in Israel." Few manufactured products are exported, due to closure and a political situation which discourages investment in industry. Since the beginning of the al-Aqsa Intifada, many small businesses have been deliberately destroyed by the Israeli army.

At Karni as at Erez, merchandise traffic is severely delayed, which adds to transportation costs and economic dependence on Israel. At Karni, trucks from Gaza are unloaded in a huge transit zone. After the contents have been inspected, they are reloaded onto "sterile" trucks belonging to Israeli companies. At Erez, the procedure is different. Palestinian trucks carrying goods for export are grouped together. After the usual search, the Palestinian transporters are made to wait several hours until the Israeli authorities decide there are enough trucks to leave; then the trucks are escorted by the army to their destination - usually the port of Ashdod. The trucks must return empty: the State of Israel maintains a monopoly on the transportation of goods to Karni.

The Gaza Strip

The Gaza Strip is a narrow belt of land approximately 45 kilometres long and 6 kilometres wide at its narrowest point. In all, it measures 165 square kilometres, the same size as Lake Tiberias or 1.3 % of the British Mandate. Up to 1948, Gaza was the administrative capital of a piece of land stretching from the Palestinian border with Egypt to Isdoud (Ashdod). Israeli military takeover has reduced its surface area by one third of that designated by the United Nations partition plan in 1947. In 1948, the southern conquest of Palestine stopped at the borders of this strip of land, which in the space of several months became a real "sanctuary." In all, between 200,000 and 250,000 refugees took refuge here. The latest refugees came in 1951, fleeing from their occupied villages or Bedouin encampments in the western part of the Negev.

This strip of land owes its existence to Zionist political offensives in 1948 and the less enthusiastic initiative of Egypt's late King Farouk. The establishment of a Jewish state in Palestine over as much land as successive military conquests permitted, forced the indigenous Palestinian population into a bare minimum of space. In fact, not a single village from Jaffa to Gaza was spared the elimination and displacement of its entire population. Egypt's political stand on the matter was motivated by fear that it would have to absorb the wave of Palestinian refugees – a threat which nearly shook the Egyptian monarchy to its foundations – in the event that the Israeli army continued its land takeover of Gaza. On February 24, 1949, the Kingdom of Egypt and the State of Israel signed an armistice establishing the boundaries of two new territorial entities: the Gaza Strip and the State of Israel.

Today, 1.4 million people live here, more than 75% being refugees. According to UNRWA statistics, the refugees living in the Gaza Strip make up more than 22% of the entire Palestinian population. Since their arrival as refugees, population density has increased, so nowadays the Gaza Strip has one of the highest densities of population in the world. Contemporary history here is marked by misery and frequent aggressions. Since the outbreak of the al-Aqsa Intifada, more than 70% of the population has lived under the poverty line. Most families depend on aid from Arab and Western countries, as well as UNRWA, for their survival.

Israel is currently talking about and planning for a "unilateral withdrawal" from the entire Gaza Strip, involving evacuating some 8,000 settlers. The settlers are not all willing to be evacuated, and are threatening to oppose the July 2005 operation. They are being offered as much as half a million dollars per family for this move, but some of the most ideological are resisting all such moves. They threaten the possibility of civil war and many soldiers have already signed as "refuseniks" to any future order to evacuate the settlers forcibly. Israel - and the world - waits to see if finally settlers will be moved from their homes, as was the case in 1982 in Yamit, which was part of the Sinai withdrawal.

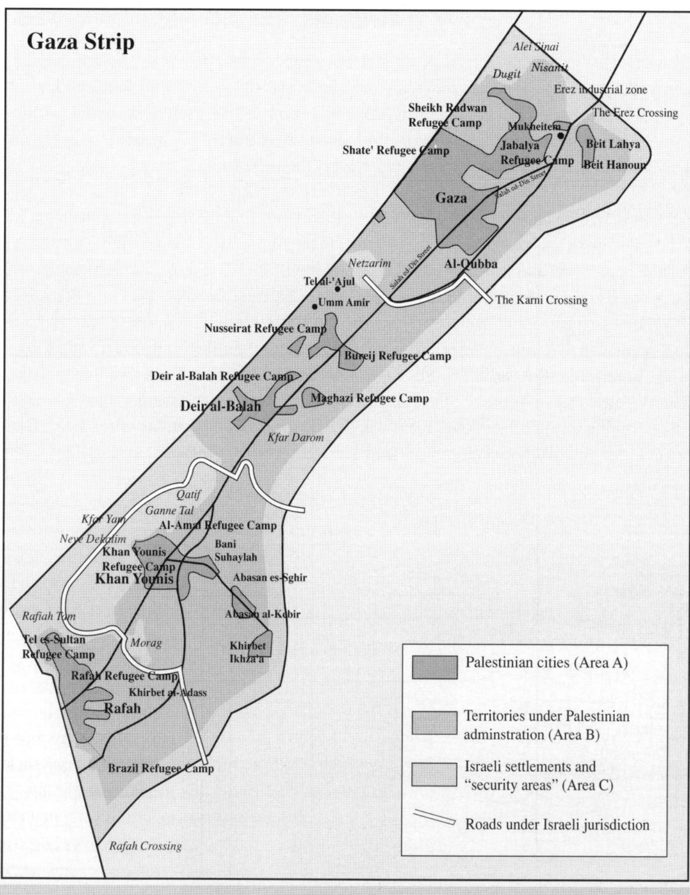

The Refugee Camps

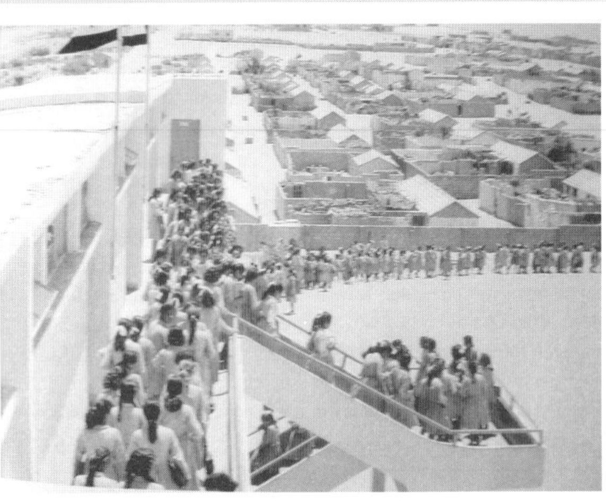

In 1948, the refugees were resettled and placed in several camps set up on uncultivated land. In December 1949, the United Nations created a unit whose purpose was to assist these refugees, called UNRWA (United Nations Relief and Work Agency for Palestinian refugees). It commenced operating in May 1950, when it took a census of the refugees, placing them on land rented for 99 years! The boundaries of these camps were also fixed in 1950. They are practically unchanged today although the population has tripled or, in certain places, quadrupled. UNRWA first tended to the most urgent needs, providing tents and food supplies as well as health and education services. As of 1954, straight rows of cramped little houses progressively replaced the old worn-out tents. Each one-room dwelling measured 3 square metres, where an average of 6.7 people (the average size of a family) lived. Two group toilets were provided for every 25 to 30 families.

When Israel occupied the heavily-populated Gaza Strip in 1967, it immediately put into action a plan for crushing the Palestinian resistance, particularly strong in the camps. By doing so, it hoped both to reduce the size of the population and to better control the situation. In 1971, under the leadership of General Ariel Sharon, roads still clearly visible today were cut across each camp on the Gaza Strip, destroying about 2,000 homes. Their inhabitants were deported to an area south of Rafah, in the Egyptian Sinai Peninsula, occupied at that time by Israel. The occupation authorities then created five areas for refugees to live in: the Brazil area (Rafah), Tel es-Sultan (Rafah), Sheikh Radwan (Gaza City), the village of Beit Lahya, and al-'Amal (Khan Younis). This initiative was taken to reduce the population density in the camps – thus gaining a firmer hand over them – and to do away with the status of refugee. The Israelis rented the land (expropriated from Palestinians landlords) for a period of 99 years and provided construction materials. In return, Palestinians who wanted to take advantage of this offer had to destroy their home inside the camp and give up their refugee card and all UNRWA assistance (food, health and education) to which it entitled them. Today, such neighbourhoods look just like the official UNRWA camps and are called camps, too.

Easy to recognize, the refugee camps are built-up areas where one building crowds upon the next. Breeze-block homes with corrugated sheet roofs line a network of tiny alleyways. Basic infrastructure such as garbage collection, piped water and sewage units are usually absent or insufficient. The water is largely unfit for consumption. Since the retreat of the Israeli army in 1994, the originally low buildings in the camps have had one or more storeys built on.

Contacts

Popular Committees in the Camps

Jamal Abu Habel (Jabalya Refugee Camp), **co-ordinator for Popular Committees of Gaza Strip Refugee Camps:** ☎0599-740961.

Salim Abu Zeid, (Khan Younis Camp) **Popular Committee:**☎ 0599-772201.

Ahmed Esa'adouni, (Khan Younis Refugee Camp) **Popular Committee:** ☎0599-791882 / 08-2054853.

The Popular Committees are happy to organise visits and contacts in the Gaza Strip refugee camps to help visitors understand daily life there, the history and aspirations of Palestinian refugees and so forth. Ali Shawish, (Nusseirat Refugee Camp), an English teacher with UNRWA is a longtime peace activist: ☎0599-843553 or 08-2558532.

Refugee camps in the Gaza Strip

Area	Refugee camps	Population in 1949	Population in 2003
North of Gaza	Jabalya	35,000	107,415
Gaza	Shate' Deir al-Balah	23,000 9,000	78,158 21,185
Centre of Gaza	Nusseirat Bureij Maghazi Khan Younis	16,000 13,000 9,000 35,000	66,691 30,756 23,503 62,928
South of Gaza	Rafah	41,000	93,928
Refugees not in camps			438,111
Total refugees in Gaza Strip			922,674

Source : UNRWA 31 December 2003

Gaza – "Israel's Soweto"

Before the First Intifada, approximately 45,000 Palestinians from the Gaza Strip worked in the State of Israel, plus 10,000 more without working papers, 30% of whom were teenagers. This meant that more than half the workforce in the Gaza Strip depended on work in Israel for its income. A Palestinian worker was paid about 36% of the amount received by an Israeli doing the same job. This was still better than what a person could earn in the Gaza Strip, where there was a record high of unemployment due to the absence of industrial infrastructure and a general stagnation of all sectors of the economy.

In 1994, the withdrawal of the occupation army from 60% of the Gaza Strip and the arrival of the Palestinian Authority brought an unprecedented urban boom. However, all investment went into the construction and equipment of public infrastructure or its renovation. Little money was invested to develop industrial or agricultural production, due to restrictions on export and repeated sieges. The Israelis prevented the construction of a truly commercial port, which Gaza desperately needed: this was referred to only in terms of a vague future. During the Oslo years, the average number of Palestinian workers going to daily jobs in Israel fell to about 30,000 and since the beginning of the al-Aqsa Intifada, the number is about 6,000. However, most of these workers do not leave the area since they work in the Israeli settlements located in the heart of the Gaza Strip or in industrial complexes on the edge of the Strip. The most important of these business complexes is at Erez, where some 3,000 Palestinians work.

■ GAZA

"Gaza remains standing today, even if its hands are tied. Its horizon is fenced off. Yet the Gaza Strip harmoniously continues the long Arab coastline south along the Mediterranean. In olden times, it was called Syrian, but its scenery already has an Egyptian air. It also went by the name of "Arab Gaza" because it was the natural terminus of the Arabian Peninsula on the Mediterranean."

Jean-Baptiste Humbert in *"Mediterranean Gaza – History and Archaeology in Palestine."*

A land rich in history and in archaeological finds (often hidden under the sand or under the camps), Gaza used to be one of the busiest crossroads in the Near East. Prehistoric man arrived here on his long trek across Asia and Europe and settled near Wadi Ghazzeh. In the 4th century BC, the domestication of the donkey started caravan trading. Commerce with Egypt developed in importance. Egypt established many market towns along the southern coast of Palestine in the second half of the 4th century BC, with Gaza as their administrative centre. In the third millennium (the First Dynasty in Egypt), the area became independent of Egypt. Several Canaanite cities raised their defences, the most prominent of these being founded on the site of Tel al-Ajul (in the south of Gaza). This city had its heyday under the Hyksos (or "rulers of foreign countries" in Egyptian), the Syro-Palestinian authorities who took political and social control of the region as far as the Nile Delta. This period came to an end when the pharaohs of the Eighteenth Dynasty conquered Palestine *circa* 1550 BC. Gaza, (*ga-da-tu* in Egyptian), became the most important urban centre in southern Palestine, where the Egyptian governor of the area had his residence. *Circa* 1200 BC, invasions from "Sea Peoples" – the Philistines in particular – increased and helped push the Egyptians out. Gaza was probably the capital of an independent confederation of five city-states. In 734 BC, Gaza was conquered by Tiglath-Pileser III, whose Assyrian name was *ha-za-ti* or *ha-zi-ti*. The Governor of Gaza quite naturally fled to Egypt. Nonetheless, Gaza flourished as the actual gateway of the Assyrian empire into Egypt. This neo-Babylonian domination did not last long, but still there were deportations, as elsewhere. Among them was the King of Gaza himself.

In *circa* 538 BC, the whole Near East fell to the Persians and became part of their great empire: Gaza benefited from the opening of trade links with the Mediterranean basin. It became the terminus for caravans of incense, myrrh and exotic animals from Yemen, slaves from the African Horn as well as spices from India and, quite probably, silks from China. Greek and Cypriot ships bound for the Levant and Egypt took on manufactured goods, olive oil and wine in Gaza, which became famous for these products until the end of the Byzantine period. Conquered by Alexander the Great in 332 BC, Gaza was one of the most renowned Greek cities in the Orient. At the crossroads of civilizations, it was truly cosmopolitan, second only to Alexandria, with people, goods, cultures and religions from everywhere.

During the Umayyad Dynasty, the city was known as "Hashem's Gaza," or the Gaza of Hashem Ibn Abdel Munaf, the Prophet Mohammed's grandfather, who was buried here. Its outstanding contributions as an intellectual and commercial centre were widely acknowledged. In the 13th century, Muslim Shafeite doctrine was developed here, by a native of Gaza, Imam el-Shafii. Gaza became a real breadbasket as well as a crossroads between two great Arab capitals – Cairo and Damascus – experiencing a new expansion under the Mamelukes until the Great Plague of 1348 AD, during which it lost many of its citizens.

Vasco de Gama's discovery of new sea routes to India in the 15th Century put an end to Gaza's maritime activities and robbed it of its privileged position on the Spice Route.

From this point on, Gaza was important for agriculture, thanks to its fertile soil. Cereal crops were its speciality and earned it the nickname "the ocean of wheat." Gaza's population increased from 16,000 inhabitants in 1885 to 40,000 in 1906. Its prosperity ended in World War I, however, when one of the war's fiercest battles between Ottoman Turk and British soldiers devastated the city of Gaza and the surrounding countryside. When the British army occupied the city on November 7, 1917, they found the old city in ruins. The 1927 earthquake later completed the destruction of any piece of land that had been spared in the war.

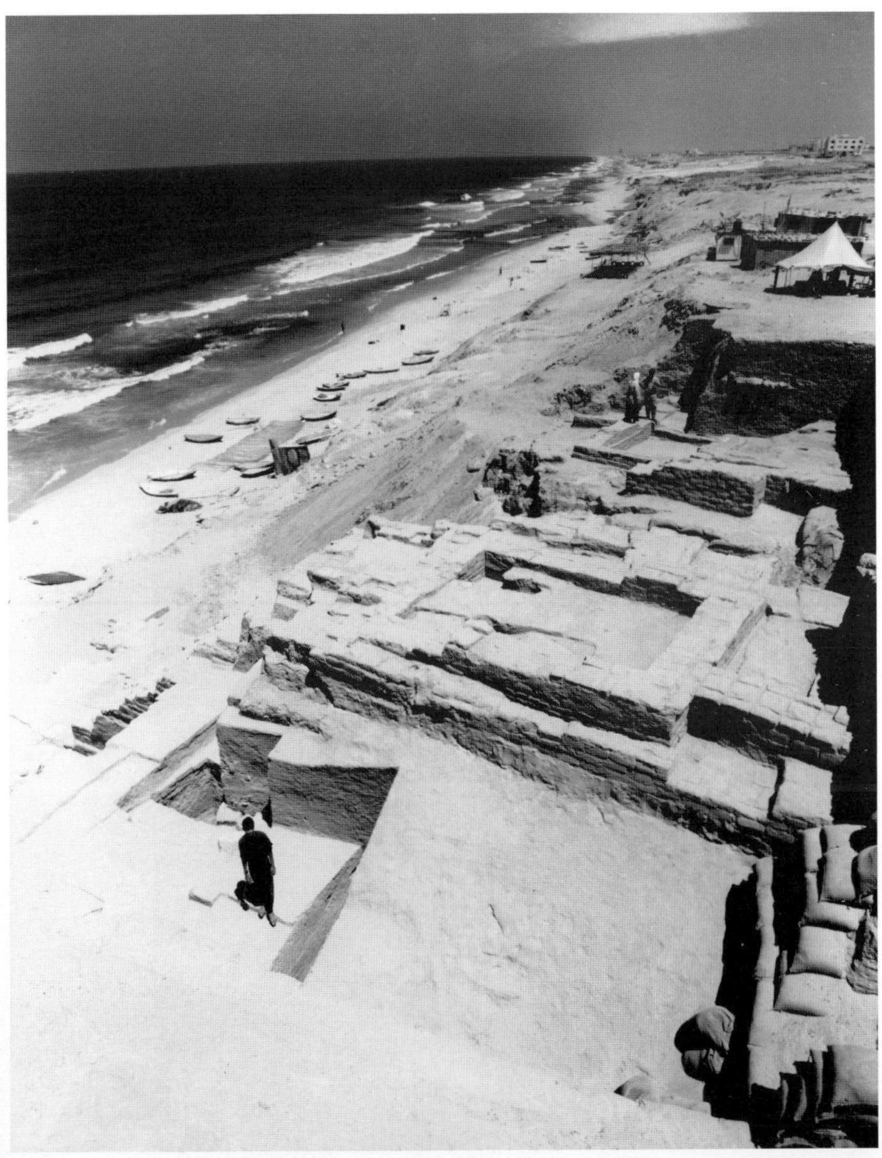

Then, in 1948, the massive influx of Palestinian refugees caused the population to explode, transforming the face of the Gaza countryside. Of 58 villages and towns in the district, 46 were evacuated and totally demolished. In a matter of months, the population of the Municipality of Gaza rose from 35,000 to 170,000 people. Unlike the West Bank, Gaza was not annexed to another country, but was given by the Arab League to Egypt to administer militarily. Most of the population depend, to this day, for their subsistence, on UNRWA assistance and money sent by refugees working in the Gulf States.

In 1956, the Gaza Strip was occupied for several months by the Israeli army. After a second occupation in 1967, resistance campaigns multiplied. Israel retaliated, executing most of the leaders of the resistance – Pan-Arab and left-wing party leaders. Twelve thousand Palestinians were arrested, some of the population was deported, the refugee camps were combed for suspects and long curfews were enforced. In order to control activities in the camps, the army razed entire areas in 1971, leaving 15,000 Palestinians again without homes. From the very beginning, Israeli strategy was to chase as much of the population as possible out of the Gaza Strip. The port of Gaza was closed and the economy put in a strangle-hold. Between 1967 and 1984, more than 100,000 Palestinians left. Some were forcibly deported to the Sinai Peninsula; others emigrated to Jordan or the Gulf States.

During these years of occupation, organizations close to the Muslim Brotherhood (an Islamic movement born in Egypt) grew in social and religious influence. Occupation authorities did not seem to mind these new movements as long as they refrained from political or armed

resistance against the Israeli presence. They were given free rein to develop, especially as they were against the Pan-Arab or leftist groups of the Palestinian Liberation Organisation (PLO). These Islamic movements claim that this period was necessary to build moral and religious strength in order to prepare for political and armed struggle against the occupation of Palestine. The First Intifada was the signal for these actors to enter the military and political arena, by the creation of the Islamic Resistance Movement (Hamas), today the most influential resistance movements in the Gaza Strip.

On December 8, 1987, a popular revolt broke out in the Jabalya Refugee Camp after the death of several Palestinian workers. It marked a new phase of opposition to the Occupation. The next day, the Uprising (Intifada) swept all Palestinian territories occupied in 1967. It would last for more than six years.

The period of the Oslo Accords brought a new rhythm to daily life in the territories. One could move around the camps and towns without fear of running into an Israeli army patrol; and yet, the Gaza Strip was steadily becoming one huge prison camp. In fact, most of its population has never left Gaza (half the people in Gaza are under 15 years of age: these children and teenagers are the first victims of this closure). At the same time, there was considerable urban expansion. After a long period of restriction, especially in the refugee camps, it was at long last possible to build or to add on to dwellings. As a result, everyone started building everywhere without any real urban planning. This boom had a short life due to economic suffocation.

The al-Aqsa Intifada has marked a new development in the struggle against occupation. As usual, the repression has been brutal, the violence, daily, and of all types (see al-Aqsa Intifada, p. 43). One extremely serious consequence of the Israeli reaction is that more than 70% of the working population of the Gaza Strip has been prevented from working.

Yes, we may die, but we will eradicate death from our land
Yes, we may die, but we will pull the oppression of our land out by its roots

Over there - far, far away - oh comrade, the soldiers will take me
They will throw me into the horrible dark, into the shackled hell

Yes, we may die, but we will eradicate death from our land
Yes, we may die, but we will pull the oppression of our land out by its roots

Oh comrade! They searched my bedroom
They found only books
Piles of bones – my brothers who wail between their mother and their father
They woke them up by kicking them awake
They set fire to the anger in their eyes

The soldiers of oppression have me now
I've been hauled down to jail
My father's face is always before me, strengthening me with hope,
My mother wails and wails and my brothers yell
There are some neighbours keeping them company, each with a son in the prisons
But no matter how the soldiers crush us, I raise my fist weighed down by chains and cry:
I will return with an army of comrades, of thunderbolts
Over there I see a worker in the street
I see the victorious leader of the revolution
Waving to me with an iron fist, the other hand throwing flashes of lightning
I am now one of hundreds of comrades
I grip their hands in mine
I feel strong, I will master my cell
Yes, we will not die, we will live even if the chains break our bones
Even if the whips tear us to pieces
Even if they throw our bodies into the fire

Yes, we may die, but we will eradicate death from our land
Yes, we may die, but we will pull the oppression of our land out by its roots

Mo'in Bsesso

Mo'in Bsesso (1928-1984)

Born in Gaza in the working class neighbourhood of Shujah'iya, Mo'in Bsesso is one of the great figures in Palestinian literature. After serving time in British and Egyptian prisons, he settled in Beirut in 1963. Sympathetic to the Arab Nationalist Movement, he contributed to several left-wing newspapers. He also kept close contact with intellectuals in the Soviet Union (a number of his works are translated into Russian). He was a member of the PLO's Palestinian National Council and of the General Secretariat of the Union of Palestinian Writers and Journalists. Mo'in Bsesso died in London in 1984 while participating in Palestinian Cultural Week.

❑ Mukheitem

Situated on the road between the Erez border and Gaza City (in the commune of Jabalya village). This site is closed at present but promises to be one of the most beautiful archaeological sites in the Gaza Strip.

In 1997, archaeologists brought to light on this site a group of Byzantine buildings including a church, a chapel, a baptistry and annexes. The site is located near the Byzantine village of Asalea (map of Madaba), today the village of en-Nasla. The walls have disappeared – stone for building is scarce in Gaza, and old abandoned monuments have always been the source of raw materials for builders – but the floors of the buildings are in an excellent state of conservation. Archaeologists have discovered mosaic floors as well as 17 inscriptions in Greek dating from 444 AD to the 8th century.

The scenes in the mosaics offer a rich variety of themes and subjects, such as a shepherd guarding his sheep while a young man brings a ram under control, large wild animals, and a man selling birds. Apart from scenes such as these, a large "carpet" of medallions illustrates gourmet delights, undoubtedly to praise the fertility of the land and divine generosity. Various receptacles (pitchers, dishes and bowls) and all sorts of food (fruit, bunches of asparagus, smoked fish, lobster, plucked chickens and sausages, to name a few) tempt the eye. Around the baptistery, the motifs symbolize the Garden of Eden – Adam is surrounded by wild animals. The animals and scenery are heavily inspired by an exotic vision of the Ethiopian countryside, highly regarded in Byzantine days. In addition to the beauty and delicacy of the floors, the site is a unique historical document. Numerous inscriptions make it possible to date the appearance of the iconoclastic movement in the eighth century; iconoclasts actually damaged a number of the heads and bodies of the human and animal figures.

❑ The Old City

Although nothing antique remains of the city, the layout of Gaza gives you a good idea of what it was like. The centre of Gaza City is located on an enormous mound from which you can easily see the old city's defined limits. At its foot to the east lies the neighbourhood of Shuja'iya and, to the west, the marketplace. Gaza's quiet years after its zenith under the Mamelukes, the destruction caused by the battle between Turkish and British forces in 1917 and the Israeli Occupation have caused the disappearance of almost all of its architectural heritage. Still, the old town holds some surprises even if its remains often seem lost today in the middle of poor, run-down constructions.

❑ The er-Radwan Fortress

Although there is no inscription indicating the date this fortress was built, the ornaments on the main entrance are definitely in the style of Mameluke architecture. The sides of the fortress are more recent, dating from the 17th century when the Governor (Pasha) of Gaza, Sheikh er-Radwan, lived here. In 1799, Napoleon established his headquarters here and stayed here himself, which is why the edifice is sometimes called Napoleon's Fort. The future national museum of Gaza is to be housed here.

❑ The al-Omari Mosque or Great Mosque

Local tradition has it that this was the site of the temple of Dagon which Samson, tied to its columns, pulled down on the faithful Philistines and himself. Other places of worship were built on the spot. One of these was the cathedral of St. John the Baptist. Built in 1149 AD, the design of the church is well preserved, particularly the western door. There are interesting parts of the church still extant: "lily flower" capitals on columns, the capitals standing on older bases taken from ancient Roman monuments. This church was converted into a mosque after the victory of Saladin in the late 10th century. Its library at the time of Mameluke Sultan Baybar contained more than 20,000 volumes, a precious

cultural heritage. In 1917, the mosque was damaged by British shelling, to be restored by the Islamic High Council in 1926.

❑ The gold market

The gold market is one of the few remaining important relics of the past to be seen in Gaza. It was built in 1476 AD by Sheikh Shams ed-Din el-Hamsi, a judge or *qadi*, and a prominent citizen. Today, this narrow marketplace is a very popular place to buy articles made of gold. Every engaged couple comes here to inspect and choose inexpensive pieces of 21 carat gold jewellery from a wide selection.

❑ St. Porphyrius Church

This church was built in the 5th century by order of Bishop Porphyrius, then Bishop of Maioumas, the port of Gaza, and later Bishop of Gaza itself between 395 AD and 420 AD. The layout and foundations of the church date from this time. The western entrance, cross-vaults and flying buttresses date from the Crusader period and the most recent restorations date from the 19th century. The bilingual Greek and Arabic inscription above the north entrance dates from restoration work undertaken in March 1856. The church belongs to the small Christian community of the Greek Orthodox Church. Saint Porphyrius, buried in the cemetery next to the church, was a staunch supporter of the decision of the Byzantine Emperor Theodosius to forbid pagan religious worship. Bishop Porphyrius closed Gaza's pagan holy sites and ordered the destruction of the Temple to Zeus Marnas (Marneion), the revered god of Gaza, which put an end to pagan Graeco-Roman worship in Gaza. The Temple to Zeus is thought to have been on the site of the Great Mosque, and not under St. Porphyrius Church.

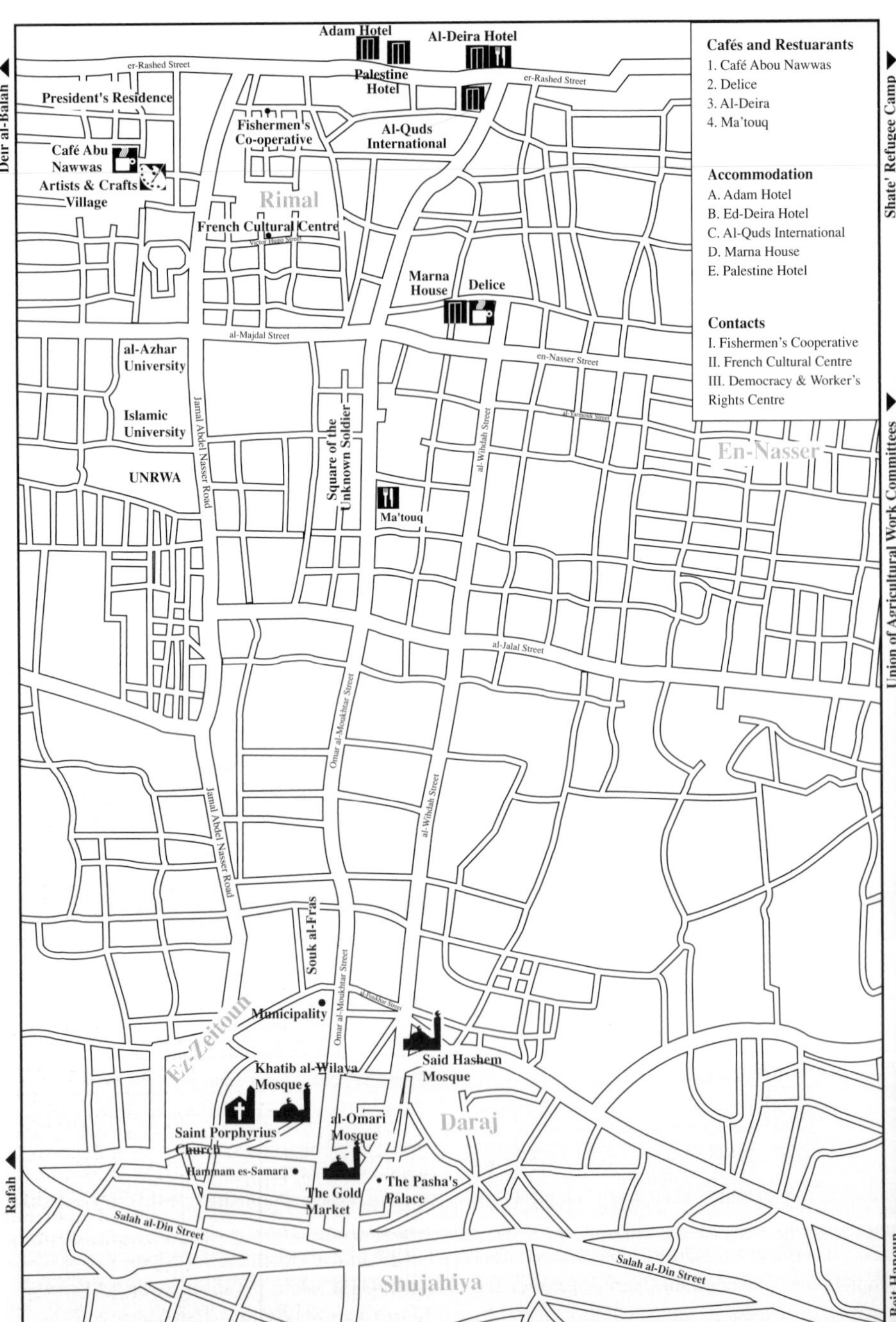
Cafés and Restuarants
1. Café Abou Nawwas
2. Delice
3. Al-Deira
4. Ma'touq
Accommodation
A. Adam Hotel
B. Ed-Deira Hotel
C. Al-Quds International
D. Marna House
E. Palestine Hotel
Contacts
I. Fishermen's Cooperative
II. French Cultural Centre
III. Democracy & Worker's Rights Centre
Deir al-Balah
Shate' Refugee Camp
Union of Agricultural Work Committees
Rafah
Beit Hanoun
Adam Hotel
Al-Deira Hotel
Palestine Hotel
er-Rashed Street
President's Residence
Fishermen's Co-operative
Al-Quds International
Café Abu Nawwas
Artists & Crafts Village
Rimal
French Cultural Centre
Victor Hugo Street
Marna House
Delice
al-Majdal Street
en-Nasser Street
al-Azhar University
Islamic University
UNRWA
Jamal Abdel Nasser Road
Square of the Unknown Soldier
al-Wihdah Street
al-Yarmouk Street
En-Nasser
Ma'touq
al-Jalal Street
Omar al-Moukhtar Street
Souk al-Fras
Municipality
Ez-Zeitoun
Said Hashem Mosque
Khatib al-Wilaya Mosque
Saint Porphyrius Church
al-Omari Mosque
Daraj
Hammam es-Samara
The Pasha's Palace
The Gold Market
Salah al-Din Street
Shujahiya

Next to the church, is the **Khatib al-Wilaya Mosque,** dating from the Mameluke dynasty, which has the following inscription dated 1337 AD at the foot of a minaret, describing the destruction of the Temple to Zeus.

❑ Hammam es-Samara

Thanks to its beautiful, polished marble floors, the Hammam, or Turkish baths, may be dated to the end of the Mameluke period. The entrance to these public baths is three metres below the present street level. The baths are still in use and currently undergoing renovation.

"Governors and soldiers went straight to the places where the idols of Gaza stood. There were eight holy places in the city: the temples to the Sun, to Aphrodite, to Apollo, to the Virgin, to the Moon, to Eros, to the wealth of the city, which was called Tychaion, and to Marneion, the god Zeus, who was born in Crete, and the most renowned sanctuary in the world (...) [Following the revelation of a child "filled with the Holy Spirit," the authorities decided that the temple to Marneion had to be burnt down to the ground.]

"After a prayer, a fire was lit, and the temple blazed and burnt down quickly. All the soldiers and foreigners took everything they could from the ashes: gold, silver, iron or lead. After this, they searched the houses (...) They also found books on sorcery which people claimed were holy books about idol worship, its mysteries and other forbidden religious practices. And they treated them as they had treated their gods (...)

The holy bishop decided to lay the pieces of marble from the Temple to Marneion in front of the temple to pave the street, so that not only men, but also women, who had until then been forbidden to enter the temple, would walk on them, desecrating them with their feet. Pigs, dogs and other animals would also tread on them. This pained the idol worshippers more than the burning of their temple. In fact, most people, especially women, avoid walking on these pieces of marble until this very day."

■ *Mark the Deacon, The life of Porphyry of Gaza (5th century)*

❑ The Said Hashem Mosque

This mosque was erected in 1850 (on the site of a 12th century edifice) near the tomb of Hashem Ibn Abd al-Munaf, grandfather of the prophet Mohammed. It is a reminder of the ancient ties between Arabia and Gaza, the Mediterranean outlet for products from the Arabian Peninsula. Bombed by British forces, the mosque was restored by the Islamic High Council at the beginning of the 1920s.

❑ The pottery workshop

Situated near the el-Faras market, the pottery workshop is unique. Pottery-making in Gaza has inherited a long tradition. From the Greek to the Byzantine period, amphorae called "Gaza jars" filled with olive oil, wine or brine could be found all over the eastern Mediterranean. Today, the jars are principally decorative in purpose. They are usually of generous proportions, but one may also find smaller versions: in particular, water coolers whose unglazed clay is perfect for keeping water fresh and cool. The techniques of fabrication, firing and storing these pieces of pottery give their workshop a character of its own.

Practical Information

Taxis are the easiest and quickest means of transportation around Gaza City. On their regular lines, they cost only one shekel. A ride in a private taxi inside Gaza City costs about six shekels. Renting a car is also reasonable; there are three rental companies: Imad *(☎ 08-286 4000)*, Palestine *(☎ 08-282 3841)*, Yafa *(☎ 08-282 5127)*.

Cafés and Restaurants

There are a number of café-restaurants along the beach. Some have straw roofs, which make them particularly charming. Almost all serve fish and have water pipes (*nargilas* or *shishas*) for their customers.

In the city itself, popular restaurants are numerous and inexpensive. There are also better known and more expensive ones in the well-to-do neighbourhood of er-Rimal. The ***Abu Nawwas café*** is one such, situated in the Artists and Crafts Village. Its architecture and décor lend it a unique charm. One may enjoy *hors d'oeuvre* and pastries here and also smoke a *nargila*.

Everybody who loves French pastries stops at the ***Délice*** café, on Sheikh Izz ed-Din-el-Qassam Street. Near the Square of the Unknown Soldier, on Omar al-Moukhtar Street, one can eat excellent traditional food at ***Ma'touq Restaurant***. There is a good selection, and the atmosphere is rhythmic with the songs of Fairouz.

Al-Deira (☎ 08-283 8100), built on the seashore in traditional sun-dried brick, is a first class hotel and restaurant, and its prices correspond. The refined setting echoes its architecture, while outside there is a splendid view of the sea. Its cuisine is amongst the best in Gaza: its fish, squid and fresh shrimp are highly recommended.

Accommodation

There are several hotels in the three-star category on the beachfront in Rimal. Among them are the ***Adam Hotel*** (*er-Rashid Street*; tel/fax ☎ 08-282 3521, single $50 or double $60), the ***Palestine Hotel*** (*er-Rashid Street*, ☎ 08-282-3355, fax ☎ 08-286 0056, single $50, double $60), the Al-Quds International Hotel (*er-Rashid Street*, 08-282 6223, single $50, double $60). In the same street a hotel which deserves attention is the recently constructed Hotel al-Deira (☎ 08-283 8100/200/300, fax 08-283 8400; single $90, double $120). It has a unique character, having been constructed in a traditional Gazan material, baked red-brick. Its architect, Rashid Abdel Hamid, also designed the Artists and Crafts Village (see p. 281). Near the Square of the Unknown Soldier, is ***Marna House*** (*Ahmed Abdel Aziz Street*; ☎ 08-282 2624, fax ☎ 08-282 3322; single $40, double $50), a friendly little hotel. Guests can use its English library and purchase several books on Gaza, also in English.

Points of Cultural Interest

The French Cultural Centre

Victor Hugo Street. Open Sunday-Thursday 9:30-18:00, Saturday 14:30-18:00. Tel: ☎ 08-286 7883 Fax ☎ 08-282 8811.

French courses are the main activity at the centre, but it is also a place for cultural exchange and social gatherings. There are regular photography and painting exhibitions as well as conferences, seminars or talks. There is also a cafeteria where one may meet francophone Palestinians as well as non-French speakers. People are eager for news of the outside world and happy to answer your questions about life on the Gaza Strip.

The Artists and Crafts Village

Jamal Abdel Nasser Street, near al-Azhar University. ☎ 08-284 6405. Open daily except Friday.

The centre contains an art gallery and handicraft workshops which offer high quality articles for sale. Don't miss the highly agreeable Café Abu Nawwas (p. 280) in the complex.

Contacts

Al-Tawfiq Co-operative Society of Fishermen

88 Ahmed Orabi Street, Mohammed Zakout (Abu Ahmed) Tel: ☎ 08-283 4144 or ☎ 08-286 5295.Visits to the port or to fishermen's families are organized by the co-operative..

There are 5,000 members of the co-operative – including 2,700 fishermen and 450 boat owners. The association offers several services to its members, including provision of nets, gas, ice, refrigerated vehicles and boat maintenance. Before the al-Aqsa Intifada, the co-operative took care of 30% of its members' living expenses and offered loans for boat maintenance. Today, families earn less than $100 a month, compared to around $450 in the year 2000, before the Intifada. Occupation authorities have forbidden deep-sea fishing in international waters, so catches are small. Now, fishermen cannot go out further than 12 miles (20,000 nautical miles) and have seen the area they can fish reduced to 6,000 nautical miles since the start of the al-Aqsa Intifada. Israeli naval aggressions are numerous and often take the form of stopping fishing boats at sea, arrests of fishermen under the pretext that they have gone out too far, and confiscation of boats and destruction of equipment.

Union of Agricultural Work Committees (UAWC)

Hassan Salameh Street, opposite en-Nasser Hospital. Tel: ☎ 08-287 9959, Fax ☎ 08-285 3075; E-mail: uawc@mtcgaza.com [see UAWC Ramallah, p. 235].

Here, one can go on an organised visit to discover rural Gaza and learn about the problems specific to farming: water scarcity, both in quantity and quality, priorities, difficulties related to export of produce, and destruction of infrastructure.

Democracy & Workers' Rights Centre in Palestine (DWRC)

Al-Quds Open University Street. ☎ 08-285 3011, fax ☎ 08-285 3010; gaza@dwrc.org; the centre offers briefings and talks with workers (by appointment).

The centre is an important source of information on labour law adopted by the Palestinian Authority and on violations of the rights of Palestinian workers in the Occupied Territories and in Israel, where they are the most vulnerable. It is extremely difficult to prosecute any employer in Israel.

Although it is theoretically possible for victims of abuse to file a complaint in the Israeli courts as to unpaid salaries, social insurance, damages for unfair dismissal, violence, etc., most people have to forego such recourse. It is in reality very hard for the person concerned to be physically present when judgment is handed down, which is required by law. One of the centre's activities is concerned with obtaining the Israeli authorities' permits to enter Israel to initiate such proceedings, as well as to provide legal assistance for the plaintiff. The most frequent violations concern non-payment of job dismissal compensation and the practical impossibility for workers to collect the social benefits deducted from their

Destruction due to Israeli army aggressions during the al-Aqsa Intifada (in the Gaza Strip and West Bank)

Agricultural depots destroyed	465
Farm homes destroyed	480
Greenhouses destroyed	1,410 dunums
Fences destroyed	303 km
Sheep, cows and cattle killed	13,871
Poultry dead in epidemics	1,179,314
Bee hives destroyed	9,863
Ponds and reservoirs destroyed	1,023
Irrigation pipelines destroyed	738 km
Wells destroyed	264
Farmland destroyed	24,188 dunums
Trees uprooted, felled or burnt	1,000,914

Source: Palestinian Ministry of Agriculture
March 31, 2004

salaries. Firstly, employers hide behind the government decision to ban access into Israel to Palestinian workers. Secondly, Palestinians who pay Israeli social insurance for themselves and their families cannot collect it as they are forbidden to enter and live in Israel. Thirdly, they receive no public services in return for money they are forced to pay for social insurance because they are not allowed to live in the 1948 Territories, but live in the Gaza Strip or the West Bank. The DWRC is waging a general campaign on this issue of rights' infringement, demanding that workers be reimbursed for their payment of taxes.

■ The Southern Gaza Strip

To see this part of the Gaza Strip, the road along the coast – between the sea and the countryside – is definitely the most scenic route. To this day, the coastline has been preserved from the building craze that has taken over the Gaza Strip since 1994. Between Gaza City and Deir al-Balah, crops grow on sandy but fertile soil, which requires little care other than watering. Farmers cultivate creeping plants here, using an ancient farming method that takes advantage of the morning dew. In Deir al-Balah, palm trees give one a foretaste of the scenery in Egypt. The coastal route ends at the Deir al-Balah Refugee Camp. Beyond this point, all land has been confiscated for a group of settlements called Gush Katif in Hebrew.

❑ Tel al-Ajul

8 kilometres south of Gaza City. Free entry.

During the first half of the second millennium BC, Tel al-Ajul was the most important Canaanite city of this southern part of Palestine and a military stronghold of the Hyksos, the rulers in Egypt. When the Eighteenth Dynasty conquered the Hyksôs and undertook a victorious military campaign against Palestine, Tel al-Ajul fell out of favour; Gaza, which Thutmose III took in 1468 BC, replaced it permanently. Today, there are no traces of its once greatness remaining, but the "tel" and its view over flourishing countryside are worth a visit.

❑ The Byzantine site of Umm Amir

Situated in the Municipality of Nusseirat, Umm Amir is 300 metres from the shore and 13 kilometres south of Gaza City. There are archaeological digs being carried out here at the moment. Do not hesitate to ask for permission to visit: you will be given a warm welcome.

The ruins here cover some two acres, constituting a group of church buildings and a monastery, which includes a chapel, baptistery, burial crypt and the monks' cells. To the north, a steam bath (*hammam*) and its annexes complete the site. At the periphery, an encircling wall protected the monastery from all intrusion. Several figurative

The Byzantine site of Umm Amir

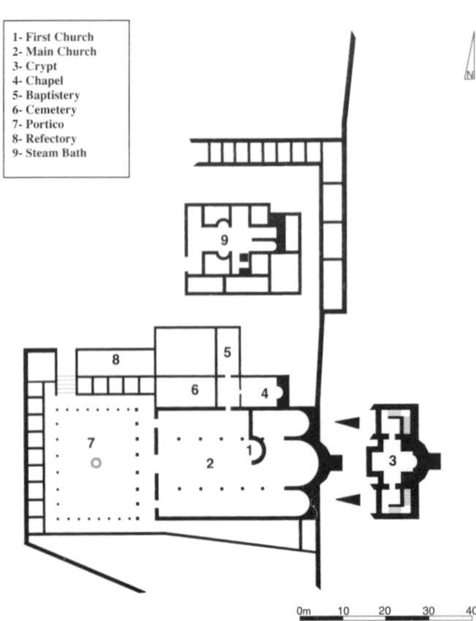

Schematic interpretation of map of remains

and geometrical mosaics decorate the floors. The finds are presumed to date from the fourth to the eighth century AD. Construction of the monastery is attributed to St. Hilarion. At the beginning of 4 AD, Hilarion, a young Gazan who had converted to Christianity in Egypt, built a hermitage on this site. Its popularity was such that after 30 years there were 400 monks living here. The community was organized around a church and several less important buildings. In 362 AD, Julian, known as the Apostate, forced Hilarion to flee to Cyprus and had the monastery destroyed. Several years later, the complex was rebuilt. Saint Hilarion's remains were buried here *circa* 371 AD. In 638 AD, the Muslim conquest brought to an end all large monastic estates. At the beginning of the eighth century, all buildings were converted under the Umayyads. The steam bath was probably added at this time. Following an earthquake, the site was abandoned and used as a stone quarry by the inhabitants of the neighbouring villages.

■ Deir al-Balah

Deir al-Balah is famous for the sarcophagi discovered here (which are now exhibited at the Israel Museum in Jerusalem). They date from the 13th century BC. At that time, Deir al-Balah was an important fortified market town under Egyptian rule. Next to the Egyptian sarcophagi, archaeologists also discovered furniture from various historical periods: Mycenaean, Cypriot and Canaanite. From a small country town in 1948, Deir al-Balah has today become one of the four urban areas on the Gaza Strip, with a population of roughly 30,000 inhabitants. The four refugee camps nearby (Deir al-Balah, Bureij, Maghazi and Nusseirat) increase its population to over 150,000 people.

Khan Younis

Khan Younis is the second largest urban centre after Gaza City. The town, including Khan Younis and al-Amal refugee camps, has more than 130,000 residents. It received its name from Emir Younis Ibn Ala'en-Nawruzi, who in 1387 AD built a huge *caravanserai* or *khan* (inn for caravans) here on the route between Cairo and Damascus; its southern façade is still preserved, 60 metres long and 10 metres high. This fortified town was also an important commercial centre, with a post office and military barracks, which earned it the name "Qala'a" (fortress).

Khan Younis Refugee Camp

Popular Committee, Ahmed Esa'adouni, ☎ 0599-791882.

The camp houses more than 58,000 refugees. Due to an insufficient number of schools, the existing schools cater daily to two separate groups of children. Despite this system of doubling up, there is an average number of 50 children per class in nursery, elementary and secondary schools. Living conditions and infrastructure are precarious. During the so-called peace process, reductions in UNRWA budgets decreased the aid assistance. The camp's water reserves are unfit to drink. Although water is in principal free for refugees, the fact is that

people must pay the Khan Younis Municipality for water, as well as electricity and secondary education. The contrast is completely scandalous when one compares the water consumption by refugees or other residents of the Gaza Strip to that of the Jewish settlements. Khan Younis is surrounded on three sides by the Israeli settlements or colonies of Gadid, Neve Dekalim and Ganne Tal – veritable oases -which represent permanent threats. Since the beginning of the al-Aqsa Intifada, the Israeli army has razed many homes on the edge of the camp and destroyed the crops in the fields separating the camp from the settlements.

Practical Information

From Deir al-Balah to the Egyptian border, the coastal road is under Israeli control. A road controlled by the Israeli army leads to the Khan Younis beaches, amongst the most beautiful beaches in Palestine. Here, there are many café-restaurants under straw roofs that invite one with a variety of leisure activities and excellent fish meals. Hospitality is the most attentive. One may swim, but in respect for dress standards in the Gaza Strip, one should remain completely covered when in the water. Feel free to ask for advice from the café owners, who can provide a place to change. They will do their best to make your visit memorable.

Accommodation

Al-Hilal al-Ahmar Hotel (tel/fax ☎ 08-205 4261, $15 per person per room). This establishment is run by the Palestinian Red Crescent (the equivalent of the Red Cross). It is the only hotel in the south of the Gaza Strip. One meets interesting people here. At present, with the Gaza Strip cut into four separate areas and due to the long delays imposed by the Israeli army at the Egyptian border, many Palestinians from the north of the Gaza Strip plan a stop in Khan Younis, on their way to the border crossing at Rafah (which is temporarily closed at time of going to press: June 2004).

The Israeli Settlements

Immediately after the Israeli Occupation in 1967, few new settlers came to live in the Gaza Strip. Only one settlement, Kfar Darom, was established in 1970. The exposure of the settlers, almost too close for comfort to Palestinian towns and their resistance, discouraged Zionist expansion. For this reason, when the Labour Party came to power at the beginning of the 1970s, it chose first of all to set up a series of new settlements not inside the Strip, but surrounding it. From 1978 onwards, the Israelis founded many settlements, responding to three principal objectives: to control the maritime border between the Gaza Strip and Egypt, to isolate each of the Palestinian towns from each other, and to thwart the possible creation of a Palestinian state in the Gaza Strip (the political context representing compromise with the Egyptian authorities).

Since the beginning of the al-Aqsa Intifada, this strategy of territorial control has permitted the occupation authorities to divide the Strip into four "regions": Gaza, Deir al-Balah, Khan Younis and Rafah.

Today, there are over 20 Israeli farming and military settlements in the Gaza Strip, representing nearly 8,000 settlers. Thus, 30% of the Gaza Strip is under Israeli domination; encircled by razor wire, electric fences and military watch-towers, the settlements of gleaming white residential houses with bright red roofs and turquoise swimming pools are spread out in lush gardens. The contrast with their neighbours is more than striking and strongly reminiscent of South Africa in its *apartheid* days.

Rafah

The gateway between Egypt and Asia, Rafah has always been a busy mercantile centre but also a strategic point for armies. Antony and Cleopatra were married here in the First Century BC. Ruins are numerous here, but buried deep under the sand dunes.

Today, the town (or, to be exact, the Rafah Refugee Camp) extends along both sides of the border, which is under Israeli control. When the Gaza Strip and Egyptian Sinai were occupied in 1967, several thousand Palestinian refugees were deported to Sinai. The camp was enlarged on the Egyptian side. In 1978, the Camp David agreements gave the Sinai, occupied since 1967, back to Egypt. The re-establishment of this border imposed a new separation on the Palestinian population. Thousands more people were cut off from their relatives. On either side of the No Man's Land under Israeli control, relatives continue to this day to talk to each other with megaphones.

Humanitarian Crisis in Gaza (June 2004)

After three years of the al-Aqsa Intifada, the situation in Gaza is disastrous: there has recently (April 2004) been a temporary cessation of emergency food aid because of Israeli refusal to allow the easy passage of food, and IDF refusal to allow empty shipping containers back into Israel from Gaza. Although international aid agencies supply humanitarian aid valued at $1 billion p.a., the UN Office Co-ordinating Humanitarian Affairs reported in November 2003:

"***Inability of humanitarian organisations to cope with the destruction***: National and international organisations face major logistic challenges dealing with the immediate aftermath of large-scale house demolition. The Rafah Municipality's Emergency Committee set up two initial transit stations in a sports hall and library on 11 October 2003 for hundreds of the homeless, providing shelter and food for the first 2-3 days. UNRWA provided a one-off cash payment for nearly 250 families and cash assistance of varying amounts was provided by the Welfare Association, Rafah Governorate, Palestine Red Crescent Society, the Health Work Committees and the President's Office. Donations of essential supplies ranging from food parcels, water, blankets, mattresses, clothes and kitchenware were given by the World Food Programme (WFP), Islamic Relief, the Union of Arab Doctors, World Vision, Save the Children (US), Catholic Relief Services, Emirates Red Crescent Society, ICRC and the Ministry of Housing including providing temporary shelter and cash payments to the families for a short period after the demolitions. Such assistance is immediate and short-term. But the central issue is that organisations cannot keep up with the current pace of home destruction. UNRWA, for example, in the last 3 years has re-built 228 shelters to accommodate 236 families. UNRWA's ability to construct new homes has been constrained by a lack of donor support. UNRWA needs over $30.5 million for re-housing, yet has only $3.2 million for 2003. Donors are reluctant to commit funds to infrastructure projects that may then be destroyed. In the past few weeks donors have publicly questioned their role in financing Israel's occupation. The growing sense of discontent has been fuelled by access restrictions faced by staff working in the OPT. Providing accommodation is the most pressing need. (...) The private rental market is becoming saturated outside of Gaza City especially in camps. Families have responded by living in small units due to the limited space. Some have migrated from Rafah. A small number of homeless have moved into houses abandoned by families living next to the buffer zone, who fled in the fear their home [would] be demolished next. The economic impact of the continuous incursions and increasing levels of dependency in Rafah is reflected in the levels of assistance provided by WFP in the last 5 months:

August 2003	3,473 families (20,838 beneficiaries)
End November 2003	8,809 families (53,454 beneficiaries)
End December 2003	expected 57,600 beneficiaries

In February 27, 2004 the UN Special Rapporteur of the Commission on Human Rights, John Dugard, reported on the situation of human rights in the Palestinian Territories, saying of Gaza:

"Death and destruction continue to be the fate of Gaza. During the visit of the Special Rapporteur 15 Palestinians, including 3 civilians, were killed and 62 wounded in gun battles with the IDF. The targeted killing of militants in densely populated areas is carried out with little regard for civilians. Innocent passers-by, often children, have consequently been killed or wounded in these attacks. Of the 95 persons killed or injured in targeted killings in Gaza since 1 January 2003, most were civilians. As pointed out in earlier reports, targeted killings and assassinations are illegal and may constitute war crimes. Moreover, the principle of distinction, a fundamental tenet of international humanitarian law, obliges States to distinguish at all times between civilians and combatants in their military operations. The IDF often fails to pay due regard to this principle and, moreover, does not in most cases investigate the killing of civilians or prosecute those responsible. Although over 2,500 Palestinians have been killed by the IDF since the start of the Second Intifada in September 2000, only 15 soldiers have been indicted for causing death or grievous injury to Palestinians. Impunity of this kind in an international order committed to accountability for international crimes and the criminal responsibility of commanders for crimes committed by their troops is a matter of serious concern."

"The demolition of houses and the destruction of property continue unabated. A total of 1,640 homes have been destroyed or damaged beyond repair in the Gaza Strip since 2000, rendering 2,705 families - about 15,000 persons - homeless. The IDF has been particularly active in its demolition of homes in Rafah, adjacent to the border with Egypt. (...) An eight-metre metal and concrete wall along the Egyptian border protects IDF patrols along the border from sniper fire. That tunnels from Egyptian territory into Rafah exist cannot be disputed. Nor can it be disputed that these tunnels are used for the smuggling of goods and arms. On the other hand, the question must be asked whether the high-tech IDF does not have the expertise to discover and destroy these tunnels in the vacant territory adjacent to the wall. Is it really necessary to destroy more and more houses in the vicinity of the boundary wall on the pretext of destroying tunnels?"

"While in Rafah the Special Rapporteur visited UNRWA schools close to the razed zone near the boundary wall. Teachers at one school told of random shooting in the direction of the school that terrorised children and disrupted school activities. Shell holes in the school walls confirmed the veracity of these statements. At another school, teenage girls at a trauma counselling session attended by the Special Rapporteur spoke with tears and pain about their experiences of military occupation: of neighbours shot by the IDF and savaged by IDF sniffer dogs; of homes destroyed without proper notice; and of their desire to live normal lives like children in other countries. To deny childhood to children is unforgivable. Moreover, to create feelings of hatred in the youth of Palestine in this way is impossible to reconcile with the security concerns that Israel claims guide its actions. From the perspective of international law it must be noted that the actions of the IDF violate many provisions of the Convention on the Rights of the Child."

THE TERRITORIES OF '48

مناطق ال ٤٨

THE TERRITORIES OF '48

مناطق ال ٤٨

XVII

THE TERRITORIES OF '48

Here we shall stay
Sentinels watching over our land
(…)
If we are thirsty,
We shall squeeze the stones.
If we are hungry,
We shall eat the earth
But we will not leave
We have a past
A present
A future
Here, we are on our land
And it is here that our roots will grow
Deep
Deep down.

■ Tawfiq Zayyad

The Palestinians of 1948

The Palestinian citizens of Israel today represent almost 20% of the population, or more than a million inhabitants (76% Muslim, 15% Christian and 9% Druze), who live mainly in three areas - the Galilee, the Triangle and the Negev. Around 10% live in encampments and unrecognised villages, some of which contain several thousand inhabitants; about 8% live in mixed towns where they are a minority: Acre, Haifa, Jaffa-(Tel Aviv), Lod, Nazareth-Upper Nazareth (*Nazrat Illit*) and Ramle. The remaining Palestinian population of Israel lives in exclusively Arab cities and villages. A third of these Palestinians of '48 are displaced persons, refugees since the 1948 war or since the early fifties. Although almost all were farmers, few now support themselves by agriculture. Most of their property was confiscated by the Israeli authorities, which invoked "the general interest," "security," or the need to manage the estates of "absentee landlords." Although Palestinians represent 20% of the population, they own only 2.5% of the territory of the State of Israel.

Palestinians of '48

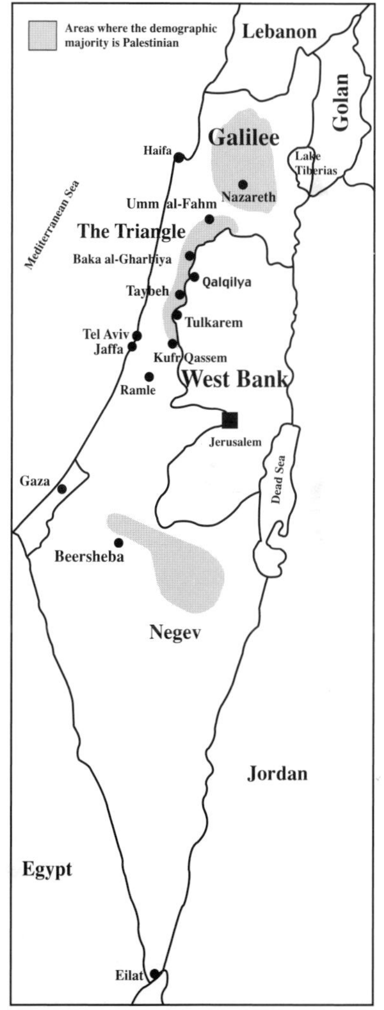

> Golda Meir claimed that there was no such thing as a Palestinian people and that they were *"an invention of Arab propaganda."* In the same vein, Yitzhak Rabin said: *"the Arabs* [of Israel] *are only a culture, not a national minority group."* In fact, the Israeli government and Jewish citizens of Israel call the Palestinian minority *"Arabs"* or *"Israeli Arabs"* but never *"Palestinians."*

The Palestinians who escaped transfer in 1948, whose families had always lived in this region as the majority, became a minority in the "Jewish democratic State" as defined in the Declaration of Independence of the State of Israel. They were confronted by a new reality of defeat, massacres, deportations, forced displacements inside the new Jewish state, the destruction of villages or urban areas, the imposition of martial law and the status of an Arab minority. Their distress and isolation from both the internal and international communities made these Palestinians the silent generation. Most Jews treated them with suspicion and hostility, especially the government, which kept them under military rule until 1966, controlling all aspects of their lives: refugee status, work, education and public expression of opinion. From their daily experience of political discrimination, humiliation and land confiscation developed the concept of *summud*, which means "perseverance" or "endurance" in Arabic; *summud* implies not giving in: staying on the land at whatever cost, in a hostile and foreign environment. Local leaders, chosen by the Israeli authorities, were placed in positions of power as intermediaries between the people they represented and the government. Any Palestinian organisation was forbidden, so the only place where Palestinians had a voice was in the Israeli Communist Party, whose members were both Jewish and Palestinian. While hoping for liberation by outside forces, the Palestinians of '48 enthusiastically welcomed the Pan-Arab movement and anti-colonial stance of Egypt's president, Gamal Abdel Nasser. When Israel, working with France and the United Kingdom, attacked Egypt in 1956, the state of emergency already in force among the Palestinian population was intensified; arrest, intimidation and curfew increased in all Arab areas. On the evening of Israel's attack on Egypt, the Israeli army massacred 49 Palestinians in the town of Kufr Qassem. (See p. 358.)

During this period, the Palestinians (a majority of whom were peasants), whose rural towns had been almost completely demolished in 1948, became - as their land was confiscated - progressively dependant on the Jewish economy; as farmers out of work, they were a cheap source of labour. During the years 1961 to 1994, the percentage of Palestinian farmers decreased from 48.8% to 4.6%. In 1966, martial law was lifted, except for the emergency laws permitting house arrest, administrative arrest, prohibition from leaving the country and other similarly repressive laws. A year later, when Israel took control of East Jerusalem, the West Bank and the Gaza Strip, the Palestinians of '48 renewed contact with a part of the Palestinian people. In the face of accelerated settlement growth during the Seventies and as blatant discrimination in the allocation of budgets to Palestinian local councils inside Israel became obvious, huge protest gatherings and strikes were organised. On March 30, 1976, the Israeli police fired on demonstrators, killing several Palestinians; this day, named "Land Day," is commemorated every year and has become a national day, symbolising the unity of the Palestinian people and the struggle against the occupation of Palestinian land.

Forced to accept various forms of discrimination and marginalisation as second-class citizens, many Palestinian Israelis believed the Oslo Accords represented a chance to improve their situation; their illusions soon faded as they faced the facts. The Oslo Accords dealt only with Palestinians in the West Bank and Gaza: the Palestinian Israelis were totally ignored.

On the contrary, the policies of land confiscation, town and village closure, underdevelopment and discrimination in every sector continued, interspersed with occasional promises during election periods. The Basic Law: Human Dignity and Freedom, a 1992 update of the 1948 Declaration of the Establishment of the State of Israel, describes the country as "a democratic, Jewish state." Palestinian citizens of Israel remark ironically that Israel is "a democratic state for Jews." The gulf between Jews and Arabs has increased in recent years: the murderous repression under Ehud Barak's government, named "Strong Wind," the attacks on Palestinian communities in Nazareth, Jaffa and Acre by waves of angry Israelis, calls to boycott businesses employing "Israeli Arabs" and cuts in the budgets of the Palestinian communities since the beginning of the al-Aqsa Intifada have contributed to that increasing gulf.

According to the 2001/2002 data published recently by the Israeli Central Bureau of Statistics (May 2004): "Some 70% of the country's poor towns are in the Arab sector." The report's main section compared welfare conditions in the Arab and Jewish populations; it showed that in 2001, only Jewish towns were classified as being high on the socio-economic scale. Furthermore, and tellingly, *in 2002, 46.8% of Palestinian Arab Israelis lived below the poverty line, as opposed to 14.9% of Jews.* Half of all Arab children and a fifth of Jewish children lived below the poverty line. The infant mortality rate among Jews was 4.1 per thousand births, compared to 8.2 per thousand among Palestinian Arab Israelis, in 2001. Similarly in education: over 90% of 17-year-old Jewish males were enrolled in educational frameworks, compared to 68.2% in the "Arab" sector. Between 1990-2002, the number of male teenagers who passed matriculation exams rose in both sectors, reaching 45% among Jews, compared to 24% among "Arabs" in 2002. "Arab" girls also lagged behind their Jewish peers in 2002, with 39% passing their exams, compared to 61%. Bearing in mind that resources are so unfairly distributed, these statistics come as no surprise: Israel recently lost its high standing in the international scales of educational matriculation results, as a direct result of the poor showing by Arab students, whose schools are under-funded in such a racist manner. Even the results of The Orr Commission, a government commission of inquiry into the killing of Palestinian Arabs during riots at the beginning of the al-Aqsa Intifada, which recommended healing the gross inequalities and treatment, have had little impact.

In 1998, of 429 localities classified as zones of national priority, only four were Arab. These four, moreover, were towns in the Negev, where the objective was to relocate the Arab population, which is currently scattered on land coveted by the Israeli authorities. Under the government of Labour Prime Minister Ehud Barak, the Minister of Trade and Industry allotted the Arab community (20% of the total population of Israel) 0.5% of its annual budget. In that ministry, only four Arabs were employed, of its manpower of 540 employees.

THE GALILEE

This fertile area extends from Haifa Bay to Lake Tiberias (the Sea of Galilee) and, to the north, to the foothills of the Golan plateau. Nazareth is located in the centre of the Galilee. In Upper Galilee, from Acre to Safad, the landscape is a succession of wooded hills between 800 to 1,000 metres high. The scenery in Lower Galilee is very different, with its vast fertile plains; the largest one, Marj Bin 'Amer (the Jezreel Valley), stretches from Mount Carmel to the hills of the northern West Bank.

For Christians everywhere, the name "Galilee" evokes the names of places both familiar yet mysterious:

"And Jesus went about all Galilee, teaching in their synagogues, and preaching the gospel of the kingdom, and healing all manner of sickness and all manner of disease among the people. And his fame went throughout all Syria (...) And there followed him great multitudes of people from Galilee, and from Decapolis, and from Jerusalem, and from Judaea, and from beyond Jordan." (Matthew 4:23-25)

Judaising the Galilee

The United Nations drew up a partition plan for Palestine in 1947 (Resolution 181) that foresaw most of the Galilee as part of a future Arab state; but at the end of the 1948 war, the whole area was integrated into Israel. In spite of the policy of ethnic cleansing, the centre and west of the Galilee remained predominantly Arab. The Israeli authorities therefore put in place certain measures designed to modify these demographic realities. (*See Confiscation of the 1948 Territories, p. 69*). The process of "judaising the Galilee" refers to these measures. The development of new residential and industrial Jewish areas was the only initiative for regional growth, deemed a national priority and therefore benefiting from central and regional state funding. Population statistics were the first consideration prior to the establishment of any development policy.

In the 1970s, the Commissioner of the Northern District (Galilee), Israel Koenig, "worried" that the Arabs constituted over 51% of the region's population (in 1978). He made a series of recommendations, which were by and large applied by his successors. In the year 2000, the Arab population represented only 31% of the inhabitants of the Northern District, but could reach 55% by the year 2020. For this reason, the government is dissatisfied with the results of its policy, and the subject regularly comes up for debate in the Knesset, the Israeli parliament, under the title "*Demographic development in Israel - risks and solutions*."

The Koenig Memorandum

The demographic problem and expressions of Arab nationalism

(1) The rate of growth of the Arab population in Israel is 5.9%, compared to 1.5% for the Jewish population.

This is a particularly acute problem in the Northern District, where a large part of the Arab population is concentrated. During mid-1975, the Arab population there totalled 250,000, while the Jewish population was 269,000. A closer look at the statistics for each district reveals that Arabs in Western Galilee represent 67% of the total population, with 48% of them residing in the Jezreel Valley (...). At this rate of growth, the Arabs could represent more than 51% of the population of this region by 1978...

(2) This wave of nationalism in the Israeli Arab population dates from the Six Day War. The policy of exchanges with the West Bank and open bridges to Jordan has encouraged contacts between the Palestinians of Judaea and Samaria, Palestinians in Jordan and the Palestinian Arabs of Israel. This contact has given them the impetus to work together in a common front using anti-Israel nationalist slogans. Recently, they have even started referring to the 1947 UN resolution concerning the borders of Israel, even stating that much of the Northern District was not included within the boundaries of Israel (...).

Prospects

(a) The rapid growth of the Arab population (from 150,000 in 1948 to 430,000 in 1975) strengthens this nationalism and gives the Arabs the impression that time is on their side. This is particularly true of the Northern District, where their physical presence over large areas is uninterrupted.

(b) There is a serious danger that, in decades to come, the Arabs will take control, demographically and politically, of St. John of Acre and the region of Nazareth.

(c) It must be taken into account that, at a certain stage of political activity hostile to the State, the Arab population in the Northern District, where it is in the majority, might demand a referendum.

(d) Arabs may already be seen acting concertedly to buy up real estate in the Northern District. This activity is obvious in Upper Nazareth (*Nazrat Illit*) and in St. John of Acre, and there are disturbing signs of the same phenomenon in the Jezreel Valley.

Proposals

(a) Expand and intensify Jewish settlement in all areas where Arabs are contiguously established and explore possibilities of thinning out the Arab communities that are already there.
Particular attention should be paid to zones adjacent to the northwest border and in the region of Nazareth. At the same time, any laws preventing the establishment of Arab settlements should be rigorously enforced in different parts of the country.

(b) At the same time, put in place, in St. John of Acre and in Upper Nazareth, Jewish leaders capable of coming to grips with these disturbing developments which we have exposed.

(c) Establish a policy of sanction and reward (with a legal base) regarding local authorities and places which show their hostility to the State or to Zionism in any way, shape or form.

(d) ..it is necessary to create a political party, which will be in symmetry with the Labour Party, which will extol concepts such as equality, humanism, culture, language and peace in the Middle East. The Israeli government institutions must prepare to exercise a secret presence and control of this party.

■ Extract from *The Koenig Memorandum*, a report published in 1976 by the Northern District Commissioner of the Interior Ministry, Israel Koenig. Quoted by Ilan Halevi in *Beneath Israel, Palestine.*

■ Acre

"About the city of Acre. May God destroy it and return it to Islam! It is the chief city of the Franks in Syria, the place where the ships that deck the sea like so many banners land, where all galleons dock. It may be compared in size to Constantinople. It is the assembly point for galleons and caravans, the meeting place of Muslim and Christian merchants from far and wide. Its streets and its roads are thronged with a crowd so dense, one cannot move."

■ Ibn Jobair, born in Valencia, twelfth century.

Mentioned in Egyptian writings of the ninth century BC and in the Old Testament (Judges 1:31) by its Semitic name, Akko, Acre later became one of numerous Phoenician ports built along the Levantine coast. In 333 BC, Alexander the Great granted it preference over Tyre, by establishing a mint here; his successors, the Ptolemites, enlarged Acre on Hellenistic lines and gave it the Greek name, Ptolemais; the Umayyads renamed it with its Semitic name, translated into Arabic as Akka. The city benefited at this time from Caesarea's decline and became the major Arab seaport in the western Mediterranean as well as the main port for Damascus (the Umayyad capital). However, it is the city's mediaeval and Ottoman history which is best known, thanks to the various writings of Crusader pilgrims, traders and Arab historians, as well as archaeological finds. Conquered by Baldwin I in 1104, St. John of Acre (as the Crusaders called it) became the besieged stronghold of the Order of St. John. Having been retaken by Saladin in 1187 AD, the town was soon reconquered by the armies of the Third Crusade under Richard the Lionheart. With the loss of Jerusalem, St. John of Acre became the capital of the Latinate Kingdom for a period (1191-1291 AD) and the most important port in the western Mediterranean. Merchants from Venice, Genoa and Amalfi each had their own part of the city where they stored precious supplies of goods from the Far East: silks, spices, cotton fabrics and other goods. The city extended over an area three times larger than as defined by its actual walls, with nearly 40,000 inhabitants. Protected by the many castles scattered throughout its hinterland, St. John of Acre finally fell, after a long siege in 1291. The Mameluke sultan, Baybar, had it destroyed and established a new capital of Galilee far away from the sea, in Safad. For more than 400 years, Acre was just a modest town, almost a village, until the Druze prince, Fakhreddin, undertook its restoration in the seventeenth century. He was responsible for the construction of the Khan al-Franj, which became the entry point to Acre for merchants and European diplomats during the entire Ottoman period. The renovation did not last long however. Fakhreddin was unable to make his domain an independent state and was beheaded in 1635.

In the middle of the eighteenth century, the new strong man of the area, Bedouin chief Sheikh Daher al-Omar, Farmer General of Galilee (which in those days meant senior tax collector), took control of Acre, which at the time belonged to the province of Saida; he used his influence to make the port of Acre the principal market for Galilee and Damascus. Keeping his distance from the centres of Ottoman power, he established a notable alliance with Maltese pirates, which inspired several unsuccessful Turkish attacks. In the end, a Bosnian sea captain, Ahmed Pasha al-Jazzar, known as "the Butcher" for his unusual cruelty, re-established the authority of the Ottoman sultan over the region and pursued the development of the city, commenced by Fakhreddin. In 1799, al-Jazzar, with some help from the English fleet, also repulsed Napoleon's troops. From this time on, foreign European powers meddled more and more in the Ottoman Empire's internal affairs, switching alliances as it pleased them, first supporting the Ottoman colonies and then areas under Ottoman jurisdiction. This policy explains the British support first for Mohammed Ali when he freed Egypt from the Turks, then their rejection of the alliance when he wanted to restore an Arab state which would have incorporated Palestine and Syria. Between 1832 and 1840, Acre came under Egyptian control; Acre was badly damaged by the prolonged fighting over it, which, above all, clearly demonstrated the incapacity of its walls to protect it against a modern army. The port of Haifa, however, proved itself better able to develop new harbour infrastructure, surpassing the capacities of neighbouring Acre. Acre concentrated on its past glories, while jealously witnessing the rise of Haifa. Nevertheless, as the major town of the frontier district bordering Lebanon, Acre became newly busy under the British Mandate. New residential areas grew up in the east outside its walls, while the population doubled between 1922 and 1945, rising from 6,420 to 12,360 (9,890 Muslims, 2,330 Christians and 50 Jews). After the city was conquered on May 18, 1948, the inhabitants were confined to the old town and placed under Israeli military jurisdiction until 1966. All movement - whether it involved return to, or exit from, the town - was subject to the Israeli authorities' permission.

The town today

Today the Municipality of Acre has over 50,000 residents, of whom 28% are Palestinian Arabs. A poor city, Acre attracts many Jewish immigrants from the former republics of the Soviet Union (25% come from Georgia or Kafkaz). For recently-arrived Jewish immigrants, Acre is a temporary stopover: it is the city with the highest rate of emigration into the interior of Israel. Over 7,000 people live in the old city alone, which represents more than half the Palestinian population of the whole municipality. Although Acre has the undeniable charm of a fortified port and a place rich in history, the rundown state of its buildings is striking. In fact, few local or national initiatives to renew and promote the historical heritage of the old city have been made, although it has a great potential for tourism. The worst of it is that the Arab Palestinian population (who represent the majority of the population inside the walls) is the group most affected by unemployment. The residents believe that the Israeli authorities have made a political decision to encourage Palestinians to settle outside the old city. This policy was most notable in 1976, by the construction of a village situated eight kilometres from the old town, designed especially for the Arab population of Acre; until now, however, it has attracted few Arab settlers. Given the low standard of living of the Arab population, few Palestinians can afford to buy property outside the old city and therefore cannot leave it On the other hand, living in an Arab neighbourhood definitely does not appeal to most of the Jewish Israeli population and the old city also has the reputation of being an active centre of drug dealing. For these reasons, there has been very little Jewish immigration into the old city.

"Acre resisted the Crusaders longer than any other inhabited place. Acre defended itself successfully against Napoleon, never gave in to the Tartars and kept its prestige long after age and decay had set in. Grass grew on its ramparts, its lighthouse threw out a light as feeble as the light from Juha's lamp, but Acre remained a metropolis even after Haifa recovered to become fashionable again. Its high school, on the top of the city ramparts, was better than the secondary school in Haifa. That's why we finished our schooling at "the soldiers' school" *[the school was located in the former headquarters of the Turkish garrison]* in Acre; we made the return journey by train, every day. And in the train, we would meet my friend Yu'ad, also from Haifa, who had her school bag under her arm, too (...)

But a classmate's jealousy would make me weep in silence.

He gave me away to my friend's school principal, who repeated the denunciation to my headmaster. The headmaster called a meeting for all students who had a pass for the Acre-Haifa train and made a terrible scene, which ended with the following words:

'Acre, Haifa, it is the sea! There is an ocean separating them! What is permitted in Haifa is not permitted in Acre: we have been the capital of the province since the days of Saladin!'"

■ Emil Habibi, *The Pessoptimist: The Secret Life of Saeed*

En-Nakba

Acre fell into the hands of Israeli forces on May 18, 1948. Terrified by the fall of Haifa, some of the population had already fled north, several weeks before, to take refuge in Lebanon. At the beginning of May, Acre was surrounded and besieged. The residents of new areas, situated outside the wall, took refuge in the old town. At the news of the conquest of Jaffa by Zionist troops on May 14, panic provoked a new exodus by the only way of escape left open, the sea. Only 3,500 of the 15,000 inhabitants of Acre escaped exile. The Israeli government seized the land and homes located outside the city walls as "absentee property" although their legal owners were not absent at all, but forced to live inside the walls, in the old city.

Ghassan Kanafani

Born in Acre in 1936, Ghassan Kanafani studied at the French missionary school until 1948. Following the Zionist conquest, he and his family took refuge in Lebanon, and then in Syria. He studied Arabic Literature at the University of Damascus, from which he was expelled in 1955 for his involvement in the Arab Nationalist Movement (ANM). He worked for several newspapers: *al-Houriya ('Liberty' or 'Freedom'),* the official organ of the ANM, then for *al-Mouharrir ('The Liberator'),* and a progressive pro-Nasser paper. He wrote many novels and literary papers, among them *The Literature of Resistance in Occupied Palestine, 1948 - 1966, The Birth of Zionist Literature, Race and Religion in Zionist Literature.* In 1967, he was one of the founders of the Popular Front for the Liberation of Palestine (PFLP), for which he became the spokesman. In 1969, he also became the editor of the *al-Hadaf ('The Target')* newspaper, the press organ of the PFLP. Ghassan Kanafani was assassinated on July 8, 1972 by a bomb placed in his car by the Israeli secret services, the Mossad.

Acre

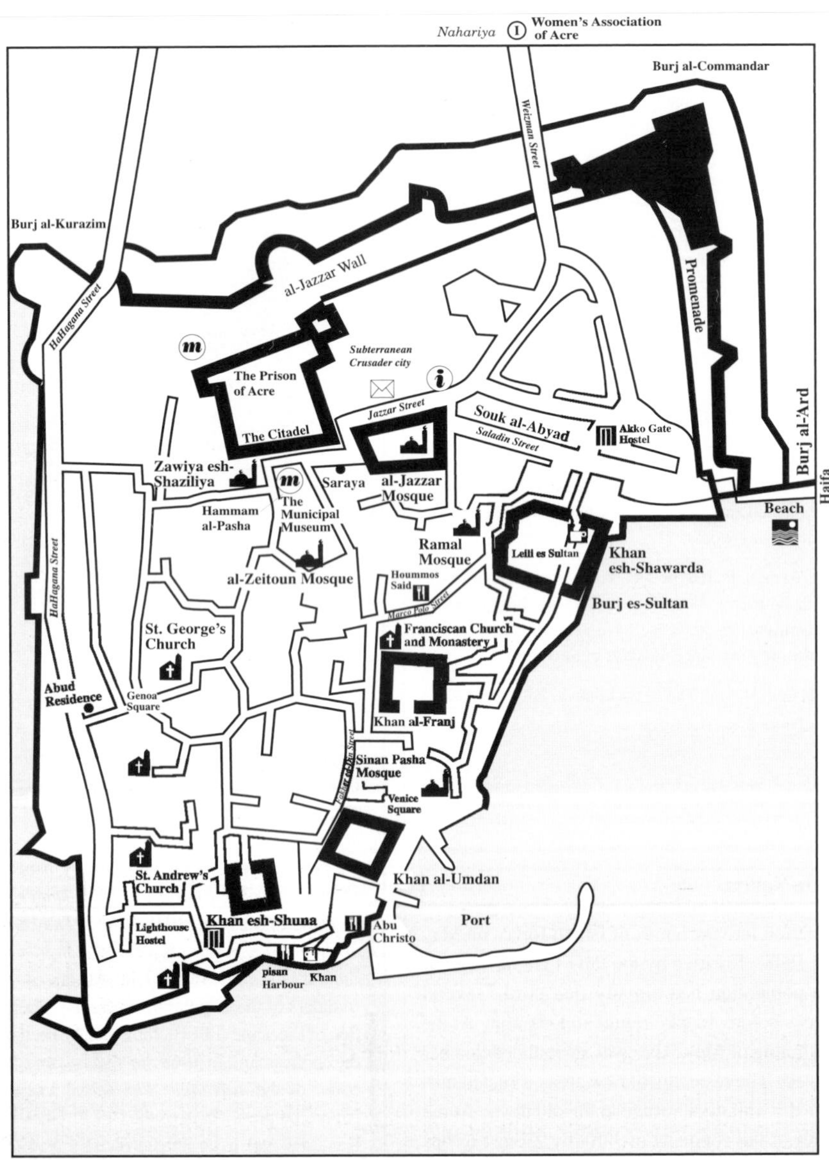

Nahariya
Women's Association of Acre
Burj al-Commandar
Weizman Street
Burj al-Kurazim
al-Jazzar Wall
Promenade
HaHagana Street
Subterranean Crusader city
The Prison of Acre
The Citadel
Jazzar Street
Souk al-Abyad
Saladin Street
Akko Gate Hostel
Burj al-'Ard
Haifa
Beach
Zawiya esh-Shaziliya
Saraya
al-Jazzar Mosque
The Municipal Museum
Hammam al-Pasha
Ramal Mosque
Leili es Sultan
Khan esh-Shawarda
Burj es-Sultan
al-Zeitoun Mosque
Hoummos Said
Marco Polo Street
Franciscan Church and Monastery
St. George's Church
Abud Residence
Genoa Square
Khan al-Franj
Sinan Pasha Mosque
Venice Square
St. Andrew's Church
Khan al-Umdan
Port
Lighthouse Hostel
Khan esh-Shuna
Abu Christo
pisan Harbour
Khan

■ The old city

❑ The walls

After the destruction of St. John of Acre in 1291, Acre remained without fortifications until Daher al-Omar provided it with a new wall seven metres high and one metre thick. To this day, it can easily be seen in the northeast corner of the town. Napoleon trusted the description of this wall by Volney, a French traveller and Oriental expert, who visited Palestine *circa* 1780. He underestimated the wall's capacity for resistance: it had also been reinforced by Ahmed Pasha al-Jazzar; the French heavy artillery was therefore able to inflict serious damage to the wall during Napoleon's siege of 1799, but the wall remained standing. After the defeat and retreat of Napoleon's army, Ahmed Pasha undertook the construction of a stout new rampart, parallel to Daher al-Omar's wall.

❑ Al-Souk al-Abyad (The White Marketplace)

This long marketplace was built on the site of Souk al-Daher, which, with 110 market-stalls, was Acre's main commercial centre. After a fire in 1817, the Governor, Suleyman Pasha, ordered its reconstruction. It was called the White Marketplace, probably because of the intensity of the light reflected from its whitewashed walls. At the beginning of the nineteenth century, people sometimes compared it to the market in Damascus. Today, it has lost some of its brilliance but is still full of activity, with several reasonably priced restaurants.

❑ The al-Jazzar Mosque

Al-Jazzar Street. Open Saturday–Thursday 8:00-12:30 and 13:15-16:00; Friday 8:00-11:00 and 14:00-16:00 (14:00-18:00 in summer), entrance fee NIS 2.

Known as the al-Jazzar Mosque or the Pasha's Mosque, this edifice was originally called the Mosque of Lights. Constructed in 1781 by Ottoman Governor Ahmed Pasha al-Jazzar, it is the largest mosque built in Palestine during the Ottoman period. Around a central courtyard, the cloister arches lead to cells reserved for the numerous students and pilgrim-travellers who visit Acre. The granite and porphyry columns are from ancient cities in the area, such as Caesarea and Tyre. The mosque's interior is an impressive example of eighteenth century Ottoman art; the walls and the mihrab are completely covered with faience, encrusted marble and Quranic calligraphy.

The minaret, built in a cylindrical shape, is also characteristic of the Anatolian period and style. Relics are reverently kept inside a small casket, which - according to local Muslim tradition - contains hairs from the beard of the Prophet Mohammed. Each year, on the 27th day of Ramadan (Sura al-Qadr 1-5 of the Quran), the open casket is put on view to the faithful.

At the entry to the mosque *(on the left)*, notice the white marble tombs of two important governors of the city: Ahmed Pasha al-Jazzar (1775-1804) and his adopted son and heir, Suleyman Pasha (1804-1818). On the right, a small staircase leads to a large vaulted room, dating from the Crusader period; it was erected during that time by the Knights Hospitaller.

❑ The Seraglio

Al-Jazzar Street. Currently left open to the elements, the building is in a state of disrepair.

The elaborately decorated main door reveals the importance of this monument. Next to its geometrical designs is an inscription describing its function: "Door of the Acre government" *('Bab Hukumat Akka')*. It dates from 1850/51 (1267 of the Hejira or Muslim calendar). The emblem (*tugra* in Turkish) of the Ottoman sultan, Abdel Majid (1839-1861), crowns the inscription. The inscription corresponds to the time of the Seraglio's renovation: it was actually built by Ahmed Pasha at the end of the eighteenth century. A century later, it became a post office, then a school under both the British Mandate and, currently, the State of Israel.

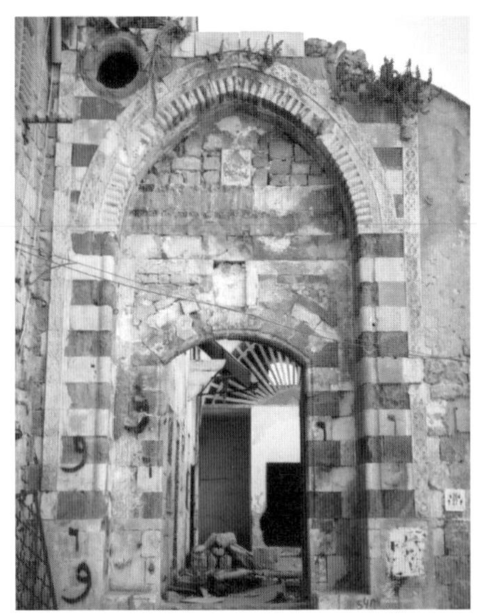

❑ The Citadel

Al-Jazzar Street, opposite al-Jazzar Mosque. Open Saturday-Thursday 9:00-16:30, Friday 9:00-12:30, entrance fee NIS 12: this includes a visit to the municipal museum. A map of subterranean Acre is available at the entrance.

The Turks built this Ottoman citadel on the thirteenth-century ruins of the Crusader city. The Druze leader, Fakhreddin, was the first to undertake restorations, *circa* 1630 AD. However, the Ottoman sultan had the work stopped, for fear that the new fortress would be taken over by Maltese pirates, allies of Fakhreddin. In the middle of the eighteenth century, Daher al-Omar completed the construction of the citadel and established his palace there, as did his successors. Ahmed Pasha al-Jazzar constructed the Divan-Khan or counsel chamber (today at the entrance to the knights' hall). **The knights' hall**: under the Citadel, archaeologists have exposed huge rooms dating from mediaeval times, including rooms and the courtyard of the Crusaders' hospice. These areas are actually three to seven metres underground, beneath al-Jazzar Street; these underground rooms are one of the major sites in the city.

❑ Acre Prison

Burj Qurayim. Open Sunday-Thursday 9:00 -16:00 and Friday 9:00-12:00, entry fee NIS 10.

Since the seventeenth century, the Citadel has housed the Acre prison. During the British Mandate, hundreds of Palestinian patriots were jailed here, "interrogated," and sometimes hung. The present day **Museum of Prisoners of the Shadow** is run by the museographic section of the Israeli Ministry of Defence! Presentation of the historical facts is completely biased: absolutely no mention is made of Palestinian resistance and patriots, who were the majority of the prisoners held in Palestine under the British Mandate. During the Palestinian Revolution, also called the Great Revolt of 1936-1939, more than 10,000 Palestinians were placed in detention camps. The Acre prison was one of the principal prisons in Palestine, used as a transit camp for other detention camps. If there were some Zionist prisoners at the beginning of the British Mandate, they belonged to the revisionist group and were very few in number; it was only after the publication of a British parliamentary White Paper in 1939 rejecting the idea of a Jewish state that paramilitary Zionist groups started a direct campaign of violence against the British authorities, leading to British military retaliation and a correspondingly large increase in the number of Jewish prisoners.

Despite these reservations, the actual museum gives an impression of conditions of imprisonment during the British Mandate: on our last visit to the room one could see a scale model of the prison, while two guards on duty there, wearing dark glasses and stony expressions, set the tone. Despite these reservations, the museum as it is permits a glimpse of what it was to be imprisoned during the British Mandate, or, equally, today under Israeli control. Popular Palestinian songs and chants about the times of Ottoman and British oppression keep the memory of the prison of Acre alive while evoking today's Israeli prisons.

From Acre Prison

From Acre Prison came the funeral processions
Of Mohammed Jamjoum and Fuad Hijazi.
Blame them, oh my people, blame them!
The High Commissioner and all his agents.
Mohammed Jamjoum, 'Ata ez-Zir,
And Fuad Hijazi are the best supplies
Witness their fate and the oppressor's decision
To execute them.
Mohammed says, "I'll go first,
I'm afraid to see your misfortune 'Ata."
Hijazi says, "I'll go first,
I have never been afraid to die.
My loving mother calls out loudly,
Every country turns to listen to her,
She cries: 'Fuad, oh my dear one,
Before they separate us, I want to bid you farewell.'
She calls to 'Ata behind the door,
She waits for him to answer,
'Oh, 'Ata, the most valiant, you who would attack soldiers without fear,
Oh, my brother Yussif, I entrust my mother to you,
And you, my sister, do not grieve after my departure,
For this country have I sacrificed my blood,
All this, for your eyes, Oh Palestine."
The three of them died like lions.
Oh, my mother, be generous [implicit subtext: give us others like them]
For the Fatherland, we sacrifice our soul,
For its freedom, they torture us.
The town crier calls for a strike,
On Tuesday, the hanging day of the young men,
The courageous 'Ata and Fuad who do not fear death.

■ Song to the memory of the three Palestinian patriots imprisoned and hung in Acre.
(See *Safad*, p. 312)

”

❑ The Municipal Museum

Entrance through the underground rooms of the Citadel or directly from al-Jazzar Street. Open Saturday–Thursday 9:00-16:30; Friday 9:00 -12.30; NIS 12, incl. a visit to the Citadel.

The museum has been established in the Hammam al-Pasha, the bathhouse of al-Jazzar. Constructed in *circa* 1780 AD for the Pasha's private use, where he would invite his friends and guests of honour, it was the official property of the al-Jazzar mosque and an important source of revenue. The bathhouse, an Islamic authorities' *(waqf)* property, was in use until May 1947, confiscated in 1948 as "absentee property" and converted into a museum in 1954. In 1801, a British navigator by the name of Clarke described the *hammam* as *"the most refined, and the construction the most carefully executed"* that he had seen in the entire Ottoman Empire. Take for example the eighteenth century Armenian tiles from Kutahya in Anatolia: certain motifs are identical to motifs in the church of Saint James (St. James Cathedral) in Jerusalem, which was restored in 1727; it is possible that these tiles were simply re-used and not specially imported from Turkey. In this beautiful setting one may see archaeological artefacts found in the town and the surrounding area (the best pieces, however, can be seen in museums in Jerusalem and Tel Aviv).

❑ Zawiya al-Shaziliya

To the west of the Hammam al-Pasha

The Sufi order and the *zawiya* al-Shaziliya were established by Sheikh Ali Nur ed-Din al-Yashruti.

He was born in Tunis in 1793 and moved to Acre in 1849, and had the *zawiya* built in 1862. The Sheikh's personality made a strong impression on the Acre Muslim community, which adhered to the movement; his popularity spread over the whole area as far as Beirut. Today, the order is still active. It has about 1,300 members: 200 in Acre, 600 in Umm al-Fahm, 300 in Jaffa and 200 in Jerusalem.

❑ The Zeituna Mosque

This mosque was built in 1754-55 by Haj Mohammed al-Sadiki. Popular local myth says that its name derived from the field of olives where it was constructed. At that time, Acre was just a small village of 200 to 300 residents. In the middle of the nineteenth century, the mosque belonged to Sheikh al-Yashruti's Sufi order, until the *Zawiya al-Shaziliya* was built next door. According to another version of local myth, the mosque was named after the *Grand Mosque ez-Zaytouna* in Tunis, from where the sheikh originally came. In its courtyard is the Tomb of Hussein Abdel Hadi; born in Nablus, he was made governor of Acre during the period of Egyptian domination, until his death in 1836.

The khans (overnight inns for caravanserais: caravans)

All the *khans* in Acre were built under the Ottomans; their construction was part of the city's renovation in the eighteenth century. They are characterised by a collection of arcaded buildings of one or two storeys in height, which surround a large quadrangle around a central well. Market-stalls, shops and storage areas lined the ground floors, with living quarters and offices on the upper levels.

❑ Khan al-Umdan

The Khan al-Umdan ('Khan of the Pillars') is the best preserved of all the *khans*. Unfortunately, it remains empty and lifeless except in September (during the Jewish Festival of Succoth), when it houses a theatre festival with plays in Hebrew. Built in 1785, it was given different names in its

time: the al-Jazzar Khan, the Corn Khan, the Cavalry Khan and in the end, the Khan of the Pillars. This imposing edifice is the best indicator of the height of Acre's economic development under Pasha Ahmed al-Jazzar. Taxes paid by the farmers of the area paid for its construction, a common practice for financing most public buildings at that time.

❑ The al-Shawarda Khan

This *khan* was built in two stages. The eastern wing was erected against the surrounding wall, under the direction of Daher al-Omar, while the other wings were built under Pasha al-Jazzar: from his time on, the inn became the property of the al-Jazzar Mosque. In its southeast angle is a thirteenth century belfry, named Burj al-Sultan. It dates from the time of Daher al-Omar and served as a watchtower. Some of its stones bear the marks of masons (a cross and triangles), which indicate that they were taken from older buildings dating from the Crusader period. Today there are several workshops here.

In the evening, when all the workshops and other shops are closed, people flock to the huge and popular café, **Leili al-Sultan**.

❑ The al-Franj Khan (Khan of the Franks or French Inn)

This *khan* was originally called Sinan Pasha's Inn but was soon nicknamed the French Inn due to the many French and Italian merchants who went there in the sixteenth century to buy cotton goods. The French buyers were given preferential treatment by a business treaty concluded between Sultan Suleyman the Magnificent and King Francis I in 1535. The French Inn was built in the Venetian quarter in Crusader times. There is a Franciscan church located in its northeast corner, dating from the eighteenth century.

❑ The al-Shuna Khan

This is the smallest of Acre's *khans* or inns and is located near Pisa Square, which was the area reserved for natives of Pisa. It was built by Daher al-Omar in 1764-65, at his own expense.

❑ The port

After the fall of Acre in 1291, the city ruins literally obstructed the port, so merchant ships were afraid to moor there without danger. When in the eighteenth century the port again became important, ships would anchor at a considerable distance from the city walls and transfer their goods onto small boats to take them in to harbour to unload. For this reason, from the nineteenth century onwards, Haifa Port on the other side of the bay was considered a superior location for shipping, and in less than a century became second only to Marseilles as a Mediterranean port. Today, the little port of Acre has no commercial significance, although it is lively with fishermen and pleasure boats.

❑ Al-Masjid al-Bahr Mosque (The Mosque of the Sea)

The Mosque of the Sea was built by Suleyman Pasha, *circa* 1816 AD. Located near the ruins of the Sinan Pasha Mosque, it is today also frequently referred to by that name, although nothing remains of the former mosque.

❑ St. Andrew's Church

This church was built by the Palestinian Greek Catholic or Melkite community, *circa* 1760 AD, at the initiative of their first bishop, Makarios Ujaymi. It was probably called St. Andrew's after an earlier church built at the time of the Crusades, situated near the lighthouse. As the congregation increased during the nineteenth century, the church was richly furnished, giving it a special charm which pervades it to this day.

❑ The Abud Residence

It was in this eighteenth century domain, constructed by Elias Abud, that the founder of the Bahai religion, Baha'ullah, was placed under house arrest after having been released from Acre prison in 1870. He lived here for seven years with his family and a group of his faithful. Amongst other works, he wrote the *Book of Laws (al-Kitab al-Akdas)* in this house. Distinguished by a beautiful white façade, the building is now a hospice for Bahai pilgrims.

❑ St. George's Church

The focal point of the Greek Orthodox community, St. George's is the oldest church in Acre. The exact date of its inception is unknown, but the Order of Saint Basil was based here *circa* 1631 AD. It was renovated at the time of Fakhreddin, in the middle of the seventeenth century. It is sometimes called St. Nicolas Church, and has the reputation of being the most beautiful church in the Middle East. It was renamed St. George's in the middle of the eighteenth century, after a young Cypriot named Georgios, who was executed in Acre. He was canonised by the Greek Orthodox patriarch in Istanbul and his body exhumed and taken to Cyprus in 1972. The Palestinian Greek Orthodox community is today the leading Christian community in Acre. It has close ties with the Christian community in Cyprus, as evidenced by the church decorations, which are typically Cypriot.

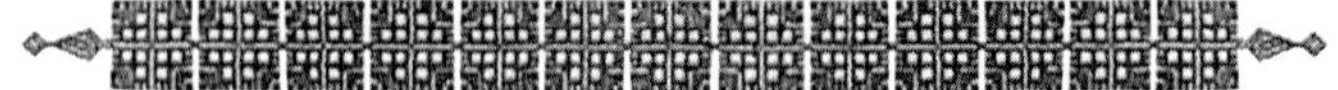

Practical Information

Opposite the main entrance to al-Jazzar Mosque are the most useful places for a passing visitor: a **tourist office** *(☎ 04-991 1764. Open Sunday-Monday 8:30-16:45, Friday 8:30-13:45, Saturday 9:00-16:45)* a **post office** and a **bank** with an automatic cash point.

Cafés

There are several terrace cafés in a row near the al-Jazzar mosque. This is an extremely active area during the day; in the evening, activities centre more around the al-Shawarda Inn and the **Leili al-Sultan café**. *Nargila* smokers are not to be disappointed here. The **Khan café** is also popular: its seaside terrace provides a lovely view over the harbour, with Haifa to be seen in the distance.

Restaurants

Fish is obviously one of Acre's specialities, and there is a wide choice of various fresh fish. These are prepared in a fairly standard manner, which may be a source of regret to fish connoisseurs. There are many simple restaurants in the White Marketplace *(Saladin Street)*, serving generous fish specialities, which are reasonably priced. Two well-known restaurants on the seaside - the **Abu Christo** and the **Pisan Harbour** or **Galileo** - specialise in fish and seafood. Their open-air décor seems to have somewhat boosted both their reputation and their prices. On the other hand, there is a superb restaurant, the **Hummus Said** (Marco Polo Street), which is definitely one of the town's best restaurants. It does not serve fish, but there are excellent *hors d'oeuvre* such as hummus, eggplant purée, grilled meats and so forth.

Accommodation

There is currently only one hostel in the old town for visitors seeking budget accommodation. Minimally equipped, it offers all the advantages of a location inside the city walls. For more comfortable accommodation, consult the tourist office's list of hotels located in the newer part of Acre; they represent better quality but are much more expensive.

Akko Gate Hostel (Saladin Street:☎ *04-991 0410, fax 04-981 5530 ; rooms with bedding and towels, Single: $45, Double: $50; rooms without bedding or towels, NIS 90 - NIS 120 per person; dormitory, NIS 30*). This hostel is inexpensive. The "equipped rooms" are spacious if austere. There is a large bar downstairs. One may rent a bicycle, which is both a practical and extremely pleasant way to get around the old town or down to the beaches. The owner of the hostel also organises day trips to the Golan.

Contacts

Acre Women's Association

4 Ben Ami Street: ☎ 04-991 2436, fax 04-990 0201

Women founded this association in 1975 in order to respond to the need for improved social infrastructure. It should be remembered that the town was just emerging then from over 20 years of isolation. The association supports several projects, which aim at reinforcing the position of women in Acre society, which is quite conservative. These projects concentrate on developing child-rearing education for parents and promoting access to the job market for women.

■ Outside the Walls

❑ The beaches

There are several beaches of variable quality in the Bay of Acre, to the south of the city.

The best known is Agarman Beach ("Purple Beach" in Hebrew, since the Romans obtained their imperial purple dye from shellfish caught here). It is about 500 metres from the Land Gate (Bab al-Ard), one of the three entrances into the old city (*NIS 10 admission fee*).

❑ Sheikh Izzedin Wali

Near the coast, about one and a half kilometres north of the walls of the old city

According to local tradition, Sheikh Izzedin was an officer in Saladin's army, who died in combat in 1191. His tomb and its annexes have been turned into an absorption centre for newly arrived Jewish immigrants.

❑ Baha'ullah Shrine and the Bahai Gardens

Three kilometres north of Acre, on the main road to Nahariya. Shrine: open Sunday-Monday, Friday-Saturday 9:00-12:00; gardens: open daily, 9:00-16:00. No entry fee.

In 1844, a young Persian from Shiraz, Ali Mohammed, announced the coming of a new prophet and began preaching a new religion. He was executed in 1850 for heresy. At his death, the movement divided into two groups: one condoned violence to oppose Persian authority (Subhi Azad, Hussein Ali's half brother, spoke for this group) and the other preached passive resistance (Hussein Ali's group). In 1863, Hussein Ali declared himself to be the Messenger of the Glory of God (Baha'ullah) (*Bab* means 'door') foreseen by Ali Mohammed. He is in fact believed by the Bahai to be the last prophet. Banished from Persia and Constantinople, the Bahai spiritual leader was deported to Acre, where he was first imprisoned in the citadel (1868-1870) and then released under house arrest. He was finally permitted to settle outside the city walls, where he lived - under house arrest - for the final twelve years of his life, in this elegant house, the ancient residence of Governor Abdallah Pasha's mother. He died there in 1892. The house and tomb have become a shrine and the second most important holy place for Bahai believers. Its delightful gardens resemble the Bahai Gardens in Haifa, sharing the same atmosphere of tranquillity and serene aesthetics. (See *Haifa, the Bahai Shrine*, p. 345)

■ North and east of Acre

Ez-Zeeb

Five kilometres north of Nahariya. Traces of former dwellings in the Israeli Akhziv National Park.

Archaeological remains attest to the early beginnings, in the eighteenth century BC, of this small maritime city. In 701 BC, the Phoenician city of Akzib fell to the Assyrians. It is mentioned by this name in the Bible (Joshua 19:29; Judges 1:31), as well as in the time of the Roman Emperor, when it was known by its Greek name, Ecdippa, as in the later Crusader period, under Casal Imbert. However, generation after generation of local people called it by its original name, ez-Zeeb. For example, in the thirteenth century, the Arab geographer Yaqut al-Hamawi described the village of ez-Zeeb as an important coastal town. In 1596 AD, there were 875 residents living as farmers: harvesting wheat, cotton, fruit trees, water buffalo herds and fish. By the end of the nineteenth century, ez-Zeeb had flourished and become a prosperous seashore village.

En-Nakba

The village numbered over 1,900 people in 1945. It was over-run between May 13 and May 14, 1948. The day after the Zionist victory and the proclamation of the State of Israel, Moshe Carmel, the commander of "Operation Ben-Ami," ordered the villagers to be "punished" for the resistance they had put up to the Zionist forces, by annihilating the village so that they "could never return." The director of the Department of Lands of the Jewish National Fund, Yosef Weiss, as he looked at the destroyed village in December 1948, speculated about the decision to demolish the village: "*I wonder if it was a good thing to destroy it, and if the revenge would not have been better if Jews were now living in the original village houses today.*"

➡ The village today

Only the **mosque** and the house of **mukhtar Hussein 'Ataya** remain of the village. Around the ruins of the mosque, the National Park Office has created a park (*open Saturday-Thursday 8:00-17:00, Friday 8:00-16:00; entrance fee NIS 10*). A sign at the entrance states, *"During the Talmudic period* [the Roman period, second - third centuries AD], *Akhziv had a flourishing Jewish community (…). Over the next centuries, it* (the town) *declined until it was just a coastal village."* Next to the national park, a private Israeli park, Akhzivland *(open April-September 8:00-17:00,*

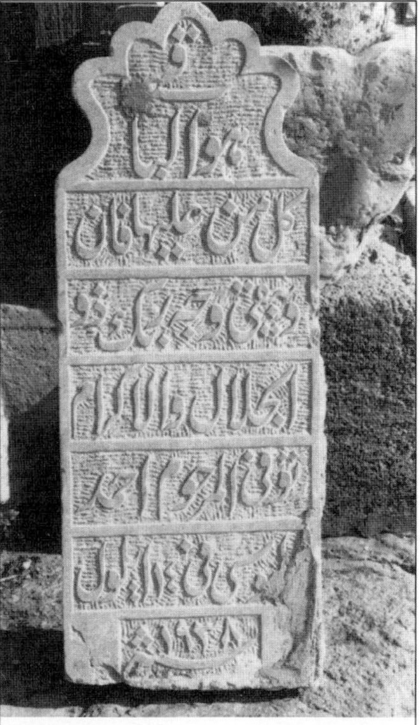

"*Whomever they carry* [an allusion to the precarious nature of seafaring] *may perish; only the Face of your Lord, majestic, worthy of veneration, endures.*" [Quran, er-Rahman, 26-27] - *Ahmed al-Moussa, deceased September 14, 1938.*

October-March 8:00-16:00; entrance fee NIS 7) occupies the house of the *mukhtar*; it contains a small museum. In it one may find Phoenician, Roman, Byzantine and Islamic works of art on display, as well as several tombstones looted from the destroyed, desecrated cemetery.

In the early 1950s, *Kibbutz Gesher HaZiv* was built on the village's land (to the southeast) by Jews from England, the United States and South Africa.

Al-Bassa and Ras en-Naqoura

Destroyed Palestinian village in the present day Israeli region of Shlomi.

Al-Bassa's name derives from the Canaanite Bissah, which signifies "marshland". In Roman days, the town was named Bezeth. In 1596, al-Bassa was a relatively important village with nearly 600 inhabitants. Pasha Ahmed Pasha gave it the status of an administrative market town of the *nihiya al-Bassa* in the eighteenth century. In 1948, the population, half Christian and half Muslim, was about 4,000; there were several schools, places of worship (churches, mosques and *maqams*), stores, cafés and also a local branch of the trade union of the National Union of Palestinian Workers, as well as a co-operative belonging to the trade union.

En-Nakba

Al-Bassa was occupied on May 14, 1948 during "Operation Ben-Ami." Many villagers, particularly women and children, had already taken refuge in Lebanon (on the other side of the hill) several weeks previously. The 300 or so armed partisans in the village decided to retreat into Lebanon, in order to join the Arab armies there. They relied on these forces to wage a counter-offensive the next day, which was the day of the official British army withdrawal from Palestine. On arrival on Lebanese soil, the partisans were disarmed, under the pretext of verifying the state of their weapons; in fact, the Lebanese offensive never materialised. Those who had stayed behind in the village took refuge inside a church. Several young men were executed, even at the church's very door; the others were chased out of the village towards Lebanon, while a group of 100 people (old men and Christians, in particular) were deported towards the village of al-Mazra'a (three kilometres south of *Nahariya*). In Lebanon, the authorities decided to separate the group into their Christian and Muslim communities. The Christian refugees from al-Bassa were placed mainly in the Dbayeh camp, near the

Christian areas of East Beirut. However, Palestinian Christian refugees never supported the Lebanese Maronite plan promoted by Patriarch Agnatius Mubarak in 1936 and again in 1947: to create a Jewish state in Palestine and a Christian state in Lebanon. The attempt to divide Palestinians into different religious backgrounds failed, and in 1976 Phalange militias completely destroyed the Dbayeh Refugee Camp.

➡ The village today

The Melkite Greek Catholic Church and the mosque have both been transformed into stables, while other houses have been occupied by Jewish residents. The Shlomi industrial estate (adjoining a Jewish settlement, *Shlomi*, founded in 1950) has grown up near the location of the old village, while many Jewish settlements now stand on the site of the village and its land: *Betzet* was established on part of the village, for Romanian and Yugoslavian Jews (in 1949); *Kfar Rosh HaNikra*, on the Palestinian hamlet of Ras en-Naqura (a small village that was part of the town of al-Bassa), for veterans of the Yiftach Zionist brigade. *Rosh HaNikra* represents the Israeli front on the Lebanese border.

Chronology of the Eviction of the Inhabitants of Iqrit and Destruction of the Village

Year	Date	Events
1948	Oct. 31	Israeli troops enter Iqrit; villagers surrender peacefully. Army officers order the people to leave, promising they can return *"two weeks later"* at the end of operations.
	Nov. 6-8	Israeli army deports inhabitants of Iqrit to Rama (west of Safad). Fifty residents, including the village priest, are allowed to stay in Iqrit to watch over the property. Six months later, they are evacuated; no one is allowed to return from Rama, as had been promised.
1949	Sept. 26	The village is declared off-limits to civilians: a "security zone."
1951	July 31	In its first ruling on Iqrit, the Israeli Supreme Court states the villagers have the legal right to return to live there and rules the *"evacuation"* illegal in the absence of an official order.
	Sept. 10	Three years after expulsion, villagers in Rama receive an "Order of Evacuation," from the Military Governor, issued retroactively.
	Nov. 26	In a second ruling, the Supreme Court rejects the villagers' appeal that the first ruling be applied.
	Dec. 24	Israeli army blows up houses in Iqrit on order of Yitzhak Rabin, commander of the Northern District (only the church and cemetery are spared). Prime Minister and Minister of Defence, David Ben-Gurion, denies issuing demolition orders: Jan. 16, 1956 he admits the IDF did it "without an order from me."
1952	Feb. 25	The third ruling of the Israeli Supreme Court reproaches the villagers for not having taken up the Court's original permission to return. Verdict mentions that Ben-Gurion (then Minister of Defence) and the Military Governor did "not fulfil their requirements."
1953	Aug. 25	Iqrit lands confiscated under law: "Confiscation for Public Needs."
1981	Dec. 23	The Supreme Court rejects villagers' appeal against confiscation of their land (August 25, 1953) and its definition as a security zone (September 26, 1949).
1998	Dec. 8	Minister of Justice Tsahi Hanegbi pleads for return of the land as a gesture to "solidify the relationship between the state and its Arab citizens and [as] a testimony to the morality of the State of Israel."
2002	June 26	Fifth Supreme Court ruling declines Iqrit Committee's appeal to return to homes and properties, concerned such an outcome would set precedent in Iqrit to influence the entire Israeli-Palestinian conflict.

Iqrit

Road 8944, near Goren. Contacts and visits to the village are available with the Iqrit Heritage Association (Haifa, ☎ 04-851 5505).

In 1944-1945, the community of Iqrit numbered 490 people (460 Christians, mainly Greek Catholic, and 30 Muslims). The church is the only building that was not demolished. Although Palestinians from this village bearing Israeli nationality are forbidden to return, several Jewish establishments now exist on village land, including *Goren* (1950) and *Gornot HaGalil* (1980). Today the population of people whose families originated in Iqrit numbers over 3,500.

❑ Monfort Castle

On Road 89, 18 kilometres from Nahariya. Follow a small stone road until Ma'ilya. There is a parking area 2 kilometres from the junction. Take the path through the woods (about 4 kilometres: a one and a half hour walk). One can also reach the terrace above the castle from the north (Golan Nature Park), from where the castle ruins are less than an hour's walk away; although the ruins are not remarkable, the site is worth a visit for the scenery and the walk itself.

The domain of Ma'ilya was the fiefdom of the Courtenay family in the twelfth century, and was then bought (in 1220 AD) by the Teutonic Order of Knights, a German monastic military order modelled in 1190 AD on the French Knights Hospitaller. When the small castle of Monfort was bought in 1228, it was enlarged and given the German name Starkenberg. Baibars twice laid siege to it, in 1266 and 1271. Finally, the Teutonic Knights capitulated and negotiated their transfer to St. John of Acre; the fortress was then razed.

Fassouta

Arab Palestinian village to the northeast of Ma'ilya. Contact: Father Fawzi Khoury (☎ 0505-414016) priest of the Fassouta parish and member of the Arab Association for Human Rights (see p. 325). It is possible to attend parish activities.

The majority of Fassouta are Christians of the Melkite Greek Catholic sect. You may contact Father Khoury, to learn about the Melkite Church and the Christian community of Galilee, and to discuss the question of human rights and the various types of discrimination to which Israeli Palestinians are subjected.

Bir'am

On Road 8967, on the Lebanese border. Committee of uprooted people of Kufr Bir'am (based in Haifa), ☎ 04-866 5276 www.birem.org

The name of this village has a Semitic origin. Archaeological remains bear witness to its ancient beginnings; a third century AD synagogue, tombs, olive presses and cisterns can be seen near the ruins of the village, which has become the National Park of Ancient Baram *(open daily April-September 8:00-17:00, Friday 8:00-16:00; October-March 8:00-16:00 Friday 8:00-15:00; NIS 10 entrance)*. Byzantine tradition has it that the synagogue was built on the tomb of Esther. The synagogue's beautiful door and the principal door that leads to it are today the best-preserved features of the site. In 1945, the population, which had long been converted to Christianity, comprised 700 Christians, mostly Maronites, and 10 Muslims. The village, a compact group of houses of stone, sealed or bonded with clay, had a view over the surrounding wooded hills and valleys. Olives, almonds and cereal crops held an essential place in village agriculture.

En-Nakba

The history of Bir'am is similar to that of the village of Iqrit (see p. 308) and Ghabsiya, a village of 700 inhabitants in the district of Acre also completely destroyed in 1948. [See *The National Committee for the Defence of the Rights of Internally Displaced Persons in Israel*, p. 325.] The village was taken in November 1948 and all the villagers were evicted for "security" reasons, according to the Israeli authorities, with the promise that they would be able to return. Some villagers who were deported to Lebanon were actually permitted to return to what had become the State of Israel, but not to their village. In 1951, the Israeli Supreme Court ruled that there was no reason to prevent their return to their own village. However, the Security Cabinet decided otherwise; following which, the village was destroyed on September 16 and 17, 1953. At this time, two Jewish settlements were established on village land: *Bar'am* in 1949 (for veterans of the Palmach, the elite force of the Israeli Hagana army) and *Dovev* in 1963. The

Palestinians who originated in Bir'am and who are now internal refugees together with their families, today number over 5,000 people. The story of Bir'am may also be read in Fr. Elias Shakour's book: *Blood Brothers.* Elias Shakour, originally from Bir'am and forced to flee - together with the entire village - is a tireless worker for peace, co-existence and the higher education of Palestinian Arabs, Muslim and Christian. To this end, he has established both Ibillin University and Ibillin High School, at Ibillin near Shfa-Amr, east of Haifa, where he is rector of both.

The village today

The village has been declared a "closed area." The extensive ruins speak for themselves. Only the church and its belfry remain intact. Palestinians originally from Bir'am meet here on many occasions throughout the year.

Since then, verdicts and counter-orders on the issue of return succeed each other:

- **1972** : Golda Meir's government rejects the villagers' request to return to live on their land.
- **1977** : Menachem Begin's government promises them an authorisation to return.
- **1995** : Yitzhak Rabin's minister of justice suggests a partial return on condition: only heads of families and a maximum of two descendants; any agricultural activity forbidden; no lands to be returned except for each family to receive a small parcel of its original land.

The cases of Bir'am and Iqrit raise fundamental issues of the Israeli - Arab conflict: the right of return of Palestinian refugees. The official reason the Israelis give for rejecting the suit of villagers of Bir'am and Iqrit is that authorising them to return would create a legal precedent for all other internally displaced refugees. In fact more than 25% of the Palestinian community in Israel (between 250,000 and 300,000 people) are refugees.

■ Safad

Reference is made to Safad as Seph in the first century AD. In 1140 AD, Crusaders occupied it and built a citadel here. First liberated by Saladin in 1188, Safad was given to the Knights Templar in 1240 by the Governor of Damascus, Salah Ishmael, who was at war with the Mamelukes. In 1266, Sultan Baybar ensured a definitive finale to the Crusader presence. He had the fortress destroyed and ordered the town to be rebuilt, turning it into a commercial and administrative centre of a province which extended from the Galilee to Mount Lebanon. The **Banat Hamad *zawiya*** (Mameluke Mausoleum) and the Red Mosque (or Baybars' Mosque) are two of the rare vestiges of buildings left from that period. Under the Mamelukes and until the eighteenth century, Safad was a high centre of Muslim mysticism. The town houses several Sufi monasteries *(zawiya)*, which were freely placed under the patronage of Damascus. In the sixteenth century, the Ottoman Sultan Selim bestowed several estates on Sheikh Mohammed al-Assad's Sufi order, amongst them Mount Canaan in Safad. After the overthrow of the Grenada Caliphate in 1492, a small Sephardi community settled next to the local Muslim population. The Jewish community in Safad revived the mystic Kabbalistic movement, which had been popular in Andalusia. Synagogues rivalled each other in their particular interpretation of the Old Testament, where each sign (letter, number or punctuation mark) is supposed to have deep hidden significance. Safad's Kabbalism spread through Europe via the main centres of Judaism (in Venice and Salonika); ever since, Kabbalist rabbis have been specially venerated. As was the case in the seventh century, in the seventeenth century many Jews converted to Islam. Amongst many celebrities who converted were two spiritual leaders of the Ari Sephardi community (Ari had been a Jewish saint from Safad), Shabbtai Ze'evi and Nathan of Gaza, who converted to the "law of mercy," which was how they referred to Islam.

Safad's economic position declined in the eighteenth century, as the epicentre of the Galilee moved from the interior of the country to the port of Acre on the coast. In addition, Safad suffered in the eighteenth and nineteenth centuries from a series of major earthquakes and epidemics. It still maintained a regional importance for its products (leather, wood, cotton and tobacco), which were to be found in the markets of Nazareth, Acre, Haifa and Damascus.

Under the British Mandate, Zionist immigration encountered strong Arab resistance. While the relatively small number of Jewish immigrants had integrated with the local population in the previous century, the new immigrants, mostly from central Europe, settled apart and kept to their distinctive life style. Conflicts grew and led to riots in 1929. It was after these disturbances that Fuad Hijazi, from Safad, was accused with two men from al-Khalil (Hebron), Mohammed Jamjoum and 'Ata Zir, of having killed a Jewish settler [see p. 301]. Although they never stopped claiming their innocence, they were condemned and hanged in Acre on June 17, 1930. This tragic day in Safad's history saw riots in all the principal urban centres of Palestine.

My dear brothers Yussif and Ahmed,

God make you prosperous!
My last wish is that you will do exactly as I say.
I ask you to help those in need and work for brotherly love.
Do this earnestly to combat the suffering in the world. (…)
I was very upset to hear you say when you visited me that you would avenge me.
My dear brother, you are not the only one concerned, because I am not only your brother.
I have become the brother of the Arab nation and the son of the entire Muslim world (…)
I formally forbid tears, wailing and shouting because I have disliked them all my life just as I also dislike the tearing of clothes.
Let there be singing and laughter.
Know that Fuad is not dead.

■ Extract from Fuad Hijazi's last letter to his family, which appeared in the *al-Yarmouk* newspaper in Haifa, June 18, 1930.

En-Nakba

In 1948, Safad had 13,000 inhabitants (80% Muslim or Christian and 20% Jewish). At the end of the month of April, Zionist forces isolated the city and forced the people of neighbouring villages out of their homes ('Arab al-Shamalina [650 inhabitants in 1944], Ein ez-Zeitoun [820 inhabitants in 1944], al-Ja'una [population of 1,150 in 1944]). The Palestinian resistance, supported by Arab volunteers from elsewhere (altogether about 600 partisans), asked in vain for reinforcements from Syria and from King Abdullah of Transjordan while they were increasingly isolated. After two weeks of fighting, Safad fell on May 12, 1948, three days before the Declaration of the Establishment of the State of Israel and its recognition by the international community. The last resistants, who had taken refuge in the citadel, were executed. The entire Palestinian population of Safad, Muslim and Christian, all 10,500 people, was forced into exile. Today, they and their descendants are estimated to number over 67,000 people. Most are refugees in Syria, where 40% of all Palestinian refugees come from the Safad district. The town today (in Hebrew, *Tzfat*) has over 16,000 inhabitants, exclusively Jewish, with a preponderance of Orthodox Jews.

■ The old city

Lying on the western side of Mount Canaan (960 metres), the old city is full of alleyways and staircases. The best way to discover Safad is by foot. Although certain areas were badly destroyed in 1948 (the ruins of many demolished houses are still visible), the historical centre of Safad has remained intact. The appearance of old private Palestinian homes and public buildings leaves no doubt as to the past economic vitality of the city, its quality of life, its mysteries and its history, all wiped out in the month of May, 1948.

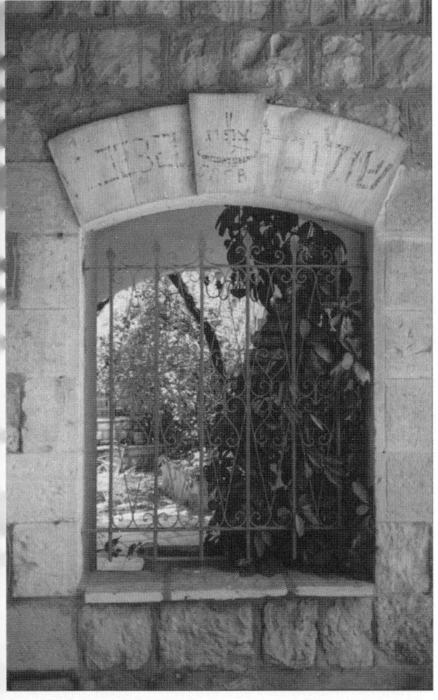

❑ The ancient market area (Harat al-Souk)

This is one of the most beautiful parts of the city. Today, it has been designated an Artists' Quarter, whose cobbled streets and charming houses are full of Jewish artists and craftsmen who have chosen it for its picturesque setting, which appeals to their artistic sensibilities, just as they have flocked to the village of Ein Hod [see p. 350]. Near *Zvi Levanon Street* is the **al-Younis Mosque** or Souk (Market) Mosque. It was built in 1902 during the reign of the Ottoman Sultan Abdel Hamid II. Today it has become the General Exhibition Hall of the Safad Artists' Colony. In the southern part of the quarter, in *Tet Zayin Street,* are two Mameluke buildings: the **Red Mosque**, dedicated to Mameluke Sultan Baybar, and the **Banat Hamad *zawiya*** (Mameluke Mausoleum) with its alternately striped walls of basalt and limestone. The

Red Mosque has not been renovated at all; it is occasionally used as a festival site. The mausoleum houses the Safad masonic lodge. Both sites are closed to the public.

❑ Es-Saraya (government palace)

This fortress-like building was a *khan* for travelling caravans, before being transformed into a public building under the Ottoman Empire. It is now the Wolfson Community Centre, named after the person who financed its renovation. It houses a music conservatory, a centre where newly arrived Jewish immigrants learn Hebrew, a synagogue, and nearby, the **Memorial Museum for Jews of Hungarian Mother Tongue.**

❑ The al-Shaar al-Sharifa Mosque (or the Cave Mosque)

Situated in the heart of the city on *HaPalmach Street*, this mosque is said to stand on the site where Jacob went to live in seclusion. After learning from his sons that his youngest son Joseph was dead, the Prophet Jacob lived in the cave here until a messenger brought the glad news that Joseph was actually alive:

"When the caravan left (Egypt)
Their father said: 'I do indeed
Scent the presence of Joseph:
Nay, think me not a dotard.
They [his sons] said; 'By God!

Truly thou art in
Thine old wandering mind.'
Then when the bearer
of the good news came,
He cast (the shirt)
Over his face, and he
Forthwith regained clear sight."
(Quran, sura Youssif, XII:93-96)

The Cave Mosque was also a holy shrine because it had conserved the relics of the Prophet Mohammed (a hair from his beard). Today, the site serves as a synagogue.

❑ The citadel (al-Qala'a)

The citadel overlooks the city and its surroundings, offers few archaeological discoveries, but the ascent is worthwhile, for the superb panorama over the roofs of the old city with **Jabal Jermaq** (Mount Meron) in the distance. Below is the old British police station at the top of a staircase *(Ma'alot Olei Hagardim)*, built after the 1929 riots in order to separate the Jewish quarter from the Arab quarters. Near the British police station is a memorial with a cannon mounted on it; this is the **Davidka Cannon**, conceived by David Liebovitch, whose name it took. It was manufactured in secret by the Hagana and was an important weapon for the Zionist forces.

❑ Sheikh 'Issa Mosque or Sueika (little market)

A short distance from the bus station, in *Jerusalem Street*, there is a lone minaret; it is all that remains of a mosque built in 1648. Three hundred years later, the neighbourhood was almost completely destroyed.

❑ Old Jewish quarter (Harat al-Yahoud)

Today, this area is also called the Quarter of Synagogues. All told, there are over thirty synagogues here, many dating from the time of the Ottomans and commemorating Safad's Kabbalist rabbis and scholars. The **Josef Caro Synagogue** in *Alkabetz Street* was rebuilt by the Italian Jewish architect Yitzhak Guetta, after the earthquake of 1837. Farther along, in *Bet Yosef Street*, is a seventeenth century synagogue dedicated to Rabbi Moussa (Moshe) al-Sheikh *(closed to the public)*.

Safad

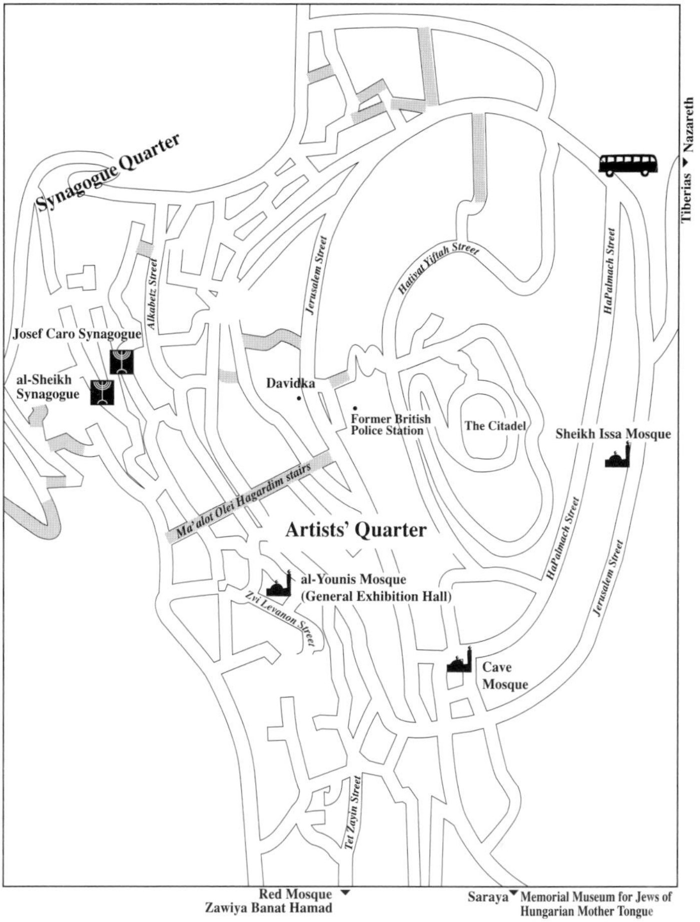

Synagogue Quarter
Tiberias ▼ Nazareth
Alkabetz Street
Jerusalem Street
Hativat Yiftah Street
HaPalmach Street
Josef Caro Synagogue
al-Sheikh Synagogue
Davidka
Former British Police Station
The Citadel
Sheikh Issa Mosque
Ma'alot Olei Hagardim stairs
Artists' Quarter
HaPalmach Street
Jerusalem Street
al-Younis Mosque (General Exhibition Hall)
Zvi Levanon Street
Cave Mosque
Tet Zayin Street
Red Mosque ▼ Zawiya Banat Hamad
Saraya ▼ Memorial Museum for Jews of Hungarian Mother Tongue

■ Northeast of Safad

❑ Tel Hazor

On Road 90, 7 kilometres north of Rosh Pinna [Jewish settlement dating from 1882, developed around 1950 on the site of the destroyed village of al-Ja'una, district of Safad. It numbered 1,150 inhabitants in 1944].

Like Meggido, Hazor was one of the principal city-states of the area. The northern gateway to Canaan, Hazor maintained close diplomatic and commercial contact with the major cities of Mesopotamia (Mari, Ugarit, Karkemish and Babylon) at its height, in the seventeenth and eighteenth centuries BC. The city progressively declined in importance after its destruction at the end of the thirteenth century BC and completely disappeared after the Assyrian conquest of 733 BC.

❑ Hazor National Park, archaeological site and museum

Open Sunday-Thursday 8:00-17:00 (16:00 in winter), Friday 8:00-13:00; NIS16 entrance fee, incl. entry to museum

The impressive excavations at this site reveal the historic importance of this ancient Canaanite city. But, as in most other archaeological sites in the area, there are few vantage points and the interpretation of the ruins is complex. The exhibits in the Hatzor Museum, at the entrance to *Kibbutz Ayelet HaShahar (just across the road)*, help you understand what you see. There is a scale model of the city on display and various excavated artefacts that reflect different aspects of the city's culture.

❑ The Hula Nature Reserve

Located on Road 90 between Rosh Pinna and Kiryat Shmona [Israeli settlement established in 1950 on the site of al-Khalisa, a destroyed village of the Safad district, which had housed 1,840 inhabitants in 1944]. Open daily from 8:00-16:00, Friday 8:00-15:00; NIS 20 entrance fee. One may buy an ornithology field guide and rent binoculars at the entrance to the park. Exhibition of flora, fauna and landscape of the area at the Visitors' Centre. It is preferable to go early before it gets too hot to walk comfortably in the swamp. Spring and autumn are the best seasons for observing migratory birds.

The Hula Nature Reserve was created in 1970 in order to save part of the swamp, which is indispensable for millions of migratory birds. All along the two-kilometre walking trail are shelters, hides and observatories in the marshes from which one may observe many species (cranes, storks and kingfishers), mammals (water buffaloes and otters), plants (papyrus and water lilies) and a variety of water turtles.

The Hula Valley

These lakes and marshes between the hills of the Upper Galilee and the Golan Heights are what remain of the Lisan Sea [See *Lake Tiberias*, p. 331]. Until 1948, the valley belonged to the Bedouin al-Ghawarna tribe ('those who live in the Ghor or Depression'). Zionists attempted to live here in the late nineteenth century but usually found it too difficult due to malaria epidemics; at the beginning of the 1940s, Jewish settlers, helped by the British authorities, instituted canal drainage systems and eliminated the mosquitoes by the use of kerosene. The Bedouins in vain protested the project, which put the entire ecosystem of the region in danger, but on May 4, 1948, the Hagana launched "Operation Matateh" (*matateh* means brush in Hebrew). All Palestinians of the Hula Valley and villages east of Safad were evicted in Operation Brush. The drainage scheme was brought to an end during the 1950s and 1960s [see *Golan*, p. 396]. Recently an area has been re-flooded, in a tacit admission that the damage to the ecosystem - as predicted by the ecologically wise Bedouin - should be ceased and the area rehabilitated by returning it to its natural state.

Nazareth (en-Na'sra)

A Canaanite village already existed here by the Middle Bronze Age (2200-1500 BC) near the present day Basilica of the Annunciation. Nazareth ("the woman who keeps watch" in Greek) was a modest village first mentioned in writings of the first century AD. It is intimately associated with the Annunciation and Jesus' boyhood. *"Now in the sixth month the angel Gabriel was sent from God to a town of Galilee called Nazareth, to a virgin betrothed to a man named Joseph, of the house of David, and the virgin's name was Mary."* (Luke 1:26-27) Curiously enough, St. Luke was the only one of the four apostles to mention this event. In any case, Nazareth seems to have indeed become the home of the Holy Family when they returned from their flight into Egypt. It is plausible that Joseph was among the many craftsmen recruited to work on building the new regional capital of Galilee, Sepphoris (Saffuriya), six kilometres away. Any evidence of a Judaeo-Christian community in the first centuries of our era is obscure. Jesus personally experienced the lack of enthusiasm of the villagers for his teachings. As he put it, *"Verily I say unto you, no prophet is accepted in his own country."* (Luke 4:24) Even so, in the third century, there were definitely Christians in Nazareth, among them St. Conon, who was subsequently martyred in Asia Minor [See: *the Grotto of the Annunciation*, p. 323]. Relations were sometimes sorely strained between Jews, Judaeo-Christians (native Jews who recognised Jesus as the Messiah but maintained their old religious traditions) and those who called themselves authentic Christians, following the official doctrine (these people were often former pagans, sometimes foreigners). In addition, after the construction *circa* 352 AD of the Byzantine basilica on the site of the Annunciation, it is quite possible that Christians of Palestinian origin were less than appreciative of the control exercised on their holy places by the Byzantine religious authorities.

In any case, by this time, Christian pilgrimages to the Holy Land had commenced. From this time on, foreign pilgrims perpetuated local traditions and added new ones of their own. Romantic, mystically-inclined pilgrims, following in the footsteps of Jesus, marvelled to see the "bench [in the synagogue] where Jesus sat with the other children," "Mary's house," now a basilica, and other sites and objects from the life of Jesus. An Italian pilgrim's comment, in the sixth century, about the exceptional beauty of local women is surprising: *"The Jewish women* [he seems to mean Judaeo - Christians because he makes reference to Mary's holiness] *of this city are more elegant than all the other Jewissh women in the whole country. They say they get this elegance from the Virgin Mary, from whom they claim to be descended"*. After the Persians had sacked Nazareth, with the help of the Jewish and Samaritan communities of Palestine, in 614 AD, written records became scarce. With the coming of the Islamic conquest, there were fewer Christian pilgrimages, but the local Christian community remained predominant. Nazareth was restored to its place of importance at the time of the Crusader Conquest; churches and monasteries were erected on the places to which ancient Byzantine tradition had linked the Holy Family and the Angel Gabriel. At the beginning of the Ottoman period, there were more Muslims than Christians, a fact that shocked Christian pilgrim-explorers from Europe. In *circa* 1767, Daher al-Omar inaugurated a policy for developing the Galilee, by encouraging Christian families originating from the south of Palestine, from Lebanon and from Transjordan to settle there. The demographics of the population soon favoured the Christians: Greek Orthodox, Roman Catholic and Greek Catholic, among others. In the nineteenth century, Nazareth once again became one of the major sites for Christian pilgrimage in Palestine. The town profited from its position, attaining the status of municipality in 1880, and then became the foremost town of the district until the end of the British Mandate period. During the British Mandate, the authorities encouraged divisions in the community, preferring to employ Christians; nevertheless, Christians and Muslims united to protest against Zionist immigration and settlement. To this end, they created a branch of the Muslim-Christian Association in 1922. Between this date and 1944 the population of Nazareth doubled, rising from 7,424 to 14,200 residents. The Christian community remained in the majority until the post-war period. After 1948, the influx of refugees, most of whom were Muslim, created a Muslim majority. As with other Palestinian localities taken over in 1948, Nazareth was placed under Israeli military jurisdiction. Nazareth became the 'spokesman' for the demands of Palestinians inside Israel. On May 1, 1958, the Israeli army quelled a demonstration organised by the Communist Party against land confiscation, by bringing it to a bloody halt. Since that day, every May 1 has been a day when groups publicly air social and national issues. The Israeli Communist Party has been at the forefront of political life in Nazareth for three decades. Combining a membership of Jews and Arabs, it has been almost the only party to put the Palestinian cause at the top of its agenda. This being the case, it has attracted a large proportion of the Palestinian voting population of Israel. Tawfiq Zayyad, mayor of Nazareth from 1976 to 1994, and also a poet, was a leading party member.

En-Nakba

On his first visit to Nazareth, Ben-Gurion looked around him with astonishment and said, 'Why are there so many Arabs here? Why didn't you chase them away?' (cited by Michael Ben-Zohar)

Until Nazareth was taken by Israeli forces, it served as an area of refuge for thousands of Palestinians chased from their homes. For most, it was merely a temporary stop *en route* to Syria, Lebanon, Transjordan or the West Bank. Some settled on the outskirts of the city. In this way, the population rose from 15,540 in 1946 to over 20,000 in 1951. Israeli troops took Nazareth on July 16, 1948. The mayor at that time, Yussif Fahoum, accompanied by two Greek Orthodox priests, signed the conditions of surrender, by which the Israelis promised that there would be no looting or destruction of public or private property. Bearing in mind its importance to the international Christian world and its ties to the Vatican, Nazareth was spared the suffering endured by every other Palestinian town. In fact, it was the only place to escape the policy of ethnic cleansing.

➡ The urban centre of Nazareth today

Upper Nazareth and my town are for me two completely different worlds. I am particularly aware of this as Nazareth is a special city in the eyes of the Christian world and the international community. I am in the habit of saying that if the city of Nazareth were in any other country than Israel, without this system of discrimination, the city would surely have a completely different physical appearance."

■ Ramez Jerayseh, Mayor of Nazareth

Nazareth is the largest Palestinian urban area in Israel and the largest city in the Galilee, with a population of more than 70,000 citizens (60% Muslim and 40% Christian).

It was a city where many took refuge in 1948, and today nearly half its citizens are internally displaced persons (some 30,000 people). The refugees have settled around the suburbs of the city, where they are sometimes grouped by their village of origin, such as villagers from Saffuriya, who live in the Safafra neighbourhood on the slopes of Nazareth. From where they live, they have a direct view onto the forest that covers the ruins of Saffuriya [See *Saffuriya*, p. 327].

The density of Nazareth's population is particularly high: although there are 70,000 residents today compared to 14,000 in 1948, the area of the municipality has not expanded at all. What is more, 1,500 hectares were confiscated to create the Jewish municipality of Upper Nazareth *(Nazrat Illit)*. Government authorities or authorities close to the government (the Jewish National Fund and the Jewish Agency, for example) as well as regional councils, constantly expressed "concern" over the concentration of Palestinians in the Galilee and the influence of Nazareth, which naturally became the capital of the area [See *The Koenig Memorandum*, p. 292]. The reality is that the policy of judaising the Galilee systematically affected Nazareth by forcing it to suffer economic underdevelopment and overpopulation. This policy aimed at preventing any geographical contiguity between Nazareth's outlying suburbs (Ein Mahel, Kufr Kana, Mash'ad, Reineh and others). It also limited any growth of the municipal territory of Nazareth and its Arab suburbs as well as general economic growth by denying land for industrial development; finally, it was intended to regulate the demographics of the region.

This policy was the reason for the establishment of a second urban centre named Upper Nazareth or *Nazrat Illit*. Dominating the ancient town, it was created in 1957 above it as its Jewish double, intended to be the new economic and administrative capital of the Galilee. Upper Nazareth has not ceased since its creation to expand to the detriment of Nazareth and its neighbouring Arab suburbs, which in other circumstances would have joined Nazareth to form one large, single agglomeration. Upper Nazareth numbers some 40,000 residents. In the 1990s, the city's population considerably soared with the arrival of waves of Jews from the ex-Soviet republics. Still, the success of this policy of judaisation of the Nazareth region was mitigated in the eyes of Israeli planners by the fact that, above all, Upper Nazareth's population is elderly: 58% of its residents are aged between 45 and 65, as opposed to only 20% in Nazareth.

The alarmist appeals of Zionist demographers are all the more virulent in warning against another trend: many Palestinians from Nazareth have moved to Upper Nazareth (approximately 6,000 people, representing 15% of the Jewish municipality's population), and they are young, with a higher birth rate than the Jewish residents. The discriminatory nature of the Jewish municipality is again evident in the absence of schools and cultural or religious centres for the Arab sector, even though it represents 15% of the population of Upper Nazareth.

The government has put Upper Nazareth high on its list of priorities. It is officially in the first category of "development priority areas." Ninety-nine percent of the constructions in Upper Nazareth belong to the government, subsidised by the Ministry of Planning & Infrastructure. Upper Nazareth has four times more land than Nazareth at its disposal, for half the number of people. Its land was confiscated from land

The urban centre of Nazareth

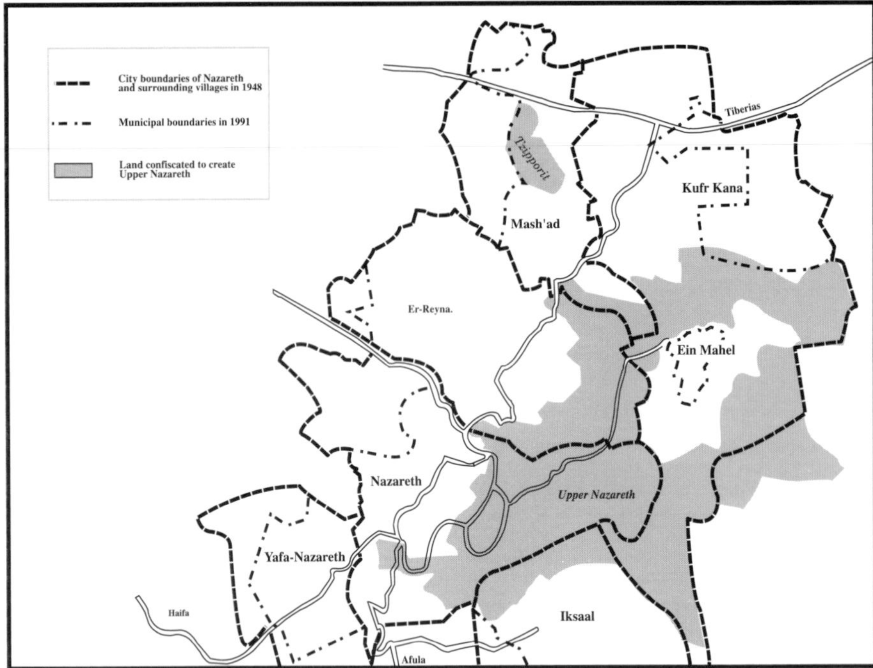

belonging to Nazareth and its suburbs, already cruelly in need of more room. At the present rate of population growth in Nazareth, there will not be enough urban space within 15 years. Lack of space for economic expansion is already a problem today. In fact, the unemployment rate is one of the highest in Israel (14% of the active population, without taking into account the low rate of women who are part of the work force). Work opportunities for this largely working class population are restricted to the Jewish industrial zones established outside the city borders after the Oslo accords (Upper Nazareth and *Karmiel*, for example). Most residents of Upper Nazareth work inside the city's borders. It is an unavoidable fact that the government's development plan for Upper Nazareth endowed it with a vast industrial zone of over 50 hectares, while Nazareth does not have more than 8 hectares for industrial use in the centre of town. What is worse, the Upper Nazareth industrial zone of Tzipporit, which constitutes an actual enclave of Upper Nazareth, stands on lands confiscated from the Arab locality of Mash'ad. This area between Mash'ad and Kufr Kana is a 34-hectare collection of polluting factories. Upper Nazareth profits well from these industries, while sparing itself from any of the disagreeable aspects they represent. Upper Nazareth owns another similar enclave in the very centre of Nazareth, a few minutes from the Basilica of the Annunciation: since 1960, the military centre of command for the Northern District has been located here, as well as a tourist complex (*Nazareth Gardens Hotel*, formerly the *Sprinzak Restaurant*).

The Palestinian town of Ein Mahel, which once fell within the city boundaries, is another example of Israeli urban planning. It, too, has become totally constricted on all sides by the municipal territory of Upper Nazareth, which has confiscated most of its land to boost its own land reserves. Today, some 140 hectares more are also threatened with confiscation.

Excluding Palestinian Nazareth from any administrative or political function, all government institutions and services have been moved to Upper Nazareth, where one finds departments of the Ministry of the Interior, the Ministry of Agriculture, the Ministry of Health, the Ministry of Education, the Nazareth District Court and so on. Administrative buildings have also been constructed on private property in Nazareth, invoking "the public interest" and then subsequently placed under the jurisdiction of Upper Nazareth.

Writing on the trunk of an olive tree

Because I am not a spinner of wool
But am every day
Under warrants for arrest
And my house threatened
By police raids
Searches
"Cleaning up" operations
Because I am unable
To buy any paper
I will write all that happens to me
I will carve all my secrets
On an olive tree
In the courtyard of my house
I will carve my story
And the successive pages of my tragedy
And my sighs
On my garden
And the tombs of my dead ones
And I will carve
All the bitterness
Which a tenth of future joys will suffice to erase
I will carve the number
Of each acre robbed from our land
The location of my village, its boundaries
The houses dynamited
My trees uprooted
Each little flower crushed
The names of those who have taken pleasure
In shattering my nerves and interfering with my breathing
The names of the prisons
The marks of all the handcuffs
Locked tight on my wrists
The boots of my guards
Each curse
Directed on my head
And I will carve
Kufr Qassem
I shall not forget
And I will carve
Deir Yassin
Your memory devours me
And I will carve
We have attained the summit of the tragedy
We have reached it
I will carve everything the sun reveals to me
And the moon murmurs to me
Everything the turtle dove
Coos to me above the well
Where the lovers no longer keep their trysts
So that I remember
I will stay standing to carve
All the successive pages of my tragedy
And every stage of the defeat
From the infinitely small
To the infinitely huge
On the trunk of an olive tree
In the courtyard
Of my house.

■ Tawfiq Zayyad, extract from *Bury Your Dead and Rise Up*. Tawfiq Zayyad (1929-1994) was mayor of Nazareth from 1975 to 1994.

■ The old city

A multicultural city, Nazareth boasts a diversity of religions, exemplified by its religious sites: mosques, churches and monasteries, which are as much places of pilgrimage for pilgrims and visitors as uncontested attractions. If religious architecture has left its mark, it has not hidden the secular buildings from the eighteenth and nineteenth centuries, which are also of architectural interest. Impressive residences today tell of the privileged economic position of important citizens in Nazareth's past; a characteristic of these buildings is that they have storage areas reserved on their ground floors, while the upper levels, reserved for living quarters, are enhanced by three beautiful archway openings. Notice the hand-carved wooden friezes, sometimes painted, under their eaves. There is now a renewed interest in this architectural heritage. One of these beautiful houses *(in the process of restoration)* is located near the *Saraya*. It will soon house a cinema and, without doubt, one of the most beautiful cafés in the city. Other public and private initiatives are equally contributing to the re-establishment of the old city's architectural value. The **Saraya** of Daher al-Omar, Governor of Galilee, constructed in *circa* 1730 AD, is currently being renovated and will serve as the municipal museum. Nearby, the ***Café Casa Palestina***, located in the former storage area of a bourgeois house of the eighteenth century and earlier, is a delightful place to take a break. (See p. 324.)

At the top of Casa Nova Street, a gate provides access to the **street market** *(open every day except Sunday)*. Thursday is the main market day. In the market, one finds the oldest mosque of Nazareth, the **White Mosque** (Masjid al-Abyad), which was built in 1812. Farther along, a warren of small pedestrian alleyways allows one to explore at a more leisurely pace.

As in Jerusalem and Bethlehem, many different Christian churches are represented in Nazareth. Each church or monastery has been built on the site of older buildings and traditions, dating from more or less ancient times. The **Sisters of Nazareth Convent**, built over a Jewish necropolis, con-

Nazareth

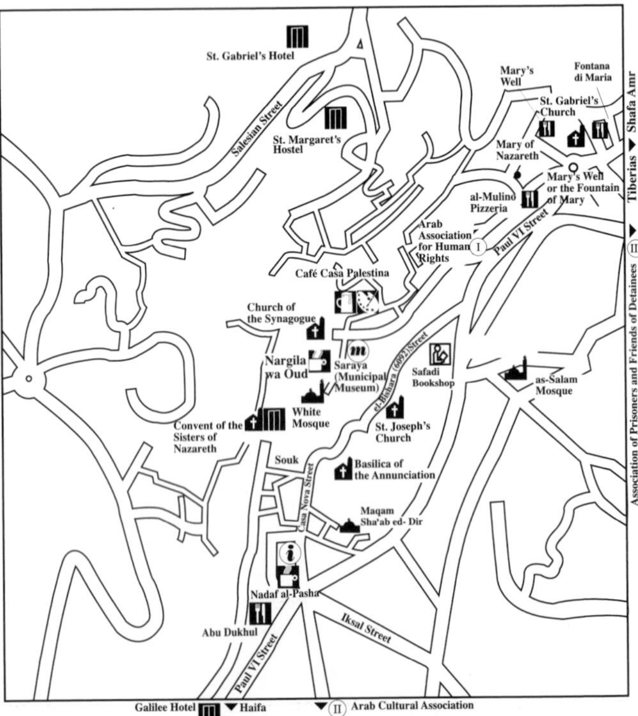

tains an excellent example of a vault closed by a rolling millstone. In the centre of the market *(souk)*, is the **Church of the Synagogue** (a Greek Catholic church), being the synagogue where Jesus preached and was driven out (Luke 4:16-30). **Mary's Well** or the Fountain of Mary, on al-Hanuq Street, is another important location for Christian pilgrims. **St. Gabriel's Greek Orthodox Church** is sited where the Angel Gabriel appeared to Mary while she was drawing water from the well (and not in her home as Catholic tradition has it). The church *(open every day 8:30-11:45 and 14:00-18:00)* is built on Byzantine and Crusader foundations. In its crypt, one may see Armenian tiles dating from the twelfth century. The iconostasis - the screen that hides the altar from view - decorated with icons and holy pictures, equally merits particular attention.

❑ St. Joseph's Church

This church, built in 1914 on the remains of a Crusader church, but with more modest dimensions, is an inviting place for meditation and prayer. There are several caves underneath it, one of which is said to be St. Joseph's workshop (according to a tradition dating from the seventeenth century, shared by the Sisters of Nazareth Convent and St. Gabriel's Church). In the crypt underneath St. Joseph's, there is a striped black and white basin of alternating basalt and limestone, believed to be a baptismal font from late Roman times (first to third century AD).

❑ Nazareth's Ancient Bathhouse

Mary's Well Square. Open Monday–Saturday 8:00-16:00
☎ 04 6578539

The remains of the only existing public bathhouse in Nazareth were uncovered by chance in 1993. The water for the bathhouse no doubt came from Mary's Well, since it was the only available water source in ancient times. The site contains artefacts dating not only from the Ottoman and Crusader period, but back to Byzantine and ancient Roman times as well.

Today, one can enjoy guided tours of the *caldarium*, the most beautiful *hypocaust* in the Middle East and the *praefurnarium* (stove) at the site. Refreshments in the arched hall of the wooden cave, where exhibitions are presented, are also available.

❑ The Basilica of the Annunciation

Casa Nova Street. Open Monday–Saturday 8:30-11:45 and 14:00-17:00, Sunday only during mass)

An imposing church, criticised for its style, the basilica was designed between 1955 and 1969 by a leading Italian architect Antonio Barluzzi. It stands on the site - recognised since Byzantine times or even earlier - of the Annunciation. *"Behold, thou shalt conceive in thy womb and shalt bring forth a son, and thou shalt call his name Jesus"*. (Luke 1:31) The Franciscan church, built here in 1730 and restored in 1877, has been superseded by this modern building. Archaeological digs, undertaken after the Franciscan church's destruction, revealed parts of the Crusader church (the north wall) and Byzantine church (the octagonal apse under the altar and mosaics). Underneath the heart of the lower church is the Grotto of the Annunciation, a holy site since the early days of Christianity. A small shrine on the left is dedicated to St. Conon, who suffered martyrdom in Asia Minor *circa* 249-251 AD. He declared before his judges: "I am from Nazareth in Galilee, I am from the family of Christ, whom I worship as did my ancestors." An unusual graffiti found in a pre-Byzantine baptismal font bears witness to the worship of the Virgin Mary: "Rejoice, Mary!" It may be seen in the **Franciscan Museum** (*the Franciscan monastery in the precincts of the basilica is open Monday-Saturday 8:00-11:30 and 14:00-17:00; access only permitted to groups, as a rule*) next to objects dating from the Crusades. Among other items on display are the exquisite marble capitals sent from France by Louis IX (1226-1279 AD). They arrived just before Nazareth was conquered by Baybars and were never mounted on the columns.

In the square in front of the church, a small field containing archaeological discoveries gives an impression of Nazareth as a village of cave dwellers in the days of Jesus Christ. A staircase to the right of the entrance to the lower church leads to the upper level of the basilica, which is used for regular services for the Christian Roman Catholic community of Nazareth. The contemporary frescoes are gifts from Roman Catholic communities around the world.

Practical Information

Nazareth has one main street, Paul VI Street. There is often heavy traffic, so it is best to leave one's car in one of the various parking areas to the east of Paul VI Street.
The **tourist information centre** (*open Monday-Friday 8:30-17:00, Saturday 8:30-14:00; ☎ 04-657 0555*) is at the junction of Paul VI Street and Casa Nova Street. They provide free maps of the city and a calendar of local events. On the way up Paul VI Street, on the left, the **Samir Safadi Bookshop** (*☎ /fax 04-655 5803*) sells newspapers and magazines in French and English. When planning a visit to Nazareth, remember that many sites and shops are closed on Sunday.

Cafés

In the heart of the old city, near the White Mosque, ***Nargila wa Oud*** is a good café to relax in and smoke a water pipe. There are always musicians on Friday and Saturday evenings. Nearby, opposite the *Saraya* (the intended municipal museum), is the ***Casa Palestina*** cultural café-restaurant (*☎ 04-602 1001*). It is situated in an ancient home, whose vaulted storerooms are warm and welcoming; one can buy a variety of Palestinian handicrafts from the display here. On Saturday evenings, there are musical or, sometimes, theatrical performances held here. Another *nargila-café* at the corner of Casa Nova Street and Paul VI Street, ***Nadaf al-Pasha***, is also located in the antique storerooms of an eighteenth century middle-class house and has a spacious setting with a view of the street.

Restaurants

There is a good selection of inexpensive restaurants around the Basilica of the Annunciation and along Paul VI Street and Casa Nova Street, offering typical Palestinian specialities such as *mezzés* or grilled meat. ***Abu Dukhul*** (also known as the ***Diana Restaurant***) is one of the best. Higher up, on al-Ein or Mary's Well Square, the ***Fontana di Maria*** (*Mary's Well Square: ☎ 04-646 0435/6*) is another highly reputed restaurant, known for its good, wide-ranged cuisine. There are also several pizzerias around the square. The ***al-Mulino Pizzeria*** has both good decor and superior cooking but is relatively expensive. Young people prefer ***Mary's Well Pizza*** for its atmosphere rather than its setting.

Accommodation

St. Margaret's Hostel (*Salesian Street: ☎ 04-657 3507, fax 04-656 7166; Single $50 Double $77*) has a splendid view over the roofs of the old town. Its tastefully renovated rooms and its outdoor café restaurant add to its charm. Nearby, the ***St. Gabriel Hotel*** (*Salesian Street; ☎ 04-646 6613, fax 04-655 4071; Single $60, Double $90, Triple $105*) also offers a fine view and its bell tower provides a reliable landmark. The rooms are simple; on the garden side, they have large bay windows looking out over the town. The hotel has been classically renovated; breakfasts are delicious and particularly generous.
Near the Basilica of the Annunciation, the ***Convent of the Sisters of Nazareth*** runs a hospice (*Casa Nova Street; ☎ 04-655 4304, fax 04-646 0741 ; private room $23 per person, dormitory $8 per person*), which is usually reserved for groups of pilgrims. A meeting room and a chapel are available for guests.
Located to the south of the Church of the Annunciation, the ***Hotel Galileo*** (*Paul VI Street; ☎ 04-657 1311, fax 04-655 6627; Single $60, Double $80, Triple $110*) has been recently renovated. It has a spacious modern lobby and large public rooms.

Contacts

Arab Cultural Association

Iksal Street. ☎ 04-608 2352; ACA1998@hotmail.com. Talks, exhibitions and shows are organised throughout the year. Check their Calendar of Events. Every May 15 (Day of the Nakba), there are visits to Palestinian villages destroyed in 1948. The ACA helps organise such visits; do not hesitate to contact them on such occasions. There is also a cafeteria and an Internet café (both are simple and pleasant).

The heritage of Palestinian Arab Israelis is absent from the Israeli school curriculum or distorted or devalued, in every aspect - cultural, geographical, historical and literary. To counter this, a group of activists created this cultural association in 1998, to promote and reaffirm the cultural and national identity of Israeli Palestinians of 1948 and equally to promote egalitarian, democratic values and social justice. The centre is active in many areas, including providing scholarships for schoolchildren, workshops where discussions take place, focusing on identity, literature, the media and so on, as well as artistic exhibitions.

(Similar aims as the Arab Cultural Association's aims are expressed by an Israeli peace organisation *Zochrot* ["Remembering"], which is dedicated to teaching Israelis their true history, by marking the sites of all demolished Palestinian villages and holding joint memorial services at such sites as Deir Yassin; they believe that peace and reconciliation will only come between the two nations once Israelis understand, acknowledge and apologise with full reparations for their past treatment of Palestinians. For further details: *Eitan Bronstein: 0506-314229.*)

Arab Association for Human Rights

Al-Bishara Street (6092 Street).☎ 04-656 1923; www.arabhra.org; Open for visits: fees applicable for study facilities.

This association is an important source of information for any study of the status of the Palestinian Arab community in Israel and the various forms of discrimination it faces. It was established in 1988 by a group of lawyers and human rights activists to advocate all the rights of the Palestinian Israeli minority (which forms 20% of the population of the State of Israel): it therefore defends all their civil, political, economic, cultural, religious or other rights. Besides providing general information, the association organises visits lasting from an hour to a day, on different themes, including the Galilee, the Triangle and the Negev. These include: 'A comparative visit to Nazareth and Upper Nazareth,' 'Demolished villages,' 'Unrecognised villages (in the Galilee and Negev),' or 'The situation of Palestinians in mixed towns.'

National Committee for the Defence of the Rights of Internally Displaced Persons in Israel

Shufr'Amr ☎ 04-986 1171/2. Visits and conferences can be arranged.

This committee was formed in 1995 in the absence of any mention of internally displaced people in the Oslo Accords. Its members represent over 30 demolished villages. Its aim is to permit Palestinians who were displaced inside the Green Line to return to their villages and to recover their land on the basis of UN Resolution 194. Committee members promote numerous activities, collecting information about demolished villages and the origin and current residence of people displaced from them, as well as the present status of the land. The committee is also concerned with reclaiming and maintaining holy sites: mosques, churches and cemeteries.

Internal refugees

The creation of the State of Israel by the Zionist movement resulted in the eviction of at least 800,000 of 1.28 million Palestinians. Only 150,000 stayed in what became Israel after the Nakba. A third of these people became internally displaced refugees, having been driven out of their villages or towns. They often live near their original homes, inside the new state. These people found themselves living in what Palestinians call The Territories of 1948 (The State of Israel) due to a combination of circumstances. All internally displaced refugees come from families broken up in 1948: most family members took refuge in the West Bank, the Gaza Strip and in the principal refugee states: Jordan, Syria and Lebanon. In 1950, UNRWA conducted a census and took on the responsibility of caring for 46,000 internal refugees. They now number between 200,000 to 250,000 people, or 20% of the Palestinian population of Israel. After 1952, UNRWA gradually stopped all its aid to internal Palestinian refugees after Israel formally annexed the territory conquered in 1948. In 1950, the State of Israel defined refugees outside its territories as "absent" according to the Absentees' Property Law. Internal refugees were defined as "present absentees" or "absent-present." Their property, just like property of refugees in exile, was expropriated. The "Development Authority" of the Ministry of Agriculture was created and given jurisdiction over lands it could declare "abandoned." It has the power to freeze development; an example of this treatment is the large number of sealed houses and apartments in Haifa. The authority can also rent or sell such properties to Israeli state bodies or to Jewish agencies such as the Jewish National Fund or the Israeli Lands Authority, for projects for the unique benefit of the Jewish community.

Association for Prisoners and Friends of Detainees

☎ 04-655 0027. Demonstrations and other expressions of solidarity are organised on Prisoners' Day (April 17).

This association was created in 1989 to support Palestinian political prisoners being held in Israel: it provides legal and material aid to prisoners and their families. The longest-serving political prisoner, Sami Younis, has just been released, having been in prison since 1982 (serving life imprisonment). Most Palestinian Israelis are jailed in Shatta Prison (near Bissan) with Syrians from the Golan and Palestinians from Jerusalem. This system of separating these individuals from prisoners from the West Bank and Gaza corresponds with Israel's formal annexation of the Golan on December 14, 1981, and East Jerusalem, on July 30, 1980, as permanent additions to the territory of the State of Israel.

Safwan Fahoum (Member of Nazareth city council)

(Nazareth Municipality. ☎ 04-657 6877. www.nazareth.muni.il)

Mr. Fahoum is happy to acquaint visitors with his city and its residents. He organises visits and meetings with citizens of Nazareth as well as talks on the situation in Nazareth and relations between the Palestinian and Jewish communities.

■ North and east of Nazareth

Saffuriya (Zippori)

Archaeological excavations in the Zippori National Park, open every day 8:00-17:00 (16:00 in winter); NIS 22 entrance fee; ☎ 04-656 8272. Detailed map of the site (NIS 10). For a visit to the demolished village and other information on internal refugees, contact the Heritage Society of Saffuriya through the National Committee for the Defence of the Rights of Internally Displaced Persons in Israel [See p. 325].

A fortified city in the first century BC, Saffuriya was raised to the status of administrative capital of the Galilee shortly after the Roman conquest of Palestine. Herod Antipas inherited it from his father after the Romans put down a revolt stirred up by the old Hasmonean nobility. He built the city of Sepphoris on the ruins of the town and called it "the jewel of the Galilee." A cosmopolitan city, it welcomed the Oriental, Graeco-Roman and Jewish religions which flourished side by side. Sepphoris remained loyal to the Roman Empire and was awarded the status of a free city under Hadrian, when it was renamed Diocaesarea. At the end of the second century AD, it became an important centre for Judaism and was the seat of the High Court (Sanhedrin). In the fourth century AD, the Christian community began to develop here. One of its main churches was built by Joseph of Tiberias, a Jewish convert to Christianity. Saffuriya remained an important market town under Islamic rule and is mentioned frequently by Arab geographers and chroniclers; it even had its own mint under the Umayyads. The Crusaders made the town their strategic base, building a citadel here, which they called La Saphorie, which was renovated in the eighteenth century by Daher al-Omar ez-Zaydani, governor of the north of Palestine. The **fortress** was made into a *kuttab* (primary school) at the end of the nineteenth century and later became a school. Among its illustrious citizens, Saffuriya can claim Jamal Ibn Abdel Hadi al-Saffuri (1436-1503), historian and theologian, who was the teacher of historian Ibn Tulun; Abu al-Baqa al-Saffuri (1574-1628), a judge in Safad and several villages of Sham; Ahmed al-Sharif, also known by the name of Ahmed Ibn Ali al-Saffuri ed-Damashqi, judge and poet (1569-1633). In 1944, Suffuriya was the most important village in the district of Nazareth, having a population of over 4,330 inhabitants (4,320 Muslims and 10 Christians).

The Sultan's gift

When the First World War broke out, the Saffuriya town council learned that Turkish troops being sent to the front were to make a stop at Saffuriya to requisition supplies. The imminent arrival of soldiers did not bode well, so the village authorities decided to prepare the best welcome possible for the troops and their horses in terms of food, drink and mounted provisions. Every villager contributed personally from his own wealth. Tents were erected in the Field of Abdel Mohti and straw mats spread on the ground. The soldiers arrived on the expected day at midday, tired and thirsty; they were well received with much respect and ate until they could eat no more. At the end of the afternoon, at the time of parting, their commanding officer thanked the village sheikh, Mohammed Sliman, and the other village dignitaries, praising their hospitality. Well-fed and rested, the soldiers continued their return march to Nazareth. The villagers accompanied them to the village boundaries.

A few days later, a small detachment of soldiers came to the village and gave the sheikh a summons from the Turkish governor of the district himself. This summons was considered a bad sign. Grim stories were told about this important military commander. People said that anyone who entered his residence was lost and that anyone who came out was reborn. Sheikh Mohammed Sliman hastily gathered two of his children and a small committee together, and they followed the soldiers back to Nazareth to the governor's residence. Everyone was silent and gloomy during the entire journey, each one wondering as to the reason for the summons. Once they had arrived at the destination, their astonishment knew no bounds at seeing the Governor take their sheikh in his arms, uttering respectful, friendly greetings! In broken Arabic, he praised the welcome his soldiers had received in the name of the sultan. The sheikh replied that the sultan's soldiers had been their guests and that the village had been honoured by their presence. The governor told them that a sign of appreciation for their hospitality had been agreed upon in the highest circles. Before the villagers left, he gave them a gift. On the orders of the sultan himself! *"An extremely precious gift,"* he stressed. "*May God grant the sultan victory*," responded the little group in unison. On the way back, everyone eyed the package and its wrappings with growing curiosity. Sheikh Mohammed Sliman was greeted by his people with great relief and recounted their adventure in great detail, ending with the moment they had received the disturbing gift, on which all eyes converged. The sheikh continued his story: "*The sultan in person decided to offer this precious gift to our village, and transmitted his order to the Wali of Beirut, who gave it to the Moutassareff of Acre, who communicated it to the governor in Nazareth. But since we are now all here together, it is high time to open the package*." The sheikh undid the knots, unwrapped the package and, from inside the box, took out a large Turkish flag. All the villagers laughed and laughed until they were out of breath and could laugh no more and gave thanks to God that their emissaries had returned from their mission safe and sound.

■ This incident, which took place at the very beginning of World War I, is related by generation to generation among the Safafra (the villagers of Saffuriya).

En-Nakba

On July 15, 1948, the village was bombed by Israeli aircraft. Some of the villagers fled into the neighbouring countryside and returned when it was over; others took refuge in Lebanon. On January 2, 1949, those who had stayed in Saffuriya were deported to nearby Palestinian localities (the outskirts of Nazareth, Illut, er-Reyna and Kufr Kanna). They filed a complaint with the Israeli Supreme Court. It was refused on the grounds that Saffuriya had been declared a closed military zone by the military governor. In 1949, two farming settlements, *Zippori* and *HaSolelim*, were established on the village's land. Hungarian Jews settled in *Zippori*. Saffuriya's evicted residents settled on the slopes of Nazareth in an area they called **Safafra** (people originating in Saffuriya). This neighbourhood has a superb view of the plain below and the site of their village, six kilometres away.

➡ The village today

The remains of the Palestinian village are lost under a pine forest planted by the Jewish National Fund (in the context of the campaign: *Plant a Tree in Israel*). The forest is dedicated to the Independence of Guatemala (September 15, 1821).

In *Moshav Zippori* there remain only a few ruins of Palestinian houses and a Catholic convent of **Saint Hannah** (☎ 04-655 5342). The convent was built in the 1920s on property put at the disposal of the nuns by the Islamic *waqf.* Local tradition (dating from the Crusader occupation period) has it that Mary's parents, St. Joachim and St. Anne, were originally from Sepphoris. The Crusaders built a church on the site of their home, and its beautifully preserved apse may be visited *(ask at the St. Hannah Convent).* Until the Nakba, the convent ran a clinic for the village and a training centre for women; today, the nuns run a boarding-school at the convent. There were close contacts between the villagers (exclusively Muslims) and the convent; during World War II, when the convent ceased to receive a subsidy from the Vatican, the municipal council financed its basic needs and made a donation to the monastic community.

The people of Saffuriya have been fighting for restitution of their lands for over fifty years. Their efforts have been partly concentrated on the protection and restoration of burial sites and holy places. In 1948, five cemeteries and several *maqams* were destroyed by Israeli forces and local Jews. The **al-Karaki graveyard**, including burial sites of children, was among them, buried under earth and debris. In 1978, the Jews of the area started to work the land in the main cemetery. The committee of the original inhabitants of Saffuriya intervened and managed to save two-thirds of the land from desecration. The rest was completely dug up. Since 1993, the committee has obtained permission to fence off the cemetery (*300 metres after the entrance to Zippori, near an enclosure for cows*).

The site of Sepphoris

Large areas of this ancient site have been excavated. Among the most impressive finds are the superb **mosaic floors** which decorated homes and places of worship. The symbolic figure "Mona Lisa of the Galilee" retains one's attention. Next to this are several scenes of celebration in honour of the Greek god of wine, Dionysos. The Roman theatre, constructed in the first century AD, had about 5,000 seats. Likewise to be seen at the site is the **Citadel**, dating from Crusader times, which now houses an exhibition centre. A short walk brings one to an impressive reservoir used in Roman and Byzantine times, as well as the remains of two aqueducts.

Sakhnin

Surrounded by hills and olive groves, Sakhnin (23,000 residents) is a good place to start a country hike. During the olive harvest (mid-October to beginning of November), there is an ***olive oil festival*** (*Ghazzal Abu Raya, Sakhnin municipality,* ☎ *04-678 8888*). In the middle of the village is the **Palestinian Folk Museum** (*above the Omar Mosque. Open every day 8:00-16:30, NIS 10 entrance fee*). It has an interesting painting of a traditional village and its social organisation. There is also a floor dedicated to handicrafts (glass from Hebron, mother-of-pearl boxes from Beit Sahour and olive-wood statuettes from Bethlehem.) as well as hand-embroidered Palestinian dresses

Land Day (Yom al-'Ard)

This is a Palestinian national holiday. On March 30, 1976, six Palestinians from Sakhnin, 'Arrabé, Kufr Kana and Taybeh were killed during a day of strikes and general protests against the confiscation of land by the Israeli authorities [See p. 69]. In the face of this resistance, Israeli authorities put a moratorium on their land confiscation projects for some time. This decision was motivated by a desire to avoid any uprising inside the State of Israel which could spread to the West Bank and Gaza while the Israeli army was busy with military operations against Palestinian refugees in Lebanon. However, land expropriations never completely stopped, and the policy intensified after signature of the Oslo Accords.

Kufr Kana

About 8 kilometres northeast of Nazareth, on Road 754. On bus route No. 431 between Nazareth and Tiberias.

This village is the site of Jesus' first miracle, His transformation of water into wine for the wedding feast of Cana (John 2:1-11). Christian pilgrimages have been recorded here since the third century AD. When there was a renewal of Christian pilgrimages from the West, the Franciscans built the **Church of the Wedding Feast** in 1879. The **Greek Orthodox Church** nearby displays the very water jars in which the miracle took place. A village of over 10,000 residents, both Christian and Muslim, Kufr Kana also includes a small Circassian community which settled in Palestine in the nineteenth century.

❑ Mount Tabor

Nine kilometres east of Nazareth. Franciscan church, open every day 8:00-11:30 and 2:30-18:00, October-March 2:00-17:00. An exceptional panorama.

Like Jabal al-Sheikh (Mount Hermon), which one can see from here on a clear day, as well as Lake Tiberias, Mount Tabor (588 metres) has been considered a sacred mountain since ancient times (Deuteronomy 19:33). Due to its proximity to Nazareth, this "high mountain" is naturally accepted as the site of extraordinary events in the life of Jesus of Nazareth: the site of the Transfiguration of Christ (Matthew 17:1-8). In the fourth century, many Christian pilgrims flocked here, which did not stop it from being an important strategic and military base. It became the symbol of the Fifth Crusade in 1217, by surviving a siege of many days and was later the setting of a particularly deadly battle between Napoleon's army and the Ottoman forces. Two churches crown its summit: the **Greek Orthodox Church of St.Elijah** *(closed to the public)* and the **Franciscan Basilica**, which is accessed through the entrance to the **Ayyubid Fortress**, Bab al-Hawa (Gateway of the Wind).

■ West and south of Nazareth

❑ Beit She'arim

On Road 75, 4 kilometres south of Nazareth. Open Saturday-Thursday 8:00-16:00, Friday 8:00-15:00, NIS 18 entrance fee. Small museum in Tomb 28.

This town, known by the Greeks as Besara, was at the heart of territory belonging to Berenice, a descendant of Herod the Great. From the second century AD on, it was one of the most important centres of Judaism and the seat of the Jewish ecclesiastical hierarchy, banished from Jerusalem after the revolt of 135 AD. The city reached its peak in the third and fourth centuries but was destroyed in 352 by the Byzantine governor, Gallus, after a revolt which had spread throughout the whole area. Among its many famous citizens was Rabbi Yehuda HaNasi (135-217 AD), who compiled the Mishna, codifying the laws Jews must follow in their daily lives (until then only an oral tradition). At his death, Beit She'arim became a holy place, and many Jews from Yemen, Antiochus and Babylon chose to be buried there; in the third century, Jerusalem was forbidden to Jews and Beit She'arim became the burial place for Jews from all over the world.

Archaeologists have uncovered a huge network of **catacombs** here, with 31 exposed tombs on view: today the principal attraction of the site. A hundred metres southeast of the basilica, **Wali (Saint) Abreik Mosque** is the only building remaining of a Palestinian village, demolished in 1948. Legend has it that a sufi of the village, Sufi Abreik, performed a miracle by making sparkling water pour out of a broken pitcher. This water spread and spread, forming a swamp whose waters were said to possess healing powers. The village took its name from Sheikh Abreik. A statue of Alexander Zaid now dominates it; Zaid was leader of the Zionist paramilitary organisation Hashomer ("the Watchman" in Hebrew), killed by Palestinian partisans in 1938.

❑ Tel Megiddo (Armageddon)

On Road 65, 20 kilometres north of Jenin, 5 kilometres southwest of Afula. Archaeological site, with a museum at its entrance. Open Saturday-Thursday 8:00-16:00, Friday 8:00-15:00, NIS 15 entrance fee.

This ancient city is on the large plain of Marj Amer (Jezreel Valley) at the crossroads of routes to Egypt, to the Mediterranean coast, to Syria and to Mesopotamia. From its geographical position, the civilisations of Mesopotamia and Egypt contributed to its cultural, philosophical, religious and technical heritage. Many battles between local and regional powers were fought over it. In the Book of the Revelation of St. John the Divine, it also became the scene of the ultimate battle between good and evil.

"And he gathered them [the demoniac spirits, the practitioners of amazements] together into a place called in the Hebrew tongue, Har-Megiddo [Armageddon] ... And there were voices, and thunders and lightnings, and there was a great earthquake (...) the Great City was divided into three parts, and the cities of the nations fell. And great Babylon came in remembrance before God, to give unto her the cup of the wine of the fierceness of his wrath." (Revelation 16:16-19) The most famous battle fought over Megiddo was between Pharaoh Thutmose III and the ruling coalition of 330 Canaanite and Syrian rulers (of the Mitanni kingdom). Egypt was victorious in 1479 BC and took no less than 924 battle-chariots as spoils.

■ Tiberias (Tabariya)

"It used to be a city of considerable importance, but now there are only simple ruins which tell of its former glory"
■ Ibn Battuta, fourteenth century

Herod Antipas, Tetrach (Ottoman governor) of the Galilee, founded this city in 18 AD in honour of the Roman Emperor Tiberius, thus taking the title 'capital of the Galilee' from Sepphoris. The city developed significantly in the second century AD. For many centuries, it was the principal theological seat of Palestinian Judaism. In 220 AD, Yohanan ben Nappaha (180-279 AD), disciple of Rabbi Yehuda HaNasi (135-217) [See *Beit She'arim* p. 330], founded the Talmudic Academy. In circa 400 AD, the Academy published his compilation of the Mishna and the commentaries (Gemara), which it inspired. This is the "Palestinian Talmud," mistakenly called the "Jerusalem Talmud." The decline of the Tiberias Academy in the fifth century was to the advantage of the Jewish religious authorities in Persia, who took the "Babylonian Talmud" as their authority. At this time Christianity had become a serious rival, with many of its faithful being converts from Judaism. Conflicting relations between Jews and Christians in Palestine worsened when the Persians invaded in 614 AD. Most Christian holy places in the region were vandalised by the Persians, actively aided by the Jews and the Samaritans. The Arab-Muslim conquest reduced these inter-religious

conflicts. Tiberias became the Umayyad capital of the province (*jund*) of al-Urdonn (more or less the same area as the Byzantine province of *Palaestina Secunda*, which covered the Galilee and the north of Transjordan). The Talmudic Academy flourished anew during the Abbassid period and produced the Jewish calendar of holy days and punctuation for the Hebrew version of the Bible, as recognised internationally by world Jewry.

A flourishing city, Tiberias was hard hit by two earthquakes: in 749 AD and in 1033 AD. After 1099, Tancred, Crusader prince of the Galilee, rebuilt Tabariya as the new administrative capital of the Galilee, north of the ancient town (where the old city now stands). In 1187, Saladin freed the city, before achieving a decisive victory over the Crusaders at the Horns of Hittin. The Crusaders regained control here temporarily, between 1240 and 1247, under a treaty signed with Salah Ismail al-Ayyubi. In the sixteenth century, Sultan Suleyman the Magnificent gave the region a new lease of life. Joseph Nassi, a Jewish Ottoman adviser on European affairs and a banker of Portuguese origin, organised the arrival from the Ottoman Empire of Jews who introduced the cultivation of silk here. In the eighteenth century, Daher al-Omar al-Zaydani (1694-1775) made Tiberias the seat of his government of the Galilee. The Ottoman central authorities were alarmed by the extent to which he made the area independent and made several attempts to crush his power by attacking his troops, until he was finally assassinated in 1775. Destroyed yet again by earthquakes in 1837, the town only started to revive at the end of the nineteenth century. In 1945, Tiberias had 11,300 residents: 5,300 Muslims and Christians and 6,000 Jews. As elsewhere in Palestine, relations between the different communities became progressively strained as Jewish residents adhered to the Zionist ideology of establishing a Jewish state in Palestine. Encouraged by the Balfour Declaration in 1917, Jewish immigrants established themselves as an ambitious foreign colonial power, overtly hostile to the original indigenous population. Zionist pressure in the region (buying land from landowners, evicting farmers, founding colonies, or "settlements") led to the active participation of Palestinians of the Tiberias district in the riots of 1920-1921, 1929 and the Palestinian Revolution (or Great Revolt) between 1936 and 1939. By 1945, Zionist organisations had already managed to acquire 38% of the land in the Tiberias district although the Jewish population was only 33% of the district's total population.

En-Nakba

The first clashes in this area took place on March 11, 1948. After a truce of several weeks negotiated by Palestinian leaders and the city's Jewish committee, on April 12, 1948 the Hagana, having evacuated civilians from the Jewish neighbourhood, recommenced its assault on Tiberias. This assault was preceded by the destruction of several nearby villages. For two days, the town was bombarded without the least intervention from British mandatory authorities, who were responsible, until their withdrawal, for the order and safety of the inhabitants of Palestine under the terms of their mandate from the United Nations. On April 16, the commander of the British forces ordered the leader of the Palestinian defence committee to declare a ceasefire and evacuate the population, guaranteeing to make sure the people could leave safely and that he would put the means of transportation at their disposal! With insufficient arms, without support from the British or the Arab world, the Palestinians resigned themselves to accepting the British offer. Tiberias was the first Palestinian town to be occupied and cleansed of its population (April 18, 1948).

"That day, the port was full. Swarms of people waited for the boat to take them to the al-Batiha beach on the eastern side of the lake. I left with my son Daher, my family and other residents, without any news of my husband. In Batiha, the Syrians picked us up and took us to different Syrian villages : Jassem, Nawa, Fiq and more. We lived there under cover of tents for a month. My father, who was an entrepreneur in the shipping business, lost many of his boats. May God punish them for what they did to us! We left our homes and everything that was in them. Even my wedding clothes were left behind in their boxes."

■ Haja Amina Sa'diyeh - Umm Daher

■ The old city

The old city was the heart of the Palestinian town, until 1948. Today, it is a seaside tourist resort. You can easily recognise the old houses, built of basalt, a material found in abundance locally, which gives the town its special charm. As for historical remains of the town - these are extremely modest and simple.

Tiberias

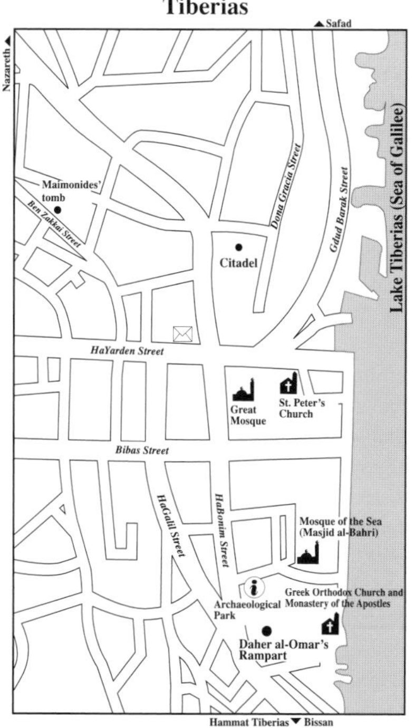

The main ruins found at the entrance to the town are the **eighteenth century ramparts**. Designed with semi-circular towers, they were built *circa* 1738 by Daher al-Omar, governor of the Galilee. The best-preserved part of the wall is at the south end of the old city, where it leads to the **Greek Orthodox Monastery of the Apostles**. The monastery was built in 1863 on ruins of a church dating from the third or fourth century AD. *(It is usually closed to the public but if you ring at the gate, you may be allowed to visit it.)*

Continuing on the promenade, one comes to the **al-Masjid al-Bahri** (Mosque of the Sea). This mosque was built in 1880, but worship has been forbidden here since 1948. To the north is the **Great Mosque** or **al-Omari Mosque**, which also

dates from the renaissance of Tiberias in the eighteenth century and which has also been closed since 1948. This is the best-preserved and most elegant historical and religious edifice in Tiberias, but has never benefited from any specific restoration project. Even worse, it was ransacked by the Israelis in October 2000. Since then, the Israeli authorities (the municipality and Ministry of the Interior, which is responsible for all Islamic property) have done nothing to restore it. Its neighbour, St. Peter's Church *(open Monday-Friday, free entry)*, commemorates the Miracle of

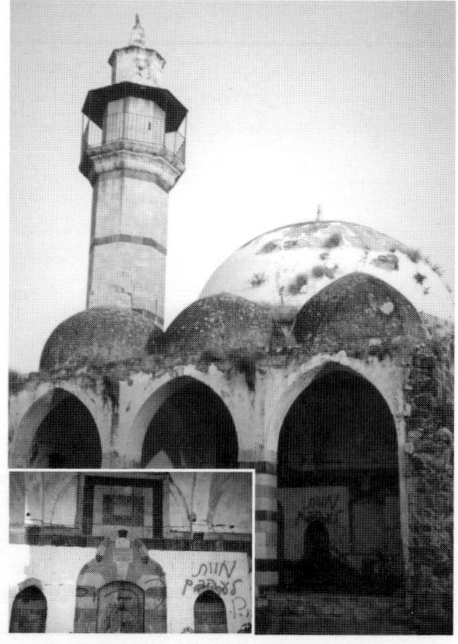

the Fishes (John 21). Built in 1870 on the remains of a Crusader church, an extension was added in the first half of the twentieth century. Two hundred metres farther along on Dona Grazia Street are ruins of a **Crusader Fortress** *(Dona Grazia Street; open every day 10:00-13:00 & 17:00-19:00, NIS 8 entrance fee)*, also known as The Citadel. The three-storey castle constructed in basalt was rebuilt by Daher al-Omar, who made it his headquarters. The Citadel has been recently restored by a local artist, who has opened an art gallery and a restaurant inside it.

❑ Maimonides' Tomb

Ancient cemetery on Yohanan Ben Zakai Street. Fourteen pillars line the path to Maimonides' cenotaph (he died in Cairo), symbolising the 14 books of his commentary on the Talmud, the Mishna Torah.

Maimonides, or Rambam, as he signed his works (an acronym of Rabbi Moshe ben Maimon), was from Cordoba in Spain, but lived most of his life in Cairo. Theologian, philosopher and medical doctor, he visited Tiberias near the end of his life, but died in Cairo. He was particularly interested in the therapeutic effects of its hot springs, rich in sulphur. A prodigious writer, he wrote many philosophical, theological and medical treatises (including one on asthma and another describing the symptoms of illnesses). His greatest work is the Mishna Torah (the first code of talmudic law), which remains an important theological reference for Judaism today. In it, he describes a very specific medical practice permitted by the Torah as he interprets it: "*As for Gentiles* [non-Jews] *with whom we are not at war (...) one must not cause their death, but it is forbidden to save them if they are in danger of dying (...) However, if you are afraid of him* [the Gentile] *or if you suspect he is hostile to you, care for him if he pays you for it, but you are forbidden to care for him if you are not reimbursed.*" Maimonides was Saladin's personal physician.

❑ Hammat Tiberias

Two kilometres south of Tiberias, on Road 90. National Park. Open Sunday-Thursday 8:00-17:00; Friday 8:00-16:00; NIS 10 entrance fee including entry to the museum.

These hot springs, rich in sodium and magnesium, were famous for their healing properties even in ancient times. Their existence was the deciding factor for Herod Antipas when he chose Tiberias as his capital. In the Byzantine and Islamic periods, the spa contributed more than ever to the town's attraction. In the tenth century, Arab historian al-Muqaddassi recorded eight different spas here. What is left of them can be seen in the Hammat Tiberias National Park. The **Great Bathhouse**, built in 1830 under Abdallah Jazzar, is now the **Lehman Museum**, dedicated to the geomorphologic origin of the hot springs and the history of the Tiberias spas. The most impressive archaeological antiquity here is the mosaic floor of a fourth century Byzantine synagogue. On the opposite side of the road, there is a thermal complex: **The Tiberias Hot Springs**, which offers a full range of therapeutic and modern recreational facilities. (*Sunday-Monday and Wednesday 8:00-20:00, Thursday 8:00-11:00, Friday 8:00-onset of Sabbath, Saturday 8:30-20:00*).

Practical Information

As a lakeside resort, Tiberias has a good selection of hotels, restaurants and cafés. A word of warning: the closer one gets to the shore, the more expensive the price. At holiday time, it becomes full, and prices rise. The **Tiberias Tourist Information Office** (*23 HaBanim Street; Sunday-Thursday 8:30-17:00, Friday 8:00-14:00, ☎ 04-672 5666*) is at the entrance of the city in the centre of a small archaeological park.

The city's main attraction remains, above all else, the lake, or Sea of Galilee. Most beaches of the town, and others nearby, are private and provide showers and changing rooms at a fee. To find natural, open beaches, one must leave the city. Roads 90 and 92 follow the coastline round the lake; it is easy to find good corners. A word of warning: most beaches are pebbly.

Lake Tiberias (Sea of Galilee)

Lake Tiberias (*Buhairet Tabariya* in Arabic and the *Kinneret* in Hebrew) is what is left of the Lisan Sea, which was formed at the end of the Tertiary Era after the collapse of the Jordan Valley. The Lisan Sea had stretched from the Hula Valley to the south of the Dead Sea. Like the Dead Sea, Lake Tiberias is below sea level, by more than 212 metres; however, it is much shallower than the Dead Sea: between only 40 to 49 metres deep. It is 21 kms. long and 12 kms. wide and covers an area of 165 sq.kms. (the same area as the Gaza Strip). The lake is associated with many of Jesus' miracles - the feeding of the multitude with five loaves and two fishes [See *Tabgha*, p. 336], His walk on the water (Matthew 14:22-33, Mark 6:45-52, John 6:16-21) - and is the place where the first Christian community sprang up dedicated to His teachings, since Capernaum was His adopted home [See *Capernaum*, p. 336].

■ North of Tiberias

❑ The Horns of Hittin

Eight kilometres west of Tiberias: take Road 77 and then Road 7717. Recommended for hiking.

The two peaks are the remnants of the interior of an ancient, extinct volcano. The large, fertile valleys served from time immemorial as a commercial way for caravans of merchants and, sometimes, armies. In the third century BC, the village there was called Kfar Hattin (the "village of the cereals"). In the fourth century BC, the village became a rabbinical seat; but the Horns of Hittin are best known for the decisive battle fought here between the Arab Muslims of Saladin and the Crusaders in 1187. Saladin's victory marked the prelude to the end of the Crusader occupation of Palestine. Historians of the day describe the enormous investment on both sides: 12,000 archers confronting 1,200 mounted troops and 16,000 foot soldiers.

> "*They* [the Franks] *looked like mountains in movement, like seas overflowing with waves hitting against each other, dragging each other down into seething hollows with their enormous weight, raising the sand from the seafloor. The atmosphere itself was infected and its light faded: the desert was in uproar; the vast space was thrown into confusion, divine order fell from heaven, the dust rose up even to the Plaeiades.*"
>
> ■ Imad al-Din al-Isfahani (1125-1201), Saladin's private secretary

Several well-known Arab personalities lived in the village here: amongst them, the historian al-Ansari ed-Damashqi (in the fourteenth century), who was called the Sheikh of Hittin, and Ali al-Dawadari, a writer, commentator on the Quran and calligrapher, who died in the village in 1302.

Hittin

In 1944, the village had a population of 1,190 residents who essentially lived by cultivating cereals and fruit trees (especially olives). The day after Nazareth was taken, during the night of July 16, 1948, the villagers left Hittin and took refuge in the village Salama. A small group of villagers tried to return at a moment of truce between the Zionists and Arabs, a short time later. They were forced back by Israeli soldiers, who shot at them. Two settlements were quickly established on the village lands: *Arbel* (1949) and *Kfar Zeitim* (1950). The village is today reduced to the minaret of the mosque, the only building left standing. Southwest of the village is the **Nabi Shu'eib *Maqam*** (the biblical Jethro), dedicated to the prophet, who was chief of the Madianites (an Arab tribe) and father-in-law of Moses. This is a sacred site for the Druze community, which makes an annual spring pilgrimage to its shrine here. Before 1948, the Druze came here from the Galilee, from Lebanon (Jabal Druze) and from Syria (the Golan and the Hauran). The site is easily recognisable by the five-coloured Druze flag hoisted over the shrine, representing the five founding fathers. [See *The Druze Doctrine*, p. 399.] Behind the tomb is a stone believed to bear the Prophet Shu'eib's footprint.

❑ The Mount of the Beatitudes

This hill offers one of the most beautiful views of the lake and its surroundings.

The Mount of the Beatitudes is the site traditionally held to be where Jesus preached His famous Sermon on the Mount (Matthew 5-7). Jesus, like the Prophet Mohammed after Him, proclaimed Himself the inheritor of past traditions: "*Think not that I am come to destroy the Law, or the Prophets: I am not come to destroy, but to fulfil.*" (Matthew 5:17) On the hill, the chapel of the Sermon on the Mount, which has an octagonal form, commemorates the eight Beatitudes (Mathew 5: 3-10). It was built in 1937, designed by the Italian architect, Barluzzi.

Tabgha (et-Tabigha)

This is very pleasant for country walks. There is a path along the lake to Capernaum (3 kms). The way up the Mt. of Beatitudes is recommended. Take a picnic. Swimming is possible all along the lake, but watch out for jagged basalt rocks, which can cut.

The name Tabgha is the Arabic version of Heptapegon (in Greek, the 'Seven Springs'). It is famous as the place where Jesus drew huge crowds to listen to His sermons and witness the miracles He wrought there. The **Church of the Multiplication of the Loaves and Fishes** (*open Monday-Saturday 8:30-17:00; Sunday 10:00-17:00, free entry; ☎ 04-672 1061*) commemorates Jesus' first miracle: His feeding of a crowd of 5,000 people with five loaves of barley bread and two fishes (Mark 6:30-44, John 6:1-15, Matthew 14:13-21). The church was built recently, in 1956, but its floors are fifth century mosaics; one theme represented is the famous basket of fishes. Nearer the lake is the **Church of the Primacy of St. Peter** (*open 8:00-12:00, 14:00-17:00*), erected in 1933 where Jesus is supposed to have made His third appearance to His apostles after his Resurrection; the Bible tells us that the apostles had fished all night, catching nothing, when Jesus appeared to them in the morning and filled their net so full that "*...they were not able to draw it for the multitude of fishes*" (John 21:6). According to tradition, Jesus then made Peter head of the Church; but the Apostle Matthew says it was in the region of Caesarea Philippi (Banyas) that Peter's primacy took place (Matthew 16:13-20). Wherever it was carried out, it is on this transmission of power that pontifical sovereignty bases its claim to legitimacy as leader of the Christian world. Constructed in 1933, in basalt, a local material found plentifully in this ancient volcanic region, the church has a most beautiful character and ambience.

The village

In 1944, Tabigha's population numbered 330 residents (310 Muslims and 20 Christians), principally peasant-farmers who supplemented their income by fishing. The houses in the village were located along the edge of the lake and on the road from Tiberias to Safad. As part of "Operation Brush" which was launched to "sweep" the area "clean," Zionist troops of the Palmach were ordered to *"evict the inhabitants and blow up their houses."* After Tiberias fell in mid-April, some villagers fled to Syria. On May 4, 1948, as a column of armoured vehicles drew near to Tabgha, the rest of the inhabitants took refuge in the neighbouring village of al-Samakiya ['Arab al-Samakiya, district of Tiberias, population 380 in 1944]. Later that day, all inhabitants fled in the direction of Syria, under fire from the Hagana. In the next days some tried to return home to recover things left behind, but Zionist army patrols prohibited all such movement. In 1983, the Israeli towns *Korazim* and *Amnon* were established on the village land. The **Korazim National Park** contains the remains of a fourth century synagogue *(open Sunday-Thursday 8:00-17:00, Friday: 8:00-16:00. NIS 10 entry).*
In the vicinity of the church in Tabgha, there are some meagre Barbary fig trees and small heaps of stones surrounded by high grass, indications that show where the village once stood.

Capernaum

Three kms. east of Tabgha. Open 8:30-16:00, NIS 4 entry. Respectful dress required (no shorts or bare arms). The beauty and calm make a leisurely visit well worthwhile.

On the northern shore of Lake Tiberias, Capernaum (Kufr Nahum in Arabic) was a small, busy port in Roman times. Here Christ took refuge after fleeing Nazareth (Matthew 4:13), considering it His "hometown." He started preaching here and recruited His first disciples from local fishermen: Simon (Peter) and his brother Andrew, as well as James and his brother John (Matthew 4:18-22).
As Jesus travelled around preaching in synagogues and performing a number of miracles, He attracted a large group of followers who converted to the new religion. These converts were given the name "Sectarians." In 1894, the Franciscan order bought land on the ruins of the ancient town, considered to be the cradle of the Revelation of Jesus, and undertook its excavation. They uncovered the foundations of houses from the first century AD, a Byzantine synagogue built *circa* 300 AD and an octagonal Byzantine church dating from the fifth century. On top of one of these foundations, they constructed the **Church of the House of St. Peter**.
On the way back to the shore, in the **domain of the Greek Orthodox Church of the Seven Apostles**, one may see what remains of a dock for small boats.

Bissan (*Beth Shean*)

We had forever owned a beautiful orange grove
And a village
And April was sleeping in its shadows
Our village was called Bissan.
Take me back to Bissan, my winter village,
There, where tenderness floods the grey riverbanks,
Take me back to the sleepy afternoons near the door to my house
There, where I opened my arms to embrace
The silence of the earth.

I remember you, Oh Bissan,
You, the playground of my infant childhood
I remember your shy shadows,
And everything there was there
A door, two windows, our house in Bissan.
Take me back, with the goldfinches in the shade
That weep and tell of yearning for home!
Take me back to Bissan ...

Poem by the Rahbani Brothers, sung by Fairouz

99

A large part of the history of Bissan (or Baysan) is in its 80 metre-high 'tel.' A Canaanite city, it was already being referred to in Egyptian records of the nineteenth century BC. Not much was known about it, however, until the Lagides from Egypt (the family of Ptolemy) founded the Greek city of Scythopolis at the foot of the *tel* in the third century BC. It probably received its name because of the Scythian mercenaries who were garrisoned there. Conquered in 107 BC by John Hyrcanus, the inhabitants had no choice but to convert to Judaism (or at least to accept circumcision) or leave. Under Pompey, it became a fully Graeco-Roman city once again and a leading city of the Decapolis. Scythopolis was known throughout the Roman world for its textile production and became the capital of the province of *Palaestina Secunda* (Galilee and north Transjordan) at the end of the fourth century AD. However, in the sixth century the textile industry which had flourished until then went into a decline, and the city lost both its power

and standing. The terrible earthquake in 749 AD devastated most of Scythopolis. In its ruins, only a small town named Bissan, the arabisation of its old Aramaic name, survived. In the twelfth century, it became the fiefdom of Adam of Bethune, lord of the barony of Bissan. Remains of its **fortress** are preserved, as well as a **Mameluke *caravanserai*** (caravan inn) *(on the edge of the main road leading to Tiberias, the Haim Struman Road)*. Bissan remained an agricultural community and a haven for travellers and merchants, who never tired of praising the exceptional beauty of daily life here.

En-Nakba

In 1944, there were approximately 6,000 Muslim and Christian residents of Bissan. After the fall of Tiberias on April 18, 1944, some of the inhabitants fled to Transjordan. On May 11, 1948, Bissan was bombarded by Zionist forces of the Golani Brigade. The villagers surrendered the next day and were taken forcibly to the Jordan crossing, from where they were expelled. On May 28, the Israelis brought their policy of ethnic cleansing to its climax: Muslims and Christians were separated by the Israeli military forces. Muslim families were deported to Transjordan and Christian families (some 300 people), to Nazareth. *"For the first time ... the Beit She'an Valley* [Bissan] *has become a purely Jewish valley."* (David Yizhar, official historian of Golani Brigade)

❑ The Museum and Byzantine Monastery of Our Lady Mary

Industrial zone, past the municipal park. Open Sunday-Thursday 8:30-15:30, Friday 8:30-13:30, entry free.

The museum is small but has an interesting collection of Roman artefacts reflecting daily life. One should ask here for the keys to the building, lodging one's passport as security, in order to visit the remains of the Byzantine monastery *(open Sunday-Friday 8:30-15:00, entry free)*. The monastery was built *circa* 567 AD and contains exquisite mosaic floors, one of which is a beautiful mosaic calendar representing the twelve months of the year, set around the sun and the moon.

❏ The archaeological site

Open Sunday–Thursday 8:00-17:00, Friday 8:00-15:00, NIS 15 entrance fee.

From the *tel*, one has a superb view of the entire ancient city and its surroundings. At its foot is the magnificent **Roman theatre**, the jewel of this site, which was built *circa* 200 BC to accommodate 8,000 spectators. One should also visit the remains of the **Byzantine thermal baths**, which incorporated elements from the upper part of the theatre and the *palaestra* (wrestling school). There is an ancient **Byzantine colonnaded way** where the basalt column bases stand on flagstones arranged in herringbone pattern. There is a pagan temple, too, dedicated to Dionysos or Nysa, his nurse, who - according to the tradition recounted by Pliny the Elder - is buried on the hill here. There is the Nymphaeum; there are ruins of a Roman hippodrome and odeons and there are other remains of what was once a renowned Romano-byzantine city.

■ North and west of Bissan

Kawkab al-Hawa (Star of the Wind) - Belvoir Castle

On Road 717. Open Saturday-Thursday 8:00-16:00, Friday 8:00-15:00, NIS 10 entrance fee. A spectacular panorama.

Several historians have identified this site as that of Yarmuta, mentioned on a thirteenth century BC Egyptian *stele* (an upright slab bearing inscriptions). At this time, there was a band of nomads living in the region, whom the Egyptians called the Habiru. The Knights Templar built Belvoir Castle itself in 1168 AD. They called it "Coquet" or the "Dandy," which became, in Arabic, "Kawkab." On July 1, 1187 AD, 12,000 of Saladin's archers marched on Belvoir; nevertheless, only after four years of repeated siege did they succeed in taking the fortress, in 1191. The Templars surrendered on condition of safe passage to Tyre. The castle was demolished at the beginning of the thirteenth century, in order to preclude it from being eventually retaken; the Crusaders did, however, return to Belvoir in 1241, but under the terms of a treaty, not by force of arms. Afterwards, the villagers settled inside the castle walls. In the nineteenth century, the village spread to the north and west of the castle walls. In 1944, there was a population of 300 souls.

En-Nakba

The village was occupied on May 18, 1948 by Israeli forces, after several days of fighting with Iraqi troops based in that area, who had intervened on May 16. In September 1948, the leader of a kibbutz in the area asked Israeli authorities for permission to demolish the village and three other local Palestinian villages. The reply is unknown, but whatever the response was, the fact is that the village was wiped out and ever since, archaeologists have been busily excavating and restoring the remains of the Crusader castle.

❏ Beit Alpha

Take Road 77, then Road 669. Open Saturday-Thursday 8:00-16:00 (Friday 8:00-15:00), NIS 7 entrance fee.

It was in 1928 that one of the most original mosaics in Palestine was discovered here, and - what is more - it is even signed. *"In honour of the two artists who created this masterpiece, Marianos and his son Hanina,"* reads the Greek inscription at the foot of the pavement which decorated the floor of a sixth century synagogue. Another inscription in Aramaic indicates that the Christian emperor, Justin I (518-527 AD) himself donated to the execution of this outstanding piece of work. The floor is a picture divided into three scenes combining Jewish, Hellenistic and pagan themes and symbols. This mixture reflects the religious syncretism typical of Palestine during the Byzantine epoch. The mosaics are remarkable because they contain human figures, a practice which was forbidden in the days of the Old Testament. There are, however, other exceptions, such as in a synagogue in Doura-Europos (Syria), which also offers such figurative scenes. The floor is nevertheless a puzzling enigma and has been the subject of much controversy.

■ Haifa

I love the countries that I shall love.
I love the women whom I love.
But one single cypress branch in the flaming Carmel
Is worth the hips of all women
And all cities of the world.
I love the seas that I shall love.
I love the fields that I shall love
But a drop of water on the feathers of a lark
Nesting in the stones of Haifa
Is worth all the seas of the world

■ Mahmoud Darwish, *The descent of the Carmel*

The oldest known ancestor of man, *Homo carmeliensis*, one hundred thousand years old, was discovered in this area; its skeleton is exhibited in the Rockefeller Museum in Jerusalem. Archaeological evidence dating from Greek and Roman times indicates that there was a small port here in those days. The name Haifa, however, appears later: it is first mentioned in the Talmud in the third century. Prosperous under the Fatimids, the port was taken in 1099 AD by the Crusaders. The local population put up fierce resistance but was either massacred or sold into slavery. Haifa suffered the same fate as several Palestinian coastal cities (Gaza, Ascalon or *Ashqelon*, and Caesarea, for example), which were all dismantled by the Ayyubids in anticipation of new Crusades. Located on the headland of the Gulf of Acre, Haifa was a haven for smugglers, which earned it the nickname of "Little Malta." In the sixteenth century, the Ottoman authorities decided to build fortifications around the port to protect it from pirates; they encouraged immigration in order to repopulate the coastal area by exempting citizens from paying taxes and by awarding them special privileges. At the end of the eighteenth century, the strongman of the Galilee, Sheikh Daher al-Omar, established the new port city where the old town now stands. Napoleon occupied it briefly, in 1799, while laying siege to Acre. At the end of the nineteenth century, the port of Haifa started to grow steadily. The entire transportation network was modernised. In 1905, Haifa was connected to Damascus by railway line, which went through Bissan. In 1919, the railway line to Cairo was completed. The port was successively enlarged in 1908, 1927 and 1933. At that time, Haifa was even busier than Beirut: it became the principal anchorage for shipping in the western Mediterranean. In 1929, *the Iraq Petroleum Company* inaugurated a pipeline between its oilfields in Kirkuk, Iraq and its refineries in Haifa. Thanks to its activity and its modern installations, Haifa became the leading port of the Mediterranean after Marseilles and the principal industrial city of Palestine, employing some 1,400 workers on a permanent basis. Within half a century, the provincial port had been transformed into a huge industrial maritime city. Both Haifa and Jaffa were the principal entry points to Palestine for Jewish immigration, which was at its most intense during the years 1930-1940. In Haifa, Jewish immigrants settled mainly on the heights of the city, while the Palestinians lived in the old town's neighbourhoods, around the port area and in working class suburbs.

Population of Haifa

Year	Total	Muslim Arabs	Christian Arabs	Jews
1922	24,634	9,377	8,863	6,230
1931	50,483	20,401	13,827	15,923
1938	99,090	*51,090		48,000
1945	138,300	35,940	26,570	75,500
1949	88,893	*3,566		85,327

*Muslim and Christian Palestinians

Social and cultural activities increased, as did political activities. Several newspapers were published in Haifa. Among them was *al-Carmel* (1908), a well-known newspaper that belonged to Najib Nassar, a Christian. From the moment it appeared on the scene in 1908, it warned of the dangers of Zionist immigration and its aims. As Haifa was always an industrial town, it was natural that it was the birthplace and centre of trade union activity in Palestine and assumed union leadership. Its railway workers started the first workers' organisation, or trade union, in 1919. The Organisation of Railway Workers of Haifa was clandestine until the foundation of the Palestinian Workers' Trade Union Movement (1925 -1948). Many newspapers representing groups of workers and farmers were published here: *Haifa* (which went into print in March 1921), *al-Ittihad* (*The Union* - first published in 1924), and *al -'Omal al-Arabi (The Arab Worker* - first published in 1945).

En-Nakba

"It seems to me that we should take advantage of this situation [the fact that many Palestinians were leaving] and drive the rest of the Arab residents out so that they do not surrender to the Hagana, but are forced to flee; for we must create our State (...) I have met with Moshe Carmel's adviser [Carmel was commanding officer of the Carmeli Brigade] *who told me that they have evacuated all residents of the Arab villages of Balad al-Sheikh and al-Yajour near Haifa (...) I was very happy that the senior leadership saw fit to push the policy of alarming the Arabs"* [so they would leave]

■ Yossef Weitz, member of the Bank of Israel and high-ranking Carmeli Brigade officer, April 22-24, 1948

In 1948, the city lay between the Arab neighbourhoods of the lower part of the city (Balad al-Qadim, Wadi Nisnas, Wadi Salib, Halissa, Abbas and others) and the Jewish areas of the upper part of the city *(Hadar HaCarmel).* On the night of April 21 1948, Zionist forces launched an attack on Haifa from their advantageous position on the heights of the city, taking advantage of the extremely ambiguous attitude of the British authorities. While a high proportion of British troops were stationed in Haifa, bound by the United Nations to maintain order until May 15, when Britain's mandate officially ended, they did practically nothing to stop the assault. Instead, they did all they could to help evacuate all the Muslim, Christian and Armenian Palestinians from the city and, indeed, the country. The Zionist military organisations *Hagana* and *Irgun Zvai Leumi* (*Etzel* or, simply, *Irgun*) mobilised some 5,000 soldiers in Haifa against 350 to 500 Palestinian partisans and members of the Arab Liberation Army. Three hundred or so Arab partisans stationed in Tira (7 kilometres from Haifa) were arrested by General Stockholm, commander of the British forces, while attempting to reach Haifa. The Arab neighbourhoods were bombarded, and when a Palestinian committee asked the British forces in Haifa to intervene, they simply refused. The British also refused repeated requests from the committee for ambulances to be sent to help evacuate the wounded. In the general panic, thousands of Palestinians took refuge on the docks, which were under British protection. The British army took them to Acre and from there to Lebanon. In less than a week, the Zionist forces' policy of ethnic cleansing had succeeded. Only 3,500 Palestinians remained of the 61,000 Palestinians who had lived in Haifa the evening before the attack. The Jewish population became the absolute majority (96%). The Hagana immediately created an organisation to confiscate Palestinian property (declaring it "enemy property" of "absentee landlords") and to allocate it to immigrant Jews (whose arrival brought the number of Jewish citizens in Haifa to 140,000 within a few years) or to declare the land and property newly zoned as "frozen" state land. Today, Haifa has 250,000 residents, approximately 10% of whom are Palestinian.

Palestinian property

In light of the systematic looting of Palestinian property (homes, shops, warehouses), the Arab committee lodged a formal complaint with the mayor. The Hagana declared that it was not responsible for Arab property or able to control the situation. So the looting continued until the Jewish municipality named a team responsible for recovering abandoned Palestinian property. On May 6, 1948, the representative of the municipal committee, lawyer Naftali Levitch, announced that all the property recovered by the team had been handed over to the Israeli army !

➡ The old city - an endangered patrimony

The historic heart of Haifa includes several different neighbourhoods that spread around the port as it expanded. The most ancient part, known by the Arabic name: al-Balad ("old city"), dates from the time of Daher al-Omar. Much of this quarter was destroyed in April 1948; some of its most beautiful historic buildings are today threatened with demolition, once again. On July 1, 1948, all Palestinians who had remained in Haifa were issued with an ultimatum: to move to Wadi Nisnas or to Wadi Salib. As a result, many Palestinians had to leave their homes in other neighbourhoods. In their new "ghettos," as they were called, the Palestinians were subjected to curfews, systematic house searches, arbitrary arrests and had to obtain authorisation from the military administration to enter Jewish neighbourhoods or simply to go from one Arab neighbourhood to another. Their "empty" homes were declared "absentee property" and handed to Jewish housing agencies, principally *Shikmona* and *Amidar,* who became responsible for their administration. By November 1948, approximately 6,000 Jewish families had been installed in these Palestinian homes. Later, many of these immigrant Jews settled on Mount Carmel and rented "their" apartments to Palestinians. However, to this day, Jewish housing agencies are the "legal owners." Today, almost 70% of the Palestinians of Haifa

rent their place of residence. Many live in decaying, partly uninhabited buildings.

The municipality and the Jewish housing agencies have done nothing to restore Haifa's urban heritage. Even worse, entire neighbourhoods,

whose architecture surpasses any other in Haifa, are actually being demolished. For the Palestinians, the policy of enclosure and destruction of Arab neighbourhoods and the Arab urban patrimony of Haifa is nothing but a continuation of a long-standing programme to evict Palestinian residents from their city, Haifa. It is yet another example (similar to the case of Palestinian East Jerusalem) of a long-standing Israeli policy of "quiet transfer" or sanitised ethnic cleansing.

Emil Habibi
(1922-1996)

Born in Haifa, Habibi was a presenter on Palestinian radio in Jerusalem in the 1940s. Before Haifa was taken in 1948, he became editor-in-chief of the local Arab daily newspaper, *al-Ittihad (The Union)*. A member of the Palestinian Communist Party from 1940 on, he became a prominent figure in the Israeli Communist party, which he represented in the Knesset from 1953 to 1972. Author of several novels, short stories and plays, his work received the Jerusalem Prize for Art and Literature in 1990.

The Streets of Haifa

As soon as the Zionist troops took Haifa, almost empty of its Arab inhabitants, the new authorities began a process of judaising, known as the "Shikmona Operation" (May-July 1948). Its principal objective was to confiscate property and land and to concentrate the remaining Palestinians in as small an area as possible, where the aim was to remove all Palestinian cultural references. In this context, almost all Arab street names were obliterated; in some cases the names were hebraicised, in other cases names were replaced by those of Zionist heroes or important figures in Judaism. The Palestinian community of Haifa still calls the main streets by their Arabic street names, but many names have been lost to memory.

"Welcome to Medinat Israel," says the soldier (...) "Get down!" says the man accompanying me [the soldier]. *I got down, and he left me with the provisional Arab Commission. Its members began showering him with thanks and then, as soon as his back was turned, overwhelmed me with reproaches: "Does he take the seat of this commission to be a hotel?" cried one. "We shall be obliged to protest to the Minister of Minority Groups!"*
I wanted them to see that I was really Arab, so they would think well of me, and so I expressed my regret that the name of Haifa had been changed to Medinat Israel. They looked at each other, dumbfounded. "And an idiot, to boot!" sighed one.
It was only at the moment of the electoral campaign that I understood why they had judged me to be an idiot: it was then that I realised that the word "medina," in Hebrew, means "state," like "dawla" in Arabic. In fact, they had left Haifa with its ancient name, because it had appeared as such in the Bible.
■ Emil Habibi, *The Pessoptimist: The Secret Life of Saeed*

■ Some historical sites

❑ al-Istiqlal Mosque (Independence Mosque)

Faysal Square. Contact the Committee for the Social Development of Haifa (Hussein Ighbarieh),☎/fax 04-851 4648

The mosque was built by the Islamic Association of Haifa, in 1923. Sheikh Izz ed-Din al-Qassam taught here from 1925 to 1935. It was here, too, that the secret organisation of resistance, instrumental in the Great Revolt of 1936-1939, was formed. The mosque was damaged in 1940 by the Italian naval forces, which bombarded Haifa.

❑ The Nassar Mosque

Closed and partially destroyed. Contact the Committee for the Social Development of Haifa (Hussein Ighbarieh),☎ /fax.04-851 4648 *[See p. 348]*

The Nassar Mosque is the most ancient in Haifa. It was constructed under Daher Omar ez-Zaydani in 1761. Located in Haifa's old *souk* (demolished in 1948), it is usually called the Mosque of the Souk. In 1955, a committee for Islamic affairs, set up

Haifa

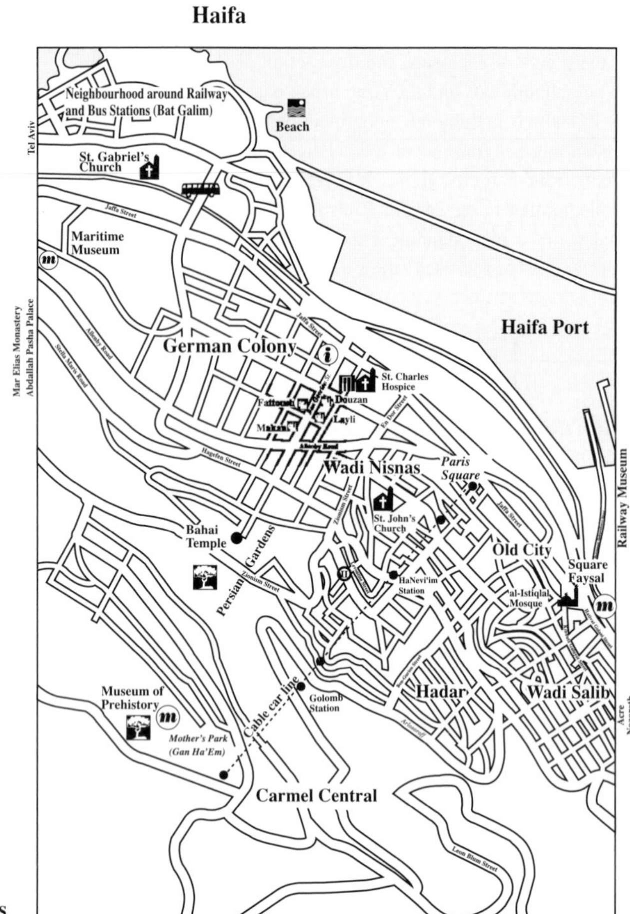

Some names of streets renamed in 1948

Arabic names (pre-1948)	Hebrew names (post-1948)
al-Hamra Square	Paris Square
Abu Bakr Street	Rasiel Street
Abu Hawam Street	HaHalutz Street
Ahmed Shawki Street	Etzion Bloc Street
Bissan Street	Beit Shean Street
al-Bassatine Street	HaGanim Street
al-Hijaz Street	Golani Brigade Street
al-Iraq Street	Kibbutz Galuyot Street
al-Jabal Street	Zionut (Zionism) Street
al-Carmel Street	Ben Gurion Street
al-Moulouk Street	HaAtzmaut (Independence) Street
al-Snober Street	HaNasi (President) Street
Khaled Ibn al-Walid Street	HaRav (Rabbi) Baruch Street
Saladin Street	HaGiborim (Heroes) Street
Siqet al-Hadid Street	Messilat HaBarzel St. (Railway St.)
Tantura Street	En Dor Street
Yafa Street	HaHagana (Defence)/Yafo Street

* In 1948, al-Jabal Street was renamed United Nations Street by the Israeli authorities after the UN recognised the State of Israel. Then, after the UN General Assembly passed Resolution 3379 on November 10, 1975, condemning Zionist ideology as "a form of racism and racial discrimination," the Municipality of Haifa re-altered the name, this time to Zionism Street (*Rehov Hatziyonut*).

up by the Israeli authorities, approved the closing of the mosque and later turned it over to the Municipality of Haifa, even though Israeli law forbids the sale of places of worship. In 1977, a part of the mosque was destroyed.

❑ St. Gabriel's Church

In the neighbourhood of the Bat Galim central train station (formerly Carmel). Closed and in a state of collapse.

Little remains of this neighbourhood except several partially or totally bricked-up houses as well as St. Gabriel's Church, which was built by Gabriel Fuad Saad in 1930 for the Greek Catholic (Melkite) community, but which ceased functioning in 1948. Cleansed of its population, the whole neighbourhood was almost entirely destroyed at that time, and families forced to move to Wadi Nisnas or Wadi Salib. The destruction of the quarter made space for the port's expansion and the construction of the Jewish neighbourhood of *Bat Galim*. The church today is classified as a site "protected" by the Israeli Ministry of Religious Affairs; lacking maintenance, the roof has collapsed.

❑ Haj Abdallah Mosque

In the Halissa neighbourhood. Contact the Committee for the Social Development of Haifa (Hussein Ighbarieh,☎/fax. 04-851 4648 [See p. 348].

Distinguished by its minaret, with three balconies surrounded by a wrought iron trellis, the mosque dates from 1932. It was originally built by Haj Abdallah Abu Younis. There was once a primary school on the first floor. When Haj Abdallah moved to Damascus in 1937, it became Islamic *(waqf)* property, under the jurisdiction of the Supreme Muslim Council of Palestine. The mosque was closed during the Nakba, and Israeli authorities then confiscated it under the terms of the Absentee Property Law. The ground and first floors were rented to private individuals. After a legal process undertaken for years by the Haifa Muslim community, the mosque was handed back to the community in 1981.

❑ Bahai Temple and Gardens

Open every day: gardens 8:00-17:00, temple 9:00-12:00, free entry. Buses 22 or 26. Modest dress mandatory; long sleeves and covered legs - no shorts.

Built on the slopes of Mount Carmel, the Bahai Temple and its terraced gardens are the symbol of Haifa. The planned beauty of its Persian gardens is unique: for Bahai believers, aesthetics and mysticism are inseparable. The temple, which was constructed in 1953, houses the tomb of the prophet recognised by the Bahai, the Bab (Ali Mohammed), executed in Persia in 1850. His body was brought to Palestine in 1909 by Abd al-Baha Abbas, also known as Abbas Effendi, the son and successor of Baha'ullah. The movement claims itself to be an independent religion and to inherit the prophetic messages of Moses, Zarathustra, Buddha, Jesus, Mohammed and Baha'ullah. It is very close, as much in its unitary message and its geographic origins as in its value for floral and aesthetic purity, to the founder of the Mahdi movement, in the fifth century. It has some five million followers, most of whom are drawn from well-to-do Westerners.

❑ Mar Elias, or the Carmelite Monastery

Stella Maris. On the feast day of Saint Elijah (July 20), a huge religious celebration is organised here, which reunites the Catholics of Haifa; on this day, several dozen children take their first Communion.

The original Mar Elias Monastery was built in the twelfth century, by the Carmelites. Its name is derived from the nearby cave, where the Prophet Elijah or Elias was said to have prayed, in the nineteenth century BC. Destroyed in 1291, a new monastery was built in 1769 with the approval of the ruling governor of the Galilee, Daher al-Omar. During the siege of Acre in 1799, the convent (there are two institutions here, a convent for nuns and a monastery for monks) became a temporary hospital for those of Napoleon's troops who were wounded.

❑ Abdallah Pasha's Palace

Stella Maris, opposite the Mar Elias Convent. Closed to the public.

This villa was constructed in 1821 as the summer residence of the former Ottoman governor of Acre, Abdallah Pasha. Before he was deported to Egypt in 1840, Abdallah Pasha entrusted it to the Carmelites, who converted it into a hospice. Under the British Mandate, a lighthouse was built next to the palace, which had only been rented to the monks, and the palace became the general headquarters of the British army. In 1948, the building was requisitioned and confiscated by the Israeli army.

❑ Maqam Nabi Khader or Magharat al-Khader (the Grotto of al-Khader)

Allenby Road. Open Sunday-Thursday 8:00-17:00, Friday 8:00-12:30.

Legend has it that wherever Khader prayed, green grass would spring up to cover the site. This *maqam* is one of several Palestinian holy places dedicated to al-Khader; it is a holy place for both Muslims and Christians. Islamic property (*waqf*) until 1948, the *maqam* was expropriated and converted into a synagogue in honour of the prophet Elijah (1 Kings 18).

■ Museums

❑ National Maritime Museum

198 Allenby Rd. Open Monday, Wednesday and Thursday 10:00-17:00; Tuesday 10:00-14:00 & 17:00-20:00; Friday 10:00-13:00; Saturday 10:00-14:00; closed Sunday. Library open Monday & Wednesday, 8:00-13:00. NIS 22 entry.

The museum has an excellent collection of models of Egyptian, Phoenician and Cypriot galleys as well as more recent vessels from the Venetian, English and French fleets of the seventeenth and nineteenth centuries. Thanks to many shipwrecks near Ashqelon, Ashdod, Atlit, Tantura (*Dor*), and other places along the Levantine coast, the museum also has a very interesting exhibition of cargoes from ancient merchant galleons; there is an equally remarkable collection of navigation instruments, too. Nevertheless, although the museography attains a high standard, the absence of almost 1,400 years of Arab naval history is regrettable: an omission all the more astonishing since the museum exhibits an important collection of Arab navigation devices, amongst them several astrolabes. On the other hand, there are impressive models of the galleons in which Christopher Columbus and his crew sailed to the "New World."

❑ Museum of Prehistory

Carmel, "Gan HaEm" Park, inside the grounds of the zoo. Sunday-Thursday & Saturday 9:00-18:00. Friday 9:00-15:00. NIS 28 for adults, NIS 23 for children.

Founded in 1961, the museum displays finds from sites throughout the Carmel Range, extending south from Haifa along the coast. Dioramas recreate scenes of daily life of Stone Age hunter-gatherers and earliest Neolithic farmers; a model of a Natufian village demonstrates the period's culture, when Early Man (circa 10,000 BC) evolved from hunting to farming activities.

❑ Railway Museum (Hijaz railway station)

Wadi Salib neighbourhood. Golani Brigade Way, near Faysal Square. Open Sunday, Tuesday and Thursday, 9:00-12:00. NIS 13 entrance fee.

The old former Hijaz (Haifa East) railway station now houses a small museum. Most of the building was destroyed when a Zionist group bombed it in 1946. The major railway station in Haifa, it had been inaugurated in 1888, and the line steadily became modernised in the first half of the century, linking Jerusalem, Cairo, Damascus, the Hijaz, Beirut and Istanbul. The railway links played a vital role in Haifa's economic development. In the first half of the twentieth century, Haifa was considered to be the economic capital and also the centre of organised labour of Palestine. Its railway workers, who created the first trade union (The Railway Workers' Organisation - 1919), were the vanguard of the Palestinian trade union movement. Apart from its interest as a site of historical importance, the museum is limited in interest to the various locomotives on display. Two of them date from the first half of the twentieth century. The presence in a carriage that dates from 1893 of equipment flying the Israeli flag is somewhat unusual.

Practical Information

Located on the side of Mount Carmel, the town is composed of various levels. Most of the streets are narrow and twisting and often full of traffic. It is more advisable to explore the city on foot, with public transportation when necessary. The underground **cable car** links the lower town to the top of Mount Carmel. It is the best means of transport *(open Sunday-Thursday 6:30 am-midnight, Friday 6:30 - 15:00, Saturday end of the Sabbath-midnight).* It starts in Wadi Salib (Paris Square or Kikar Paris in Hebrew, Hamra in Arabic) and stops at six stations. *HaNevi'im* is in the Hadar neighbourhood. *Golomb* is a short distance from the Bahai Shrine *(10 minutes walking distance).* The Central Carmel area is the terminus. This is a residential area inhabited by the wealthy of Haifa; it is an area that dominates the rest of the city. There are also open green spaces, museums (for example, the Museum of Prehistory in the grounds of the Zoo, and the Shtekelis Museum), restaurants and chic cafés, which make it a busy, popular place.
There is a **tourist office** *(open Sunday-Thursday 8:00-18:00, Friday 8:00-15:00; ☎ 04-853 5606)* at the foot of the Bahai Gardens at 48, Ben-Gurion Avenue (German Colony). Negligible mention is made there of the city's Arab heritage, but information is available about museums, walks and hotels, etc.

Cafés and restaurants

There are many popular restaurants in the Palestinian quarters of Wadi Nisnas and Wadi Salib. On the menu: traditional *hors d'oeuvre* and grilled meats.
The German Colony, at the foot of the Persian Gardens, is a popular area with a unique ambience and is very much in fashion. On either side of Ben-Gurion Street (formerly al-Carmel Street), Palestinian cafés and restaurants have recently opened in renovated houses of the German Colony. This is a new phenomenon and a reaffirmation of identity. The first café-restaurant to open in the area was ***Fattoush*** (Arab salad is served here on toasted bread sprinkled with olive oil and lemon juice). It has been built in an old workshop. Others have followed its example: ***Layli*** *("The Night"),* ***Makan*** *("A Place"),* and others. They all have open terraces outside on the airy street, which is especially delightful at dusk, when the Bahai Temple and gardens are illuminated. The ***Douzan*** *("Tuning the lute")* is the most original of all. Its antique furniture, art books and photos of pre-1948 Haifa evoke a golden age; a paradise lost which seeks to cling to it ever after.

The German Colony

At the foot of the terraces of the Bahai Temple and gardens, this area has recently been renovated. It was inaugurated in 1869 by the Society of the Knights Templar on the initiative of a German theologian, Christophe Hoffmann (1815-1885). The German community then numbered up to 1,700 members in Palestine, divided between Jerusalem, Jaffa and Haifa.

Accommodation

Bed & Breakfast *(Wadi Nisnas, near St. John's Church. ☎/fax 04-851 4648).* **The Committee for Social Development in Haifa** arranges rooms with local people, an excellent way to learn about the Arab culture of Palestinian Israelis and to experience the old city of Haifa.

St. Charles Hospice *(105 Jaffa Road. ☎ 04-855 3705, fax 04-851 4919. Single: $35; double: $60; triple: $75. Television in a common room. Children's beds available. Curfew at 10 p.m., but this is flexible. A splendid view.)* The hospice is run by Catholic nuns of the Order of the Sisters of the Rosary. The rooms are simple but very comfortable with modern bathrooms. The hospice is a stone's throw from the German Colony and near Wadi Nisnas, an excellent location for tourists. It has its own orange grove, perfectly delightful when the orange blossom is in flower (but off limits in the evening). The rooms on the garden side have a beautiful view of the Bahai Temple and its gardens.

Contacts

Al-Balad (The Land) Cultural Association

29 Ben Yehuda Street.☎*04-8667491/2; jeel_jadeed@yahoo.com; visits to historic Palestinian towns (mixed towns) and to demolished and unrecognised villages.*

This association was created in 1993 to preserve the collective memory of the Palestinians of the 1948 Territories and to promote a national and social awareness among the younger generations. It also encourages a more active and equal participation of women in its project. Amongst its cultural activities, it organises special classes for schoolchildren, literacy courses, literary workshops and discussions on society and history. It publishes a monthly information magazine in Arabic, *Jeel al-Jadeed (The New Generation).*

Iqrit Heritage Association

☎*0544-833228 / 0577-673665 / 04-851-5505, www.iqrit.org. The association organises contacts with Palestinians originally from Iqrit and visits to the demolished village.* [See *Iqrit*, p. 308]

Committee for the Social Development of Haifa

Wadi Nisnas, 21 St. John's Street. ☎*/fax. 04-851 4648. Meetings and guided tours in and around Haifa. Arrangements for lodging with Palestinian families in Haifa* *[See Bed & Breakfast, p. 347].*

The association started in 1986 to fill a need for better public services for Haifa's Palestinian community and to work against discrimination in education, employment, housing, health and so on. Sensitive to Haifa's multicultural identity, the association has also spearheaded information campaigns about the city's endangered cultural heritage.

Ittijah - Union of Associations of the Arab Community

19 Levontin Street. ☎ *04-850 7110, www.ittijah.org; here one may organise tours, visits or contacts with members of Ittijah and other Palestinian Israelis.*

The Arabic word *Ittijah* means "direction." It is also the acronym for the Union of Arab Non-Governmental Organisations - of which there are more than a hundred in the State of Israel. Its objectives: to raise the status of Palestinian Arab citizens of Israel, to co-ordinate the activities and strategies of member associations and to inform the international world about the systematic discrimination with which Palestinian Israeli citizens live. *Ittijah* is a key reference for information and contact with associations working in the areas of education, human rights, child rights, health, economic and social development, unrecognised villages, political prisoners, women's rights, etc.

■ East Haifa

Balad al-Sheikh

7 kms. east of Haifa, in the direction of Nazareth, below the present Jewish town of Nesher, on the outskirts of Haifa.

The village's name refers to a famous Sufi who lived there, Sheikh Abdallah al-Sahli (fifteenth-sixteenth century). In 1944, there were 4,120 villagers; most of the men worked in the refineries and factories of Haifa.

En-Nakba

On December 31, 1947, a unit of the Hagana surrounded Balad al-Sheikh. Sixty Palestinian men, women and children were massacred and many houses damaged (12 were totally demolished). After the killings, some residents evacuated the village and fled. The conquest of Haifa by Zionist forces on April 22, 1948 provoked a further exodus. On April 24, military forces once more surrounded Balad al-Sheikh. The villagers asked for a cease-fire, but the next morning, the town was bombarded. The British authorities negotiated with the Zionist forces, in order to evacuate the remaining population and escort them some of the way to Acre. Several days later, panic gripped Acre, too, provoking a new exodus towards Lebanon.

The town today

In 1949, the settlement of *Tel Chanan* grew up on the ruins of Balad al-Sheikh. Then the Jewish town of *Nesher*, a suburb, gradually covered the Carmel slopes. Only a few Palestinian homes escaped destruction. The **cemetery** remains the main surviving trace of Balad al-Sheikh. Although partially destroyed, its surface area and the remaining tombs suggest the importance of the extinct village. A large elevated bypass road cuts through it: to enter the graveyard, which is frequently desecrated, one must pass under the road. The stonemasonry of the entrance, like the cemetery, has been vandalised. It bears the following inscription: *"All that is on earth will perish: but will abide forever the Face of the Lord, Full of Majesty, Worthy of Veneration."* (Quran, er-Rahman, 55:26). The cemetery is home to a famous **tomb**, that of **Sheikh Izz ed-Din al-Qassam**. After frequent acts of vandalism, a metal grille has now been placed around his tomb, to protect it.

Sheikh Izz ed-Din al-Qassam

Born in Syria (1871-1935), al-Qassam moved to Palestine in 1921 to escape from a French military tribunal. An active, sociable person and a devout Muslim, he opened a school for illiterates and was the president of the Young Men's Muslim Association [See *al-Istiklal Mosque*, p. 343]. At the end of the 1920s, he created an underground resistance movement, mainly recruiting for it among peasants and workers. This movement advocated armed struggle and the development of self-confidence in order to establish its fixed goals: an independent state in the whole of Palestine, the expulsion of the British forces and an end to Zionist immigration. After calling on his followers to revolt, he was martyred on November 21, 1935 in an ambush near Haifa, set up by British soldiers. Most of the Palestinian political organisations, at the time in the hands of the leading families, rejected his approach, at the command of the Mufti of Jerusalem who preferred a politically negotiated solution. However, when the British and the Zionists refused to consider Palestinian proposals, particularly the creation of a Palestinian Legislative Council in which all the religious communities would be represented, there was a national uprising and popular support for armed struggle.

South of Haifa

Atlit

Thirteen kilometres south of Haifa. Neither the ruins of the Crusader castle, nor those of the demolished village are accessible, as this is a military zone.

An ancient Phoenician mercantile city, Atlit counted as one of many centres of trade on the Syro-Palestinian coast. The Templars built a fortress here *circa* 1118 AD and then a castle, the Castle of the Pilgrims. Atlit remained in the hands of the Crusaders until 1291 AD. In 1296, descendants of the 'Uwayrat tribe (a Tartar tribe), and companions in arms of the Mameluke Sultan Baybar, settled in and around Atlit. At the end of the nineteenth century, Atlit was a small hamlet of some 200 inhabitants who lived in the centre of the Crusader fortress. In 1903, Jewish immigrants from various European countries founded a settlement with the same name near the village. In 1939, a second settlement (named *Newe Yam*) was established next to the first. In the 1920s, the Palestinian village of Atlit was a member of a regional co-operative organised to improve the lives of the farmers. In 1938, Atlit numbered 508 residents and the Jewish settlement of *Atlit*, 224 people. But in 1944-45 there was an inversion of the population statistics: the village population fell to only 150 (90 Muslims and 60 Christians) while the Jewish population steadily increased. In the 1930s and 40s, the settlement of *Atlit* was an important clandestine military base, affiliated to the Hagana.

During the First Intifada, the old British detention camp near Atlit (originally used to hold many Palestinian prisoners during the Great Revolt of 1936-39, and then used for illegal Jewish immigrants in the 1940s) became a prison for Palestinians and Lebanese.

Ein Houd

Fifteen kilometres south of Haifa.

Local tradition has it that this village was founded by Hamdan Abu al-Haija', an officer in the army of Saladin. In 1944-45, there were 650 people living in the village. It was famous throughout the region for its honey and its carob trees; the carob tree yields a type of molasses, which is made into popular syrup.

En-Nakba

On two occasions, the village was attacked: on April 11, and then at the end of May, 1948. However, Ein Houd was only actually occupied on July 15 in an operation in which Israeli naval forces also participated. The inhabitants were deported and made transit through several internment camps before their final expulsion to the West Bank and Transjordan. Most of the original inhabitants of Ein Houd now live in the Jenin Refugee Camp or in the region of Irbid (Jordan).

The old village

Ein Houd is one of few Palestinian villages to have escaped demolition in 1948; its population, however, was all forced out. Since 1953, it has been progressively transformed into an artists' colony and its name has been hebraicised into *Ein Hod.* The dozens of artists' studios, galleries and cafes have been installed in the Palestinian homes, which have been redesigned to answer individual needs. The serenity of the landscape and the sea, which surround the village, are amongst its dominant themes. One of the houses is now the **Janco-Dada Museum**, dedicated to Marcel Janco (originally Austrian and founder of the artistic colony here) and to the Dadaist movement. As for the mosque: today it houses a café-restaurant.

Ein Houd al-Jadida

Access to the village: When you leave Ein Houd (the old village), drive straight up until you reach a hairpin bend. There, leave the asphalt road, continuing on a path that will take you to the Carmel National Park. On your right, you will see a cow pasture that belongs to the Jewish neigh-

bourhood of Nir Etzion (a settlement built in 1949 on the village's lands), and shortly after that, on your right, you will see the new village of Ein Houd appear. You are on the right track, but the way is still quite far. Although the way is a little steep at the end, any car can manage the road. In all, one must explore more than 3 kms of the track. Village council, ☎ 04-984 3335 and the home of ***The Association of the 40s****, an association for the recognition of unrecognised villages, ☎ 04-836 2381/2. Guest rooms are available for visitors. Production and sale of honey.*

Ein Houd includes a second village, improvised by the only villagers who were not expelled from the region. Today, there are few more than 250 people living here. In 1948, a small branch of the Abu al-Haija' family fled into the area near their village (now the Carmel Nature Reserve). They then set up a small tent encampment less than one kilometre, as the crow flies, from their home, which they named New Ein Houd *("Ein Houd al-Jadida")*. In the Galilee the village is also known as Kawkab Abu Haija (the Fortress of the Abu al-Haija' family). The Israeli authorities have "tolerated" the village for more than 40 years, while denying it any legal or official existence: it has remained an unrecognised village. As a consequence, its inhabitants have been deprived of all basic public services: water, electricity, roads, etc. The necessary construction material was transported to the village on the backs of donkeys, until the 1980s. In 1987, the village committee started to put pressure on the Israeli authorities to recognise the village and grant it normal rights. The response was immediate: the application of a policy of intimidation. Demolition orders were posted on each "illegal" house (they were all illegal, as the village was unrecognised!); bulldozers and army patrols made frequent forays into the village, creating a constant state of alert. From then on, the urgency felt by the committee was no longer a case of having the village recognised but of succeeding to have the demolition orders frozen and thereby save it from destruction. The village was finally granted official recognition in 1994. However, nothing changed! In 1996, the area of land granted to the village was fixed at 1,7 hectares. After the Israeli government was replaced that same year, this area was cut in half, whilst the Defence Minister expressed his opposition to any road construction. The result was that, by 2002, the only infrastructure to have been undertaken was access to water and the beginnings of a road through the national park (asphalt has been laid down in the steepest parts).

The Association of the 40s

Ein Houd. ☎ 04-836 2381/2; www.assoc40.org. The association organises visits and contacts on the theme of the unrecognised villages.

Created in 1988, the Association of the 40s actively advocates for the recognition of unrecognised villages and the improvement of living conditions in those villages, especially the development of infrastructure and basic services. One of its main projects, underway at present, is the drawing up of a land development zoning plan to propose to the Israeli authorities; this plan takes into account the needs of the Israeli Palestinian population, such as recognition, development project, equipment and so on.

Unrecognised villages

Some 10% of all Palestinian citizens of the State of Israel (about 100,000 people) live in unrecognised villages. [See *Negev*, p. 387.] These villages are not on the map and have no local official representative body or basic facilities: water, sewage systems, health services, electricity, roads, telephones, schools, rubbish collection, etc. One of the Israeli Government's repeated claims to justify its refusal to recognise these villages and so refuse to provide services is the low number of their residents and the extremely high cost of linking them to existing infrastructure. However, the government does officially recognise 85 other localities with fewer than 100 residents: 83 of those recognised villages being exclusively Jewish.

Today, there are 149 unrecognised encampments, villages and urban neighbourhoods (117 in the Negev, 32 in the Galilee and centre of the country), having a population of 70,000 in the South (Negev) and 30,000 in the North (Galilee), central region and mixed villages; in all, a total of 100,000 citizens. Most of these sites have existed since the 1950s. Since the threat of demolition hangs over each new dwelling, which is automatically considered illegal, there is an extremely high density of population. The population of these villages is variable and ranges from between 60 to 6,000 people. As was the case with Ein Houd, some villages have recently received official recognition without any improvement whatsoever to their basic infrastructure.

❑ Carmel Caves *(Nahal Me'arot Reserve)*

Just off Road 4, 3 kilometres south of the Ein Hod junction, one kilometre east of the Old Coastal Highway (Road 4), 20 kms. south of Haifa. Open Saturday-Thursday 8:00-16:00, Friday 8:00-13:00; NIS 13 to visit the caves. After visiting the prehistoric caves, a picnic and a hike in the park are recommended.

The geological formation of these cliffs is over 100 million years old. This beautiful countryside allows one, besides, to discover the natural habitat of Palaeolithic man, who lived here in communities. The **Skhul Cave** *(on the left of the kiosk)* contained 16 skeletons of Cro-Magnon man, who lived from 100,000 to 40,000 BE. This discovery was a landmark in prehistoric research because it proved the existence of *Homo sapiens sapiens* during the same long period as *Homo sapiens neanderthalensis* (now extinct), of whom remains were found in the **Tabun Cave**. Many prehistorians believe that the disappearance of Neanderthal man was due to genetic assimilation. Three other prehistoric caves superseded the Skhul Cave. The **Tabun Cave** (*Tanur* in Hebrew) was inhabited from 200,000 to 40,000 BE. It was probably near the riverbank. There are no signs of life inside the **Gamal Cave**. However, in here one may see a rather mediocre reconstruction of a typical household of a Middle Palaeolithic family (between 100,000 and 40,000 BE). An animated cartoon in the next cave, the **d'al-Wad Cave** (*Nahal* in Hebrew) suggests a better idea of life at this time. With a depth of 70 metres, this cave was inhabited during the Upper Palaeolithic period, between 40,000 and 20,000 years ago, and again during the Natoufian period, between 12,000 and 9,000 years ago. At this time, people started to grow crops. The cave housed a more significant population than previously and this was the period when sedenterisation commenced: the cave dwellers did not simply arrange the interior, but also built circular huts in the protection of the rocky walls. If one passes by the closed site, towards the wadi, one also finds the famous **Kebara Cave** [See *Prehistory*, p. 25].

The findings from these caves are housed in the Rockefeller Museum in East Jerusalem, near the Damascus Gate, and date back 130,000 years. Remains of Neanderthal Man and his palaeolithic tools were found here; also discovered were bones of 60 animal species, including elephant, rhinoceros and a 60,000 year-old donkey.

■ Tantura (Dor)

Two kilometres north of Furaydis ["Paradise"], on the way to Nahsholim-Dor.

The village Tantura is near the remains of the ancient Canaanite port city mentioned in an ancient Egyptian papyrus of the thirteenth century BC by the name Dor (the Canaanite god of the sea). In the eleventh century BC, an Egyptian tale says the Sikils (who were at that time also found in Sicily, which derived its name from them), or Tjekers, a people originally from the Aegean Sea, were to be found here. Like the Philistines, these people were the business and military elite of the city. A feudal city of the Phoenician kingdom of Sidon, and then a city of the first order during the Hellenistic period, Dor declined when Caesarea,

Marlboro

15 kilometres away, became capital of Roman Palestine. Two shipwrecks in the Tantura Lagoon (dating from the fifth and ninth centuries BC) prove the perennial importance of its port in the Byzantine and then Abbassid periods. The port was conquered by the Crusaders in the twelfth century and renamed Merle. Yet another conquest and more catastrophes came in August, 1799 AD, when Napoleon's retreating army laid waste to the village. Nevertheless, Tantura recovered and by 1944 had a population of 1,500 people. The village economy depended on agriculture and fishing, which were prosperous branches of the economy in the 1930s and 40s.

The Massacre of Tantura

At the beginning of the month of May, 1948, the villagers of Tantura were one of the last groups of people on the Palestinian coast between Haifa and Jaffa not to have been driven out. A Zionist committee of Hagana officers and their Arab Affairs' administrators took the decision on May 9, 1948 *"..to expel or to subdue"* the people of Tantura. The decision was acted upon during the night of May 22. Captured during the assault, the village fell after a battle lasting several hours. In the morning, more than 200 unarmed villagers, mostly young men aged 13 to 30, were executed after they had surrendered to the Hagana forces. An Israeli officer investigating *"the irregularities committed at Tantura"* learned that *"an overwhelming enthusiasm at the victorious outcome"* of the operation had led to some damage inflicted *"directly after our people entered the place* [the village]." After the massacre, the women, infants, children and old people were deported to the outskirts of Furaydis before being moved towards Tulkarem. The men were deported to prisoners' camps (Ijlil, Umm Khalil, Sarafand el'Amar and others) and then transferred to the West Bank between a year to eighteen months later. Most refugees from Tantura finally sought asylum in Syria.

"I was then 21. They took a group of ten men and lined them up against the wall of the cemetery and shot them. Then they took another group and shot them so they fell on the first bodies and continued like that. (...) I was waiting my turn to be shot in cold blood when I saw the men facing me lower their arms." The massacre, continued Fawzi Tanji, stopped after the intervention of the leader of the Jewish settlement of Zichron Yaacov.

Fawzi Mahmoud Ahmed Tanji, refugee in the town of Tulkarem

"From the moment the village Kufr Lam [a demolished village in the Haifa district, population 340 in 1944] *was captured, after the fall of Haifa, we feared an attack on Tantura. The night of the assault, men were guarding several entrances to the village, but they were poorly armed. (...) Then, at dawn, right in front of our eyes, they took a first group of men and executed them, all except one to whom they said, 'Take a good look, and tell everybody what you have seen.'*
They even looked for money and gold inside our children's nappies, and when a little girl fumbled while trying to take an earring out of her ear, a woman soldier tore it out. (...)"

Amina al-Masri (Umm Mustafa), Tamam al-Masri (Umm Suleyman), born respectively in 1925 and 1927, refugees in Qabun, a neighbourhood of Damascus

" Several days later, they transferred us to an Arab village that had been cleansed of its population [Umm Khalil, village demolished in the district of Tulkarem, a population of 970 in 1944] *and surrounded by barbed wire! From there, we were taken to a big camp for prisoners in the village of Ijlil* [Ijlil al-Qibliya, a demolished village in the district of Jaffa; 470 Palestinian villagers in 1944] *near Jaffa. We were given 150 grams of bread and a ladleful of lentils or chickpeas every day. They put us to work. If you were between 15 and 17 years old, you had to work as a cleaner or work in the camp workshops; as for the older ones, they had to carry construction materials to build fortifications and dig trenches to bury the dead of the armed Arabs. We were the ones who buried the martyrs of the Iraqi army in Qaqun village* [a demolished village in the district of Tulkarem, population of 1,970 villagers in 1944] *after it was taken by the Israelis [June 5, 1948]. Later, I was transferred with others from Tantura to the prison camp at Sarafand* [Sarafand al-'Amar, a demolished village in the district of Ramle, 1,950 residents in 1944]. *This was after some 25 villagers from Tantura escaped from the camp at Ijlil. I spent a whole year in Sarafand."*

Salim Zeidan Omar al-Sarafandi, born in 1932, refugee in Yarmouk camp, Syria

➡ Tantura today

Immediately after the massacre and the deportation of the people of Tantura, in May 1948, two settlements were founded on the site of Tantura: the first was *Kibbutz Nahsholim* (established by Jews from the United States and Poland, in June 1948); the second *Moshav Dor* (established by Greek Jews in 1949). *Dor* is known today for the quality of its beach and the beauty of its lagoon, the Tantura Lagoon. There are several Palestinian houses still standing, but as for the burial ground... it has been buried somewhere under the huge parking lot which serves the beach.

■ The Archaeological Park

If one follows the beach to its northern end, one comes across the site of the antique seafaring port of Dor (Tel Dor). The history of the site and its remains are well documented: archaeological excavations are undertaken here each summer. On the other hand, it is not easy to decipher the ruins. However, one may find docks which date back to the eleventh century BC, to the south of the *tel*, as well as ruins of a fourth century Byzantine church. At the north of the *tel*, archaeologists have found a workshop, which manufactured purple dye. Its manufacture was a speciality of the Phoenicians, who reigned over the entire Palestinian coast (except for Gaza) during most of the first millennium BC. The Greek word "phoenix," used for the first time in Homer's *Iliad* to describe this Canaanite people who lived on the Levantine coast, in fact means "purple of the sea." This purple dye, a precious pigment, was extracted from a marine shellfish, the *murex*. Religious and political officials sported the colour as the symbol of their power; the purple robes of Roman senators were equally famous.

To complete one's tour of the site, one should go to the **Marine Archaeology Museum** *(open Sunday-Thursday 8:30-14:00,Friday 8:30-13:00, Saturday 10:00-15:00; NIS 10 entrance fee)*, in *Kibbutz Nahsholim*. Moreover, in order to learn something about the marine archaeology of the site, one should really start at the museum, housed in an old glass factory once belonging to Baron de Rothschild. There are now photographs of the different archaeological digs on display, particularly the underwater excavations, as well as artefacts found in the port or exposed or washed up along the shore.

> "There is no city more beautiful, no city better stocked with all wares"
>
> ■ al-Muqaddassi
> Tenth century

■ Caesarea (Qissarya)

In the fourth century BC, a Phoenician trade harbour was recorded here, later called Strato's Tower. Strato, its founder, was the king, or at least a governor, of Sidon. Masters of the sea, many royal Phoenicians shared the coastal ports as far as Ascalon and even beyond, into the Sinai Peninsula. In 96 BC, Alexander Yannai occupied the city and forced the population either to convert or go into exile. Between 22 and 10 BC, Herod the Great founded the city of Maritime Caesarea and the port of Sebastos ('Augustus' in the Greek) here, in honour of the Roman emperor, Augustus Caesar. The fastest ships could connect Caesarea within 10 days with Rome. With his grandiose building project for the city and the huge scope of its harbour, Herod surely dreamed of surpassing the greatest ports of the eastern Mediterranean: Alexandria and Piraeus (the port of Athens). As the commercial and cultural capital of the area, Caesarea became the seat of the Roman governor, shortly after the death of King Herod. Life in Caesarea attracted indebted farmers from the hinterland and mountains, or even just citizens who wanted to improve their social standing, but also the Jewish, Samaritan and pagan elites of the province. Little by little, the city became a centre of resistance against the Roman Empire. There was a widespread revolt in 66 AD, sparked by a Roman provocation in one of the city's synagogues. In the third century, with a population more than 50,000 strong, Caesarea became an important centre of Christianity. Born in Caesarea in 260 AD, Eusebius of Caesarea became the first bishop; he became notably famous as the first historian of the churches and the first person to compile a geography of Biblical places.

Caesarea, the Byzantine administrative and political seat, was the last city of Palestine to fall to the Arab Muslims in 640 AD. First Lydd (or 'Lydda' as it was known in ancient times), then Ramle, took over the city's functions as provincial capital. Nevertheless, the city remained the principal Palestinian port. Its flourishing commerce was accompanied by a culture of arts and humanities, making it the cultural centre of Palestine as well. In the eighth century, Abdel Hamid al-Khatib, a native son, was considered one of the great Arab rhetoricians, thus perpetuating the city's proud literary tradition.

Conquered by King Baldwin in the twelfth century, Caesarea became a leading Crusader port. Sturdily fortified, it remained a military outpost until the Mameluke Sultan Baybar took it and dismantled it to prevent its capture by future Crusades. After a lengthy period of abandon, Caesarea was resettled in 1878 by Bosnian Muslims fleeing the Austrian occupation. In 1945, the population of Caesarea had reached 960 people - 930 Muslims and 30 Christians, most of whom were rural peasants.

En-Nakba

Caesarea was the first village in Palestine where the deportation of the population was planned and put into effect. Occupied on February 15, 1948 by the Hagana, Caesarea was destroyed five days later; the British mandatory forces did nothing to protect the villagers or repatriate or re-establish them on their lands. The devastation of Caesarea inaugurated the process of systematic ethnic cleansing of the Palestinian population elsewhere all along the coast and then on the land in the interior; the customary Zionist tactic was to attack and drive the inhabitants out during the assault. To this end, conquered villages and towns were never completely surrounded: there would always be an open "door" a passage to the east, to the sea or to the north - which would remain open, a way out which people would inevitably choose. Of 64 villages on the way connecting Haifa with Jaffa, only two villages were spared, after pressure by the settlers of the region, who employed some of the men from these villages, to whom they paid low wages. These villages were Jisr ez-Zarqa *(on the coast, 35 kilometres south of Haifa)* and Furaydis *(at the foot of Mount Carmel, 28 kilometres south of Haifa).*

Archaeological Site at Caesarea

Two entries: one near the Roman theatre, the other 500 metres to the north through the eastern gate of the Crusader city. Open Saturday-Thursday 8:00-17:00 (October-March, 16:00), Friday 8:00-15:00; entrance fee NIS 22; maps of the site available. Do not hesitate to explore beyond the marked limits to discover the boundaries of the Roman and Byzantine cities, their remains and the aqueducts.

The only remains of **the village**, located inside the ancient Crusader fortifications, are the mosque

and several houses, which have been transformed into a restaurant and its supporting infrastructure. The mosque has been converted into a café-restaurant *(Charlie's Bar).*

In the Crusader City, the entire city rampart has been excavated. This structure dates from the reconstruction of the city's defences, undertaken by Louis IX in 1251-52 AD. The main gate to the east is one of the best-preserved features of the mediaeval city, whose population has been estimated at circa 12,000 people. Recent restoration work has enabled the reinforcing or rebuilding of the vaulted rooms and the arches built on to the ramparts. To the south of the Crusader city are the ruins of St. Paul's Cathedral, itself built over both the Roman podium and a mosque dating from the beginning of the Islamic period.

The ancient city in Byzantine days extended over a surface ten times the size of the Crusader city, and it may have had as many as 100,000 inhabitants. Herod was the first to build public monuments here. The temple to Augustus has disappeared, replaced by successive places of worship, but remains of the podium on which it rested may still be discerned inside the fortifications of the

Crusader city. Herod also built a hippodrome, with a capacity for some 15,000 spectators: it may still be seen between the Crusader city and the Roman amphitheatre.

South of the archaeological site, the **theatre** is the best-preserved Roman monument. A dedication plaque found there enables the theatre to be attributed to Pontius Pilate, whose existence was otherwise only known from stories in the New Testament. The inscription states: *"Pontius Pilate, Prefect of Judaea, dedicated a temple in honour of Tiberius to the people of Caesarea."* The amphitheatre, which overlooks the sea, seats over 5,000 spectators.

Outside the Park

The Roman and Byzantine cities extend much farther than the present boundaries of the archaeological site. One finds relics to be explored to the east and to the north of the park, too. Near the entrance to the Crusader city and near the cafeteria are the remains of a Byzantine way. Farther east, a hippodrome erected under the Emperor Hadrian is visible in the middle of a large ploughed field. What remains of the *spina* (the structure that divided the racetrack in two) reveals where it once stood. Along the northern beach, two aqueducts run along the length of the shoreline.

Swimming

One may swim near the Roman theatre. There is also a small private beach near the Crusader citadel, but access is expensive. A third beach to the north of the site is to be found, near the aqueducts. It is huge and sandy and runs along the Coastal Road for many kilometres.

The Triangle

The region named the Triangle, or Small Triangle, contains more than 17 Arab localities, situated along the Green Line. Before 1948, most fell under the jurisdiction of the districts of Jenin, Tulkarem or Ramle. Today, each has a population of between 10,000 to 20,000 people, while some have over 30,000 (Umm al-Fahm, Taybeh). Before 1948, they were agricultural towns or villages, but now they are densely populated, semi-urban areas, among the poorest in the country (in Tira, a town of more than 20,000, 60% of the children live below the poverty line). The policy of land confiscation - 75% of the land belonging to these people has been appropriated by the Israeli authorities - forced Palestinian farmers living here in the 1950s to take up work in the factories of the industrial zones of the new Jewish areas. There is no vacant land around the Arab villages and towns, which thereby prevents economic growth and poses serious housing problems. In fact, the population density is very heavy, and some places resemble Palestinian refugee camps. While a great deal of the land was confiscated in the 50s, the process of expropriation has never stopped. The judaisation of the Triangle has even stepped up its pace since the period of the Oslo "Peace" Accords. Its most "efficient" instrument is the new highway system being built at this moment.

Territory belonging to local Arab Palestinian localities in the Triangle before and after the creation of the State of Israel

Arab villages	Area in 1947*	Area in 1990*
Jaljulia	2,700	450
Kufr Qassem	1,080	810
Taibeh	4,050	1,170
Tira	5,400	882
Umm al-Fahm	11,250	2,250

* Area in hectares

The Trans-Israel Highway Project (Highway No. 6)

This highway, still under construction, is designed to link the Jewish regions of Nahariya (north of Acre) to *Tlallim* (south of Beersheba). A second branch starting at *Yoqne'am Illit* (southeast of Haifa) will hook up with the system north of Lake Tiberias. Officially, this road system is intended to lighten the traffic load of the coastal roads (A2 and A4) and to encourage urban development along the eastern border with Jordan and in the Galilee.

There are, however, other concerns involved, besides traffic density. This system is in reality an excellent way to continue the judaisation of the Galilee and the Triangle *[See The Koenig Memorandum, p. 292]*, as well as to implement the policy of unifying Israeli territory (inside the 1949 armistice line - the "Green Line") and the Occupied Palestinian Territories ("OPT"), occupied in 1967. The Palestinian localities of the Triangle inside the Green Line are already terribly cramped in terms of open space. This system robs them of every remaining piece of land. In fact, these regions have been totally overlooked by the Israeli urban development master plan for the area, which foresees considerable development of Jewish areas on the edge of the West Bank as well as the creation of new Jewish towns. In Wadi'Ara (where Umm al-Fahm is located), a new Jewish town called *Iron*, which will have 100,000 inhabitants, is planned. The small Jewish towns of *Katzir* and *Harish* will absorb 15,000 new residents; more than 50,000 are planned for *Kokhav Ya'ir, Tzur Yigal* and *Kfar Yona;* the projected population for *Modi'in* is 250,000 (in only its intermediate stage). Each Jewish locality has a good reserve of land available for absorbing new Israeli residents and for extending industrial development, while taking advantage of the new highway system. Officially considered the new "spine" of the country, the highway moves the country's centre of gravity eastward along and over the Green Line. In fact, this urban development plan simply completes the "Seven Star Plan" [See p. 71]. The highway system plan, adopted by the Rabin government in 1994, also foresees the economic "integration" of the West Bank. Highway No. 6 integrates the settlements of the Occupied Territories with mainstream Israel on the other side of the Green Line. The Trans-Israel Highway Project is the core link in a road network that redefines the settler communities of the entire West Bank as part of Israel proper. Needless to say, those settler-only by-pass roads are inaccessible to Palestinians of the West Bank, unless they receive special travel permits, which are extremely difficult to obtain. Strategically placed military checkpoints monitor vehicles on all such roads.

Oh Kufr Qassem
From down in the victims' coffins
A flag will go up
Halt! Stop, it will say
Make them stop.
No, no, you will be humiliated no longer!
The debt of torments, you have paid it in full!
- The shadows have fallen -
Oh Kufr Qassem! We shall not sleep as long as in you
Reign the graveyard and night,
The indisputable testament of blood!
This testament of blood is not for sale.
This testament of blood begs us to resist
And resist we will.

■ Tawfiq Zayyad

The massacre of Kufr Qassem

Kufr Qassem

On Road No. 5, 30 kilometres northeast of Jaffa/Tel Aviv. Every year on October 29, the People's Committee of Kufr Qassem (☎ 03-937 0110) organises a day of commemoration. This contact is also interesting for anyone wanting to know more about the town's contemporary situation and the life of its inhabitants.

On October 29, 1956, Israeli military forces declared a curfew on the villages in the south of the Triangle, on the first day of the tripartite attack carried out by Britain, France and Israel on the Suez Canal, Egypt. The curfew was declared without warning at the end of the afternoon when many farmers were still in their fields and therefore completely ignorant of it. On their way home to Kufr Qassem after work, the villagers met Israeli military forces, who executed in cold blood 49 Palestinian men, women, children and elderly people. The State of Israel condemned the massacre as "an isolated incident." Yizhar Shedmi, the officer who ordered his men to fire on any person not respecting the curfew and not to take any prisoners, was condemned with his soldiers to long prison terms. However, the sentences were shortened: the last soldier left prison in 1960 (four years after the massacre). Like his superior officer Yizhar Shedmi, he had to pay one lire (a merely symbolic fine) for his release!

The Central Plains

■ Jaffa (Yaffa)

Jaffa

I remember a day when I was in Jaffa
(chorus)
Tell us, tell us about Jaffa
My sail was in the port of Jaffa,
Oh, the days of fishing in Jaffa
The sea called to us and, at dusk, we prepared to row out,
We see ghosts now, in the present day
Nostalgia took us back to Jaffa
We took to the sea at dawn, covered with wounds,
Like a drop of water, we lost our way
And the coastline disappeared
Was the fishing good?
We filled our holds to overflowing
Playing with the water from morning to evening, but at night …
But at night?
At night, the wind blew,
Oh mad tempest, you who united the water and sky,
The sea in a fury, the night, like packs of sea wolves
We lowered the sails and took up the oars,
Death surrounded us but we resisted the raging waves and
We subdued the angry sea,
Hands squeezed tight, the rowboat held fast,
That day, they said that we were lost, that we were dead in cold eternity,
But we came back in the morning like the giant,
And we returned to the port of Jaffa.
How beautiful is the return to Jaffa
We filled the shore with shellfish
Oh beautiful days of Jaffa
To the wild howling wind, we replied
We shall return to Jaffa,
And today, to the wild howling wind
We shall return to Jaffa…
We shall return to Jaffa…

■ poem by the Rahbani Brothers, sung by Fairouz

The first historical reference made to Jaffa was recorded when Pharaoh Thutmose III conquered it in 1468 BC; the city at that time was named Yapu. The port seems to have stayed under Egyptian control until the Philistines settled there circa 1200 BC. The Philistines originally came from islands in the Aegean Sea and settled in the central Palestinian port cities, which they already knew from longstanding commercial and cultural exchanges. Conquered and reconquered in the first millennium BC, Jaffa remained a bridge between the Mediterranean and the Near East for whoever controlled it. At the end of the eighth century, this is how the Assyrian victory of Sennacherib was described: "*… as my campaign continued,* [Jaffa], *Bene-Berak, Asor, cities belonging to Sidqia* [king of the kingdom of Ascalon], which had taken a while to bend low before me; I took them and all their riches." (Sennacherib's Prism, p. 701).

Later, it was called in the Bible by its Hebrew name Yafo (the official name of the town since its conquest in 1948). Under Alexander the Great (ca. 332 BC), it was named Joppa. It became a Greek (Hellenistic) colony, a city built on the model of the Greek city-state and strongly imbued with Greek culture. During the following centuries, it was either governed by local rulers (Maccabeans or Hasmoneans) or by regional governors (Ptolemites and Seleucids). Once the Romans had conquered the city in 63 BC, it gained a comparative amount of independence under Roman domination. As he had with Jericho, Marc Antony offered Jaffa in "tribute" to Cleopatra. When she died (30 BC), the city became part of the kingdom of Herod. As Herod put all his energy into the construction of Caesarea, Jaffa remained a second-class port, although it was an active one. During the Umayyad period and then under the Abbassid rulers, Jaffa became the port of Ramle, capital of the province of Palestine (Jund Falistine). In the twelfth century, the Crusaders awarded Jaffa official status as the port of Jerusalem; being the port nearest to Jerusalem, Jaffa has thus always received visitors and pilgrims of all religions. In 1799 AD, it was the scene of a terrible massacre carried out by Napoleon's troops.

In the nineteenth century, the city experienced an awakening and unprecedented growth. Under Egyptian rule, from *circa* 1830-1840 AD, an economic revival took place in trade, and in development of agriculture on Jaffa's fertile lands, while Jaffa's population also developed. Since Jaffa was situated at the head of the quickest route to Jerusalem from the Mediterranean coast, it also benefited from a growing interest in Jerusalem on the part of foreign diplomatic authorities and also from the new waves of pilgrims travelling to Jerusalem. Several religious orders took up residence there in order to look after the pilgrims once they arrived in Palestine. In 1882, Jaffa had a population of 25,000 and was rapidly becoming an extremely dynamic urban, industrial, cultural and political centre. Its growth continued under the British Mandate. However, the separate development of the young settlement of Tel Aviv cast an ominous shadow. Jaffa, one of the main Palestinian political centres, mounted strong resistance to the British policy of encouraging Jewish immigration. In Jaffa on May 8, 1936, a general strike was called for, as well as a boycott of British and Zionist institutions and products. In June 1936, when British repression came to a climax, a section of the old working-class neighbourhoods of Jaffa, near the port and a bastion of Palestinian resistance, was destroyed by the British.

Shortly before the Zionist forces captured Jaffa in 1948, its population (Muslim and Christian) numbered nearly 70,000. Following the United Nations partition plan of 1947, Jaffa was made part of an Arab enclave within the Jewish state, with borders set by the UN. Only in the wake of events of May 1948 and the war that followed did the area partitioned to Israel undergo considerable expansion, adding, amongst other areas, the Western Galilee (including Acre), the Negev and the Arava. And Jaffa.

En-Nakba

As soon as the UN partition plan was announced on November 29, 1947, Zionist terror attacks began. Among others, one took place against the palace *(seraglio)* of Jaffa on January 4, 1948, in which 26 Palestinians were killed. On April 22, the day Haifa was attacked, armed forces stationed in Tel Aviv launched an operation called "Hametz," or "yeast" in Hebrew, against the villages around Jaffa. The operation started on the first day of the Jewish Passover ("Pesach"), after a month of purification, at which time Jewish believers rigorously clean their homes of all traces of yeast, considered during this period to be impure; the scarcely veiled allusion to "cleaning" Jaffa of its Arabs is obvious. Even though the Hagana was planning to lay siege to Jaffa, the Irgun group took the initiative of carrying out a pre-emptive strike. Indiscriminate bombing followed, which speeded the mass exodus of the population. The neighbourhood of al-Manshiya was the first to fall to the Zionists; its conquest was followed by systematic looting of all belongings that had been left behind. The Palestinian commander of the resistance in Jaffa, Michel al-'Issa, was unable to hold out, so he used the British authorities to communicate his agreement to the Zionists for Jaffa to be an "open city." The Zionists, however, refused to let the British negotiate the Palestinian surrender of the city. On May 13, 1948, the surrender was signed by the Palestinian national committee and witnessed by leaders of the Hagana. The next day, the British Mandate in Palestine ended, as the Governor and the final contingent of British soldiers left. The British Governor's final official act, as stipulated by the terms of the UN partition plan, was to hand the keys of the public buildings to the Palestinian National Committee. The city was in the hands of the Hagana, while the 4,000 or so Palestinians who had escaped were grouped together in the districts of Old Jaffa and al-Ajami, which were declared "closed military zones."

The night that the United Nations published their Partition Plan [Resolution 181], *there were rifles fired in the air and demonstrations all over Jaffa. From that moment on, everything changed. I was 10 years old, with four sisters and one brother. My parents and the rest of my family decided to leave the district where we lived, al-Manshiya, which was very near Tel Aviv, and which stood on the front line. We went to live in the al-Inshireh Hotel, in the centre of the city, and we stayed there for four months until the fighting worsened in April. Jewish families which found themselves on the front line also moved out. Both sides immediately took up positions in these deserted neighbourhoods. Between the night we left al-Manshiya and the moment the fighting started again, Jaffa had become a ghost city. (...) When the Zionists renewed their assault on Jaffa, they surrounded it on three sides, leaving the fourth open; it was the side facing the port ..."*

■ Abdel Khader Yassin

■ Jaffa from 1948 onwards, until today

Jaffa today has 35,000 residents, including 20,000 Palestinians, who represent 57% of the population of Jaffa. However, as a percentage of the population of the entire Tel Aviv-Jaffa municipality, they constitute no more than 3.7%.

In mid-May 1948, the Palestinian population of Jaffa had been depleted to less than 4,000 individuals. The towns and villages in the Jaffa area had been completely cleansed of their inhabitants. There was no survivor who had not lost almost all his relatives as refugees in the Gaza Strip, Lebanon or elsewhere. Wearing haggard faces, Palestinian survivors were forced to stay inside certain areas and were subjected to many forms of harassment, whilst each empty house was looted by soldiers and by new Jewish immigrants who settled in the city. Other, still inhabited houses were requisitioned by the army, then declared "absentee property." In fact, today only 36% of the Palestinians living in Jaffa own their property. The others rent their apartments or shops from the custodian bodies established by the Absentee Property Law: *Amidar* and *Halamish*. One of the most important property owners in Jaffa is the Israeli Ministry of Defence. On April 24, 1950, Jaffa was integrated into the Municipality of Tel Aviv under the name Tel Aviv-Yafo.

During the 1960s, the municipality set up a vast construction project along the coast to the south of Jaffa, in the neighbourhoods of Ajami and Jabalya, where most of Jaffa's Palestinians lived. Over half this area, which had been spared the first wave of destruction, was demolished between 1957 and 1997, most of the time supposedly because it was collapsing and therefore a public danger. It had been deliberate policy over the years to allow the area to fall into ruin, by forbidding home improvement and boarding up absent refugees homes. Prices of the land soared

due to over-demand, so that the original inhabitants could not afford to buy property, suffering also as they did a double discrimination: both class and ethnic discrimination. Today, overpopulation affects 17% of Jaffa's Palestinian families as against 2% of its Jewish families, even though the average Palestinian family in Jaffa has no more than four members. The Palestinian community also views plans to develop luxurious residences with apprehension, not only because they do not faithfully reflect the Arab character of Jaffa, but also because Palestinian residents may be seen as being of a lower class and an undesirable community, thereby jeopardising their presence.

▪ Old Jaffa (Yaffa al-Qadima)

The entry to the Old City is marked by several monuments: one of the most striking is at **clock tower square**, formerly Midan al-Shouhada - Martyrs' Square. The **belfry** was built in 1906 in honour of the 25th year of the reign of Sultan Abdel Hamid II. It was renovated in 1965 in a style reminiscent of Russian Orthodox bell towers. Until 1874, this square was located inside the main entrance gate to the city; however, when the ramparts of Jaffa were destroyed, the square remained its business and administrative heart. One of its pre-eminent buildings is the **Great Mosque** or **al-Mahmoudiya Mosque**. It was built *circa* 1814 AD under Governor Mohammed Agha, nicknamed Abu Nabout ("Father Cudgel").

Until 1948, the law courts and the main Islamic administrative *(Wakf)* office were located here. Next to the building was the former **Ottoman Kishleh**, which served as the police station and its prison. In 1948, the Israeli police occupied the premises.

Nearby (slightly to the south-east) is the present-day **flea market**, a huge area dealing in second-hand goods, which is located in the old **vegetable market** and in the **al-Salahi market**. This is one of Jaffa's oldest neighbourhoods. At the end of *Beit Eshel Street* (formerly Siksek Street) is the former **Siksek Mosque**, now transformed into a plastics factory. Jaffa Palestinians have made numerous overtures to the Israeli authorities in order to secure the return of the mosque to the jurisdiction of the Muslim community and to have it restored to its original use. To this day, those demands have been made in vain.

From the top of the hill, Old Jaffa appears to contain large areas of open space. However, until 1936, this empty space was the most densely populated neighbourhood in the city, and also the oldest. This area was one of the bastions of Palestinian opposition and resistance. British occupation forces destroyed most of the area between June 18 and 21, 1936. This destruction was made under the pretext of implementing a new urban development plan. In the middle of the 1960s, Israeli municipal authorities working with the Old Jaffa Development Company undertook a project to build a centre for tourism here. Jaffa Palestinians refer to it ironically as "the new Jaffa." Today it is full of many artists' studios and galleries, a park and expensive cafés and restaurants. Visitors come across several historical sites and "historical" information panels conceived by the Israeli municipality in which the original population of Jaffa is either simply excluded or described in disparaging terms. These comments eloquently illustrate how the Palestinian minority of Jaffa is considered.

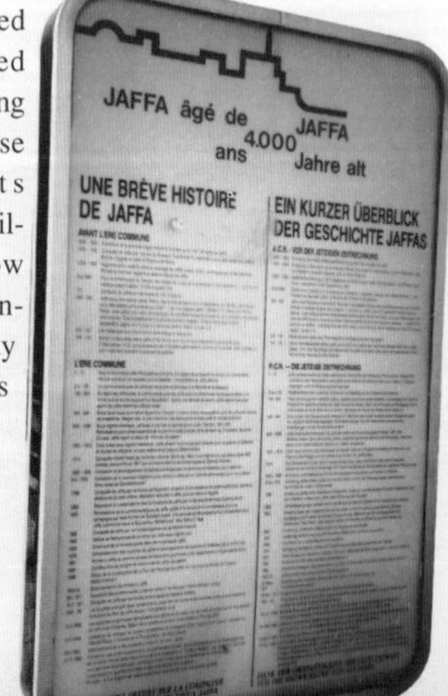

" (...)and this was the beginning of the British Mandate. At that time, there, the port of Jaffa was the principal port of Israel and was also recognised as the port for Jerusalem. It was in Jaffa that conquering pilgrims and Jewish immigrants came each in their turn to settle in Israel. The Jews suffered from Arab persecution throughout the first part of the [twentieth] century; these attacks reached their most violent height at the moment of the creation of the State of Israel, towards the middle of the century. The defensive counter-attacks of the Jews put to rout the majority of Jaffa's Arabs. (...)

In 1960, the Israeli government and the Municipality of Tel Aviv–Jaffa decided to found the Old Jaffa Development Company, which was given the mandate of saving the dignity of the ancient city and its glorious past from annihilation. (...) As for Jaffa's Old City, with its past, its history, its architecture, its geographical location, its marvellous sunsets, its verdant footpaths, its narrow alleys, by daylight or by night, it awakens keen feelings in every visitor sensitive to its beauty and serenity."

■ Extract from the brochure published by the Old Jaffa Development Company

❑ The Jaffa Museum of Antiquities

Open Sunday-Tuesday and Thursday 9:00-14:00, Wednesday 9:00-19:00, Saturday 10:00-14:00. (Currently closed).

The museum is located in a wing of the palace *(al-Saraya)* - the administrative residence of the Ottoman governors, constructed in the eighteenth century. Archaeological finds made on the *tel* are exhibited here. One of the most beautiful pieces in the museum is a lintel, which was in place above the main entrance of the Egyptian fortress in Jaffa in the days of Ramses II (thirteenth century BC).

❑ View

Behind the **Mosque of the Sea** and St. **Nicolas' Armenian Church,** one can see the Tel Aviv shoreline to its most northern limit. In the distance, high-rise towers (one of which houses the Hilton Hotel) have been established on an ancient Jaffa cemetery, the **Abdel Nabi cemetery**. Nearer to our lookout point stands an isolated mosque. This is the **Hassan Bek Mosque**; until 1948 it was situated in the heart of one of the liveliest neighbourhoods of Jaffa, al-Manshiya.

❑ The Franciscan Church and St. Peter's Monastery (Kanissa al-Qal'a - the Church of the Citadel).

The Roman Catholic Church of St. Peter was built by the Franciscans in 1891, according to the plans of two Italian architects, Serafino of Palermo and Bernardino of Rome. Its style is arresting. The church was also dedicated to Saint Louis, King of France (Louis IX), to remind people that it was built on the ruins of the Crusader citadel. Local tradition has it that Napoleon stayed here during his military campaign in 1799.

❑ The Visitors' Centre

The Visitors' Centre is situated below present-day **Kedumim Square**; it is easily accessible by a lateral ramp, descending under the square. Here, archaeologists have uncovered foundations of houses from Roman times. Free brochures on the "history" of Jaffa, published by the Old Jaffa Development Company, are also available here.

❑ The House of Simon the Tanner

Closed.

This is said to be where the Apostle Peter, hosted by Simon, received the revelation telling him that the Christian faith must also be open to non-Jews (Acts 10:9-16). Summoned to Caesarea by a Roman centurion, Peter declared, *"Ye know how that it is an unlawful thing for a man that is a Jew to keep company, or come unto one of another nation; but God hath shewed me that I should not call any man common or unclean."* (Acts 10:28) Christianity thereby changed from being a regional and exclusive religion, and became universal. The house of Simon the Tanner belonged until 1948 to an Armenian family, Zakarian.

❑ The port of Jaffa

From Jaffa harbour, there is a unique view of the old city, an image straight out of the old lithographs of the town. The port, full of life though it is, with fishing boats and pleasure craft coming and going, is nevertheless unpretentious. However, it was the most important harbour in Palestine until Haifa took its place in 1934. Too small a dock for cargo boats, the merchandise was transported by small craft, which rowed out, through treacherous reefs, to larger ships anchored at sea. One product more than any other made the reputation and fortune of Jaffa: citrus fruit.

During the general strike of 1936, the colony of *Tel Aviv* developed its own port with the approval of the British authorities. In 1948, the port witnessed the tragic departure of the people of Jaffa.

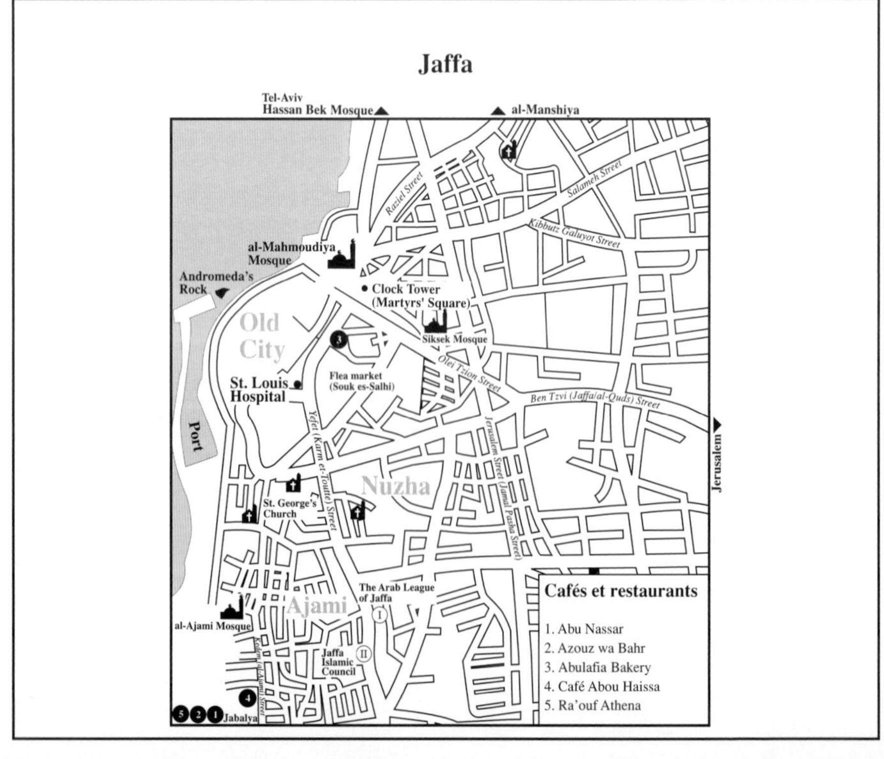

Since 1965, it has no longer been a port of call for merchant vessels, but has been refurbished as a leisure area, with many shops, cafes and fashionable restaurants.

Jaffa oranges

The orange groves of Jaffa made it one of the most popular Arab cities in this part of the world. Orange growing developed in the 1850s, when the oranges were exported to Egypt and Turkey and, from 1875 on, to Europe. Their export was helped by the discovery of a local variety of oranges, which had an especially thick skin and a good size that permitted relatively long transportation by sea, to arrive in maximal state of preservation. Jaffa in fact rapidly became the main port for orange exports, while orange groves sprang up on the outskirts of the city and in the surrounding countryside. In about 1880, there were some 800,000 orange groves in and around Jaffa. The production of oranges continued to expand until 1948. Jaffa's oranges had such a worldwide reputation that when the Israelis had cleansed the region of its people, they took over their orange groves and the name *Jaffa Oranges* for their own commercial benefit.

❑ Andromeda's Rock (Sakhret Andromeda)

Located at the end of the harbour pier, the rock is associated with the myth in Greek mythology written by the Greek geographer Strabo in the first century BC: an oracle predicted that if Andromeda, a young woman who was a great beauty, was sacrificed to a sea monster that was laying waste to the area, the local people would be liberated. So Andromeda was chained to this rock. She was rescued just in time by Perseus, a demi-god born of the union between a king's daughter, Danae, and the god Zeus. Perseus, with the help of the goddess Athena and the god Hermes, killed the monster and married Andromeda. This myth was a favourite with the inhabitants of Jaffa and people throughout the Mediterranean. In 58 BC, huge bones were discovered washed up on the coast - probably belonging to a stranded whale - and were exhibited in Rome as the remains of the monster that would have devoured Andromeda. In the fourth century, St. Jerome referred to the ongoing, curious commerce still taking place around the monster's remains.

❑ St. Louis Hospital

Constructed in the nineteenth century under the auspices of the Sisters of the Order of St. Joseph of the Revelation, this was the first modern hospital in Jaffa. An imposing building, it mixes neo-Gothic and neo-Renaissance styles, typical of European religious foundations established in Palestine in the nineteenth century. This old French hospital was recently bought by the Hilton Hotel chain.

■ Jaffa's neighbourhoods

"I can tell you the names of 50 famous cafés at the time [pre-1948]: al-Halawani, al-Halabi, Abu Chakchouk, and others. But also the names of cinemas: al-Hamra (the Red), King Farouk, er-Rashid, al-Sharq, Apollo; discotheques: Tartous, al-Bosta, Abdel Massih or ez-Zarakiya. And many other clubs where the greatest Egyptians singers, such as Farid al-Atrash, Umm Kolthoum and Mohammed Abdel Wahab performed. I will always remember the two plays written by Yussif Wahbi, which ran here in the 1940s: "The Chair of the Confession" and "The Children of the Poor."

Of course, there were a number of cultural centres in the city, which never left any place for boredom or unfilled time. Every neighbourhood had its centre: al-Manshiya, in the Old City, al-Nuzha, Abu Kabir, Karm et-Toutte, Ajami and so on.

One mustn't forget that there were dozens of schools in the town and national daily newspapers, such as Falastine (Palestine), ed-Difah (The Defence), and al-Jamea al-Islamiya (the Islamic University), and dozens of other papers and periodical magazines."

■ Haj Abdel Fatah al-Masharawi - Abu Salim

Most of Jaffa's Palestinians today live in the **Ajami, Jabalya, Nuzha** and **al-Manshiya** neighbourhoods. The Ajami Quarter could be considered the heart of social, cultural and fun activities for the Arab community. In the 1960s, and again in about 1987, Ajami and Jabalya were targeted by a municipal project of luxury housing construction. At the same time, private housing construction and the huge increase in the price of land in these areas led many of their Palestinian residents to look for homes elsewhere. Low-income housing projects financed by the city and targeted at Palestinians are exceptional. Finally, in 1996, the municipal authorities agreed to build 400 units for Palestinian families. To this day, however, only 100 units have been built.

Tel Aviv

Until the nineteenth century, the Jewish community of Jaffa was limited to a few families. Towards 1941, a small community of Jews, originally from North Africa, settled here. Their culture was Arabic and they were looking for new business opportunities in a booming cosmopolitan city. Since the 1880s, European Jewish immigration to Palestine has followed a completely different logic, one that would bring about the city's tragic destiny. Strangers to the town's culture, influenced by racial theories popular at that time (the superiority of *Judaeo-Christians* and the rebirth of the *Jewish race*), established the settlement of Tel Aviv in 1909 on land acquired by the Jewish National Fund, two kilometres north of Jaffa. Following the revolts of 1920 and 1921, the British authorities granted an autonomous urban status to the settlement of Tel Aviv. This was the principal place of arrival of many new Jewish immigrants to Palestine, so that Tel Aviv in the 1930s and 40s expanded considerably to become the headquarters for Zionist political, military and cultural organisations.

Practical Information

Coming from Jerusalem, take the first exit off the highway, to a road called *Kibbutz Galuyot Road*. From there, the road takes one directly to Jaffa across what remains of the al-Manshiya neighbourhood. From the Central Bus Station, take Bus No. 46. It will take you to the Clock Tower (the ancient Square of the Martyrs). The Bus No. 10 takes you to this part of Jaffa from the Arlosorov Railway Station, through Tel Aviv and up to Jaffa along the coast.

Cafés and restaurants

Most Palestinian restaurants and cafés are found in the Ajami Quarter. Ajami Road (now called **Kedem Road**) has a monopoly of the best fish restaurants. **Ra'ouf Athena, Azouz wa Bahr** (Azouz), and **Abu Nassar** (next to the Jabalya Mosque) are almost a ritual for all visitors to Jaffa. The meals are generous and there is a varied choice of fish. The **Abu Haissa café**, a quiet outdoor venue, is also on Ajami Road. Other cafés and inexpensive restaurants with less charm may be found along **Yefet Street**, including a new activists' bookshop and cafe **Yafa**, on the corner of **Yehuda MeRaguza Street** and Yefet. At Yefet Street is also **Abulafia Bakery**, in business since 1879. Today, it sells a variety of garnished breads — sprinkled in traditional Palestinian style with *za'atara* (a local herb), eggs, mushrooms, or minced beef, or filled with cheese.

Contacts

The Islamic Council of Jaffa

110 Yefet Street (formerly Karm et-Toutte Road - Road of the Mulberry Trees in Arabic). ☎ 03-682 7761 / 0545-692798 (Wael Mohammed). It is possible to visit Muslim holy sites, whether destroyed or now in danger of destruction. Presentation of the situation of Jaffa's Palestinians.

The objectives of the council are to restore and preserve the Muslim holy places of Jaffa and its outlying catchment area (mosques, *maqams* and cemeteries), which are totally unprotected and often desecrated. As a single example, one of Jaffa's cemeteries in the north of Tel Aviv was demolished in order to build the Hilton Hotel. The council is equally active in social affairs, for instance, by granting study scholarships to young Palestinian students.

League for Arab Jaffa (Rabita)

73 Yefet Street (formerly Karm et-Toutte Road). ☎ 03-682 7172. Meetings and guided tours of Jaffa and the sites of ancient villages in the Jaffa region. For anyone who wants to know about the city and its historical inheritance as well as the current situation of Palestinians living there, a visit here is fundamental.

The league was founded in 1979 in response to the isolation of the Palestinian community in Jaffa and to improve its living conditions. The association plays a social and cultural role by organising cultural events and providing social support. It is also active in preserving Jaffa's heritage, which is threatened by many municipal projects for luxury housing construction.

Near Jaffa

Al-Abbassiya

Twelve kilometres east of Jaffa, beneath the present Jewish town of Yehud.

Known in the Bible as Yahud, and Iudaea in its Latinised form under the Romans, then changed to the Arabic al-Yahudiya in the Islamic era, this town was renamed again in 1932 when its residents named it al-Abbassiya after a local dignitary, Sheikh Abbas. Until its demolition in 1948, al-Abbassiya was one of the most important towns in the Jaffa region. It had a population of 3,258 in 1931, which had increased to 5,800 by 1944 (5,650 Palestinians and 150 Jews). From the end of 1947 onwards, al-Abbassiya was the target of many Zionist attacks: on December 13, 1947, the paramilitary group Irgun placed several bombs in the village, killing more than seven Palestinians. On February 24, 1948, a bomb was thrown from a moving car, killing two people. Al-Abbassiya was completely cleansed of its population in the "clean-up" operation of the district of Jaffa undertaken by the Hagana at the end of April 1948. On May 4, 1948, al-Abbassiya was occupied by the Irgun. On June 11, the village was retaken by Arab troops, but the Israeli army retook it on July 10. On September 13, 1948, Prime Minister David Ben Gurion asked the Cabinet to approve the destruction of al-Abbassiya. The Cabinet apparently refused, because ten days later immigrant Jews were settled in the empty homes.

The town today

Many buildings still stand, among them the **al-Abbas Mosque** in the heart of the village, today bearing the name "Shalom Shebdi Synagogue." Five settlements have grown up on the land belonging to al-Abbassiya: *Yehud* (on the site of the village; 1948), *Magshimim* (1949), *Ganei Yehuda* (1951), *Ganei Tikva* (1953) and *Savyon* (1954).

Nabi Rubin

Twenty kilometres south of Jaffa. Drive towards Kibbutz Palmahim. It is visible from the road, but one must continue for more than a kilometre until a bridge over a small stream, which separates it. From there, one must walk fifteen minutes by foot on a sandy path to reach the ruins of the Nabi Rubin mosque.

"Either Rubin, or you divorce me," Jaffa ladies would say to their husbands as a joke, not wanting to miss the annual festivities here.

The village owes its name and popularity to the tomb of the Prophet Rubin (Reuben) who, the Bible says, was the first son of Jacob and Leah (Genesis 29:32). The origins of the *mawsim* celebrations are obscure, but it seems that this great regional festivity is a tradition dating back to ancient days. In the first half of the twentieth century it attracted as many as 30,000 people from the centre of Palestine (Jaffa, Ramle, Gaza and Beersheba) and even farther afield. The festivities continued from July to September; the pilgrimage was both religious and secular in expression: the days were passed in religious chanting (plainsong), but also with folk music and folk dancing (*dabkeh*). In 1944, there were 1,420 people living in the village.

The Mosque and Nabi Rubin's Tomb

The mosque is the only remaining trace of Nabi Rubin: it is beautiful despite its state of neglect. Located in a field of sand dunes, one can only reach it by foot. The *maqam*, located inside the mosque, has become a place of Jewish worship, but is visited infrequently. If one looks carefully, the places for the stands for the annual celebrations may be detected under the thick layer of sand.

■ Lydd (Lydda or Lod)

Prehistoric artefacts, particularly from the Natoufian (Epipalaeolithic) era, abound in this entire area. The town of Lydd itself, according to the Bible, was founded by Samad. *"And of Hushim he begot Abitub and Elpaal. The sons of Elpaal; Eber, and Misham, and Shamed, who built Ono, and Lod, with the towns thereof."* (I Chronicles 8:11-12) However, the city's origins pre-date biblical times: the Canaanite city was cited among Thutmose III's conquests, in the middle of the second millennium. During the Roman Empire, it was an important staging post on the road between Caesarea and Jerusalem. The early conversion of the city to Christianity came immediately after Peter's miracle there, according to the New Testament: *"And Peter said unto him: 'Aeneas, Jesus Christ maketh thee whole; arise, and make thy bed.' And he arose immediately that dwelt at Lydda and Saron saw him, and turned to the Lord."* (Acts 9:32-35) During the Byzantine period the town was called Georgopolis, in honour of St. George who, legend has it, was born of a Cappadocian father and a mother from Lydd, the city where he spent part of his childhood. In the first centuries of the Islamic Empire the town became one of the most important urban centres in Palestine. Its Arabicised name was Lydd. Less than a century after the Crusaders left, the Mongols invaded as far as Lydd and ravaged the city. Under the Ottomans, it remained an important town but was removed, in the same way as its neighbour, Ramle, from the main trade routes and so its commerce was seriously reduced.

Economic activity picked up at the end of the nineteenth century, when (in 1882) Lydd was linked to the railway system and once again became an important focal point of Palestine. The labour movement commenced early here and was highly active. One campaign led by Palestinian unionists was in protest at the discriminatory British system of salaries, in which they paid Jewish municipal workers more than Palestinian employees.

Population of Lydd

Year	Total	Muslim Arabs	Christian Arabs	Jews
1922	8,103	7,166	926	11
1931	11,250	10,012	1,210	18
1947	18,250	*18,250		0
1950	10,450	*1,050		9,400
1973	33,200	*3,400		29.800
1992	**41,600			

*Muslim and Christian Palestinians
**Jewish and Arab Israelis

En-Nakba

Lydd and Ramle were defended by a contingent of the Arab Legion of Transjordan, auxiliary forces of the Arab Liberation Army, and Palestinian partisans, who resisted repeated attacks during the months of May and June. The Arab troops even managed to liberate several occupied villages. During the night of July 9, 1948, a massive Israeli offensive ("Operation Dani") commenced against Lydd and Ramle. King Abdullah ordered his troops to retreat on July 11 although the two towns were encircled and under heavy shelling, which was followed by the massacre on July 12 of civilians taking refuge in the Dahamash Mosque. This provoked a mass exodus of residents from the entire region. This flight of thousands of Palestinians was an arm of the war which General Yigal Allon (in mid-July 1948) viewed as desirable: "...[it] *slowed down the progress of the Legion* [the Arab Legion of Transjordan] *and gave the Arab economy the problem of maintaining 45,000 additional souls ... What is more, the arrival of tens of thousands* [of refugees] *will indubitably demoralise all the Arab regions concerned ...This victory will have a great influence on other sectors."* This "victory" caused the exile of almost 18,000 of Lydd's 19,000 citizens, as refugees.

George Habash (*al-Hakim* - the Wise One)

Born in Lydd on August 2, 1926 to a Greek Orthodox family, George Habash lived there until July 1948. A refugee, he studied in Beirut and in 1951 received a diploma in paediatrics (graduating first in his class). In 1952, convinced that only a united Arab world could attain the liberation of Palestine, he founded the Arab Nationalist Movement with Dr. Wadi Haddad (a Palestinian from Safad), Hani al-Hindi (a Syrian) and Ahmed al-Khatib (from Kuwait). At the same time he opened a clinic and a school for Palestinian refugees in Amman. In 1957, he went underground after the proclamation of martial law in the Kingdom of Jordan. After the defeat of 1967 and the intensification of the role of Palestinian resistance, he continually called for armed struggle as the sole means of defending the Palestinian people and their land. It was in this context that he founded the Popular Front for the Liberation of Palestine (PFLP) of which he became Secretary-General. His sharp criticism of the Arab states earned him a prison term in Syria in 1968, which he escaped in November of the same year. On his return to Amman, he firmly rejected United Nations' Resolution 242. (In 1967 in UN Resolution 242, the Palestinians were offered only 22% of the land of historic Palestine, as opposed to the terms of Resolution 181 of 1947, in which a proposed Palestinian state as defined in the Partition Plan represented some 44% of Palestine.) He also denounced the American peace plan (the Roger Plan), supported by Jordan's King Hussein, which ordered a halt to Palestinian resistance activities. Confrontation with the Kingdom of Jordan led to a state of open warfare: "Black September". Habash was opposed to the Oslo Accords and he helped organise the opposition based in Damascus, which included Islamic parties that were not PLO members. He resigned from his position as Secretary General of the PFLP in 2000 to devote himself to setting up a centre for research on Palestine.

➡ Lydd today

Tuesday is the best day to visit the old town, as it is market day.

Lydd, or Lod (the name given to it under the British Mandate), is an unrecognisable town, a ghost emerging from some cultivated farmland, vacant lots and huge urban developments, typical of urban suburbs everywhere. A poor suburb of Tel Aviv, the city numbers over 40,000 residents, of whom 9,000 are Palestinian. Russian and Ethiopian new immigrants make up the majority of the population. The social and economic situation is very similar to that of its neighbour, Ramle. But Lydd had its moments of glory and there remain some vestiges of proof to witness, places of interest ignored both by the municipal authorities and the Israeli Ministry of Tourism.

❑ Church of St. George

If the door is locked, ask the Greek priest who lives just opposite the church to open it for you. The church has an interesting collection of icons. St. George is considered the most important Christian saint in Palestine, and on his feast day (April 23) and the day of his burial (November 15), the Christian community of Lydd/Lod organises processions.

Local Christian and Muslim tradition has it that St. George (*al-Khader* in Arabic) was born in Lydd, where his bones were brought after his martyrdom; his tomb should therefore be found in the crypt. As for the church itself, it was built in the nineteenth century by the Greek Orthodox community. Several Byzantine and mediaeval architectural elements have been reintegrated into the more recent structure. As with most oriental churches dedicated to St. George, this one has iron rings in the walls *(on the right of the main entrance)*, used to chain insane people in the hope of curing them [See *al-Khader Church*, p. 200]. Next to the church is the **Omar Mosque**, built *ca.*1268, and also dedicated to al-Khader (St. George). Nearby, two *caravanserais* (inns serving camel caravans) reveal the historic importance of Lydd as a centre for pilgrims and trade; upkeep of these *caravanserais* has been totally neglected by the Jewish municipality. **Khan al-Helou** (the Beautiful Caravanserai), still well conserved, is in the middle of a field; without doubt, it merits a visit – and also, full restoration. In today's *Herzl Street*, the **Dahamash Mosque** re-opened its doors on April 12, 1996, almost exactly 48 years after Israeli troops, under the command of Moshe Dayan (who went on to become Israel's commander in chief during the 1967 War) and subsequently was known as a peacemaker in negotiations with Egypt), bombarded it while the citizens of Lydd had taken refuge in it.

■ Ramle

"I was on my way to the town of Ramle, also called Palestine [the administrative capital of Jund Falastine]. It is a large town, with abundant wealth and adorned with beautiful marketplaces. One notices the principal mosque, named the White One, of which it is said that in its qibla three hundred prophets are interred".

■ Ibn Battuta

Al-Ramle was founded in 715 AD, by the Umayyad Caliph Suleyman Ibn Abd al-Malik (674-717 AD) at the crossroads of the principal trade routes. It soon became the administrative and commercial capital of the province of Palestine *(Jund Falastine)*, roughly the equivalent of the Byzantine provinces of *Palaestina Prima* and *Palaestina Tertia*. Its entire area, endowed with public buildings (mosques, bathhouses and caravanserais), marketplaces and homes, exceeded even that of Jerusalem. The eleventh and twelfth centuries were terrible for Ramle: earthquakes in 1033 and 1067, the Crusader conquest in 1099, a fire in 1177, and a battle between the Crusader force and Saladin's army in 1191. Ramle was restored to life under the Mameluke Sultan Baybar, to become one of the most important urban centres of Palestine. The Mamelukes were responsible for this revitalisation, by constructing much public utility infrastructure, especially reservoirs and bridges. Ramle then became famous for its cotton cloth. No longer situated at an important commercial axis during the Ottoman era, Ramle gradually declined into a small provincial administrative town until the beginning of the twentieth century, when it became a principal town of the district.

Population in the district of Ramle

Year	Total	Arabs*	Jews
1922	49,075	45,149	3,926
1931	70,579		
1945	127,270	97,998	29,272

* Muslim and Christian Arabs

En-Nakba

Shortly after the release of the UN Partition Plan of November 1947, which recommended that Ramle be included in an Arab state, a Zionist commando placed a bomb in the city's main marketplace (February 1948). In all, seven Palestinians were killed and 45 others were injured. In the month of April, Zionist forces launched "cleansing" operations against villages in the west of the district of Ramle. Ramle itself fell on July 12. *"I couldn't get to my house,"* Aissa Dabit remembers. *"There was chaos everywhere, houses in flames, tanks firing machine guns, crowds of people fleeing with babies and bundles under their arms..."* About 500 Palestinians took refuge in the Italian Terra Sancta monastery. They were practically the only original residents of Ramle, out of 16,000 Palestinians, who were allowed to stay in the town together with a thousand villagers who had just arrived as refugees. The National Housing Bureau *(Amidar)* (which means in Hebrew "my people dwell") appropriated all the refugees' property (land, churches, mosques, cemeteries, shops, homes, etc.), which they allocated to new-immigrant Jews, most of whom were Oriental Jews (from Yemen, North Africa and Iraq). Of the fourteen mosques existing in 1948, five were destroyed and six converted into apartments. The original Palestinian citizens of Ramle who had managed to stay after 1948 saw most of their property confiscated by Amidar (the National Housing Bureau). Paradoxically, they themselves were moved into "absentee property" after paying rent to the housing bureau. *"That's how I, myself a 'present absentee,' in official jargon, ended up living in the house of another absentee. (...) See what has become of me, at my age. After a half century of work, I still don't have a roof to call my own, and the only one I would be able to buy belongs to another Palestinian who hopes to return and who perhaps dreams of it every night!"* (Aissa Dabit)

Population of Ramle

Year	Total	Muslim Arabs	Christian Arabs	Jews
1922	7,312	5,837	2,184	35
1931	10,347	8,156	3,260	5
1945	15,160	11,900		
1950	10,592	*168		9,224
1973	36,000	*400		31,200
1998	60,600	*10,700		49,900

* Muslim and Christian Palestinians

A deplorable economic and social situation

Ramle is one of the poorest cities in the State of Israel. Located in the middle of a vast fertile plain, it has all the allure of a huge low-income housing development, where Arab Jewish immigrants and, since 1989, Russian and Ethiopian immigrants live. As soon as their economic situation allows them, the Jewish immigrants move away to pleasanter quarters, often to Israeli settlements in East Jerusalem and the West Bank. It has to be said that Ramle, like Lod, has a bad reputation. Drug trafficking and social crime regularly feature on the front pages of local newspapers.

Ramle Palestinians constitute a population of third class citizens, but they would not dream of leaving: this would only play into the hands of the Zionists and betray their rights to exist here in this city. In any case, economic considerations and the housing shortage in all Palestinians cities and towns in Israel prevent other solutions. Called by the generic term "Arabs," Palestinians live in three different neighbourhoods: the old town ("the ghetto"), Jawarish and Jan Hakal. The Jawarish quarter is mainly inhabited by Palestinian Bedouins originally from the Negev, who were either expelled from their lands or came to seek better job opportunities in Ramle. The neighbourhood speaks for itself as to municipal urban policy: Jawarish is completely walled in on three sides. Since 1948, absolutely no public urban development project has been initiated for the Palestinian Israeli Arab community, whilst in only the last 10 years; urban projects have allowed the city to house some 18,000 Russian and Ethiopian Jews. Moreover, the Palestinian habitat is precarious - rooms have been illegally added to family dwellings, both anaesthetic and overcrowded. The lack of basic infrastructure is blatant: street surfaces, cleaning services, public street lighting, and social services - all are reduced to an inadequate minimum. The level of education is also one of the worst: 15% of the young people are illiterate. The schools are old and the teachers - often selected in a discriminatory way - are poorly qualified. To add to the negative atmosphere of the area, the government of Yitzhak Rabin settled 450 families of Palestinian collaborators from the West Bank and Gaza Strip here, before inaugurating the autonomous zones.

Khalil al-Wazir (Abu Jihad) (1935-1988)

Born into one of the leading families of Ramle, Khalil al-Wazir took refuge in 1948 in what became the al-Bureij Refugee Camp (Gaza Strip). He was one of the close companions of Yasser Arafat (Abu Amar) in the Struggle and one of the founders of the Palestinian resistance movement, *Fatah* (1959) and its military branch *al-Assifa* ("the Storm"), for which he recruited and trained the *fedayin* ("fighters who sacrifice themselves"). He advocated close ties with Algeria (Fatah's main training base after its liberation from France in 1962) and the communist bloc (China, Eastern Europe, Vietnam and North Korea), sharing their ideal of a people's war for liberation. In spite of the relations he had with these countries, he grew ideologically ever closer to the Islamic movement of the Muslim Brotherhood. The defeat of 1967 confirmed his aspiration for a people's war and helped build the popularity of his movement. After the Israeli invasion of Lebanon, he put his efforts into supporting the Struggle inside the Occupied Territories, and especially through the committees of young people who were the vanguard of the *Intifada* (Uprising). A principal figure of the United National Leadership of the Uprising, he was assassinated in his home in Tunis by an Israeli commando on April 16, 1988.

■ The old city

Ramle today is a melting pot of all the different people one sees at the busy market in the heart of the old city. The area, which is quite run-down, has been called a "ghetto" since 1948. Palestinians were in effect confined to the old city under martial law, until 1966. Once a historic centre of Palestine, the old city is lacking neither in charm nor historical ruins.

Next to buildings built in the first half of the twentieth century, one finds magnificent Mameluke and Ottoman dwellings (around the Great Mosque), today the property of *Amidar*, the National Housing Bureau. Notice especially the architectural and decorative details. The state of dilapidation of these Islamic buildings, and the lack of interest invested in the Arab-Islamic heritage of the town is obvious. Elsewhere in the country, however, one sees crumbling foundations of antique stone walls which have been conserved, with no expense spared! Overpopulation, poverty, disregard by the Palestinian population as to its cultural heritage and Israeli municipal and state policy towards it, all have contributed to the sad state of this historic centre.

❑ Hammam al-Wazir

The site of the old public bathhouse has been a victim of municipal policy, as the city recently allowed a restaurant to extend its rooms here, to the detriment of the older buildings. What remains, in the middle of the crossroads, is now less eloquent a statement than before…

❑ The town hall

The town hall is housed in the former residence of a wealthy Palestinian gold dealer, Choukri Rezeq. He had it built for his son shortly before Israeli troops took the city in 1948. The residence and all its brand new furniture, prepared for the newlyweds whose wedding was to be in the summer of 1948, was confiscated. Today it has been turned into Ramle's town hall. Notice the original carpets inside the building.

❑ The Great Mosque (Masjid al-Kebir)

The mosque is near a market. It was originally a Roman Catholic cathedral, St. John's Cathedral, built by the Crusaders. Its beautiful façade, Cistercian capitals and roof are distinctive. Sultan Baybar had it transformed into a mosque in 1268, and it was endowed with its exquisite minaret in 1314.

❑ Birket al-Anzia or Pool of St. Helena

HaHagana Street. Open Sunday-Thursday 8:00-15:00, Friday 8:00-12:00, Saturday 8:00-16:00. NIS5 entrance fee.

One may take small boats around this underground cistern, built under the palace of Abbassid Caliph Haroun er-Rashid (766-809 AD). Notice the pointed arch vaults - among the most ancient examples of this technique. This style was copied by the Crusaders and incorporated into the Gothic style of architecture.

❑ Franciscan Church of St. Joseph of Arimathea

Open Monday-Friday 9:00-11:30. Visitors are requested to respect the silence.

The Crusaders mistakenly identified Ramle as the Biblical site of Rama, the hometown of the saint, Joseph of Arimathea, and so they built a church here in his honour. According to the New Testament (John 19:38-42), St. Joseph of Arimathea, with Nicodemus, laid Jesus' crucified body in a tomb. Today's church is on the site of the mediaeval church. Napoleon slept in the adjacent St. Joseph and St. Nicodemus hospice in 1799, before his conquest of Jaffa. Local tradition has it that Napoleon had the *muezzin* of the nearest mosque executed because he woke him, when calling the faithful to the morning prayer *(sala't al-fajer)*. The adjacent monastery dates from 1750 AD. It served in July 1948 as refuge for those citizens of the town who were almost the only ones not to have been chased out and forced to flee from Ramle.

❑ The White Mosque

"People say that forty of the Prophet's first companions are buried under this mosque."

■ Al-Harawi

The famous Arab geographer al-Harawi died in 1214. He was the author of *The Book of Visits*, a complete description of religious sites: holy places, tombs where important people in Islamic history were buried, the *zawiya* of mystics, and Quranic schools. This guide was something of a forerunner to later guides to pilgrimages in the Holy Land (in Arabic: *'Ard al-Mouqadassa*).

The minaret of the White Mosque, or the Square Tower, always fulfilled both religious and military functions. A superb lookout tower *(closed to*

visitors at present), its view encompasses the entire surrounding plain, as far as the Mediterranean. The minaret was built in 1318 by Mameluke Sultan Nasser ed-Din Ibn Qalaoun (1309-1340). As Ramle declined under the Ottomans, the White Mosque, an Umayyad monument hitherto often restored, progressively disintegrated. However, several original archways are still intact. Islamic property (as is the cemetery next door), the Israeli authorities confiscated the land and monument as "abandoned property." Although Jewish archaeologists have conducted digs here since then, no restoration work at all has been undertaken. The cemetery, declared "untransferable property of the Jewish people," is today a vacant lot used as a public rubbish dump, more or less sanctioned by the authorities. The minaret remains the only building still preserved, a contemporary symbol of the city's "desecration," a symbol crowned by a Jewish ritual emblem, a *menora*. (The menora is the multi-branched ceremonial candelabrum, especially used at Hanukka, and also found on Israeli coins, Roman artefacts or wall-inscriptions - such as in the Beit She'arim catacombs, and used as a state symbol.) Whilst no effort has been made to restore or reinforce the White Mosque, it must be said that a tiled floor recently installed at the base of the minaret is in the worst possible taste.

Practical Information

Buses run regularly between Ramle and other cities. The Central Bus Station is very near the Great Mosque and the marketplace. The market is a wonderful place to browse for hardware and many other goods. The town has many small Arab restaurants and also some Indian ones.

Samir Restaurant (☎ 08-922 0195), near the Church of St. Joseph of Arimathea, serves excellent *mezzes*. At the back of the restaurant, see a bas-relief representation of the town.

Contacts

To learn about the Palestinian community in Ramle, its local opinions and daily life, as well as its cultural heritage and urban Israeli policy (including building of a wall isolating Palestinians from their Jewish neighbours, with NIS3 million government finance), contact the **Residents' Association** - a committee of Ramle citizens *(Busayna Dabit, 0525-345937 or BusaynaD@shatil.nif.org.il; introduction and visit. www.palestineremembered.com/al-Ramle).*

■ East and south of Ramle

❑ The Soreq Caves

20 kilometres west of Jerusalem on Ein Karem Road. Open Sunday-Thursday 8:30-12:00; NIS20 entrance fee.

The Soreq caves are in the Absalom Nature Reserve. An interesting diorama explains the geological formation of the site, especially stalagmite and stalactite formations inside the caves. Besides, the lovely scenery makes it a perfect place for highly enjoyable country rambles.

❑ Monastery of our Lady of the Assumption and St. Bruno (Beit Gemal) Monastery

On Road 38, 3 kilometres south of Beit Shemesh. Open Monday-Saturday 8:30-17:00. ☎ *02-991 7672/02-9911889.*

The monastery was founded at the end of the nineteenth century by the Salesian order. Like the Trappists of Latroun *(Latrun)*, the Salesians started an agricultural school, which provided the manpower necessary for vineyards. The school closed in 1948 for lack of students and replaced the vines with olive trees, which are less labour intensive except during the harvest. The estate provides a wonderful opportunity for highly agreeable walks. From the rooftop of the monastery, one may appreciate the serenity of the surroundings. What has equally made the monastery's reputation: many visitors come here to taste the much-vaunted Cremisan wines produced by the Salesian monastery in Beit Jala. Three institutions are represented in this compound, in different buildings: two male orders (Silesian and Monial) and a female order of Moniale nuns, the Nuns of Bethlehem, of the Assumption of the Virgin and of St. Bruno. The latter are famous for the beautiful quality and distinctive Palestinian designs on ceramics they produce in their workshops; their gift shop, set in these delightful surroundings, provides a wide range of charming articles, well worth a visit for connoisseurs.

Beit Jibrin and Marissa

On Road 35. From Sunday-Thursday 8:00 -15:00, Friday 8:00 -15:00, NIS15 entrance fee. Sites of Beit Jibrin and the Hellenistic city of Marissa (Beit Guvrin and Maresha in Hebrew). The Marissa site is 2 kilometres south of the demolished village of Beit Jibrin. Follow the marked trails, because of the many caves and holes. Wear shoes with a good grip and remember the flash for your camera. To explore those caves that have not been adapted for tourists, a torch (flashlight) is recommended.

Located at the foot of the Hebron Hills, Beit Jibrin (the "Strong House" in Arabic) is mentioned for the first time by Flavius Josephus under its Latin derivative, Betogsabra. This small town was built in the first century BC after the destruction of the city of Marissa *(2 kms south)*, by the Hasmonean King John Hyrcanus I and then by the Parthians in

40 BC. Under Emperor Septimus Severus (193-211AD), the city was granted the status of a Roman colony and called Eleutheropolis - the city of free men. Oriental and Graeco-Roman religions coexisted peacefully here. In the fourth century, Christianity took precedence over all other religions and the city became the seat of a bishopric. It was conquered by Caliph Abu Bakr (632-634 AD). A companion of the Prophet Mohammed, Tamim Abu Ruqaya, is buried here. The Arab geographer from Jerusalem, al-Muqaddassi (tenth century) mentioned the town as one of the main places for trade in the region. The conquering Crusaders fortified it ca.1136, but Saladin destroyed those fortifications, fifty years later. In the thirteenth century, Baybar finally ended the period of the Crusader presence in the region. Beit Jibrin remained a prosperous town and a postal relay station between Gaza and al-Karak (Jordan). During the Ottoman period, its population grew from 275 people in 1596 AD to 1,000 residents in 1912, then to 2,430 in 1944. Until 1948, it fell under the Hebron district.

En-Nakba

At the beginning of May 1948, Palestinians from the Jaffa area took refuge in the caves all around Beit Jibrin. The day after May 14, 1948, the Egyptian army entered the military arena and took up position in Beit Jibrin along the demarcation line between Egyptian and Israeli troops. In mid-October, the Israeli Cabinet broke the second Israeli-Arab truce (in force from July 18 until mid-October) by launching "Operation Yoav" in the region of Beit Jibrin and Majdal. The offensive was commanded by Yigal Allon, a distinguished commando *"who in his earlier campaigns had left not a single Arab civilian community in his wake"* (Benny Morris). The village was shelled from both land and air, provoking the flight of most of the inhabitants. *"With the victory of 'Operation Yoav,' the region was liberated by the Israeli army on October 27, 1948,"* says the Israeli tourist brochure of Beit Guvrin-Maresha. The inhabitants of Beit Jibrin have given their name to a refugee camp in Bethlehem *[*See *Beit Jibrin or 'Azza Refugee Camp*, p. 190*]*.

The village today

Of the 369 houses officially registered (1,430 residents), there are only a few Palestinian homes left - reoccupied or deserted. One of these has been converted into a restaurant. An inscription on the house reads, in Arabic, *"al-Bustan,"* or "the garden." The village school has been transformed into the secretariat of *Beit Guvrin*, a kibbutz founded there in 1949.

Archaeologists working on remains of the village have brought to light the Crusader fortress, built by the Duke of Anjou in the twelfth century, and a pretty little amphitheatre of the Roman period.

The Site of Marissa

This city of the Old Testament was called Mareshah; the city was fortified, according to the Bible, by Rehoboam, King of Judah (Joshua 15:44; II Chronicles 11:8) together with other cities over which he strengthened his control. Integrated into the province of Idumaea in the Persian and Hellenistic periods, Marissa (its Greek name) was the hub of the slave trade. The Ptolemites established a Sidonian settlement here in the third century BC, which was dependent on the port of Ascalon, also ruled by the maritime city of Sidon (today, the city of Saida, Lebanon). Sidon then controlled a vast area ranging from the shores of the Mediterranean, to south of the Dead Sea *(Palaestina Prima)*. The extension of the Hasmonean kingdom at the end of the second century BC accompanied the conquest of the city and the forced conversion of the inhabitants to Judaism. Some historians identify Marissa as the birthplace of King Herod, which would explain its destruction by the Parthians, sworn enemies of Herod the Great, in 40 BC. In any case, the town was then rebuilt on the site of Beit Jibrin.

The ruins

If the antiquities above ground are modest, the underground site is an exceptional revelation. There is a huge network of artificial and natural caves underneath the Hellenistic city open today to visitors. Here one may see **bathhouses, oil presses** (no fewer than 20 have been discovered), **cisterns** and **storage areas,** constituting the underground, conserved part of the site. There is also a **dovecote** *(colombarium)* with more than 2,000 small pigeonholes. The intensive use of pigeons, then recorded throughout the whole of Palestine, was of multiple purpose: they were used as messengers, offerings of food, libations in pagan rites

and their droppings were used as fertiliser.

Ancient burial chambers were easily carved in this soft limestone and chalk. One of these, known as the **Sidonian tomb**, dates from the third century BC. It contains 41 funerary chambers, including that of Apollophanes, the son of Sesmaios, who was governor of the city for 33 years; paintings and original inscriptions have survived. In the **Tomb of the Musicians**, the painting of a flute player and a harp player decorate the cave.

Returning to the surface, if one walks along a path, one comes upon the ruins of the Crusader **Church of St. Anne**, which gave its name to the Tel Sandakhanna (in Arabic). Farther along is a series of **bell-shaped caves**. In all, some 800 of such caves exist in this region. In 1948, exiled Palestinians took shelter in some of them. Their heights range from 12 to 25 metres; most were carved out of the rock between the seventh and tenth centuries AD. The soft rock was used in construction work and in the manufacture of whitewash. The extraction was made through a shaft dug on the surface in the form of a bell to ensure that the ceiling would not cave in. The discovery of graffiti in Arabic and crosses on the walls indicates that the workers were Palestinian Christians, who no doubt lived in the town of Beit Jibrin.

Yibna

Southeast of the present-day Jewish town of Yavne.

The name Yavne has several variations in ancient references: Jabneel or Jabneh (Philistine town, II Chronicles 26:6-8); Yammia in the Persian period, inhabited by seafaring Phoenicians and Greeks, Iamnia under the Romans, and then Yibne (seat of a Jewish religious council at the end of the first century BC); Yibna in Arabic. In the ninth century, it was described by the Arab geographer al-Ya'qubi as one of the oldest towns in Palestine, a town inhabited by Samaritans. Yibna was the site of a Crusader victory against the Fatimids in 1123 (at which time they called the town "Ibline"). It was at Yibna in 1265 that the Mameluke Sultan Baybar received the news of the victory over the Tartars in northern Syria.

En-Nakba

In 1944, there were over 5,400 people living in Yibna; in addition, 1,500 Bedouins lived on the outskirts of the town. Israeli military forces occupied Yibna on June 5, 1948. The entire population then took refuge in what became the Gaza Strip.

The village today

Today, only the lower half of the minaret of the Mameluke mosque (1386 AD) is visible on the hill in the middle of a field of ruins. The town, which surrounded the mosque, was completely devastated, although one can still make out where several houses once stood. In 1931, the British authorities had registered 794 buildings!

The tomb of Rabbi Gamliel of Yibne ('The Ramban', a Jewish theologian of the first century AD)

In reality a Roman sepulchre, the tomb is an ancient *maqam* dedicated to a Muslim saint, probably a companion of the Prophet Mohammed, possibly Abu Hureira, but nothing has been decisively proved. As far back as the thirteenth century, geographer Yaqut al-Hamawi, in his Dictionary of the Country *(Mu'jam al-Buldan)*, wrote that Yibna was the place of "*...the tomb of one of the companions of the Prophet Mohammed (May Prayer and Peace Be Upon Him!), whose identity is subject to controversy.*" The identification of the maqam, after the establishment of the State of Israel, as the tomb of a Jewish personality of the first century, is a prize example of the appropriation of the Arab Palestinian historical heritage by the Jews.

Ashdod (Isdoud)

A small Canaanite town is recorded on this spot as far back as the seventeenth century BC. *Circa* 1000 BC, Ashdod was one of the confederate cities of the Philistine Pentapolis; in 712 BC, it was destroyed by the Assyrian troops of Sargon II. Although the city itself was landlocked, it had its own port, which was called Azotos Paralios in the Hellenistic period. The Maccabeans destroyed the town anew in the second century BC, but it was revived during the Roman era. The port of Azotus developed to the detriment of its mother city. Isdoud, as it was known at the beginning of the Islamic period, was mentioned in the tenth century by the Persian geographer Ibn Khurdadhbi as a station for the postal service between Gaza and al-Ramle. In 1596, 413 people lived in Isdoud. It had its own *caravanserai* where the famous Egyptian sufi, As'ad al-Luqaymi, made a stop in 1730. In 1944-45, there were 4,910 townsfolk (4,620 Muslims and 290 Jews).

En-Nakba

Egyptian troops entered Palestine after May 15, 1948. The Egyptian Sixth Battalion took position in Isdoud (Ashdod) during the second half of May. Gamal Abdel Nasser, future president of Egypt, was then a battalion officer. On June 2 and 3, Israeli military forces shelled the town heavily, putting several thousand people to flight. During the Israeli offensive, Egyptian troops, Palestinian partisans and the remaining civilian population retreated towards Gaza. The town finally fell on October 28, 1948. About 300 Palestinians remained in the city, waving white flags. They were immediately expelled southwards. An Israeli military communiqué announced, on the day of the Israeli occupation of Ashdod, that Israeli forces had entered Ashdod at the request of a delegation of the local Arab population!

The town today

Four kilometres southeast of the present-day city of Ashdod, directly west of Road No. 4.

Almost nothing remains of the town of Isdoud. A dilapidated mosque, some school buildings, a *maqam* and ruins of houses line what was once the main street of the town.

Ashdod today

Except for the beaches, there is little to see or do. To the south of the city, the modest ruins of a tenth-century Fatimid castle, **Qalet al-Mina** ('the Citadel of the Port' but known in Hebrew as: *Ashdod Yam*), lie scattered along the shore.

Ascalon (Asqalan)

Mentioned as early as the nineteenth century BC in the Egyptian Execration Texts, Ascalon was subsequently regularly cited in Egyptian sources. In the eleventh century, according to the Old Testament, it was one of the Philistine Pentapolis cities. In the Persian era, the city fell under the jurisdiction of the powerful Phoenician kingdom of Tyre. Embattled against the Maccabean and then the Hasmonean dynasties, the city was later placed under the protection of the Roman Empire in the first century BC. Herod built several remarkable public edifices here (bathhouses, fountains and colonnades), doubtless dedicated to the memory of his grandfather, who served the temple of Apollo. The town prospered in the Roman, Byzantine and Islamic periods. Under the Umayyad Caliph Abdel Malik (685-705), new monuments were built in Ascalon. Protected by a powerful fortress, it resisted the Crusaders in 1153, despite a five-month siege. A truce was brokered to permit the people to leave unharmed; nevertheless, the Crusaders broke their agreement and massacred the population. At that time, the city was under Fatimid administration. In 1187, a short time after its conquest, it was liberated by Saladin. At the time of the Third Crusade (1189-1192), led by Frederick Barbarossa, Philip Augustus and Richard the Lionheart, Saladin made the decision - not without regret - to destroy the city or its ramparts, at the very least. Its most beautiful works of art were first taken to safety. This explains how Saladin offered the *minbar* of the Ascalon mosque to the Haram of Hebron. Richard the Lionheart managed to take control of it, but his troops, deprived of the solid city walls, were defeated by the Arab-Muslim soldiers. Since the Eighth Crusade of 1270 AD, under the command of Louis IX (St. Louis), was looming, the Mameluke Sultan Baybar destroyed what was left of the town and founded al-Majdal, farther away from the sea.

The ancient town of Ascalon - an archaeological park

To the south of the town. Open Saturday-Thursday 8:00-16:00, Friday 8:00-15:00, NIS 15 entrance fee. The beach, accessible from the archaeological site, is the principal attraction.

This vast site has been the object of frequent archaeological excavations. Every historical period is represented here by more or less convincing artefacts; for example, a door of sun-dried brick from the Middle Bronze Age (*circa* 2000 BC), a portion of the walls of the Philistine port, the Roman forum and remains of Byzantine and Crusader churches, among others.

Al-Majdal

Al-Majdal has been erased from the map by the new Jewish town of Ashkelon. Its remains are located in a quarter known by the hebraicised name Migdal, or the Old City.

The town of al-Majdal was established at the end of the thirteenth century after Baybar had destroyed the port city of Ascalon. In 1945, the small town had over 11,000 inhabitants. Ascalon was at that time one of the most important corn granaries in Palestine; it was equally famous for its textile production, especially the manufacture of school uniforms.

En-Nakba

Al-Majdal was taken by Israeli troops with the help of air and naval forces between July 9 and July 18, 1948. Most of the population fled before or during the shelling to the Gaza area. Some 1,500 inhabitants remained in the city; they were placed in three closed areas by the Israeli authorities under a series of military and administrative measures, which culminated in the total eviction of every Palestinian occupant of al-Majdal at the beginning of 1951.

The city today

Several homes and shops still exist around what is now called *Herzl Street*. In the 1950s, many Moroccan and Iraqi Jews took possession here. An **old mosque**, renamed the Khan, now houses some shops and a small museum (with an exhibition of archaeological finds from the area). Those whose roots are originally in al-Majdal are today estimated at 71,000 people; UNRWA has registered 52,000 of them as refugees. Most of them live in refugee camps in the Gaza Strip, less than 20 kilometres from their town of origin.

Al-Jura

Demolished Palestinian village northwest of the present-day city of Ashkelon.

The village of al-Jura was built on a ridge of tufa (a porous limestone, *kukar* in Arabic). Under the Romans, the village was known as Jagur, and in written records of the sixteenth century as Jawra or Jawrit al-Haja. A village of fishermen and farmers, al-Jura had more than 2,400 inhabitants in 1944-45. Some of the people living in al-Majdal, which was 5 kilometres from the sea, had a summer residence here at al-Jura, where they could enjoy the breeze from the sea during the hottest months of the year. A *mawsim* here every spring was an important occasion for a gathering of Palestinians from cities, villages and Bedouin camps from all over central Palestine. Like al-Majdal, al-Jura was shelled in mid-October 1948; its people all fled to the Gaza area. On November 5, Israeli soldiers occupied the village.

Sheikh Ahmed Yassin born in 1936 killed by Israel in 2004

In 1948, as a 12-year old refugee, he took refuge in the Gaza Strip. He studied from 1957 to 1964 at the Egyptian University of Ain Shams, in Cairo, where he joined the Muslim Brotherhood. Later, he was one of the founders of the Islamic Centre of Gaza (1973) and then founder of the Islamic Resistance Movement (Hamas) in 1987, of which he was both the spiritual and functional head, serving as its leader, spiritual authority and strategic planner, politically and militarily. He was imprisoned at the beginning of the first Intifada, then released ten years later in exchange for two Mossad agents in possession of false Canadian passports who had failed in an attempt to assassinate a leader of Hamas in Jordan. After a stay in Jordan for medical reasons (he was paraplegic and always seen in a wheelchair), he returned in 1997 to Gaza, where he received a triumphal welcome. Sheikh Yassin was assassinated in the early hours of March 22, 2004, by an Israeli helicopter gunship, while leaving the Omari Mosque in Gaza City, near the refugee camp in which he lived a life of simplicity, starkly contrasting the lifestyle of many high-level Palestinian politicians of the Authority. His entire entourage was also killed in the same attack (seven bodyguards and Hamas operatives) while 15 others, including two sons, were wounded. At Sheikh Yassin's death, Dr. Abdel Aziz Rantisi was elected his successor as leader of Hamas but he, too, was killed in the same way, by Israeli Apache helicopter-borne missile strike, in April 2004.

The Negev (en-Naqab)

Getting to the Negev
There are several buses daily from ***Jerusalem*** *or* ***Tel Aviv*** *via* ***Bet Shemesh*** *or* ***Kiryat Gat*** *to the bus station in* ***Beersheba****, which is at* ***Eilat Street, near the Canion Mall****. The journey takes about an hour and a half. (Note: There are no buses on Friday afternoons or Saturdays until the end of the Sabbath.) One can also get to* ***Beersheba from Jerusalem via Hebron*** *(service taxi in Musrara Square), which is the shortest route from Jerusalem. In terms of mobility, a rented car is the ideal way to travel.*

■ The Bedouin Population of the Negev

Pre-1948, the Bedouin populations of the Negev were more often known as Arabs of Bir es-Saba' or Beersheba *(Arab es-saba')*. Even the Bedouins called themselves *arab* and not *bedu* (Bedouins), and referred to Arab peasants in the area as *fellahin* (peasants); *bedu*, which means "inhabitants of the desert," was a term used more by the peasants. In 1946, the estimated number of Bedouins in the Negev ranged from 57,000 to 95,500, belonging to 96 different tribes. At the time, a pastoral, semi-nomadic lifestyle was still the main way of life, although the majority of the population was already involved in dry agriculture, and some men worked in road construction or building other infrastructure developed by the British. When the area came under Turkish control, at the end of the nineteenth century, its pacification and the creation of international borders contributed to the progressive sedenterisation of the Bedouin, who dedicated themselves to farming and developing commercial ties with the merchants of Gaza.

The Zionist conquest of 1948 and the creation of the State of Israel at that time triggered upheavals and brutal traumas for this population. In 1953, the number of Bedouins remaining in the Negev was estimated at only 11,000 people. All others had been expelled by Israeli troops or had fled to the West Bank, Gaza Strip, or Sinai. Those who remained in the Negev were forced to live in a closed area to the north and east of Beersheba, an area representing only 10% of the Negev Desert. This zone, like all zones populated by Arabs in the new Jewish state, was subject to military administration until 1966. The land of

those who had fled the Negev was confiscated until, by the end of the 1950s, the new state had succeeded in appropriating over 90% of all land in the Negev, including 50% of the closed zone. Until 1966, the Bedouins were regrouped into 19 tribes, which were hastily created and then transformed into different administrative units led by "sheikhs" appointed by the military government. Excluded from the Israeli work force, the Bedouins were forced to restrict themselves to animal breeding and agriculture; as for some privileged people who had lived in Beersheba or in stone houses, they were forced to return once again to life under tents or in shacks.

Society and Life Styles

In the space of 50 years, the Bedouins who stayed in the Negev have witnessed profound upheavals. Their life style and economic activities have become increasingly urban, oriented around paid employment in surrounding cities. Civil administrations that have taken the place of the military regime have, since the late 1980s, steadily given more autonomy to the Bedouins in the new Israeli townships, which has thus played a role in developing an elite class and thereby totally undermining traditional hierarchies. Today the tribe *('ashîra)* has only symbolic value; the relevant socio-political unit today is patrilineal *(â'ila)*. Members of the immediate family maintain firm solidarity with each other in matters of honour and the family's social status, on the basis of family genealogy. Nevertheless, even when extended families of the same lineage remain as economic units, their mutual support system loses its significance with their society's increased access to the social welfare system.

The Bedouins of the Negev have developed new practices, ideas, and ways of organising, very different to those practised pre-1948. Their integration into Israeli society operates only in a model of spatial, economic and social segregation. The fact that some individuals have chosen to settle in Beersheba does not change the fact that Bedouins live there completely separated from the Jews, who make up 75% of the total population of the subdistrict of Beersheba. Even if they have daily contacts with their Jewish neighbours in the context of economic activities, these contacts are always maintained as relationships of subordination. Although the standard of living for the Bedouin community has improved in the last fifty years, it remains one of the lowest levels in the country, compared to the national average income: 50% of all families and 60% of all children live below the poverty line. A survey carried out by the Israeli Central Bureau of Statistics at the beginning of the year 2000 revealed that the seven new recognised Bedouin townships were the poorest of all the 200 population centres listed in the Negev, and have the highest unemployment rate in Israel, whilst various Jewish towns in the suburbs of Beersheba were listed amongst the richest.

■ Beersheba (Bir es Saba')

The city of Bir es-Saba' was established by the Ottoman authorities in 1900 for administrative reasons. The Bedouin sheikhs of the region, wise and pragmatic, were not slow to settle there, in order to be closer to the authorities. It was also during this period that the first stone constructions appeared among the Bedouin, as storage places for agricultural products and then later as dwellings. Farms were also built in the 1920s and 30s in the northwest Negev; yet these constructions remained in the hands of a privileged minority. The Partition Plan of 1947 recommended that Beersheba be administered by an Arab state, but Israeli military forces conquered the town on October 20, 1948. The city today is an essentially Jewish cosmopolitan city (comprising over 70 ethnicities) and has more than 150,000 residents. The founding of a university in the Negev, in 1969, had the desired effect of making Beersheba one of the principal Israeli urban areas. The university was named The Ben-Gurion University of the Negev, after David Ben-Gurion, a leading Zionist leader and the first prime minister of the State of Israel; he had a residence at *Kibbutz Sde Boker (50 kms south of Beersheba)*, to which he retired and where he later died, in 1973.

▪ The old city

Beersheba is a relatively spread-out and airy city with many large stately residences; in 1948 these were taken over by Rumanian and Moroccan Jewish immigrants. Several historic buildings in the old town have been conserved, although often dwarfed by contemporary buildings. At the junction of *Ha'azmaut (Independence) Street* and *Herzl Street*, the **governor's residence** will soon house the **Israeli Museum of the Negev** *(work in progress)*. Opposite the governor's house is the **house of 'Aref al-'Aref** (a Palestinian historian), built in 1938. It has been transformed these days into a coffee house and soft drinks café. Continuing up *Ha'azmaut Street*, one arrives at the **Bir Es-Saba' Mosque**, built in 1901. Since October 1948, it has been declared *"inalienable property of the Jewish people"* and Moslems are prohibited from entering it. Since the 1970s, the Muslim community has been claiming it, but the Israeli authorities refuse to give it up for "reasons of security," under the pretext that the minaret has a view over a military base on the other side of *Ha'azmaut Street.*

Since Beersheba was the regional capital of the Negev, under the Ottomans a market was established in the city as a weekly meeting place. Every Thursday *(yom il-khamis)*, the Bedouins and the villagers from the local region (the districts of Gaza and Hebron) would always gather there to sell their products, and then, the next day, attend Friday prayers in the mosque. The size of the area then set aside for the trade in livestock suggests the past importance of pastoral production in the region. The **Bedouin covered market** *(on the Hebron road; open 6:00-1300)* today has nothing in common with it except its name. Until the First Intifada, villagers and Bedouins from the Negev, the Gaza Strip and Hebron ensured the liveliness of the place and the supply of a wide variety of merchandise. Today, the market provides only feeble interest. The Thursday market still offers an opportunity to acquire various handicrafts labelled "Bedouin," which are actually mostly produced in the villages of the Hebron region. It is preferable to get there at dawn to get the best bargains; prices are generally higher than in Hebron, but still less than in tourist shops in other towns.

'Aref al-'Aref (1892-1973)

Born in Jerusalem into a leading family in Palestinian society, 'Aref al-'Aref was an active member of three government administrations in Palestine: Ottoman, British and Jordanian. An officer in the Ottoman Army during the First World War, he was imprisoned in Siberia from 1915 to 1917, but escaped under cover of the Russian Revolution. On his return to Palestine, al-'Aref worked for the Arab nationalist newspaper, *Suriya al-Janubiya (South Syria).* Following the anti-colonialist demonstrations at the time of the *mawsim* of Nabi Moussa in April 1920, he was arrested by the British authorities and exiled to Syria, and subsequently to Transjordan, after the French colonisation of Syria. Out of respect for the Transjordanian administration, he was rehabilitated and worked with the British administration in several Palestinian districts, one of which was Beersheba. After the Nakba, he served under the Jordanian military administration, before becoming Mayor of East Jerusalem in 1949 (until 1955). A short time before the occupation of 1967, he was appointed director of the Palestinian archaeological museum of Jerusalem (Rockefeller Museum). In parallel to his career as a government official, al-'Aref was a respected historian. Amongst his well-known writings are a *History of the Nakba* ("Catastrophe") and the *History of Beersheba and its Tribes.*

❑ Tel es-Saba'

On the road to Tel es-Saba' (Tel Sheva in Hebrew), 6 kilometres northeast of Beersheba. Open daily 9:00-17:00. NIS 10 entrance fee.

The oldest traces of human occupation here date back to the Chalcolithic Age (fourth millennium BC), but the ruins seen today may be ascribed to the Iron Age. According to biblical tradition, the name Bir es–Saba' ("the well of the seven") originates from the seven ewes Abraham gave to King Abimelech in return for his hospitality (Genesis 21:22-34). A fortified town was built here during the reign of King David, *circa* 1000 BC, and then apparently destroyed at the time of the incursion by Pharaoh Shishak in 925 BC. Thanks to its strategic position on the trans-Arabian trade route, on which Gaza was the principal terminus, the small city revived and prospered until its destruction by the Assyrians. Situated on the edge of the desert, the site's fortress was an outpost for the Arab kingdoms to the north (in those day, semi-nomads), and a frontier for the Persian, Hellenistic and Roman empires to the south. Large areas of the site have been excavated, and it offers a relatively complete picture of a small administrative city in the Iron Age, with its **triple tenaille gate** (attributed to the beginning of the tenth century BC), its warehouses, streets and four-room houses. At the eastern end of the city, a **monumental quadrangular well** allowed water to be stored as a safeguard in case of siege. Although anaesthetic, the observation tower on the hill affords a wide panorama of the surrounding plains, while the small museum describes the utilisation of the semi-desert environment in ancient times.

■ North of Beersheba

Rahat, Lagiyya ... recognised townships

In the 1960s, the Israeli authorities decided to urbanise the Bedouins. This policy was motivated by the desire of the State of Israel for more land in order to develop projects for the unique benefit of the Jewish population. Officially, the authorities presented this policy as a means of giving the Bedouins access to "modern" resources and services, claiming that it was not feasible to provide them to a scattered population. The first two recognised new townships to be established were Tel es-Saba' in 1965 and Rahat in 1970. During the 1980s, five other new townships were inaugurated in the following order: Ksifa *(Kuseifa)* and *'Ar`ara,* Shgib as-Salam *(Shgeib as-Salam),* then Hura and Lagiyya *(Lakiya).*
Most of these recognised townships are failures and the Bedouins (whose total number in the Negev today is over 140,000) have refused to settle in them; their reticence comes, above all, from the fear that their lands will be confiscated if they stop living on them, and nothing in the difficult social and economic aspects of life in the new townships appeals to them. Even though the Israelis have resorted to repeated, ongoing intimidation to "persuade" them to move: large-scale confiscation of livestock, house demolitions in unrecognised villages and wanton crop destruc-

tion (including regular aerial spraying with chemicals to destroy crops), despite all this terrorising, only half of the Negev's Bedouins have settled in the new townships. A recent government Plan for the Development of the Negev has proved equally controversial; whilst the government has pledged increased funding for Bedouin townships to entice the Bedouins into them, nothing has actually been done to ameliorate their real needs, whether in employment, education, municipal facilities, health services or other infrastructure. The government's intentions to grab more land have been fairly transparent, since it has committed much of the increased budget to beefing up the Green Patrol and other police forces whose agenda is to prevent the Bedouins from "stealing" their own land! House demolitions recently have become so widespread that they are no longer newsworthy; the authorities have even recently set up a department devoted solely to this issue. Houses are demolished because they are built without building permits, but the government refusal to give permits forces most Bedouin (and Palestinians elsewhere, especially in East Jerusalem) into unwilling criminality. If the Israeli settlements in Gaza are evacuated by Israel, it is highly likely that many of those settlers will relocate to the nearby Negev, thus putting the already vulnerable Bedouins under even more pressure.

Today, the recognised townships are bedroom suburbs on the outskirts of Beersheba. Rahat, with a population of 30,000, is the most important township, while Lagiyya has a scant 4,000 residents. The infrastructure here is totally inadequate and is in no way adapted to the needs of the population. There is distressingly little business or industrial activity. This lack of business activity, coupled with the low level of qualified manpower, make the population dependent on economic centres controlled by the Jewish population of the surrounding cities, and the Bedouins are particularly vulnerable to economic recession. During the late 1990s, the unemployment rate reached 29% for men and 83% for women. Bedouins serve in the Israeli army and police force, often for want of an alternative income, although their strong traditions make them excellent soldiers and trackers.

Contacts

To become better acquainted with contemporary Bedouin society in the Negev, contact **The Association for Arab Youth** *(Rahat, Hara Street 24, House No. 134. Director: Abdel Karim el-'Ata'ika; ☎ 08-991 7796)*. The association also organises an annual folklore festival from May 1 to May 5. Also contact: *Tallal Belgarawi* of the **Rahat Municipality** *(☎ 08-991 4915)*, or **The Regional Council for Palestinian Bedouins of Unrecognised Villages** *(Rahat,☎, 08-6283043, www.arabhra.org)*, **The Forum for Coexistence in the Negev** *(Sleiman Abu Zaid: 0507-701119 sliman_abozaed@yahoo.com* who is also active in Rahat at **The Centre for the Rights of the Unemployed)**, *Amal Elsana Alhjooj*, a Bedouin woman community leader (married to a Bedouin lawyer fluent in Italian & English: *Anwar Alhjooj*: ☎ *0507-250191*) working at NISPED: Negev Institute for Strategies of Peace & Development: *amals@nisped.org.il*: ☎ *08-640-5432*; *Amer Abu Hani* of "Together" an organisation also co-ordinating the unrecognised villages, is at ☎ *0544-745625* and speaks fluent German and English. These groups can arrange informative sessions and visits to unrecognised villages or the Bedouin townships, with guides fluent in a range of languages.

Unrecognised Villages and Encampments

In the Negev, more than 60,000 Bedouins (a good half of the Bedouin population of this region) live in villages and encampments on sites that have become permanent. The existence of these unrecognised villages represent a living opposition to Israeli policy to concentrate the Bedouins into the new townships which take into account neither the particular needs of Bedouin society (such as living quarters adequate for family and tribal members to live together in a big group), nor the right of the Palestinian Arab population to live on its land, nor infrastructure or employment opportunities. Knowing that this policy's corollary is confiscation of land and eviction of its Arab dwellers, most Bedouins prefer, whenever possible, a precarious lifestyle to one of deportation into the new townships. A significant example of the policy of confiscation of land is the case of the Azazmeh tribe; part of its land was confiscated in 1990, for military purposes. After its seizure, the land was immediately transformed into an agricultural kibbutz for the exclusive use of Jews. As for the Azazmeh, they have been forcibly transferred to live next to the industrial zone of *Ramat Hovav (500 metres away)*, where chemical and toxic waste is stored or recycled. Living down-wind of a toxic site, and in the shadow of a main electricity power-generating station, it is no surprise that serious illnesses (cancers, spontaneous abortions or miscarriages, asthma, respiratory diseases, birth defects) are increasing in this community and are even double the national average. A recent Ben-Gurion University study has found the mortality rate 65% higher than elsewhere in Israel. Visitors will be impressed by the chemical quality of the air, which makes breathing difficult! Nothing speaks more volumes of the situation of today's Bedouins in the Negev-a people whose close contact with the land and nature make them so aware of their own plight. [Should one view this as an exception, one only has to go north to East Jerusalem to visit the Jahalin Bedouins - refugees originally from the Negev - who have been forcibly relocated next to Jerusalem's main garbage dump, so that Jewish settlers of Ma'ale Adumim could occupy land originally allocated to the Jahalin. The land's original and rightful owners are actually the Palestinians of nearby al-Azaria.]

Although 134 agricultural communities have been developed for the exclusive use of the Jewish population of the Negev, no Arab village or farming community has been authorised since 1948. Most Bedouin shanty-town villages are located along the highways. Some consist of only a few families, others, hundreds or even thousands of people. None of these villages are recognised by Israeli authorities, and consequently do not appear on any map. Deprived of essential services and infrastructure, the inhabitants themselves have improvised their own network of water distribution and use generators to provide electricity. The construction of permanent stone or concrete homes is illegal, so the only alternative is to use light materials (sheet metal, canvas, or plastic sheeting). The Israeli authorities regularly destroy these dwellings. Approximately 6,000 houses are currently slated for demolition.

Lakiya Negev Bedouin Weaving

Lagiyya (Lakiya). Open Sunday-Thursday 8:00-13:00. Sale of carpets, cushions, and woven bags. A medium-size carpet costs about US$100.

Founded in Lagiyya in 1991, the project intends to bring about social change by building a foundation for local economic development as a vehicle for empowerment. It channels traditional skills into a profitable cottage industry in a long-term sustainable way, thus restoring the women's contribution to family earning power. Formerly, the women wove the canvas and carpets made for their tents. Today the centre controls each phase of production, from spinning of wool to its weaving; the original four traditional colours have given way to a scale of 33 colours, offering a wide variety of tones.

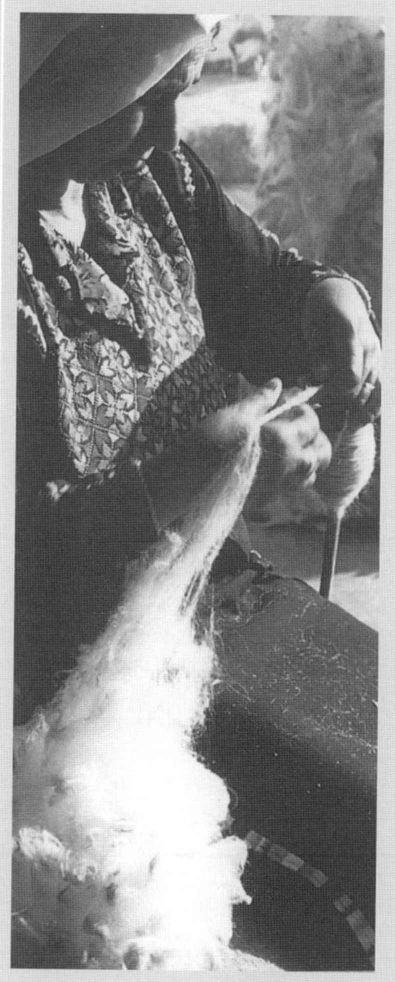

Guided Tours, or Activities

☎ *08-651 9883; lakiya@netvision.net.il www.lakiya.org.*

Lakiya Negev Weaving offers an interesting introductory programme on the Negev and its population, providing a window for outsiders into the lives and unique heritage of the Negev Bedouins. This consists of tours, which include visits (including to the Women's Embroidery Project in Lagiyya, where Bedouin women hand-embroider very beautiful and inexpensve products, or to unrecognised villages and typical landscapes) as well as many activities such as weaving and cooking. Bedouin society is in acute crisis, especially its womenfolk, who have been especially marginalised to the periphery of Israeli society. 96.5% of women in the Negev are unemployed, and because of strict traditions still obtaining, very often are restricted to the home. In the past, these women were full partners in the building and weaving of tents, the caring for flocks, raising crops or creating handiwork. Modernisation of Bedouin society has increased their dependence on men, both socially and within the family, reducing their status and thereby undermining it. These women's projects (including a literacy project for mature women), therefore, are radical as a means to support both the women and their daughters, who otherwise would receive no education.

■ East of Beersheba

❑ Massada

Open: daily 8:00-sunset, NIS15 entrance fee, on Road 90, which runs alongside the Dead Sea. Access by cable car (every 15 minutes). Two paths to the summit: one, the Snake Path (45 minutes), open from 4:00-8:00 a.m.: departure from the path under the cable car; the other, the Roman Ramp, takes 10 minutes to walk to the summit. Allow for an additional 30 minutes to reach the foot of the ramp, after parking your car in the cable car parking area. An alternative route by car: from Arad (Road 3199). There are eight buses every day between Jerusalem bus station and Massada. A detailed brochure about the ruins is available at the entrance to the site. ***Be sure to carry plenty of water with you.***

Massada is both the name given to a spectacular mountain dominating the Dead Sea, and also the name of the citadel initially built here by Alexander Yannai in the first century BC; it is on this mountain that Herod the Great built one of his majestic palace-fortresses. Abandoned now, the site served as a refuge during the years 66 BC to 73 BC for a Jewish messianic sect *(Sicarii)* who took their name from their dagger, the *sica*. It took an army of thousands of Roman soldiers and months of siege to capture the citadel; according to Flavius Josephus (the sole source for this event), the zealots preferred collective suicide to execution or slavery. The episode is recorded in a speech attributed to Elazar, leader of the Sicarii, who, having recognised the defeat as divine retribution, declared: *"Let us not receive this punishment from the Romans, but from God himself, by executing ourselves with our own hands."* (The War of the Jews against the Romans 7:333.) This story is, however, considered by most historians as pure rhetoric inspired by the tragic Graeco-Roman tradition. In the fourth and fifth centuries, monks settled in Massada and built a church here. In whatever manner the zealots or Sicarii met their death, Massada has since 1948 become a national religious symbol of the State of Israel, where soldiers of certain elite units of the army take a solemn oath: "Massada shall not fall again."

■ South of Beersheba

On the way to the archaeological site, Kunurb *(Mamshit)*, on Road 25, it is possible that the radio in your car may stop working; this is because you have entered a zone under high surveillance (the area around **Dimona**). Israel's Atomic Research Centre for the research and development of nuclear arms is located here under the greatest secrecy, as revealed to the London *Sunday Times* newspaper in 1986, by a nuclear technician, Mordechai Vanunu. Vanunu, kidnapped by the Mossad in Rome, was sentenced to 18 years' imprisonment and was placed under the harshest conditions of solitary confinement. He was re-

leased on April 21, 2004 amid much speculation as to his future; amongst his worldwide anti-nuclear supporters he remains a hero, he has spoken to journalists, especially Peter Hounam and the BBC, but there are those in Israel who remain extremely vengeful. An online poll by Maariv, one of Israel's leading newspapers, asked people to vote for various options as to his future, one of which was for Vanunu to be killed. During the days leading up to his release, there were those who speculated that maybe he would meet his death. The General Security Services have forbidden him to talk to foreigners, including the foreign press, he is not allowed to go near the sea, he is not allowed within 100 metres of any foreign embassy and his passport has been withheld so that he may not travel abroad. [For more information, contact *Alternative Information Centre* in Jerusalem, p. 168]

Nature Reserves and the Green Patrol

In 1976, the Labour Party founded the Green Patrol (Ha-sayeret ha-yeroka in Hebrew). It falls under the National Parks Authority, but operates under the orders of a committee directed by the Ministry of Agriculture, the Ministry of Security, the Ministry of the Interior and the Ministry of Housing & Infrastructure. In a document published by the National Parks Authority, the role of this patrol is defined as to defend state land against the "invasion" of herds or people who might illegally settle and erect infrastructure on this land in defiance of the law. The only population to which this document dedicates several pages is the Bedouin, who are specifically singled out as a potential danger.

"Until the beginning of the 1990s, the Green Patrol did all it could to discourage Bedouins from raising livestock and farming and to accelerate their urbanisation. Since 1977, the guards of the Negev unit have been particularly active. In order to intimidate the Bedouins, they do not hesitate to use many forms of harassment: they burn tents, conduct night raids during which they fire guns, sometimes they slaughter domestic animals, or undertake countless humiliations. (...) Animal herds are particularly targeted. Having decided to reduce greatly the movement of herds of livestock, Ariel Sharon, Minister of Agriculture in 1977, applied the 1950 law against black goats, prohibiting the breeding of this animal, which was presented as being extremely damaging to the environment. (...) The number of these goats in herds fell from

220,000 head in 1976 to 70,000. These strategies of intimidation were pursued into the mid-nineties, albeit less energetically. However, Bedouins are still subjected to numerous confiscations of their livestock and fines for taking their herds onto land transformed into nature reserves or used for military training. In the 1980s, house demolitions increased at encampments built on campsites that had become permanent settlements. (...) In addition to these measures of demolition, the state awarded itself other legal tools to gain control over the lands of the Negev. The creation of nature parks is, in this region - as in the Galilee - a decisive means to prevent expansion of the Palestinian population on the confiscated land. Even more, it has supplied a group of arguments that legitimise that control by converging the specific interests of the environmental movement with those of the State of Israel. Most of these reserves in the Negev are situated on lands belonging to the Bedouin; but these parks are often concessions given to powerful pressure groups such as the army, certain industrial groups or state institutions (such as Israel's nuclear power station in Dimona)."

■ Cedric Parizot: *The Month of Welcome. (Reappropriation of electoral mechanisms and readjustment of power proportions affecting the Bedouins of the Negev, Israel.) (Doctoral thesis.)*

❑ Kunurb *(Mamshit)*

Road 25, 5 kms east of Dimona. Open April-September, Saturday-Thursday 8:00-17:00 (Friday 8:00-16:00); October-March, Saturday-Thursday 8:00-16:00 (Friday 8:00-15:00); NIS10 entrance fee.

The city was founded by the Nabataeans (a confederation of Arab tribes) in the first century, along the principal road leading from the Gulf of Aqaba to Gaza. After the Roman conquest of the region in 106 AD, a garrison was stationed there (see the Latin inscriptions on tombs in the north-east corner of the site). At the beginning of the fourth century, walls were built around the city to protect it from raids by nomads. The intensification of such forays disrupted commercial activities and led to the decline of the city, which seems to have died out towards the end of the fifth century. Strangely enough, Kunurb is still on the Madaba map, which dates from the sixth century. Many archaeologists believe that this is an intentional anachronism, paying tribute to the city's past glory; since no sixth century church or coins from that period have been discovered on the site, this hypothesis seems the most probable. The site has been carefully excavated and restored: see, in particular, the **Nabataean stables**, the **Church of Nilos** and the **fresco of Psyche and Cupid.**

❑ Subeita (Shivta)

Approx. 50 kms southwest of Beersheba; take Road 40, then at the Telalim crossroads take Road 211.

Subeita (Shivta) is one of the most impressive ruins of an antique city in the heart of the Negev. Founded by the Nabataeans in the first century AD, the city knew its apogee during the fourth and fifth centuries. With the introduction of Islam into Palestine, the city acquired a pluri-religious character, in which small mosques and churches were perfectly good neighbours. The city survived until the ninth century. The quality of the public and private buildings' masonry reflects its prosperity. Around it, the fields - now desert - were once all cultivated. Although there seems to have been somewhat more rainfall at that time, water remained a rare and precious commodity. Ingenious systems for recuperating water were engineered in the city itself (using pipes and tanks) and in the surrounding hills. Amongst the most efficient techniques utilised were the removal of rocks from hills so that water could run freely down into valleys and the building of terraces along those valleys.

❑ Ein Obdah (Ein Avdat)

Fifty-two kilometres south of Beersheba. Open April-September, Saturday-Thursday 8:00-16:00 (Friday 8:00-15:00); October-March, Saturday–Thursday 8:00-15:00, (Friday 8:00-14:00); NIS10 entrance fee. There are two entrances: the northern entrance is just before the sign to (i.e. to the south of) Kibbutz Sde Boker, where you can park your car. From there, there is a spectacular two to three hour hike (without including the return journey) along a marked pathway. Certain places have steep climbs (take care if you suffer from vertigo) and are therefore equipped with metal ladders. The southern entrance is just off Road 40, 7 kms. from the top of the walk from the northern entrance. A small Bedouin café under a tent offers visitors rest and refreshments and an opportunity to retrieve one's energy. One can walk or take the next bus (information at the café) back to the parking area.

Ein Obdah is the name of a spring which gushes as a waterfall into a deep canyon. The cliffs reach a height of 200 metres. After this waterfall, there are two lakes of icy water. A word of advice to nature lovers: remember your botanical and animal guides, for the site is rich in vegetation and animal life (gazelles, ibex, damans, porcupines, eagles…).

❑ Obdah *(Avdat)*

Sixty kilometres south of Beersheba, 15 kms south of Sde Boker. Open April-September, Saturday-Thursday 8:00-16:00 (Friday 8:00-15:00); October-March, Saturday-Thursday 8:00-15:00 (Friday 8:00-14:00); NIS 12 entrance fee. Display at Reception of archaeological objects found on the site.

Built as a caravan station serving the Nabataean trade routes, and founded in the second century AD, Obdah was named in homage to King Abdos II (30-9 BC), an eminent individual, elevated to the status of divinity. The city's population numbered around 3,000 people before it was abandoned, following the Persian expedition of incursion at the beginning of the seventh century. Like all other cities in the Negev at that time, Obdah owed its prosperity to the trans-Arabian trade and to agriculture. One sees around the city ruins of its sophisticated irrigation network that watered gardens and orchards.

❑ Makhtesh Ramon (The Ramon Crater)

On Road 40, 80 kilometres south of Beersheba. Bus. There is an exhibition of the geology, flora and fauna at the Visitors' Centre (☎ 08-658 8691) in the small tourist town of Mitzpe Ramon, on the edge of the crater. There are several hostels and camping areas in the vicinity of Mitzpe Ramon. Available activities include: hiking (maps are on sale), guided tours, camel, jeep, ATV (all-terrain vehicles) or mountain bike tours. **Make sure to take enough water with you.**

A spectacular geological phenomenon, the makhtesh is an enormous crevasse extending 40 kilometres in length, with a width of 9 kilometres and a depth of 300 metres. Formed by the movement of tectonic plates and by erosion, the crater seems to represent a genuine textbook of geological history covering 245 million years. This way was the traditional route for Arab caravans, which connected Arabia to Palestine via Beersheba.

❑ The Hai Bar Biblical Wildlife Reserve

Forty kms. north of Eilat. Open Sunday-Thursday 8:30-17:00, Friday-Saturday 8:30-16:00; NIS 15 entrance fee, NIS 5 extra for vehicle. Predators' Section: NIS 26 entrance fee. Safari tour by jeep.

Like other animal parks in Israel, this nature reserve seeks a biblical connection. Animal species mentioned in the Bible have been reintroduced here. The park has more than 450 wild species (not all mentioned in the Bible), among them the white oryx, the wild ass of Somalia, the twisted-horned addax and the ostrich. A special section is reserved for predators: wolves, lynxes, wild cats, leopards and hyaenas.

❑ The Copper Mines of Timna

Road 90, 30 kilometres north of Eilat. Open daily 7:30 a.m.-sunset; NIS 15 entrance fee. Video and diagrams available at the entrance to the site, describing Timna's geology, history and methods of extracting copper. Hikes are possible; there are two itineraries: one for three hours, the other for seven. The Nubian sandstone mountains (red sandstone) as well as the strange geological formations, such as rocks in the form of mushrooms, are particularly beautiful at sunrise and sunset, which explains the park's visiting hours.

Since the Ancient Bronze Age (circa 3000 BC) onwards, seams of copper at Timna were exploited. The Egyptian rule of the region, from the fifteenth to the twelfth century BC, accompanied intensive exploitation of copper mining under the auspices of the goddess Hathor, to whom a temple was consecrated. A papyrus attributed to Pharoah Ramses III (1184-1153 BC) permits us to imagine the importance of this activity: *"I sent my messengers to the land of Atika (Wadi Araba) to the large copper mines found there. They travelled by bark or on land by donkey. The mines there were full of copper: tens of thousands [of ingots] were loaded into the holds of the barks. They were sent to Egypt and arrived safely."* (Harris Papyrus 1:78, 2) The Midianites continued mining copper here after the Egyptians had retreated. After the Midianites, there was only a little mining activity. In fact, the discovery of iron made this distant source of copper a poor investment, although it was temporarily reopened by the Roman Cyrenaic Third Legion.

The Occupied Syrian Golan

الجولان السوري المحتل

The Golan

الجولان

The Golan

Getting to the Golan

Given the minimal public transportation available, the best way to travel in the Golan is by rented car. The Alternative Tourism Group (see *ATG, Beit Sahour*, p.209) organises visits but only for groups.

■ Historical Background

The etymology of the term "Golan" (pronounced "julan" in Arabic) has different sources and meanings; its Semitic root indicates a land full of dust. The name "Golan" could also relate to the root of the verb "jala" which in Arabic means *"to move from one place to another."* In this case, it could refer to the movement of herds or, there again, to the wind that is very much present in winter.

At the crossroads of the Sham Countries (Bilad esh-Sham is the name often still used to describe the group of countries of this region of the Near East [Syria, Palestine, Lebanon and Jordan] or Greater Syria [Souria al-Koubra]), the Golan Heights was always a bridge throughout history

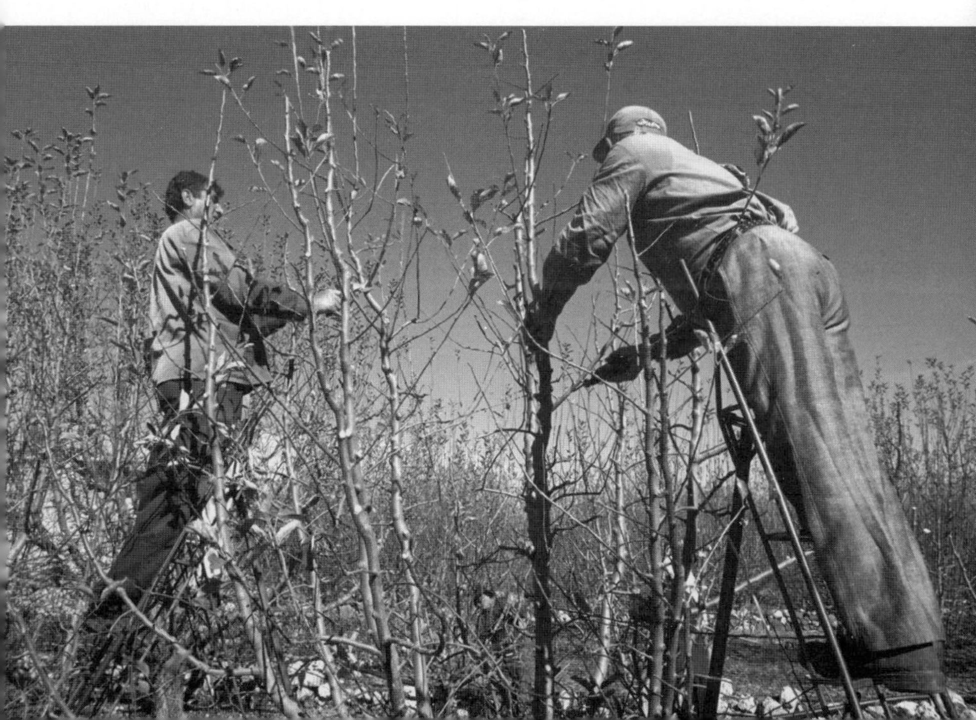

between Mesopotamia and Egypt or the Mediterranean and later between the two great capitals of the Arab world: Damascus and Cairo. It is also traditionally a place of refuge: thus in the tenth century the mountains of central Lebanon and of the Syrian Hauran constituted a favourable place for the development of the Druze Muslim sect which settled there. At the beginning of the twentieth century, the population of the Golan took an active part in Arab struggles for independence. While the Arab national movement called for establishing one united and independent Arab state, or at least the re-establishment of Greater Syria (the entire historical region), the European colonial powers divided the area into several separate mandates. The Golan was placed under French mandate, despite British and Zionist pressure to include it in British mandatory Palestine.

Ben-Gurion declared, moreover, in 1920: *"We have continually asserted that Israel should include the southern bank of the Litani River and the Hauran region, south of Damascus."* During the French Mandate, the northern area of the Golan was one of the principal Syrian hotbeds of resistance to French colonialism. In reprisal, the French army burned and demolished several villages, including Majdal Shams.

When Syrian independence was gained on April 17, 1946, the Golan, whose first foothills are only some thirty kilometres from Damascus, remained a Syrian province. In 1948, the Syrian army impeded the Zionist conquest of several Palestinian villages, which were placed in a "demilitarised zone" or "DMZ" under Syrian authority. Some 9,000 Palestinian refugees from the Galilee settled in the Golan. From 1949 to 1967, the State of Israel continuously claimed the DMZ under the pretext that these territories were inside the borders of Mandatory Palestine and that the partition plan had allocated these territories to the Jewish state! Israel adopted an offensive policy towards the DMZ, increasing its provocations and aggressions. In violation of the 1949 Armistice Treaty, the State of Israel began a programme of draining Lake Hula (DMZ). This programme had three objectives: to impose Israeli sovereignty over the DMZ, to add 100 million cu.m. of water to its water resources, and to deport the Palestinian population which was present in this zone (a decision which was made in a secret memorandum, issued at a meeting of the Israeli cabinet on April 5, 1951). The UN held Israel fully responsible for the military clashes that ensued and called for an immediate halt to the drainage. At the end of the 1950s, Syria adopted a more aggressive policy vis-à-vis the gradual Israeli assimilation of the DMZ and the passivity of the UN in implementing its resolutions. Syrian policy always limited itself to not tolerating any violation of its frontiers and permitting the Palestinian resistance (Fatah and the Arab nationalist movement) to launch operations of sabotage on the State of Israel. In April 1967, the Israeli government reasserted its intention to farm the "demilitarised zones." On April 7, 1967, an Israeli armoured tractor took up a position on the eastern shore of Lake Tiberias (DMZ). The regular Syrian army shot at the tractor with light weaponry. That same day, Israeli forces bombarded both Syrian military positions and villages and flew over Damascus. Then, following Israel's lightning victory over Egypt and Jordan, the assault turned on the Syrian Golan, which on June 9 received a rain of bombs and napalm. On June 10, the Golan was in Israeli control. A cease-fire agreement was signed, only to be broken two days later by the Israelis, who also conquered Jabal al-Sheikh (Mount Hermon).

During the war of 1973, the Syrian army temporarily liberated the Golan Heights, but a unilateral accord between the State of Israel and Egyptian President Anwar Sadat, under the auspices of American Secretary of State, Henry Kissinger, allowed Israel to mobilise its full military force to re-conquer the Golan. Under an agreement signed on May 31, 1974, Israel returned 8% of the Golan occupied in 1967, in return for a cease-fire.

The Golan

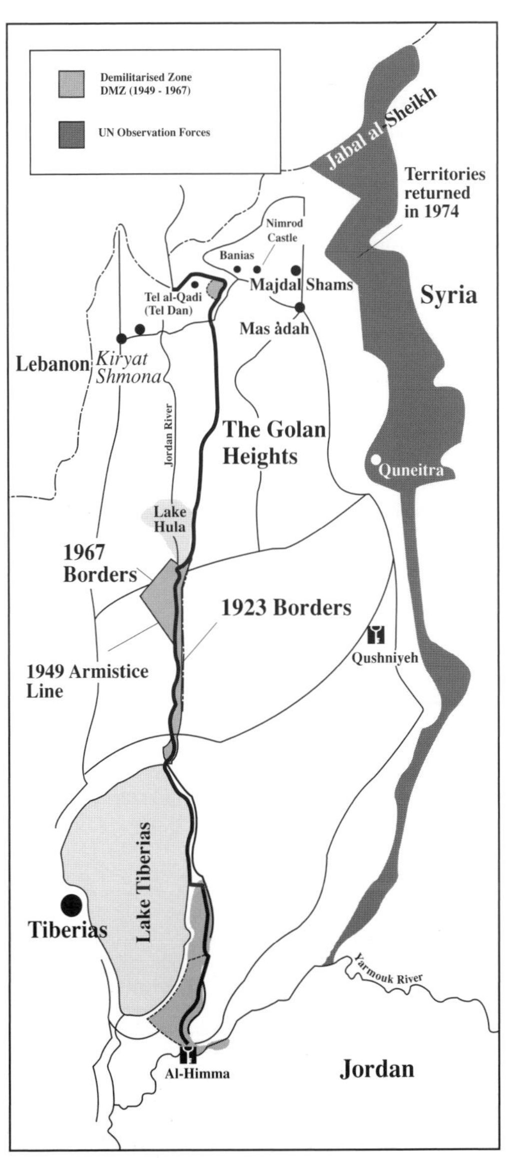
Demilitarised Zone
DMZ (1949 - 1967)
UN Observation Forces
Jabal al-Sheikh
Territories
returned
in 1974
Nimrod
Castle
Banias
Majdal Shams
Syria
Tel al-Qadi
(Tel Dan)
Mas àdah
Lebanon
Kiryat
Shmona
Jordan River
The Golan
Heights
Quneitra
Lake
Hula
1967
Borders
1923 Borders
Qushniyeh
1949 Armistice
Line
Lake Tiberias
Tiberias
Yarmouk River
Al-Himma
Jordan

Occupation and Annexation of the Golan

Before the occupation of the Golan, 130,000 Syrian and Palestinian Arabs lived here in 139 villages or encampments and on 61 farms. The intensive bombardments (both bombs and napalm) on June 9 and June 10, 1967 threw almost the entire population of the Golan into an exodus of exile. In total, 133 of those 139 locations were demolished, thereby prohibiting any return of refugees.

Only a minority of the population (6,396 people), mostly Muslim Druze, but also some Sunni Muslims and Christians, was allowed to remain. Why were these few villages (Majdal Shams, Buqatha, Mas'adah and Ain Qinya Ghajar) not destroyed in the same way as others? Many theories have been advanced. Their location, at a distance from the principal battle-fronts, saved them from the systematic shelling suffered on the rest of the heights. In addition, the experience of their engagement in Syrian resistance to French colonialism in the 1920s had reinforced the determination of the population to remain and defend their lands. Finally, the Israeli government was hoping to enlist the Golan Druze to collaborate with the State of Israel by encouraging them especially to reinforce their ties with their co-religionists, the Druze of Galilee. But the attachment of the Golan Druze to their Arab Syrian culture and their refusal to permit their national identity to be reduced to mere religious affiliation showed the Israeli authorities that this idea was ill-conceived. The Israeli authorities then put into place the usual repressive measures on the occupied population: curfews, administrative detentions, land confiscations and restrictions on water consumption, to name but a few.

On December 14, 1981, the Israeli parliament (Knesset) passed a law annexing the occupied Syrian Golan. From now on *".. the laws, jurisdiction and administration of the State* [of Israel] *apply to the Golan Heights .."* replacing the military jurisdiction in force in the Occupied Territories. The local inhabitants rejected Israeli nationality and intensified their national movement, ostracising anyone who collaborated with the occupier. Today, these five villages that escaped destruction in 1967 have a population of some 19,000 people, while the number of Jewish settlers, who live in 34 settlements, has risen to 17,000.

The General Strike of 1982

Following the Israeli annexation, the local population organised a general strike in an appeal to the international community to assume its responsibilities; it should be noted that the UN had rejected the annexation. The strike lasted five months, during which time the Israeli army laid siege to the villages and made many arrests. Israel's subsequent invasion of Lebanon in 1982 (originally named "Operation Peace for Galilee") distracted the attention of the international community; the UN resolutions were not implemented, and the Arab Syrian population of the Golan was forced to carry an identity card *(hawiya)* similar to that of Palestinians of East Jerusalem. However, faced with fierce resistance by the Arab population of the Golan, Israel was unable to impose Israeli nationality on them.

▪ The Golan Plateau (Heights)

Extending over a basalt plateau, at an average altitude of 1,000 metres, the Golan region covers an area of 1,750 sq. kms. To the north, Jabal al-Sheikh (Mount Hermon) rises to an altitude of 2,814 metres. It has a geo-strategic position dominating the south of Lebanon and Syria, the Golan Heights and the Hula Valley. In June 1967, the State of Israel conquered 1,250 sq. kms that comprised 80% of this Syrian territory. In 1974, around 100 sq. kms were returned to Syria.

Demolished Syrian Villages

Over the entire plateau

Until 1967, a population of diverse religious followings: Sunni Muslim or Druze, Circassian, Christian Greek Orthodox (whether Syriac or Armenian) peopled the Golan, an excellent, fertile territory thanks to ancient volcanic activity, cultivated by peasants on their small-holdings. Today, piles of stones and dilapidated huts dot the countryside; these ruins are unique testimony

to the tragic expulsion of the population by Israeli military forces. In all, 133 villages, encampments or hamlets were partially or completely demolished.

At the end of Road 98 are the ruins of the **demolished village of Qushniyeh**. It is easy to identify, for it was not completely destroyed, but converted for some time into an Israeli military training centre. The mosque and some buildings, riddled with bullet-holes, remain standing. Before its destruction, Qushniyeh had nearly 3,000 inhabitants, a majority of whom were Circassian; the villagers were generally farmers, craftsmen or office workers.

Quneitra

A lookout point from Road 98.

Pre-1967, the city, with a population of 30,000, was the regional capital of the Golan. Occupied in 1967, it was returned to Syria after an agreement was concluded and signed on May 31, 1974 under American auspices. Before withdrawing, the Israeli army destroyed most of the buildings, cisterns and lines of communication, a deliberate destruction condemned at the time by the UN. A sad souvenir from this time may be seen at a distance, from the vicinity of the Jewish settlement *Mitzpe Quneitra* (Road 98): *"If you want to have Quneitra, you can have it - in ruins."* So says a graffiti left by Israeli soldiers in 1974.

■ Majdal Shams

Situated at the foot of Jabal al-Sheikh, Majdal Shams ("Tower of the Rising Sun") is a village on an escarpment rising 1,100 to 1,300 metres; with a population of over 8,000 souls, it is the most important Arab village in the Golan. In the village, two monumental bronze statues vigorously express the people's deep attachment to their Arab Syrian identity and their determination to free themselves from the Israeli Occupation. These statues are the work of Hassan Khater, a native artist of the Golan, who studied sculpture at the University of Fine Arts in Damascus. They are a barely concealed message to the Israeli occupier. The statue situated at the entrance of the village is dedicated to As'ad Kanj Abu Saleh and to the freedom fighters who fought French colonialism during the Great Revolt of 1925. The people of the Golan played a major role in the insurrection, and when the French army re-occupied the region, Majdal Shams was completely devastated. The second statue, erected in the centre of the village in 1987, is called "al-Massira" which means in Arabic "a march" or "an action which continues." Sultan al-Atrash, a national leader of the revolution of Greater Syria in 1925, is represented brandishing his sword. The work reaffirms the message of civil disobedience, in the words of the Tunisian bard of the anti-colonial struggle, Abu al-Qassem al-Shabi:

"If the people one day demand life,
Surely destiny will respond,
The night will disappear,
And the chains will break asunder."

Golan Apples

The Majdal Shams region is crowned by the apple; more than 80% of the agriculture here is dedicated to it. Although less than 10% of the people are exclusively farmers, apple growing is an activity and second source of income for many. Introduced to the area in 1945, apple growing has not ceased to develop ever since; in 1967, farmers of the Golan increased the size of their orchards to prepare for a new generation of trees and to protect the land from confiscation (learning from the Palestinian experience of 1948). The land surface dedicated to apple cultivation has increased from 640 hectares in 1967 to 1,500 today; at the same time, farmers have had to face an increasingly urgent problem: water shortage. While irrigated agriculture is highly subsidized in Jewish settlements, the Arab population has to deal with severe water restrictions. At the beginning of the 1980s, a local engineer devised an alternative solution: the method consisted of building large cisterns in the orchards to collect rainwater; between 1982 and 1984, 650 cisterns were built. The Israeli authorities reacted by imposing new restrictive measures: before building a cistern, a farmer first has to obtain five permits: (from the Ministry of Defence, the Ministry of the Environment, the Ministry of Planning, the Antiquities Authority and the National Water Carrier. Not a single new reservoir has been built since! These new regulations could not apply retroactively to the cisterns already installed, so the Israeli authorities decided to tax the rainwater collected in the cisterns, in compensation for the loss caused to Israel!

The Druze Doctrine

The Druze community constitutes the majority of the Arab population of the Occupied Golan. The Druze people live primarily in the mountains of Syria and Lebanon, but there are also important Druze communities in the United States and in West Africa. In all, they total about 500,000 people.

The origin of Druze doctrine emanates from the Ismaeli movement (a Shiite branch of Islam), and dates back to the end of the reign of the Fatimid caliph, al-Hakim (996-1021 AD). Originally from North Africa, the Fatimids had founded Cairo, capital of the Fatimid caliphate in 969 AD, then conquered the countries of al-Sham (Palestine, Syria, Lebanon and Jordan). The first leader of the rebellion against the Abbassid (Sunni) power was the Persian al-Darazi, who gave his name to the new religion and its followers. Caliph al-Hakim, who claimed to be the seventieth and last incarnation of Allah, gave his conquest a religious basis to distance himself from both the Sunnis and the Shiites. After al-Hakim's death and the death of Hamza, a spiritual leader (writer of the principal tenets of the Druze religion), the movement, which was both mystical and political, progressively faded in Egypt. Nevertheless, it survived in Greater Syria (together with the sect of the Assassins) among the peasantry and mountain dwellers, who were all opposed to the central governing power. Until then it had been a proselytising movement seeking to convert people, but now it turned inwards, refusing to make conversions and isolating itself in the most remote mountainous areas. The religion is especially mysterious, even to its own followers: most Druze do not know the theological foundations of their religion. The Druze community is divided into two groups: the initiated *('oukkal)* and the uninitiated *(juhal)*. Initiated Druze devote themselves entirely to a spiritual life (study of holy texts and secret rituals based on the truths of their faith), while the uninitiated lead a more secular life, based on the religious and moral principles set by Hamza (the oneness of God and abstention from lying). Uninitiated Druze are exempted from most of the obligations set down in the Quran, particularly the daily prayers.

Practical Information

Cafés and Restaurants

Abuliz Restaurant *(in the middle of the village; ☎ 04-698 5277)* serves good *mezzeh* and grilled meat. There is a live music performance on Thursday evenings. **Ein al-Tineh café-restaurant** *(☎ 04-698 3292)* is located at the end of the village within range of Syrian voices, and dominates the "Valley of the Cries," which owes its name to the system invented by Syrian families separated since 1967, who communicate from each side of the border with megaphones: an irregular contact sometimes prohibited by the Israeli authorities.

Accommodation

The opening of a hostel in Majdal Shams is under discussion at the moment. Contact the association: **The Golan for Development**.

Contacts

The Golan for Development

Majdal Shams. ☎ 04-698 2825. For any contacts or information, don't hesitate to contact Dr. Taiseer Maray ☎ 050-831 6174 / 04-698 2672. taiser@jawlan.org It is possible to organise guided tours for groups (cost open to negotiation). A hostel is also planned.

The Golan for Development is a community association. It is involved in many areas, from the improvement of social and medical services for the Arab Syrian community, to denouncing Israeli occupation and all the measures accompanying it: land confiscation, restrictions on housing and obstacles to economic development, and the denial of basic human rights, etc. For all these reasons, the association is a centre of information and indisputable documentation.

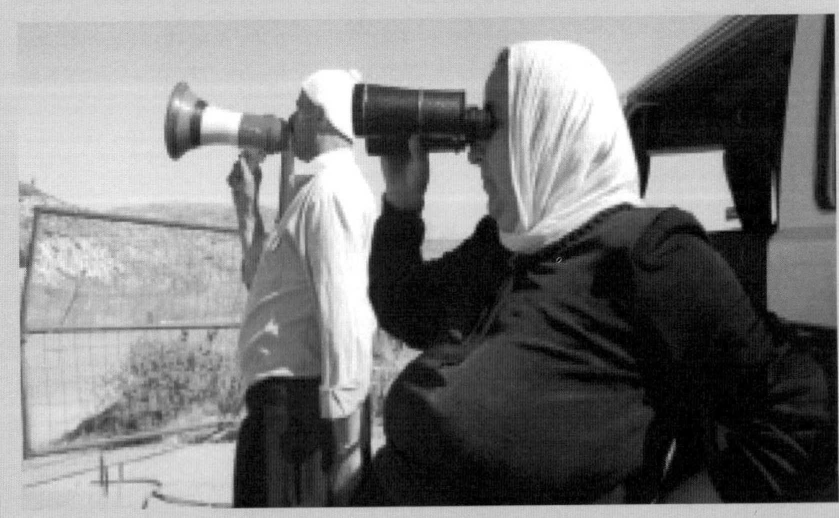

■ North and west of Majdal Shams

❒ Jabal al-Sheikh (Mount Hermon)

Rising to an altitude of 2,814 metres, Jabal al-Sheikh is the highest mountain in the Near East. Its Arabic name probably refers to a local sheikh, Rashid ed-Din es-Sinan, leader of a sect (the Assassins); he was also called the "Sheikh of the Mountain" or "Old Man of the Mountain." Founded in 1090 AD by the Persian, Hassan Sabbah, the Assassins (*assas* means "the watcher") professed a secret doctrine, firmly hostile to the reigning power. Their *fedayin* ("those who sacrifice themselves for the cause") killed even high-ranking Moslem and Frankish dignitaries. The Franks kept a bitter souvenir from that period: a new word in their vocabulary.

The mountain summit has not been accessible since it was returned to Syria in 1974. The slopes of Jabal al-Sheikh *(open end-December to mid-April)* are regularly snow-covered in the winter months; a small ski resort has been established here by Jewish settlers as part of the Jewish settlement, *Neve Ativ*. Located between Majdal Shams and Nimrod Castle, the settlement has the attraction of a prefabricated alpine village. It was built on the ruins of the village Jubatha ez-Zeit, demolished in 1967.

The Waters of the Golan

The Golan's abundance of water is legendary. It is true that it rains frequently between the months of October to May, while its mountain heights are regularly covered with snow from January to March. The entire territory collects 1.5 billion cu.m of water per year. However, because of the nature of the basalt rock (which is impermeable), 81% of the water evaporates, and only 10% is absorbed, while 9% swells the riverbeds and lakes, particularly Lake Tiberias and the Jordan River. The Golan supplies 30% of Israel's water supply.

❒ Nimrod Castle (Qala'at es-Subeibeh)

Road 99, then Road 989. Open Saturday-Thursday 8:00-17:00 and 8:00-16:00 in winter, Friday 8:00-15:00 (8:00-14:00 in winter), NIS 16 entrance fee. Hike recommended from Banias (approximately 1hr 30).

Legend has it that this was the site of the palace of Nimrod, a grandson of Ham (son of Noah), known as *"a mighty one in the earth"* (Genesis 10:8). In the Muslim tradition, Nimrod is regarded as the prototype of a proud tyrant who revolted against God, and who was the persecutor of the Prophet Abraham. Perched on a crag 3 kms north-east of Banias, Nimrod Castle is one of the best-

preserved mediaeval fortifications in the region. An ancient fortress, it was built by the Assassins in the eleventh century; they hoped that the castle would ensure their independence from the central Sunni Abbassid rulers. In fact, the fortress was captured by the Crusaders, in 1129 AD. It then fell successively into the hands of the Emir of Damascus (1132), the Seljuks (1137), the Hospitallers, and finally into the hands of Nur ed-Din (Saladin's uncle) in 1164. Each time, the castle was restored and enlarged. The Ayyubids and Mamelukes gave it its definitive architecture. The excellent state of conservation of the castle and its rich architecture make it a major historical site of the Golan.

❒ Banias (Nahal Hermon Nature Reserve)

Road 99. Open Saturday-Thursday 8:00-18:00, (8:00-17.00 in winter), Friday 8:00-16:00, NIS 12 entrance fee. To find your way around, ask for a brochure and a map of the reserve at Reception, as most of the site's signs are in Hebrew.

Since ancient times, Banias has been a sacred site where one cult succeeded another. In fact, its name is the Arabic version of a Greek divinity "Paneas," or the place of Pan (the god of nature, shepherds and herds). Niches carved in the rocky walls next to the cave contained statues of him as well as the nymph Echo and the god of music. Philip, Herod's son, built a town here called Caesarea Philippi, in the first century BC.

Christian tradition maintains that Jesus handed over the keys of the Church to Saint Peter (Simon Peter, the son of Yona) in Banias. *"And I say also unto thee, that thou art Peter, and upon this rock I will build my Church..."* (Matthew 16:13-18). The Roman and mediaeval ruins of the town are still visible to the southwest of the Pan grotto; so are other ruins of a Syrian village demolished in 1967. On the hill stands a small Muslim shrine to Weli al-Khader, which succeeded, in the Middle Ages, a chapel dedicated to Saint George.

Al-Khader - St. George

Witness to cultural and cult continuity, the names of al-Khader, St. George and the Prophet Elijah usually signify a single and unique personality, whose origin came out of Babylonian mythology. It is the symbolic representation of eternal youth and of the invisible world, appearing at will in his human form to rescue virtuous people. A central figure for Christian Palestinians, he is equally venerated by Muslims; there is a shrine consecrated to him in Jerusalem *(al-Quds)*, in the northwest corner of the Haram al-Sharif (outside the Dome of the Rock, or Mosque of Omar). In the village of al-Khader (see *Bethlehem*, p.200), an annual celebration has always reunited Muslims and Christians for a joint ceremony; in the current "situation" of closures, such traditions are seriously threatened.

Excursions and the Banias Waterfall

From Banias all the way to the cascades (the paths are signposted), there are some beautiful hikes to be made. On the way, you will come upon the only flourmill in Palestine; it is 700 years old and used to run on water-power. According to legend, King Nimrod, as tall as the mountain, only had to stretch out his arm to take a little water from the river. Swimming is possible here, but the water is cold. For hikers, the climb up to Nimrod Castle (an hour) is highly recommended.

❑ Tel al-Qadi (Tel Dan)

Road 99, 4 kms from Banias. In the heart of the Hurshat Tal (the Hebrew name) Nature Reserve. Open Sunday-Thursday 8:00-17:00, Friday 8:00-16:00; NIS 20 entrance fee. Guidebook available at the entrance.

The Canaanite city was mentioned by the name of Laish in ancient Egyptian historical texts of the nineteenth century BC. It appeared again, mid-fifteenth century BC, on the list of cities of Canaan conquered by Pharaoh Thutmose III, and in many other documents discovered in Mari (Syria). In the ninth century BC it was one of the fortified cities of the Kingdom of Israel or the Kingdom of Samaria, before it was destroyed in the Assyrian conquest of 732 BC.

▪ The ruins

There are several gates and sections of successive ramparts from the Bronze Age and Iron Age here, discovered by archaeologists. Note in particular the gate of sun-dried brick (one of the rare specimens preserved in the Near East), dating from the ninth century BC, as well as a quadrangular platform of the ninth century BC, built for religious rituals.

Practical Information

PRACTICAL INFORMATION

Customs Formalities

■ Visas and passports

Citizens of the United Kingdom, United States, Australia, Canada and South Africa need a passport valid for at least 6 months from the entry date. Citizens of EU countries and Switzerland do not generally require a visa in advance, but check this rule remains in force. Visitors must hold onward or return tickets and sufficient funds to cover their intended period of stay. Upon arrival, visitors receive an entry card to fill in and hand over with their passport. Half of it is returned and must be presented on leaving the country. Keep it!

No visa is required unless a stay longer than 3 months is planned. In this case, you need to ask for a visa for the desired length of time at the Israeli consulate in your country or request an extension or other appropriate visa in one of the offices of the Israeli Ministry of the Interior, which can be found in most major towns and cities. You must ask for the extension in the town in which you are staying. At this time, you need to establish that you have sufficient funds for the requested period. An extension costs NIS120, and you will need one passport-sized photo.

*If you intend to visit any Arab country other than Egypt, Jordan or the United Arab Emirates after leaving Israel, you **must** avoid having any Israeli stamp or visa on your passport: remember to ask officials when you enter Israel to stamp your entry card, not your passport. Repeat this request when you hand your passport over when leaving the country.*

Formalities on arrival and departure

On departure, you may be closely questioned by one or more male or female security personnel, who will ask in detail about "your stay in Israel" - why you came, what you did, where you have been, with whom you have spent time. For this, obey a golden rule: stay calm. Answer the questions calmly, as briefly as possible, without answering more than you were asked. Many travellers who have spent the better part of their time in the Occupied Territories or with Palestinian Israelis inside Israel are apprehensive about this moment, but there is no need; simply say where you were without going into details. If you have been to Gaza, you may prefer to remove the paper indicating this visit from your passport before you arrive at the airport. The Israelis are justified in their security-awareness, but then tend to view ordinary visitors as security threats, which can be off-putting.

After being questioned, you are usually asked to have your baggage carefully inspected. Absolutely everything is usually subjected to close examination if you have been in the Occupied Territories. Electric appliances, cameras and video cameras may be taken to a separate room to be examined. After reclaiming your luggage after it has been inspected, you will take it to the check-in and proceed to the departure area, possibly accompanied by security personnel. Remember to ask the airport customs officer not to stamp your passport, but rather the optional paper put there for that purpose, if you do not want a trace of your visit in your passport. In the departure hall you will find the Duty Free zone, where usually there is hardly any time left for making any purchases.

Lengthy security checks - especially when departing - must be expected, whether travelling by air (Ben Gurion-Lod Airport), land or sea. For this reason, it is advisable to arrive at the airport at least 2+ hours before take-off. These checks are generally somewhat disagreeable.

Borders

The Egyptian border

Rafah

Open every day 9:00-17:00 except Friday: 8:00-15:00 (closed during Yom Kippur and Eid al-Adha): ☎ 08-674 9444 or 08-671 3683.

To enter Egypt via Rafah, you must be in possession of an Egyptian visa, previously obtained from an Egyptian Embassy or Consulate (Tel Aviv at 54 Basel Street: ☎ 03-546 4151/2 or Gaza: Thowra Street, Rimal: ☎ 08-282 4290/74) Egypt requires passports to have validity for a minimum of three months before expiry, so do not travel if your passport is due to expire within that time. Most international passport holders receive visas on the same day, at a price of about NIS80.

To enter the Occupied Palestinian Territories or Israel, a visa can be obtained from the Israeli authorities at the border itself.

Taba

Open every day around the clock (except closed during Yom Kippur).☎ 08-637 3110.

To enter Sinai via Taba a visa is not necessary in advance; a Sinai 14-day visa for the entire Sinai coast is available at the border. This visa is not valid for Cairo and other parts of Egypt, or Ras Mohammed National Marine Park so if you wish to dive there, make sure to get a full Egyptian visa in advance. Israeli passport holders do not receive that visa on the same day.

The Jordanian border

There are three crossing points between Jordan and Israel: **Allenby Bridge** or **King Hussein Bridge**, (Palestinian territories, occupied in 1967); **Sheikh Hussein Bridge** or ***Beth Shean***, farther north, and **Aqaba** or ***Arava***, to the south, next to Eilat.

Coming from Jordan

Allenby Bridge is the only point at which West Bank Palestinians may enter Israel. East Jerusalem Palestinians, any Israeli citizen (Palestinian or Jewish) and foreigners may enter at the three border posts, all under Israeli jurisdiction Allenby Bridge is the most frequented. After the customary search and questioning, it is easy to get a service taxi to East Jerusalem, Bethlehem (via Abu Dis) or Ramallah (at the present moment, to the Kalandia check-point). The fare is about NIS40, but checkpoints sometimes make it easier to change car, which increases the fare slightly.

Although in 1988 the Hashemite Kingdom of Jordan renounced its sovereignty over the West Bank and East Jerusalem (Palestinian territories it had annexed in 1949), you can enter Palestine by the Allenby Bridge without officially leaving Jordan. This means that you can go back over the bridge to Jordan without asking for a new entry visa for Jordan. To put it simply, your Jordanian entry visa is still valid even after a stay in Palestine - but only if you have already used the bridge to enter Palestine.

From the **Sheikh Hussein Bridge *(Beit Shean)*** or **Aqaba** (***Arava*** in Hebrew), where traffic is quite light, you will probably have to take a private taxi to the nearest bus station or bus stop: in the north, to *Beth Shean* and in the south, to *Eilat*.

Going to Jordan

The kingdom of Jordan recognises the State of Israel on the basis of the borders defined by the Armistice Treaty in 1949, but regards the Israeli occupation of East Jerusalem, the West Bank and the Gaza Strip as illegal. Consequently, foreigners have to request a visa at the Jordanian Embassy in Tel Aviv *(14 Abba Hillel Silver Street, Ramat Gan,Tel Aviv: ☎ 03-751 7722)* or the Consulate in Gaza *(An-Naser*

Street: ☎ *08-282-5134/104)* in order to cross the Allenby Bridge or obtain the visa directly from passport control at Sheikh Hussein or *Eilat*. Fees at the three passport controls can differ slightly, as does the cost of transport. The fee for visas generally depends on the passport held: prices are fixed according to the cost of a visa in those countries as charged to entering Jordanians. They can be quite expensive.

■ Allenby Bridge (near Jericho)

Open (for travellers coming from Jordan) Sunday-Thursday 8:00-17:00; Friday-Saturday 8:00-15:00; (for travellers going to Jordan) Sunday-Thursday 8:00-14:30, Friday-Saturday 8:00-10:30 (closed during Yom Kippur and Eid al-Adha); ☎ *02-994 3358.*

Going to Jordan: One must have a Jordanian visa to cross the Allenby Bridge to Jordan. If you already entered Palestine from Jordan over the Allenby Bridge, your Jordanian visa is still valid and will permit you to return to Jordan across the bridge. As stated above, Jordanian visas can be relatively expensive.

Going to the Occupied Palestinian Territories: the Israeli authorities will issue a visa on the spot.

■ Sheikh Hussein Bridge (near Bissan – *Beit Shean*)

Open Sunday-Thursday 6:00-22:00, Friday-Saturday 8:00-20:00 (closed during Yom Kippur and Eid al-'Adha) ☎ *04-609 3400/410.*

Going to Jordan: the Jordanian border authorities issue visas on the spot.

Going to Israel: Israeli officials issue visas on the spot.

■ Aqaba (near Eilat - *Arava* in Hebrew)

Open Sunday-Thursday 6:30-22:00, Friday-Saturday 8:00-20:00 (closed during Yom Kippur and Eid al-Adha). ☎ *08-630 0550.*

Going to Jordan: visas are issued on the spot by passport control (immigration authorities).

Going to the State of Israel: visas are issued on the spot by the immigration authorities.

OFFICIAL ADDRESSES

In the United Kingdom

Palestinian General Delegation: 5 Galena Road, Hammersmith, London W6 OLT (☎ + 44 208 563-0008, Fax: + 44 208 563-0058)
Embassy of Israel: 2 Palace Green, London W8 4QB (☎ : + 44 207 957-9500, Fax: 1 44 207 957-9555)

In the United States

PLO Office: 1730 K Street N.W., #1004, Washington DC 20006 (☎ : + 202 785 8391, Fax: + 202 887 5337)
Embassy of Israel: 3514 International Drive N.W., Washington DC 20008 (☎ + 202 364 5527, Fax: + 202 364 5429)

In Australia

Palestinian General Delegation: 19 Carnegie Crescent, Narrabundah, PO Box 4646, Kingston ACT 2604 (☎ + 81 2-6295-0222, Fax: + 61 2-6295-0021)

In Canada

Palestinian General Delegation: 45 Country Club Drive, Ottawa, Ontario K1 V9 W1 (☎ + 613 736-0053, Fax: + 613 736-0535)

Embassy of Israel: 1005-50 O'Connor Street, Ottawa, Ontario ON KIP 4H9 (☎ + 613 567-6450)

In South Africa

Embassy of Palestine: Sudhof Bldg. 472 Walker Street, Flat No. 5, Pretoria (☎ + 27 12 342 6411, Fax: + 27 12 342 6412

Embassy of Israel: 339 Hilda Street, Hatfield 0083, Pretoria (☎ + 27 12 342 2693)

■ Transportation at the borders

■ From the airport to Jerusalem

By bus: On buses run by the Egged Israeli bus company: buses for Jerusalem (the terminus is at the Jerusalem Central Bus Station) leave about every half hour. This ride - the cheapest available - lasts three quarters of an hour, and a ticket costs NIS20. However, these buses do not go to East Jerusalem or to the Old City.
By service taxi: The last stops are at Damascus Gate and Jaffa Gate, after the taxi has let passengers off in different neighbourhoods in West Jerusalem. In fact, these Israeli taxis let you off near Damascus Gate, but not at the gate. All passengers, regardless of their destination, pay the same NIS45 for a trip that takes about 2 hours in all. There may be an extra charge for any particularly cumbersome luggage. Nesher Taxi Co. *(☎ 02-625-7227)* takes travellers in a minibus to West Jerusalem and other addresses and can be found at the airport.
In a private taxi: Any taxi parked in front of the airport will be an Israeli vehicle and, as such, will not go to East Jerusalem, with the exceptions of Jaffa Gate, the New Gate or Israeli settlements. If your destination is in the heart of East Jerusalem, get in touch beforehand with a Palestinian taxi company to have a taxi waiting for you at the airport. The journey costs approx. NIS200, and there is an additional charge if the taxi has to wait, for example if you are delayed by a baggage search. (This is not standard practice but may occur.)

For Tel-Aviv and other destinations

United Tours Airport Shuttle Service Bus 22 runs to the main hotels along the beach *(length of trip, about an hour and a half; NIS20)*. For other destinations, ask at the United Tours' desk inside the airport.

From Jerusalem to the airport

By bus : Egged buses leave the Central Bus Station and go to the airport approx. every half hour. The journey lasts about forty minutes and costs NIS20.
By service taxi: The *Nesher taxi company (21 King George Street ☎ 02-623 1231)* goes regularly from Jerusalem to the airport. It has the best rates for a person travelling alone: NIS45 for around 2 hours. You need to reserve a day in advance. The taxi will pick you up where you are staying unless it is in East Jerusalem, where it will only stop at Jaffa Gate, the New Gate, the Jerusalem Hotel or the American Colony Hotel. Indicate precisely where you will be when you make your reservation by telephone, and be sure to be punctual.
By private taxi: The journey takes about thirty minutes and costs NIS120 in the daytime and NIS150 at night [See *Private taxis for East Jerusalem*, p. 421].

■ Taxi Service to Allenby Bridge or Sheikh Hussein Bridge

From Palestine to Jordan

East Jerusalem: ***Abdo Taxis*** *(opposite Damascus Gate, on the corner of Sultan Suleiman Street and al-Musrara Square; ☎ 02-628 3281)*. Taxis leave for Allenby

Bridge when they are full (7 places in a large-Mercedes, fare: NIS30, or passengers make up the difference for vacant seats. For Sheikh Hussein Bridge, a private taxi through the Jordan Valley costs NIS250.
Ramallah: ***Darwish Taxis*** *(al-Manara Square; ☎ 02-295 6150).* Service taxi to Allenby Bridge: NIS30 (since the beginning of the al-Aqsa Intifada, the fare has doubled due to the impossibility of using the main roads). For Sheikh Hussein Bridge, there is a change of vehicle shortly before the Green Line (the boundary between the West Bank and the State of Israel), south of Bissan - *Beth Shean.*
Bethlehem: ***Shaab Taxis*** *(Manger Square Street; ☎ 02-274 1923).* Service taxis to Allenby Bridge *(NIS35).*

From Jordan to Palestine

From Amman
Abdali Station (King Hussein Street). This is the main station for buses and for service taxis. Transport is available here for Jerusalem and all the neighbouring Arab capitals.
Bus: *Jett bus* (King Hussein Street, 500 metres above Abdali Station).
Private taxis: The fare for Allenby Bridge is about 35 Euros and 55 Euros for Sheikh Hussein Bridge.

■ Airlines

■ Flight information

Gaza Airport: ☎ 08-213 4289 [Gaza Airport has been out of service since the beginning of the al-Aqsa Intifada, i.e. since September 2000.]
Ben Gurion-Lod Airport: ☎ 03-972 3344

Airline Companies

Air France
27, Ez-Zahra Street.☎ 02-628 2535 (East Jerusalem)

Egypt Air
Jerusalem Street. ☎ 02-298 6950/49 (Ramallah)

KLM
Ez-Zahra Street. ☎ 02-628 4896/7

Lufthansa
Soufian Street. ☎ 09-238 2065 (Nablus)

Palestinian Airlines
Jamal Abdel Nasser Street. ☎ 08-282 2800 (Gaza)

Royal Jordanian Airlines
Salah al-Din Street. ☎ 02-628 2365 (East Jerusalem)
Ramallah City Centre ☎ 02-240-5060

SAS Scandinavian
☎ 02-628 3235

Turkish Airlines
Manger Street. ☎ 02-277 0130 (Bethlehem)

■ Maritime Travel

The Gaza Strip's western boundary is the Mediterranean Sea; its waters are under Israeli military control, and no boat may dock at, or leave from, Gaza. On the entire Mediterranean coastline, Haifa is the only port of debarkation (☎ 04-851 8111). Weekly services are provided between Haifa and Athens via Limassol, Cyprus, and between Haifa and Rhodes, Greece, by *Poseidon Lines*. It takes two and a half days to reach Piraeus (the port for Athens), 33 hours to Rhodes and 10 hours to Limassol. Fares range from NIS 360 for a seat on the bridge to over NIS 1000 for meals and a cabin complete with bunk bed, shower and toilet.

Poseidon Lines

Greece - 32 Alkyonidhon, 16673 Kavouri Voulas (near Athens) (☎ + 30 (0)1-965 8300)

Cyprus - c/o Amathus Navigation, 2 Sindgmatos (old port), Limassol. (☎ + 357 (0) 5-341 043)

Israel - c/o Jacob Caspi, 1 Nathan, Haifa (☎ 04-867 4444)

Salamis Lines -

Greece - 9 Filellinon

Cyprus - Avenue 28 October, POB 531, Limassol (☎ +357 (0)-5-355-555

Israel - c/o Allalouf Shipping, 40 HaNemal, Haifa (☎ 04-867-1743)

Communications

Telephone

Calls inside Israel or Palestine (same procedure for both the Palestinian territories and the State of Israel): dial «0» and then the area code for the city you are calling (for example, «02» for Bethlehem).

Local Calls (in the same town or telephone area): dial the number you are calling without the area code. For example, when you make a call to Bethlehem from Jerusalem, do not dial «02».

Phone rates are much less expensive daily in Israel after 7 pm until 7 am (19:00-07:00), and on Friday afternoon and on Saturdays and Israeli holidays. In Palestine, cheaper calls are available after 10 pm until 6 am (22:00-06:00) and on Fridays and Palestinian holidays.

Calling Palestine Dial 00-972, followed by the area code (without the «0» , used only for calls inside), then the number you are calling, which should have 7 digits.

- [From the U.S., dial «01 972», + the area code (omitting the«0», which is only used for inter-city calls inside Israel or Palestine), then the number you are calling, which should have 7 digits.]
- Note: for West Bank and Gaza Strip,«972» can also be «970» (both function).

Calls to Other Countries

- From places in the West Bank or the Gaza Strip, dial 00 (the international call number), then the number for the country you are calling (for example, «1» for Canada and the U.S.), then the area code followed by the number you are calling.
- From Jerusalem or places in the State of Israel, dial 012, 013 or 014, depending on which phone company's rates you prefer.

Mobile Telephones

- To call a mobile phone from a standard phone or other mobile phone inside Israel or Palestine, dial the 4-digit code of the phone company you are using and then the number you are calling, which will have 6 digits. For example, dial 0599 and the 6-digit number.
- To call a mobile inside Israel or Palestine from another country, dial the company code without the first «0».For example: 00-972-599+6-digits.

Public Telephones

- For the Palestinian telephone system (in the West Bank and the Gaza Strip), phone cards of 10, 15, 30 or 50 units are sold in post offices and many grocery shops. One needs at least 30 units for a call to another country. For local information, dial 144.

- For the Israeli telephone system (inside the State of Israel and its annexed territories - East Jerusalem and the Golan Heights), phone cards of 20, 50 or 120 units are sold in post offices and grocery shops or newstands. To call another country, one needs at least 50 units.

- For **international information**, dial 188.
- For **local information**, dial 144.
- To **reverse charges**, dial 1-800-94-94-33-00 (Ask the operator for an *«outgoing collect call»*. One can make a collect call from any public phone booth.)

■ Postal Services

In 1995, the autonomous Palestinian cities established their own postal service: mail and stamps. Thus, you can send mail from all the urban centres in the West Bank and Gaza. In East Jerusalem, the postal system is Israeli. Telegrams, faxes and international calls are all handled at the post office.
In the West Bank and the Gaza Strip, post offices are open from 8:00-14:00 and are closed on Friday.
The main Israeli post offices are open from 8:00-18:00 and closed on Friday afternoon and all day Saturday. Branch post offices open from 8:00-14:00.

■ During Your Stay

■ Living Arrangements

There are numerous possibilities for accommodation, in all price ranges: *Bed & Breakfast, guesthouses,* Christian hospices and all categories of hotels. There is no official star system of classification of lodgings, so a good indication of the quality offered is the price, although this is not always a guarantee. In general, most of the hotels lack imaginative decor and share a certain banality in decor.

This Week in Palestine publishes a detailed but not exclusive list of hotels in East Jerusalem, the West Bank and the Gaza Strip. This free monthly brochure is available in many Palestinian tourist locations.
Israeli tourist offices also publish a brochure entitled ***Israel Tourist Hotels***, which lists different Israeli hotels and their rates in dollars.
The ***Christian Information Centre*** at Omar Ibn al-Khattab Square at Jaffa Gate provides a list of Christian hospices. You can also get information from the ***YMCA*** *(Young Men's Christian Association) in Nablus Road, East Jerusalem (☎ 02-628 6888 - fax: 02-627 6301) and the YWCA (Young Women's Christian Association) Ibn Jubayr Street, Sheikh Jarrah, East Jerusalem ☎ 02-628 2593, Fax 02-628 4654)*: most of their establishments provide accommodation for pilgrims or budget tourists.

Due to the decline in the number of visitors since the beginning of the al-Aqsa Intifada, one can benefit from lowered rates below the published prices.

■ Restaurants and Cafés

Next to the restaurants - often combined café-restaurants - there are many small fast food places. They usually sell cheap, delicious, filling sandwiches *(shawarma* and *falafel).*
Travellers on a limited budget will find these establishments a real boon.

Tipping

In most Palestinian restaurants and cafés, service is included. A tip is not necessary, but you may leave something extra as thanks for special attention or a special favour. As a reminder: do not forget the guide!

■ Money

The currency in Israel and the Occupied Palestinian Territories (OPT) is the "Shekel" or "New Israeli shekel" (NIS), since the shekel replaced the "Israeli pound" or "lira" in 1980. The exchange rates for dollars or euros have fallen since the end of the year 2000, to the advantage of European visitors. The shekel is not the only acceptable currency: dollars are also accepted, especially for large amounts. Prices are often quoted in dollars, especially in hotels and car rental companies and Israeli rents. The euro is likewise accepted everywhere.

In the West Bank, in East Jerusalem and in the Gaza Strip, the Jordanian dinar (JD) is also often used to make large payments such as rents. In fact, rents are often listed in dollars or Jordanian dinars (which is less good for people who receive salaries in shekels). Palestinian Authority employees are paid in JD. In the Gaza Strip, the Egyptian pound is also accepted.

Exchange rate (January 2005)
1 Euro = 5.67 shekels
1 U.S. dollar = 4.36 shekels
1 pound sterling = 8.82 shekels

Exchange Bureaux

Avoid changing money at borders, the airport and even banks, for the simple reason that the rates in such places are not the best, and you will usually be asked to pay a commission.
On the other hand, all main cities have moneychangers with better rates and more flexible hours than the banks; they are often open until 18h or 19h.

Banks

In the West Bank and the Gaza Strip, banks rarely have automatic cash distributors. Places where you may withdraw money with one of the internationally recognised cards (Visa, Mastercard, Eurocard, etc.) are indicated, if they exist, throughout this guide in the «Practical Information» sections.
If you with to make a banking transaction, take careful note of the opening hours, which are generally 8:30-12:30. Banks generally re-open a few hours in late afternoon (16:00-17:30).

Money-Savers

International student card: this card can be used to qualify for reductions in museums, inter-city Israeli buses and some hotels and restaurants.

Israeli national park: there are over 30 national parks, some in the Palestinian Territories occupied in 1967. A «Green Card» (NIS 102) entitles you to tour any of the parks during a 2-week period. Another 70-shekel pass entitles the bearer to visit any 6 parks in a 2-week period. These special tickets are available in any national park.

Foreign currency to cover certain expenses: larger expenses (hotel stays or car rentals) are best paid in foreign currency (e.g. euros), which permits exemption from the 17% VAT (service charges). Consequently, when you stay at a hotel, charge telephone calls, meals and drinks to your bill rather than paying for them on the spot in shekels.

Time Differences

Local time is two hours ahead of Greenwich Mean Time (GMT+2), seven hours ahead of American Eastern Standard Time and eight hours behind Australian Eastern Standard Time. There is often a period of a week in autumn and spring when there is a difference of an hour between Israel and the Palestinian territories, as both countries do not co-ordinate their daylight savings time (the "summer clock").

■ Health

- No special vaccinations are needed. However, sunstroke or sunburn are risks if you are exposed to the sun for long periods, for example along the Dead Sea. It is important to remember to drink water (or other liquids, such as fruit juice or soft drinks) in summer. For hikes, plan on taking several litres per person. You may find this weighs you down when you start off, but you will be grateful for it later on. If your head develops a feeling of heaviness, it is because you have not drunk enough. Drink, and your headaches will quickly disappear. Avoid long walks under the sun at midday, and cover your head.
- Travelling means a change in diet, and a classic case of "travel bug" (diarrhoea) is a common problem many anticipate. In Palestine, the Mediterranean diet, with rice as an important staple food, minimizes this risk. Simply wash vegetables and fruit well, as you usually do, before cooking or eating raw; do not develop a psychosis about them.
- The water is safe to drink in most places. However, where there are severe water shortages (villages, refugee camps), the quality is not good. In the Gaza Strip, the water is sometimes unfit for consumption. In this case, do not hesitate to buy mineral water. The Palestinian "Jericho" bottled mineral water is excellent.

Medical Services

If you are ill, you will find pharmacies open late into the evening. If you want to see a doctor, ask at your hotel. Most doctors (either "doctor" or "tabib" in Arabic) speak English.

In an emergency, **dial 101** (the ambulance service).

■ The Media

There are various newspapers and magazines on sale: daily, weekly, fortnightly or monthly.

■ Israeli magazines and newspapers in English

Ha'aretz: daily (liberal) newspaper in English - sold as a supplement inside the daily ***International Herald Tribune***, published by ***The New York Times***, and read by intellectuals.
Jerusalem Post: daily Israeli newspaper representing the political position of Likud.
Jerusalem Report: published every two weeks, covering Israel, Middle East and the Jewish World, with a mainstream Zionist position, somewhat similar to The Jerusalem Post.

■ Palestinian magazines

Jerusalem Times: published weekly, positions close to those of the Palestinian Authority.
This Week in Palestine: Monthly guide for tourists, with some excellent articles, available free at all hotels.

■ Information independent of connection to sources of power:

Between the Lines: A monthly publication put out by the Beit Jibrin Cultural Centre covering Palestinian resistance inside the State of Israel and in the territories occupied since 1967. To see their archives, go to their website: www.between-lines.org

News from Within: Monthly magazine with analysis and information on Palestinians in the Occupied Territories and Israeli Palestinians and Israeli society as well; published by the Alternative Information Centre [See *AIC*, p. 168].
Al-Majdal: Magazine about Palestinian refugees published every three months by the Badil Centre [See p. 205].
Palestine-Israel Journal A quarterly joint Israeli-Palestinian academic journal of politics, economics and culture focusing on "a deeper insight into the issues dividing the two peoples, as seen by prominent writers, political figures, scholars, journalists, artists and experts from Palestine, Israel and around the world."
Palestine Monitor: An online news service focusing on reporting Occupation news [See www.palestinemonitor.org]
Electronic Intifada: An online magazine based in America covering a wide spectrum of issues about Palestine, including arts, culture, media, human rights, news, events and politics [See www.electronicintifada.net]

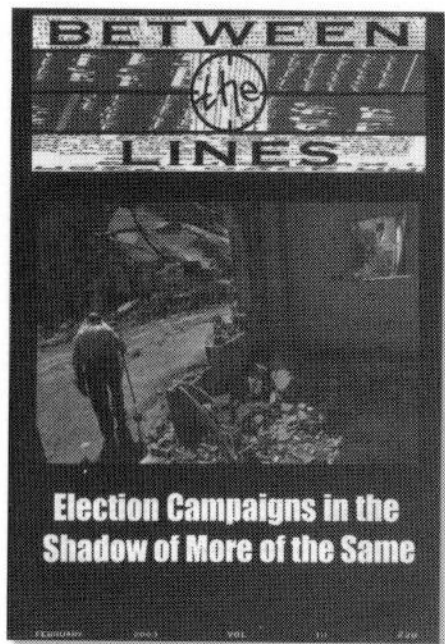

BETWEEN
the
LINES
Election Campaigns in the
Shadow of More of the Same

■ Getting Around

Service Taxis

These taxis are only a bit more expensive than public buses, rapid and practical - you can take one at the beginning of its run or anywhere along the line, getting out wherever you want.
The advantage of service taxis is their frequency: when departing, you only wait until one fills, unless you pay the driver for any empty seats and leave immediately. Palestinian taxis in the West Bank and Gaza are chrome-yellow (7 seater Mercedes or 9 seater Ford Transit). In East Jerusalem, most white Ford Transit service taxis are recycled Israeli police vans!

Buses

- **Palestinian bus companies.** In East Jerusalem, there are buses in the various Palestinian neighbourhoods and their vicinity (Abu Dis, Bethlehem and Ramallah). Small Palestinian buses have only operated in East Jerusalem since the state of siege imposed on the West Bank since the beginning of the al-Aqsa Intifada.
  In the West Bank and Gaza Strip, some buses run between the main urban centres or between checkpoints. They are cheaper than service taxis but not as fast, especially when stopped at "flying checkpoints" when all IDs are slowly checked by soldiers or Border Police.
- **Israeli bus companies.** In West Jerusalem, Israeli buses (Egged is the main Israeli bus company) connect the different neighbourhoods and connect the city with the many Jewish settlements in the territories occupied in 1967 and such sites as Rachel's Tomb in Bethlehem or the Ibrahimi Mosque in Hebron. Egged buses also regularly link all the cities. Each city also has a very dense internal bus network.

Private Taxis

Always ask a private taxi how much the trip will cost before getting in! In Palestinian cities in the West Bank and the Gaza Strip, taxis do not have a meter. The fare depends on the destination. Not every taxi driver is out to cheat - far from it - ! but caution is recommended in the tourist cities (Bethlehem and Jerusalem).
In East Jerusalem and the State of Israel, ask the driver to start the meter. Rates go up at night (between 21:00-05:30).

Renting a Car

Hiring a car is simple; you must have a driving licence (one issued by your country is sufficient) and make a deposit of 1000 Euros which you can pay with a cheque or banking card. You must be over 21, sometimes over 23.
If you rent a car from an Israeli company, the insurance may be invalid in the West Bank, where there will be no accident coverage. Bearing this in mind, you may prefer to hire a vehicle in East Jerusalem; you will be free to drive to Haifa as well as Bethlehem.
To drive in the Gaza Strip, you must rent a car there. Rates are lower than other parts of Palestine, but the distances are obviously also shorter.

If you plan on driving long distances in the summer, especially in the Negev, ask for a car with air conditioning. Only the more expensive cars have air conditioning, and the rental fee will be proportionately higher.

Car Rental Agencies

East Jerusalem

AutoNation : ☎ 02-585 1666 (Beit Hanina) / 0505-414 449

Dallah al-Baraka : ☎ 02-656 4150 (A-Ram)

Good Luck : ☎ 02-532 7126 (Beit Hanina)

Green Peace : ☎ 02-585 9756 (Shu'fat) / 0505-522 619

Orabi : ☎ 02-585 3101 (Beit Hanina)

Petra : ☎ 02-582 0716 (Shu'fat) / 0505-511 105

Bethlehem

Murad : ☎ 02-274 7092

Orabi : ☎ 0505-372 687

Petra : ☎ 0505-511 105

Hebron

Holy Land : ☎ 02-222 0811

Jericho

Orabi : ☎ 0505-405 095

Petra/Allenby Bridge Branch : ☎ 02-940 0494, Fax 02-940 0493

Nablus

Orabi : ☎ 09-238 3383

Ramallah & al-Bireh

Good Luck : ☎ 02-234 2160

Mena : ☎ 02-296 5744

Orabi : ☎ 02-240 3521

Shkoukany : ☎ 02-295 4764

Shorouq : ☎ 02-298 6154

Twins : ☎ 02-296 4688

Gaza

Imad : ☎ 08-286 4000

Palestine : ☎ 08-282 3841

Yafa : ☎ 08-282 5127

The Highway Code

Israeli road laws do not apply in the West Bank cities or the Gaza Strip. For example, it is not compulsory to wear a seat belt, but Israeli traffic police are strict on West Bank major roads.

The roads vary greatly in quality. In the State of Israel, they are generally good. In the West Bank, the huge settler only (apartheid) by-pass roads, which link settlements to each other or settlements to the State of Israel, are in excellent condition. They are all practically new; most were built after the Oslo Accords, costing over $3 billion (US taxpayers' money).

Palestinian roads are in much worse shape. They have been repaired many times by the Palestinian Authority but have suffered enormous damage since late 2000 (deliberate destruction by Israeli military forces or by Israeli army tanks using them).

You must switch your headlights on, even during the day, from 1 November to 31 March, outside towns. Watch the speed limit: there are frequent checks, especially in the Galilee, and on the main road between Tel Aviv and Haifa and in the Negev.

A few private taxi companies in East Jerusalem

Jaber taxi, ☎ 02-585 5566

Ash-Sham, ☎ 02-656 9222

Ummeh, ☎ 02-234 0378

Star 2000, ☎ 0505-394 838 (Israel and Bethlehem and West Bank)

Private taxi company in Gaza City

Sendebad Taxi Service, ☎ 0599 746719

Licence Plates

Yellow: vehicles registered with the civilian Israeli authorities - the State of Israel and annexed Palestinian (East Jerusalem) and Syrian (Golan Heights) territories.

Green: vehicles from territories under Palestinian administration (the West Bank and the Gaza Strip – Areas A, B and C)

Black: Israeli military vehicles

White: Foreign diplomatic vehicles

Calendars

Calendar of Religious Holidays

Muslim Holidays*

	2005	2006
Eid al-Adha	January 1 (4 days)	January 10 (4 days)
Hijra'	February 10	January 31
Mawled en-Nabi	April 21	April 11
Al-Isra' wa al-Miraj	September 1	August 22
First day of Ramadan	October 4	September 24
Eid al-Fitr	November 3	October 24

* Dates calculated according to the lunar calendar. Every year, they change by 10 or 11 days compared to the previous year's Gregorian calendar. In this way, the religious holidays rotate around the Gregorian calendar.

- **Eid al-Adha** (The Feast of the Sacrifice): celebrates the Prophet Abraham's will power and obedience to God.
- **Al-Isra' wa al-Miraj:** celebrates the Prophet Mohammed's Night Journey from Mecca to Jerusalem, where he ascended to paradise (miraj = Ascension) (Quran al-Isra' XVII:1).
- **Mawled en-Nabi:** the birth of the Prophet Mohammed.
- **First day of Ramadan:** celebrates the first Revelation of the Quran, ushering in a month's period of fasting (Quran al-Baqara II: 182-187).
- **Eid al-Fitr:** three days to celebrate the end of the Ramadan time of fasting
- **Hijra':** the commemoration of the Prophet Mohammed's emigration and of the establishmentof the first Muslim community near Yatrib (now Medina) in July 622. This event marked the beginning of the teaching of Islam and of the Islamic period in history.

Christian holidays

	Dates* 2005/2006	Main holidays
Christmas	Orthodox: January 7 Catholic (Latin): December 25 Armenian: January 19	Services on December 24th in Saint Catherine's Church (Bethlehem) and Church of the Holy Sepulchre (Jerusalem), procession from Shepherds' Field (Beit Sahour).
Easter	March 27, 2005 April 16, 2006	There are many different processions during Holy Week along the Via Dolorosa. One goes from Bethphage to the Mount of Olives, ending at the Church of the Holy Sepulchre.
Saint George (al-Khader)	May 5	Celebrations in village of al-Khader (outside Bethlehem), Lydda (Lod) and Jaffa.
Ascension	Orthodox: June 9, 2005 May 31, 2006 Catholic: May 5, 2005 May 25, 2006	Celebration on Mount of Olives (site of the Ascension)
Saint John	June 24	Celebration in Church of the Visitation (village of Ein Karem) and in Church of Saint John the Baptist.
Mar Elias	July 20	Religious celebrations at the monasteries dedicated to Saint Elias in Haifa and in Bethlehem.
Saint Joseph	March 19	Special service at St. Joseph's Church (Nazareth)
Feast of the Annunciation	March 25	Service in Basilica of the Annunciation (Nazareth)
Saint Nicholas	December 19	Patron saint of Beit Jala, where main celebration is held.

* Most of the above-mentioned dates are from the Gregorian calendar.
For more information, contact the *Christian Information Centre (☎02-627 2692).*

Samaritan and Jewish holidays

	Name of Holidays (Old Hebrew)	2005	2006
Yom al-'Nbi'ah (Day of the Prophets)	Taba	Dec. 22, 2004	
Eid al-Fissah (Easter)	Pessach	April 24-May 1	April 13-20
Al-Hajj (Mt. Jarzim pilgrimage)	Hag Hamasol	April 30	April 19
Al-Hassad/Al-Khamsin (a warm sandy wind that is frequent this time of year)	Shavuot	June 13	June 2
Eid es-Sana (New Year's Day) **Eid es-Soum** (Day of Fasting) **Eid al'Orsh** (Feast of the Tabernacles)	Rosh Hashana Yom Kippur Sukkot	October 4 October 13 Oct. 18-24	Sept. 22 October 1 Oct. 6-13
Firha et-Toura (Joy of the Torah)	Simchat Torah	October 25	October 14
Hannuka	Hannuka	Dec. 26-Jan. 2	Dec. 16-23

■ Special Events

January 15. Tree Day

End February-beginning March. Jericho Winter Festival

End March. Lettuce Festival (Artas)

April 15-30. Mawled Nabi Moussa

May 1 -7. Festival of Nabi Saleh (vicinity of Ramallah)
May 1-15. Apricot Festival
May 5. Al-Khader or St. George's Day

June 21. Music Day

July. Jerusalem Festival (Tomb of the Kings)
End July- beginning August. Summer night in Ramallah

August 1. Mar Elias procession (Bethlehem)
August 1-5. Sebastiya Festival
August 5-10. Marj Ibn Amer Festival (Jenin)
August 10-15. Grape Festival (Hebron)

October 7. Palestinian Folklore Heritage Day
October 15-30. Olive-Picking Festival (in several different Palestinian localities)

December 17-19. Popular festival of St. Nicolas (Beit Jala)

■ Key Dates

January 1, 1965. Official birth of Palestinian resistance movement Fatah: first operation of its military branch al-'Assifa

February 14, 1982. General Strike in the Golan

March 8. International Women's Day (UN)
March 21, 1968. Battle of Karameh (Jordan)
March 21. International Day for Elimination of Racial Discrimination
March 30, (1976). Land Day

April 17. Palestinian Prisoners' Day
April 17, 2004. Death of Abdul Aziz Rantisi of Hamas

May 1. Labour Day
May 15, 1948. Al-Nakba (the Catastrophe)

June 1. International Day of the Child
June 5-10, 1967. Six Day War
June 6, 1982. Israeli Invasion of Lebanon
June 21, 1969. Fatal fire in al-Aqsa Mosque
June 26. International Day in support of Victims of Torture (UN)
June 26, 1936. Martyr Fatmeh Ghazzal becomes first female combatant killed in a guerrilla operation

Sept. 15-17, 1982. Sabra and Shatila Massacre
September 16, 1970. Black September
September 21. International Day of Peace
September 28, 2000. Al-Aqsa Intifada commences with Sharon visit to al-Aqsa

October 2, 1187. Jerusalem liberated by Saladin al-Ayoubi al-Kurdi
October 29, 1956. Kufr Qassem Massacre

November 2, 1917. Balfour Declaration: Day of Protest
November 10, 1975. Adoption of UN Resolution 3359: Zionism is a form of racism and racial discrimination
November 15, 1988. Palestinian National Day: Declaration of Independence by Palestinian National Council in meeting in exile in Algiers
November 19, 1935. Sheikh Izz ed-Din al-Qassam killed in combat by British colonial forces
November 29, 1947. UN Partition Resolution 181
November 29. Jerusalem (al-Quds) Day - Intnl. Day of Solidarity with the Palestinian People, initiated by Iran, declared by UN

December 9, 1987. Outbreak of First Intifada
December 11, 1967. Creation of the Popular Front for the Liberation of Palestine (PFLP)
December 11, 1948. Declaration of UN Resol. 194, declaring Right of Return
December 14, 1981. Golan Heights annexed by Israel
December 14, 1987. Teachers' Day
December 14, 1987. Creation of the Islamic Resistance Movement (Hamas)

APPENDIX

Language

■ Greetings

Hello or **Peace be with you :**
As-Salam 'alekoum
Response: Wa 'aleykoum as-Salam

Morning greeting :
Sabah al-Khair Response: *Sabah-al-Nour*

Good evening:
Massa' al-Khair Response: *Massa' al-Nour*

Hello (informal):
Marhaba Response: *Marhabten*

How are you (familiar form)?
For a man: *Keef halak?*
For a woman: *Keef halek?*

Response:**Fine, thanks be to God.**
Al-Hamdulillah

Welcome !
Ahlan wa sahlan

Goodbye or **Go in Peace:**
Ma'assalam

Good night:
Leila Saida

What's your name (familiar form)?
For a man: *Esh (or Chou) esmak?*
For a woman: *Esh (or Chou) esmek?*

Je m'appelle (...) et toi ?
Esmi (...) wa enta (enti pour une femme) ?

My name is ... and you?
Esmi (...), wa enta (for a man)? *wa enti* (for a woman)?

Thank you:
Shukran
Response: *Afwan*

Please:
To a man: *Min fadlak,*
To a woman: *Min fadlek*

Yes:
Na'am or Aywa

No:
La'

Congratulations:
Mabrouk

■ Orientation

Where are you from ?
Min wein enta (for a man ?
Min wein enti (for a woman)?

I'm from ( ) Canada, England, United States, Australia ... Jerusalem, Palestine, Hebron
Ana min (...) Canada, Britanya, al-wilayat al-Muttaheda al-Amrikiya, Australia ... al-Quds, Falastine, al-Khalil

Where are the taxis for Nablus?
Wein al-taxiat ila Nablus?

Where is the hotel (...) ?
Wein al-funduk (...)?

Here:
hon

There:
honak

On the right:
Al-yamin

On the left:
Ash'mal

Straight ahead:
dughri or alatoul

Omar al-Mukhtar Street:
shariat Omar al-Mukhtar

■ Numbers

1	wahad	١
2	etnen	٢
3	talata	٣
4	arba'	٤
5	chamsa	٥
6	sitta	٦
7	sab'a	٧
8	tamanya	٨
9	tis'a	٩
10	'ashara	١٠
11	ihda'sh	١١
12	itna'sh	١٢
13	talatta'sh	١٣
20	'ishreen	٢٠
21	wahad wa 'ishreen	٢١
22	etnen wa 'ishreen	٢٢
30	talateen	٣٠
31	wahad wa talateen	٣١
40	arba'een	٤٠
50	chamseen	٥٠
100	miyya	١٠٠
200	miteyn	٢٠٠
300	talatmiyya	٣٠٠
400	arba'miyya	٤٠٠
1000	alf	١٠٠٠
2000	alfeyn	٢٠٠٠
3000	talat-talaf	٣٠٠٠
10 000	'ashar-talaf	١٠٠٠٠

■ General Vocabulary

Airport	matar
Bank	bank
Bus station	mahatat al-basat
Car	sayara
Church	kaneesah
Church	kaneesah
Consulate	consuliya
Delicious	zaki
Hotel	otel / funduk
House	beit
How much does it cost?	(q)addeish es-se'er
I want	biddi
Market	souk
Mosque	jame'/masjid
Museum	mathaf
Passport	passport/jawaz safer
Please!	itfaddal
Police	police / shurta
Post office	barid / bosta
Private taxi	taxi khususi
Restaurant	mat'am
Service taxi	taxi umumi/servis
Ticket	tazkara
Toilet	hammam

■ Food

Almond	loz
Apple	tuffah
Apricot	abocado
Banana	mouz
Bread	khubiz
Breakfast	iftour
Carrot	jazzar
Cheese	jibna
Chicken	(lahem) djaj
Coffee	kahwa
Fish	samak
French fried potatoes	batata
Fruit juice	asir fawakih
Ice cream	buza
Lamb (meat)	lahem kharouf
Lemon	lamone
Olive	zeitoun
Olive oil	zeit zeitoun
Orange (fruit)	asir burtukal
Salad	salata
Tea	shai
Water	maye

Glossary

Acanthus: Architectural decoration typically found in Corinthian columns.

Amarna Letters: Diplomatic correspondence between the Canaanite princes (vassals of the Pharoah) and Pharoah Amenhotep III and Pharoah Akhen-aten-Amenhotep IV, his successor, around 1350 BC. Written in cuneiform script in the Babylonian language, the letters (on clay tablets) were kept in the royal archives in Akhenaton's capital of Tel al-Amarna, where they were discovered in 1887.

Ashkenazi *(Hebrew)*: Member of the central European Jewish community.

Atrium *(Latin)*: Inside courtyard enclosed by a portico supported by columns.

Bab *(Arabic)*: Door.

Baptistry: Building or basin in which baptisms are performed.

Basilica: Oblong Roman construction ending in an apse. Church built on the same lines.

Bilad esh-Sham *(Arabic)*: Literally «the Country of Sham», term used to designate the historical territory of Greater Syria, a geographical whole encompassing Syria, Palestine, Lebanon and Jordan.

Caimacam *(Turkish)*: High-ranking Ottoman official in charge of a district.

Checkpoint: Military control post, stationary or "flying" (i.e.any jeep).

Coenobite: Monk living in a religious community.

Cufic or Kufic: Type of Arabic calligraphy used in the writing of the first centuries of the Islamic period, originating in the town of Kufa (Iraq).

Decapolis: Confederacy of 10 cities in the first century BC in the northeast part of ancient Palestine.

Derech *(Hebrew)*: Avenue.

Dunum *(Arabic)*: Unit of land measure. 1 dunum = 919 m2 = 0.090 hectares, or + acre, approximately.

Eschatological: Relating to any system of doctrines and beliefs concerning the last moments of mankind and the universe.

Fedayin or feddayin (Arabic): Literally «those who make the sacrifice of their life» in defence of the Palestinian cause; Palestinian resistant in a guerilla movement.

Hagana *(Hebrew)*: Paramilitary organisation of the left wing of the Zionist party, created in 1920 and controlled by the Jewish Agency. After the establishment of the State of Israel, it was renamed *Tsahal*, the acronym of the Israeli Defence Force, in Hebrew.

Hajj *(Arabic)*: Traditional annual pilgrimage to Mecca - one of the pillars of Islam. In a wider sense, the term Hajj is used to describe all pilgrimages important to all faiths in the Arab world; for example, the pilgrimage the Samaritans make up Mount Jarzim.

Hassidim *(Hebrew)*: Jewish sect stressing mysticism founded in Russia and Poland in the eighteenth century.

Hegira *(Arabic: Hijra)*: The Prophet Mohammed's forced departure from Mecca to the oasis of Yathrib in September 622, which marks the start of the Muslim calendar.

Hierodule: Slave in an ancient Greek temple, dedicated to the service of a deity.

Iconostasis: In Eastern churches, a partition or screen on which icons are places which serves as a separation between the nave from the sanctuary reserved for officiating priests.

Intifada ***(Arabic)*****:** The Uprising or literally "shaking off."

Jabal ***(Arabic)*****:** Mountain or prominent hill.

Kabbalah ***(Hebrew)*****:** Jewish mystical interpretation of holy texts, developed in Spain during the thirteenth century.

Khan ***(Arabic)*****:** Caravanserai. Inn with storage areas for overnight accommodation of caravans, located along principal routes or at the entrance to towns .

Kibbutz ***(Hebrew)*****:** Zionist agricultural farming collective.

Kippa ***(Hebrew)*****:** Skull-cap worn by practicing Jews.

Kuttab ***(Arabic)*****:** Elementary school formerly run by mosques.

Laura: Monastery where hermit monks occasionally meet for a meal or worship.

Levite: Subordinate religious official of the Jewish faith responsible for the upkeep of a synagogue or temple, a duty transmitted from father to son, as descendants of the Biblical tribe of Levi.

Liwa' ***(Turkish)*****:** Ottoman administrative division under the jurisdiction of the *wilaya.*

Madrasa ***(Arabic)*****:** Literally «place of study». Islamic educational institution which traditionally transmitted religious and legal teachings. Today, the term designates any elementary or secondary school, religious or secular, public or private.

Maqam ***(pl. maqamat, Arabic)*****:** Literally «place where someone is kept». Edifice in memory of a prophet, usually a copy of his mausoleum.

Masjid ***(Arabic)*****:** Literally, «place where one prostrates oneself (in worship)» . Mosque.

Mawled ***(Arabic)*****:** See *mawsim.*

Mawsim ***(Arabic)*****:** Literally «seasons». Religious and secular festival. A mawsim can last for several weeks or months. It is also the term used to describe a fair where city-dwellers, farmers and Bedouins exchange their wares, also the name for a fun fair.

Mihrab ***(Arabic)*****:** Decorative architectural element which points towards the Ka'aba in Mecca.

Minbar ***(Arabic)*****:** Pulpit from which the Friday prayer (Muslim sermon) is preached.

Mishna ***(Hebrew)*****:** The section of Jewish codes in the Talmud that sets down the rules that regulate daily life. Transcribed in the second century AD.

Moutassaref ***(Arabic)*****:** Governor of a *liwa.*

Muqarnas ***(Arabic)*** **or stalactites:** Honey-combed, three-dimensional vaults of the Mameluke period (1250-1516).

Nahiya ***(Turkish)*****:** The smallest administrative area for tax purposes established by the Ottomans, subordinate to the *liwa.*

Narthex: Enclosed passage between the main entrance to a church and the churchbody.

Nymphaenum: Small temple of Greek origin built around a natural cave or spring, sacred to nymphs, the goddesses of woods, streams and mountains.

Palaestra ***(Greek)*****:** A public place for physical exercise.

Pentapolis ***(Greek)*****:** Group of five cities. For example, the Philistine *pentapolis.*

Peristyle: Colonnade enclosing a building or an interior courtyard.

Qadi *(Arabic)*: Judge responsible for civil and criminal affairs in a given district.

Qala'a *(Arabic)*: Fortress.

Qasr (Arabic): Palace or castle.

Qibla *(Arabic)*: Orientation for Muslim prayer directed by the *mihrab*.

Rak'a *(pl. rakat, Arabic)*: Prostrations made during Muslim prayer.

Rehov *(Hebrew)*: Street.

Revisionist Zionism: The Revisionist movement was founded in 1925 by Polish Zionist leader Vladimir Jabotinsky as an alternative to the World Zionist Organisation, which accepted the boundaries of the Palestinian Mandate as the physical limits of a future Jewish state. The movement was called «Revisionist» because it wanted to «revise» the Mandate boundaries to include Transjordan in the future state. The military group Irgun, responsible for numerous attacks on Palestinian civilians, originated within this movement.

Sanjak *(Turkish)*: Literally, «flag, standard». Ottoman administrative district.

Seraglio: Ottoman palace and administrative or military government building in a province.

Sfaradi: In the Middle Ages, a Jew from Spain or Portugal. In a wider sense, an Arab Jew.

Sha'ra *(Arabic)*: Street.

Soloman's Seal *(Khatem Suleiman in Arabic)*: Decorative motif in the form of a six-pointed star characteristic of buildings erected by Sultan Suleiman the Magnificent at the beginning of the Ottoman period. In Palestine, this motif was a common feature in civil buildings until the nineteenth century. It became a mystic symbol of the kabbalist movement and, thousands of miles away, in the seventeenth century, gradually spread over central and eastern Europe as the emblem of Jewish communities there. In the nineteenth century, the Zionist political movement chose this sign to symbolise their movement as the «Star of David» or «Shield of David», endowing it with religious and nationalist significance.

Syncretism: Combination of several religious practices from several different cultures.

Tariq *(Arabic)*: Path or small street.

Tel: Mound formed by the accumulation of the remains of ancient cities.

Triclinium *(Latin)*: Dining room with three couches on which meals were eaten in a semi-reclining position (Roman period).

UNRWA: United Nations Relief and Works Agency for Palestinian Refugees.

Wadi *(Arabic)*: Valley.

Wali (Arabic): Muslim holy man or saint, and sanctuary to his or her memory; also governor of a *wilaya* (Ottoman province).

Waqf *(pl. awqaf, Arabic)*: Property or foundation whose revenues are donated to charitable works. Organisation of Muslim charities and the religious foundations administering them. In the State of Israel, all Awqaf property is under the jurisdiction of the Israeli Ministry of the Interior.

Wilaya *(Arabic)*: Ottoman administrative province.

Zawiya *(Arabic)*: Muslim foundation established on the site of the tomb of a holy mystic. A *zawiya* can be a large monastery or a simple room where Sufi groups meet.

Recommended Reading List

[Most of these books are available at The Bookshop, American Colony Hotel, Sheikh Jarrah, East Jerusalem (02-627 9731 - usbooks@palnet.com) or The Educational Bookshop in Salah ed-Din Street, East Jerusalem

■ Geography, History and Society

Abu-Zayyad, Ziad
Land: The Core of the Conflict. Palestine-Israel Journal 1997
Aruri, Nasser
Dishonest Broker, The US Role in Israel & Palestine. South End, 2003
Bazbaz, Marwan
Settlement in the West Bank & Gaza Strip. *Palestine-Israel Journal.* 1997
Beit-Hallahmi, Benjamin
Israeli Connection: Who Israel Arms & Why. New York: Pantheon. 1987
Original Sins: Reflections On the History of Zionism & Israel. 1996
Benvenisti, Eyal
Legal Dualism: Absorption of the Occupied Territories into Israel. 1989
Benveniste, Meron
Sacred Landscape: The Buried History of the Holy Land. Univ. Calif. 2000
City of Stone: The Hidden History of Jerusalem. University of California Press. 1996
Intimate Enemies: Jews and Arabs in a Shared Land. Univ. of Calif. 1996
Bollens, Scott
On Narrow Ground: Urban Policy & Ethnic Conflict In Jerusalem & Belfast. Albany: SUNY. 2000
Brubaker, Matthew
The Jerusalem Ring Road. News From Within 2001
Campbell, Elizabeth
'Maximum Territory, Minimum Population' - Jerusalem: The Laboratory for the Policies of Zionist Colonization. News From Within. 1998
Carey, Roane (ed)
The New Intifada: Resisting Israel's Apartheid. New York: Verso. 2001
Carey, Roane and Jonathan Shanon (eds.)
The Other Israel: Voice of Refusal and Dissent. NY: New Press. 2002
Cheshin, Amir S., Bill Hutman, Avi Melamed
*Separate and Unequal: The Inside Story of Israeli Rule in East Jerusalem.*Harvard, 1999
Chomsky, Noam
Fateful Triangle: The United States, Israel and the Palestinians. Boston: S. End Press. 1983
Cohen, Shaul Ephraim
The Politics of Planting: Israeli-Palestinian Competition for Control of Land in the Jerusalem Periphery. Chicago: University of Chicago Press. 1993
Collections:
Jerusalem in History, Olive Branch Press, 2000
de Jong, Jan
Israel's Greater Jerusalem Engulfs the West Bank's Core. Jerusalem. 2000
Doumani (Beshara)
Rediscovering Palestine, Merchants and Peasants in Jabal Nablus 1700-1900, Univ. of California Press, 1995.
Enderlin, Charles
Shattered Dreams: The Failure of the Peace Process in the Middle East, 1995-2002 Other Press, New York, 2003

Falah, Ghazi
The 1948 Israeli-Palestinian War and its Aftermath: the Transformation and De-Signification of Palestine's Cultural Landscape. Annals of the Association of American Geographers, 1996
Finkelstein, Norman
Image and Reality of the Israel-Palestine Conflict. London: Verso. 2003
Beyond Chutzpah: On the Misuse of Anti-Semitism & the Abuse of History.
Flapan, Simcha
Zionism and the Palestinians. London: Croom Helm. 1979
The Birth of Israel: Myths and Realities. New York: Pantheon. 1987
Fromkin, David
A Peace to End All Peace: The Fall of the Ottoman Empire and the Creation of the Modern Middle East. Owl Books. 1989
Goya, Nick
The Absence of Peace. Zed Books. 1998
Halper, Jeff
Obstacles to Peace; a Reframing of the Palestinian-Israeli Conflict, 2005 (available on CD).
Israel in a Middle East Union: A "Two-stage" Approach to the Conflict. Tikkun. 2005
Paralysis Over Palestine: Questions of Strategy. Journal of Palestine Studies (Fall). 2004
The Three Jerusalems: Planning & Colonial Control. J"m Quarterly. 2002
The Road to Apartheid: Trans-Israel Highway. News From Within. 2000
The 94 Percent Solution: A Matrix of Control. M. East Report. 2000
Dismantling the Matrix of Control. News From Within. 1999
Israel's War on Palestinians: Campaign of House Demolitions.Tikkun.1998
Hirst, David
The Gun And The Olive Branch: The Roots of Violence In The Middle East. New York: Nation Books. 1977
Kaminer, Reuven 1995 *Politics of Protest: The Israeli Peace Movement and the Palestinian Intifada*. Brighton: Sussex Academic Press.
Ibrahim, Nassar and Dr. Majed Nassar
The Stupidity of Power vs. the Palestinian Resistance, Bailasan, 2004
Small Dreams. Short Stories from Palestine. Bailasan, Ramallah 2003
The Palestinian Intifada: Cry Freedom. Bailasan, Ramallah 2002
Ir Shalem
East Jerusalem: The Current Planning Situation. Jerusalem. n.d.
Kaminker, Sarah
E. Jerusalem: Case Study in Political Planning Palestine/Israel Journ. 1995.
Kanafani, Ghassan
Palestine's Children: Returning to Haifa and Other Stories, Lynne Rienner Publishers, 2000.
Khalidi, Mohammed Ali, & Elmusa, Sharif,
All that Remains: The Palestinian Villages Occupied and Depopulated by Israel in 1948, The Institute for Palestinian Studies, 1992.
Khalidi, Rashid
Palestinian Identity: The Construction of Modern National Consciousness. New York: Columbia University Press. 1997
Khalidi, Walid
All That Remains. Washington: Institute for Palestine Studies. 1992
Khamaisi, Rassem and Rami Nasrallah (eds.)
The Jerusalem Urban Fabric. Jerusalem 2003
Khamaisi, Rassem, Rami Nasrallah and Michael Younan
Jerusalem on the Map. Jerusalem: IPCC. 2003

Kimmerling, Baruch
Land, *Conflict and Nation Building: A Sociological Study of the Territorial Factors in the Jewish-Arab Conflict*. Hebrew University. 1976
Zionism And Territory. Berkeley: Institute of International Studies. 1983
Politicide: Ariel Sharon's War Against the Palestinians. London: Verso. 2003
Kolatt, Israel
The Zionist Movement and The Arabs. In Shmuel Almog (ed). *Zionism and the Arabs*. Jerusalem: Zalman Shazar Center. 1983
La Guardia, Anton
Holy Land Unholy War: Israelis and Palestinians. John Murray, London, 2001.
Matar, Ibrahim
The Quiet War: Land Expropriation in the Occupied Territories. *Palestine-Israel Journal*. 1997
Makovsky, David
Taba Mythchief. The National Interest (Spring), 2003
Mansour, Atallah
Arab Lands in Israel: A Festering Wound. Palestine-Israel Journal. 1997
Morris, Benny
The Birth of the Palestinian Refugee Problem, 1947-1949. Cambridge, 1979
1948 And After: Israel and the Palestinians. Oxford: 1994
Nasrallah, Rami, Michael Younan et al.
Envisioning the Future of Jerusalem. Jerusalem: IPCC. 2003
Pappe, Ilan
The Making of the Arab-Israeli Conflict, 1948-1951. Macmillan. 1988
A Modern History of Palestine. Cambridge. 2004
Raheb, Mitri
I am a Palestinian Christian, Fortress Press, 1995
Bethlehem Besieged: Stories of Hope in Times of Trouble, Fortress, 2004
Reporters Without Borders
Israel/Palestine - The Black Book. Pluto Press, 2003
Ron, James
Frontiers and Ghettos: State Violence in Serbia & Israel. California. 2003
Rummel, R.J.
Death By Government. New Brunswick: Transaction Books. 1994
Said, Edward
Orientalism (1978)
The Question of Palestine. New York, Vintage Books 1979
Covering Islam, 1981
The World, the Text and the Critic, 1983
Representations of the Intellectual, 1994
Culture of Imperialism, 1994
The End of the Peace Process: Oslo & After. New York: Vintage. 2001
Savir, Uri
The Process. New York: Vintage. 1998
Sayigh, Yezid
Armed Struggle and the Search for a State: The Palestinian National Movement, 1949-1993. Oxford University Press. 1997
Segev, Tom
1949: The First Israelis. New York: The Free Press. 1986
One Palestine Complete. Owl Books 2001
Shavit, Ari
The Big Freeze. Ha'aretz Magazine, Oct. 8. 2004
Eyes Wide Shut. Ha'aretz Magazine, Sept. 6. 2002

Shehadeh, Raja
Strangers in the House: Coming of Age in Occupied Palestine. Steerforth Press. 2001
Land and Occupation: A Legal Review. Palestine-Israel Journal 4(2) 1997:
Shlaim Avi,
The Iron Wall: Israel and the Arab World. Penguin, 2000
Collusion Across the Jordan: King Abdullah, the Zionist Movement, and Partition of Palestine. Oxford: Clarendon. 1988
Sluka, Jeffrey
Death Squad: The Anthropology of State Terror. Philadelphia: Univ. of Pennsylvania Press. 2000
Sternhell, Zeev
The Founding Myths Of Israel. Princeton: Princeton University Press. 1998
Swisher, Clayton E.
The Truth About Camp David: The Untold Story about the Collapse of the Middle East Peace Process.
Tamari, Salim (ed.)
Jerusalem 1948: The Arab Neighbourhoods and Their Fate in the War. Jerusalem: Institute of Jerusalem Studies, 1999.
Whitelaw, Keith W.
The Invention of Ancient Israel - the silencing of Palestinian history, Routledge, 1996.
Yiftachel, Oren
Judaize and Divide: Shaping Spaces in the Israeli Ethnocracy. News From Within. 1999
Zunes, Stephen
Congress to Sharon: Take All You Want. www.anti-war.com (June 26) 2004

■ Palestinian Literature

[See *Literature*, pp. 62]

■ Personal Narratives

Abu-Sharif, Bassam & Mahnaimi, Uzi
Best of Enemies, Little Brown & Co USA, 1995.
Amiry, Suad:
Sharon and My Mother-in-law: Ramallah Diaries. Granta, UK, 2005
Ashrawi, Hanan
This Side of Peace, Touchstone, New York, 1996, first edition 1995.
Boullata, Kamal
Faithful Witnesses; Palestinian Children Recreate Their World, Olive Branch Press, New York, 1990.
Chacour, Elias, David Hazard & James A. Baker III
Blood Brothers, Chosen Books, USA, 2003 (new edition).
Chacour, Elias & Jensen, Mary E.
We Belong to the Land, 2001.
Grossman, David
The Yellow Wind. New York: Farrar, Straus and Giroux. 1988
Hamzeh, Muna
Refugees in our Own Land: Chronicles from a Palestinian Refugee Camp in Bethlehem, Pluto Books, 2001
Sandercock, Josie, Nicholas Blincoe and others
Peace under Fire: Israel/Palestine and the International Solidarity Movement, Verso, 2004.

■ Internet Sites

Alternative Tourism Group <www.patg.org>
Al-Haq: Palestinian human rights and legal service <www.alhaq.org>
Al Ahram Weekly (news including focus on Palestine) <www.ahram.com.eg>
Alternative Information Centre, incl. magazine: <www.alternativenews.org>
Applied Research Inst. of Jerusalem (esp. colonisation and settlements) <www.arij.org>
Arab Association for Human Rights: <www.arabhra.org>
Ariga: <www.ariga.com>
Badil: Resource Centre for Palestinian Residency & Refugee Rights <www.badil.org>
Bat Shalom: Israeli feminist peace organisation <www.batshalom.org>
Bitter Lemons (online political magazine): <www.bitterlemons.org>
B'Tselem: Israeli human rights organization working in OPT: <www.btselem.org>
Christian Peacemakers Team: <www.prairienet.org>
Defense for Children International <www.dci-pal.org>
Electronic Intifada: <www.electronicintifada.net>
Foundation for Middle East Peace: <www.fmep.org>
Golan-Syria: (Syria and the occupied territories in Syria) <www.golan-syria.org>
Gush Shalom: <www.gush-shalom.org>
Ha'aretz newspaper: <www.haaretzdaily.com>
Indymedia: <www.indymedia.org.il>
International Center of Bethlehem <www.annadwa.org>
Israeli Committee Against House Demolitions (ICAHD): <www.icahd.org>
Jerusalem Centre for Economic and Social Rights: <www.jcser.org/english>
Jerusalem Centre for Women: <www.j-c-w.org>
Jerusalem Media and Communication Centre: <www.jmcc.org>
Jerusalem Report: <www.jrep.com>
Jewish Voice For Peace: <www.jewishvoiceforpeace.org>
Ottoman and contemporary history of Jerusalem: <www.jqf-jerusalem.org>
New Profile (anti-militarism): <www.newprofile.org>
Palestine Liberation Organisation (Negotiations Dept.) <www.nad-plo.org>
Palestine Monitor: <www.palestinemonitor.org>
Palestinian Academic Society for Study of International Affairs <www.passia.org>
Palestinian Centre for Human Rights (PCHR) <www.pchrgaza.org>
Palestinian Hydrology Group (PHG): <www.phg.org>
Palestinian Initiative for Promotion of Global Dialogue and Democracy: <www.miftah.org>
Palestinian towns and villages destroyed in 1948; including documents, eye-witness accounts, photographs, and other information: <www.palestinremembered.com>
PalMap: Palestine Mapping Centre <www.palmap.org>
PENGON (Palestine Environmental NGO Network): <www.pengon.org>
<www.stopthewall.org>
<www.shammout.com> (Palestinian art)
Ta'ayush (Israeli-Palestinian direct action peace group): <www.taayush.org>
UNRWA: (Palestinian refugees) <www.un.org/unrwa/refugees>
UN Office Co-ordinating Humanitarian Affairs (excellent maps): <www.ochaopt.org>
Yesh Gvul (Refuseniks) <www.yeshgvul.org>
YMCA www.ej-ymca.org

■ Further Resources

Alternative Information Centre (AIC)
– *Occupation in Hebron,* 2004
– *A Wall on the Green Line?* 2004
– *Cleansing and Apartheid in Jerusalem,* 2004
– *From Communal Strife to Global Struggle,* 2004
– *Globalisation and International Advocacy,* 2004

Amnesty International
– *Under the Rubble: House Demolition and Destruction of Land and Property.* 2004
– *Shielded from Scrutiny: IDF Violations in Jenin and Nablus.* 2002
– Without *Distinction: Attacks on Civilians by Palestinian Armed Groups.* 2002
– *Demolition and Dispossession: The Destruction of Palestinian Homes.* 1999

ARIJ
Geopolitical Atlas of Palestine, October 2004

B'tselem
–*Through No Fault of Their Own: Israel's Punitive House Demolitions in the al-Aqsa Intifada.* 2004
– *Land Grab: Israel's Settlement Policy in the West Bank.* 2002
– *Not Even A Drop: Water Crisis in Palestinian Villages.* 2001
– *The Quiet Deportation Continues.* 1998

Christian Aid
– *Facts on the Ground: The End of the Two-State Solution?* 2004
– *Losing Ground: Israel, Poverty and the Palestinians.* 2003

Defence for Children International (DCI)
– *Fragile Childhood, April* 2004
– *Stolen Youth, Pluto Press January* 2004

Human Rights Watch
– *Razing Rafah: Mass Home Demolitions in the Gaza Strip.* 2004

Israeli Committee Against House Demolitions
– 2004 *A Destructive Policy: House Demolitions in East Jerusalem: Facts, Intents and Implications* (Hebrew).

Palestinian Centre for Human Rights
– 2003 *Demolition of Palestinian Houses by Israeli Occupying Forces as a Means of Punishment and Determent* 2003.

Palestine Monitor
– (for statistical up-dates, see <www.palestinemonitor.org>).

PENGON
– *Stop The Wall in Palestine.* 2003

Index

Index

CATERPILLA

Café (without alcohol)

Café (with alcohol)

Restaurant

Hotel, hospice

Viewing point

Mosque

Maqam

Church

Bus station

Taxis

Information

Post office

Museum

Library

Gallery

Public Park

Beach

Destroyed quarter

T

Z

P

Q

R

S

M

I

J

D

E

F

G

H